IST 100: Fundamentals of Computing

Owens Community College

Beskeen | Cram | Duffy | Friedrichsen | Reding

CENGAGE
Learning·

Australia • Brazil • Japan • Korea • Mexico • Singapore • Spain • United Kingdom • United States

IST 100: Fundamentals of Computing
Owens Community College

Illustrated Microsoft Office 365 & Office 2016 - Introductory
Beskeen | Cram | Duffy | Friedrichsen | Reding

© 2017 Cengage Learning. All rights reserved.

For product information and technology assistance, contact us at
Cengage Learning Customer & Sales Support, 1-800-354-9706

For permission to use material from this text or product,
submit all requests online at **cengage.com/permissions**
Further permissions questions can be emailed to
permissionrequest@cengage.com

This book contains select works from existing Cengage Learning resources and was produced by Cengage Learning Custom Solutions for collegiate use. As such, those adopting and/or contributing to this work are responsible for editorial content accuracy, continuity and completeness.

Compilation © 2016 Cengage Learning

ISBN: 978-1-337-04044-0

WCN: 01-100-101

Cengage Learning
20 Channel Center Street
Boston, MA 02210
USA

Cengage Learning is a leading provider of customized learning solutions with office locations around the globe, including Singapore, the United Kingdom, Australia, Mexico, Brazil, and Japan. Locate your local office at:
www.international.cengage.com/region.

Cengage Learning products are represented in Canada by Nelson Education, Ltd.

For your lifelong learning solutions, visit **www.cengage.com/custom.**

Visit our corporate website at **www.cengage.com.**

Brief Contents

Productivity Apps for School and Work

Corinne Hoisington

OneNote
Sway
Office Mix
Edge

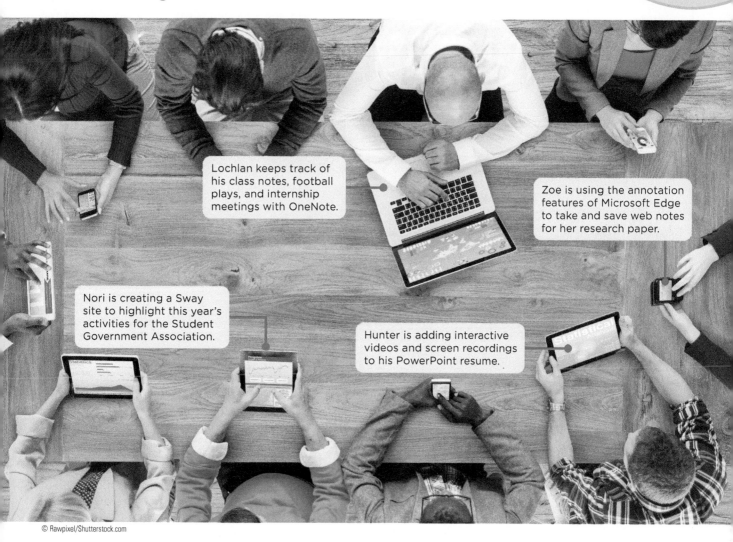

Lochlan keeps track of his class notes, football plays, and internship meetings with OneNote.

Zoe is using the annotation features of Microsoft Edge to take and save web notes for her research paper.

Nori is creating a Sway site to highlight this year's activities for the Student Government Association.

Hunter is adding interactive videos and screen recordings to his PowerPoint resume.

© Rawpixel/Shutterstock.com

Being computer literate no longer means mastery of only Word, Excel, PowerPoint, Outlook, and Access. To become technology power users, Hunter, Nori, Zoe, and Lochlan are exploring Microsoft OneNote, Sway, Mix, and Edge in Office 2016 and Windows 10.

In this Module

Learn to use productivity apps!
Links to companion **Sways**, featuring **videos** with hands-on instructions, are located on www.cengagebrain.com.

Introduction to OneNote 2016

notebook | section tab | To Do tag | screen clipping | note | template | Microsoft OneNote Mobile app | sync | drawing canvas | inked handwriting | Ink to Text

As you glance around any classroom, you invariably see paper notebooks and notepads on each desk. Because deciphering and sharing handwritten notes can be a challenge, Microsoft OneNote 2016 replaces physical notebooks, binders, and paper notes with a searchable, digital notebook. OneNote captures your ideas and schoolwork on any device so you can stay organized, share notes, and work with others on projects. Whether you are a student taking class notes as shown in Figure 1 or an employee taking notes in company meetings, OneNote is the one place to keep notes for all of your projects.

Figure 1: OneNote 2016 notebook

Each **notebook** is divided into sections, also called **section tabs**, by subject or topic.

Use **To Do tags**, icons that help you keep track of your assignments and other tasks.

Type on a page to add a **note**, a small window that contains text or other types of information.

Personalize a page with a **template**, or stationery.

Write or draw directly on the page using drawing tools.

Pages can include pictures such as **screen clippings**, images from any part of a computer screen.

Attach files and enter equations so you have everything you need in one place.

Creating a OneNote Notebook

OneNote is divided into sections similar to those in a spiral-bound notebook. Each OneNote notebook contains sections, pages, and other notebooks. You can use One-Note for school, business, and personal projects. Store information for each type of project in different notebooks to keep your tasks separate, or use any other organization that suits you. OneNote is flexible enough to adapt to the way you want to work.

When you create a notebook, it contains a blank page with a plain white background by default, though you can use templates, or stationery, to apply designs in categories such as Academic, Business, Decorative, and Planners. Start typing or use the buttons on the Insert tab to insert notes, which are small resizable windows that can contain text, equations, tables, on-screen writing, images, audio and video recordings, to-do lists, file attachments, and file printouts. Add as many notes as you need to each page.

Syncing a Notebook to the Cloud

OneNote saves your notes every time you make a change in a notebook. To make sure you can access your notebooks with a laptop, tablet, or smartphone wherever you are, OneNote uses cloud-based storage, such as OneDrive or SharePoint. **Microsoft OneNote Mobile app**, a lightweight version of OneNote 2016 shown in Figure 2, is available for free in the Windows Store, Google Play for Android devices, and the AppStore for iOS devices.

If you have a Microsoft account, OneNote saves your notes on OneDrive automatically for all your mobile devices and computers, which is called **syncing**. For example, you can use OneNote to take notes on your laptop during class, and then open OneNote on your phone to study later. To use a notebook stored on your computer with your OneNote Mobile app, move the notebook to OneDrive. You can quickly share notebook content with other people using OneDrive.

Figure 2: Microsoft OneNote Mobile app

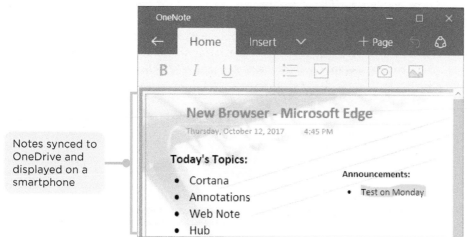

Notes synced to OneDrive and displayed on a smartphone

Taking Notes

Use OneNote pages to organize your notes by class and topic or lecture. Beyond simple typed notes, OneNote stores drawings, converts handwriting to searchable text and mathematical sketches to equations, and records audio and video.

OneNote includes drawing tools that let you sketch freehand drawings such as biological cell diagrams and financial supply-and-demand charts. As shown in Figure 3, the Draw tab on the ribbon provides these drawing tools along with shapes so you can insert diagrams and other illustrations to represent your ideas. When you draw on a page, OneNote creates a **drawing canvas**, which is a container for shapes and lines.

On the Job Now

OneNote is ideal for taking notes during meetings, whether you are recording minutes, documenting a discussion, sketching product diagrams, or listing follow-up items. Use a meeting template to add pages with content appropriate for meetings.

Figure 3: Tools on the Draw tab

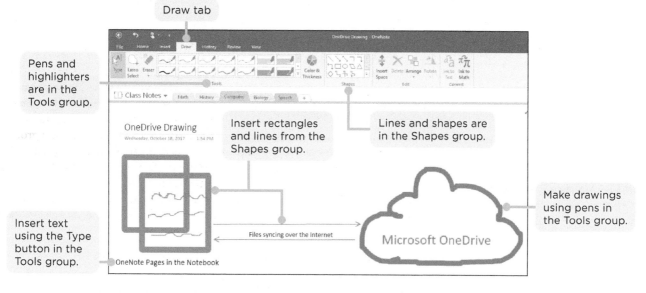

Draw tab

Pens and highlighters are in the Tools group.

Insert rectangles and lines from the Shapes group.

Lines and shapes are in the Shapes group.

Make drawings using pens in the Tools group.

Insert text using the Type button in the Tools group.

Converting Handwriting to Text

When you use a pen tool to write on a notebook page, the text you enter is called **inked handwriting**. OneNote can convert inked handwriting to typed text when you use the **Ink to Text** button in the Convert group on the Draw tab, as shown in Figure 4. After OneNote converts the handwriting to text, you can use the Search box to find terms in the converted text or any other note in your notebooks.

Figure 4: Converting handwriting to text

Ink to Text button

Women's Suffrage

Writing inserted with a fingertip

Handwriting converted to searchable text

Suffrage Movement: effort to get right to vote for women

On the Job Now

Use OneNote as a place to brainstorm ongoing work projects. If a notebook contains sensitive material, you can password-protect some or all of the notebook so that only certain people can open it.

Recording a Lecture

If your computer or mobile device has a microphone or camera, OneNote can record the audio or video from a lecture or business meeting as shown in Figure 5. When you record a lecture (with your instructor's permission), you can follow along, take regular notes at your own pace, and review the video recording later. You can control the start, pause, and stop motions of the recording when you play back the recording of your notes.

Figure 5: Video inserted in a notebook

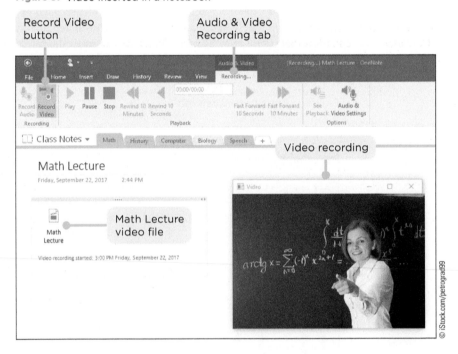

Record Video button

Audio & Video Recording tab

Video recording

Math Lecture video file

© iStock.com/petrograd99

Try This Now

Learn to use OneNote!

Links to companion **Sways**, featuring **videos** with hands-on instructions, are located on www.cengagebrain.com.

1: Taking Notes for a Week

As a student, you can get organized by using OneNote to take detailed notes in your classes. Perform the following tasks:

a. Create a new OneNote notebook on your Microsoft OneDrive account (the default location for new notebooks). Name the notebook with your first name followed by "Notes," as in **Caleb Notes**.

b. Create four section tabs, each with a different class name.

c. Take detailed notes in those classes for one week. Be sure to include notes, drawings, and other types of content.

d. Sync your notes with your OneDrive. Submit your assignment in the format specified by your instructor.

2: Using OneNote to Organize a Research Paper

You have a research paper due on the topic of three habits of successful students. Use OneNote to organize your research. Perform the following tasks:

a. Create a new OneNote notebook on your Microsoft OneDrive account. Name the notebook **Success Research**.

b. Create three section tabs with the following names:

- **Take Detailed Notes**
- **Be Respectful in Class**
- **Come to Class Prepared**

c. On the web, research the topics and find three sources for each section. Copy a sentence from each source and paste the sentence into the appropriate section. When you paste the sentence, OneNote inserts it in a note with a link to the source.

d. Sync your notes with your OneDrive. Submit your assignment in the format specified by your instructor.

3: Planning Your Career

Note: This activity requires a webcam or built-in video camera on any type of device.

Consider an occupation that interests you. Using OneNote, examine the responsibilities, education requirements, potential salary, and employment outlook of a specific career. Perform the following tasks:

a. Create a new OneNote notebook on your Microsoft OneDrive account. Name the notebook with your first name followed by a career title, such as **Kara - App Developer**.

b. Create four section tabs with the names **Responsibilities, Education Requirements, Median Salary**, and **Employment Outlook**.

c. Research the responsibilities of your career path. Using OneNote, record a short video (approximately 30 seconds) of yourself explaining the responsibilities of your career path. Place the video in the Responsibilities section.

d. On the web, research the educational requirements for your career path and find two appropriate sources. Copy a paragraph from each source and paste them into the appropriate section. When you paste a paragraph, OneNote inserts it in a note with a link to the source.

e. Research the median salary for a single year for this career. Create a mathematical equation in the Median Salary section that multiplies the amount of the median salary times 20 years to calculate how much you will possibly earn.

f. For the Employment Outlook section, research the outlook for your career path. Take at least four notes about what you find when researching the topic.

g. Sync your notes with your OneDrive. Submit your assignment in the format specified by your instructor.

Introduction to Sway

Sway site | responsive design | Storyline | card | Creative Commons license | animation emphasis effects | Docs.com

Expressing your ideas in a presentation typically means creating PowerPoint slides or a Word document. Microsoft Sway gives you another way to engage an audience. Sway is a free Microsoft tool available at Sway.com or as an app in Office 365. Using Sway, you can combine text, images, videos, and social media in a website called a **Sway site** that you can share and display on any device. To get started, you create a digital story on a web-based canvas without borders, slides, cells, or page breaks. A Sway site organizes the text, images, and video into a **responsive design**, which means your content adapts perfectly to any screen size as shown in Figure 6. You store a Sway site in the cloud on OneDrive using a free Microsoft account.

Figure 6: Sway site with responsive design

You can display a Sway presentation in a web browser.

Sway uses responsive design to make sure pages fit perfectly on any device.

© iStock.com/marinello, © iStock.com/marekuliasz

Creating a Sway Presentation

You can use Sway to build a digital flyer, a club newsletter, a vacation blog, an informational site, a digital art portfolio, or a new product rollout. After you select your topic and sign into Sway with your Microsoft account, a **Storyline** opens, providing tools and a work area for composing your digital story. See Figure 7. Each story can include text, images, and videos. You create a Sway by adding text and media content into a Storyline section, or **card**. To add pictures, videos, or documents, select a card in the left pane and then select the Insert Content button. The first card in a Sway presentation contains a title and background image.

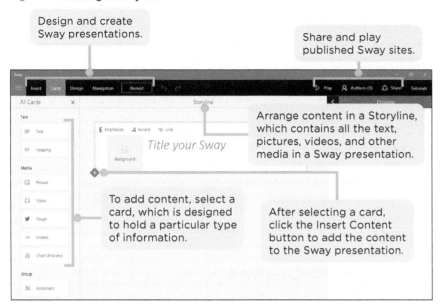

Design and create Sway presentations.

Share and play published Sway sites.

Arrange content in a Storyline, which contains all the text, pictures, videos, and other media in a Sway presentation.

To add content, select a card, which is designed to hold a particular type of information.

After selecting a card, click the Insert Content button to add the content to the Sway presentation.

Adding Content to Build a Story

As you work, Sway searches the Internet to help you find relevant images, videos, tweets, and other content from online sources such as Bing, YouTube, Twitter, and Facebook. You can drag content from the search results right into the Storyline. In addition, you can upload your own images and videos directly in the presentation. For example, if you are creating a Sway presentation about the market for commercial drones, Sway suggests content to incorporate into the presentation by displaying it in the left pane as search results. The search results include drone images tagged with a **Creative Commons license** at online sources as shown in **Figure 8**. A Creative Commons license is a public copyright license that allows the free distribution of an otherwise copyrighted work. In addition, you can specify the source of the media. For example, you can add your own Facebook or OneNote pictures and videos in Sway without leaving the app.

On the Job Now

If you have a Microsoft Word document containing an outline of your business content, drag the outline into Sway to create a card for each topic.

Figure 8: Images in Sway search results

Select the source of media objects

Information about Creative Commons licenses

Storyline title

The Market for Commercial Drones

Drag an image to the picture placeholder box

Suggested images in the search results

Designing a Sway

Sway professionally designs your Storyline content by resizing background images and fonts to fit your display, and by floating text, animating media, embedding video, and removing images as a page scrolls out of view. Sway also evaluates the images in your Storyline and suggests a color palette based on colors that appear in your photos. Use the Design button to display tools including color palettes, font choices, **animation emphasis effects**, and style templates to provide a personality for a Sway presentation. Instead of creating your own design, you can click the Remix button, which randomly selects unique designs for your Sway site.

Publishing a Sway

Use the Play button to display your finished Sway presentation as a website. The Address bar includes a unique web address where others can view your Sway site. As the author, you can edit a published Sway site by clicking the Edit button (pencil icon) on the Sway toolbar.

Sharing a Sway

When you are ready to share your Sway website, you have several options as shown in Figure 9. Use the Share slider button to share the Sway site publically or keep it private. If you add the Sway site to the Microsoft **Docs.com** public gallery, anyone worldwide can use Bing, Google, or other search engines to find, view, and share your Sway site. You can also share your Sway site using Facebook, Twitter, Google+, Yammer, and other social media sites. Link your presentation to any webpage or email the link to your audience. Sway can also generate a code for embedding the link within another webpage.

Figure 9: Sharing a Sway site

Share button

| ▷ Play | ♂ Authors (1) | ⌂ Share |

Share ◉ Just me

Drag the slider button to Just me to keep the Sway site private

Share with the world

Post the Sway site on Docs.com

Docs.com - Your public gallery

Share with friends

Options differ depending on your Microsoft account

Send friends a link to the Sway site

https://sway.com/JQDFrUaxmg4lEbbk

◢ More options

☑ Viewers can duplicate this Sway

Stop sharing

Try This Now

1: Creating a Sway Resume

Learn to use Sway!
Links to companion **Sways**, featuring **videos** with hands-on instructions, are located on www.cengagebrain.com.

Sway is a digital storytelling app. Create a Sway resume to share the skills, job experiences, and achievements you have that match the requirements of a future job interest. Perform the following tasks:

a. Create a new presentation in Sway to use as a digital resume. Title the Sway Storyline with your full name and then select a background image.
b. Create three separate sections titled **Academic Background, Work Experience**, and **Skills**, and insert text, a picture, and a paragraph or bulleted points in each section. Be sure to include your own picture.
c. Add a fourth section that includes a video about your school that you find online.
d. Customize the design of your presentation.
e. Submit your assignment link in the format specified by your instructor.

2: Creating an Online Sway Newsletter

Newsletters are designed to capture the attention of their target audience. Using Sway, create a newsletter for a club, organization, or your favorite music group. Perform the following tasks:

a. Create a new presentation in Sway to use as a digital newsletter for a club, organization, or your favorite music group. Provide a title for the Sway Storyline and select an appropriate background image.
b. Select three separate sections with appropriate titles, such as Upcoming Events. In each section, insert text, a picture, and a paragraph or bulleted points.
c. Add a fourth section that includes a video about your selected topic.
d. Customize the design of your presentation.
e. Submit your assignment link in the format specified by your instructor.

3: Creating and Sharing a Technology Presentation

To place a Sway presentation in the hands of your entire audience, you can share a link to the Sway presentation. Create a Sway presentation on a new technology and share it with your class. Perform the following tasks:

a. Create a new presentation in Sway about a cutting-edge technology topic. Provide a title for the Sway Storyline and select a background image.
b. Create four separate sections about your topic, and include text, a picture, and a paragraph in each section.
c. Add a fifth section that includes a video about your topic.
d. Customize the design of your presentation.
e. Share the link to your Sway with your classmates and submit your assignment link in the format specified by your instructor.

Introduction to Office Mix

add-in | clip | slide recording | Slide Notes | screen recording | free-response quiz

Bottom Line

- Office Mix is a free PowerPoint add-in from Microsoft that adds features to PowerPoint.
- The Mix tab on the PowerPoint ribbon provides tools for creating screen recordings, videos, interactive quizzes, and live webpages.

To enliven business meetings and lectures, Microsoft adds a new dimension to presentations with a powerful toolset called Office Mix, a free add-in for PowerPoint. (An **add-in** is software that works with an installed app to extend its features.) Using Office Mix, you can record yourself on video, capture still and moving images on your desktop, and insert interactive elements such as quizzes and live webpages directly into PowerPoint slides. When you post the finished presentation to OneDrive, Office Mix provides a link you can share with friends and colleagues. Anyone with an Internet connection and a web browser can watch a published Office Mix presentation, such as the one in Figure 10, on a computer or mobile device.

Figure 10: Office Mix presentation

Learn to use Office Mix!

Links to companion **Sways**, featuring **videos** with hands-on instructions, are located on www.cengagebrain.com.

Adding Office Mix to PowerPoint

To get started, you create an Office Mix account at the website mix.office.com using an email address or a Facebook or Google account. Next, you download and install the Office Mix add-in (see Figure 11). Office Mix appears as a new tab named Mix on the PowerPoint ribbon in versions of Office 2013 and Office 2016 running on personal computers (PCs).

Figure 11: Getting started with Office Mix

Capturing Video Clips

A **clip** is a short segment of audio, such as music, or video. After finishing the content on a PowerPoint slide, you can use Office Mix to add a video clip to animate or illustrate the content. Office Mix creates video clips in two ways: by recording live action on a webcam and by capturing screen images and movements. If your computer has a webcam, you can record yourself and annotate the slide to create a **slide recording** as shown in Figure 12.

Figure 12: Making a slide recording

When you are making a slide recording, you can record your spoken narration at the same time. The **Slide Notes** feature works like a teleprompter to help you focus on your presentation content instead of memorizing your narration. Use the Inking tools to make annotations or add highlighting using different pen types and colors. After finishing a recording, edit the video in PowerPoint to trim the length or set playback options.

The second way to create a video is to capture on-screen images and actions with or without a voiceover. This method is ideal if you want to show how to use your favorite website or demonstrate an app such as OneNote. To share your screen with an audience, select the part of the screen you want to show in the video. Office Mix captures everything that happens in that area to create a **screen recording**, as shown in Figure 13. Office Mix inserts the screen recording as a video in the slide.

Figure 13: Making a screen recording

Inserting Quizzes, Live Webpages, and Apps

To enhance and assess audience understanding, make your slides interactive by adding quizzes, live webpages, and apps. Quizzes give immediate feedback to the user as shown in Figure 14. Office Mix supports several quiz formats, including a **free-response quiz** similar to a short answer quiz, and true/false, multiple-choice, and multiple-response formats.

Figure 14: Creating an interactive quiz

Sharing an Office Mix Presentation

When you complete your work with Office Mix, upload the presentation to your personal Office Mix dashboard as shown in Figure 15. Users of PCs, Macs, iOS devices, and Android devices can access and play Office Mix presentations. The Office Mix dashboard displays built-in analytics that include the quiz results and how much time viewers spent on each slide. You can play completed Office Mix presentations online or download them as movies.

Figure 15: Sharing an Office Mix presentation

Try This Now

1: Creating an Office Mix Tutorial for OneNote

Note: This activity requires a microphone on your computer.

Office Mix makes it easy to record screens and their contents. Create PowerPoint slides with an Office Mix screen recording to show OneNote 2016 features. Perform the following tasks:

a. Create a PowerPoint presentation with the Ion Boardroom template. Create an opening slide with the title **My Favorite OneNote Features** and enter your name in the subtitle.
b. Create three additional slides, each titled with a new feature of OneNote. Open OneNote and use the Mix tab in PowerPoint to capture three separate screen recordings that teach your favorite features.
c. Add a fifth slide that quizzes the user with a multiple-choice question about OneNote and includes four responses. Be sure to insert a checkmark indicating the correct response.
d. Upload the completed presentation to your Office Mix dashboard and share the link with your instructor.
e. Submit your assignment link in the format specified by your instructor.

2: Teaching Augmented Reality with Office Mix

Note: This activity requires a webcam or built-in video camera on your computer.

A local elementary school has asked you to teach augmented reality to its students using Office Mix. Perform the following tasks:

a. Research augmented reality using your favorite online search tools.
b. Create a PowerPoint presentation with the Frame template. Create an opening slide with the title **Augmented Reality** and enter your name in the subtitle.
c. Create a slide with four bullets summarizing your research of augmented reality. Create a 20-second slide recording of yourself providing a quick overview of augmented reality.
d. Create another slide with a 30-second screen recording of a video about augmented reality from a site such as YouTube or another video-sharing site.
e. Add a final slide that quizzes the user with a true/false question about augmented reality. Be sure to insert a checkmark indicating the correct response.
f. Upload the completed presentation to your Office Mix dashboard and share the link with your instructor.
g. Submit your assignment link in the format specified by your instructor.

3: Marketing a Travel Destination with Office Mix

Note: This activity requires a webcam or built-in video camera on your computer.

To convince your audience to travel to a particular city, create a slide presentation marketing any city in the world using a slide recording, screen recording, and a quiz. Perform the following tasks:

a. Create a PowerPoint presentation with any template. Create an opening slide with the title of the city you are marketing as a travel destination and your name in the subtitle.
b. Create a slide with four bullets about the featured city. Create a 30-second slide recording of yourself explaining why this city is the perfect vacation destination.
c. Create another slide with a 20-second screen recording of a travel video about the city from a site such as YouTube or another video-sharing site.
d. Add a final slide that quizzes the user with a multiple-choice question about the featured city with five responses. Be sure to include a checkmark indicating the correct response.
e. Upload the completed presentation to your Office Mix dashboard and share your link with your instructor.
f. Submit your assignment link in the format specified by your instructor.

Introduction to Microsoft Edge

Reading view | Hub | Cortana | Web Note | Inking | sandbox

Microsoft Edge is the default web browser developed for the Windows 10 operating system as a replacement for Internet Explorer. Unlike its predecessor, Edge lets you write on webpages, read webpages without advertisements and other distractions, and search for information using a virtual personal assistant. The Edge interface is clean and basic, as shown in Figure 16, meaning you can pay more attention to the webpage content.

Figure 16: Microsoft Edge tools

Forward button · New tab button · Web address in the Address bar · Add to favorites or reading list button · Back button · Reading view button · More button · Refresh (F5) button · Hub (Favorites, reading list, history, and downloads) button · Share Web Note button · Make a Web Note button

Browsing the Web with Microsoft Edge

One of the fastest browsers available, Edge allows you to type search text directly in the Address bar. As you view the resulting webpage, you can switch to Reading view, which is available for most news and research sites, to eliminate distracting advertisements. For example, if you are catching up on technology news online, the webpage might be difficult to read due to a busy layout cluttered with ads. Switch to Reading view to refresh the page and remove the original page formatting, ads, and menu sidebars to read the article distraction-free.

Consider the Hub in Microsoft Edge as providing one-stop access to all the things you collect on the web, such as your favorite websites, reading list, surfing history, and downloaded files.

On the Job Now

Locating Information with Cortana

Cortana, the Windows 10 virtual assistant, plays an important role in Microsoft Edge. After you turn on Cortana, it appears as an animated circle in the Address bar when you might need assistance, as shown in the restaurant website in Figure 17. When you click the Cortana icon, a pane slides in from the right of the browser window to display detailed information about the restaurant, including maps and reviews. Cortana can also assist you in defining words, finding the weather, suggesting coupons for shopping, updating stock market information, and calculating math.

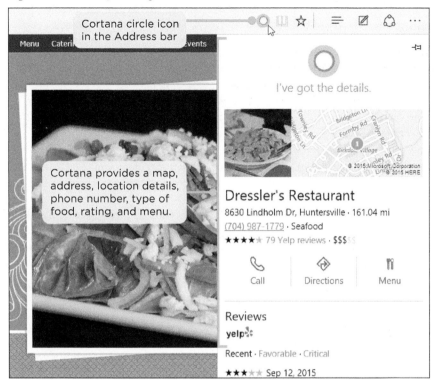

Annotating Webpages

One of the most impressive Microsoft Edge features are the **Web Note** tools, which you use to write on a webpage or to highlight text. When you click the Make a Web Note button, an **Inking** toolbar appears, as shown in **Figure 18**, that provides writing and drawing tools. These tools include an eraser, a pen, and a highlighter with different colors. You can also insert a typed note and copy a screen image (called a screen clipping). You can draw with a pointing device, fingertip, or stylus using different pen colors. Whether you add notes to a recipe, annotate sources for a research paper, or select a product while shopping online, the Web Note tools can enhance your productivity. After you complete your notes, click the Save button to save the annotations to OneNote, your Favorites list, or your Reading list. You can share the inked page with others using the Share Web Note button.

On the Job Now

To enhance security, Microsoft Edge runs in a partial sandbox, an arrangement that prevents attackers from gaining control of your computer. Browsing within the **sandbox** protects computer resources and information from hackers.

Figure 18: Web Note tools in Microsoft Edge

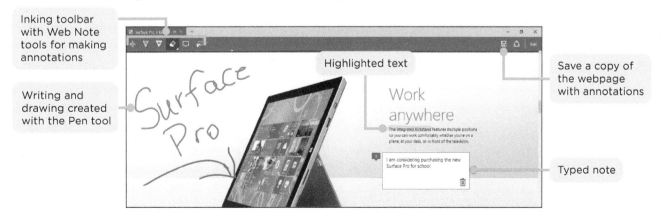

Inking toolbar with Web Note tools for making annotations

Writing and drawing created with the Pen tool

Highlighted text

Save a copy of the webpage with annotations

Typed note

Try This Now

1: Using Cortana in Microsoft Edge

Note: This activity requires using Microsoft Edge on a Windows 10 computer.

Cortana can assist you in finding information on a webpage in Microsoft Edge. Perform the following tasks:

a. Create a Word document using the Word Screen Clipping tool to capture the following screenshots.

- Screenshot A—Using Microsoft Edge, open a webpage with a technology news article. Right-click a term in the article and ask Cortana to define it.
- Screenshot B—Using Microsoft Edge, open the website of a fancy restaurant in a city near you. Make sure the Cortana circle icon is displayed in the Address bar. (If it's not displayed, find a different restaurant website.) Click the Cortana circle icon to display a pane with information about the restaurant.
- Screenshot C—Using Microsoft Edge, type **10 USD to Euros** in the Address bar without pressing the Enter key. Cortana converts the U.S. dollars to Euros.
- Screenshot D—Using Microsoft Edge, type **Apple stock** in the Address bar without pressing the Enter key. Cortana displays the current stock quote.

b. Submit your assignment in the format specified by your instructor.

2: Viewing Online News with Reading View

Note: This activity requires using Microsoft Edge on a Windows 10 computer.

Reading view in Microsoft Edge can make a webpage less cluttered with ads and other distractions. Perform the following tasks:

a. Create a Word document using the Word Screen Clipping tool to capture the following screenshots.

- Screenshot A—Using Microsoft Edge, open the website **mashable.com**. Open a technology article. Click the Reading view button to display an ad-free page that uses only basic text formatting.
- Screenshot B—Using Microsoft Edge, open the website **bbc.com**. Open any news article. Click the Reading view button to display an ad-free page that uses only basic text formatting.
- Screenshot C—Make three types of annotations (Pen, Highlighter, and Add a typed note) on the BBC article page displayed in Reading view.

b. Submit your assignment in the format specified by your instructor.

3: Inking with Microsoft Edge

Note: This activity requires using Microsoft Edge on a Windows 10 computer.

Microsoft Edge provides many annotation options to record your ideas. Perform the following tasks:

a. Open the website **wolframalpha.com** in the Microsoft Edge browser. Wolfram Alpha is a well-respected academic search engine. Type **US$100 1965 dollars in 2015** in the Wolfram Alpha search text box and press the Enter key.
b. Click the Make a Web Note button to display the Web Note tools. Using the Pen tool, draw a circle around the result on the webpage. Save the page to OneNote.
c. In the Wolfram Alpha search text box, type the name of the city closest to where you live and press the Enter key. Using the Highlighter tool, highlight at least three interesting results. Add a note and then type a sentence about what you learned about this city. Save the page to OneNote. Share your OneNote notebook with your instructor.
d. Submit your assignment link in the format specified by your instructor.

Understanding Essential Computer Concepts

CASE ▶ Computers are essential tools for all kinds of activity in virtually every type of business. In this module, you learn about computers, their components, and the software they run. You learn about input and output, how a computer processes data and stores information, how information is transmitted, and ways to secure that information.

Module Objectives

After completing this module, you will be able to:

- Recognize you live and work in the digital world
- Distinguish types of computers
- Identify computer system components
- Compare types of memory
- Summarize types of storage media
- Differentiate between input devices

- Explain output devices
- Describe data communications
- Define types of networks
- Assess security threats
- Understand system software
- Describe types of application software

Files You Will Need

No files needed.

Recognize You Live and Work in the Digital World

The Internet, computers, and mobile devices such as smartphones and tablets provide us with a world of information, literally at our fingertips. **CASE** *You'll look at some ways in which this "always-on" society is transforming your life.*

DETAILS

Over the last 25 years, the Internet has become an indispensable tool for businesses and for people's everyday needs. Just think of all the ways this time-saving technology serves us:

- Instantly communicate with friends and coworkers across town or on the other side of the planet.
- Store music and movies, and access them anywhere.
- Search and apply for jobs without leaving home.
- Quickly access information, instructions, and advice on almost anything.
- Shop for anything from clothing to food to cars to vacation deals.
- Manage your finances, deposit checks, and pay at the cash register using a mobile device.
- Get directions, view maps, and find nearby restaurants and theaters.

Here are several important ways you can use the Web to get your work done:

- **Search for information**

  Modern search engines are so powerful that you can type in anything from a person's name to a desired flight to a question like, "what time does the game start?" and see hundreds or even thousands of results. A **search engine** is an online tool that allows you to enter keywords or terms; the engine then presents a list of sites that match those terms, organized so the most relevant ones appear first. You've probably used search engines such as Google, Yahoo!, or Bing.

- **Communicate with others**

  Email, an electronic message sent from one person to another, is one of the oldest and most basic forms of Internet communication. Your company may provide email service, or you might use a service such as Microsoft's Outlook.com or Google's Gmail. You can share documents or images with coworkers and friends by sending them as attachments to email messages. FIGURE 1-1 shows an email being composed in Mail.

  Videoconferencing allows simultaneous two-way transmission of audio and video over the Internet. With a service such as Skype, users can talk to one another directly, as well as send and receive files. For example, the couple in FIGURE 1-2 is using videoconferencing to stay in touch.

QUICK TIP

Many devices come with a built-in camera and microphone for use in videoconferencing.

- **Telecommuting**

  One of the biggest changes brought about by the Internet is the ability for a company's employees to work remotely, as shown in FIGURE 1-3. If you work out of your home office your company doesn't have to spend as much money on office space—and you can get right to work instead of sitting through rush hour.

QUICK TIP

Some companies use a virtual private network (VPN) that allows users to log in from a remote location and easily access documents or communicate with coworkers.

- **Cloud computing**

  This is a friendly term for the way in which data, applications, and resources can be accessed over the Internet (in "the cloud") rather than on your individual computer. Put simply, cloud computing is Internet-based computing. The push toward the cloud has been fueled by reliable high-speed Internet connections combined with less expensive Web-based computing power and online storage. Cloud services such as Microsoft OneDrive, Apple iCloud, and Dropbox give you access to your documents from any device that has an Internet connection, including your phone.

FIGURE 1-1: Email being composed in Mail for Windows 10

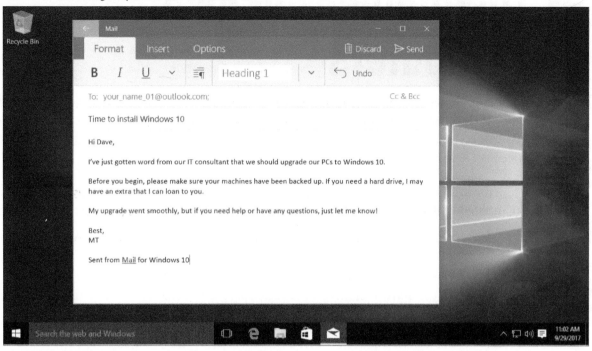

FIGURE 1-2: Couple using videoconferencing to communicate

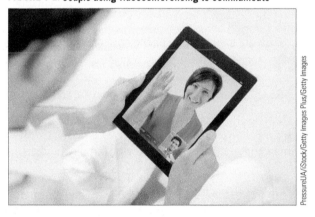

FIGURE 1-3: Employee telecommuting from home

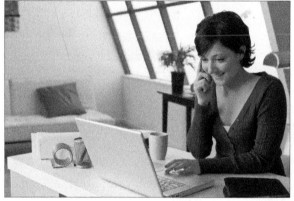

How to be a good online citizen

It's important to understand that your Internet activities can have lasting repercussions on your work and life. For instance, while social networks such as Facebook and Instagram let you hang out with your friends online, some employers are known to keep an eye on employee accounts.

Because the Web is an easy source of photos, illustrations, and text, many people assume this content is free to copy for use in their own work. However, if you plan to use an item that you didn't personally create, it's important to know that copyright laws may protect it. For help with understanding copyright issues, and for sources of "public domain" content, visit Creative Commons at creativecommons.org.

Distinguish Types of Computers

Learning Outcomes
• Define a computer
• Distinguish types of computers

A **computer** is an electronic device that accepts information and instructions from a user, manipulates the information according to the instructions, displays the information in some way, and stores the information for later retrieval. Computers are classified by their size, speed, and capabilities. **CASE** ▶ *You'll look at the most common types of computers.*

DETAILS

The following list describes various types of computers:

- **Personal computers (PCs)** are typically used by a single user at home or in the office. Personal computers are used for general computing tasks such as word processing, manipulating numbers, working with images or video, exchanging email, and accessing the Internet. The following are types of personal computers:

    - **Desktop computers** are designed to remain in one location and require a constant source of electricity. FIGURE 1-4 shows a desktop computer's monitor, CPU, keyboard, and mouse.

    - **Laptop computers** like the one shown in FIGURE 1-5 have a hinged lid that contains the computer's display and a lower portion that contains the keyboard. Laptops, also called **Notebook computers**, are powered by rechargeable batteries, and they easily slip into a bag or briefcase. (**Ultraportable computers** are smaller and generally less powerful than laptops.)

    - **Tablets** are thin computers that do not require a keyboard or a mouse. To interact with a tablet, the user touches the screen or uses a stylus (most tablets also allow you to connect an external keyboard, or other input device). Tablets are ideal for surfing the Web, checking email, delivering presentations, reading electronic books, watching video, and creating artwork. See FIGURE 1-5.

    - **Smartphones**, like the one shown in FIGURE 1-5, are used to make phone calls, maintain an address book and calendar, send email and text messages, connect to the Internet, play music, and take photos or video. They've become so powerful that for most common computing tasks some users find they don't need a traditional desktop or laptop. Like tablets, most modern smartphones are controlled by touching the screen.

    - The most personal of computers, **wearables** are devices that may be worn on a person's wrist or incorporated into clothing. Smartwatches, fitness and health monitors, and virtual reality headsets are all examples of this emerging category.

- **Mainframe computers** and **supercomputers** like the one shown in FIGURE 1-6 are used by large businesses, government agencies, and in science and education. They provide centralized storage and processing, and can manipulate tremendous amounts of data.

Touchscreens

In addition to traditional PCs, Microsoft Windows 10 was developed to work with touchscreen monitors, tablets, and smartphones. So, if you have a touchscreen device, you'll find that many tasks are easier to accomplish because they are designed for use with gestures instead of a mouse. A **gesture** is an action you take with your finger (or fingers) directly on the screen, such as tapping or swiping. For example, to switch between different apps in Windows, you can swipe in from the left edge of the touchscreen.

FIGURE 1-4: **Desktop computer**

Mmaxer/Shutterstock.com

FIGURE 1-5: **Laptop computer, smartphone, and tablet**

Laptop computer

Tablet

Smartphone

Daboost/Shutterstock.com

FIGURE 1-6: **Supercomputer**

iStockphoto.com/Senticus

Identify Computer System Components

Learning
Outcomes
• Define hardware
  and software
• Define mother-
  board and
  processor
• Define input and
  output

A **computer system** includes computer hardware and software. **Hardware** refers to the physical components of a computer. **Software** refers to the intangible components of a computer system, particularly the **programs**, or data routines, that the computer uses to perform a specific task. **CASE** ▸ *You'll look at how computers work and describe the main components of a computer system.*

DETAILS

The following list provides an overview of computer system components and how they work:

The design and construction of a computer is referred to as its **architecture** or **configuration**. The technical details about each hardware component are called **specifications**. For example, a computer system might be configured to include a printer; a specification for that printer might be a print speed of eight pages per minute or the ability to print in color.

The hardware and software of a computer system work together to process data. **Data** refers to the numbers, words, sounds, and graphics that describe people, events, things, and ideas. Modifying data is referred to as **processing**.

Processing tasks occur on the **motherboard**, the main electronic component inside the computer. See FIGURE 1-7. The motherboard is a **circuit board**, which is a rigid piece of non-conducting material with **circuits**—electrical paths—that control specific functions. Motherboards typically contain the following processing hardware:

- The **microprocessor**, also called the **processor** or the **central processing unit (CPU)**, consists of transistors and electronic circuits on a silicon chip (an integrated circuit embedded in semiconductor material). The processor is responsible for executing instructions. It is the "brain" of the computer. FIGURE 1-8 shows where the CPU sits in the flow of information through a computer.

- **Cards** are removable circuit boards that are inserted into slots in the motherboard to expand its capabilities. For example, a sound card translates digital audio information into analog sounds the human ear can hear.

A **System on a Chip (SoC)** consolidates the functions of the CPU, graphics and sound cards, memory, and more onto a single silicon chip. This miniaturization allows devices to become increasingly compact.

Input is the data or set of instructions you give to a computer. You use an **input device**, such as a keyboard or a mouse, to enter data and issue commands. **Commands** are input instructions that tell the computer how to process data. For example, if you want to enhance the color of a photo in a graphics program, you input the appropriate commands that instruct the computer to modify the data in the image.

Output is the result of the computer processing the input you provide. Output can take many different forms, including printed documents, pictures, audio, and video. Computers produce output using **output devices**, such as a monitor or printer. The output you create may be stored inside the computer itself or on an external storage device, such as a USB flash drive.

The computer itself takes care of the processing functions, but it needs additional components, called **peripheral devices**, to accomplish the input, output, and storage functions. You'll learn more about these devices later in this module.

FIGURE 1-7: Motherboard

Memory slots

CPU

Slots for graphics
and expansion cards

AndreyBrusov/Shutterstock.com

FIGURE 1-8: Flow of information through a computer system

Input → **Process** (CPU/Microprocessor) → Output

Storage

About microprocessor speeds

How fast a computer can process instructions depends partially on the speed of the microprocessor. Among other factors, the speed of the microprocessor is determined by its clock speed, word size, and whether it is single or multicore. **Clock speed** is measured in **megahertz (MHz)**, millions of cycles per second, or in **gigahertz (GHz)**, billions of cycles per second. **Word size** refers to the number of bits—the smallest unit of information in a computer—that are processed at one time; for example, a 32-bit processor processes 32 bits at a time. A computer with a large word size can process faster than a computer with a small word size. Most PCs sold today come with 64-bit processors. Finally, a **dual-core processor**, which has two processors on a single chip, can process information up to twice as fast as a **single-core processor**. Likewise, a **quad-core processor**, with four processors on a chip, processes information up to four times as fast as a single-core processor. Other multicore processors, such as hexacore and octacore, are also available.

Compare Types of Memory

One of the most important components of personal computer hardware is the **memory**, which stores instructions and data. **CASE** *You'll explore the different types of memory found in a typical computer: random access memory, cache memory, virtual memory, read-only memory, and complementary metal oxide semiconductor memory.*

DETAILS

Types of memory include the following:

QUICK TIP
When the computer
is off, RAM is empty.

Random access memory (RAM) holds information only while the computer is on. Whenever you're using a computer, the microprocessor temporarily loads the necessary programs and data into RAM so it can quickly access them. The information present in RAM can be accessed in a different sequence from which it was stored, hence its name. RAM typically consists of chips mounted on cards that are plugged into the motherboard.

- RAM is considered **volatile memory** or **temporary memory** because it's constantly changing or being refreshed. RAM is cleared when the computer is turned off.

- Most personal computers use **synchronous dynamic random access memory (SDRAM)**, which allows faster access to data by synchronizing with the clock speed of the computer's system bus.

QUICK TIP
You can often add
more RAM to a com-
puter by installing
additional memory
cards on the mother-
board. You cannot
add ROM; it is per-
manently installed
on the motherboard.

- **Memory capacity** is the amount of data the computer can handle at any given time and is usually measured in gigabytes. For example, a computer that has 4 GB of RAM has the capacity to temporarily use more than four billion bits of data at one time.

Cache memory, sometimes called **RAM cache** or **CPU cache**, is special, high-speed memory located on or near the microprocessor itself. Cache memory sits between the CPU and relatively slow RAM and stores frequently accessed and recently accessed data and commands. See FIGURE 1-9.

Virtual memory is space on the computer's storage devices (usually the hard disk drive) that simulates additional RAM. It enables programs to run as if your computer had more RAM by moving data and commands from RAM to the computer's permanent storage device and swapping in the new data and commands. Virtual memory, however, is much slower than RAM.

Read-only memory (ROM), also known as **firmware**, is a chip on the motherboard that permanently stores the **BIOS (basic input/output system)**. The BIOS is activated when you turn on the computer; it initializes the motherboard, recognizes any devices connected to the computer, and starts the boot process. The **boot process**, or **booting up**, includes loading the operating system software and preparing the computer so you can begin working.

- ROM never changes, and it remains intact when the computer is turned off; it is therefore called **nonvolatile memory** or **permanent memory**.

- Some computers allow ROM to be reprogrammed via a **firmware update**, which allows a manufacturer to fix bugs and add features.

Complementary metal oxide semiconductor (CMOS, pronounced "SEE-moss") **memory** is a chip on the motherboard that stores the date, time, and system parameters. Often referred to as **semipermanent memory**, a small rechargeable battery powers CMOS so its contents are saved when the computer is turned off.

FIGURE 1-10 shows the basic relationships between the different types of computer memory.

FIGURE 1-9: **Microprocessor with CPU cache**

Microprocessor (CPU)

Cache memory

FIGURE 1-10: **Relationships between types of computer memory**

CPU
⇕
Cache
Very Fast - Temporary
⇕
RAM
Fast - Temporary

ROM/BIOS
Fast - Permanent

Disk storage
Virtual memory
Slow - Temporary

Upgrading RAM

One of the easiest ways to make your computer run faster is to add more RAM. The more RAM a computer has, the more instructions and data can be stored there. You can often add more RAM to a computer by installing additional memory cards on the motherboard, as shown in FIGURE 1-11. Currently, you can buy 128 MB to 32 GB RAM cards, and usually, you can add more than one card. Check your computer's specifications to see what size RAM cards the slots on your motherboard will accept. Note that if your computer has a 32-bit processor, it can't use more than 4 GB of RAM, even if the computer has places to plug in more cards.

FIGURE 1-11: **Installing RAM on a motherboard**

Concepts

Summarize Types of Storage Media

Learning
Outcomes
- Define storage media
- Distinguish types of storage media

Since RAM retains data only while the power is on, your computer must have a more permanent storage option. As FIGURE 1-12 shows, a storage device receives data from RAM and places it on a storage medium, some of which are described below. The data can later be read back to RAM to use again. All data and programs are stored as files. A computer **file** is a named collection of stored data. An **executable file** is a type of computer file that contains the instructions that tell a computer how to perform a specific task; for instance, the files that are used when the computer starts are executable. Another type of computer file is a **data file**. This is the kind of file you create when you use software. For instance, a report that you write with a word-processing program is data, and it must be saved as a data file if you want to access it later. **CASE** ▶ *You'll explore some common types of storage media.*

DETAILS

The types of storage media are discussed below:

Magnetic storage devices use various patterns of magnetization to store data on a magnetized surface. The most common type of magnetic storage device is the **hard disk drive (HDD)**, also called a **hard disk** or a **hard drive**. It contains several spinning platters on which a magnetic head writes and reads data. Most personal computers come with an internal hard drive on which the operating system, programs, and files are all stored. You can also purchase external hard drives for additional storage and for backing up your computer.

QUICK TIP

Optical storage devices, such as CDs and DVDs, are much more durable than magnetic storage media.

Optical storage devices use laser technology to store data in the form of tiny pits or bumps on the reflective surface of a spinning polycarbonate disc. To access the data, a laser illuminates the data path while a read head interprets the reflection.

- Originally developed to store audio recordings, the **CD (compact disc)** was later adapted for data storage; the **CD-ROM** then became the first standard optical storage device available for personal computers. One CD can store 700 MB of data.

- A **DVD** is the same physical size as a CD, but it can store between 4.7 and 15.9 GB of data, depending on whether the data is stored on one or two sides of the disc, and how many layers of data each side contains. **Blu-ray** discs store 25 GB of data per layer. They are used for storing high-definition video.

QUICK TIP

Some companies and organizations consider flash drives to be a significant security risk, due to their small size and portability.

Flash memory (also called **solid-state storage**) is similar to ROM except that it can be written to more than once. Small **flash memory cards** are used in digital cameras, handheld computers, video game consoles, and many other devices.

- A popular type of flash memory is a **USB flash drive**, also called a **USB drive** or a **flash drive**. See FIGURE 1-13. USB drives are available in a wide range of capacities, from one to 512 GB. They are popular for use as a secondary or backup storage device.

- USB drives plug directly into the USB port of a computer where it is recognized as another disk drive. USB ports are usually found on the front, back, or side of a computer.

A **solid-state drive (SSD)** is based on flash memory, but is intended as a replacement for a traditional hard disk drive. Per gigabyte, SSDs are still more expensive than hard drives, but use less power and offer much faster data access and increased reliability.

A **solid-state hybrid drive (SSHD)** economically combines the speed of an SSD with the high capacity and lower cost of a traditional HDD.

FIGURE 1-12: **Storage devices and RAM**

A storage device receives information from RAM, writes it on the storage medium, and then reads and sends it back to RAM

Store (write to storage)

Retrieve (read from storage)

FIGURE 1-13: **USB flash drive being inserted into a laptop**

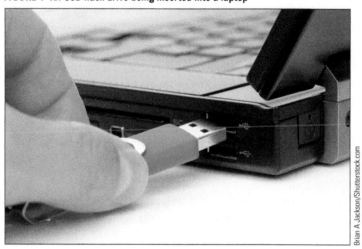

Brian A Jackson/Shutterstock.com

Storage in the Cloud

With Internet connections ever more available, Cloud storage can give you easy access to all your documents and photos from any device. Services such as Microsoft OneDrive, Apple iCloud, Dropbox, Google Drive, and Box offer both free and paid storage of your data. Typically, these services copy data stored on your computer and automatically sync it with the data on their remote servers, which are spread around the globe. For instance, when you edit a note in Microsoft OneNote on your PC, the changes are immediately sent to the version in the Cloud (via OneDrive), and then propagate to other devices such as your phone. You can also share a file or folder with colleagues so that everyone has access to the most current version, and most services offer the ability to restore a file to an earlier version. Cloud storage can also serve as an effective **off-site backup**, where your data is backed up to a remote location other than your home or office, protecting it from events like theft or fire. If you decide to use a Cloud service, remember to protect your data by creating a secure password that is difficult for others to guess.

Concepts
Module 1

Learning
Outcomes
• Define input
  device
• Identify various
  input devices

Differentiate Between Input Devices

To accomplish a task, a computer first needs to receive the data and commands you input. In a typical personal computer system, you provide this information using an **input device** such as a keyboard or a mouse. Most input devices are hardware peripherals that connect to a computer either with cables or wirelessly. Wired devices typically connect with a USB cable, or using a specialized connector. Most wireless input devices connect using radio frequency technology, while some use the same infrared technology found in a television remote control. **CASE** *You'll look at some common input devices.*

DETAILS

There are many types of input devices, as described below:

QUICK TIP

You may be able to avoid repetitive motion injuries by taking frequent breaks from computer work and by carefully stretching your hands, wrists, and arms.

The most frequently used input device is a **keyboard**, which allows you to input text and issue commands by typing. The keyboard on the right in FIGURE 1-14 is a standard keyboard, but the keyboard on the left is **ergonomic**, meaning that it has been designed to fit the natural placement of your hands and may reduce the risk of repetitive-motion injuries. Many keyboards have additional shortcut keys that are programmed to issue frequently used commands.

Another common input device is a **pointing device**, which controls the **pointer**—a small arrow or other symbol—on the screen. Pointing devices are used to select commands and manipulate text or graphics on the screen.

- The most popular pointing device for a desktop computer is a **mouse**, such as the one shown on the left in FIGURE 1-15. You control the pointer by sliding the mouse across a flat surface; this motion is tracked by either a roller ball or by infrared or laser light. A mouse usually has two or more buttons used for clicking objects on the screen. A mouse might also have a **scroll wheel** that you roll to scroll through the page or pages on your screen.

- A **trackball**, shown in the middle of FIGURE 1-15, is similar to a mouse except that it remains stationary while you control the motion of the pointer by moving a rolling ball on the top of the device.

- Laptop computers are usually equipped with a touchpad like the one shown on the right in FIGURE 1-15. A **touchpad**, also called a **trackpad**, detects the motion of your fingers. Buttons are usually located at the bottom of the touchpad, but many also allow you to click by simply tapping or pressing the pad.

QUICK TIP

Tablets and smartphones typically feature a "virtual keyboard" for inputting text.

A **touchscreen** like the one in FIGURE 1-16 accepts commands from your fingers (or a stylus), while it simultaneously displays the output. Touchscreens are found on ATMs, smartphones, and tablets. Many newer desktop and laptop computers also have hardware that supports touchscreen technology.

A **microphone** can be used to record sound or communicate with others using audio or video conferencing software. Many devices also have **voice-recognition software** that allows you to input text and commands via the microphone.

A **scanner** is a device that captures the image on a photograph or piece of paper and stores it digitally. If you scan a text document, you can use **optical character recognition** (OCR) software to translate it into text that can be edited in a word-processing program. If you scan a photo, it can be saved as an image file.

FIGURE 1-14: **Ergonomic keyboard and standard keyboard**

FIGURE 1-15: **Personal computer pointing devices: mouse, trackball, and touchpad**

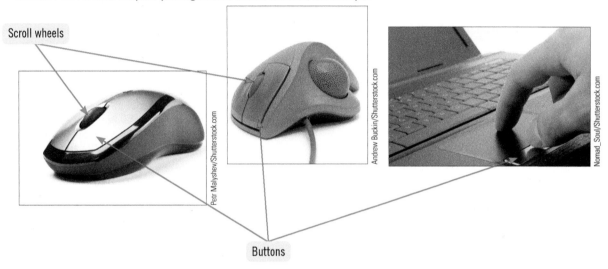

Scroll wheels

Buttons

FIGURE 1-16: **Touchscreen**

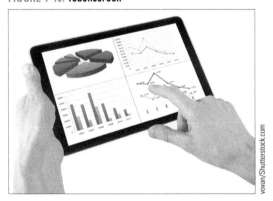

Understanding assistive devices

Advances in **computer accessibility** mean that people with physical impairments or disabilities can use computers. For example, people who cannot use their arms or hands to operate a mouse may be able to use foot, head, or eye movements to control a specialized assistive device.

Those with poor vision can use keyboards with large keys, screen enlargers that increase the size of objects on a monitor, or screen readers that speak on-screen content aloud. Experiments involving neural implants are already allowing people with disabilities to control robotic limbs.

Explain Output Devices

Learning
Outcomes
• Define output
  device
• Identify different
  output devices

An **output device** is any hardware peripheral that communicates the results of data processing. As with input devices, output devices may connect to a computer using a cable, or wirelessly via Wi-Fi or Bluetooth. **Bluetooth** is a type of wireless technology that uses short range radio waves. A Bluetooth device must first be "paired" with a computer so that it knows to trust that particular device. **CASE** ▶ *You'll explore the most commonly used output devices: monitors, printers, and speakers.*

DETAILS

Output devices are described below:

The **monitor**, sometimes called the **display** or simply the **screen**, uses video technology to display the output from a computer.

- The **flat panel monitor** shown in FIGURE 1-17 uses **LCD (liquid crystal display)** technology to create an image by modulating light within a layer of liquid crystal. LCD monitors require a backlight for illumination. Older monitors typically use a fluorescent backlight, while newer ones use **LED (light emitting diode)** technology, which is more energy efficient.

- Monitor **screen size** is the diagonal measurement from one corner of the screen to the other. In general, monitors on desktop computers range in size from 15" to 30", whereas monitors on laptop computers range in size from 10" to 20".

- A monitor's screen is divided into a matrix of small dots called **pixels. Display resolution** is the number of pixels the monitor displays in each dimension, typically expressed as width × height. Common standard resolutions range from 640 × 480 to 5120 × 2880.

- To display graphics, a computer must have a **graphics card**, also called a **video display adapter** or **video card**, or a built-in **graphics processor** (sometimes called a **built-in graphics card**). The graphics card or processor controls the signals the computer sends to the monitor.

A **printer** produces a paper copy, often called a **hard copy**, of the text and graphics processed by a computer. Print quality, or resolution, is measured by the number of **dots per inch (dpi)** that a printer can produce. The speed of a printer is determined by how many **pages per minute (ppm)** it can output.

- **LED printers** and **laser printers**, like the one shown on the left in FIGURE 1-18, are popular for business use because they produce high-quality output quickly and reliably. Each type uses its light source to temporarily transfer an image onto a rotating drum, which attracts a powdery substance called **toner**. The toner is then transferred from the drum onto paper. Laser and LED printers typically feature print resolutions of 600 to 2400 DPI and can print in black and white or color. However, they're generally better at producing sharp text and simple graphics than they are at printing clear photographs.

- **Inkjet printers**, such as the one shown on the right in FIGURE 1-18, are popular for home and small business use. These printers spray ink onto paper, producing quality comparable to that of a laser printer, though at much slower speeds. Inkjets can also print on a wide variety of paper types, though use of plain paper may result in fuzzy text. Most inkjets sold today print in color, and they excel at producing photos with smooth color, especially when using special glossy photo paper.

Speakers (and **headphones**) allow you to hear sounds generated by your computer. Speakers can be separate peripheral devices, or they can be built into the computer case or monitor. For speakers to work, a sound card must be present on the motherboard. The sound card converts the digital data in an audio file into analog sound that can be played through the speakers.

FIGURE 1-17: LCD monitor

robert_s/Shutterstock.com

FIGURE 1-18: Laser printer and inkjet printer

Maksym Dykha/Shutterstock.com

StockPhotosArt/Shutterstock.com

About 3D printers

A **3D printer** is essentially a robot that deposits multiple layers of material (typically heated plastic) onto a surface. To achieve the desired shape, the tool head may travel in a different direction as each layer is applied. A designer may use a 3D printer to create prototypes of new products, or a doctor could print prosthetic limbs. 3D "bio" printers could someday be used to create living tissue or replacement organs.

Describe Data Communications

Learning
Outcomes
• Define data com-
  munications terms
• Identify PC slots
  and ports

Data communications is the transmission of data from one computer to another or to a peripheral device. The computer that originates the message is the **sender**. The message is sent over some type of **channel**, such as a telephone or coaxial cable, or wirelessly. The computer or device at the message's destination is the **receiver**. The rules that establish an orderly transfer of data between the sender and the receiver are called **protocols**. A **device driver**, or simply **driver**, handles the transmission protocols between a computer and its peripheral devices. A driver is a computer program that can establish communication because it understands the characteristics of your computer and of the device. **CASE** ▷ *You'll look at some common ways that computers communicate.*

DETAILS

The following describes some of the ways that computers communicate:

The path along which data travels between the microprocessor, RAM, and peripherals is called the **data bus**.

QUICK TIP
An internal
peripheral device
such as a hard disk
drive or CD drive
may plug directly
into the mother-
board, or it may
have an attached
controller card.

An external peripheral device must have a corresponding **expansion port** and **cable** that connect it to the computer. Inside the computer, each port connects to a **controller card**, sometimes called an **expansion card** or **interface card**. These cards plug into connectors on the motherboard called **expansion slots** or **slots**. Personal computers can have several types of ports, including parallel, serial, USB, MIDI, Ethernet, and Thunderbolt. FIGURE 1-19 shows the ports on one desktop computer.

USB (Universal Serial Bus) is a data communications standard which has simplified and largely replaced the need for earlier interfaces such as parallel and serial ports. Many devices have a USB connector, a small rectangular plug that you insert into a USB port on a computer. Printers, keyboards, mice, cameras, smartphones, disk drives, and network adapters all commonly connect using USB. For many USB devices, power is supplied via the port, so there's no need for an extra power supply or cables.

An **Ethernet port**, which resembles a telephone jack, allows data to be transmitted at high speeds over a **local area network (LAN)**. You can use Ethernet to connect to another computer, to a LAN, or to a modem. A **modem** (short for modulator-demodulator) is a device that connects your computer to the Internet via a standard telephone jack or cable connection.

Monitors are connected to computers through HDMI, DVI, or VGA ports. Both **HDMI (high-definition multimedia interface)** and **DVI (digital video interface)** digitally transmit both video and audio. The older **VGA (video graphics array)** only allows analog transmission of video.

Understanding USB types and connectors

When you purchase USB cables, pay special attention to the type of USB your device requires. The USB specification has evolved over the years, resulting in a wide array of speeds and capabilities. USB 1.1 (introduced in 1998) supports a data rate (speed) of 12 megabits per second (Mbit/s). In 2000, USB 2.0 increased that to 480 Mbit/s. The release of USB 3.1, in 2013, further increased it to 10 gigabits per second (Gbit/s), allowing full-quality transmission of audio and video data. Also make sure you purchase the right connector for your device. Common connectors include Type A, Type B, Micro-A, Micro-B, and older Mini-A and Mini-B. There are even USB 3.0 Type-A, Type-B, and Micro-B connectors. The most recent, Type C, features a plug that can be inserted both ways.

FIGURE 1-19: Computer expansion ports

Power connection

Sound card ports

Ethernet port

1394 interface port

VGA port

Microphone port

USB ports

DVI port

Digital audio port

How computers represent and interpret data

A computer sees the world as a series of **binary digits or bits**. A bit can hold one of two numerical values: 1 for "on" or 0 for "off." You might think of bits as miniature light switches. Of course, a single bit doesn't hold much information, so eight of them are combined to form a **byte**, which can be used to represent 256 values. Integer value 1 equals 00000001 (only 1 bit is "flipped" on), while the byte that represents 255 is 11111111 (all the bits are flipped on). A kilobyte (KB or **K**) is 1024 bytes, or about a thousand bytes. A **megabyte (MB)** is 1,048,576 bytes (about a million bytes). A **gigabyte (GB)** is about a billion bytes, and a **terabyte (TB)** is about a trillion bytes.

Define Types of Networks

Learning
Outcomes
• Define networking
terms
• Identify network
types

A **network** connects one computer to other computers and peripheral devices, enabling you to share data and resources with others. There is a wide a variety of network types; however, any type of network has some basic characteristics and requirements that you should know. **CASE** *You'll look at the components that make up some different types of networks.*

DETAILS

Components of networks and the types of networks are described below:

To connect with a network via Ethernet, a computer must have a **network interface card (NIC)** which creates a communications channel between the computer and the network. Many desktop PCs and laptops come with a NIC built-in, and an Ethernet cable is used to make the connection to a router or modem. A **router** is a device that controls traffic between network components.

Network software is also essential, establishing the communications protocols that will be observed on the network and controlling the data "traffic flow."

Some networks have one or more computers, called **servers**, that act as the central storage location for programs and provide mass storage for most of the data used on the network. A network with a server and computers dependent on the server is called a **client/server network**. The dependent computers are the clients.

When a network does not have a server, all the computers are essentially equal, with programs and data distributed among them. This is called a **peer-to-peer network**.

A personal computer that is not connected to a network is called a **stand-alone computer**. When it is connected to the network, it becomes a **workstation**. Any device connected to the network, from computers to printers to routers, is called a **node**. FIGURE 1-20 illustrates a typical network configuration.

In a **local area network (LAN)**, the nodes are located relatively close to one another, usually in the same building.

A **wide area network (WAN)** is more than one LAN connected together. The **Internet** is the largest example of a WAN.

In a **wireless local area network (WLAN)**, devices communicate using radio waves instead of wires. **Wi-Fi** (short for **wireless fidelity**) is the term created by the nonprofit Wi-Fi Alliance to describe networks connected using a standard radio frequency established by the Institute of Electrical and Electronics Engineers (IEEE). Most Wi-Fi routers can transmit over distances of up to about 200 feet; a technique called **bridging** can be used to increase this range by using multiple routers.

A **personal area network (PAN)** allows two or more devices located close to each other to communicate directly via cables or wirelessly. A PAN can also be used to share one device's Internet connection with another.

Infrared technology uses infrared light waves to "beam" data from one device to another. The devices must be compatible, and they must have their infrared ports pointed at each other to communicate. This is also the technology used in TV remote controls.

Bluetooth uses short range radio waves (up to about 30 feet) to connect devices wirelessly to one another or to the Internet. Bluetooth is often used to connect wireless headsets to cell phones or computers, and for connecting some wireless pointing devices and keyboards.

FIGURE 1-20: **Typical network configuration**

Understanding telecommunications

Telecommunications means communicating over a relatively long distance using a phone line or other data conduit. To make this connection, you must use a modem, a device that converts the digital signals that your computer understands into analog signals that can travel over ordinary phone lines or cable lines. Though less common today, some PCs still come with a built-in 56K modem that can send and receive about 56,000 **bits per second (bps)** over a phone line. This is slow, so many people opt for a high-speed connection using **DSL (digital subscriber line)**, which also operates over a phone line, or using a cable connection. If you go this route, you may need to purchase or rent an external DSL or cable modem. DSL and cable modems typically connect to a computer's **NIC (network interface card)** via an Ethernet cable or using Wi-Fi. High-speed connections are often called **broadband connections**.

Assess Security Threats

Learning
Outcomes
• Define types of
security threats
• Establish impor-
tance of good
security

Once a computer is connected to a network, it is essential that it be protected against the threat of someone stealing information or causing malicious damage. **Security** refers to the steps a computer user takes to prevent unauthorized use of or damage to a computer. **CASE** ▶ *You'll look at how important it is to be vigilant about keeping your computers secure and you'll review ways to do this.*

DETAILS

QUICK TIP
Some specific types
of viruses are called
worms; another type
is a Trojan horse.
Antivirus software
usually protects
against both types.

Malware is a broad term that describes any program designed to cause harm or transmit information without the permission of the computer owner.

Unscrupulous programmers deliberately construct harmful, self-replicating programs called **viruses** which instruct your computer to perform destructive activities, such as corrupting or erasing data. Some viruses may spread themselves by hijacking your email program and emailing your friends and coworkers. **Antivirus software**, sometimes called **virus protection software**, searches executable files for sequences of characters that may cause harm, and then disinfects files by erasing or disabling those commands. FIGURE 1-21 shows the dialog box that appears when Windows Defender is scanning a computer for potential threats.

QUICK TIP
Adware is software
installed with
another program,
often with the user's
permission, that
generates advertising
revenue for the
program's creator by
displaying ads.

Spyware is software that secretly gathers information from your computer and then sends this data to the company or person that created it. Spyware may be installed by a virus, though it may also be installed along with other software without the user's permission or knowledge. **Anti-spyware software** can detect these programs and delete them.

A **firewall** is like a locked door on your computer or network. It prevents other computers on the Internet from accessing your computer and prevents access to the Internet without your permission.

- A hardware firewall provides strong protection against incoming threats. Many routers come with built-in firewalls.

- Software firewalls, installed directly on your computer, track all incoming and outgoing traffic. If a program that never previously accessed the Internet attempts to do so, the user is notified and can choose to forbid access. There are several free software firewall packages available, including Microsoft Firewall.

Criminals are relentlessly searching for new and aggressive ways of accessing computer users' personal information and passwords.

- A **spoofed** site is a website that's been set up to look exactly like another website, with the intention of convincing customers to enter their personal information. For example, a criminal site developer might create a **URL** (address on the Web) that looks similar to the URL of a legitimate site such as a bank's. If a customer isn't paying attention, he or she may inadvertently enter information such as credit card numbers, Social Security numbers, or passwords. Once a thief has this information, it can be used to steal the customer's money or identity. FIGURE 1-22 shows the alert displayed in the Microsoft Edge browser when a known spoofed site is visited.

QUICK TIP
If you suspect you've
received a phishing
message, don't click
any links in the email.
Instead, open your
browser and type the
correct URL into the
address bar.

- **Phishing** refers to the practice of sending email to customers or potential customers of a legitimate website encouraging them to click a link in the email. When clicked, the user's **browser** (the software program used to access websites) displays a spoofed site where the user is asked to provide personal information.

- A **DNS server** is one of the many computers distributed around the world that's responsible for directing Internet traffic. Using a practice called **pharming**, a criminal can sometimes break into a DNS server and redirect any attempts to access a particular website to the criminal's spoofed site.

FIGURE 1-21: Windows Defender scan in progress

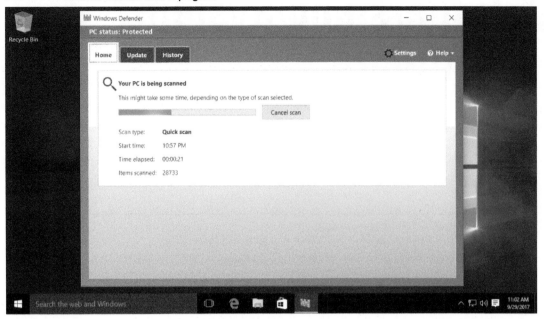

FIGURE 1-22: Microsoft Edge browser when visiting a known spoofed site

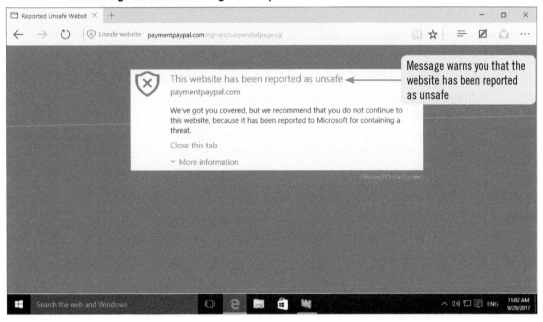

Message warns you that the website has been reported as unsafe

Understanding two-factor authentication

You've probably gotten used to logging in to a website by entering a username and password; this is called **single-factor authentication** because you're entering a single credential, your password. **Two-factor authentication (2FA)** adds another step to the process by requiring an additional credential. For example, when you log in to your bank's website, it may send a text message to your mobile phone that consists of a randomly-generated code.

The code is unique to you and to this moment in time. You then enter the code along with your username and password to gain access to the site. 2FA is considered more secure because it's likely that you're the only person in possession of your phone. Biometric devices, such as the fingerprint ID sensors on some smartphones, can also function as a second level of authentication.

Understand System Software

Learning
Outcomes
• Define system
  software
• Identify types of
  system software

The term *software* often refers to a single program, but it can also refer to a collection of programs and data that are packaged together. **System software** allocates system resources, manages storage space, maintains security, and detects equipment failure. It provides the basic platform for running specialized application software, which you'll learn about in the next lesson. **CASE** ▶ *You'll look at the components of system software and how they help the computer perform its basic operating tasks.*

DETAILS

The components of system software are described below:

System software (see FIGURE 1-23) manages the fundamental operations of your computer, such as loading programs and data into memory, executing programs, saving data to storage devices, displaying information on the monitor, and transmitting data through a port to a peripheral device. There are four basic types of system software: operating systems, utility software, device drivers, and programming languages.

QUICK TIP

As part of its security
responsibilities, your
computer's operating
system may require
you to enter a user-
name and password,
or it may scan the
computer to protect
against viruses.

- The **operating system** manages the system resources of a computer so programs run properly. A **system resource** is any part of the computer system, including memory, storage devices, and the microprocessor. The operating system controls basic data **input and output**, or **I/O**, which is the flow of data from the microprocessor to memory to peripherals and back again.

- The operating system also manages the files on your storage devices. It opens and saves files, tracks every part of every file, and lets you know if any part of a file is missing.

- The operating system is always on the lookout for equipment failure. Each electronic circuit is checked periodically, and the user is notified whenever a problem is detected.

- Microsoft Windows, used on many personal computers, and OS X, used exclusively on Apple's Macintosh computers, are referred to as **operating environments** because they provide a **graphical user interface** (**GUI**, pronounced "goo-ey") that acts as a liaison between the user and all of the computer's hardware and software. FIGURE 1-24 shows the Start menu on a computer using Microsoft Windows 10.

Utility software helps analyze, optimize, configure, and maintain a computer. Examples of utilities include anti-virus software, backup tools, and disk tools that allow you to analyze a hard drive or compress data to save space.

As you learned in the discussion of hardware ports, device drivers handle the transmission protocol between a computer and its peripherals. When you add a new device to a computer, the installation process typically involves loading a driver that updates the computer's configuration.

While most of us have no contact with them, it's important to know that computer **programming languages** allow a programmer to write instructions, or code, that a computer can understand. Programmers typically write software in a particular language and then compile the code to create a program that the computer then executes. Popular programming languages include C, C++, Objective-C, Swift, Java, Ruby, and Python.

Protecting information with passwords

You can protect data on your computer by using passwords. You can set up multiple user accounts on your computer and require that users sign in with a username and password before they can use it. This is known as **logging in** or **logging on**. You can also protect individual files on your computer so anyone who tries to access a file must type a password. Many websites, especially e-commerce and banking sites, require a username and password to access the information stored there. To prevent anyone from guessing your passwords, always create and use strong passwords. A **strong password** consists of at least eight characters of upper- and lowercase letters and numbers. Avoid using easy to obtain personal information in your passwords, such as birthdays and addresses, and always create different passwords that are unique to each website you use.

FIGURE 1-23: Relationships between system software and other system components

FIGURE 1-24: Windows 10 desktop with Start menu open

Examining Windows 10 hardware requirements

Windows 10, the newest version of the Windows operating system, requires a computer with at least a 1 GHz processor, 1 GB of RAM for the 32-bit version or 2 GB of RAM for the 64-bit version, a DirectX 9 graphics processor, and 16 GB of hard disk space for the 32-bit version or 20 GB for the 64-bit version. Keep in mind that these are the minimum recommendations. To prevent your computer from slowing to a crawl, you should consider upgrading the amount of RAM and the processor speed.

Learning
Outcomes
• Define application
  software
• Identify types of
  application
  software

Describe Types of Application Software

Application software enables you to perform specific tasks such as writing letters, creating presentations, analyzing statistics, creating graphics, enhancing photos, and much more. **CASE** ▶ *You'll look at some of the most common application software.*

DETAILS

Typical application software includes the following:

Document production software, which includes word-processing software (such as Microsoft Word) and desktop publishing software (Microsoft Publisher), allows you to write and format text documents. As shown in FIGURE 1-25, these tools offer automatic spell checking. You can also customize the look of a document by changing its **font** (the design of the typeface in which text is set) or by adding color and images.

QUICK TIP

In Excel, a workbook is a file made up of multiple worksheets. The terms spreadsheet and worksheet are often used interchangeably.

Spreadsheet software is a numerical analysis tool that displays data in a grid of **cells** arranged in columns and rows. This grid is called a **worksheet**. You can type data into the worksheet's cells, and then enter mathematical formulas that reference that data. FIGURE 1-26 shows a typical worksheet in Microsoft Excel that includes a simple calculation along with a graph that represents the data in the spreadsheet.

Database management software, such as Microsoft Access, lets you collect and manage data. A **database** is a collection of information organized in a uniform format of fields and records. A **field** contains one piece of information, such as a person's first name. A **record** contains multiple fields and can therefore store a person's full name and address. The online catalog of books at a library is a database that contains one record for each book; each record contains fields that identify the title, the author, and the subjects under which the book is classified.

Presentation software allows you to create a visual slide show to accompany a lecture, demonstration, or training session. In Microsoft PowerPoint, each presentation slide can contain text, illustrations, diagrams, charts, audio, and video. Slide shows can be projected in front of an audience, delivered over the Web, or transmitted to remote computers.

Multimedia authoring software allows you to record and manipulate image files, audio files, and video files. **Graphics software**, such as Microsoft Paint, lets you create illustrations, diagrams, graphs, and charts. **Photo-editing software** allows you to manipulate digital photos; you can make images brighter, add special effects, or crop photos to include only important parts of the image. Examples include Microsoft Photos and Adobe Photoshop. **Video-editing software**, such as Windows Movie Maker or Adobe Premiere, allows you to edit video by clipping it, adding captions and a soundtrack, or rearranging clips.

Information and task management software helps you schedule appointments, manage your address book, and manage projects. Microsoft Outlook is email software that also helps you maintain a contact list and calendar, and allows you to synchronize information between a smartphone and your computer. Microsoft OneNote lets you capture ideas, create To Do lists, and share notes with others.

Website creation and management software allows you to build websites and mobile apps using technologies that include **HTML (Hypertext Markup Language)** and **CSS (Cascading Style Sheets)**, the primary languages of Web design. Adobe Dreamweaver allows you to see how the site will appear as you create it.

FIGURE 1-25: Automatic spell checking in Microsoft Word

FIGURE 1-26: Editing a worksheet in Microsoft Excel

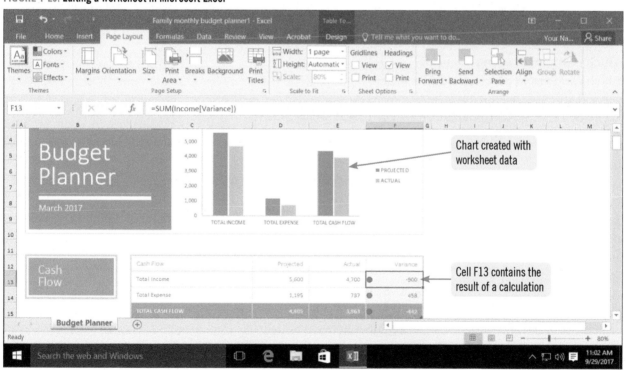

Understanding Essential Computer Concepts

Concepts 25

Practice

Concepts Review

Answer the following questions based on the elements labeled in FIGURE 1-27.

FIGURE 1-27

Oleksiy Mark/Shutterstock.com

1. Which component is used to enter text?
2. Which component is used to point to items on the screen?
3. Which component displays output?
4. Which component processes data?

Match each term with the statement that best describes it.

5. Spyware
6. Commands
7. Expansion slot
8. RAM
9. Hard disk
10. Virtual memory
11. Server
12. Operating system
13. SSD
14. Database

a. computer on a network that acts as the central storage location for programs and data used on the network
b. Based on flash memory and intended as a replacement for a traditional hard disk drive
c. Location on the motherboard into which a controller card for a peripheral device is inserted
d. Secretly gathers information from a computer and sends it without the user's permission
e. Space on the computer's storage devices that simulates additional RAM
f. Software that allocates resources, manages storage space, maintains security, and controls I/O
g. Magnetic storage media that is usually sealed in a case inside the computer
h. A collection of information stored on one or more computers organized in a uniform format of records and fields
i. Temporarily holds data and programs while the computer is on
j. Input instructions that tell the computer how to process data

Select the best answer from the list of choices.

15. Which of the following is considered volatile or temporary memory?
    a. RAM
    b. SSD
    c. HDD
    d. ROM

16. To display graphics, a computer needs a monitor and a:
    a. Network card (NIC).
    b. Sound card.
    c. Graphics card or graphics processor.
    d. USB cable.

17. What part of the computer is responsible for executing instructions to process information?
    a. ROM
    b. Card
    c. Motherboard
    d. CPU

18. What are the technical details about each hardware component called?
    a. Configuration
    b. Specifications
    c. Circuits
    d. Architecture

19. What do you call each 1 or 0 used in the representation of computer data?
    a. A bit
    b. A quark
    c. A kilobyte
    d. A byte

20. Which of the following is a pointing device that allows you to control the pointer by moving the entire device around on a desk?
    a. Scroll wheel
    b. Trackpad
    c. Mouse
    d. Trackball

21. The programs and data routines that a computer uses to perform tasks are called:
    a. Specifications.
    b. Peripherals.
    c. Hardware.
    d. Software.

22. What is a megabyte?
    a. About a million bytes
    b. About a million bits
    c. About half of a gigabyte
    d. 100 kilobytes

23. Keyboards, monitors, and printers are all examples of which of the following?
    a. Peripheral devices
    b. Input devices
    c. Output devices
    d. Data communications

24. Which of the following permanently stores the set of instructions that the computer uses to activate the software that controls the processing function when you turn the computer on?
    a. CPU cache
    b. RAM
    c. The hard disk
    d. ROM

25. Which of the following acts as a locked door on a computer?
    a. DNS server
    b. Firewall
    c. Antivirus software
    d. Browser

26. Which one of the following would not be considered a personal computer?
    a. Mainframe
    b. Desktop
    c. Laptop
    d. Tablet

27. Which of the following is not a permanent storage medium?
    a. DVD
    b. CD-ROM
    c. Hard disk
    d. RAM

28. Which of the following is the data path between the microprocessor, RAM, and the peripherals?
    a. Data channel
    b. Motherboard
    c. Data bus
    d. Cable

29. **The transmission protocol between a computer and a peripheral device is handled by a:**
   a. Data bus
   c. Controller card
   b. Channel
   d. Driver

30. **The computer that originates a message to send to another computer is called the:**
   a. Sender
   c. Firewall
   b. Receiver
   d. Server

31. **Any device connected to a network is called a:**
   a. Node
   c. Workstation
   b. Router
   d. Modem

32. **Which of the following is space on the computer's storage devices that simulates additional RAM?**
   a. Solid-state memory
   c. Volatile memory
   b. Cache memory
   d. Virtual memory

33. **A _____ consists of connected computers and peripheral devices that are located relatively close to each other.**
   a. WLAN
   c. LAN
   b. WAN
   d. PAN

34. **When data, applications, and resources are stored on servers rather than on users' computers, it is referred to as:**
   a. Shared computing
   c. Leased computing
   b. Cloud computing
   d. Cluster computing

35. **A website that's been set up to look exactly like another website, with the intention of convincing customers to enter their personal information, is a _____ site.**
   a. Phished
   c. Spoofed
   b. Malware
   d. Pharmed

Independent Challenge 1

To run the newest software, many people need to upgrade their existing computer system or purchase a brand new one. But what do you do with your old computer if you buy a new one? Most municipalities have enacted laws regulating the disposal of electronics. Research these laws in your city and state, and write a brief report describing them.
Note: To complete the Independent Challenge, your computer must be connected to the Internet.

   a. Start your browser, go to your favorite search engine, and then search for information about laws regarding the disposal of electronics in your city and state. Try searching your city's official Web site for the information, or use **electronics disposal laws** followed by your city name as a search term and then repeat that search using your state's name.
   b. Open each website that you find in a separate browser tab or window.
   c. Read the information on each website. Can some components be thrown away? Are there laws that apply only to display monitors? Are the laws different for individuals and businesses? Does the size of the business matter? Are manufacturers or resellers required to accept used components they manufactured or sold?
   d. Search for organizations you can donate your computer to. How do these organizations promise to protect your privacy? Can you take a deduction on your federal income tax for your donation?
   e. Write a short report describing your findings. Include the URLs for all relevant websites. (*Hint:* If you are using a word processor to write your report, you can copy the URLs from your browser and paste them into the document. Drag to select the entire URL in the Address or Location bar in your browser. Right-click the selected text, then click Copy on the shortcut menu. Position the insertion point in the document where you want the URL to appear, then press [Ctrl][V] to paste it.)

Independent Challenge 2

New instances of malware and hacks are reported on an almost daily basis. If you surf the Internet or exchange e-mail, it's important to use antivirus software and to keep it updated. Research the most current malware threats, and create a table that lists them along with details about each threat. *Note: To complete the Independent Challenge, your computer must be connected to the Internet.*

a. Start your browser, go to **www.microsoft.com**, then in the Search text box, type "Malware Protection Center" and press Enter. In the list of search results, select "Microsoft Malware Protection Center Home Page" and then read about the MMPC and its mission.

b. Click the Malware encyclopedia menu, click the "Top threats" link, and then read about some prevalent threats, including the Summary and Technical information provided for each threat.

c. Open a new word-processing document, and create a table that lists five different threats (may include ransomware, families, rogues, exploits, etc.). Include a description of what each threat does, and how damaging it is considered to be (the alert level). Also note any steps you can take to prevent the threat, along with ways to recover an infected computer.

d. Use your search engine to find three different antivirus programs that can be installed on your computer. In your word-processing document, create a new section that lists the programs you found. Include the benefits and costs of using each program.

Independent Challenge 3

You've decided to buy a new desktop or laptop computer to run Windows 10 and Microsoft Office. *Note: To complete the Independent Challenge, your computer must be connected to the Internet.*

a. To help you organize your search, create the table shown below.

	Your Requirements	Computer Retailer 1	Computer Retailer 2	Computer Retailer 3
Windows 10 (Edition)				
Office 2016 (Edition)				
Brand of computer				
Model number				
Processor speed				
RAM (amount)				
Video RAM/Graphics specifications				
Hard disk/SSD (capacity and speed)				
Display (type and size)				
Printer (type and speed)				
Antivirus software				
Firewall (software or router with built-in firewall)				
System price				
Additional costs				
Total price				

b. Decide which edition of Windows 10 you want, and enter it in the Your Requirements column of the table. To read a description of the available editions, go to **www.microsoft.com** and search the site for information about the different editions (Windows 10 Home or Pro).

c. Research the hardware requirements for running the edition of Windows 10 you selected. Search the Microsoft Web site again for features that may require specific hardware (such as a fingerprint reader).

d. Decide which edition of Office you want, and enter it in the first column of the table. Search the Microsoft Web site to find a description of the software titles included with each edition of Office, and then search for the hardware requirements for running the edition of Office that you chose. If necessary, change the hardware requirements in the table.

Independent Challenge 3 (continued)

e. Research the cost of your new computer. To begin, visit local stores, look at advertisements, or search the Web for computer retailers. Most retailers sell complete systems that come with all the necessary hardware, an operating system, and additional software already installed. In the Computer Retailer 1 column of the table, fill in the specifications for the system you chose. If any item listed as a minimum requirement is not included with the system you chose, determine the cost of adding that item and enter the price in the table. Repeat this process with systems from two other retailers, entering the specifications in the Computer Retailer 2 and Computer Retailer 3 columns.

f. If the system you chose does not come with a printer, search the Web for a color inkjet printer.

g. Research the capabilities of the antivirus software that comes with Windows 10. If the system you chose does not come with additional antivirus software, search the Web for the cost, if any, of an antivirus software package. Make sure you look up reviews of the package you choose. Decide whether to purchase this software or use a free one, and enter this cost in the table.

h. Decide whether you need a separate router with a built-in firewall, or if you can use your computer's firewall. Search the Web for the price of routers with firewalls. Enter this information in the table.

i. Determine the total cost for each of the three systems in your table. If the costs exceed your budget, think about items you can downgrade. Can you get a less expensive printer or share someone else's printer? Would a less expensive display still provide the room you need to work? On the other hand, if the total costs come in under your budget, you may be able to upgrade your system; perhaps you can afford a larger display with better resolution or a better mouse or keyboard.

Independent Challenge 4: Explore

As you have learned, Cloud storage allows you to store documents and images on remote servers. You then have access to these items from any compatible device that is connected to the Internet. You need to decide which cloud service is best for you. *Note: To complete this Independent Challenge, your computer must be connected to the Internet.*

a. Use your favorite search engine to locate the sites for Microsoft OneDrive, Apple iCloud, Google Drive, and Dropbox. If there is another service you'd like to investigate, include it as well (e.g., Amazon Cloud Drive).

b. To help you compare the different services, create the table shown below.

	OneDrive	iCloud	Google Drive	Dropbox
Free storage capacity				
Paid storage capacity				
Paid storage cost				
Maximum file size				
Syncs to all your devices? (PC/Mac, mobile)				
Supports version tracking?				
Mobile apps provided*				
Additional features/notes				

*List all known mobile operating systems for which the service provides an app, such as Android, iOS, or Windows Phone.

c. Enter details in the table using the information available on each service's website.

d. Search for online reviews and comparisons of each cloud service, and note any additional information that you feel is important. For example, if you have a large music collection on your computer, is it compatible with each service?

e. Based on your research, explain which service would best serve your needs and why.

Getting Started with Windows 10

You are about to start a new job, and your employer has asked you to get familiar with Windows 10 to help boost your productivity. You'll need to start Windows 10 and Windows apps, work with on-screen windows and commands, get help, and exit Windows. *Note: With the release of Windows 10, Microsoft now provides ongoing updates to Windows instead of releasing new versions periodically. This means that Windows features might change over time, including how they look and how you interact with them. The information provided in this text was accurate at the time this book was published.*

Module Objectives

After completing this module, you will be able to:

- Start Windows 10
- Navigate the desktop and Start menu
- Point, click, and drag
- Start an app
- Work with a window

- Manage multiple windows
- Use buttons, menus, and dialog boxes
- Get help
- Exit Windows 10

Files You Will Need

No files needed.

Start Windows 10

Learning
Outcomes
• Power on a
  computer
• Log into
  Windows 10

Windows 10 is an **operating system**, a type of program that runs your computer and lets you interact with it. A **program** is a set of instructions written for a computer. If your computer did not have an operating system, you wouldn't see anything on the screen after you turned it on. Windows 10 reserves a special area called a **Microsoft account** where each user can keep his or her files. In addition, a Microsoft account lets you use various devices and services such as a Windows Phone or Outlook.com. You may have more than one Microsoft account. When the computer and Windows 10 start, you need to **sign in**, or select your Microsoft account name and enter a password, also called **logging in**. If your computer has only one Microsoft account, you won't need to select an account name. But all users need to enter a **password**, a special sequence of numbers and letters. Users cannot see each other's account areas or services without the other person's password, so passwords help keep your computer information secure. After you sign in, you see the Windows 10 desktop, which you learn about in the next lesson. **CASE** ▶ *You're about to start a new job, so you decide to learn more about Windows 10, the operating system used at your new company.*

STEPS

1. **Press your computer's** power button, **which might look like** 🔵 **or** ⬛ , **then if the monitor is not turned on, press its** power button

   On a desktop computer, the power button is probably on the front panel. On a laptop computer it's likely at the top of the keys on your keyboard. After a few moments, a **lock screen**, showing the date, time, and an image, appears. See FIGURE 1-1. The lock screen appears when you first start your computer and also if you leave it unattended for a period of time.

2. **Press [Spacebar], or click once to display the sign-in screen**

   The **sign-in screen** shows your Windows account picture, name, and e-mail address, as well as a space to enter your Microsoft account password. The account may have your name assigned to it, or it might have a general name like "Student" or "Lab User."

3. **Type your** password, **as shown in** FIGURE 1-2, **using uppercase and lowercase letters as necessary**

   If necessary, ask your instructor or technical support person what password you should use. Passwords are **case sensitive**, which means that if you type any letter using capital letters when lowercase letters are needed, or vice versa, Windows will not let you use your account. For example, if your password is "booklet43+", typing "Booklet43+" or "BOOKLET43+" will not let you enter your account. For security, Windows substitutes bullets for the password characters you type.

4. **Click or tap the** Submit button →

   The Windows 10 desktop appears. See FIGURE 1-3.

Using a touch screen with Windows

Windows 10 was developed to work with touch-screen computers, including tablets and smartphones. See FIGURE 1-4. So if you have a touch-screen device, you'll find that you can accomplish many tasks with gestures instead of a mouse. A **gesture** is an action you take with your fingertip directly on the screen, such as tapping or swiping. For example, when you sign into Windows 10, you can tap the Submit button on the screen, instead of clicking it.

FIGURE 1-4: **Touch-screen device**

© vovan/Shutterstock.com

FIGURE 1-1: Lock screen with time and date

Your lock screen contents may differ →

10:49
Friday, July 31

FIGURE 1-2: Typing your password

Your_Name@outlook.com
Your_Name@outlook.com

Your_Name@outlook.com
Your_Name@outlook.com

FIGURE 1-3: Windows 10 desktop

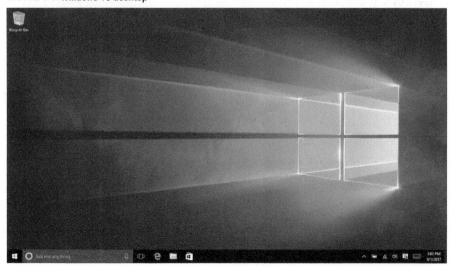

Navigate the Desktop and Start Menu

Learning
Outcomes
• Examine the
desktop
• Open the Start
menu
• View Start menu
apps
• Close the Start
menu

Every time you start your computer and sign in, the Windows 10 desktop appears. The **Windows 10 desktop** is an electronic work area that lets you organize and manage your information, much like your own physical desktop. The desktop contains controls that let you interact with the Windows 10 operating system. These controls are called its **user interface (UI)**. The Windows 10 user interface is called the **Windows 10 UI.** **CASE** ▶ *To become better acquainted with Windows 10, you decide to explore the desktop and Start menu.*

STEPS

1. **Examine the Windows 10 desktop**

   As shown in FIGURE 1-5, the desktop currently contains one item, an icon representing the **Recycle Bin**, an electronic wastepaper basket. You might see other icons, files, and folders placed there by previous users or by your school lab. The desktop lets you manage the files and folders on your computer. A **file** is a collection of stored information, such as a letter, video, or program. A **folder** is a container that helps you organize your files. A file, folder, or program opens in a window. You can open multiple windows on the desktop at once, and you can move them around so you can easily go back and forth between them. You work with windows later in this module. At the bottom of the screen is a bar called the **taskbar**, with buttons representing commonly used programs and tools. In a default Windows installation, the taskbar contains four buttons, described in TABLE 1-1. Also on the taskbar is the search box, which you can use to find an item on your computer or the Internet. On the right side of the status bar you see the **Notification area**, containing the time and date as well as icons that tell you the status of your computer. At the left side of the taskbar, you see the Start button. You click the **Start button** to display the **Start menu**, which lets you start the programs on your computer.

2. **Move the pointer to the left side of the taskbar, then click or tap the** Start button ⊞

   The Start menu appears, as shown in FIGURE 1-6. Your user account name and an optional picture appear at the top. The menu shows a list of often-used programs and other controls on the left, and variously-sized shaded rectangles called **tiles** on the right. Each tile represents an **app**, short for **application program**. Some tiles show updated content using a feature called **live tile**; for example, the Weather app can show the current weather for any city you choose. (Your screen color and tiles may differ from the figures shown here. Note that the screens in this book do not show live tiles.)

3. **Move the pointer near the bottom of the Start menu, then click or tap the** All apps button

   You see an alphabetical listing of all the apps on your computer. Only some of the apps are visible.

4. **Move the pointer into the list, until the gray scroll bar appears on the right side of the list, place the pointer over the** scroll box, **press and hold down the** mouse button, **then drag to display the remaining programs; on a touch screen, swipe the list to scroll**

5. **Click or tap the** Back button **at the bottom of the Start menu**

   The previous listing reappears.

6. **Move the pointer back up over the desktop, then click or tap once to close the Start menu**

FIGURE 1-5: Windows 10 desktop

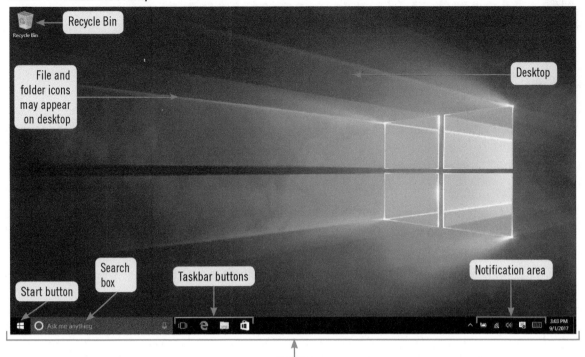

Recycle Bin

File and folder icons may appear on desktop

Desktop

Search box

Taskbar buttons

Notification area

Start button

Taskbar

FIGURE 1-6: Start menu

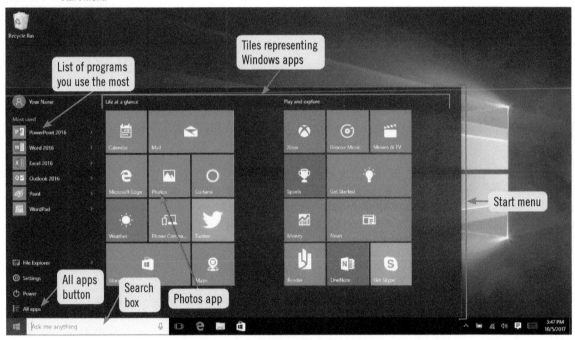

Tiles representing Windows apps

List of programs you use the most

Start menu

All apps button

Search box

Photos app

TABLE 1-1: Windows taskbar buttons

button	looks like	what it does
Task View		Shows miniatures of all open windows and lets you create multiple desktops, so you can switch from one to another
Microsoft Edge		Opens the Microsoft Edge web browser
File Explorer		Lets you explore the files in your storage locations
Store		Opens the Windows Store featuring downloadable apps, games, music, movies, and TV

Point, Click, and Drag

Learning
Outcomes
• Point to, select,
and deselect a
desktop icon
• Move a desktop
icon

You communicate with Windows 10 using a variety of pointing devices (or, with a touch-screen device, your finger). A **pointing device** controls the movement of the **pointer**, a small arrow or other symbol that moves on the screen. Your pointing device could be a mouse, trackball, graphics tablet, or touchpad. There are five basic **pointing device actions** you use to communicate with your computer; see TABLE 1-2. Touch-screen users can tap, press, and tap and hold. **CASE** *You practice the basic pointing device actions.*

STEPS

QUICK TIP
A pointing device
might be attached to
your computer with
a cable, connected
wirelessly, or built
into your computer.

1. **Locate the pointer � on the desktop, then move your pointing device left, right, up, and down (or move your finger across a touch pad or screen)**
   The pointer shape � is the **Select pointer**. The pointer moves in the same direction as your device.

2. **Move your pointing device so the Select pointer is over the Recycle Bin (if you are using a touch screen, skip this step)**
   You are **pointing to** the Recycle Bin icon. The icon becomes **highlighted**, looking as though it is framed in a box with a lighter color background. (Note that touch-screen users cannot point to items.)

QUICK TIP
If you are using a
pointing device, the
pointer's shape
changes depending
on both where you
point and the
options available to
you when you point.

3. **While pointing to the Recycle Bin icon, press and quickly release the left mouse button once (or tap the icon once), then move the pointer away from the Recycle Bin icon**
   You click or tap a desktop icon once to **select** it, which signals that you intend to perform an action. When an icon is selected, its background changes color and maintains the new color even when you point away from it.

4. **With a pointing device, point to (don't click) the Microsoft Edge button 🗨 on the taskbar**
   The button becomes highlighted and an informational message called a **ScreenTip** identifies the program the button represents. ScreenTips are useful because they help you to learn about the tools available to you. **Microsoft Edge** is the new Microsoft web browser that lets you display and interact with webpages.

5. **If you are using a pointing device, move the pointer over the time and date in the notification area on the right side of the taskbar, read the ScreenTip, then click or tap once**
   A pop-up window appears, containing the current time and date and a calendar.

TROUBLE
If a window didn't
open, try again with a
faster double-click.

6. **Click or tap on the desktop, point to the Recycle Bin icon, then quickly click or tap twice**
   You **double-clicked** (or double-tapped) the icon. You need to double-click or double-tap quickly, without moving the pointer. A window opens, showing the contents of the Recycle Bin, as shown in FIGURE 1-7. The area at the top of the window is the title bar, which displays the name of the window. The area below the title bar is the **Ribbon**, which contains tabs, commands, and the Address bar. **Tabs** are groupings of **buttons** and other controls you use to interact with an object or a program.

7. **Click or tap the View tab**
   The buttons on that tab appear. Buttons act as **commands**, which instruct Windows to perform tasks. The **Address bar** shows the name and location of the item you have opened.

8. **Point to the Close button ✕ on the title bar, read the ScreenTip, then click or tap once**

QUICK TIP
You use dragging to
move folders, files,
and other objects on
the desktop.

9. **Point to the Recycle Bin icon, hold down the left mouse button, or press and hold the Recycle Bin image with your finger, move the mouse or drag so the object moves right as shown in FIGURE 1-8, release the mouse button or lift your finger, then drag the Recycle Bin back to its original location**

FIGURE 1-7: Recycle Bin window

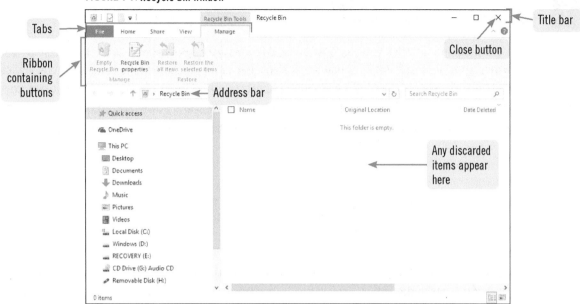

Tabs

Ribbon containing buttons

Address bar

Title bar

Close button

Any discarded items appear here

FIGURE 1-8: Dragging the Recycle Bin icon

Releasing mouse button moves object to this location

TABLE 1-2: Basic pointing device actions

action	with a mouse	with a touch pad	use to
Point	Move mouse to position tip of pointer over an item	Move your finger over touch pad to position tip of pointer over an item	Highlight items or display small informational boxes called ScreenTips
Click	Press and release left mouse button once	Tap touch pad once	Select objects or commands, open menus or items on the taskbar
Double-click	Quickly press and release left mouse button twice	Tap touch pad twice in quick succession	Open programs, folders, or files represented by desktop icons
Drag	Point to an object, press and hold down left mouse button, move object to a new location, then release mouse button	Slide finger across touch pad to point to an object, press and hold left touch pad button, drag across touch pad to move object to new location, then release button	Move objects, such as icons, on the desktop
Right-click	Point to an object, then press and release right mouse button	Point to an object, then press and release right touchpad button	Display a shortcut menu containing options specific to the object

Selecting and moving items using touch-screen devices

If you use a touch-screen computer, a tablet, or a smartphone, you click desktop items by tapping them once on the screen. Tap an icon twice quickly to double-click and open its window. Press and hold an icon, then drag to move it. A touch-screen device does not let you point to an object without selecting it, however, as mice and touchpads do.

Start an App

Apps are programs that let you perform tasks. Windows 10 runs Windows apps and desktop apps. **Windows apps** are small programs that are available free or for purchase in the Windows Store, and can run on Windows desktops, laptops, tablets, and phones. Windows apps are also called **universal apps**. They are specially designed so they can stay open as you work without slowing down your computer, and often have a single purpose. Examples include the Photos app, which lets you view your photographs, and the OneDrive app, which lets you connect to files and programs you have stored on the Microsoft OneDrive website. **Desktop apps** are fully-featured programs; they may be available at an online store or on disk. For example, Microsoft Word allows you to create and edit letters, reports, and other text-based documents. Some smaller desktop apps called **Windows accessories**, such as Paint and Notepad, come already installed in Windows 10. **CASE** *To prepare for your new job, you start three apps.*

STEPS

1. **Click or tap the Start button ⊞, then click or tap the Weather tile, shown in FIGURE 1-9**
   The Weather app opens, letting you find the current weather in various locations.

2. **If you are asked to choose a location, begin typing your city or town, then click the full name if it appears in the drop-down list**
   The current weather for your selected city appears in Summary view. FIGURE 1-10 shows a forecast for Boston, MA.

3. **Click or tap the Weather app window's Close button ☒**

4. **Click or tap ⊞, then type onenote**
   Typing an app name is another way to locate an app. At the top of the Start menu, you see the OneNote Trusted Windows Store app listed, as shown in FIGURE 1-11. OneNote is a popular app that lets you create tabbed notebooks where you can store text, images, files, and media such as audio and video.

5. **Click or tap the OneNote Trusted Windows Store app name**
   The OneNote app opens, showing a blank notebook (or a notebook you have previously created).

6. **Click or tap the Close button ☒ in the upper right corner of the OneNote app window**
   You have opened two Windows apps, Weather and OneNote.

7. **Click or tap ⊞, then type paint**
   The top of the Start menu lists the Paint Desktop app, shown in FIGURE 1-12. Paint is a simple accessory that comes installed with Windows and lets you create simple illustrations.

8. **Click or tap the Paint Desktop app name at the top of the Start menu**
   Other accessories besides Paint and Notepad include the Snipping Tool, which lets you capture an image of any screen area, and Sticky Notes, that let you create short notes.

Using the Windows Store

The Windows Store is an app that lets you find all kinds of apps for use on Windows personal computers, tablets, and phones. You can open it by clicking or tapping its tile on the Start menu or by clicking or tapping the Store button on the taskbar. To use the Windows Store, you need to be signed in to your Microsoft account. You can browse lists of popular apps, games, music, movies, and TV including new releases; you can browse the top paid or free apps. Browse app categories to find a specific type of app, such as Business or Entertainment. To locate a specific app, type its name in the Search box. If an app is free, you can go to its page and click the Free button to install it on your computer. If it's a paid app, you can click or tap the Free trial button to try it out, or click or tap its price button to purchase it. Any apps you've added recently appear in the Recently added category of the Start menu.

FIGURE 1-9: Weather tile on the Start menu

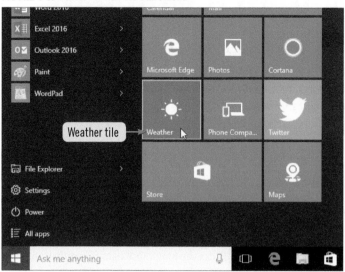

Weather tile

FIGURE 1-10: Weather app

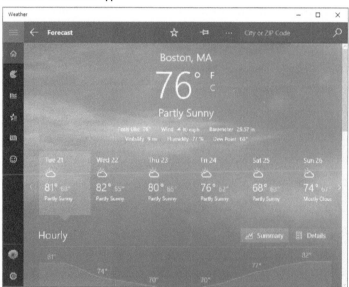

FIGURE 1-11: OneNote Windows app name on Start menu

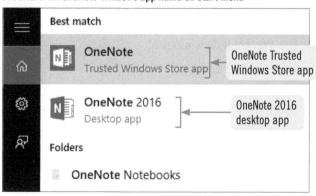

OneNote Trusted
Windows Store app

OneNote 2016
desktop app

FIGURE 1-12: Paint Desktop app name on Start menu

Paint Desktop app

Work with a Window

Learning
Outcomes
• Minimize, restore,
  and maximize a
  window
• Scroll a window
• Move a window

When you start an app, its **window**, a frame displaying the app's tools, opens. In many apps, a blank file also opens so you can start creating a new document. For example, in Paint, a blank document opens so you can start drawing right away. All windows in the Windows 10 operating system have similar window elements. Once you can use a window in one app, you will know how to work with windows in many other apps. **CASE** *To become more familiar with the Windows 10 user interface, you explore elements in the Paint window.*

DETAILS

Many windows have the following common elements. Refer to FIGURE 1-13:

- At the top of the window, you see a **title bar**, a strip that contains the name of the document and app. This document has not been saved, so it has the temporary name "Untitled" and the app name is "Paint."

TROUBLE
If your Ribbon looks
different from the
figure, your window
might be slightly
wider or narrower. A
narrow window
collapses some
buttons so you can
only see group
names; in that case,
you might need to
click or tap a group
name to see buttons.

- On the right side of the title bar, the **Window control buttons** let you control the app window. The **Minimize button** ⊟ temporarily hides the window, making it a button on the taskbar. The app is still running, but its window is temporarily hidden until you click its taskbar button or its miniature window in Task view to reopen it. The **Maximize button** ☐ enlarges the window to fill the entire screen. If a window is already maximized, the Maximize button changes to the **Restore Down button** ⧉, which reduces it to the last non-maximized size. Clicking or tapping the **Close button** ✕ closes the app.

- Many windows have a **scroll bar** on the right side and/or the bottom of the window. You click (or press) and drag scroll bar elements to show additional parts of your document. See TABLE 1-3.

- Just below the title bar is the Ribbon, a bar containing tabs as well as a Help icon. The Paint window has three tabs: File, Home, and View. Tabs are divided into **groups** of buttons and tool palettes. The Home tab has five groups: Clipboard, Image, Tools, Shapes, and Colors. Many apps also include **menus** you click to show lists of commands, as well as **toolbars** containing buttons.

- The **Quick Access toolbar** lets you quickly perform common actions such as saving a file.

STEPS

TROUBLE
If you don't see a
scroll bar on the right
side of your screen,
drag the window's
lower-right corner
to make the window
smaller.

1. **Click or tap the Paint window** Minimize button ⊟
   The app is reduced to a taskbar button, as shown in FIGURE 1-14. The contrasting line indicates the app is still open.

2. **Click or tap the taskbar button representing the** Paint app 🖌 **to redisplay the app**

3. **Drag the gray** scroll box **down, notice the lower edge of the work area that appears, then click or tap the** Up scroll arrow ⌃ **until you see the top edge of the work area**

QUICK TIP
To quickly restore
down the selected
window, press and
hold down the ⊞
key, then press the
down arrow key on
your keyboard.

4. **Point to the** View tab, **then click or tap the** View tab **once**
   Clicking or tapping the View tab moved it in front of the Home tab. This tab has three groups containing buttons that let you change your view of the document window.

5. **Click the** Home tab, **then click or tap the Paint window** Maximize button ☐
   The window fills the screen, and the Maximize button becomes the Restore Down button ⧉.

6. **Click the window's** Restore Down button ⧉ **to return it to its previous size**

7. **Point to the** Paint window title bar **(if you are using a pointing device), then drag about an inch to the right to move it so it's centered on the screen**

FIGURE 1-13: Typical app window elements

Quick Access toolbar

Ribbon with tabs

Click arrow to display a menu

Groups

Title bar

Windows control buttons

Scroll bar

Canvas

FIGURE 1-14: Taskbar with minimized Paint program button

Buttons without contrasting lines represent programs that are not open

Your buttons may differ

Paint program button with contrasting line indicating program is open

TABLE 1-3: Parts of a scroll bar

name	looks like		to use
Scroll box	☐	(Size may vary)	Drag to scroll quickly through a long document
Scroll arrows	⋀ ⋁		Click or tap to scroll up, down, left, or right in small amounts
Shaded area	(Above, below, or to either side of scroll box)		Click or tap to move up or down by one screen

Using the Quick Access toolbar

On the left side of the title bar, the Quick Access toolbar lets you perform common tasks with just one click. The Save button 🖫 saves the changes you have made to a document. The Undo button 🖒 lets you reverse (undo) the last action you performed.

The Redo button 🖒 reinstates the change you just undid. Use the Customize Quick Access Toolbar button ▼ to add other frequently used buttons to the toolbar, move the toolbar below the Ribbon, or minimize the Ribbon to show only tabs.

Manage Multiple Windows

You can work with more than one app at a time by switching among open app windows. If you open two or more apps, a window opens for each one. You can work with app windows individually, going back and forth between them. The window in front is called the **active window**. Any open window behind the active window is called an **inactive window**. For ease in working with multiple windows, you can move, arrange, make them smaller or larger, minimize, or restore them so they're not in the way. To resize a window, drag a window's edge, called its **border**. You can use the taskbar to switch between windows. See TABLE 1-4 for a summary of taskbar actions. **CASE** *Keeping the Paint app open, you open the OneNote app and then work with both app windows.*

STEPS

1. **With Paint open, click or tap the Start button ⊞, then the OneNote tile**

   The OneNote window appears as a second window on the desktop, as shown in FIGURE 1-15. The OneNote window is in front, indicating that it is the active window. The Paint window is the inactive window. On the taskbar, the contrasting line under the OneNote and Paint app buttons tell you both apps are open.

2. **Point to a blank part of the OneNote window title bar on either side of the app name (if you are using a pointing device), then drag the OneNote window down slightly so you can see more of the Paint window**

3. **Click or tap once on the Paint window's title bar**

   The Paint window is now the active window and appears in front of the OneNote window. You can make any window active by clicking or tapping it, or by clicking or tapping an app's icon in the taskbar.

4. **Point to the taskbar if you are using a pointing device, then click or tap the OneNote window button**

   The OneNote window becomes active. When you open multiple windows on the desktop, you may need to resize windows so they don't get in the way of other open windows.

5. **Point to the lower-right corner of the OneNote window until the pointer changes to ⬉, if you are using a pointing device, or tap and press the corner, then drag down and to the right about an inch to make the window larger**

   You can also point to any edge of a window until you see the ⟷ or ↕ pointer, or tap and press any edge, then drag to make it larger or smaller in one direction only.

6. **Click or tap the Task View button ▣ on the taskbar, click or tap the Paint window, click or tap ▣ again, then click or tap the OneNote window**

   The **Task View button** is another convenient way to switch among open windows.

7. **Point to the OneNote window title bar if you are using a pointing device, drag the window to the left side of the screen until the pointer or your finger reaches the screen edge and you see a vertical line down the middle of the screen, then release the mouse button or lift your finger from the screen**

   The OneNote window instantly fills the left side of the screen, and any inactive windows appear on the right side of the screen. This is called the **Snap Assist** feature. You can also drag to any screen corner to snap open app windows to quarter-screen windows.

8. **Click or tap anywhere on the reduced-size version of the Paint window**

   The Paint window fills the right side of the screen. Snapping makes it easy to view the contents of two windows at the same time. See FIGURE 1-16.

9. **Click or tap the OneNote window Close button ✕, then click or tap the Maximize button ☐ in the Paint window's title bar**

   The OneNote app closes. The Paint app window remains open.

FIGURE 1-15: Working with multiple windows

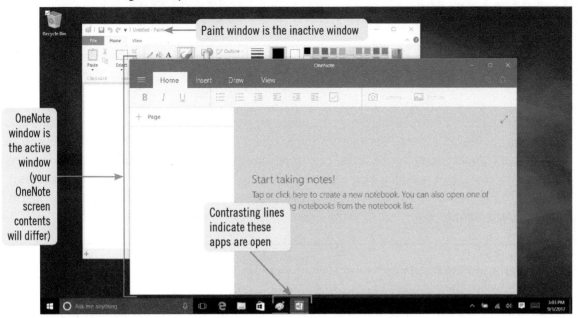

FIGURE 1-16: OneNote and Paint windows snapped to each side of the screen

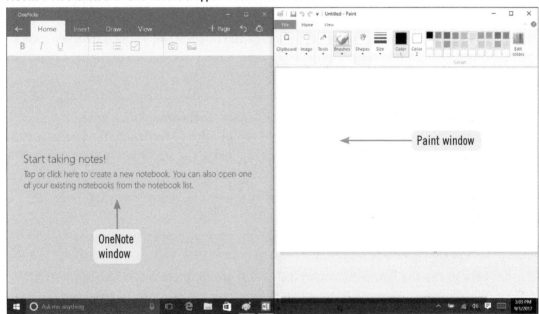

TABLE 1-4: Using the taskbar

to	do this
Add buttons to taskbar	Open an app, right-click or press its icon on the taskbar, then click or tap Pin this program to taskbar
Change order of taskbar buttons	Drag any icon to a new taskbar location
See a list of recent documents opened	Right-click or press taskbar app button
Close a document using the taskbar	Point to taskbar button, point to document image, then click its Close button
Minimize/Redisplay all open windows	Click or press Show desktop button (the thin bar) to the right of taskbar date and time
See preview of documents in taskbar	With a pointing device, point to taskbar button for open app
Bring a minimized window to the front	Click or press the Task View button, then click or tap the window or desktop you want in front
Rearrange windows on the desktop	Right-click taskbar, click Cascade Windows, Show windows stacked, or Show windows side by side

Use Buttons, Menus, and Dialog Boxes

Learning Outcomes
• Use a button and a menu
• Work in a dialog box

When you work in an app, you communicate with it using buttons, menus, and dialog boxes. **Buttons** let you issue instructions to modify app objects. Buttons are often organized on a Ribbon into tabs, and then into groups like those in the Paint window. Some buttons have text on them, and others show only an icon that represents what they do. Other buttons reveal **menus**, lists of commands you can choose. And some buttons open up a **dialog box**, a window with controls that lets you tell Windows what you want. TABLE 1-5 lists the common types of controls you find in dialog boxes. **CASE** *You practice using buttons, menus, and dialog boxes to create some simple graphics in the Paint app.*

STEPS

1. **In the Shapes group, click or tap the** More button ▼ **just to the right of the shapes, then click the** Triangle button △

2. **Click or tap the** Turquoise button ■ **in the Colors group, move the pointer or your finger over the white drawing area, then drag down and to the right, to draw a** triangle **similar to the one in** FIGURE 1-17
   The white drawing area is called the **canvas**.

3. **In the Shapes group, click or tap** ▼, **click the** down scroll arrow **if necessary, click or tap the** Five-point star button, **click or tap the** Indigo color button ■ **in the Colors group, then drag a star shape near the triangle, using** FIGURE 1-17 **as a guide**
   Don't be concerned if your object isn't exactly like the one in the figure, or in exactly the same place.

4. **Click or tap the** Fill with color button ⬧ **in the Tools group, click or tap the** Light turquoise color button ■ **in the Colors group, click or tap inside the** triangle, **click or tap the** Purple color button ■, **click or tap inside the** star, **then compare your drawing to** FIGURE 1-17

5. **Click or tap the** Select list arrow **in the Image group, then click or tap** Select all, **as shown in** FIGURE 1-18
   The Select all command selects the entire drawing, as indicated by the dotted line surrounding the white drawing area. Other commands on this menu let you select individual elements or change your selection.

6. **Click or tap the** Rotate button **in the Image group, then click or tap** Rotate 180°
   You often need to use multiple commands to perform an action—in this case, you used one command to select the items you wanted to work with, and another command to rotate them.

7. **Click or tap the** File tab, **then click or tap** Print
   The Print dialog box opens, as shown in FIGURE 1-19. This dialog box lets you choose a printer, specify which part of your document or drawing you want to print, and choose how many copies you want to print. The **default**, or automatically selected, number of copies is 1, which is what you want.

8. **Click or tap** Print, **or if you prefer not to print, click or tap** Cancel
   The drawing prints on your printer. You decide to close the app without saving your drawing.

9. **Click or tap the** File tab, **click or tap** Exit, **then click or tap** Don't Save
   You closed the file without saving your changes, then exited the app. Most apps include a command for closing a document without exiting the program. However, Paint allows you to open only one document at a time, so it does not include a Close command.

FIGURE 1-17: **Triangle and star shapes filled with color**

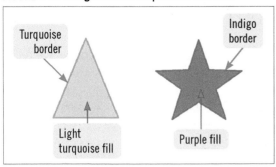

Turquoise border

Indigo border

Light turquoise fill

Purple fill

FIGURE 1-18: **Select menu options**

Select list arrow

Select menu

Select all command

FIGURE 1-19: **Print dialog box**

Your default printer will be highlighted here

Specify number of copies to print here

TABLE 1-5: **Common dialog box controls**

element	example	description
Text box	1 - 27	A box in which you type text or numbers
Spin box	1	A box with up and down arrows; you can click or tap arrows or type to increase or decrease value
Option button	◉	A small circle you click or tap to select the option; only one in a set can be selected at once
Check box	☑	A small box that turns an option on when checked or off when unchecked; more than one in a set can be selected at once
List box		A box that lets you select from a list of options
Button	Save	A button you click or tap to issue a command

Get Help

Learning
Outcomes
• Explore the
  Getting Started
  app
• Search for
  Windows help
  using Cortana

As you use Windows 10, you might feel ready to learn more about it, or you might have a problem and need some advice. You can use the Windows 10 Getting Started app to learn more about help options. You can also search for help using Cortana, which you activate by using the search box on the taskbar. **CASE** *You explore Windows 10 help using the Get Started app and Cortana.*

STEPS

Note: Because Help in an online resource, topics and information are liable to change over time. If your screen choices do not match the steps below exactly, be flexible by exploring the options that are available to you and searching for the information you need.

1. **Click or tap the** Start button ⊞, **then in the Explore Windows section click or tap the** Get Started tile; **if the Explore Windows section does not appear on your Start menu, begin typing** Get Started, **then click or tap** Get Started Trusted Windows Store app **in the list**

   The Get Started app window opens. The window contains a menu expand button ☰ in the upper left and a bar containing buttons on the left side.

2. **Click or tap the** Menu Expand button ☰, **move the pointer over the list of topics, then scroll down to see the remaining topics**

3. **Click or tap the** Search and help topic, **click the** Search for anything, anywhere tile, **then read the information, as shown in** FIGURE 1-20, **scrolling as necessary**

4. **Click or tap the** Back button ← **in the top-left corner of the window, click the** Search for help tile, **then read the Search for help topic and watch any available videos**

5. **Click or tap** ☰, **click or tap a topic that interests you, then read the information or click or tap one of the tiles representing a subtopic if one is available**

QUICK TIP
Depending on your
current settings, the
prompt text in the
search box reads,
"Ask me anything" or
"Search the web and
Windows."

6. **After you have read the information, click or tap the Get started window's** Close button ✕

   As the Help topic explained, you can also search the web for help with Windows using Cortana.

7. **Click in the** search box **on the taskbar, then type** windows help

   As you type, Cortana begins a search, and shows results on the Start menu. See FIGURE 1-21. Your results may also include topics from the Microsoft Store, the web, Store apps, and OneDrive, your online storage location.

QUICK TIP
You learn more
about OneDrive in
Module 2.

8. **Click any web option that interests you**

9. **When you are finished, click or tap the window's** Close button ✕ **to return to the desktop**

FIGURE 1-20: **Get Started Search and Help topic**

Menu Expand button

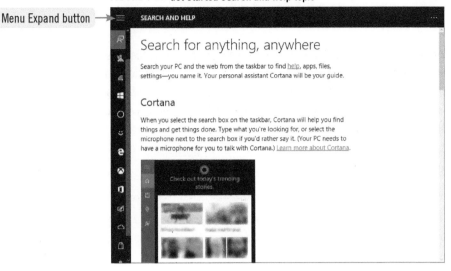

FIGURE 1-21: **Search results information**

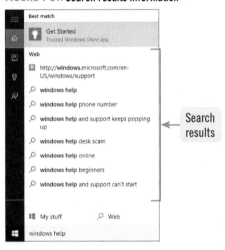

Search results

Using Cortana

Cortana is the digital personal assistant that comes with Windows 10 and Windows phones. You can interact with Cortana typing or using your voice. Use Cortana to search the web, remind you of events or appointments, set alarms, change computer settings, get directions, get current news and weather, track airline flights, play, and even identify music. FIGURE 1-22 shows Cortana's response to "What's the weather in New York?" which may also give a voice response. You call Cortana by saying, "Hey Cortana," or by clicking or tapping the microphone icon on the right side of the taskbar search box, and then asking a question or saying a command. Depending on your request, Cortana may reply out loud, display results in the Start menu, or display results in a Microsoft Edge web browser window. You may need to set up Cortana on your computer and answer security questions before you use it. The first time you use Cortana, you may be asked to answer questions to help the assistant recognize your voice or solve issues with your computer's microphone.

FIGURE 1-22: **Using Cortana to check the weather**

Symbol indicates Cortana is standing by

Cortana's response to a request for the weather

Information requested

Voice request appears in search box

Exit Windows 10

When you finish working on your computer, you should close any open files, exit any open apps, close any open windows, and exit (or **shut down**) Windows 10. TABLE 1-6 shows options for ending your Windows 10 sessions. Whichever option you choose, it's important to shut down your computer in an orderly way. If you turn off or unplug the computer while Windows 10 is running, you could lose data or damage Windows 10 and your computer. If you are working in a computer lab, follow your instructor's directions and your lab's policies for ending your Windows 10 session. **CASE** ▶ *You have examined the basic ways you can use Windows 10, so you are ready to end your Windows 10 session.*

STEPS

QUICK TIP
Instead of shutting
down, you may be
instructed to sign out,
or log out, of your
Microsoft account.
Click or tap Start,
click or tap your
account name, then
click or tap Sign out.

1. **Click or tap the** Start button ⊞, **then click or tap** Power

   The Power button menu lists shut down options, as shown in FIGURE 1-23.

2. **If you are working in a computer lab, follow the instructions provided by your instructor or technical support person for ending your Windows 10 session; if you are working on your own computer, click or tap** Shut down **or the option you prefer for ending your Windows 10 session**

QUICK TIP
If you are using a
Windows 10 tablet,
press the lock button
on your tablet to
bring up the lock
screen, swipe the lock
screen, then click or
tap the Shut down
button to power off
your computer.

3. **After you shut down your computer, you may also need to turn off your monitor and other hardware devices, such as a printer, to conserve energy**

FIGURE 1-23: **Shutting down your computer**

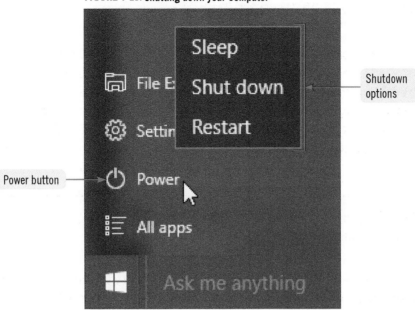

Shutdown options

Power button

TABLE 1-6: **Power options**

option	description
Sleep	Puts computer in a low-power state while keeping any open apps open so you can return immediately to where you left off
Shut down	Closes any open apps and completely turns off the computer
Restart	Closes any open apps, shuts down the computer, then restarts it

Installing updates when you exit Windows

Sometimes, after you shut down your machine, you might find that your machine does not shut down immediately. Instead, Windows might install software updates. If you see an option on your Power menu that lets you update, you can click or tap it to update your software. If you see a window indicating that updates are being installed, do not unplug or press the power switch to turn off your machine. Let the updates install completely. After the updates are installed, your computer will shut down, as you originally requested.

Practice

Concepts Review

Label the elements of the Windows 10 window shown in FIGURE 1-24.

FIGURE 1-24

Match each term with the statement that best describes it.

9. **Cortana**

10. **Snap Assist**

11. **Desktop app**

12. **Microsoft account**

13. **User interface**

14. **Operating system**

15. **Windows app**

a. A special area of the operating system where your files and settings are stored

b. Controls that let you interact with an operating system

c. The personal digital assistant in Windows 10

d. Full-featured program that is installed on a personal computer

e. Feature that displays windows at full height next to each other on the screen

f. Available from the Windows store, it runs on Windows laptops, tablets, and phones

g. A program necessary to run your computer

Select the best answer from the list of choices.

16. **The bar containing buttons and other elements at the bottom of the Windows 10 desktop is called the _____.**

   a. title bar

   b. address bar

   c. scroll bar

   d. taskbar

17. **Paint is an example of a(n) _____.**

   a. group

   b. accessory

   c. active window

   d. operating system

18. **Which of the following is in the upper-left corner of a program window, and lets you perform common actions?**
   a. Application program
   b. Quick Access toolbar
   c. Operating system
   d. Accessory program

19. **The new Microsoft web browser is called Microsoft _____.**
   a. Paint
   b. WordPad
   c. Edge
   d. File Explorer

Skills Review

1. **Start Windows 10.**
   a. If your computer and monitor are not running, press your computer's and (if necessary) your monitor's power buttons.
   b. If necessary, select the user name that represents your user account.
   c. Enter your password, using correct uppercase and lowercase letters.

2. **Navigate the desktop and Start menu.**
   a. Examine the Windows 10 desktop.
   b. Open the Start menu.
   c. Display all the apps using a command on the Start menu, and scroll the list.
   d. Return to the Start menu.
   e. Close the Start menu.

3. **Point, click, and drag.**
   a. On the Windows 10 desktop, click or tap to select the Recycle Bin.
   b. Point to display the ScreenTip for Microsoft Edge in the taskbar, and then display the ScreenTip for each of the other icons on the taskbar.
   c. Double-click or double-tap to open the Recycle Bin window, then close it.
   d. Drag the Recycle Bin to a different corner of the screen, then drag it back to its original location.
   e. Click or tap the Date and Time area to display the calendar and clock, then click or tap it again to close it.

4. **Start an app.**
   a. Open the Start menu, then start the Maps app. (If asked to allow Windows to access your location, do so if you like.)
   b. Click or tap the icons on the left side of the Maps app window and observe the effect of each one.
   c. Close the Maps app.
   d. Reopen the Start menu, then type and click or tap to locate and open the Sticky Notes accessory.
   e. Click or tap the Sticky Notes Close button, clicking or tapping Yes to delete the note.
   f. Open the Weather Windows app.

5. **Work with a window.**
   a. Minimize the Weather window, then use its taskbar button to redisplay the window.
   b. Use the Weather app window's scroll bar or swiping to view the information in the lower part of the window, and then scroll or swipe up to display the top of it. (*Hint*: You need to move the pointer over the Weather app window, or swipe it, in order to display the scroll bar.)
   c. Click or tap the menu expand button, then click Historical Weather.
   d. Read the contents of the window, then click or tap two other menu buttons and read the contents.
   e. Maximize the Weather window, then restore it down.

6. **Manage multiple windows.**
   a. Leaving the Weather app open, go to the Start menu and type to locate the Paint app, open Paint, then restore down the Paint window if necessary.
   b. Click or tap to make the Weather app window the active window.
   c. Click or tap to make the Paint window the active window.
   d. Minimize the Paint window.

Skills Review (continued)

  e. Drag the Weather app window so it's in the middle of the screen.

  f. Redisplay the Paint window.

  g. Drag the Paint window so it automatically fills the right side of the screen.

  h. Click or tap the Weather app window image so it snaps to the left side of the screen.

  i. Close the Weather app window, maximize the Paint window, then restore down the Paint window.

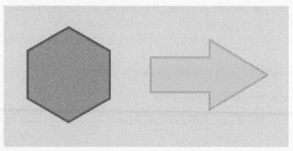

FIGURE 1-25

7. Use buttons, menus, and dialog boxes.

  a. In the Paint window, draw a Dark red Hexagon shape, similar to the one shown in FIGURE 1-25.

  b. Use the Fill with color button to fill the hexagon with a brown color.

  c. Draw an Orange right arrow to the right of the hexagon shape, using the figure as a guide.

  d. Use the Fill with color button to fill the orange arrow with a lime color.

  e. Fill the drawing background with Light turquoise color, as shown in the figure.

  f. Use the Select list arrow and menu to select the entire drawing, then use the Rotate command to rotate the drawing 180°.

  g. Open the Print dialog box, print a copy of the picture if you wish, then close the Paint app without saving the drawing.

8. Get help.

  a. Open the Get Started app, then use the menu expand button to display the available help topics.

  b. Use the Menu button to display help for Cortana.

  c. Click or tap a tile representing a Cortana help topic that interests you, read the help text, scrolling or swiping as necessary.

  d. Display the Search and Help topic, then close the Get Started window.

  e. In the search box on the taskbar, type Help Microsoft Account, then click the help Microsoft account result to search the web.

  f. In the Microsoft Edge browser window, select a help topic that interests you, read the information (ignore any commercial offers), then click or tap the Microsoft Edge window's Close button.

9. Exit Windows 10.

  a. Sign out of your account, or shut down your computer using the Shut down command in the Start menu's Power command or the preferred command for your work or school setting.

  b. Turn off your monitor if necessary.

Independent Challenge 1

You work for Chicago Instruments, a manufacturer of brass instruments. The company ships instruments and supplies to music stores and musicians in the United States and Canada. The owner, Emerson, wants to know an easy way for his employees to learn about the new features of Windows 10, and he has asked you to help.

  a. Start your computer if necessary, sign in to Windows 10, then use the search text box to search for **what's new in Windows 10**.

  b. Click or tap the Search the web link in the Best match section at the top of the Help menu, then in the Microsoft Edge browser window, click or tap a search result that interests you.

  c. Open the Getting Started app and review the new features listed there.

  d. Using pencil and paper, or the Notepad accessory if you wish, write a short memo to Emerson summarizing, in your own words, three important new features in Windows 10. If you use Notepad to write the memo, use the Print button to print the document, then use the Exit command on the File tab to close Notepad without saving your changes to the document.

Independent Challenge 1 (continued)

e. Close the browser window, then sign out of your account, or shut down your computer using the preferred command for your work or school setting. Turn off your monitor if necessary.

Independent Challenge 2

You are the new manager of Katharine Anne's Garden Supplies, a business that supplies garden tools to San Diego businesses. Some of their tools are from Europe and show metric sizes. For her American customers, Katharine Anne wants to do a simple calculation and then convert the result to inches.

a. Start your computer and log on to Windows 10 if necessary, then type to locate the Windows app called Calculator, and start it.

b. Click or tap to enter the number 96 on the Calculator.

c. Click or tap the division sign (÷) button.

d. Click or tap the number 4.

e. Click or tap the equals sign button (=), and write down the result shown in the Calculator window. (*Hint*: The result should be 24.)

f. Select the menu expand button in the Calculator window, then under CONVERTER, select Length.

g. Enter 24 centimeters, and observe the equivalent length in inches.

h. Start Notepad, write a short memo about how Calculator can help you convert metric measurements to inches and feet, print the document using the Print command on the File tab, then exit Notepad without saving.

i. Close the Calculator, then sign out of your account, or shut down your computer using the preferred command for your work or school setting. Turn off your monitor if necessary.

Independent Challenge 3

You are the office manager for Erica's Pet Shipping, a service business in Dallas, Texas, that specializes in air shipping of cats and dogs across the United States and Canada. It's important to know the temperature in the destination city, so the animals won't be in danger from extreme temperatures when they are unloaded from the aircraft. Erica has asked you to find a way to easily monitor temperatures in destination cities. You decide to use a Windows app so you can see current temperatures in Celsius on your desktop. (Note: To complete the steps below, your computer must be connected to the Internet.)

a. Start your computer and sign in to Windows 10 if necessary, then on the Start menu, click or tap the Weather tile.

b. Click or tap the Search icon in the location text box, then type **Toronto**.

c. Select Toronto, Ontario, Canada, in the drop-down list to view the weather for Toronto.

d. Search on and select another location that interests you.

e. Close the app.

f. Open Notepad, write Erica a memo outlining how you can use the Windows Weather app to help keep pets safe, print the memo if you wish, close Notepad, then sign out, or shut down your computer.

Independent Challenge 4: Explore

Cortana, the Windows 10 personal digital assistant, can help you with everyday tasks. In this Independent Challenge, you explore one of the ways you can use Cortana.

a. Click or tap the microphone icon, to the right of the search box in the Windows 10 taskbar, to activate Cortana and display its menu. (*Note*: If you have not used Cortana before, you will not see the microphone icon until you answer some preliminary questions and verify your user account; you may also need to first help Cortana to understand your speaking voice.) Cortana displays a pulsating circle, indicating that she is listening for speech, and then shows you a greeting and some general information.

Independent Challenge 4: Explore (continued)

FIGURE 1-26

b. In the list of icons on the left side of the menu, click the menu expand button to show the names of each one, as shown in FIGURE 1-26.

c. Click or tap the Reminders button, then click the plus sign at the bottom of the menu. Click or tap Remember to…, then enter information for a to-do item, such as "Walk the dog." Click or tap the time box and use the spin boxes to set the time for one or two minutes from now. Click or tap the check mark, then click Remind to set the reminder. Click or tap the Reminders icon again to see your reminder listed, then click the desktop. When the reminder appears, click Complete.

d. Click or tap the microphone icon again, and when you see the pulsating circle, speak into your computer microphone and tell Cortana to remind you to do something in one minute. Click or tap Remind, then close the Cortana window. When the reminder appears, click or tap Complete.

e. Click or tap the Close button on the Cortana menu, then sign out of your account, or shut down your computer.

Visual Workshop

Using the skills you've learned in this module, open and arrange elements on your screen so it looks similar to FIGURE 1-27. Note the position of the Recycle Bin, and the size and location of the Notepad and Weather app windows, as well as the city shown. In Notepad, write a paragraph summarizing how you used pointing, clicking (or tapping), and dragging to make your screen look like the figure. Print your work if you wish, close Notepad and the Weather app without saving changes, then sign out or shut down your computer.

FIGURE 1-27

Understanding File Management

CASE ▶ Now that you are familiar with the Windows 10 operating system, your new employer has asked you to become familiar with file management, or how to create, save, locate and delete the files you create with Windows apps. You begin by reviewing how files are organized on your computer, and then begin working with files you create in the WordPad app. *Note: With the release of Windows 10, Microsoft now provides ongoing updates to Windows instead of releasing new versions periodically. This means that Windows features might change over time, including how they look and how you interact with them. The information provided in this text was accurate at the time this book was published.*

Module Objectives

After completing this module, you will be able to:

- Understand files and folders
- Create and save a file
- Explore the files and folders on your computer
- Change file and folder views

- Open, edit, and save files
- Copy files
- Move and rename files
- Search for files and folders
- Delete and restore files

Files You Will Need

No files needed.

Understand Files and Folders

Learning Outcomes
- Analyze a file hierarchy
- Examine files and folders

As you work with apps, you create and save files, such as letters, drawings, or budgets. When you save files, you usually save them inside folders to help keep them organized. The files and folders on your computer are organized in a **file hierarchy**, a system that arranges files and folders in different levels, like the branches of a tree. FIGURE 2-1 shows a sample file hierarchy. **CASE** ▶ *You decide to use folders and files to organize the information on your computer.*

DETAILS

Use the following guidelines as you organize files using your computer's file hierarchy:

- **Use folders and subfolders to organize files**

  As you work with your computer, you can add folders to your hierarchy and name them to help you organize your work. As you've learned, folders are storage areas in which you can group related files. You should give folders unique names that help you easily identify them. You can also create **subfolders**, which are folders that are inside other folders. Windows 10 comes with several existing folders, such as Documents, Music, Pictures, and Videos, that you can use as a starting point.

QUICK TIP

When you open File Explorer, you see a list of recently opened files and frequently used folders in the Quick Access area that helps you go directly to files and locations.

- **View and manage files in File Explorer**

  You can view and manage your computer contents using a built-in program called **File Explorer**, shown in FIGURE 2-2. A File Explorer window is divided into **panes**, or sections. The **Navigation pane** on the left side of the window shows the folder structure on your computer. When you click a folder in the Navigation pane, you see its contents in the **File list** on the right side of the window. To open File Explorer from the desktop, click the File Explorer button ▣ on the taskbar. To open it from the Start menu, click the File Explorer shortcut.

QUICK TIP

The name "File Explorer" only appears in the title bar when you first open it. As you navigate, you'll see the current folder name instead.

- **Understand file addresses**

  A window also contains an **Address bar**, an area just below the Ribbon that shows the address, or location, of the files that appear in the File list. An **address** is a sequence of folder names, separated by the ▶ symbol, which describes a file's location in the file hierarchy. An address shows the folder with the highest hierarchy level on the left and steps through each hierarchy level toward the right; this is sometimes called a **path**. For example, the Documents folder might contain subfolders named Work and Personal. If you clicked the Personal folder in the File list, the Address bar would show Documents ▶ Personal. Each location between the ▶ symbols represents a level in the file hierarchy. If you see a file path written out, you'll most likely see it with backslashes. For example, in FIGURE 2-1, if you wanted to write the path to the Brochure file, you would write "Documents\Reason2Go\Marketing\Brochure.xlsx. File addresses might look complicated if they may have many levels, but they are helpful because they always describe the exact location of a file or folder in a file hierarchy.

QUICK TIP

Remember that in the Address bar and Navigation pane you single-click a folder or subfolder to show its contents, but in the File list you double-click it.

- **Navigate up and down using the Address bar and File list**

  You can use the Address bar and the File list to move up or down in the hierarchy one or more levels at a time. To **navigate up** in your computer's hierarchy, you can click a folder or subfolder name to the left of the current folder name in the Address bar. For example, in FIGURE 2-2, you can move up in the hierarchy three levels by clicking once on This PC in the Address bar. Then the File list would show the subfolders and files inside the This PC folder. To **navigate down** in the hierarchy, double-click a subfolder in the File list. The path in the Address bar then shows the path to that subfolder.

- **Navigate up and down using the Navigation pane**

  You can also use the Navigation pane to navigate among folders. Move the mouse pointer over the Navigation pane, then click the small arrows to the left of a folder name to show ▶ or hide ✔ the folder's contents under the folder name. Subfolders appear indented under the folders that contain them, showing that they are inside that folder.

FIGURE 2-1: **Sample folder and file hierarchy**

FIGURE 2-2: **File Explorer window**

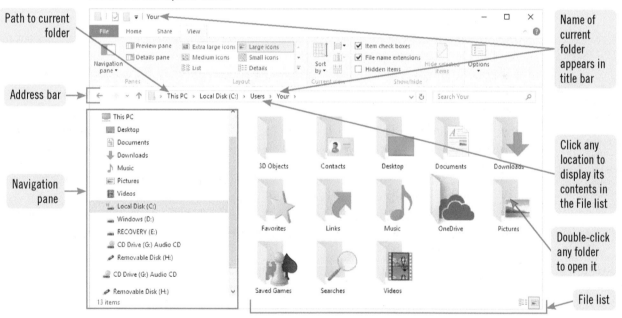

Path to current folder

Address bar

Navigation pane

Name of current folder appears in title bar

Click any location to display its contents in the File list

Double-click any folder to open it

File list

Plan your file organization

As you manage your files, you should plan how you want to organize them. First, identify the types of files you work with, such as images, music, and documents. Think about the content, such as personal, business, clients, or projects. Then think of a folder organization that will help you find them later. For example, you can use subfolders in the Pictures folder to separate family photos from business photos or to group them by location or by month. In the Documents folder, you might group personal files in one subfolder and business files in another subfolder. Then create additional subfolders to further separate sets of files. You can always move files among folders and rename folders. You should periodically reevaluate your folder structure to make sure it continues to meet your needs.

Create and Save a File

Learning Outcomes
- Start WordPad
- Create a file
- Save a file

After you start a program and create a new file, the file exists only in your computer's **random access memory (RAM)**, a temporary storage location. RAM contains information only when your computer is on. When you turn off your computer, it automatically clears the contents of RAM. So you need to save a new file onto a storage device that permanently stores the file so you can open, change, and use it later. One important storage device is your computer's hard drive built into your computer. You might want to store your files online in an online storage location like Microsoft OneDrive. Or you might use a **USB flash drive**, a small, portable storage device that you plug into a USB port on your computer. **CASE** ➤ *You create a document, then save it.*

STEPS

1. **Click or tap the Start button, then type** word

   Available apps with "word" in their names are listed. See FIGURE 2-3.

2. **Click the** WordPad Desktop app listing, **then maximize the WordPad window if necessary**

   Near the top of the WordPad window you see the Ribbon containing buttons, similar to those you used in Paint in Module 1. The Home tab appears in front. A new, blank document appears in the document window. The blinking insertion point shows you where the next character you type will appear.

3. **Type** Company Overview, **then press** [Enter] **twice, type** Conservation, **press** [Enter], **type** Community Work, **press** [Enter], **type** Research, **press** [Enter] **twice, then type your name**

   See FIGURE 2-4.

4. **Click the** File tab, **then click** Save

   The first time you save a file using the Save button, the Save As dialog box opens. You use this dialog box to name the file and choose a storage location for it. The Save As dialog box has many of the same elements as a File Explorer window, including an Address bar, a Navigation pane, and a File list. Below the Address bar, the **toolbar** contains buttons you can click to perform actions. In the Address bar, you can see the Documents folder, which is the **default**, or automatically selected, storage location. But you can easily change it.

   QUICK TIP
   On a laptop computer, the USB port is on the left or right side of your computer.

5. **If you are saving to a USB flash drive, plug the drive into a USB port on your computer, if necessary**

   TROUBLE
   If you don't have a USB flash drive, you can save the document in the Documents folder on OneDrive, or you can ask your instructor which storage location is best.

6. **In the Navigation pane scroll bar, click the** down scroll arrow ✔ **as needed to see This PC and any storage devices listed under it**

   Under This PC, you see the storage locations available on your computer, such as Local Disk (C:) (your hard drive) and Removable Disk (H:) (your USB drive name and letter might differ). Above This PC, you might see your OneDrive listed. These storage locations are like folders in that you can open them and store files in them.

7. **Click the name of your USB flash drive, or the folder where you store your Data Files**

   The files and folders in the location you chose, if any, appear in the File list. The Address bar shows the location where the file will be saved, which is now Removable Disk (H:) or the name of the location you clicked. You need to give your document a meaningful name so you can find it later.

   TROUBLE
   If your Save As dialog box does not show the .rtf file extension, click Cancel, open File Explorer, click the View tab, then in the Show/hide group, click the File name extensions check box to select it.

8. **Click in the** File name text box **to select the default name** Document.rtf, **type** Company Overview, **compare your screen to** FIGURE 2-5, **then click** Save

   The document is saved as a file on your USB flash drive. The filename Company Overview.rtf appears in the title bar. The ".rtf" at the end of the filename is the file extension that Windows added automatically. A **file extension** is a three- or four-letter sequence, preceded by a period, which identifies a file to your computer, in this case **Rich Text Format**. The WordPad program creates files in RTF format.

9. **Click the** Close button ☒ **on the WordPad window**

   The WordPad program closes. Your Company Overview document is now saved in the location you specified.

FIGURE 2-3: **Results at top of Start menu**

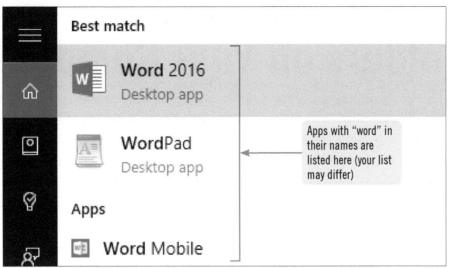

Apps with "word" in their names are listed here (your list may differ)

FIGURE 2-4: **WordPad document**

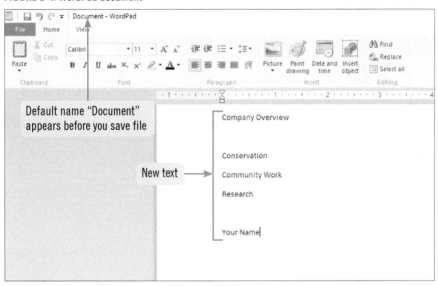

Default name "Document" appears before you save file

New text

FIGURE 2-5: **Save As dialog box**

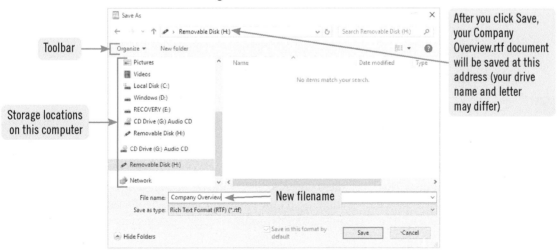

Toolbar

Storage locations on this computer

New filename

After you click Save, your Company Overview.rtf document will be saved at this address (your drive name and letter may differ)

Explore the Files and Folders on Your Computer

In a File Explorer window, you can navigate through your computer contents using the File list, the Address bar, and the Navigation pane. Examining your computer and its existing folder and file structure helps you decide where to save files as you work with Windows 10 apps. **CASE** *In preparation for organizing documents at your new job, you look at the files and folders on your computer.*

STEPS

1. **At the Windows desktop, click the File Explorer button 🗔 on the taskbar, then in the File Explorer Navigation pane, click This PC**

TROUBLE

If you don't see the colored bars, click the View tab, click Tiles in the Layout group.

2. **If you do not see a band of buttons near the top of the window, double-click the View tab**

   The band containing buttons is called the **Ribbon**. Your computer's storage devices appear in a window, as shown in FIGURE 2-6. These include hard drives; devices with removable storage, such as CD and DVD drives or USB flash drives; portable devices such as smartphones or tablets; and any network storage locations. Colored bars shows you how much space has been taken up on your drives. You decide to move down a level in your computer's hierarchy and see what is on your USB flash drive.

3. **In the File list, double-click Removable Disk (H:) (or the drive name and letter for your USB flash drive)**

   You see the contents of your USB flash drive, including the Company Overview.rtf file you saved in the last lesson. You decide to navigate one level up in the file hierarchy.

TROUBLE

If you do not have a USB flash drive, click the Documents folder instead.

4. **In the Address bar, click This PC, or if This PC does not appear, click the far-left address bar arrow ⯈ in the Address bar, then click This PC**

   You return to the This PC window showing your storage locations.

5. **In the File list, double-click Local Disk (C:)**

   The contents of your hard drive appear in the File list.

6. **In the File list, double-click the Users folder**

   The Users folder contains a subfolder for each user account on this computer. You might see a folder with your user account name on it. Each user's folder contains that person's documents. User folder names are the names that were used to log in when your computer was set up. When a user logs in, the computer allows that user access to the folder with the same user name. If you are using a computer with more than one user, you might not have permission to view other users' folders. There is also a Public folder that any user can open.

7. **Double-click the folder with your user name on it**

   Depending on how your computer is set up, this folder might be labeled with your name; however, if you are using a computer in a lab or a public location, your folder might be called Student or Computer User or something similar. You see a list of folders, such as Documents, Music, and OneDrive. See FIGURE 2-7.

QUICK TIP

In the Address bar, you can click ⯈ to the right of a folder name to see a list of its subfolders; if the folder is open, its name appears in bold in the list.

8. **Double-click Documents in the File list**

   In the Address bar, the path to the Documents folder is This PC ⯈ Local Disk (C:) ⯈ Users ⯈ *Your User Name* ⯈ Documents.

9. **In the Navigation pane, click This PC**

   You once again see your computer's storage locations. You can also move up one level at a time in your file hierarchy by clicking the Up arrow ⬆ on the toolbar, or by pressing [Backspace] on your keyboard. See TABLE 2-1 for a summary of techniques for navigating through your computer's file hierarchy.

FIGURE 2-6: File Explorer window showing storage locations

Click this arrow if necessary to navigate to a different location

Storage locations on this PC

Colored bars show how full drives are

FIGURE 2-7: Your user name folder

Path to your user name folder contents

OneDrive

Your user name folder contents and view may differ

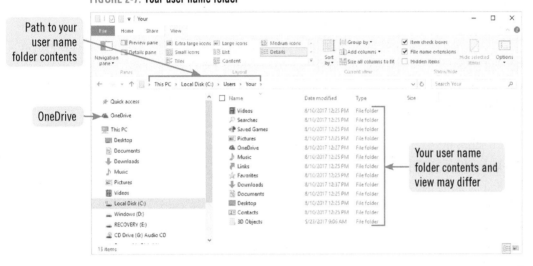

TABLE 2-1: Navigating your computer's file hierarchy

to do this	Navigation pane	Address bar	File list	keyboard
Move up in hierarchy	Click a drive or folder name	Click an item to the left of ▶ or Click the **Up to** button ↑		Press [**Backspace**]
Move down in hierarchy	Click a drive or folder name that is indented from the left	Click an item to the right of ▶	Double-click a folder	Press ↑ or ↓ to select a folder, then press [**Enter**] to open the selected folder
Return to previously viewed location		Click the **Back to** button ← or **Forward** button →		

Using and disabling Quick Access view

When you first open File Explorer, you see a list of frequently-used folders and recently used files, called Quick access view. Quick Access view can save you time by giving you one-click access to files and folders you use a lot. If you want File Explorer to open instead to This PC, you can disable Quick Access View. To do this, open a File Explorer window, click the View tab, click the Options button on the right side of the Ribbon, then click Change folder and search options. On the General tab of the Folder Options dialog box, click the Open File Explorer to list arrow, click This PC, then click OK.

Change File and Folder Views

Learning
Outcomes
• View files as large
  icons
• Sort files
• Preview files

As you view your folders and files, you can customize your **view**, which is a set of appearance choices for files and folders. Changing your view does not affect the content of your files or folders, only the way they appear. You can choose from eight different **layouts** to display your folders and files as different sized icons, or as a list. You can change the order in which the folders and files appear, and you can also show a preview of a file in the window. **CASE** ▶ *You experiment with different views of your folders and files.*

STEPS

1. **In the File Explorer window's Navigation pane, click** Local Disk (C:); **in the File list double-click** Users, **then double-click the** folder **with your user name**
   You opened your user name folder, which is inside the Users folder.

2. **Click the** View tab **on the Ribbon if necessary, then if you don't see eight icons in the Layout list, click the** More button ⤓ **in the Layout group**
   The list of available layouts appears, as shown in FIGURE 2-8.

3. **Click** Extra large icons **in the Layout list**
   In this view, the folder items appear as very large icons in the File list. This layout is especially helpful for image files, because you can see what the pictures are without opening each one.

4. **On the View tab, in the Layout list, point to the other layouts while watching the appearance of the File list, then click** Details
   In Details view, shown in FIGURE 2-9, you can see each item's name, the date it was modified, and its file type. It shows the size of any files in the current folder, but it does not show sizes for folders.

5. **Click the** Sort by button **in the Current view group**
   The Sort by menu lets you **sort**, or reorder, your files and folders according to several criteria.

6. **Click** Descending **if it is not already selected with a check mark**
   Now the folders are sorted in reverse alphabetical order.

7. **Click** Removable Disk (H:) **(or the location where you store your Data Files) in the Navigation pane, then click** Company Overview.rtf **in the File list**

8. **Click the** Preview pane button **in the Panes group on the View tab if necessary**
   A preview of the selected Company Overview.rtf file you created earlier appears in the Preview pane on the right side of the screen. The WordPad file is not open, but you can still see the file's contents. See FIGURE 2-10.

9. **Click the** Preview pane button **again to close the pane, then click the window's** Close button ✕

Using the Windows Action Center

The Windows Action Center lets you quickly view system notifications and selected computer settings. To open the Action Center, click the Notifications button on the right side of the taskbar. The Action Center pane opens on the right side of the screen. Any new notifications appear in the upper part of the pane, including messages about apps, Windows tips, and any reminders you may have set. In the lower part of the pane, you see Quick Action buttons, shown in FIGURE 2-11, for some commonly-used Windows settings. For example, click Note to open the OneNote app; click the Brightness button repeatedly to cycle though four brightness settings; click the Airplane mode button to place your computer in airplane mode,

which turns off your computer's wireless transmission; click Quiet hours to silence your computer's notification sounds. Clicking the All settings button opens the Settings windows, where you can access all Windows settings categories. Note that the buttons available will vary depending on your hardware and software configuration.

FIGURE 2-11: **Quick Action buttons**

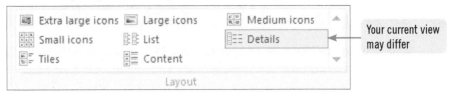

FIGURE 2-8: Layout options for viewing folders and files

Windows 10

FIGURE 2-9: Your user name folder contents in Details view

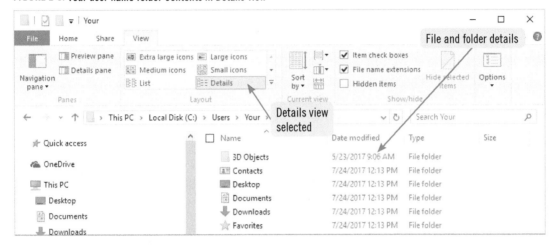

FIGURE 2-10: Preview of selected Company Overview.rtf file

Customizing Details view

When you use File Explorer to view your computer contents in Details view, you see a list of the files and folders in that location. At the top of the list you see each item's Name, Size, Type, and Date Modified. If the list of file and folder details doesn't show what you need, you can customize it. To change a column's location, drag a column heading to move it quickly to a new position. To change the order of, or **sort**, your files and folders, click any column header to sort the list by that detail; click it a second time to reverse the order. To show only a selected group of, or **filter**, files, click the ☑ icon to the right of the Name, Size, Type, or Date Modified, column headers, and select the check boxes for the type of items you want to include. To change the kind of details you see, right-click or tap-hold a column heading in Details view, then click or tap the detail you want to show or hide. To see more details or to change the list order, right-click or tap-hold a column title, then click or tap More.

Open, Edit, and Save Files

Learning Outcomes
• Open a file
• Edit a file
• Save a file

Once you have created a file and saved it with a name to a storage location, you can easily open it and **edit** (make changes to) it. For example, you might want to add or delete text or add a picture. Then you save the file again so the file contains your latest changes. Usually you save a file with the same filename and in the same location as the original, which replaces the existing file with the most up-to-date version. To save a file you have changed, you use the Save command. **CASE** ▶ *You need to complete the company overview list, so you need to open the new Company Overview file you created earlier.*

STEPS

QUICK TIP
When you double-click a file in a File Explorer window, the program currently associated with that file type opens the file; to change the program, right-click a file, click Open with, click Choose another app, click the program name, select the Always use this app to open [file type] files check box, then click OK.

1. **Click the** Start button, **begin typing** wordpad, **then click the** WordPad program **if it is not selected or, if it is, simply press** [Enter]
   The WordPad program opens on the desktop.

2. **Click the** File tab, **then click** Open
   The Open dialog box opens. It contains a Navigation pane and a File list like the Save As dialog box and the File Explorer window.

3. **Scroll down in the Navigation pane if necessary until you see This PC and the list of computer locations, then click** Removable Disk (H:) **(or the location where you store your Data Files)**
   The contents of your USB flash drive (or the file storage location you chose) appear in the File list, as shown in FIGURE 2-12.

QUICK TIP
You can also double-click a file in the File list to open it.

4. **Click** Company Overview.rtf **in the File list, then click** Open
   The document you created earlier opens.

5. **Click to the right of the "h" in Research, press** [Enter], **then type** Outreach
   The edited document includes the text you just typed. See FIGURE 2-13.

QUICK TIP
To save changes to a file, you can also click the Save button 🖫 on the Quick Access toolbar (on the left side of the title bar).

6. **Click the** File tab, **then click** Save, **as shown in** FIGURE 2-14
   WordPad saves the document with your most recent changes, using the filename and location you specified when you previously saved it. When you save changes to an existing file, the Save As dialog box does not open.

7. **Click the** File tab, **then click** Exit
   The Company Overview document and the WordPad program close.

Comparing Save and Save As

Many apps, including Wordpad, include two save command options—Save and Save As. The first time you save a file, the Save As dialog box opens (whether you choose Save or Save As). Here you can select the drive and folder where you want to save the file and enter its filename. If you edit a previously saved file, you can save the file to the same location with the same file-name using the Save command. The Save command updates the stored file using the same location and filename without opening the Save As dialog box. In some situations, you might want to save a copy of the existing document using a different filename or in a different storage location. To do this, open the document, click the Save As command on the File tab, navigate to the location where you want to save the copy if necessary, and/or edit the name of the file.

FIGURE 2-12: **Navigating in the Open dialog box**

USB flash drive selected

Contents of selected drive (your contents will differ)

FIGURE 2-13: **Edited document**

Company Overview

Conservation

Community Work

Research

Outreach   ← Added text

Your Name

FIGURE 2-14: **Saving the updated document**

Save button on Quick Access toolbar

Save command

Using Microsoft OneDrive

Microsoft OneDrive is a location on the World Wide Web where you can store your files. Because OneDrive is an online location instead of a disk or USB device, it's often called a **cloud storage location**. When you store your files on OneDrive, you can access them from different devices, including laptops, tablets, and smartphones. Any changes you make to a file stored "in the cloud" are automatically made on OneDrive; this is known as **file syncing**. For example, if you make changes to a file from your laptop, and then open it on your tablet, you will see the changes. You can share OneDrive folders with others so they can view or edit files using a web browser such as Microsoft Edge or Internet Explorer. You can even have multiple users edit a document simultaneously. In Windows 10, OneDrive appears as a storage location in the navigation bar in File Explorer, and in the Open and Save As dialog boxes in Windows apps, so you can easily open, modify, and save files stored there. You can also download the free OneDrive Windows app from the Windows Store to help manage your OneDrive files from all your devices.

Copy Files

Learning Outcomes
• Create a new folder
• Copy and paste a file

Sometimes you need to make a copy of an existing file. For example, you might want to put a copy on a USB flash drive so you can open the file on another machine or share it with a friend or colleague. Or you might want to create a copy as a **backup**, or replacement, in case something happens to your original file. You can copy files and folders using the Copy command and then place the copy in another location using the Paste command. You cannot have two copies of a file with the same name in the same folder. If you try to do this, Windows asks you if you want to replace the first one, and then gives you a chance to give the second copy a different name. **CASE** *You want to create a backup copy of the Company Overview document that you can store in a folder for company publicity items. First you need to create the folder, then you can copy the file.*

STEPS

1. **On the desktop, click the** File Explorer button 📁 **on the taskbar**

QUICK TIP

You can also create a new folder by clicking the New folder button on the Quick Access toolbar (on the left side of the title bar).

2. **In the Navigation pane, click** Removable Disk (H:) **(or the location where you store your Data Files)**

   First you create the new folder you plan to use for storing publicity-related files.

3. **In the New group on the Home tab, click the** New folder button

   A new folder appears in the File list, with its default name, New folder, selected.

4. **Type** Publicity Items, **then press** [Enter]

   Because the folder name was selected, the text you typed, Publicity Items, replaced it. Pressing [Enter] confirmed your entry, and the folder is now named Publicity Items.

QUICK TIP

You can also copy a file by right-clicking the file in the File list and then clicking Copy, or you can use the keyboard by pressing and holding [Ctrl], pressing [C], then releasing both keys.

5. **In the File list, click the** Company Overview.rtf **document you saved earlier, then click the** Copy button **in the Clipboard group, as shown in** FIGURE 2-15

   After you select the file, its check box becomes selected (the check box appears only if the Item check boxes option in the Show/Hide group on the View tab is selected). When you use the Copy command, Windows places a duplicate copy of the file in an area of your computer's random access memory called the **clipboard**, ready to paste, or place, in a new location. Copying and pasting a file leaves the file in its original location.

6. **In the File list, double-click the** Publicity Items folder

   The folder opens. Nothing appears in the File list because the folder currently is empty.

QUICK TIP

To paste using the keyboard, press and hold [Ctrl] and press [V], then release both keys.

7. **Click the** Paste button **in the Clipboard group**

   A copy of the Company Overview.rtf file is pasted into the Publicity Items folder. See FIGURE 2-16. You now have two copies of the Company Overview.rtf file: one on your USB flash drive in the main folder, and another in your new Publicity Items folder. The file remains on the clipboard until you end your Windows session or place another item on the clipboard.

Copying files using Send to

You can also copy and paste a file using the Send to command. In File Explorer, right-click the file you want to copy, point to Send to, then in the shortcut menu, click the name of the device you want to send a copy of the file to. This leaves the original file on your hard drive and creates a copy in that location. You can send a file to a compressed file, the desktop, your Documents folder, a mail recipient, or a drive on your computer. See TABLE 2-2.

FIGURE 2-15: Copying a file

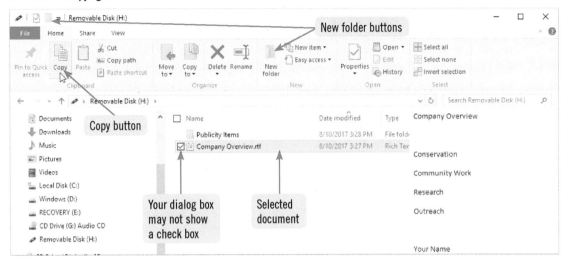

FIGURE 2-16: Duplicate file pasted into Publicity items folder

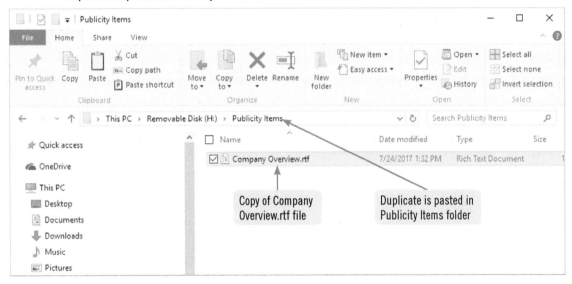

TABLE 2-2: Selected Send to menu commands

menu option	use to
Compressed (zipped) folder	Create a new, compressed (smaller) file with a .zip file extension
Desktop (create shortcut)	Create a shortcut (link) for the file on the desktop
Documents	Copy the file to the Documents library
Fax recipient	Send a file to a fax recipient
Mail recipient	Create an e-mail with the file attached to it (only if you have an e-mail program on your computer)
DVD RW Drive (D:)	Copy the file to your computer's DVD drive (your drive letter may differ)
CD Drive (G:) audio CD	Copy the file to your computer's CD drive (your drive letter may differ)
Removable Disk (H:)	Copy the file to a removable disk drive (your drive letter may differ)

Move and Rename Files

Learning Outcomes
- Cut and paste a file
- Rename a file

As you work with files, you might need to move files or folders to another location. You can move one or more files or folders at a time, and you can move them to a different folder on the same drive or to a different drive. When you **move** a file, the file is transferred to the new location, and unlike copying, it no longer exists in its original location. You can move a file using the Cut and Paste commands. Before or after you move a file, you might find that you want to change its name. You can easily rename it to make the name more descriptive or accurate. **CASE** *You decide to move your original Company Overview.rtf document to your Documents folder. After you move it, you edit the filename so it better describes the file contents.*

STEPS

QUICK TIP
You can also cut a file by right-clicking it in the File list, then clicking Cut, or by clicking it, pressing and holding [Ctrl] on the keyboard, pressing [X], then releasing both keys.

1. **In the Address bar, click** Removable Disk (H:) **(or the name of the location where you store your Data Files) if necessary**

2. **Click the** Company Overview.rtf **document to select it**

3. **Click the** Cut button **in the Clipboard group on the Ribbon, as shown in** FIGURE 2-17

4. **In the Navigation Pane, under This PC, click** Documents
   You navigated to your Documents folder.

5. **Click the** Paste button **in the Clipboard group**
   The Company Overview.rtf document appears in your Documents folder and remains selected. See FIGURE 2-18. The filename could be clearer, to help you remember that it contains a list of company goals.

QUICK TIP
You can also paste a file by right-clicking an empty area in the File list and then clicking Paste, or by pressing and holding [Ctrl] on the keyboard, pressing [V], then releasing both keys.

6. **With the Company Overview.rtf file selected, click the** Rename button **in the Organize group**
   The filename is highlighted. The file extension isn't highlighted because that part of the filename identifies the file to WordPad and should not be changed. If you deleted or changed the file extension, WordPad would be unable to open the file. You decide to change the word "Overview" to "Goals."

7. **Move the** I **pointer after the "w" in "Overview", click to place the insertion point, press** [Backspace] **eight times to delete** Overview, **type** Goals **as shown in** FIGURE 2-19, **then press** [Enter]
   You changed the name of the pasted file in the Documents folder. The filename now reads Company Goals.rtf.

8. **Close the File Explorer window**

Using Task View to create multiple desktops

As you have learned in Module 1, you can have multiple app windows open on your desktop, such as WordPad, Paint, and OneNote. But you might need to have a different set of apps available for a different project. Instead of closing all the apps and opening different ones, you can use Task View to work with multiple desktops, each containing its own set of apps. Then, when you need to work on another project, you can switch to another desktop to quickly access those apps. To open Task View, click the **Task View** button on the taskbar. The current desktop becomes smaller and a New desktop button appears in the lower-right corner of the screen. Click the New desktop button. A new desktop appears in a bar at the bottom of the screen, which you can click to activate and work with its

apps. See FIGURE 2-20. To switch to another desktop, click the Task View button and click its icon.

FIGURE 2-20: Working with multiple desktops in Task view

Desktop #2 is displayed

New Desktop button

Desktops

FIGURE 2-17: Cutting a file

FIGURE 2-18: Pasted file in Documents folder

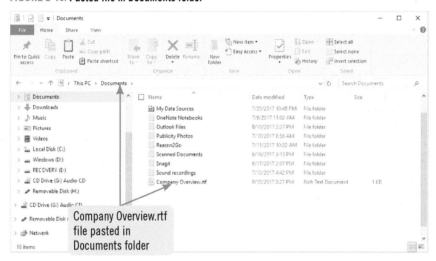

FIGURE 2-19: Renaming a file

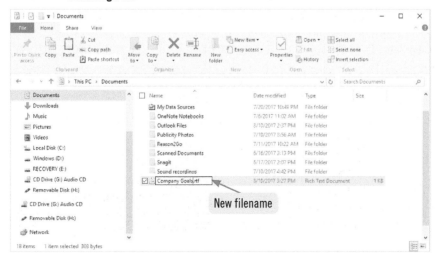

Search for Files and Folders

Learning Outcomes
• Search for a file
• Open a found file

Windows Search helps you quickly find any app, folder, or file. You can search from the Search box on the taskbar to locate applications, settings, or files. To search a particular location on your computer, you can use the Search box in File Explorer. You enter search text by typing one or more letter sequences or words that help Windows identify the item you want. The search text you type is called your **search criteria**. Your search criteria can be a folder name, a filename, or part of a filename. **CASE** *You want to locate the Company Overview.rtf document so you can print it for a colleague.*

STEPS

1. **Click in the search box on the taskbar**
   The Cortana menu opens.

2. **Type company**
   The Search menu opens with a possible match for your search at the top, and some other possible matches below it. You may see results from The Windows Store, the Internet, or your computer settings.

3. **Click My stuff, near the bottom of the menu**
   This limits your search to the files and folders in your storage locations on this device. It includes documents with the text "company" in the title or in the document text.

> **QUICK TIP**
> If you navigate to a specific folder in your file hierarchy, Windows searches that folder and any subfolders below it.

4. **Scroll down if necessary to display search results under This Device, including the Company Goals.rtf file you stored in your Documents folder**
   See FIGURE 2-21. It does not find the Company Overview.rtf file stored on your Flash drive because it's searching only the items on this device. To open the found file, you could click its listing. You can also search using File Explorer.

5. **Click the File Explorer button ⊞ on the taskbar, then click This PC in the Navigation pane**

> **QUICK TIP**
> Windows search is not case-sensitive, so you can type upper- or lowercase letters, and obtain the same results.

6. **Click in the Search This PC box to the right of the Address bar, type company, then press [Enter]**
   Windows searches your computer for files that contain the word "company" in their title. A green bar in the Address bar indicates the progress of your search. After a few moments, the search results, shown in FIGURE 2-22, appear. Windows found the renamed file, Company Goals.rtf, in your Documents folder, and the original Company Overview.rtf document on your removable drive, in the Publicity Items folder. It may also locate shortcuts to the file in your Recent folder. It's good to verify the location of the found files, so you can select the right one.

7. **Click the View tab, click Details in the Layout group then look in the Folder column to view the path to each file, dragging the edge of the Folder column header with the ⟷ pointer to widen it if necessary**

> **TROUBLE**
> If you see a message asking how you want to open the file, click WordPad.

8. **Double-click the Company Overview.rtf document in your file storage location**
   The file opens in WordPad or in another word-processing program on your computer that reads RTF files.

9. **Click the Close button ⊠ on the WordPad (or other word-processor) window**

Using the Search Tools tab in File Explorer

The **Search Tools tab** appears in the Ribbon as soon as you click the Search text box, and it lets you narrow your search criteria. Use the commands in the Location group to specify a particular search location. The Refine group lets you limit the search to files modified after a certain date, or to files of a particular kind, size, type, or other property. The Options group lets you repeat previous searches, save searches, and open the folder containing a found file.

FIGURE 2-21: **Found file**

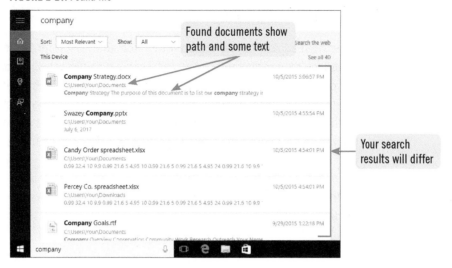

FIGURE 2-22: **Apps screen and Search pane**

Using Microsoft Edge

When you search for files using the search box on the Windows taskbar and click Web, the new web browser called **Microsoft Edge** opens. You can also open Edge by clicking its icon ![e] on the taskbar. Created to replace the older Internet Explorer browser, Edge is a Windows app that runs on personal computers, tablets, and smartphones. Edge features a reading mode that lets you read a webpage without ads. It also lets you annotate pages with markup tools such as a pen or highlighter, and add typed notes, as shown in FIGURE 2-23. You can also add pages to a Reading list or share them with OneNote or a social networking site.

FIGURE 2-23: **Web page annotated in Microsoft Edge**

Windows 10

Delete and Restore Files

Learning Outcomes
• Delete a file
• Restore a file
• Empty the Recycle Bin

If you no longer need a folder or file, you can delete (or remove) it from the storage device. By regularly deleting files and folders you no longer need and emptying the Recycle Bin, you free up valuable storage space on your computer. Windows places folders and files you delete from your hard drive in the Recycle Bin. If you delete a folder, Windows removes the folder as well as all files and subfolders stored in it. If you later discover that you need a deleted file or folder, you can restore it to its original location, as long as you have not yet emptied the Recycle Bin. Emptying the Recycle Bin permanently removes deleted folders and files from your computer. However, files and folders you delete from a removable drive, such as a USB flash drive, do not go to the Recycle Bin. They are immediately and permanently deleted and cannot be restored. **CASE** *You decide to delete the Company Goals document that you stored in your Documents folder.*

STEPS

1. **Click the Documents folder in the File Explorer Navigation pane**
   Your Documents folder opens.

2. **Click Company Goals.rtf to select it, click the Home tab, then click the Delete list arrow ⊠ in the Organize group; if the Show recycle confirmation command does not have a check mark next to it, click Show recycle confirmation (or if it does have a check mark, click ⊠ again to close the menu)**
   Selecting the Show recycle confirmation command tells Windows that whenever you click the Delete button, you want to see a confirmation dialog box before Windows deletes the file. That way you can change your mind if you want, before deleting the file.

3. **Click the Delete button ⊠ in the Organize group**
   The Delete File dialog box opens so you can confirm the deletion, as shown in FIGURE 2-24.

4. **Click Yes**
   You deleted the file. Because the file was stored on your computer and not on a removable drive, it was moved to the Recycle Bin.

5. **Click the Minimize button — on the window's title bar, examine the Recycle Bin icon, then double-click the Recycle Bin icon on the desktop**
   The Recycle Bin icon appears to contain crumpled paper, indicating that it contains deleted folders and/or files. The Recycle Bin window displays any previously deleted folders and files, including the Company Goals.rtf file.

6. **Click the Company Goals.rtf file to select it, then click the Restore the selected items button in the Restore group on the Recycle Bin Tools Manage tab, as shown in FIGURE 2-25**
   The file returns to its original location and no longer appears in the Recycle Bin window.

7. **In the Navigation pane, click the Documents folder**
   The Documents folder window contains the restored file. You decide to permanently delete this file after all.

8. **Click the file Company Goals.rtf, click ⊠ in the Organize group on the Home tab, click Permanently delete, then click Yes in the Delete File dialog box**

9. **Minimize the window, double-click the Recycle Bin, notice that the Company Goals.rtf file is no longer there, then close all open windows**

FIGURE 2-24: **Delete File dialog box**

FIGURE 2-25: **Restoring a file from the Recycle Bin**

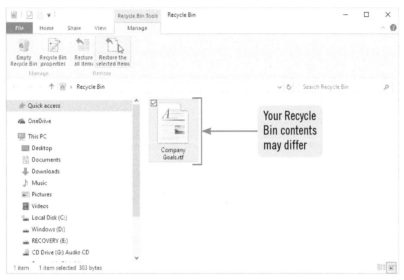

Your Recycle
Bin contents
may differ

More techniques for selecting and moving files

To select a group of items that are next to each other in a window, click the first item in the group, press and hold [Shift], then click the last item in the group. Both items you click and all the items between them become selected. To select files that are not next to each other, click the first file, press and hold [Ctrl], then click the other items you want to select as a group. Then you can copy, cut, or delete the group of files or folders you selected. **Drag and drop** is a technique in which you use your pointing device to drag a file or folder into a different folder and then drop it, or let go of the mouse button, to place it in that folder. Using drag and drop does not copy your file to the clipboard. If you drag and drop a file to a folder on a different drive, Windows *copies* the file. However, if you drag and drop a file to a folder on the same drive, Windows *moves* the file into that folder

instead. See FIGURE 2-26. If you want to move a file to another drive, hold down [Shift] while you drag and drop. If you want to copy a file to another folder on the same drive, hold down [Ctrl] while you drag and drop.

FIGURE 2-26: **Moving a file using drag and drop**

ScreenTip
confirms action

Image of file appears
as you drag

Practice

Concepts Review

Label the elements of the Windows 10 window shown in FIGURE 2-27.

FIGURE 2-27

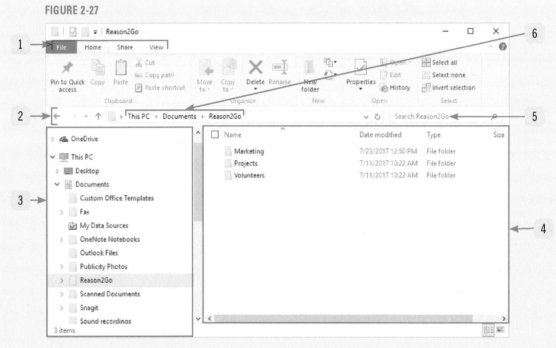

Match each term with the statement that best describes it.

7. View
8. File extension
9. Address bar
10. Path
11. Clipboard
12. Snap Assist

a. A series of locations separated by small triangles or backslashes that describes a file's location in the file hierarchy
b. A feature that helps you arrange windows on the screen
c. An area above the Files list that contains a path
d. A three- or four-letter sequence, preceded by a period, that identifies the type of file
e. A set of appearance choices for files and folders
f. An area of a computer's RAM used for temporary storage

Select the best answer from the list of choices.

13. Which part of a window lets you see a file's contents without opening the file?
   a. File list
   b. Address bar
   c. Navigation pane
   d. Preview pane

14. The new Microsoft web browser is called Microsoft _____.
   a. View
   b. Task
   c. Edge
   d. Desktop

15. The text you type in a Search text box is called:
   a. Sorting.
   b. RAM.
   c. Search criteria.
   d. Clipboard.

16. Which of the following is not a visible section in a File Explorer window?
   a. Clipboard
   b. Navigation pane
   c. File list
   d. Address bar

Skills Review

1. Understand files and folders.

a. Create a file hierarchy for an ice cream manufacturing business, using a name that you create. The business has departments for Product Development, Manufacturing, and Personnel. Product development activities include research and testing; manufacturing has facilities for ice cream and frozen yogurt; and Personnel handles hiring and payroll. How would you organize your folders and files using a file hierarchy of three levels? How would you use folders and subfolders to keep the documents related to these activities distinct and easy to navigate? Draw a diagram and write a short paragraph explaining your answer.

b. Use tools in the File Explorer window to create the folder hierarchy in the Documents folder on your computer.

c. Open NotePad and write the path of the Hiring folder, using backslashes to indicate levels in the hierarchy. Do the same for the Testing folder.

2. Create and save a file.

a. Connect your USB flash drive to a USB port on your computer, then open WordPad from the Start menu.

b. Type **Advertising Campaign** as the title, then start a new line.

c. Type your name, press [Enter] twice, then create the following list:

Menu ads

Email customers

Web page specials

Local TV spots

d. Save the WordPad file with the filename **Advertising Campaign.rtf** in the location where you store your Data Files, view the filename in the WordPad title bar, then close WordPad.

3. Explore the files and folders on your computer.

a. Open a File Explorer window.

b. Use the Navigation pane to navigate to your USB flash drive or the location where you store your Data Files.

c. Use the Address bar to navigate to This PC.

d. Use the File list to navigate to your local hard drive (C:).

e. Use the File list to open the Users folder, and then open the folder that represents your user name.

f. Open the Documents folder. (*Hint*: The path is This PC\Local Disk (C:) \Users\Your User Name\Documents.)

g. Use the Navigation pane to navigate back to This PC.

4. Change file and folder views.

a. Navigate to your Documents folder or the location of your Data Files using the method of your choice.

b. Use the View tab to view its contents as large icons.

c. View the folder's contents in the seven other views.

d. Sort the items in this location by date modified in ascending order.

e. Open the Preview pane, view a selected item's preview, then close the Preview pane.

5. Open, edit, and save files.

a. Start WordPad, then use the Open dialog box to open the Advertising Campaign.rtf document you created.

b. After the text "Local TV spots," add a line with the text **Social media**.

c. Save the document and close WordPad.

6. Copy files.

a. In the File Explorer window, navigate to the location where you store your Data Files if necessary.

b. Copy the Advertising Campaign.rtf document.

c. Create a new folder named **Advertising** on your USB flash drive or the location where you store your Data Files (*Hint*: Use the Home tab), then open the folder.

d. Paste the document copy in the new folder.

7. Move and rename files.

a. Navigate to your USB flash drive or the location where you store your Data Files.

b. Select the Advertising Campaign.rtf document located there, then cut it.

Skills Review (continued)

c. Navigate to your Documents folder, then paste the file there.

d. Rename the file **Advertising Campaign - Backup.rtf**.

8. Search for files and folders.

a. Use the search box on the taskbar to search for a file using the search text **backup**. (*Hint*: Remember to select My stuff.)

b. If necessary, scroll to the found file, and notice its path.

c. Open the Advertising Campaign - Backup document from the search results, then close WordPad. (*Hint*: Closing the program automatically closes any open documents.)

d. Open a File Explorer window, click in the search box, search your USB flash drive using the search text **overview**.

e. Open the found document from the File list, then close WordPad.

9. Delete and restore files.

a. Navigate to your Documents folder.

b. Verify that your Delete preference is Show recycle confirmation, then delete the Advertising Campaign - Backup.rtf file.

c. Open the Recycle Bin, and restore the document to its original location.

d. Navigate to your Documents folder, then move the Advertising Campaign - Backup.rtf file to the Advertising folder on your USB flash drive (or the location where you store your Data Files).

Independent Challenge 1

To meet the needs of gardeners in your town, you have opened a vacation garden care business named GreenerInc. Customers hire you to care for their gardens when they go on vacation. To promote your new business, your website designer asks you to give her selling points to include in a web ad.

a. Connect your USB flash drive to your computer, if necessary.

b. Create a new folder named **GreenerInc** on your USB flash drive or the location where you store your Data Files.

c. In the GreenerInc folder, create two subfolders named **Handouts** and **Website**.

d. Use WordPad to create a short paragraph or list that describes three advantages of your business. Use **GreenerInc Selling Points** as the first line, followed by the paragraph or list. Include your name and email address after the text.

e. Save the WordPad document with the filename **Selling Points.rtf** in the Website folder, then close the document and exit WordPad.

f. Open a File Explorer window, then navigate to the Website folder.

g. View the contents in at least three different views, then choose the view option that you prefer.

h. Copy the Selling Points.rtf file, then paste a copy in the Documents folder.

i. Rename the copied file **Selling Points Backup.rtf**.

j. Cut the Selling Points Backup.rtf file from the Documents folder, and paste it in the GreenerInc\Website folder in the location where you store your Data Files, then close the File Explorer window.

Independent Challenge 2

As a freelance webpage designer for nonprofit businesses, you depend on your computer to meet critical deadlines. Whenever you encounter a computer problem, you contact a computer consultant who helps you resolve the problem. This consultant has asked you to document, or keep records of, your computer's available drives.

a. Connect your USB flash drive to your computer, if necessary.

b. Open File Explorer and go to This PC so you can view information on your drives and other installed hardware.

c. View the window contents using three different views, then choose the one you prefer.

d. Open WordPad and create a document with the text **My Drives** and your name on separate lines. Save the document as **My Drives.rtf**.

Independent Challenge 2 (continued)

e. Use Snap Assist to view the WordPad and File Explorer windows next to each other on the screen. (*Hint*: Drag the title bar of one of the windows to the left side of the screen.)

f. In WordPad, list the names of the hard drive (or drives), devices with removable storage, and any other hardware devices installed on the computer as shown in the Devices and Drives section of the window.

g. Switch to a view that displays the total size and amount of free space on your hard drive(s) and removable storage drive(s), and edit each WordPad list item to include the amount of free space for each one (for example, 22.1 GB free of 95.5 GB).

h. Save the WordPad document with the filename **My Drives** on your USB flash drive or the location where you store your Data Files.

i. Close WordPad, then maximize the File Explorer window. Navigate to your file storage location, then preview your document in the Preview pane, and close the window.

Independent Challenge 3

You are an attorney at Garcia and Chu, a large accounting firm. You participate in the company's community outreach program by speaking at career days in area schools. You teach students about career opportunities available in the field of accounting. You want to create a folder structure to store the files for each session.

a. Connect your USB flash drive to your computer (if necessary), then open the window for your USB flash drive or the location where you store your Data Files.

b. Create a folder named **Career Days**.

c. In the Career Days folder, create a subfolder named **Valley Intermediate**. Open this folder, then close it.

d. Use WordPad to create a document with the title **Accounting Jobs** at the top of the page and your name on separate lines, and the following list of items:
Current Opportunities:
Bookkeeper
Accounting Clerk
Accountant
Certified Public Accountant (CPA)

e. Save the WordPad document with the filename **Accounting Jobs.rtf** in the Valley Intermediate folder. (*Hint*: After you switch to your USB flash drive in the Save As dialog box, open the Career Days folder, then open the Valley Intermediate folder before saving the file.) Close WordPad.

f. Open WordPad and the Accounting Jobs document again, add **Senior Accountant** after Accountant, then save the file and close WordPad.

g. Store a copy of the file using the Save As command to your Documents folder, renaming it **Accounting Jobs - Copy.rtf**, then close WordPad.

h. In File Explorer, delete the document copy in your Documents folder so it is placed in the Recycle Bin, then restore it.

i. Open the Recycle Bin window, snap the File Explorer to the left side of the screen and the Recycle in to the right side, then verify that the file has been restored to the correct location.

j. Cut the file from the Documents folder and paste it in the Career Days\Valley Intermediate folder in your Data File storage location, then close all windows.

Independent Challenge 4: Explore

Think of a hobby or volunteer activity that you do now, or one that you would like to start. You will use your computer to help you manage your plans or ideas for this activity.

a. Using paper and pencil, sketch a folder structure with at least two subfolders to contain your documents for this activity.

b. Connect your USB flash drive to your computer, then open the window for your USB flash drive.

Independent Challenge 4: Explore (continued)

c. In File Explorer, create the folder structure for your activity, using your sketch as a reference.

d. Think of at least three tasks that you can do to further your work in your chosen activity.

e. Start a new WordPad document. Add the title **Next Steps** at the top of the page and your name on the next line.

f. Below your name, list the three tasks. Save the file in one of the folders created on your USB flash drive, with the title **To Do.rtf**.

g. Close WordPad, then open a File Explorer window and navigate to the folder where you stored the document.

h. Create a copy of the file, place the copied file in your Documents folder, then rename this file with a name you choose.

i. Delete the copied file from your Documents folder, restore it, then cut and paste the file into the folder that contains your To Do.rtf file, ensuring that the filename of the copy is different so it doesn't overwirte the To Do.rtf file.

j. Open Microsoft Edge using its button on the taskbar, click in the search text box, then search for information about others doing your desired hobby or volunteer activity.

k. Click the Make a Web Note button ![icon] at the top of the window, click the Highlighter tool, then highlight an item that interests you.

l. Click the Share button ![icon], click Mail, choose your desired email account, then send the annotated page to yourself. You will receive an email with an attachment showing the annotated page.

m. Close Edge, your email program, and any open windows.

Visual Workshop

Create the folder structure shown in FIGURE 2-28 on your USB flash drive (or in the location where you store your Data Files). Create a WordPad document containing your name and today's date, type the path to the Midsize folder, and save it with the filename **Midsize.rtf** in a Midsize folder on your USB Flash drive or the location where you store your Data Files.

FIGURE 2-28

Getting Started with Microsoft Office 2016

CASE This module introduces you to the most frequently used programs in Office, as well as common features they all share.

Module Objectives

After completing this module, you will be able to:

- Understand the Office 2016 suite
- Start an Office app
- Identify Office 2016 screen elements
- Create and save a file
- Open a file and save it with a new name
- View and print your work
- Get Help, close a file, and exit an app

Files You Will Need

OF 1-1.xlsx

Understand the Office 2016 Suite

Learning Outcomes
• Identify Office suite components
• Describe the features of each app

Microsoft Office 2016 is a group of programs—which are also called applications or apps—designed to help you create documents, collaborate with coworkers, and track and analyze information. You use different Office programs to accomplish specific tasks, such as writing a letter or producing a presentation, yet all the programs have a similar look and feel. Microsoft Office 2016 apps feature a common, context-sensitive user interface, so you can get up to speed faster and use advanced features with greater ease. The Office apps are bundled together in a group called a **suite**. The Office suite is available in several configurations, but all include Word, Excel, PowerPoint, and OneNote. Some configurations include Access, Outlook, Publisher, Skype, and OneDrive. **CASE** *As part of your job, you need to understand how each Office app is best used to complete specific tasks.*

DETAILS

The Office apps covered in this book include:

• **Microsoft Word 2016**

  When you need to create any kind of text-based document, such as a memo, newsletter, or multipage report, Word is the program to use. You can easily make your documents look great by using formatting tools and inserting eye-catching graphics. The Word document shown in FIGURE 1-1 contains a company logo and simple formatting.

• **Microsoft Excel 2016**

  Excel is the perfect solution when you need to work with numeric values and make calculations. It puts the power of formulas, functions, charts, and other analytical tools into the hands of every user, so you can analyze sales projections, calculate loan payments, and present your findings in a professional manner. The Excel worksheet shown in FIGURE 1-1 tracks checkbook transactions. Because Excel automatically recalculates results whenever a value changes, the information is always up to date. A chart illustrates how the monthly expenses are broken down.

• **Microsoft PowerPoint 2016**

  Using PowerPoint, it's easy to create powerful presentations complete with graphics, transitions, and even a soundtrack. Using professionally designed themes and clip art, you can quickly and easily create dynamic slide shows such as the one shown in FIGURE 1-1.

• **Microsoft Access 2016**

  Access is a relational database program that helps you keep track of large amounts of quantitative data, such as product inventories or employee records. The form shown in FIGURE 1-1 can be used to generate reports on customer invoices and tours.

Microsoft Office has benefits beyond the power of each program, including:

• **Note-taking made simple; available on all devices**

  Use OneNote to take notes (organized in tabbed pages) on information that can be accessed on your computer, tablet, or phone. Share the editable results with others. Contents can include text, web page clips (using OneNote Clipper), email contents (directly inserted into a default section), photos (using Office Lens), and web pages.

• **Common user interface: Improving business processes**

  Because the Office suite apps have a similar **interface**, your experience using one app's tools makes it easy to learn those in the other apps. Office documents are **compatible** with one another, so you can easily **integrate**, or combine, elements—for example, you can add an Excel chart to a PowerPoint slide, or an Access table to a Word document.

  Most Office programs include the capability to incorporate feedback—called **online collaboration**—across the Internet or a company network.

FIGURE 1-1: Microsoft Office 2016 documents

Letter created in Word

Checkbook register created in Excel

Tourism presentation created in PowerPoint

Form created in Access

Photos courtesy of Elizabeth Eisner Reding

What is Office 365?

Until recently, most consumers purchased Microsoft Office in a traditional way: by buying a retail package from a store or downloading it from Microsoft.com. You can still purchase Microsoft Office 2016 in this traditional way—but you can also now purchase it as a subscription service called Microsoft Office 365, which is available in a wide variety of configurations.

Depending on which configuration you purchase, you will always have access to the most up-to-date versions of the apps in your package and, in many cases, can install these apps on multiple computers, tablets, and phones. And if you change computers or devices, you can easily uninstall the apps from an old device and install them on a new one.

Start an Office App

Learning
Outcomes
• Start an Office app
• Explain the purpose
  of a template
• Start a new blank
  document

To get started using Microsoft Office, you need to start, or **launch**, the Office app you want to use. An easy way to start the app you want is to press the Windows key, type the first few characters of the app name you want to search for, then click the app name In the Best match list. You will discover that there are many ways to accomplish just about any Windows task; for example, you can also see a list of all the apps on your computer by pressing the Windows key, then clicking All Apps. When you see the app you want, click its name. **CASE** *You decide to familiarize yourself with Office by starting Microsoft Word.*

STEPS

1. **Click the Start button ⊞ on the Windows taskbar**

   The Start menu opens, listing the most used apps on your computer. You can locate the app you want to open by clicking the app name if you see it, or you can type the app name to search for it.

2. **Type word**

   Your screen now displays "Word 2016" under "Best match", along with any other app that has "word" as part of its name (such as WordPad). See FIGURE 1-2.

3. **Click Word 2016**

   Word 2016 launches, and the Word **start screen** appears, as shown in FIGURE 1-3. The start screen is a landing page that appears when you first start an Office app. The left side of this screen displays recent files you have opened. (If you have never opened any files, then there will be no files listed under Recent.) The right side displays images depicting different templates you can use to create different types of documents. A **template** is a file containing professionally designed content and formatting that you can easily customize for your own needs. You can also start from scratch using the Blank Document template, which contains only minimal formatting settings.

Enabling touch mode

If you are using a touch screen with any of the Office 2016 apps, you can enable the touch mode to give the user interface a more spacious look, making it easier to navigate with your fingertips. Enable touch mode by clicking the Quick Access toolbar list arrow, then clicking Touch/Mouse Mode to select it. Then you'll see the Touch Mode button 🔁 in the Quick Access toolbar. Click 🔁, and you'll see the interface spread out.

Using shortcut keys to move between Office programs

You can switch between open apps using a keyboard shortcut. The [Alt][Tab] keyboard combination lets you either switch quickly to the next open program or file or choose one from a gallery. To switch immediately to the next open program or file, press [Alt][Tab]. To choose from all open programs and files, press and hold [Alt], then press and release [Tab] without releasing [Alt]. A gallery opens on screen, displaying the filename and a thumbnail image of each open program and file, as well as of the desktop. Each time you press [Tab] while holding [Alt], the selection cycles to the next open file or location. Release [Alt] when the program, file, or location you want to activate is selected.

FIGURE 1-2: **Searching for the Word app**

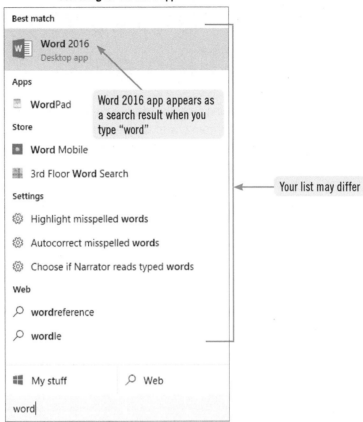

FIGURE 1-3: **Word start screen**

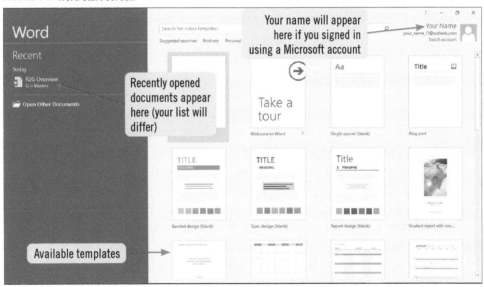

Using the Office Clipboard

You can use the Office Clipboard to cut and copy items from one Office program and paste them into others. The Office Clipboard can store a maximum of 24 items. To access it, open the Office Clipboard task pane by clicking the dialog box launcher 🖻 in the Clipboard group on the Home tab. Each time you copy a selection, it is saved in the Office Clipboard. Each entry in the

Office Clipboard includes an icon that tells you the program it was created in. To paste an entry, click in the document where you want it to appear, then click the item in the Office Clipboard. To delete an item from the Office Clipboard, right-click the item, then click Delete.

Identify Office 2016 Screen Elements

Learning Outcomes
• Identify basic components of the user interface
• Display and use Backstage view
• Adjust the zoom level

One of the benefits of using Office is that its apps have much in common, making them easy to learn and making it simple to move from one to another. All Office 2016 apps share a similar user interface, so you can use your knowledge of one to get up to speed in another. A **user interface** is a collective term for all the ways you interact with a software program. The user interface in Office 2016 provides intuitive ways to choose commands, work with files, and navigate in the program window. **CASE** ▸ *Familiarize yourself with some of the common interface elements in Office by examining the PowerPoint program window.*

STEPS

1. **Click the Start button ⊞ on the Windows taskbar, type** pow, **click** PowerPoint 2016, **then click** Blank Presentation

   PowerPoint starts and opens a new file, which contains a blank slide. Refer to FIGURE 1-4 to identify common elements of the Office user interface. The **document window** occupies most of the screen. At the top of every Office program window is a **title bar** that displays the document name and program name. Below the title bar is the **Ribbon**, which displays commands you're likely to need for the current task. Commands are organized onto **tabs**. The tab names appear at the top of the Ribbon, and the active tab appears in front. The **Share button** in the upper-right corner lets you invite other users to view your cloud-stored Word, Excel, or Powerpoint file.

2. **Click the** File tab

   The File tab opens, displaying **Backstage view**. It is called Backstage view because the commands available here are for working with the files "behind the scenes." The navigation bar on the left side of Backstage view contains commands to perform actions common to most Office programs.

3. **Click the** Back button ⊙ **to close Backstage view and return to the document window, then click the** Design tab **on the Ribbon**

   To display a different tab, click its name. Each tab contains related commands arranged into **groups** to make features easy to find. On the Design tab, the Themes group displays available design themes in a **gallery**, or visual collection of choices you can browse. Many groups contain a **launcher**, which you can click to open a dialog box or pane from which to choose related commands.

4. **Move the mouse pointer ⊠ over the** Ion Boardroom theme **in the Themes group as shown in** FIGURE 1-5, **but** *do not click* **the mouse button**

   The Ion Boardroom theme is temporarily applied to the slide in the document window. However, because you did not click the theme, you did not permanently change the slide. With the **Live Preview** feature, you can point to a choice, see the results, then decide if you want to make the change. Live Preview is available throughout Office.

5. **Move ⊠ away from the Ribbon and towards the slide**

   If you had clicked the Ion theme, it would be applied to this slide. Instead, the slide remains unchanged.

6. **Point to the** Zoom slider ▬▬▬▬▮▬▬▬ + 100% **on the status bar, then drag to the right until the Zoom level reads** 166%

   The slide display is enlarged. Zoom tools are located on the status bar. You can drag the slider or click the Zoom In or Zoom Out buttons to zoom in or out on an area of interest. **Zooming in** (a higher percentage), makes a document appear bigger on screen but less of it fits on the screen at once; **zooming out** (a lower percentage) lets you see more of the document at a reduced size.

7. **Click the** Zoom Out button ▬ **on the status bar to the left of the Zoom slider until the Zoom level reads** 120%

FIGURE 1-4: PowerPoint program window

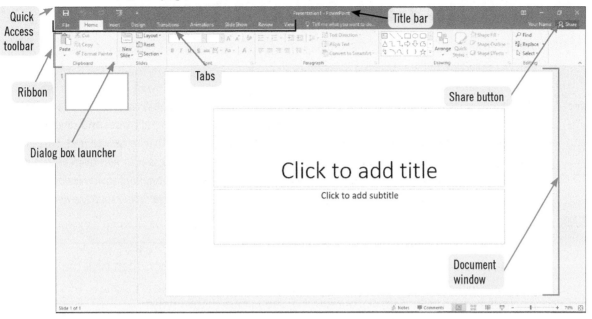

FIGURE 1-5: Viewing a theme with Live Preview

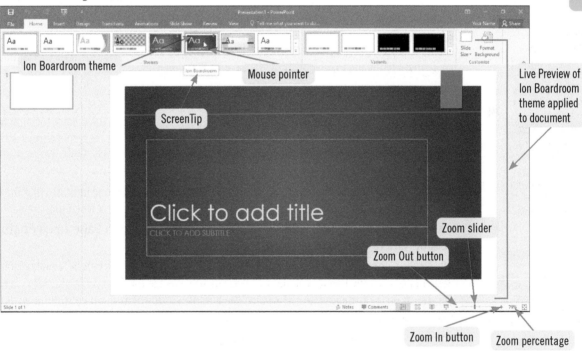

Using Backstage view

Backstage view in each Microsoft Office app offers "one stop shopping" for many commonly performed tasks, such as opening and saving a file, printing and previewing a document, defining document properties, sharing information, and exiting a program. Backstage view opens when you click the File tab in any Office app, and while features such as the Ribbon, Mini toolbar, and Live Preview all help you work *in* your documents, the File tab and Backstage view help you work *with* your documents. You can click commands in the navigation pane to open different places for working with your documents, such as the Open place, the Save place, and so on. You can return to your active document by clicking the Back button.

Create and Save a File

**Learning
Outcomes**
• Create a file
• Save a file
• Explain OneDrive

When working in an Office app, one of the first things you need to do is to create and save a file. A **file** is a stored collection of data. Saving a file enables you to work on a project now, then put it away and work on it again later. In some Office programs, including Word, Excel, and PowerPoint, you can open a new file when you start the app, then all you have to do is enter some data and save it. In Access, you must create a file before you enter any data. You should give your files meaningful names and save them in an appropriate location, such as a folder on your hard drive or OneDrive so they're easy to find. **OneDrive** is a Microsoft cloud storage system that lets you easily save, share, and access your files from anywhere you have Internet access. **CASE** *Use Word to familiarize yourself with creating and saving a document. First you'll type some notes about a possible location for a corporate meeting, then you'll save the information for later use.*

STEPS

1. **Click the Word button ▥ on the taskbar, click Blank document, then click the Zoom In button ⊞ until the level is 120%, if necessary**

2. **Type Locations for Corporate Meeting, then press [Enter] twice**
   The text appears in the document window, and the **insertion point** blinks on a new blank line. The insertion point indicates where the next typed text will appear.

3. **Type Las Vegas, NV, press [Enter], type Chicago, IL, press [Enter], type Seattle, WA, press [Enter] twice, then type your name**

4. **Click the Save button 🖫 on the Quick Access toolbar**
   Because this is the first time you are saving this new file, the Save place in Backstage view opens, showing various options for saving the file. See FIGURE 1-6. Once you save a file for the first time, clicking 🖫 saves any changes to the file *without* opening the Save As dialog box.

5. **Click Browse**
   The Save As dialog box opens, as shown in FIGURE 1-7, where you can browse to the location where you want to save the file. The Address bar in the Save As dialog box displays the default location for saving the file, but you can change it to any location. The File name field contains a suggested name for the document based on text in the file, but you can enter a different name.

6. **Type OF 1-Possible Corporate Meeting Locations**
   The text you type replaces the highlighted text. (The "OF 1-" in the filename indicates that the file is created in Office Module 1. You will see similar designations throughout this book when files are named.)

7. **In the Save As dialog box, use the Address bar or Navigation Pane to navigate to the location where you store your Data Files**
   You can store files on your computer, a network drive, your OneDrive, or any acceptable storage device.

8. **Click Save**
   The Save As dialog box closes, the new file is saved to the location you specified, and the name of the document appears in the title bar, as shown in FIGURE 1-8. (You may or may not see the file extension ".docx" after the filename.) See TABLE 1-1 for a description of the different types of files you create in Office, and the file extensions associated with each.

TABLE 1-1: Common filenames and default file extensions

file created in	is called a	and has the default extension
Word	document	.docx
Excel	workbook	.xlsx
PowerPoint	presentation	.pptx
Access	database	.accdb

FIGURE 1-6: Save place in Backstage view

Saves to your OneDrive account

Click to display a list of recently accessed locations on this PC

Click to open the Save As dialog box

FIGURE 1-7: Save As dialog box

Address bar; your location may differ

Navigation pane; your links and folders may differ

File name field; your computer may not display file extensions

Save as type list

FIGURE 1-8: Saved and named Word document

Save button

File name appears in title bar

Your name should appear here

Insertion point

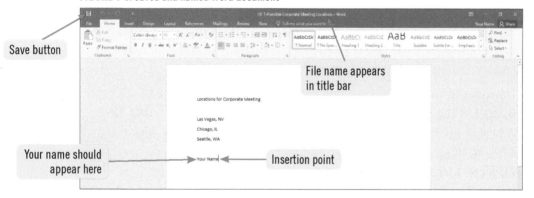

Saving files to OneDrive

All Office programs include the capability to incorporate feedback—called **online collaboration**—across the Internet or a company network. Using **cloud computing** (work done in a virtual environment), you can store your work in the cloud. Using OneDrive, a file storage service from Microsoft, you and your colleagues can create and store documents in the cloud and make the documents available anywhere there is Internet access to whomever you choose. To use OneDrive, you need a Microsoft Account, which you obtain at onedrive.live.com. Pricing and storage plans vary based on the type of Microsoft account you have. When you are logged into your Microsoft account and you

save a file in any of the Office apps, the first option in the Save As screen is your OneDrive. Double-click your OneDrive option, and the Save As dialog box opens displaying a location in the address bar unique to your OneDrive account. Type a name in the File name text box, then click Save and your file is saved to your OneDrive. To sync your files with OneDrive, you'll need to download and install the OneDrive for Windows app. Then, when you open Explorer, you'll notice a new folder called OneDrive has been added to your folder. In this folder is a sub-folder called Documents. This means if your Internet connection fails, you can work on your files offline.

Open a File and Save It with a New Name

Learning
Outcomes
• Open an existing file
• Save a file with a new name

In many cases as you work in Office, you need to use an existing file. It might be a file you or a coworker created earlier as a work in progress, or it could be a complete document that you want to use as the basis for another. For example, you might want to create a budget for this year using the budget you created last year; instead of typing in all the categories and information from scratch, you could open last year's budget, save it with a new name, and just make changes to update it for the current year. By opening the existing file and saving it with the Save As command, you create a duplicate that you can modify to suit your needs, while the original file remains intact. **CASE** *Use Excel to open an existing workbook file, and save it with a new name so the original remains unchanged.*

STEPS

1. **Click the Start button on the Windows taskbar, type exc, click Excel 2016, click Open Other Workbooks, This PC, then click Browse**

   The Open dialog box opens, where you can navigate to any drive or folder accessible to your computer to locate a file.

2. **In the Open dialog box, navigate to the location where you store your Data Files**

   The files available in the current folder are listed, as shown in FIGURE 1-9. This folder displays one file.

3. **Click OF 1-1.xlsx, then click Open**

   The dialog box closes, and the file opens in Excel. An Excel file is an electronic spreadsheet, so the new file displays a grid of rows and columns you can use to enter and organize data.

4. **Click the File tab, click Save As on the navigation bar, then click Browse**

   The Save As dialog box opens, and the current filename is highlighted in the File name text box. Using the Save As command enables you to create a copy of the current, existing file with a new name. This action preserves the original file and creates a new file that you can modify.

5. **Navigate to where you store your Data Files if necessary, type OF 1-Corporate Meeting Budget in the File name text box, as shown in FIGURE 1-10, then click Save**

   A copy of the existing workbook is created with the new name. The original file, OF 1-1.xlsx, closes automatically.

6. **Click cell A18, type your name, then press [Enter], as shown in FIGURE 1-11**

   In Excel, you enter data in cells, which are formed by the intersection of a row and a column. Cell A18 is at the intersection of column A and row 18. When you press [Enter], the cell pointer moves to cell A19.

7. **Click the Save button on the Quick Access toolbar**

   Your name appears in the workbook, and your changes to the file are saved.

Exploring File Open options

You might have noticed that the Open button in the Open dialog box includes a list arrow to the right of the button. In a dialog box, if a button includes a list arrow you can click the button to invoke the command, or you can click the list arrow to see a list of related commands that you can apply to the currently selected file. The Open list arrow includes several related commands, including Open Read-Only and Open as Copy.

Clicking Open Read-Only opens a file that you can only save with a new name; you cannot make changes to the original file. Clicking Open as Copy creates and opens a copy of the selected file and inserts the word "Copy" in the file's title. Like the Save As command, these commands provide additional ways to use copies of existing files while ensuring that original files do not get changed by mistake.

FIGURE 1-9: Open dialog box

FIGURE 1-10: Save As dialog box

FIGURE 1-11: Your name added to the workbook

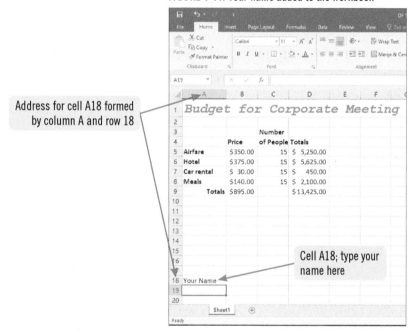

Working in Compatibility Mode

Not everyone upgrades to the newest version of Office. As a general rule, new software versions are **backward compatible**, meaning that documents saved by an older version can be read by newer software. To open documents created in older Office versions, Office 2016 includes a feature called Compatibility Mode. When you use Office 2016 to open a file created in an earlier version of Office, "Compatibility Mode" appears in the title bar, letting you know the file was created in an earlier but usable version of the program. If you are working with someone who may not be using the newest version of the software, you can avoid possible incompatibility problems by saving your file in another, earlier format. To do this in an Office program, click the File tab, click Save As on the navigation bar, then click Browse. In the Save As dialog box, click the Save as type list arrow in the Save As dialog box, then click an option in the list. For example, if you're working in Excel, click Excel 97-2003 Workbook format in the Save as type list to save an Excel file so it can be opened in Excel 97 or Excel 2003.

View and Print Your Work

Each Microsoft Office program lets you switch among various **views** of the document window to show more or fewer details or a different combination of elements that make it easier to complete certain tasks, such as formatting or reading text. Changing your view of a document does not affect the file in any way, it affects only the way it looks on screen. If your computer is connected to a printer or a print server, you can easily print any Office document using the Print button in the Print place in Backstage view. Printing can be as simple as **previewing** the document to see exactly what the printed version will look like and then clicking the Print button. Or, you can customize the print job by printing only selected pages. You can also use the Share place in Backstage view or the Share button on the Ribbon (if available) to share a document, export to a different format, or save it to the cloud. **CASE** ▶ *Experiment with changing your view of a Word document, and then preview and print your work.*

STEPS

1. **Click the** Word program button 🗐 **on the taskbar**
   Word becomes active, and the program window fills the screen.

2. **Click the** View tab **on the Ribbon**
   In most Office programs, the View tab on the Ribbon includes groups and commands for changing your view of the current document. You can also change views using the View buttons on the status bar.

3. **Click the** Read Mode button **in the Views group on the View tab**
   The view changes to Read Mode view, as shown in FIGURE 1-12. This view shows the document in an easy-to-read, distraction-free reading mode. Notice that the Ribbon is no longer visible on screen.

4. **Click the** Print Layout button 🗐 **on the Status bar**
   You return to Print Layout view, the default view in Word.

5. **Click the** File tab, **then click** Print **on the navigation bar**
   The Print place opens. The preview pane on the right displays a preview of how your document will look when printed. Compare your screen to FIGURE 1-13. Options in the Settings section enable you to change margins, orientation, and related options before printing. To change a setting, click it, and then click a new setting. For instance, to change from Letter paper size to Legal, click Letter in the Settings section, then click Legal on the menu that opens. The document preview updates as you change the settings. You also can use the Settings section to change which pages to print. If your computer is connected to multiple printers, you can click the current printer in the Printer section, then click the one you want to use. The Print section contains the Print button and also enables you to select the number of copies of the document to print.

6. **If your school allows printing, click the** Print button **in the Print place (otherwise, click the** Back button ⊙ **)**
   If you chose to print, a copy of the document prints, and Backstage view closes.

Customizing the Quick Access toolbar

You can customize the Quick Access toolbar to display your favorite commands. To do so, click the Customize Quick Access Toolbar button 🔽 in the title bar, then click the command you want to add. If you don't see the command in the list, click More Commands to open the Quick Access Toolbar tab of the current program's Options dialog box. In the Options dialog box, use the Choose commands from list to choose a category, click the desired command in the list on the left, click Add to add it to the Quick Access toolbar, then click OK. To remove a button from the toolbar, click the name in the list on the right in the Options dialog box, then click Remove. To add a command to the Quick Access toolbar as you work, simply right-click the button on the Ribbon, then click Add to Quick Access Toolbar on the shortcut menu. To move the Quick Access toolbar below the Ribbon, click the Customize Quick Access Toolbar button, and then click Show Below the Ribbon.

FIGURE 1-12: Read Mode view

Print Layout button

View buttons on status bar

FIGURE 1-13: Print settings on the File tab

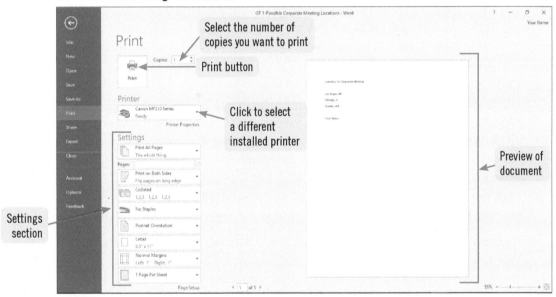

Select the number of copies you want to print

Print button

Click to select a different installed printer

Settings section

Preview of document

Creating a screen capture

A **screen capture** is a digital image of your screen, as if you took a picture of it with a camera. For instance, you might want to take a screen capture if an error message occurs and you want a Technical Support person to see exactly what's on the screen. You can create a screen capture using the Snipping Tool, an accessory designed to capture whole screens or portions of screens. To open the Snipping Tool, click the Start button on the Windows taskbar, type "sni", then click the Snipping Tool when it appears in the left panel. On the Snipping Tool toolbar, click New, then drag the pointer on the screen to select the area of the screen you want to capture. When you release the mouse button, the screen capture opens in the Snipping Tool window, and you can save, copy, or send it in an email. In Word, Excel, and PowerPoint 2016, you can capture screens or portions of screens and insert them in the current document using the Screenshot button in the Illustrations group on the Insert tab. Alternatively, you can create a screen capture by pressing [PrtScn]. (Keyboards differ, but you may find the [PrtScn] button in or near your keyboard's function keys.) Pressing this key places a digital image of your screen in the Windows temporary storage area known as the **Clipboard**. Open the document where you want the screen capture to appear, click the Home tab on the Ribbon (if necessary), then click the Paste button in the Clipboard group on the Home tab. The screen capture is pasted into the document.

Get Help, Close a File, and Exit an App

You can get comprehensive help at any time by pressing [F1] in an Office app or clicking the Help button on the title bar. You can also get help in the form of a ScreenTip by pointing to almost any icon in the program window. When you're finished working in an Office document, you have a few choices for ending your work session. You close a file by clicking the File tab, then clicking Close; you exit a program by clicking the Close button on the title bar. Closing a file leaves a program running, while exiting a program closes all the open files in that program as well as the program itself. In all cases, Office reminds you if you try to close a file or exit a program and your document contains unsaved changes. **CASE** *Explore the Help system in Microsoft Office, and then close your documents and exit any open programs.*

STEPS

1. **Point to the Zoom button in the Zoom group on the View tab of the Ribbon**

   A ScreenTip appears that describes how the Zoom button works and explains where to find other zoom controls.

2. **Click the Tell me box above the Ribbon, then type Choose a template**

   As you type in the Tell me box, a Smart list anticipates what you might want help with. If you see the task you want to complete, you can click it and Word will take you to the dialog box or options you need to complete the task. If you don't see the answer to your query, you can use the bottom two options to search the database.

3. **Click Get Help on "choose a template"**

   The Word Help window opens, as shown in FIGURE 1-14, displaying help results for choosing a template in Word. Each entry is a hyperlink you can click to open a list of topics. The Help window also includes a toolbar of useful Help commands such as printing and increasing the font size for easier readability, and a Search field. Office.com supplements the help content available on your computer with a wide variety of up-to-date topics, templates, and training.

4. **Click the Where do I find templates link in the results list Word Help window**

   The Word Help window changes, and a more detailed explanation appears below the topic.

5. **If necessary, scroll down until the Download Microsoft Office templates topic fills the Word Help window**

   The topic is displayed in the Help window, as shown in FIGURE 1-15. The content in the window explains that you can create a wide variety of documents using a template (a pre-formatted document) and that you can get many templates free of charge.

6. **Click the Keep Help on Top button ⊣ in the lower-right corner of the window**

   The Pin Help button rotates so the pin point is pointed towards the bottom of the screen: this allows you to read the Help window while you work on your document.

7. **Click the Word document window, notice the Help window remains visible**

8. **Click a blank area of the Help window, click ⊤ to Unpin Help, click the Close button ✕ in the Help window, then click the Close button ✕ in the Word program window**

   Word closes, and the Excel program window is active.

9. **Click the Close button ✕ in the Excel program window, click the PowerPoint app button 🗗 on the taskbar if necessary, then click the Close button ✕ to exit PowerPoint**

   Excel and PowerPoint both close.

FIGURE 1-14: **Word Help window**

FIGURE 1-15: **Create a document Help topic**

Search field

Help toolbar

Word 2016 Help

Choose a template

Click to learn how to find templates

Where do I find **templates?**
In Microsoft templates all the formatting is complete; ... click My Templates or Personal, and then choose your template. ... Download Microsoft Office templates.

Edit **templates**
Edit templates. Whether you're starting from a built-in template or updating one of your own, Word's built-in tools help you update templates to suit your needs.

Create forms that users complete or print in Word
Create forms that users complete or print in Word. You can create a form in Microsoft Word by starting with a template and ... you want people to choose a ...

Zoom in or out of a document
Choose a particular zoom setting. You can choose how

Help topics are updated frequently; your list may differ

Print button

Word 2016 Help

Choose a template

templates.

Download Microsoft Office templates

Do you want to create a resume, mailing label, budget, fax cover sheet, presentation, or invitation? To get free templates like these, go to **File > New** in your Office program, and then click a category under **Office.com Templates**, such as **Letters**, **Business**, or **Form** (In Office 2013 or Office 2016, try one of the **Suggested searches** links).

Or, type what you're looking for in the search box, such as **avery** for labels.

TIP   If you're on the web, try the free online templates at templates.office.com. You can use them right in your browser, in the Office Online programs.

Drag scroll bar to read more

Keep Help on Top button

Office 2016

Using sharing features and co-authoring capabilities

If you are using Word, Excel, or PowerPoint, you can take advantage of the Share feature, which makes it easy to share your files that have been saved to OneDrive. When you click the Share button, you will be asked to invite others to share the file. To do this, type in the name or email addresses in the Invite people text box. When you invite others, you have the opportunity to give them different levels of permission. You might want some people to have read-only privileges; you might want others to be able to make edits. Also available in Word, Excel, and PowerPoint is real-time co-authoring capabilities for files stored on OneDrive. Once a file on OneDrive is opened and all the users have been given editing privileges, all the users can make edits simultaneously. On first use, each user will be prompted to automatically share their changes.

Recovering a document

Each Office program has a built-in recovery feature that allows you to open and save files that were open at the time of an interruption such as a power failure. When you restart the program(s) after an interruption, the Document Recovery task pane opens on the left side of your screen displaying both original and recovered versions of the files that were open. If you're not sure which file to open (original or recovered), it's usually better to open the recovered file because it will contain the latest information. You can, however, open and review all versions of the file that were recovered and save the best one. Each file listed in the Document Recovery task pane displays a list arrow with options that allow you to open the file, save it as is, delete it, or show repairs made to it during recovery.

Practice

Concepts Review

Label the elements of the program window shown in FIGURE 1-16.

FIGURE 1-16

Match each project with the program for which it is best suited.

8. Microsoft PowerPoint
9. Microsoft Word
10. Microsoft Excel
11. Microsoft Access

a. Corporate convention budget with expense projections
b. Presentation for city council meeting
c. Business cover letter for a job application
d. Department store inventory

Independent Challenge 1

You just accepted an administrative position with a local independently owned insurance agent who has recently invested in computers and is now considering purchasing a subscription to Office 365. You have been asked to think of uses for the apps and you put your ideas in a Word document.

a. Start Word, create a new Blank document, then save the document as **OF 1-Microsoft Office Apps Uses** in the location where you store your Data Files.
b. Change the zoom factor to 120%, type **Microsoft Access**, press [Enter] twice, type **Microsoft Excel**, press [Enter] twice, type **Microsoft PowerPoint**, press [Enter] twice, type **Microsoft Word**, press [Enter] twice, then type your name.
c. Click the line beneath each program name, type at least two tasks you can perform using that program (each separated by a comma), then press [Enter].
d. Save the document, then submit your work to your instructor as directed.
e. Exit Word.

Creating Documents with Word 2016

CASE ▶ You have been hired to work in the Marketing Department at Reason2Go (R2G), a company that provides adventurous travelers with meaningful project options for giving back to the global community. Shortly after reporting to your new office, Mary Watson, the vice president of sales and marketing, asks you to use Word to create a memo to the marketing staff and a letter to one of the project hosts.

Module Objectives

After completing this module, you will be able to:

- Understand word processing software
- Explore the Word window
- Start a document
- Save a document
- Select text
- Format text using the Mini toolbar and the Ribbon
- Use a document template
- Navigate a document

Files You Will Need

WD 1-1.docx

Understand Word Processing Software

Learning Outcomes
- Identify the features of Word
- State the benefits of using a word processing program

A **word processing program** is a software program that includes tools for entering, editing, and formatting text and graphics. Microsoft Word is a powerful word processing program that allows you to create and enhance a wide range of documents quickly and easily. FIGURE 1-1 shows the first page of a report created using Word and illustrates some of the Word features you can use to enhance your documents. The electronic files you create using Word are called **documents**. One of the benefits of using Word is that document files can be stored on a hard disk, flash drive, or other physical storage device, or to OneDrive or another Cloud storage place, making them easy to transport, share, and revise. **CASE** *Before beginning your memo to the marketing staff, you explore the editing and formatting features available in Word.*

DETAILS

You can use Word to accomplish the following tasks:

- **Type and edit text**

  The Word editing tools make it simple to insert and delete text in a document. You can add text to the middle of an existing paragraph, replace text with other text, undo an editing change, and correct typing, spelling, and grammatical errors with ease.

- **Copy and move text from one location to another**

  Using the more advanced editing features of Word, you can copy or move text from one location and insert it in a different location in a document. You also can copy and move text between documents. This means you don't have to retype text that is already entered in a document.

- **Format text and paragraphs with fonts, colors, and other elements**

  The sophisticated formatting tools in Word allow you to make the text in your documents come alive. You can change the size, style, and color of text, add lines and shading to paragraphs, and enhance lists with bullets and numbers. Creatively formatting text helps to highlight important ideas in your documents.

- **Format and design pages**

  The page-formatting features in Word give you power to design attractive newsletters, create powerful résumés, and produce documents such as research papers, business cards, brochures, and reports. You can change paper size, organize text in columns, and control the layout of text and graphics on each page of a document. For quick results, Word includes preformatted cover pages, pull quotes, and headers and footers, as well as galleries of coordinated text, table, and graphic styles. If you are writing a research paper, Word makes it easy to manage reference sources and create footnotes, endnotes, and bibliographies.

- **Enhance documents with tables, charts, graphics, screenshots, and videos**

  Using the powerful graphics tools in Word, you can spice up your documents with pictures, videos, photographs, screenshots, lines, preset quick shapes, and diagrams. You also can illustrate your documents with tables and charts to help convey your message in a visually interesting way.

- **Use Mail Merge to create form letters and mailing labels**

  The Word Mail Merge feature allows you to send personalized form letters to many different people. You can also use Mail Merge to create mailing labels, directories, e-mail messages, and other types of documents.

- **Share documents securely**

  The security features in Word make it quick and easy to remove comments, tracked changes, and unwanted personal information from your files before you share them with others. You can also add a password or a digital signature to a document and convert a file to a format suitable for publishing on the web.

FIGURE 1-1: A report created using Word

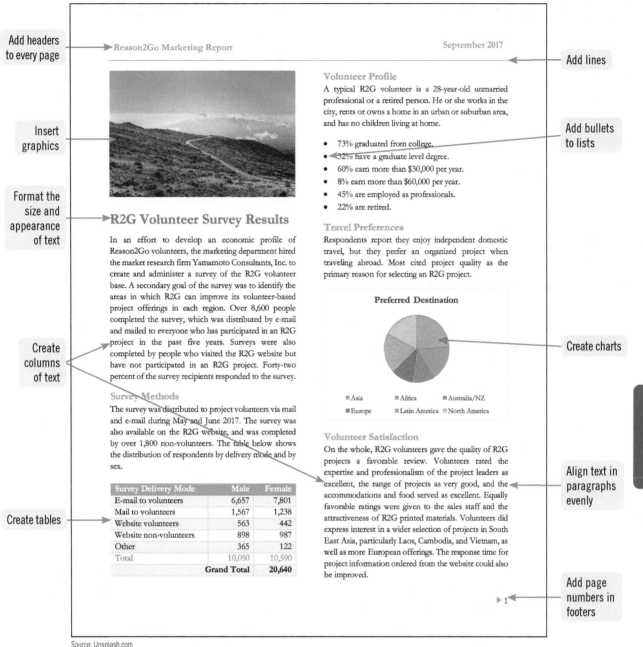

Add headers to every page

Insert graphics

Format the size and appearance of text

Create columns of text

Create tables

Add lines

Add bullets to lists

Create charts

Align text in paragraphs evenly

Add page numbers in footers

Source: Unsplash.com

The following text appears within the figure:

Reason2Go Marketing Report   September 2017

R2G Volunteer Survey Results

In an effort to develop an economic profile of Reason2Go volunteers, the marketing department hired the market research firm Yamamoto Consultants, Inc. to create and administer a survey of the R2G volunteer base. A secondary goal of the survey was to identify the areas in which R2G can improve its volunteer-based project offerings in each region. Over 8,600 people completed the survey, which was distributed by e-mail and mailed to everyone who has participated in an R2G project in the past five years. Surveys were also completed by people who visited the R2G website but have not participated in an R2G project. Forty-two percent of the survey recipients responded to the survey.

Survey Methods

The survey was distributed to project volunteers via mail and e-mail during May and June 2017. The survey was also available on the R2G website, and was completed by over 1,800 non-volunteers. The table below shows the distribution of respondents by delivery mode and by sex.

Survey Delivery Mode	Male	Female
E-mail to volunteers	6,657	7,801
Mail to volunteers	1,567	1,238
Website volunteers	563	442
Website non-volunteers	898	987
Other	365	122
Total	10,050	10,590
	Grand Total	20,640

Volunteer Profile

A typical R2G volunteer is a 28-year-old unmarried professional or a retired person. He or she works in the city, rents or owns a home in an urban or suburban area, and has no children living at home.

- 73% graduated from college.
- 32% have a graduate level degree.
- 60% earn more than $30,000 per year.
- 8% earn more than $60,000 per year.
- 45% are employed as professionals.
- 22% are retired.

Travel Preferences

Respondents report they enjoy independent domestic travel, but they prefer an organized project when traveling abroad. Most cited project quality as the primary reason for selecting an R2G project.

Preferred Destination

■ Asia   ■ Africa   ■ Australia/NZ
■ Europe   ■ Latin America   ■ North America

Volunteer Satisfaction

On the whole, R2G volunteers gave the quality of R2G projects a favorable review. Volunteers rated the expertise and professionalism of the project leaders as excellent, the range of projects as very good, and the accommodations and food served as excellent. Equally favorable ratings were given to the sales staff and the attractiveness of R2G printed materials. Volunteers did express interest in a wider selection of projects in South East Asia, particularly Laos, Cambodia, and Vietnam, as well as more European offerings. The response time for project information ordered from the website could also be improved.

1

Word 2016

Planning a document

Before you create a new document, it's a good idea to spend time planning it. Identify the message you want to convey, the audience for your document, and the elements, such as tables or charts, you want to include. You should also think about the tone and look of your document—are you writing a business letter, which should be written in a pleasant, but serious, tone and have a formal appearance, or are you creating a flyer that must be colorful, eye-catching, and fun to read? The purpose and audience for your document determine the appropriate design. Planning the layout and design of a document involves deciding how to organize the text, selecting the fonts to use, identifying the graphics to include, and selecting the formatting elements that will enhance the message and appeal of the document. For longer documents, such as newsletters, it can be useful to sketch the layout and design of each page before you begin.

Explore the Word Window

When you start Word, the Word start screen opens. It includes a list of recently opened documents and a gallery of templates for creating a new document. **CASE** ▸ *You open a blank document and examine the elements of the Word program window.*

STEPS

1. **Start Word, then click Blank document**

   A blank document opens in the **Word program window**, as shown in FIGURE 1-2. The blinking vertical line in the document window is the **insertion point**. It indicates where text appears as you type.

TROUBLE

If the Ribbon is hidden, click the Ribbon Display Options button on the title bar, then click Show Tabs and Commands.

2. **Move the mouse pointer around the Word program window**

   The mouse pointer changes shape depending on where it is in the Word program window. You use pointers to move the insertion point or to select text to edit. TABLE 1-1 describes common pointers in Word.

3. **Place the mouse pointer over a button on the Ribbon**

   When you place the mouse pointer over a button or some other elements of the Word program window, a ScreenTip appears. A **ScreenTip** is a label that identifies the name of the button or feature, briefly describes its function, conveys any keyboard shortcut for the command, and includes a link to associated help topics, if any.

DETAILS

QUICK TIP

You can modify the Quick Access toolbar to include the commands you use frequently.

Using FIGURE 1-2 **as a guide, find the elements described below in your program window:**

• The **title bar** displays the name of the document and the name of the program. Until you give a new document a different name, its temporary name is Document1. The left side of the title bar contains the **Quick Access toolbar**, which includes buttons for saving a document and for undoing, redoing, and repeating a change. The right side of the title bar contains the **Ribbon Display Options button**, which you use to hide or show the Ribbon and tabs, the resizing buttons, and the program Close button.

QUICK TIP

To display a different tab, you simply click its name on the Ribbon.

• The **File tab** provides access to **Backstage view** where you manage files and the information about them. Backstage view includes commands related to working with documents, such as opening, printing, and saving a document. The File tab also provides access to your account and to the Word Options dialog box, which is used to customize the way you use Word.

• The **Ribbon** contains the Word tabs. Each **tab** on the Ribbon includes buttons for commands related to editing and formatting documents. The commands are organized in **groups**. For example, the Home tab includes the Clipboard, Font, Paragraph, Styles, and Editing groups. The Ribbon also includes the **Tell Me box**, which you can use to find a command or access the Word Help system, and the **Share button**, which you can use to save a document to the Cloud.

• The **document window** displays the current document. You enter text and format your document in the document window.

TROUBLE

Click the View tab, then click the Ruler check box in the Show group to display the rulers if they are not already displayed.

• The rulers appear in the document window in Print Layout view. The **horizontal ruler** displays left and right document margins as well as the tab settings and paragraph indents, if any, for the paragraph in which the insertion point is located. The **vertical ruler** displays the top and bottom document margins.

• The **vertical** and **horizontal scroll bars** are used to display different parts of the document in the document window. The scroll bars include **scroll boxes** and **scroll arrows**, which you use to scroll.

• The **status bar** displays the page number of the current page, the total number of pages and words in the document, and the status of spelling and grammar checking. It also includes the view buttons, the Zoom slider, and the Zoom level button. You can customize the status bar to display other information.

• The **view buttons** on the status bar allow you to display the document in Read Mode, Print Layout, or Web Layout view. The **Zoom slider** and the **Zoom level button** provide quick ways to enlarge and decrease the size of the document in the document window, making it easy to zoom in on a detail of a document or to view the layout of the document as a whole.

Creating Documents with Word 2016

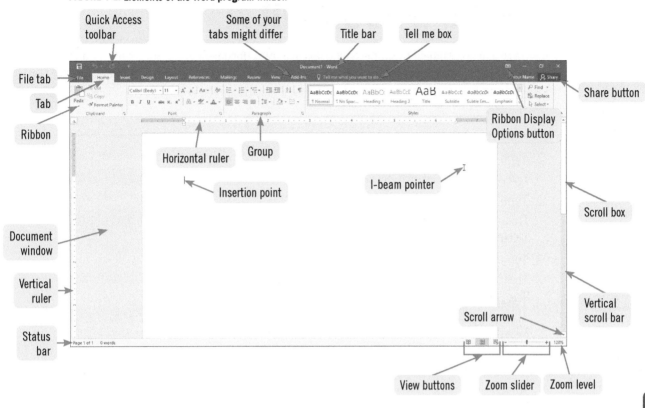

FIGURE 1-2: Elements of the Word program window

TABLE 1-1: Common mouse pointers in Word

name	pointer	use to
I-beam pointer	I	Move the insertion point in a document or to select text
Click and Type pointers, including left-align and center-align	I ≡I ⊥I	Move the insertion point to a blank area of a document in Print Layout or Web Layout view; double-clicking with a Click and Type pointer automatically applies the paragraph formatting (alignment and indentation) required to position text or a graphic at that location in the document
Selection pointer	↖	Click a button or other element of the Word program window; appears when you point to elements of the Word program window
Right-pointing arrow pointer	⇗	Select a line or lines of text; appears when you point to the left edge of a line of text in the document window
Hand pointer	☝	Open a hyperlink; appears when you point to a hyperlink in a task pane or when you press [Ctrl] and point to a hyperlink in a document
Hide white space pointer	⊣⊢	Hide the white space in the top and bottom margins of a document in Print Layout view
Show white space pointer	⊤⊥	Show the white space in the top and bottom margins of a document in Print Layout view

Word 2016

Start a Document

You begin a new document by simply typing text in a blank document in the document window. Word uses **word wrap**, a feature that automatically moves the insertion point to the next line of the document as you type. You only press [Enter] when you want to start a new paragraph or insert a blank line. **CASE** ▸ *You type a quick memo to the marketing staff.*

STEPS

TROUBLE
If you press the wrong key, press [Backspace] to erase the mistake, then try again.

1. **Type** Reason2Go, **then press** [Enter] **twice**

   Each time you press [Enter] the insertion point moves to the start of the next line.

2. **Type** TO:, **then press** [Tab] **twice**

   Pressing [Tab] moves the insertion point several spaces to the right. You can use the [Tab] key to align the text in a memo header or to indent the first line of a paragraph.

3. **Type** R2G Managers, **then press** [Enter]

   The insertion point moves to the start of the next line.

QUICK TIP
Wavy lines and other automatic feature markers appear on screen but do not print.

4. **Type:** FROM: [Tab] [Tab] Mary Watson [Enter]

   DATE: [Tab] [Tab] March 13, 2017 [Enter]

   RE: [Tab] [Tab] Marketing Meeting [Enter] [Enter]

   Red or blue wavy lines may appear under the words you typed, indicating a possible spelling or grammar error. Spelling and grammar checking is one of the many automatic features you will encounter as you type. TABLE 1-2 describes several of these automatic features. You can correct any typing errors you make later.

TROUBLE
To reverse an AutoCorrect adjustment, immediately click the Undo button ⤺ on the Quick Access toolbar.

5. **Type** The next marketing staff meeting will be held on the 17th of March at 2 p.m. in the conference room on the ground floor., **then press** [Spacebar]

   As you type, notice that the insertion point moves automatically to the next line of the document. You also might notice that Word automatically changed "17th" to "17th" in the memo. This feature is called **AutoCorrect**. AutoCorrect automatically makes typographical adjustments and detects and adjusts typing errors, certain misspelled words (such as "taht" for "that"), and incorrect capitalization as you type.

6. **Type** Heading the agenda will be the launch of our new Sea Turtle Conservation Project, a rewarding opportunity to supervise hatcheries, count and release baby turtles, and patrol the nighttime shores of Costa Rica. The project is scheduled for September 2017.

   When you type the first few characters of "September," the Word AutoComplete feature displays the complete word in a ScreenTip. **AutoComplete** suggests text to insert quickly into your documents. You can ignore AutoComplete for now. Your memo should resemble FIGURE 1-3.

QUICK TIP
If you want uniform spacing between lines and paragraphs, apply the No Spacing style to the document by clicking the No Spacing button in the Styles group on the Home tab before you begin to type. Alternatively, select the text and then click the No Spacing button.

7. **Press** [Enter], **then type** Sam Roiphe is in Tamarindo hammering out the details. A preliminary draft of the project brochure is attached. Bring your creative ideas to the meeting.

   When you press [Enter] and type the new paragraph, notice that Word adds more space between the paragraphs than it does between the lines in each paragraph. This is part of the default style for paragraphs in Word, called the **Normal style**.

8. **Position the** I **pointer after** for **(but before the space) in the last sentence of the first paragraph, then click to move the insertion point after "for"**

9. **Press** [Backspace] **three times, then type** to begin in

   Pressing [Backspace] removes the character before the insertion point.

10. **Move the insertion point before** staff **in the first sentence, then press** [Delete] **six times to remove the word "staff" and the space after it**

    Pressing [Delete] removes the character after the insertion point. FIGURE 1-4 shows the revised memo.

FIGURE 1-3: Memo text in the document window

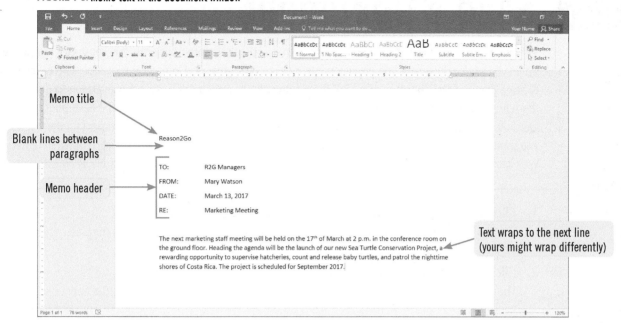

Memo title

Blank lines between paragraphs

Memo header

Text wraps to the next line (yours might wrap differently)

FIGURE 1-4: Edited memo text

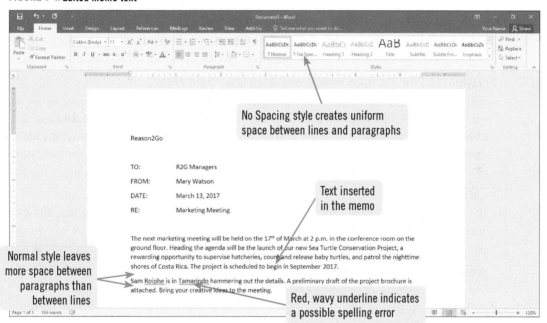

No Spacing style creates uniform space between lines and paragraphs

Text inserted in the memo

Normal style leaves more space between paragraphs than between lines

Red, wavy underline indicates a possible spelling error

TABLE 1-2: Automatic features that appear as you type in Word

feature	what appears	to use
AutoComplete	A ScreenTip suggesting text to insert appears as you type	Press [Enter] to insert the text suggested by the ScreenTip; continue typing to reject the suggestion
AutoCorrect	A small blue box appears when you place the pointer over text corrected by AutoCorrect; an AutoCorrect Options button appears when you point to the blue box	Word automatically corrects typos, minor spelling errors, and capitalization, and adds typographical symbols (such as © and ™) as you type; to reverse an AutoCorrect adjustment, click the AutoCorrect Options list arrow, then click the option that will undo the action
Spelling and Grammar	A red wavy line under a word indicates a possible misspelling or a repeated word; a blue wavy line under text indicates a possible grammar error	Right-click red- or blue-underlined text to display a shortcut menu of correction options; click a correction option to accept it and remove the wavy underline

Save a Document

Learning Outcomes
- Save a file using a descriptive filename
- Use the Save As dialog box

To store a document permanently so you can open it and edit it at another time, you must save it as a **file**. When you **save** a document you give it a name, called a **filename**, and indicate the location where you want to store the file. Files created in Word 2016 are automatically assigned the .docx file extension to distinguish them from files created in other software programs. You can save a document using the Save button on the Quick Access toolbar or the Save command on the File tab. Once you have saved a document for the first time, you should save it again every few minutes and always before printing so that the saved file is updated to reflect your latest changes. **CASE** ▶ *You save your memo using a descriptive filename and the default file extension.*

STEPS

1. **Click the Save button 🖫 on the Quick Access toolbar**

   The first time you save a document, the Save As screen opens. The screen displays all the places you can save a file to, including OneDrive, your PC, or a different location.

TROUBLE

If you don't see the extension .docx as part of the filename, the setting in Windows to display file extensions is not active.

2. **Click Browse in the Save As screen**

   The Save As dialog box opens, similar to FIGURE 1-5. The default filename, Reason2Go, appears in the File name text box. The default filename is based on the first few words of the document. The default file type, Word Document, appears in the Save as type list box. TABLE 1-3 describes the functions of some of the buttons in the Save As dialog box.

3. **Type WD 1-Sea Turtle Memo in the File name text box**

   The new filename replaces the default filename. Giving your documents brief descriptive filenames makes it easier to locate and organize them later. You do not need to type .docx when you type a new filename.

4. **Navigate to the location where you store your Data Files**

   You can navigate to a different drive or folder in several ways. For example, you can click a drive or folder in the Address bar or the navigation pane to go directly to that location. You can also double-click a drive or folder in the folder window to change the active location. When you are finished navigating to the drive or folder where you store your Data Files, that location appears in the Address bar. Your Save As dialog box should resemble FIGURE 1-6.

5. **Click Save**

   The document is saved to the drive and folder you specified in the Save As dialog box, and the title bar displays the new filename, WD 1-Sea Turtles Memo.docx.

6. **Place the insertion point before conference in the first sentence, type large, then press [Spacebar]**

   You can continue to work on a document after you have saved it with a new filename.

7. **Click 🖫**

   Your change to the memo is saved. After you save a document for the first time, you must continue to save the changes you make to the document. You also can press [Ctrl][S] to save a document.

FIGURE 1-5: **Save As dialog box**

Active folder or drive (yours might differ)

Folders and files in the active folder or drive (yours might differ)

Default filename and file extension are selected

Click to change the file type

FIGURE 1-6: **File to be saved to the Mod 1 folder**

Click to create a new folder in the active folder or drive

Save location (yours might differ)

Your dialog box might list the files and folders in the active drive or folder here

New filename

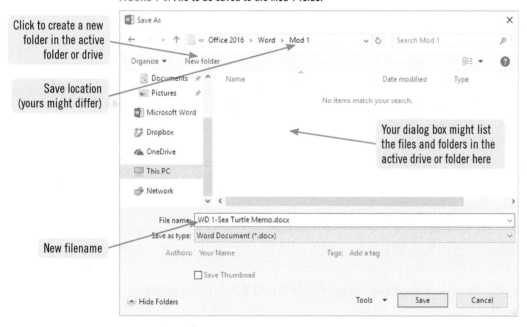

TABLE 1-3: **Save As dialog box buttons**

button	use to
Back	Navigate back to the last location shown in the Address bar
Forward	Navigate to the location that was previously shown in the Address bar
Up to	Navigate to the location above the current location in the folder hierarchy
Organize	Open a menu of commands related to organizing the selected file or folder, including Cut, Copy, Delete, Rename, and Properties
New folder	Create a new folder in the current folder or drive
Change your view	Change the way folder and file information is shown in the folder window in the Save As dialog box; click the Change your view button to toggle between views, or click the list arrow to open a menu of view options

Word 2016

Select Text

Learning
Outcomes
• Select text using
the mouse
• Use formatting
marks

Before deleting, editing, or formatting text, you must **select** the text. Selecting text involves clicking and dragging the I-beam pointer across the text to highlight it. You also can click in the margin to the left of text with the 𝄃 pointer to select whole lines or paragraphs. TABLE 1-4 describes the many ways to select text. **CASE** ▶ *You revise the memo by selecting text and replacing it with new text.*

STEPS

1. **Click the** Show/Hide ¶ **button** ⟦¶⟧ **in the Paragraph group**

   Formatting marks appear in the document window. **Formatting marks** are special characters that appear on your screen but do not print. Common formatting marks include the paragraph symbol (¶), which shows the end of a paragraph—wherever you press [Enter]; the dot symbol (·), which represents a space—wherever you press [Spacebar]; and the arrow symbol (▲), which shows the location of a tab stop—wherever you press [Tab]. Working with formatting marks turned on can help you to select, edit, and format text with precision.

2. **Click before** R2G Managers, **then drag the** 𝖨 **pointer over the text to select it**

   The words are selected, as shown in FIGURE 1-7. For now, you can ignore the floating toolbar that appears over text when you first select it.

3. **Type** Marketing Staff

   The text you type replaces the selected text.

4. **Double-click** Mary, **type your first name, double-click** Watson, **then type your last name**

   Double-clicking a word selects the entire word.

5. **Place the pointer in the margin to the left of the RE: line so that the pointer changes to** 𝄃, **click to select the line, then type** RE: [Tab] [Tab] Launch of new Sea Turtle Conservation Project

   Clicking to the left of a line of text with the 𝄃 pointer selects the entire line.

6. **Select** supervise **in the third line of the first paragraph, type** build, **select** nighttime shores, **then type** moon-lit beaches

7. **Select the sentence** Sam Roiphe is in Tamarindo hammering out the details. **in the second paragraph, then press** [Delete]

   Selecting text and pressing [Delete] removes the text from the document.

8. **Click** ⟦¶⟧, **then click the** Save **button** 🖫 **on the Quick Access toolbar**

   Formatting marks are turned off, and your changes to the memo are saved. The Show/Hide ¶ button is a **toggle button**, which means you can use it to turn formatting marks on and off. The edited memo is shown in FIGURE 1-8.

FIGURE 1-7: **Text selected in the memo**

FIGURE 1-8: **Edited memo with replacement text**

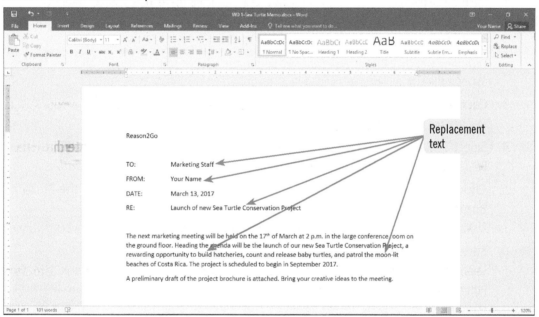

TABLE 1-4: **Methods for selecting text**

to select	use the pointer to
Any amount of text	Drag over the text
A word	Double-click the word
A line of text	Move the pointer to the left of the line, then click
A sentence	Press and hold [Ctrl], then click the sentence
A paragraph	Triple-click the paragraph or double-click with the pointer to the left of the paragraph
A large block of text	Click at the beginning of the selection, press and hold [Shift], then click at the end of the selection
Multiple nonconsecutive selections	Select the first selection, then press and hold [Ctrl] as you select each additional selection
An entire document	Triple-click with the pointer to the left of any text; press [Ctrl][A]; or click the Select button in the Editing group on the Home tab, and then click Select All

Learning
Outcomes
• Apply bold to text
• Increase the font
  size of text
• Print a document

Format Text Using the Mini Toolbar and the Ribbon

Formatting text is a fast and fun way to spruce up the appearance of a document and highlight important information. You can easily change the font, color, size, style, and other attributes of text by selecting the text and clicking a command on the Home tab. The **Mini toolbar**, which appears above text when you first select it, also includes commonly used text and paragraph formatting commands. **CASE** *You enhance the appearance of the memo by formatting the text using the Mini toolbar. When you are finished, you preview the memo for errors and then print it.*

STEPS

1. **Select Reason2Go**

   The Mini toolbar appears over the selected text, as shown in FIGURE 1-9. You click a formatting option on the Mini toolbar to apply it to the selected text. TABLE 1-5 describes the function of the buttons on the Mini toolbar. The buttons on the Mini toolbar are also available on the Ribbon.

2. **Click the Increase Font Size button Å on the Mini toolbar six times, then click the Bold button B on the Mini toolbar**

   Each time you click the Increase Font Size button the selected text is enlarged. Applying bold to the text makes it thicker.

3. **Click the Center button in the Paragraph group on the Home tab**

   The selected text is centered between the left and right margins.

4. **Select TO:, click B, select FROM:, click B, select DATE:, click B, select RE:, then click B**

   Bold is applied to the memo header labels.

5. **Click the blank line between the RE: line and the body text, then click the Bottom Border button ⊞ in the Paragraph group**

   A single-line border is added between the heading and the body text in the memo.

6. **Save the document, click the File tab, then click Print**

   Information related to printing the document appears on the Print screen in Backstage view. Options for printing the document appear on the left side of the Print screen and a preview of the document as it will look when printed appears on the right side, as shown in FIGURE 1-10. Before you print a document, it's a good habit to examine it closely so you can identify and correct any problems.

7. **Click the Zoom In button ⊞ on the status bar five times, then proofread your document carefully for errors**

   The document is enlarged in print preview. If you notice errors in your document, you need to correct them before you print. To do this, press [Esc] or click the Back button in Backstage view, correct any mistakes, save your changes, click the File tab, and then click the Print command again to be ready to print the document.

8. **Click the Print button on the Print screen**

   A copy of the memo prints using the default print settings. To change the current printer, change the number of copies to print, select what pages of a document to print, or modify another print setting, you simply change the appropriate setting on the Print screen before clicking the Print button.

9. **Click the File tab, then click Close**

   The document closes, but the Word program window remains open.

FIGURE 1-9: Mini toolbar

FIGURE 1-9: **Mini toolbar**

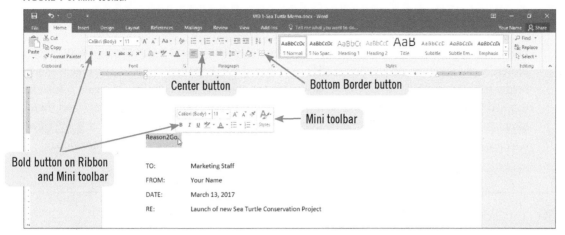

FIGURE 1-10: **Preview of the completed memo**

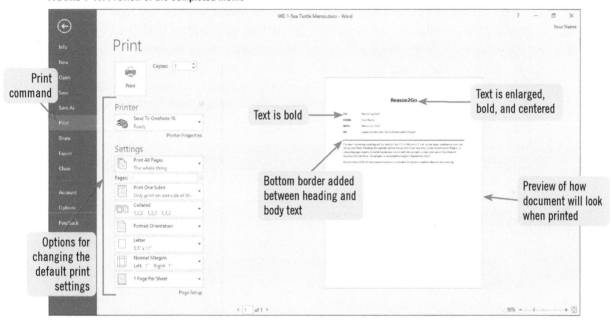

TABLE 1-5: **Buttons on the Mini toolbar**

button	use to	button	use to
Calibri (Body) ⌄	Change the font of text	**B**	Apply bold to text
11 ⌄	Change the font size of text	*I*	Apply italic to text
A⌃	Make text larger	U	Apply an underline to text
A⌄	Make text smaller	aꞵ ⌄	Apply colored highlighting to text
✎	Copy the formats applied to selected text to other text	A ⌄	Change the color of text
A⌄	Apply a style to text	≣ ⌄	Apply bullets to paragraphs
		≣ ⌄	Apply numbering to paragraphs

Use a Document Template

Learning Outcomes
• Search for templates
• Customize a template
• Use content controls

Word includes many templates that you can use to create letters, reports, brochures, calendars, and other professionally designed documents quickly. A **template** is a formatted document that contains place-holder text and graphics, which you replace with your own text and graphics. To create a document that is based on a template, you use the New command on the File tab in Backstage view, and then select a template to use. You can then customize the document and save it with a new filename. **CASE** *You use a template to create a cover letter for a contract you will send to the Rainforest Hotel in Tamarindo.*

STEPS

QUICK TIP
You must have an active Internet connection to search for templates.

1. **Click the File tab, then click New**

   The New screen opens in Backstage view, as shown in FIGURE 1-11. You can select a template from the gallery shown in this window, or use the search box and links in the Suggested Searches section to find other templates.

TROUBLE
Templates change over time. If this tem-plate is not available, select another Cover Letter template or just read the steps to understand how to work with templates.

2. **Scroll down until you find the Cover Letter (blue) thumbnail on the New screen, click it, preview the template in the preview window that opens, then click Create**

   The Cover Letter (blue) template opens as a new document in the document window. It contains placeholder text, which you can replace with your own information. Your name might appear at the top of the document. Don't be concerned if it does not. When a document is created using this template, Word automatically enters the username from the Word Options dialog box at the top of the document and in the signature block.

3. **Click [Date] in the document**

   The placeholder text is selected and appears inside a content control. A **content control** is an interactive object that you use to customize a document with your own information. A content control might include placeholder text, a drop-down list of choices, or a calendar.

4. **Click the [Date] list arrow**

   A calendar opens below the content control. You use the calendar to select the date you want to appear on your document—simply click a date on the calendar to enter that date in the document.

5. **Click the Today button on the calendar**

   The current date replaces the placeholder text.

QUICK TIP
You can delete any content control by right-clicking it, and then clicking Remove Content Control on the menu that opens.

6. **Click [Recipient Name], type Ms. Yana Roy, press [Enter], type Manager, press [Enter], type Rainforest Lodge, press [Enter], type P.O. Box 4397, press [Enter], then type Tamarindo 50309, COSTA RICA**

   You do not need to drag to select the placeholder text in a content control, you can simply click it. The text you type replaces the placeholder text.

7. **Click [Recipient], then type Ms. Roy**

   The text you type replaces the placeholder text in the greeting line.

8. **Click the File tab, click Save As, then save the document as WD 1-Rainforest Letter to the location where you store your Data Files**

   The document is saved with the filename WD 1-Rainforest Letter, as shown in FIGURE 1-12.

Creating Documents with Word 2016

FIGURE 1-11: **New screen in Backstage view**

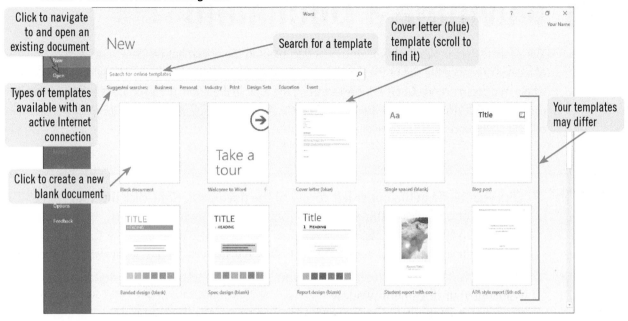

Click to navigate to and open an existing document

Search for a template

Cover letter (blue) template (scroll to find it)

Types of templates available with an active Internet connection

Your templates may differ

Click to create a new blank document

FIGURE 1-12: **Document created using the Cover Letter (blue) template**

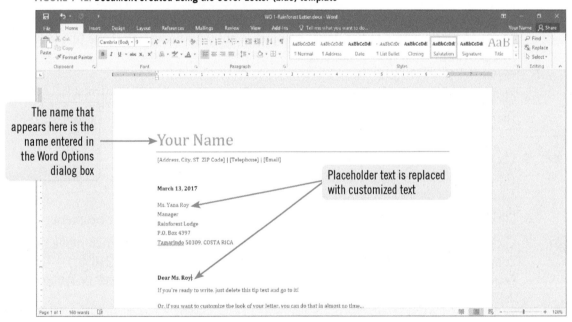

The name that appears here is the name entered in the Word Options dialog box

Placeholder text is replaced with customized text

Using the Undo, Redo, and Repeat commands

Word remembers the editing and formatting changes you make so that you can easily reverse or repeat them. You can reverse the last action you took by clicking the Undo button ⤺ on the Quick Access toolbar, or you can undo a series of actions by clicking the Undo list arrow ⤺ ▾ and selecting the action you want to reverse. When you undo an action using the Undo list arrow, you also undo all the actions above it in the list—that is, all actions that were performed after the action you selected. Similarly, you can keep the change you just reversed by using the Redo button ⤻

on the Quick Access toolbar. The Redo button appears only immediately after clicking the Undo button to undo a change.

If you want to repeat an action you just completed, you can use the Repeat button ⟳ on the Quick Access toolbar. For example, if you just typed "thank you," clicking ⟳ inserts "thank you" at the location of the insertion point. If you just applied bold, clicking ⟳ applies bold to the currently selected text. You also can repeat the last action you took by pressing [F4].

Navigate a Document

The Zoom feature in Word lets you enlarge a document in the document window to get a close-up view of a detail or reduce the size of the document in the document window for an overview of the layout as a whole. You zoom in and out on a document using the tools in the Zoom group on the View tab or you can use the Zoom level buttons and Zoom slider on the status bar. **CASE** *You find it is helpful to zoom in and out on the document as you finalize the letter.*

STEPS

1. **Click your name in the upper-left corner of the document, right-click the** Your Name content control, **click** Remove Content Control **on the menu that opens, select your name, then type** Reason2Go

   Removing the content control changes the text to static text that you can then replace with other text.

2. **Drag the** vertical scroll box down **until the body of the letter and the signature block are visible in your document window**

   You **scroll** to display different parts of the document in the document window. You can also scroll by clicking the scroll arrows above and below the scroll bar, or by clicking the scroll bar.

3. **Select the** four paragraphs **of placeholder body text, type** Enclosed please find a copy of our contract for the Sea Turtle Conservation Project. We look forward to working with you., **then, if the name in the signature block is not your name, select the text in the content control and type your name**

   The text you type replaces the placeholder text, as shown in FIGURE 1-13.

4. **Click the** View tab, **then click the** Page Width button **in the Zoom group**

   The document is enlarged to the width of the document window. When you enlarge a document, the area where the insertion point is located appears in the document window.

5. **Click the** Zoom level button `154%` **on the status bar**

   The Zoom dialog box opens. You use the Zoom dialog box to select a zoom level for displaying the document in the document window.

6. **Click the** Whole page option button, **then click** OK **to view the entire document**

7. **Click** Reason2Go **to move the insertion point to the top of the page, then move the Zoom slider to the right until the Zoom percentage is approximately 230%**

   Dragging the Zoom slider to the right enlarges the document in the document window. Dragging the zoom slider to the left allows you to see more of the page at a reduced size.

8. **Click the** [Address...] **content control, type** Travel, **click** [Telephone], **type** Volunteer, **click** [Email], **type** www.r2g.com, **then press** [Tab]

   You can replace placeholder text with information that is different from what is suggested in the content control.

9. **Click the** Read Mode button 📖 **on the status bar**

   The document appears in the document window in Read Mode view. Read Mode view hides the tabs and ribbon to make it easier to read documents on screen. Read Mode view is useful for reading long documents.

10. **Click the** Print Layout view button 🖺 **on the status bar, click the** Zoom Out button ➖ **on the status bar until the zoom level is 100%, then save the document**

    The completed cover letter is displayed at 100% zoom level in Print Layout view, as shown in FIGURE 1-14.

11. **Submit the document to your instructor, close the file, then exit Word**

FIGURE 1-13: Replacement text and Zoom slider

Replace placeholder text with this text

Zoom slider at 120% (your zoom level may differ)

Zoom level button at 120% (your zoom level may differ)

FIGURE 1-14: Completed letter

Using Word document views

Document **views** are different ways of displaying a document in the document window. Each Word view provides features that are useful for working on different types of documents. The default view, **Print Layout view**, displays a document as it will look on a printed page. Print Layout view is helpful for formatting text and pages, including adjusting document margins, creating columns of text, inserting graphics, and formatting headers and footers. Also useful is **Read Mode view**, which displays document text so that it is easy to read on screen. Other Word views are helpful for performing specialized tasks. **Web Layout view** allows you to format webpages or documents that will be viewed on a computer screen. In Web Layout view,

a document appears just as it will when viewed with a web browser. **Outline view** is useful for editing and formatting longer documents that include multiple headings. Outline view allows you to reorganize text by moving the headings. Finally, **Draft view**, shows a simplified layout of a document, without margins, headers and footers, or graphics. When you want to quickly type and edit text, it's often easiest to work in Draft View. You switch between views by clicking the view buttons on the status bar or by using the commands on the View tab. Changing views does not affect how the printed document will appear. It simply changes the way you view the document in the document window.

Practice

Concepts Review

Label the elements of the Word program window shown in FIGURE 1-15.

FIGURE 1-15

Match each term with the statement that best describes it.

7. **Ribbon**	**a.** A formatted document that contains placeholder text
8. **AutoCorrect**	**b.** Suggests text to insert into a document
9. **AutoComplete**	**c.** Fixes certain errors as you type
10. **Zoom slider**	**d.** Provides access to Word commands
11. **Status bar**	**e.** Special characters that appear on screen but do not print
12. **Horizontal ruler**	**f.** Displays tab settings and paragraph indents
13. **Template**	**g.** Enlarges and reduces the document in the document window
14. **Formatting marks**	**h.** Displays the number of pages in the current document

Select the best answer from the list of choices.

15. **Which of the following shows the number of words in the document?**
   a. The title bar
   b. The Ribbon
   c. The status bar
   d. The Mini toolbar

16. **Which tab includes buttons for formatting text?**
   a. View
   b. Page Layout
   c. Insert
   d. Home

17. **Which element of the Word window shows the top and bottom document margins settings?**
   a. Status bar
   b. View tab
   c. Vertical ruler
   d. Vertical scroll bar

18. **What is the default file extension for a document created in Word 2016?**
   a. .doc
   b. .dot
   c. .dotx
   d. .docx

Creating Documents with Word 2016

19. **Which of the following is not included in a ScreenTip for a command?**
   a. Link to a help topic on the command
   c. Keyboard shortcut for the command
   b. Alternative location of the command
   d. Description of the function of the command

20. **Which view is best for reading text onscreen?**
   a. Print Layout view
   c. Read Mode view
   b. Outline view
   d. Draft view

Skills Review

1. **Explore the Word program window.**
   a. Start Word and open a new, blank document.
   b. Identify as many elements of the Word program window as you can without referring to the module material.
   c. Click the File tab, then click the Info, New, Save, Open, Save As, Print, Share, and Export commands.
   d. Click the Back button in Backstage view to return to the document window.
   e. Click each tab on the Ribbon, review the groups and buttons on each tab, then return to the Home tab.
   f. Point to each button on the Home tab and read its ScreenTip.
   g. Click the view buttons to view the blank document in each view, then return to Print Layout view.
   h. Use the Zoom slider to zoom all the way in and all the way out on the document, then return to 120%.

2. **Start a document.**
   a. In a new blank document, type **Summer of Music Festivals** at the top of the page, then press [Enter] two times.
   b. Type the following, pressing [Tab] as indicated and pressing [Enter] at the end of each line:
   To: [Tab] [Tab] **Michael Mellon**
   From: [Tab] [Tab] **Your Name**
   Date: [Tab] [Tab] **Today's date**
   Re: [Tab] [Tab] **Reservation confirmation**
   Pages: [Tab] [Tab] **1**
   Fax: [Tab] [Tab] **(603) 555-5478**
   c. Press [Enter] again, then type **Thank you for your interest in our summer music festival weekend package, which includes accommodations for three nights, continental breakfast, and a festival pass. Rooms are still available during the following festivals: International Jazz Festival, Americana Festival, Classical Fringe Festival, and the Festival of Arts. Please see the attached schedule for festival dates and details.**
   d. Press [Enter], then type **To make a reservation, please call me at (617) 555-7482 or visit our website. Payment must be received in full by the 3rd of June to hold a room. No one knows how to celebrate summer like music-lovers!**
   e. Insert **Summer Strings Festival,** before International Jazz Festival.
   f. Using the [Backspace] key, delete **1** in the Pages: line, then type **2**.
   g. Using the [Delete] key, delete **festival** in the last sentence of the first paragraph.

3. **Save a document.**
   a. Click the Save button on the Quick Access toolbar.
   b. Save the document as **WD 1-Mellon Fax** with the default file extension to the location where you store your Data Files.
   c. After your name, type a comma, press [Spacebar], then type **Reservations Manager**
   d. Save the document.

4. **Select text.**
   a. Turn on formatting marks.
   b. Select the **Re:** line, then type **Re:** [Tab] [Tab] **Summer Music Festival Weekend Package**

Skills Review (continued)

c. Select **three** in the first sentence, then type **two**.

d. Select **3rd of June** in the second sentence of the last paragraph, type **15th of May**, select **room**, then type **reservation**.

e. Delete the sentence **No one knows how to celebrate summer like music-lovers!**

f. Turn off the display of formatting marks, then save the document.

5. Format text using the Mini toolbar.

a. Select **Summer of Music Festivals**, click the Increase Font Size button on the Mini toolbar six times, then apply bold.

b. Center **Summer of Music Festivals** on the page.

c. Apply a bottom border under **Summer of Music Festivals**.

d. Apply bold to the following words in the fax heading: **To:**, **From:**, **Date:**, **Re:**, **Pages:**, and **Fax:**.

e. Read the document using the Read Mode view.

f. Return to Print Layout view, zoom in on the document, then proofread the fax.

g. Correct any typing errors in your document, then save the document. Compare your document to FIGURE 1-16.

h. Submit the fax to your instructor, then close the document.

FIGURE 1-16

Summer of Music Festivals

To:	Michael Mellon
From:	Your Name, Reservations Manager
Date:	April 11, 2017
Re:	Summer Music Festival Weekend Package
Pages:	2
Fax:	(603) 555-5478

Thank you for your interest in our summer music festival weekend package, which includes accommodations for two nights, continental breakfast, and a festival pass. Rooms are still available during the following festivals: Summer Strings Festival, International Jazz Festival, Americana Festival, Classical Fringe Festival, and the Festival of Arts. Please see the attached schedule for dates and details.

To make a reservation, please call me at (617) 555-7482 or visit our website. Payment must be received in full by the 15th of May to hold a reservation.

6. Create a document using a template.

a. Click the File tab, click New, then scroll the gallery of templates.

b. Create a new document using the Fax cover sheet (Professional design) template.

c. Click the "Company Name" placeholder text, type **Summer of Music Festivals**, delete the "Street Address" and "City..." content controls, click the "Phone number" placeholder text, type **Tel: 617-555-7482**, click the "Fax number" placeholder text, type **Fax: 617-555-1176**, click the website placeholder text, then type **www.summerofmusic.com**.

d. Type **Jude Lennon** to replace the "To:" placeholder text; type **555-2119** to replace the "Fax:" placeholder text; click the "Phone:" placeholder text, then press [Delete]; then type **Summer of Music Festivals** to replace the "Re:" placeholder text.

e. If your name is not on the From line, select the text in the From content control, then type your name.

f. Insert today's date using the date content control.

g. Delete the "Pages:" and "cc:" placeholder text.

h. Save the document with the filename **WD 1-Lennon Fax** to the location where you store your Data Files, clicking OK if a warning box opens.

7. View and navigate a document.

a. Scroll down until Comments is near the top of your document window.

b. Replace the Comments placeholder text with the following text: **Packages for the following summer music festivals are sold out: Chamber Music Festival, Solstice Festival, and Dragonfly Festival. We had expected these packages to be less popular than those for the bigger festivals, but interest has been high. Next year, we will increase our bookings for these festivals by 30%.**

Skills Review (continued)

c. Use the Zoom dialog box to view the Whole Page.

d. Use the Zoom slider to set the Zoom percentage at approximately 100%.

e. Read the document using the Read Mode view.

f. Return to Print Layout view, zoom in on the document, then proofread the fax.

g. Preview the document, then correct any errors, saving changes if necessary. Compare your document to FIGURE 1-17. Submit the document to your instructor, close the file, then exit Word.

FIGURE 1-17

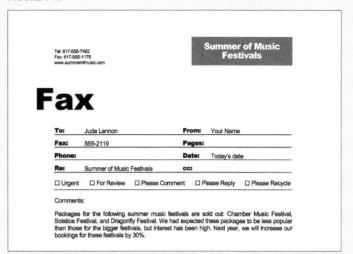

Independent Challenge 1

Yesterday you interviewed for a job as marketing director at Rose Design Services. You spoke with several people at the company, including Yuko Picard, chief executive officer, whose business card is shown in FIGURE 1-18. You need to write a follow-up letter to Ms. Picard, thanking her for the interview and expressing your interest in the company and the position. She also asked you to send her some samples of your marketing work, which you will enclose with the letter.

a. Start Word and save a new blank document as **WD 1-Picard Letter** to the location where you store your Data Files.

b. Begin the letter by clicking the No Spacing button in the Styles group. You use this button to apply the No Spacing style to the document so that your document does not include extra space between paragraphs.

c. Type a personal letterhead for the letter that includes your name, address, telephone number, and e-mail address. If Word formats your e-mail address as a hyperlink, right-click your e-mail address, then click Remove Hyperlink. (*Note: Format the letterhead after you finish typing the letter.*)

FIGURE 1-18

d. Three lines below the bottom of the letterhead, type today's date.

e. Four lines below the date, type the inside address, referring to FIGURE 1-18 for the information. Include the recipient's title, company name, and full mailing address.

f. Two lines below the inside address, type **Dear Ms. Picard:** for the salutation.

g. Two lines below the salutation, type the body of the letter according to the following guidelines:

- In the first paragraph, thank her for the interview. Then restate your interest in the position and express your desire to work for the company. Add any specific details you think will enhance the power of your letter.

- In the second paragraph, note that you are enclosing three samples of your work, and explain something about the samples you are enclosing.

- Type a short final paragraph.

h. Two lines below the last body paragraph, type a closing, then four lines below the closing, type the signature block. Be sure to include your name in the signature block.

i. Two lines below the signature block, type an enclosure notation. (*Hint*: An enclosure notation usually includes the word "Enclosures" or the abbreviation "Enc." followed by the number of enclosures in parentheses.)

j. Format the letterhead with bold, centering, and a bottom border.

k. Save your changes, preview the letter, submit it to your instructor, then close the document and exit Word.

Independent Challenge 2

Your company has recently installed Word 2016 on its company network. As the training manager, it's your responsibility to teach employees how to use the new software productively. Now that they have begun working with Word 2016, several employees have asked you about sharing documents with colleagues using OneDrive. In response, you wrote a memo to all employees explaining the Share feature. You now need to format the memo before distributing it.

a. Start Word, open the file **WD 1-1.docx** from the location where you store your Data Files, clicking the Enable Editing button if prompted to do so, then read the memo to get a feel for its contents. Switch to Print Layout view if the document is not already displayed in Print Layout view.

b. Save the file as **WD 1-Share Memo** to the location where you store your Data Files.

c. Replace the information in the memo header with the information shown in FIGURE 1-19. Make sure to include your name in the From line and the current date in the Date line.

d. Apply bold to **To:**, **From:**, **Date:**, and **Re:**.

e. Increase the size of **WORD TRAINING MEMORANDUM** to match FIGURE 1-19, center the text on the page, add a border below it, then save your changes.

f. Preview the memo, submit it to your instructor, then close the document and exit Word.

FIGURE 1-19

WORD TRAINING MEMORANDUM

To:	All employees
From:	Your Name, Training Manager
Date:	Today's date
Re:	Sharing documents

Independent Challenge 3

You are an expert on climate change. The president of the National Parks Association, Isabella Meerts, has asked you to be the keynote speaker at an upcoming conference on the impact of climate change on the national parks, to be held in Grand Teton National Park. You use one of the Word letter templates to write a letter to Ms. Meerts accepting the invitation and confirming the details. Your letter to Ms. Meerts should reference the following information:

- The conference will be held September 17–19, 2017, at the Jackson Lake Lodge in the park.
- You have been asked to speak for an hour on Saturday, September 18, followed by one-half hour for questions.
- Ms. Meerts suggested the lecture topic "Melting Glaciers, Changing Ecosystems."
- Your talk will include a 45-minute slide presentation.
- The National Parks Association will make your travel arrangements.
- Your preference is to arrive at Jackson Hole Airport on the morning of Friday, September 17, and to depart on Monday, September 20. You would like to rent a car at the airport for the drive to the Jackson Lake Lodge.
- You want to fly in and out of the airport closest to your home.

a. Start Word, click the File tab, click New, and then search for and select an appropriate letter template. Save the document as **WD 1-Meerts Letter** to the location where you store your Data Files.

b. Replace the placeholders in the letterhead with your personal information. Include your name, address, phone number, and e-mail address. Delete any placeholders that do not apply. (*Hints:* Depending on the template you choose, the letterhead might be located at the top or on the side of the document. You can press [Enter] when typing in a placeholder to add an additional line of text. You can also change the format of text typed in a placeholder. If your e-mail address appears as a hyperlink, right-click the e-mail address and click Remove Hyperlink.)

Independent Challenge 3 (continued)

c. Use the [Date] content control to select the current date.

d. Replace the placeholders in the inside address. Be sure to include Ms. Meerts title and the name of the organization. Make up a street address and zip code.

e. Type **Dear Ms. Meerts:** for the salutation.

f. Using the information listed previously, type the body of the letter:
- In the first paragraph, accept the invitation to speak.
- In the second paragraph, confirm the important conference details, confirm your lecture topic, and provide any relevant details.
- In the third paragraph, state your travel preferences.
- Type a short final paragraph.

g. Type **Sincerely,** for the closing, then include your name in the signature block.

h. Adjust the formatting of the letter as necessary. For example, remove bold formatting or change the font color of text to a more appropriate color.

i. Proofread your letter, make corrections as needed, then save your changes.

j. Submit the letter to your instructor, close the document, then exit Word.

Independent Challenge 4: Explore

Word includes a wide variety of templates that can help you create professional-looking documents quickly, including business letters, business cards, résumés, calendars, faxes, memos, labels, reports, blog posts, posters, invitations, certificates, newsletters, and holiday and party cards. In this independent challenge, you will explore the variety of Word templates available to you, and use a template to make a document that is helpful to you in your business or personal life. You might create business cards for yourself, a poster for an event, a letter for a job search, a new résumé, or an invitation to a party. Choose a template that allows you to personalize the text.

a. Start Word, click the File tab, click New, then click each link after Suggested searches: (Business, Personal, Industry, Print, Design Sets, Education, Event) to explore the templates available to you.

b. Preview all the templates for the type of document you want to create, and then select one to create a new document.

c. Save the document as **WD 1-Template Document** to the location where you store your Data Files.

d. Replace the placeholders in the document with your personal information. Delete any placeholders that do not apply. (*Hints*: You can press [Enter] when typing in a placeholder to add an additional line of text. If an e-mail or web address appears as a hyperlink in your document, right-click the e-mail or web address and then click Remove Hyperlink.)

e. Use the [Pick the date] content control to select a date if your document includes a date placeholder.

f. Experiment with changing the font of the text in your document by using the Font list arrow on the Mini toolbar or in the Font group on the Home tab. (*Note:* Remember to use the Undo button immediately after you make the change if you do not like the change and want to remove it.)

g. Experiment with changing the font size of the text in your document by using the Font Size list arrow on the Mini toolbar or in the Font group on the Home tab.

h. Experiment with changing the color of text in your document using the Font Color button on the Mini toolbar or in the Font group on the Home tab.

i. Make other adjustments to the document as necessary, using the Undo button to remove a change you decide you do not want to keep.

j. Save your changes to the document, preview it, submit it to your instructor, then close the document and exit Word.

Visual Workshop

Create the cover letter shown in FIGURE 1-20. Before beginning to type, click the No Spacing button in the Styles group on the Home tab. Add the bottom border to the letterhead after typing the letter. Save the document as **WD 1-Davidson Cover Letter** to the location where you store your Data Files, submit the letter to your instructor, then close the document and exit Word.

FIGURE 1-20

Your Name
82 Genesee Street, Madison, WI 53701
Tel: 608-555-7283; E-mail: yourname@gmail.com

November 8, 2017

Ms. Marta Davidson
Davidson Associates
812 Jefferson Street
Suite 300
Madison, WI 53704

Dear Ms. Davidson:

I read of the opening for a public information assistant in the November 4 edition of wisconsinjobs.com, and I would like to be considered for the position. I am a recent graduate of the University of Wisconsin-Madison (UW), and I am interested in pursuing a career in public relations.

My interest in a public relations career springs from my publicly acknowledged writing and journalism abilities. For example, at UW, I was a reporter for the student newspaper and frequently wrote press releases for campus and community events.

I have a wealth of experience using Microsoft Word in professional settings. Last summer, I worked as an office assistant for the architecture firm Mason & Greenbush, where I used Word to create newsletters, brochures, and financial reports. During the school year, I also worked part-time in the UW Office of Community Relations, where I used the Word mail merge feature to create form letters and mailing labels.

My enclosed resume details my skills and experience. I welcome the opportunity to discuss the position and my qualifications with you. I can be reached at 608-555-7283.

Sincerely,

Your Name

Enc.

Editing Documents

CASE You have been asked to edit and finalize a press release for an R2G promotional lecture series. The press release should provide information about the series so that newspapers, radio stations, and other media outlets can announce it to the public. R2G press releases are disseminated via the website and by e-mail. Before distributing the file electronically to your lists of press contacts and local R2G clients, you add several hyperlinks and then strip the file of private information.

Module Objectives

After completing this module, you will be able to:

- Cut and paste text
- Copy and paste text
- Use the Office Clipboard
- Find and replace text

- Check spelling and grammar
- Research information
- Add hyperlinks
- Work with document properties

Files You Will Need

WD 2-1.docx	WD 2-5.docx
WD 2-2.docx	WD 2-6.docx
WD 2-3.docx	WD 2-7.docx
WD 2-4.docx	

Cut and Paste Text

Learning Outcomes
- Open a document and save it with a new filename
- Edit text using formatting marks
- Cut and paste text

The editing features in Word allow you to move text from one location to another in a document. Moving text is often called **cut and paste**. When you **cut** text, it is removed from the document and placed on the **Clipboard**, a temporary storage area for text and graphics that you cut or copy from a document. You can then **paste**, or insert, text that is stored on the Clipboard in the document at the location of the insertion point. You cut and paste text using the Cut and Paste buttons in the Clipboard group on the Home tab. You also can move selected text by dragging it to a new location using the mouse. This operation is called **drag and drop**. **CASE** *You open the press release, save it with a new filename, and then reorganize the information in the press release using the cut-and-paste and drag-and-drop methods.*

STEPS

QUICK TIP
You can also click Open Other Documents at the bottom of the Recent list on the Word start screen to open the Open dialog box.

1. **Start** Word, **click** Blank document, **click the** File tab, **click** This PC **on the Open screen, click** Browse **to open the Open dialog box, navigate to the location where you store your Data Files, click** WD 2-1.docx, **then click** Open

   The document opens in Print Layout view. Once you have opened a file, you can edit it and use the Save or the Save As command to save your changes. You use the **Save** command when you want to save the changes you make to a file, overwriting the stored file. You use the **Save As** command when you want to leave the original file intact and create a duplicate file with a different filename, file extension, or location.

TROUBLE
Click the Enable Editing button if necessary.

2. **Click the** File tab, **click** Save As, **click** Computer, **click** Browse **to open the Save As dialog box, type** WD 2-Lecture PR **in the File name text box, then click** Save

   You can now make changes to the press release file without affecting the original file.

TROUBLE
If the headline and all six paragraphs of body text do not display in your document window, use the Zoom slider to change the zoom level.

3. **Replace** Mary Watson **with your name, scroll down until the headline "Pedro Soares to Speak..." is at the top of your document window, then click the** Show/Hide ¶ **button** ¶ **in the Paragraph group on the Home tab to display formatting marks**

4. **Select** Alaskan guide Michael Coonan, **(including the comma and the space after it) in the third body paragraph, then click the** Cut button **in the Clipboard group**

   The text is removed from the document and placed on the Clipboard. Word uses two different clipboards: the **system clipboard**, which holds just one item, and the **Office Clipboard** (the Clipboard), which holds up to 24 items. The last item you cut or copy is always added to both clipboards.

5. **Place the insertion point before** African **(but after the space) in the first line of the third paragraph, then click the** Paste button **in the Clipboard group**

   The text is pasted at the location of the insertion point, as shown in FIGURE 2-1. The Paste Options button appears below text when you first paste it in a document. For now you can ignore the Paste Options button.

QUICK TIP
As you drag, the pointer changes to ▯ and a black vertical line, which is the insertion point, moves with the pointer.

6. **Press and hold** [Ctrl], **click the sentence** Ticket prices include lunch. **in the fourth paragraph, then release** [Ctrl]

   The entire sentence is selected. You will drag the selected text to a new location using the mouse.

QUICK TIP
If you make a mistake, click the Undo button ↶ on the Quick Access toolbar, then try again.

7. **Press and hold the mouse button over the selected text, then drag the** pointer's vertical line **to the end of the fifth paragraph (between the period and the paragraph mark) as shown in** FIGURE 2-2

   You drag the insertion point to where you want the text to be inserted when you release the mouse button.

8. **Release the mouse button**

   The selected text is moved to the location of the insertion point. Text is not placed on the Clipboard when you drag and drop it.

9. **Deselect the text, then click the** Save button 🖫 **on the Quick Access toolbar**

FIGURE 2-1: Moved text with Paste Options button

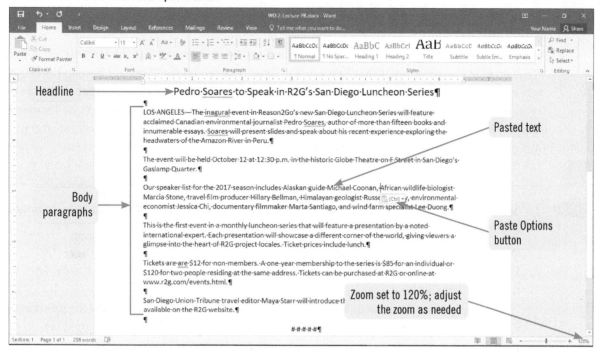

Headline

Pedro·Soares·to·Speak·in·R2G's·San·Diego·Luncheon·Series¶

Body paragraphs

Pasted text

Paste Options button

Zoom set to 120%; adjust the zoom as needed

FIGURE 2-2: Dragging and dropping text in a new location

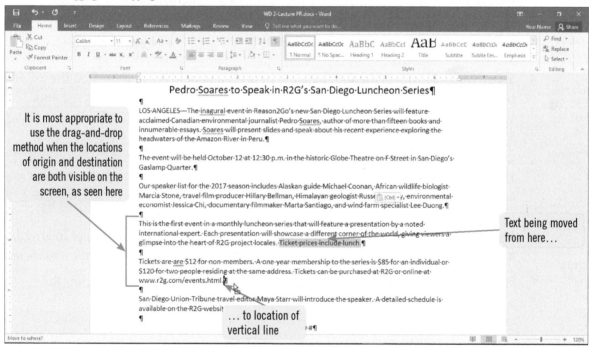

It is most appropriate to use the drag-and-drop method when the locations of origin and destination are both visible on the screen, as seen here

Text being moved from here...

... to location of vertical line

Using keyboard shortcuts

A **shortcut key** is a function key, such as [F1], or a combination of keys, such as [Ctrl][S], that you press to perform a command. For example, instead of using the Cut, Copy, and Paste commands on the Ribbon or the Mini toolbar, you can use the **keyboard shortcuts** [Ctrl][X] to cut text, [Ctrl][C] to copy text, and [Ctrl][V] to paste text. You can also press [Ctrl][S] to save changes to a document instead of clicking the Save button on the Quick Access toolbar or clicking Save on the File tab. Becoming skilled at using keyboard shortcuts can help you quickly accomplish many of the tasks you perform in Word. If a keyboard shortcut is available for a command, then it is listed in the ScreenTip for that command.

Copy and Paste Text

Learning Outcomes
- Copy and paste text
- Format pasted text with the Paste Options button

Copying and pasting text is similar to cutting and pasting text, except that the text you **copy** is not removed from the document. Rather, a copy of the text is placed on the Clipboard, leaving the original text in place. You can copy text to the Clipboard using the Copy button in the Clipboard group on the Home tab, or you can copy text by pressing [Ctrl] as you drag the selected text from one location to another. **CASE** *You continue to edit the press release by copying text from one location to another using the copy-and-paste and drag-and-drop methods.*

STEPS

1. **Select** San Diego Luncheon **in the headline, then click the** Copy button **in the Clipboard group on the Home tab**

   A copy of the selected text is placed on the Clipboard, leaving the original text you copied in place.

2. **Place the insertion point before** season **in the third paragraph, then click the** Paste button **in the Clipboard group**

   "San Diego Luncheon" is inserted before "season," as shown in FIGURE 2-3. Notice that the pasted text is formatted differently than the paragraph in which it was inserted.

3. **Click the** Paste Options button, **move the mouse over each button on the menu that opens to read its ScreenTip, then click the** Keep Text Only (T) button

   The formatting of "San Diego Luncheon" is changed to match the rest of the paragraph. The buttons on the Paste Options menu allow you to change the formatting of pasted text. You can choose to keep the original formatting (Keep Source Formatting), match the destination formatting (Merge Formatting), or paste as unformatted text (Keep Text Only).

4. **Select** www.r2g.com **in the fifth paragraph, press and hold** [Ctrl]**, then drag the** pointer's vertical line **to the end of the last paragraph, placing it between** site **and the period**

   As you drag, the pointer changes to ▯, indicating that the selected text is being copied and moved.

5. **Release the mouse button, then release** [Ctrl]

   The text is copied to the last paragraph. Since the formatting of the text you copied is the same as the formatting of the destination paragraph, you can ignore the Paste Options button. Text is not copied to the Clipboard when you copy it using the drag-and-drop method.

6. **Place the insertion point before** www.r2g.com **in the last paragraph, type** at **followed by a space, then save the document**

   Compare your document with FIGURE 2-4.

Splitting the document window to copy and move items in a long document

If you want to copy or move items between parts of a long document, it can be useful to split the document window into two panes. This allows you to display the item you want to copy or move in one pane and the destination for the item in the other pane. To split a window, click the Split button in the Window group on the View tab, and then drag the horizontal split bar that appears to the location you want to split the window. Once the document window is split into two panes, you can use the scroll bars in each pane to display different parts of the document. To copy or move an item from one pane to another, you can use the Cut, Copy, and Paste commands, or you can drag the item between the panes. When you are finished editing the document, double-click the split bar to restore the window to a single pane, or click the Remove Split button in the Window group on the View tab.

FIGURE 2-3: Text pasted in document

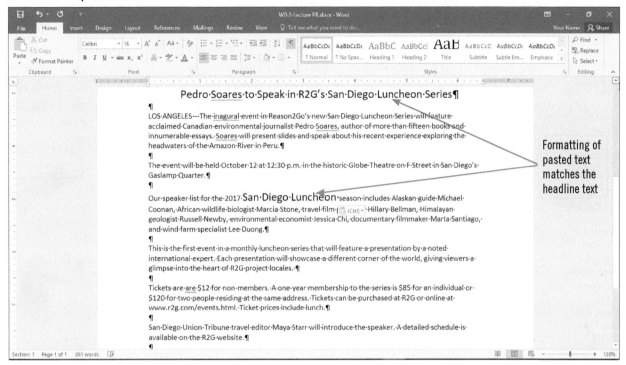

Formatting of pasted text matches the headline text

FIGURE 2-4: Copied text in document

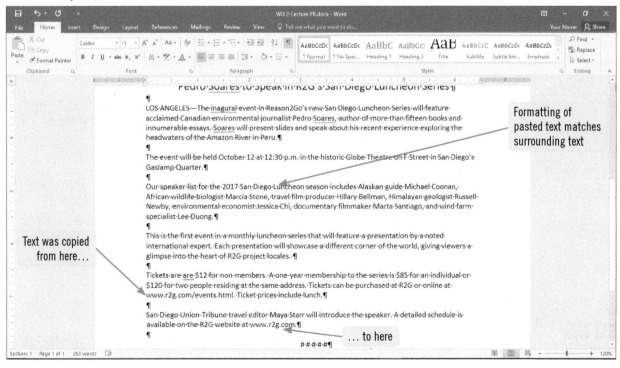

Formatting of pasted text matches surrounding text

Text was copied from here...

... to here

Use the Office Clipboard

Learning Outcomes
• Copy and cut items to the Clipboard
• Paste items from the Clipboard

The Office Clipboard allows you to collect text and graphics from files created in any Office program and insert them into your Word documents. It holds up to 24 items and, unlike the system clipboard, the items on the Office Clipboard can be viewed. To display the Office Clipboard (the Clipboard), you simply click the launcher in the Clipboard group on the Home tab. You add items to the Office Clipboard using the Cut and Copy commands. The last item you collect is always added to both the system clipboard and the Office Clipboard. **CASE** ➤ *You use the Office Clipboard to move several sentences in your press release.*

STEPS

QUICK TIP

You can set the Clipboard pane to open automatically when you cut or copy two items consecutively by clicking Options on the Clipboard pane, and then selecting Show Office Clipboard Automatically.

1. **Click the launcher 🔲 in the Clipboard group on the Home tab**

   The Office Clipboard opens in the Clipboard pane. It contains the San Diego Luncheon item you copied in the last lesson.

2. **Select the sentence San Diego Union-Tribune travel editor... (including the space after the period) in the last paragraph, right-click the selected text, then click Cut on the menu that opens**

   The sentence is cut to the Clipboard.

3. **Select the sentence A detailed schedule is... (including the ¶ mark), right-click the selected text, then click Cut**

   The Clipboard displays the items you cut or copied, as shown in FIGURE 2-5. The icon next to each item indicates the items are from a Word document. The last item collected is displayed at the top of the Clipboard pane. As new items are collected, the existing items move down the Clipboard.

QUICK TIP

If you add a 25th item to the Clipboard, the first item you collected is deleted.

4. **Place the insertion point at the end of the second paragraph (after "Quarter." but before the ¶ mark), then click the San Diego Union-Tribune... item on the Clipboard**

   Clicking an item on the Clipboard pastes the item in the document at the location of the insertion point. Items remain on the Clipboard until you delete them or close all open Office programs.

5. **Place the insertion point at the end of the third paragraph (after "Duong."), then click the A detailed schedule is... item on the Clipboard**

   The sentence is pasted into the document.

6. **Select the fourth paragraph, which begins with the sentence This is the first event... (including the ¶ mark), right-click the selected text, then click Cut**

   The paragraph is cut to the Clipboard.

7. **Place the insertion point at the beginning of the third paragraph (before "Our..."), click the Paste button in the Clipboard group on the Home tab, then press [Backspace]**

   The sentences from the "This is the first..." paragraph are pasted at the beginning of the "Our speaker list..." paragraph. You can paste the last item collected using either the Paste command or the Clipboard.

8. **Place the insertion point at the end of the third paragraph (after "www.r2g.com." and before the ¶ mark), then press [Delete] twice**

   Two ¶ symbols and the corresponding blank lines between the third and fourth paragraphs are deleted.

QUICK TIP

To delete an individual item from the Clipboard, click the list arrow next to the item, then click Delete.

9. **Click the Show/Hide ¶ button 🔳 on in the Paragraph group**

   Compare your press release with FIGURE 2-6. Note that many Word users prefer to work with formatting marks on at all times. Experiment to see which method you prefer.

10. **Click the Clear All button on the Clipboard pane to remove the items from the Clipboard, click the Close button ✖ on the Clipboard pane, press [Ctrl][Home], then save the document**

    Pressing [Ctrl][Home] moves the insertion point to the top of the document.

FIGURE 2-5: Office Clipboard in Clipboard pane

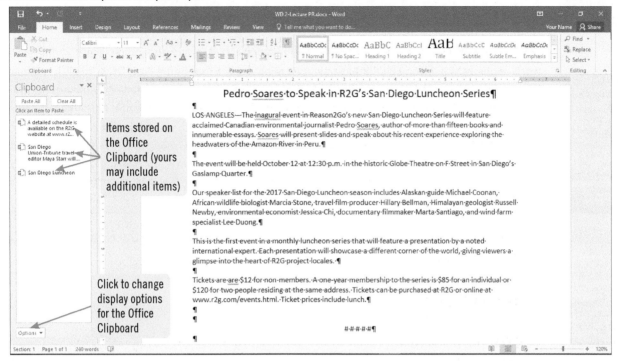

FIGURE 2-6: Revised press release

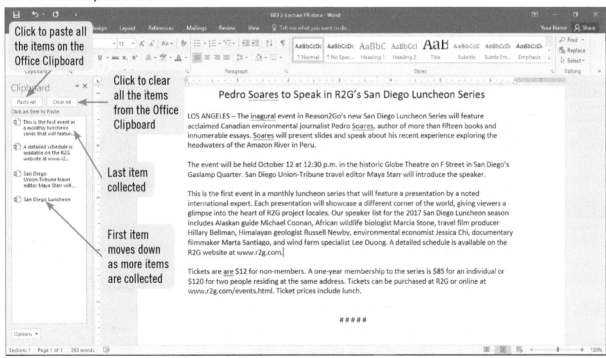

Copying and moving items between documents

You can also use the Clipboard to copy and move items between documents. To do this, open both documents and the Clipboard pane. With multiple documents open, copy or cut an item from one document and then switch to the other document and paste the item. To switch between open documents, point to the Word icon 📄 on the taskbar, and then click the document you want to appear in the document window. You can also display more than one document at the same time by clicking the Arrange All button or the View Side by Side button in the Window group on the View tab.

Find and Replace Text

Learning Outcomes
- Replace text
- Find text with the Navigation pane
- Navigate a document

The Find and Replace feature in Word allows you to automatically search for and replace all instances of a word or phrase in a document. For example, you might need to substitute "tour" for "trip." To manually locate and replace each instance of "trip" in a long document would be very time-consuming. Using the Replace command, you can find and replace all occurrences of specific text at once, or you can choose to find and review each occurrence individually. Using the Find command, you can locate and highlight every occurrence of a specific word or phrase in a document. **CASE** *R2G management has decided to change the name of the lecture series from "Travel Luncheon Series" to "Travel Lecture Series." You use the Replace command to search the document for all instances of "Luncheon" and replace them with "Lecture."*

STEPS

TROUBLE
If any of the Search Options check boxes are selected in your Find and Replace dialog box, deselect them. If Format appears under the Find what or Replace with text box, click in the text box, then click the No Formatting button.

1. **Click the Replace button in the Editing group, then click More in the Find and Replace dialog box**

   The Find and Replace dialog box opens and expands, as shown in FIGURE 2-7.

2. **Type Luncheon in the Find what text box**

   "Luncheon" is the text that will be replaced.

3. **Press [Tab], then type Lecture in the Replace with text box**

   "Lecture" is the text that will replace "Luncheon."

4. **Click the Match case check box in the Search Options section to select it**

   Selecting the Match case check box tells Word to find only exact matches for the uppercase and lowercase characters you entered in the Find what text box. You want to replace all instances of "Luncheon" in the proper name "San Diego Luncheon Series." You do not want to replace "luncheon" when it refers to a lunchtime event.

QUICK TIP
To find, review, and replace each occurrence individually, click Find Next.

5. **Click Replace All**

   Clicking Replace All changes all occurrences of "Luncheon" to "Lecture" in the press release. A message box reports three replacements were made.

6. **Click OK to close the message box, then click the Close button in the Find and Replace dialog box**

   Word replaced "Luncheon" with "Lecture" in three locations, but did not replace "luncheon."

QUICK TIP
Alternately, you can also use the Find tab in the Find and Replace dialog box to find text in a document.

7. **Click the Find button in the Editing group**

   Clicking the Find button opens the Navigation pane, which is used to browse a longer document by headings, by pages, or by specific text. The Find command allows you to quickly locate all instances of text in a document. You use it to verify that Word did not replace "luncheon."

8. **Type luncheon in the search text box in the Navigation pane, then scroll up until the headline is at the top of the document window**

   The word "luncheon" is highlighted and selected in the document, as shown in FIGURE 2-8.

9. **Click the Close button in the Navigation pane**

   The highlighting is removed from the text when you close the Navigation pane.

10. **Press [Ctrl][Home], then save the document**

FIGURE 2-7: Find and Replace dialog box

FIGURE 2-8: Found text highlighted in document

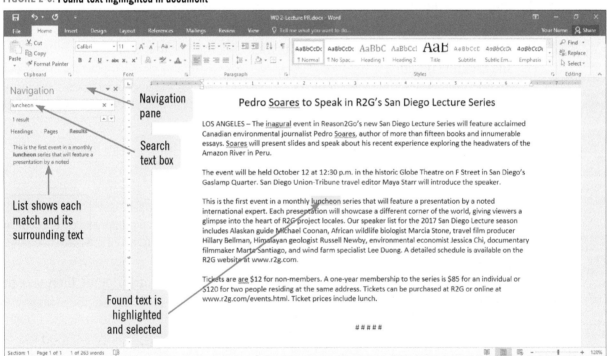

Word 2016

Navigating a document using the Navigation pane and the Go To command

Rather than scrolling to move to a different place in a longer document, you can use the Navigation pane to quickly move the insertion point to a specific page or a specific heading. One way to open the Navigation pane is by clicking the Page number button on the status bar, then clicking the link in the Navigation pane for the type of item you want to use to navigate the document.

To move to a specific page, section, line, table, graphic, or other item in a document, you use the Go To tab in the Find and Replace dialog box. On the Go To tab in the Find and Replace dialog box, select the type of item you want to find in the Go to what list box, enter the relevant information about that item, and then click Next to move the insertion point to the item.

Check Spelling and Grammar

Learning
Outcomes
• Ignore correctly
spelled words
• Correct spelling
errors
• Correct grammar
errors

When you finish typing and revising a document, you can use the Spelling and Grammar command to search the document for misspelled words and grammar errors. The Spelling and Grammar checker flags possible mistakes, suggests correct spellings, and offers remedies for grammar errors such as subject–verb agreement, repeated words, and punctuation. **CASE** ▶ *You use the Spelling and Grammar checker to search your press release for errors. Before beginning the search, you set the Spelling and Grammar checker to ignore words, such as Soares, that you know are spelled correctly.*

STEPS

1. **Right-click Soares in the headline**

   A menu that includes suggestions for correcting the spelling of "Soares" opens. You can correct individual spelling and grammar errors by right-clicking text that is underlined with a red or blue wavy line and selecting a correction. Although "Soares" is not in the Word dictionary, it is spelled correctly in the document.

2. **Click Ignore All**

   Clicking Ignore All tells Word not to flag "Soares" as misspelled.

3. **Press [Ctrl][Home], click the Review tab, then click the Spelling & Grammar button in the Proofing group**

   The Spelling pane opens, as shown in FIGURE 2-9. The pane identifies "inagural" as misspelled and suggests a possible correction for the error. The word selected in the suggestions box is the correct spelling.

4. **Click Change**

   Word replaces the misspelled word with the correctly spelled word. Next, the pane indicates that "are" is repeated in a sentence.

5. **Click Delete**

   Word deletes the second occurrence of the repeated word, and the Spelling pane closes. Keep in mind that the Spelling and Grammar checker identifies many common errors, but you cannot rely on it to find and correct all spelling and grammar errors in your documents, or to always suggest a valid correction. Always proofread your documents carefully.

6. **Click OK to complete the spelling and grammar check, press [Ctrl][Home], then save the document**

Using Smart Lookup

The Smart Lookup feature gives you quick access to information about document text, including definitions, images, and other material from online sources. For example, you might use Smart Lookup to see the definition of a word used in a document or to hear the word pronounced. To use Smart Lookup, select the text you want to look up in your document, then click the Smart Lookup button in the Insights group on the Review tab. The Insights pane opens and includes the Explore and Define tabs. The Explore tab includes images and web links related to the selected text. The Define tab includes a dictionary definition of the selected text and a link you can click to hear the selected text pronounced.

Editing Documents

FIGURE 2-9: **Spelling pane**

Inserting text with AutoCorrect

As you type, AutoCorrect automatically corrects many commonly misspelled words. By creating your own AutoCorrect entries, you can set Word to insert text that you type often, such as your name or contact information, or to correct words you misspell frequently. For example, you could create an AutoCorrect entry so that the name "Mary T. Watson" is automatically inserted whenever you type "mtw" followed by a space. You create AutoCorrect entries and customize other AutoCorrect and AutoFormat options using the AutoCorrect dialog box. To open the AutoCorrect dialog box, click the File tab, click Options, click Proofing in the Word Options dialog box that opens, and then click AutoCorrect Options. On the AutoCorrect tab in the AutoCorrect dialog box, type the text you want to be corrected automatically in the Replace text box (such as "mtw"), type the text you want to be inserted in its place automatically in the With text box (such as "Mary T. Watson"), and then click Add. The AutoCorrect entry is added to the list. Click OK to close the AutoCorrect dialog box, and then click OK to close the Word Options dialog box. Word inserts an AutoCorrect entry in a document when you press [Spacebar] or a punctuation mark after typing the text you want Word to correct. For example, Word inserts "Mary T. Watson" when you type "mtw" followed by a space. If you want to remove an AutoCorrect entry you created, simply open the AutoCorrect dialog box, select the AutoCorrect entry you want to remove in the list, click Delete, click OK, and then click OK to close the Word Options dialog box.

Research Information

Learning Outcomes
- Find synonyms using the Thesaurus
- Check word count

The Word research features allow you to quickly search reference sources and the web for information related to a word or phrase. Among the reference sources available are a Thesaurus, which you can use to look up synonyms for awkward or repetitive words, as well as dictionary and translation sources. **CASE** *After proofreading your document for errors, you decide the press release would read better if several adjectives were more descriptive. You use the Thesaurus to find synonyms.*

STEPS

QUICK TIP
To look up synonyms for a different word, type the word in the search text box, then click the search button.

1. **Scroll until the headline is displayed at the top of your screen**

2. **Select** noted **in the first sentence of the third paragraph, then click the** Thesaurus button **in the Proofing group on the Review tab**

   The Thesaurus pane opens, as shown in FIGURE 2-10. "Noted" appears in the search text box, and possible synonyms for "noted" are listed under the search text box.

3. **Point to** prominent **in the list of synonyms**

   A shaded box containing a list arrow appears around the word.

4. **Click the** list arrow, **click** Insert **on the menu that opens, then close the Thesaurus pane**

   "Prominent" replaces "noted" in the press release.

5. **Right-click** innumerable **in the first sentence of the first paragraph, point to** Synonyms **on the menu that opens, then click** numerous

   "Numerous" replaces "innumerable" in the press release.

6. **Select the four paragraphs of body text, then click the** Word Count button **in the Proofing group**

   The Word Count dialog box opens, as shown in FIGURE 2-11. The dialog box lists the number of pages, words, characters, paragraphs, and lines included in the selected text. Notice that the status bar also displays the number of words included in the selected text and the total number of words in the entire document. If you want to view the page, character, paragraph, and line count for the entire document, make sure nothing is selected in your document, and then click Word Count in the Proofing group.

7. **Click** Close, **press [Ctrl][Home], then save the document**

8. **Click the** File tab, **click** Save As, **navigate to the location where you store your files, type** WD 2-Lecture PR Public **in the File name text box, then click** Save

   The WD 2-Lecture PR file closes, and the WD 2-Lecture PR Public file is displayed in the document window. You will modify this file to prepare it for electronic release to the public.

Publishing a blog directly from Word

A **blog**, which is short for weblog, is an informal journal that is created by an individual or a group and available to the public on the Internet. A blog usually conveys the ideas, comments, and opinions of the blogger and is written using a strong personal voice. The person who creates and maintains a blog, the **blogger**, typically updates the blog regularly. If you have or want to start a blog, you can configure Word to link to your blog site so that you can write, format, and publish blog entries directly from Word.

To create a new blog post, click the File tab, click New, then double-click Blog post to open a predesigned blog post document that you can customize with your own text, formatting, and images. You can also publish an existing document as a blog post by opening the document, clicking the File tab, clicking Share, and then clicking Post to Blog. In either case, Word prompts you to log onto your personal blog account. To blog directly from Word, you must first obtain a blog account with a blog service provider. Resources, such as the Word Help system and online forums, provide detailed information on obtaining and registering your personal blog account with Word.

FIGURE 2-10: Thesaurus pane

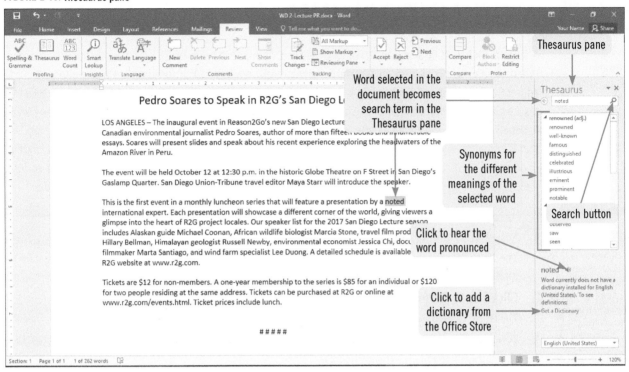

FIGURE 2-11: Word Count dialog box

Using a dictionary and other add-ins for Word

Instead of a built-in dictionary, Word includes the ability to install a free dictionary add-in from the Office Store that you can use to see definitions of words. A dictionary add-in is just one of many add-ins that are available in Word. **Add-ins** are small programs embedded in Word that allow you to access information on the web without having to leave Word. For example, you can look up something on Wikipedia, insert an online map in one of your documents, or access dictionaries and other reference sources, all from within Word using an add-in. To install a free dictionary add-in from the Office Store, click the Thesaurus button In the Proofing group on the Review tab, click the Get a Dictionary link

to open the Dictionaries pane, decide which dictionary you want, review the Terms & Conditions as well as the Privacy Policy associated with the add-in you want, and then click the Download button associated with the dictionary you want in order to install that dictionary. If you want to download other dictionaries or other add-ins, click the Store button in the Add-ins group on the Insert tab, find the add-in you want, and then follow the prompts to install the add-in. Some add-ins are free, and some require purchase. To use an add-in, click the My Add-ins button in the Add-ins group to see your list of add-ins, and then click the add-in you want to use.

Add Hyperlinks

Learning Outcomes
- Insert a hyperlink
- Test hyperlinks
- E-mail a document from Word

A **hyperlink** is text or a graphic that, when clicked, "jumps" the viewer to a different location or program. When a document is viewed on screen, hyperlinks allow readers to link (or jump) to a webpage, an e-mail address, a file, or a specific location in a document. When you create a hyperlink in a document, you select the text or graphic you want to use as a hyperlink and then you specify the location you want to jump to when the hyperlink is clicked. You create a hyperlink using the Hyperlink button in the Links group on the Insert tab. Text that is formatted as a hyperlink appears as colored, underlined text. **CASE** *Hundreds of people on your lists of press and client contacts will receive the press release by e-mail or view it on your website. To make it easier for these people to access additional information about the series, you add several hyperlinks to the press release.*

STEPS

1. **Select your name, click the Insert tab, then click the Hyperlink button in the Links group**

   The Insert Hyperlink dialog box opens, as shown in FIGURE 2-12. You use this dialog box to specify the location you want to jump to when the hyperlink—in this case, your name—is clicked.

2. **Click E-mail Address in the Link to section**

   The Insert Hyperlink dialog box changes so you can create a hyperlink to your e-mail address.

3. **Type your e-mail address in the E-mail address text box, type San Diego Lecture Series in the Subject text box, then click OK**

   As you type, Word automatically adds mailto: in front of your e-mail address. After you close the dialog box, the hyperlink text—your name—is formatted in blue and underlined.

4. **Press and hold [Ctrl], then click the your name hyperlink**

   An e-mail message addressed to you with the subject "San Diego Lecture Series" opens in the default e-mail program. People can use this hyperlink to send you an e-mail message.

5. **Close the e-mail message window, clicking No if you are prompted to save**

   The hyperlink text changes to purple, indicating the hyperlink has been followed.

6. **Scroll down, select Gaslamp Quarter in the second paragraph, click the Hyperlink button, click Existing File or Web Page in the Link to section, type www.gaslamp.org in the Address text box, then click OK**

   As you type the web address, Word automatically adds "http://" in front of "www." The text "Gaslamp Quarter" is formatted as a hyperlink to the Gaslamp Quarter Association home page at www.gaslamp.org. When clicked, the hyperlink will open the webpage in the default browser window. If you point to a hyperlink in Word, the link to location appears in a ScreenTip. You can edit ScreenTip text to make it more descriptive.

7. **Right-click Quarter in the Gaslamp Quarter hyperlink, click Edit Hyperlink, click ScreenTip in the Edit Hyperlink dialog box, type Map, parking, and other information about the Gaslamp Quarter in the ScreenTip text box, click OK, click OK, save your changes, then point to the Gaslamp Quarter hyperlink in the document**

   The ScreenTip you created appears above the Gaslamp Quarter hyperlink, as shown in FIGURE 2-13.

8. **Press [Ctrl], click the Gaslamp Quarter hyperlink, verify the link opened in your browser, then click the Word icon [W] on the taskbar to return to the press release**

   Before distributing a document, it's important to test each hyperlink to verify it works as you intended.

Editing Documents

FIGURE 2-12: Insert Hyperlink dialog box

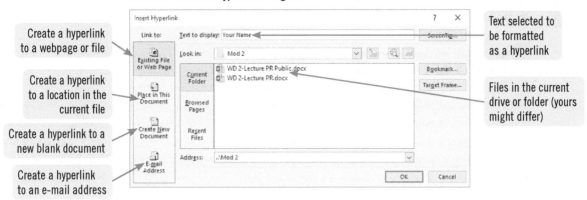

Create a hyperlink to a webpage or file

Create a hyperlink to a location in the current file

Create a hyperlink to a new blank document

Create a hyperlink to an e-mail address

Text selected to be formatted as a hyperlink

Files in the current drive or folder (yours might differ)

FIGURE 2-13: Hyperlinks in the document

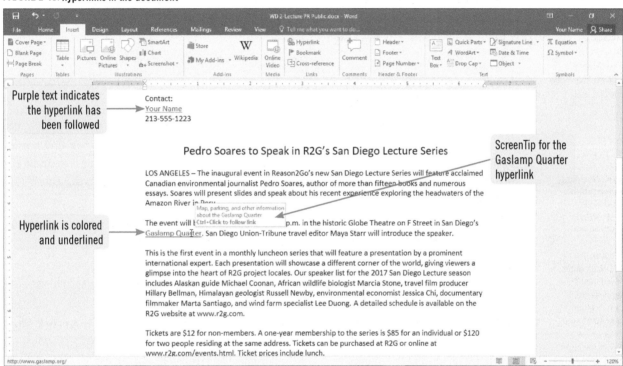

Purple text indicates the hyperlink has been followed

ScreenTip for the Gaslamp Quarter hyperlink

Hyperlink is colored and underlined

Sharing documents directly from Word, including e-mailing

Word includes several options for distributing and sharing documents over the Internet directly from within Word, including saving a document to OneDrive for others to view and edit, e-mailing a document, presenting a document online so others can view it in a web browser, sending it by Instant Message, and posting a document to a blog. To share a document, open the file in Word, click the File tab, click Share, and then click one of the Share options. You can also use the Share button on the title bar to save a document to an online location.

When you e-mail a document from within Word, the document is sent as an attachment to an e-mail message using your default e-mail program. You can choose to attach the document as a Word file, a .pdf file, or an .xps file, or to send it as an Internet fax. When you click an option, a message window opens that includes the filename of the current file as the message subject and the file as an attachment. Type the e-mail address(es) of the recipient(s) in the To and Cc text boxes, any message you want in the message window, and then click Send to send the message. The default e-mail program sends a copy of the document to each recipient. Note that faxing a document directly from Word requires registration with a third-party Internet fax service.

Work with Document Properties

Learning
Outcomes
• Edit document
properties
• Remove document
properties
• Modify advanced
document
properties

Before you distribute a document electronically to people outside your organization, it's wise to make sure the file does not include embedded private or confidential information. The Info screen in Backstage view includes tools for stripping a document of sensitive information, for securing its authenticity, and for guarding it from unwanted changes once it is distributed to the public. One of these tools, the Document Inspector, detects and removes unwanted private or confidential information from a document. **CASE** *Before sending the press release to the public, you remove all identifying information from the file.*

STEPS

QUICK TIP

To create or modify document properties for a file, move the pointer over a property value on the Info screen, then type in the text box.

1. **Press [Ctrl][Home], then click the File tab**

   Backstage view opens with the Info screen displayed. The left side of the Info screen includes options related to stripping the file of private information. See TABLE 2-1. The right side of the Info screen displays basic information about the document. Notice that the file contains document properties. You want to remove these before you distribute the press release to the public.

2. **Click the Show All Properties link at the bottom of the Info screen**

   The Properties section expands on the Info screen. It shows the document properties for the press release. **Document properties** are user-defined details about a file that describe its contents and origin, including the name of the author, the title of the document, and keywords that you can assign to help organize and search your files. You decide to remove this information from the file before you distribute it electronically.

QUICK TIP

A document property, such as author name, might appear automatically in a content control in a document. Stripping a file of document properties does not remove information from a content control.

3. **Click the Check for Issues button on the Info screen, then click Inspect Document, clicking Yes if prompted to save changes**

   The Document Inspector dialog box opens. You use this dialog box to indicate which private or identifying information you want to search for and remove from the document.

4. **Make sure all the check boxes are selected, then click Inspect**

   After a moment, the Document Inspector dialog box indicates the file contains document properties, as shown in FIGURE 2-14.

5. **Click Remove All next to Document Properties and Personal Information, then click Close**

   The document property information is removed from the press release document, but the change will not be reflected on the Info screen until you close the document and reopen it.

6. **Click Save on the Info screen, close the document, open the document again in Word, then click the File tab**

   The Info screen shows the document properties have been removed from the file.

7. **Save the document, submit it to your instructor, close the file, then exit Word**

   The completed press release is shown in FIGURE 2-15.

TABLE 2-1: Options on the Info screen

option	use to
Protect Document	Mark a document as final so that it is read-only and cannot be edited; encrypt a document so that a password is required to open it; restrict what kinds of changes can be made to a document and by whom; restrict access to editing, copying, and printing a document and add a digital signature to a document to verify its integrity
Check for Issues	Detect and remove unwanted information from a document, including document properties and comments; check for content that people with disabilities might find difficult to read; and check the document for features that are not supported by previous versions of Microsoft Word
Manage Document	Browse and recover draft versions of unsaved files

FIGURE 2-14: **Results after inspecting a document**

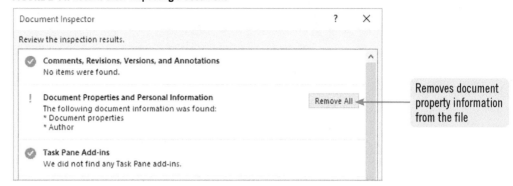

FIGURE 2-15: **Completed press release for electronic distribution**

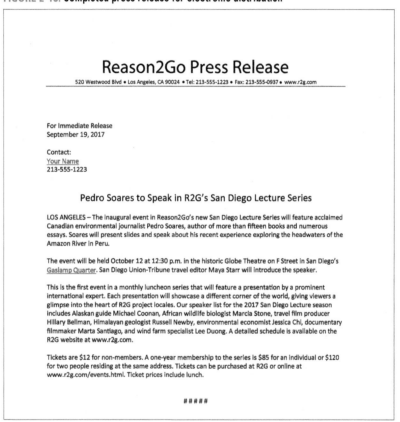

Viewing and modifying advanced document properties

The Properties section of the Info screen includes summary information about the document that you enter. To view more detailed document properties, click the Properties button on the Info screen, and then click Advanced Properties to open the Properties dialog box. The General, Statistics, and Contents tabs of the Properties dialog box display information about the file that is automatically created and updated by Word. The General tab shows the file type, location, size, and date and time the file was created and last modified; the Statistics tab displays information about revisions to the document along with the number of pages, words, lines, paragraphs, and characters in the file; and the Contents tab shows the title of the document.

You can define other document properties using the Summary and Custom tabs in the Properties dialog box. The Summary tab shows information similar to the information shown on the Info screen. The Custom tab allows you to create new document properties, such as client, project, or date completed. To create a custom property, select a property name in the Name list box on the Custom tab, use the Type list arrow to select the type of data you want for the property, type the identifying detail (such as a project name) in the Value text box, and then click Add. When you are finished viewing or modifying the document properties, click OK to close the Properties dialog box.

Practice

Concepts Review

Label the elements of the Word program window shown in FIGURE 2-16.

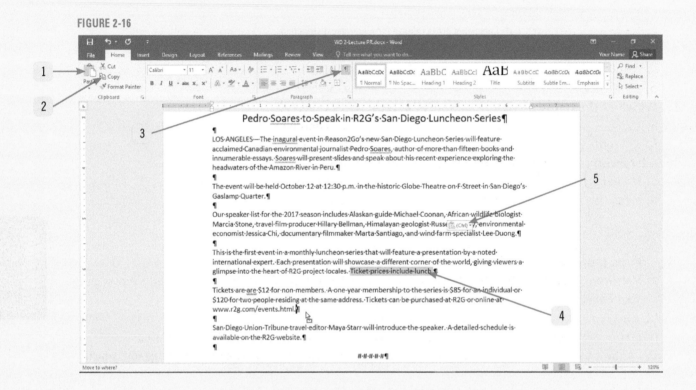

FIGURE 2-16

Match each term with the statement that best describes it.

6. Office Clipboard
7. Paste
8. Hyperlink
9. Thesaurus
10. Shortcut Key
11. Smart Lookup
12. Cut
13. System clipboard
14. Document properties

a. Command used to insert text stored on the Clipboard into a document
b. Temporary storage area for up to 24 items collected from Office files
c. Temporary storage area for only the last item cut or copied from a document
d. A function key or a combination of keys that perform a command when pressed
e. Text or a graphic that jumps the reader to a different location or program when clicked
f. A program that accesses information on the web from within Word
g. User-defined details about a file that describe its contents and origin
h. Feature used to suggest synonyms for words
i. Command used to remove text from a document and place it on the Clipboard

Select the best answer from the list of choices.

15. **What is the keyboard shortcut for the Cut command?**
    a. [Ctrl][V]   c. [Ctrl][P]
    b. [Ctrl][C]   d. [Ctrl][X]

16. **Which command is used to display a document in two panes in the document window?**
    a. Split   c. Arrange All
    b. New Window   d. Two pages

17. **Which of the following statements is *not* true?**
    a. You can view the contents of the Office Clipboard.
    b. The last item cut or copied from a document is stored on the system clipboard.
    c. The Office Clipboard can hold more than one item.
    d. When you move text by dragging it, a copy of the text you move is stored on the system clipboard.

18. **To locate and select all instances of a word in a document, which command do you use?**
    a. Highlight   c. Find
    b. Show/Hide   d. Search

19. **Which of the following is an example of a document property?**
    a. URL   c. Permission
    b. Keyword   d. Language

20. **A hyperlink *cannot* be linked to which of the following?**
    a. Document   c. ScreenTip
    b. E-mail address   d. Webpage

Skills Review

1. **Cut and paste text.**
    a. Start Word, click the Open Other Documents link, open the file WD 2-2.docx from the location where you store your Data File, then save the document with the filename **WD 2-MATOS 2017 PR**.
    b. Select **Your Name** and replace it with your name.
    c. Display paragraph and other formatting marks in your document if they are not already displayed.
    d. Use the Cut and Paste buttons to switch the order of the two sentences in the fourth body paragraph (which begins New group shows...).
    e. Use the drag-and-drop method to switch the order of the second and third paragraphs.
    f. Adjust the spacing if necessary so that there is one blank line between paragraphs, then save your changes.

2. **Copy and paste text.**
    a. Use the Copy and Paste buttons to copy **MATOS 2015** from the headline and paste it before the word **map** in the third paragraph.
    b. Change the formatting of the pasted text to match the formatting of the third paragraph, then insert a space between **2015** and **map** if necessary.
    c. Use the drag-and-drop method to copy **MATOS** from the third paragraph and paste it before the word **group** in the second sentence of the fourth paragraph, then save your changes.

3. **Use the Office Clipboard.**
    a. Use the launcher in the Clipboard group to open the Clipboard pane.
    b. Scroll so that the first body paragraph is displayed at the top of the document window.
    c. Select the fifth paragraph (which begins Studio location maps...) and cut it to the Clipboard.
    d. Select the third paragraph (which begins Manchester is easily accessible...) and cut it to the Clipboard.
    e. Use the Clipboard to paste the Studio location maps... item as the new fourth paragraph.
    f. Use the Clipboard to paste the Manchester is easily accessible... item as the new fifth paragraph.
    g. Adjust the spacing if necessary so there is one blank line between each of the six body paragraphs.
    h. Turn off the display of formatting marks, clear and close the Clipboard pane, then save your changes.

Skills Review (continued)

4. **Find and replace text.**

   a. Using the Replace command, replace all instances of **2015** with **2017**.

   b. Replace all instances of **tenth** with **twelfth**.

   c. Replace all instances of the abbreviation **st** with **street**, taking care to replace whole words only when you perform the replace. (*Hint*: Deselect Match case if it is selected.)

   d. Click the Find tab, deselect the Find whole words only check box, click the Reading Highlight button, click Highlight All, close the dialog box, then view all instances of **st** in the document to make sure no errors occurred when you replaced st with street.

   e. Click the Find button to open the Navigation pane, notice the results and the highlighted text, close the Navigation pane, then save your changes to the press release. (*Note: You can see the highlighted results using either the Reading Highlight button in the Find and Replace dialog box or the Navigation pane.*)

5. **Check spelling and grammar and research information.**

   a. Switch to the Review tab.

   b. Move the insertion point to the top of the document, then use the Spelling & Grammar command to search for and correct any spelling and grammar errors in the press release.

   c. Use the Thesaurus to replace **thriving** in the second paragraph with a different suitable word, then close the Thesaurus pane.

   d. Check the word count of the press release.

   e. Proofread your press release, correct any errors, then save your changes.

6. **Add hyperlinks.**

   a. Save the document as **WD 2-MATOS 2017 PR Public**, then switch to the Insert tab.

   b. Select your name, then open the Insert Hyperlink dialog box.

   c. Create a hyperlink to your e-mail address with the subject **MATOS 2017**.

   d. Test the your name hyperlink, then close the message window that opens and click No if a message window opens. (*Hint*: Press [Ctrl], then click the hyperlink.)

   e. Select **NEA** in the last paragraph of the press release, then create a hyperlink to the webpage with the URL **www.nea.gov**.

   f. Right-click the NEA hyperlink, then edit the hyperlink ScreenTip to become **Information on the National Endowment for the Arts**.

   g. Point to the NEA hyperlink to view the new ScreenTip, then save your changes.

   h. If you are working with an active Internet connection, press [Ctrl], click the NEA hyperlink, view the NEA home page in the browser window, then close the browser window and return to Word. The finished press release is shown in FIGURE 2-17.

FIGURE 2-17

PRESS RELEASE

FOR IMMEDIATE RELEASE
September 7, 2017

Contact:
Your Name
910-555-2938

MATOS 2017
Manchester Artists Open Their Studios to the Public

MANCHESTER, NH – The fall 2017 Open Studios season kicks off with Manchester Art/Tech Open Studios (MATOS) on Saturday and Sunday, October 13 and 14, from 11 a.m. to 6 p.m. More than 60 Manchester artists will open their studios and homes to the public for this annual event, now in its twelfth year.

Manchester is a historic and diverse city, long home to a flourishing community of artists. Quiet residential streets lined with charming Victorians edge a vibrant commercial and industrial zone, all peppered with the studios of printmakers, sculptors, painters, glass and jewelry makers, illustrators, potters, photographers, watercolorists, and other artists working in a wide range of digital mediums.

Internationally celebrated sculptor Mara Currier will display her new work in the rotunda of City Library. New MATOS group shows will open at the Art 5 Gallery and at the Fisher Café, both on Hanover Street.

Studio location maps will be available prior to the opening at businesses and public libraries, and on the days of the event in Victory Park. Victory Park is located at the junction of Amherst Street and Chestnut Street in downtown Manchester.

Manchester is easily accessible from all points in New England by car or bus, and from other cities by air. On Saturday, non-Manchester residents may park in permit-only areas provided they display a copy of the MATOS 2017 map on the dashboard. There are no parking restrictions on Sundays in Manchester.

MATOS 2017 receives funds from participating artists and from the Manchester Arts Council, the North Hampshire Cultural Council, and the NEA, with valuable support from local universities and businesses.

#####

7. Work with document properties.

a. Click the File tab, click the Properties button on the Info screen, then click Advanced Properties to open the Properties dialog box and view the document properties for the press release on the Summary tab.

b. Close the Properties dialog box, then use the Check for Issues command to run the Document Inspector.

c. Remove the document property and personal information data, close the Document Inspector, save your changes, then close the file.

d. Open the file WD 2-MATOS 2017 PR Public, then verify that the document propertes have been removed both on the Info screen and in the Properties dialog box. Save the document, submit it to your instructor, close the file, then exit Word.

Independent Challenge 1

Because of your success in revitalizing a historic theatre in Auckland, New Zealand, you were hired as the director of The Adelaide Opera House in Adelaide, Australia, to breathe life into its revitalization efforts. After a year on the job, you are launching your first major fund-raising drive. You'll create a fund-raising letter for The Adelaide Opera House by modifying a letter you wrote for the Lyric Theatre in Auckland.

a. Start Word, open the file WD 2-3.docx from the location where you store your Data Files, then save it as **WD 2-Fundraising Letter**.

b. Replace the theatre name and address, the date, the inside address, and the salutation with the text shown in FIGURE 2-18.

c. Use the Replace command to replace all instances of **Auckland** with **Adelaide**.

d. Use the Replace command to replace all instances of **Lyric Theatre** with **Opera House**.

e. Use the Replace command to replace all instances of **New Zealanders** with **Australians**.

f. Use the Find command to locate the word **considerable**, then use the Thesaurus to replace the word with a synonym.

FIGURE 2-18

The Adelaide Opera House
32 King William Street, Adelaide SA 5001, Australia

March 12, 2017

Ms. Georgina Fuller
12-34 Wattle Street
Adelaide SA 5006

Dear Ms. Fuller:

g. Move the fourth body paragraph so that it becomes the second body paragraph.

h. Create an AutoCorrect entry that inserts **Executive Director** whenever you type **exd**.

i. Replace Your Name with your name in the signature block, select Title, then type **exd** followed by a space.

j. Use the Spelling and Grammar command to check for and correct spelling and grammar errors.

k. Delete the AutoCorrect entry you created for exd. (*Hint*: Open the AutoCorrect dialog box, select the AutoCorrect entry you created, then click [Delete].)

l. Open the Properties dialog box, add your name as the author, change the title to **Adelaide Opera House**, add the keyword **fund-raising**, then add the comment **Letter for the capital campaign**.

m. Review the paragraph, line, word, and character count on the Statistics tab.

n. On the Custom tab, add a property named **Project** with the value **Capital Campaign**, then close the dialog box.

o. Proofread the letter, correct any errors, save your changes, submit a copy to your instructor, close the document, then exit Word.

Independent Challenge 2

An advertisement for job openings in Chicago caught your eye and you have decided to apply. The ad, shown in FIGURE 2-19, was printed in last weekend's edition of your local newspaper. Instead of writing a cover letter from scratch, you revise a draft of a cover letter you wrote several years ago for a summer internship position.

FIGURE 2-19

ThinkPoint Technologies

Career Opportunities in Detroit

ThinkPoint Technologies, an established software development firm with offices in North America, Asia, and Europe, is seeking candidates for the following positions in its Detroit facility:

Instructor
Responsible for delivering software training to our expanding Midwestern customer base. Duties include delivering hands-on training, keeping up-to-date with product development, and working with the Director of Training to ensure the high quality of course materials. Successful candidate will have excellent presentation skills and be proficient in Microsoft PowerPoint and Microsoft Word. Position B12C6

Administrative Assistant
Proficiency with Microsoft Word a must! Administrative office duties include making travel arrangements, scheduling meetings, taking notes and publishing meeting minutes, handling correspondence, and ordering office supplies. Must have superb multitasking abilities, excellent communication, organizational, and interpersonal skills, and be comfortable working with e-mail and the Internet. Position B16F5

Copywriter
The ideal candidate will have marketing or advertising writing experience in a high tech environment, including collateral, newsletters, and direct mail. Experience writing for the Web, broadcast, and multimedia is a plus. Fluency with Microsoft Word required. Position C13D4

Positions offer salary, excellent benefits, and career opportunities.

Send resume and cover letter referencing position code to:

Selena Torres
Director of Recruiting
ThinkPoint Technologies
700 Woodward Ave.
Detroit, MI 48226

a. Read the ad shown in FIGURE 2-19 and decide which position to apply for. Choose the position that most closely matches your qualifications.

b. Start Word, open WD 2-4.docx from the location where you store your Data Files, then save it as **WD 2-ThinkPoint Cover Letter**.

c. Replace the name, address, telephone number, and e-mail address in the letterhead with your own information.

d. Remove the hyperlink from the e-mail address.

e. Replace the date with today's date, then replace the inside address and the salutation with the information shown in FIGURE 2-19.

f. Read the draft cover letter to get a feel for its contents.

g. Rework the text in the body of the letter to address your qualifications for the job you have chosen to apply for in the following ways:

- Delete the third paragraph.
- Adjust the first sentence of the first paragraph as follows: specify the job you are applying for, including the position code, and indicate where you saw the position advertised.
- Move the first sentence in the last paragraph, which briefly states your qualifications and interest in the position, to the end of the first paragraph, then rework the sentence to describe your current qualifications.
- Adjust the second paragraph as follows: describe your work experience and skills. Be sure to relate your experience and qualifications to the position requirements listed in the advertisement. Add a third paragraph if your qualifications are extensive.
- Adjust the final paragraph as follows: politely request an interview for the position and provide your phone number and e-mail address.

h. Include your name in the signature block.

i. When you are finished revising the letter, check it for spelling and grammar errors, and correct any mistakes. Make sure to remove any hyperlinks.

j. Save your changes to the letter, submit the file to your instructor, close the document, then exit Word.

Independent Challenge 3

As administrative director of continuing education, you drafted a memo to instructors asking them to help you finalize the course schedule for next semester. Today, you'll examine the draft and make revisions before distributing it as an e-mail attachment.

a. Start Word, open the file WD 2-5.docx from the drive and folder where you store your Data Files, then save it as **WD 2-Business Courses Memo**.

Independent Challenge 3 (continued)

b. Replace Your Name with your name in the From line, then scroll until the first body paragraph is at the top of the screen.

c. Use the Split command on the View tab to split the window under the first body paragraph, then scroll until the last paragraph of the memo is displayed in the bottom pane.

d. Use the Cut and Paste buttons to move the sentence **If you are planning to teach...** from the first body paragraph to become the first sentence in the last paragraph of the memo.

e. Double-click the split bar to restore the window to a single pane.

f. Use the [Delete] key to merge the first two paragraphs into one paragraph.

g. Use the Clipboard to reorganize the list of twelve-week courses so that the courses are listed in alphabetical order, then clear and close the Clipboard.

h. Use drag-and-drop to reorganize the list of one-day seminars so they are in alphabetical order.

i. Select the phrase "website" in the first paragraph, then create a hyperlink to the URL **www.course.com** with the ScreenTip **Spring 2018 Business Courses**.

j. Select "e-mail me" in the last paragraph, then create a hyperlink to your e-mail address with the subject **Final Business Course Schedule**.

k. Use the Spelling and Grammar command to check for and correct spelling and grammar errors.

l. Use the Document Inspector to strip the document of document property information, ignore any other content that is flagged by the Document Inspector, then close the Document Inspector.

m. Proofread the memo, correct any errors, save your changes, submit a copy to your instructor, close the document, then exit Word.

Independent Challenge 4: Explore

Reference sources—dictionaries, thesauri, style and grammar guides, and guides to business etiquette and procedure—are essential for day-to-day use in the workplace. Much of this reference information is available on the World Wide Web. In this independent challenge, you will locate reference sources that might be useful to you, including the Office Add-ins resources that are available for Word. Your goal is to familiarize yourself with online reference sources and Office Add-ins for Word so you can use them later in your work. You will insert a screenshot of an Office Add-in webpage in your document.

a. Start Word, open the file WD 2-6.docx from the location where you store your Data Files, then save it as **WD 2-References**. This document contains the questions you will answer about the web reference sources you find and Office Add-ins. You will type your answers to the questions in the document.

b. Replace the placeholder text at the top of the WD 2-References document with your name and the date.

c. Use your favorite search engine to search the web for grammar and style guides, dictionaries, and thesauri. Use the keywords **grammar**, **usage**, **dictionary**, **glossary**, or **thesaurus** to conduct your search.

d. Complete question 1 of the WD 2-References document, making sure to format each website name as a hyperlink to that website.

e. Read question 2 of the WD 2-References document, then move the insertion point under question 2.

f. Click the Store button in the Add-ins group on the Insert tab. Explore the add-ins available through the Office Add-ins window, click one add-in to select it, then click the hyperlink for that add-in to open it in a new browser window. (*Hint:* The hyperlink for an add-in is located under the icon for the add-in.)

g. Switch to the WD 2-References document in Word. Close the Office Add-ins window if it is still open.

h. With the insertion point below question 2, click the Screenshot button in the Illustrations group on the Insert tab. The Available Windows gallery opens.

i. Read the ScreenTip for each thumbnail in the gallery, find the Add-in browser window thumbnail in the gallery, click it, then click Yes in the dialog box that opens. A screenshot of the Add-in you selected is inserted in the WD 2-References document.

j. Save the document, submit a copy to your instructor, close the document, then exit Word.

Visual Workshop

Open WD 2-7.docx from the drive and folder where you store your Data Files, then save the document as **WD 2-Visa Letter**. Replace the placeholders for the date, letterhead, inside address, salutation, and closing with the information shown in FIGURE 2-20, then use the Office Clipboard to reorganize the sentences to match FIGURE 2-20. Correct spelling and grammar errors, remove the document property information from the file, then submit a copy to your instructor.

FIGURE 2-20

Your Name

863 East 18th Street, Apt. 4, New York, NY 20211; Tel: 212-555-9384

1/12/2017

Embassy of the Republic of Korea
2320 Massachusetts Avenue NW
Washington, DC 20008

Dear Sir or Madam:

I am applying for a long-stay tourist visa to South Korea, valid for four years. I am scheduled to depart for Seoul on March 9, 2017, returning to Chicago on September 22, 2017.

During my stay in South Korea, I will be interviewing musicians and recording footage for a film I am making on contemporary Korean music. I would like a multiple entry visa valid for four years so I can return to South Korea after this trip to follow up on my initial research. I will be based in Seoul, but I will be traveling frequently to record performances and to meet with musicians and producers.

Included with this letter are my completed visa application form, my passport, a passport photo, a copy of my return air ticket, and the visa fee. Please contact me if you need further information.

Sincerely,

Your Name

Enc: 5

Formatting Text and Paragraphs

CASE You have finished drafting the text for a two-page flyer advertising last minute specials for R2G October projects. Now, you need to format the flyer so it is attractive and highlights the significant information.

Module Objectives

After completing this module, you will be able to:

- Format with fonts
- Use the Format Painter
- Change line and paragraph spacing
- Align paragraphs
- Work with tabs

- Work with indents
- Add bullets and numbering
- Add borders and shading
- Insert online pictures

Files You Will Need

WD 3-1.docx	WD 3-4.docx
WD 3-2.docx	WD 3-5.docx
WD 3-3.docx	WD 3-6.docx

Format with Fonts

Formatting text with fonts is a quick and powerful way to enhance the appearance of a document. A **font** is a complete set of characters with the same typeface or design. Arial, Times New Roman, Courier, Tahoma, and Calibri are some of the more common fonts, but there are hundreds of others, each with a specific design and feel. Another way to change the appearance of text is to increase or decrease its **font size**. Font size is measured in points. A **point** is 1/72 of an inch. **CASE** *You change the font and font size of the body text, title, and headings in the flyer. You select fonts and font sizes that enhance the positive tone of the document and help to structure the flyer visually for readers.*

STEPS

1. **Start Word, open the file** WD 3-1.docx **from the location where you store your Data Files, save it as** WD 3-October Projects, **then change the zoom level to 120%**

   Notice that the name of the font used in the document, Calibri, is displayed in the Font list box in the Font group. The word "(Body)" in the Font list box indicates Calibri is the font used for body text in the current theme, the default theme. A **theme** is a related set of fonts, colors, styles, and effects that is applied to an entire document to give it a cohesive appearance. The font size, 11, appears in the Font Size list box in the Font group.

2. **Scroll the document to get a feel for its contents, press** [Ctrl][Home], **press** [Ctrl][A] **to select the entire document, then click the** Font list arrow **in the Font group**

   The Font list, which shows the fonts available on your computer, opens as shown in FIGURE 3-1. The font names are formatted in the font. Font names can appear in more than one location on the Font list.

3. **Drag the pointer slowly down the font names in the Font list, drag the scroll box to scroll down the Font list, then click** Garamond

   As you drag the pointer over a font name, a preview of the font is applied to the selected text. Clicking a font name applies the font. The font of the flyer changes to Garamond.

4. **Click the** Font Size list arrow **in the Font group, drag the pointer slowly up and down the Font Size list, then click** 12

   As you drag the pointer over a font size, a preview of the font size is applied to the selected text. Clicking 12 increases the font size of the selected text to 12 points.

5. **Select the title** Reason2Go October Projects, **click the** Font list arrow, **scroll to and click** Trebuchet MS, **click the** Font Size list arrow, **click** 22, **then click the** Bold button B **in the Font group**

   The title is formatted in 22-point Trebuchet MS bold.

6. **Click the** Font Color list arrow A ⋅ **in the Font group**

   A gallery of colors opens. It includes the set of theme colors in a range of tints and shades as well as a set of standard colors. You can point to a color in the gallery to preview it applied to the selected text.

7. **Click the** Green, Accent 6 **color as shown in** FIGURE 3-2, **then deselect the text**

   The color of the title text changes to green. The active color on the Font Color button also changes to green.

8. **Scroll down, select the heading** Animal Care Rajasthan, **then, using the Mini toolbar, click the** Font list arrow, **click** Trebuchet MS, **click the** Font Size list arrow, **click** 14, **click** B, **click** A, **then deselect the text**

   The heading is formatted in 14-point Trebuchet MS bold with a green color.

9. **Press** [Ctrl][Home], **then click the** Save button **on the Quick Access toolbar**

   Compare your document to FIGURE 3-3.

Formatting Text and Paragraphs

FIGURE 3-1: Font list

FIGURE 3-2: Font Color Palette

Fonts used in the default theme

Font Size list arrow

List of recently used fonts (your list may differ)

Font list arrow

Alphabetical list of all fonts on your computer (your list may differ)

Font Color list arrow

Name of color appears as a ScreenTip

Click to create a custom color

FIGURE 3-3: Document formatted with fonts

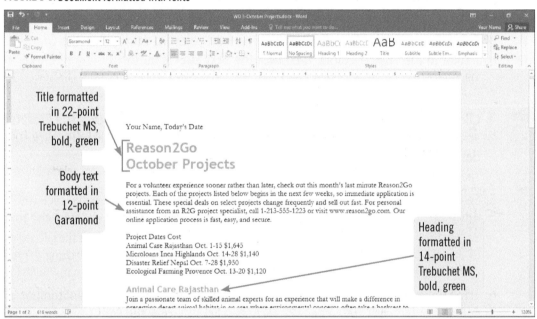

Title formatted in 22-point Trebuchet MS, bold, green

Body text formatted in 12-point Garamond

Heading formatted in 14-point Trebuchet MS, bold, green

Adding a drop cap

A fun way to illustrate a document with fonts is to add a drop cap to a paragraph. A **drop cap** is a large initial capital letter, often used to set off the first paragraph of an article. To create a drop cap, place the insertion point in the paragraph you want to format, click the Insert tab, and then click the Drop Cap button in the Text group to open a menu of Drop cap options. Preview and select one of the options on the menu, or click Drop Cap Options to open the Drop Cap dialog box, shown in FIGURE 3-4. In the Drop Cap dialog box, select the position, font, number of lines to drop, and the distance you want the drop cap to be from the paragraph text, and then click OK. The drop cap is added to the paragraph as a graphic object.

Once a drop cap is inserted in a paragraph, you can modify it by selecting it and then changing the settings in the Drop Cap dialog box. For even more interesting effects, you can enhance a drop cap with font color, font styles, or font effects. You can also fill the graphic object with shading or add a border around it. To enhance a drop cap, first select it, and then experiment with the formatting options available in the Font dialog box and in the Borders and Shading dialog box.

FIGURE 3-4: Drop Cap dialog box

Use the Format Painter

Learning Outcomes
- Apply font styles and effects
- Add a shadow to text
- Change character spacing

You can dramatically change the appearance of text by applying different font styles, font effects, and character-spacing effects. For example, you can use the buttons in the Font group to make text darker by applying **bold** or to make text slanted by applying *italic*. When you are satisfied with the formatting of certain text, you can quickly apply the same formats to other text using the Format Painter. The **Format Painter** is a powerful Word feature that allows you to copy all the format settings applied to selected text to other text that you want to format the same way. **CASE** *You spice up the appearance of the text in the document by applying different font styles and text effects.*

STEPS

QUICK TIP

To change the case of selected text from lowercase to uppercase—and vice versa—click the Change Case button Aa ▾ in the Font group, and then select the case style you want to use.

1. **Select** immediate application is essential **in the first body paragraph, click the** Bold **button** B **on the Mini toolbar, select the entire** paragraph, **then click the** Italic button I

   The phrase "immediate application is essential" is bold, and the entire paragraph is italic.

2. **Select** October Projects, **then click the** launcher ▣ **in the Font group**

   The Font dialog box opens, as shown in FIGURE 3-5. You can use the options on the Font tab to change the font, font style, size, and color of text, and to add an underline and apply font effects to text.

3. **Scroll down the Size list, click** 48, **click the** Font color list arrow, **click the** Orange, Accent 2 **color in the Theme Colors, then click the** Text Effects button

   The Format Text Effects dialog box opens with the options for Text Fill & Outline active. You can also use this dialog box to apply text effects, such as shadow, reflection, and 3-D effects to selected text.

QUICK TIP

You can also apply text effects using the Text Effects and Typography button in the Font group.

4. **Click the white** Text Effects icon **in the dialog box, click** Shadow, **click the** Presets list arrow, **click** Offset Diagonal Bottom Right **in the Outer section, click** OK, **click** OK, **then deselect the text**

   The text is larger, orange, and has a shadow effect.

5. **Select** October Projects, **right-click, click** Font **on the menu that opens, click the** Advanced tab, **click the** Scale list arrow, **click** 80%, **click** OK, **then deselect the text**

   You use the Advanced tab in the Font dialog box to change the scale, or width, of the selected characters, to alter the spacing between characters, or to raise or lower the characters. Decreasing the scale of the characters makes them narrower and gives the text a tall, thin appearance, as shown in FIGURE 3-6.

6. **Scroll down, select the subheading** Wildlife Refuge, **then, using the Mini toolbar, click the** Font list arrow, **click** Trebuchet MS, **click** B, **click** I, **click the** Font Color list arrow ▲ ▾, **click the** Orange, Accent 2 **color in the Theme Colors, then deselect the text**

   The subheading is formatted in Trebuchet MS, bold, italic, and orange.

7. **Select** Wildlife Refuge, **then click the** Format Painter button **in the Clipboard group**

   The pointer changes to 🖌I.

8. **Scroll down, select** Animal Shelter **with the** 🖌I **pointer, then deselect the text**

   The subheading is formatted in Trebuchet MS, bold, italic, and orange, as shown in FIGURE 3-7.

9. **Scroll up, select** Animal Care Rajasthan, **then double-click the** Format Painter button

   Double-clicking the Format Painter button allows the Format Painter to remain active until you turn it off. By keeping the Format Painter active, you can apply formatting to multiple items.

10. **Scroll down, select the headings** Microloans Inca Highlands, Disaster Relief Nepal, **and** Ecological Farming Provence **with the pointer, click the** Format Painter **button to turn off the Format Painter, then save your changes**

    The headings are formatted in 14-point Trebuchet MS bold with a green font color.

FIGURE 3-5: Font tab in Font dialog box

Font, font style, and font size options

Font color, underline style, and underline color options

Preview of selected font and font effects

Font effects options

Text effects

FIGURE 3-6: Font and character spacing effects applied to text

Title formatted in 48-point, orange, with a shadow effect and a character scale of 80%

Paragraph formatted in italic

FIGURE 3-7: Formats copied and applied using the Format Painter

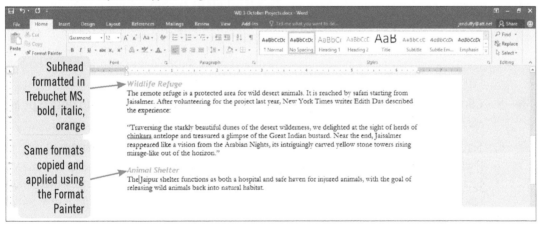

Subhead formatted in Trebuchet MS, bold, italic, orange

Same formats copied and applied using the Format Painter

Underlining text

Another creative way to call attention to text and to jazz up the appearance of a document is to apply an underline style to words you want to highlight. The Underline list arrow in the Font group displays straight, dotted, wavy, dashed, and mixed underline styles, along with a gallery of colors to choose from. To apply an underline to text, simply select it, click the Underline list arrow, and then select an underline style from the list. For a wider variety of underline styles, click More Underlines in the list, and then select an underline style in the Font dialog box. You can change the color of an underline at any time by selecting the underlined text, clicking the Underline list arrow, pointing to Underline Color, and then choosing from the options in the color gallery. If you want to remove an underline from text, select the underlined text, and then click the Underline button.

Learning Outcomes
- Add spacing under paragraphs
- Change line spacing in paragraphs
- Apply styles to text

Change Line and Paragraph Spacing

Increasing the amount of space between lines adds more white space to a document and can make it easier to read. Adding space before and after paragraphs can also open up a document and improve its appearance. You use the Line and Paragraph Spacing list arrow in the Paragraph group on the Home tab to quickly change line spacing. To change paragraph spacing, you use the Spacing options in the Paragraph group on the Layout tab. Both line and paragraph spacing are measured in points. **CASE** *You increase the line spacing of several paragraphs and add extra space under each heading to give the flyer a more open feel. You work with formatting marks turned on, so you can see the paragraph marks (¶).*

STEPS

1. **Press [Ctrl][Home], click the** Show/Hide ¶ button ¶ **in the Paragraph group, place the insertion point in the italicized paragraph under the title, then click the** Line and Paragraph Spacing list arrow ≣▾ **in the Paragraph group on the Home tab**

   The Line Spacing list opens. This list includes options for increasing the space between lines. The check mark on the Line Spacing list indicates the current line spacing.

2. **Click** 1.15

   The space between the lines in the paragraph increases to 1.15 lines. Notice that you do not need to select an entire paragraph to change its paragraph formatting; simply place the insertion point in the paragraph.

QUICK TIP
Word recognizes any string of text that ends with a paragraph mark as a paragraph, including titles, headings, and single lines in a list.

3. **Scroll down, select the** five-line list **that begins with "Project Dates Cost", click** ≣▾**, then click** 1.5

   The line spacing between the selected paragraphs changes to 1.5. To change the paragraph-formatting features of more than one paragraph, you must select the paragraphs.

4. **Scroll down, place the insertion point in the heading** Animal Care Rajasthan**, then click the** Layout tab

   The paragraph spacing settings for the active paragraph are shown in the Before and After text boxes in the Paragraph group on the Layout tab.

QUICK TIP
You can also type a number in the Before and After text boxes.

5. **Click the** After up arrow **in the Spacing section in the Paragraph group until 6 pt appears**

   Six points of space are added after the Animal Care Rajasthan heading paragraph.

TROUBLE
If your [F4] key does not work, use the After up arrow to apply 6 pts of space to the headings listed in Steps 6 and 7, then continue with Step 8.

6. **Scroll down, place the insertion point in** Microloans Inca Highlands**, then press [F4]**

   Pressing [F4] repeats the last action you took. In this case, six points of space are added after the Microloans Inca Highlands heading. Note that using [F4] is not the same as using the Format Painter. Pressing [F4] repeats only the last action you took, and using the Format Painter applies multiple format settings at the same time.

7. **Scroll down, select** Disaster Relief Nepal**, press and hold [Ctrl], select** Ecological Farming Provence**, release [Ctrl], then press [F4]**

   When you press [Ctrl] as you select items, you can select and format multiple items at once. Six points of space are added after each heading.

QUICK TIP
Adjusting the space between paragraphs is a more precise way to add white space to a document than inserting blank lines.

8. **Press [Ctrl][Home], place the insertion point in** October Projects**, then click the** Before up arrow **in the Spacing section in the Paragraph group twice so that 12 pt appears**

   The second line of the title has 12 points of space before it, as shown in FIGURE 3-8.

9. **Click the** Home tab**, click** ¶**, then save your changes**

FIGURE 3-8: Line and paragraph spacing applied to document

12 points of space added before October Projects heading

Spacing section shows paragraph spacing for the paragraph where the insertion point is located

Insertion point (your placement may vary)

Line spacing is 1.15

Line spacing is 1.5

6 points of space added after the heading

Formatting with Quick Styles

You can also apply multiple format settings to text in one step by applying a style. A **style** is a set of formats, such as font, font size, and paragraph alignment, that is named and stored together. Formatting a document with styles is a quick and easy way to give it a professional appearance. To make it even easier, Word includes sets of styles, called **Quick Styles**, that are designed to be used together in a document to make it attractive and readable. A Quick Style set includes styles for a title, several heading levels, body text, quotes, and lists. The styles in a Quick Style set use common fonts, colors, and formats so that using the styles together in a document gives the document a cohesive look.

To view the active set of Quick Styles, click the More button ⬇ in the Styles group on the Home tab to expand the Quick Styles gallery, shown in FIGURE 3-9. As you move the pointer over each style in the gallery, a preview of the style is applied to the selected text. To apply a style to the selected text, you simply click the style in the Quick Styles gallery. To remove a style from

FIGURE 3-9: Quick Styles gallery

selected text, you click the Clear All Formatting button ⬛ in the Font group or the Clear Formatting command in the Quick Styles gallery.

If you want to change the active set of Quick Styles to a Quick Style set with a different design, click the Design tab, click the More button ⬇ in the Document Formatting group, and then select the Quick Style set that best suits your document's content, tone, and audience. When you change the Quick Style set, a complete set of new fonts and colors is applied to the entire document. You can also change the color scheme or font used in the active Quick Style set by clicking the Colors or Fonts buttons, and then selecting from the available color schemes or font options.

Formatting Text and Paragraphs

Align Paragraphs

Changing paragraph alignment is another way to enhance a document's appearance. Paragraphs are aligned relative to the left and right margins in a document. By default, text is **left-aligned**, which means it is flush with the left margin and has a ragged right edge. Using the alignment buttons in the Paragraph group, you can **right-align** a paragraph—make it flush with the right margin—or **center** a paragraph so that it is positioned evenly between the left and right margins. You can also **justify** a paragraph so that both the left and right edges of the paragraph are flush with the left and right margins. **CASE** *You change the alignment of several paragraphs at the beginning of the flyer to make it more visually interesting.*

STEPS

1. **Replace** Your Name, Today's Date **with your name, a comma, and the date**

2. **Select your name, the comma, and the date, then click the** Align Right button ≣ **in the Paragraph group**

   The text is aligned with the right margin. In Page Layout view, the place where the white and shaded sections on the horizontal ruler meet shows the left and right margins.

TROUBLE
Click the View tab, then click the Ruler check box to display the rulers if they are not already displayed.

3. **Place the insertion point between your name and the comma, press** [Delete] **to delete the comma, then press** [Enter]

   The new paragraph containing the date is also right-aligned. Pressing [Enter] in the middle of a paragraph creates a new paragraph with the same text and paragraph formatting as the original paragraph.

4. **Select the** two-line title, **then click the** Center button ≣ **in the Paragraph group**

   The two paragraphs that make up the title are centered between the left and right margins.

QUICK TIP
Click the Align Left button ≣ in the Paragraph group to left-align a paragraph.

5. **Scroll down as needed, place the insertion point in the** Animal Care Rajasthan **heading, then click** ≣

   The Animal Care Rajasthan heading is centered.

6. **Place the insertion point in the italicized paragraph under the title, then click the** Justify button ≣ **in the Paragraph group**

   The paragraph is aligned with both the left and right margins, as shown in FIGURE 3-10. When you justify a paragraph, Word adjusts the spacing between words so that each line in the paragraph is flush with the left and the right margins.

7. **Scroll down, place the insertion point in** Animal Care Rajasthan, **then click the** launcher ⌟ **in the Paragraph group**

   The Paragraph dialog box opens, as shown in FIGURE 3-11. The Indents and Spacing tab shows the paragraph format settings for the paragraph where the insertion point is located. You can check or change paragraph format settings using this dialog box.

8. **Click the** Alignment list arrow, **click** Left, **click** OK, **then save your changes**

   The Animal Care Rajasthan heading is left-aligned.

FIGURE 3-10: Modified paragraph alignment

FIGURE 3-11: Indents and Spacing tab in the Paragraph dialog box

Formatting a document using themes

Changing the theme applied to a document is another powerful and efficient way to tailor a document's look and feel, particularly when a document is formatted with a Quick Style set. By default, all documents created in Word are formatted with the default Office theme—which uses Calibri as the font for the body text—but you can change the theme at any time to fit the content, tone, and purpose of a document. When you change the theme for a document, a complete set of new theme colors, fonts, and effects is applied to the whole document.

To preview how various themes look when applied to the current document, click the Themes button in the Document Formatting group on the Design tab, and then move the pointer over each theme in the gallery and notice how the document changes. When you click the theme you like, all document content that uses theme colors, all text that is formatted with a style,

including default body text, and all table styles and graphic effects change to the colors, fonts, and effects used by the theme. In addition, the gallery of colors changes to display the set of theme colors, and the active Quick Style set changes to employ the theme colors and fonts. Note that changing the theme does not change the non-theme-based font formatting that has already been applied. For example, if you changed the font of text, applied bold to text, or changed the font color of text to a standard or custom color, that formatting remains in place.

If you want to tweak the document design further, you can modify it by applying a different set of theme colors, heading and body text fonts, or graphic effects. To do this, simply click the Colors, Fonts, or Effects button in the Document Formatting group, move the pointer over each option in the gallery to preview it in the document, and then click the option you like best.

Work with Tabs

Learning Outcomes
- Set tab stops and tab leaders
- Modify tabs
- Use tabs to align text

Tabs allow you to align text at a specific location in a document. A **tab stop** is a point on the horizontal ruler that indicates the location at which to align text. By default, tab stops are located every 1/2" from the left margin, but you can also set custom tab stops. Using tabs, you can align text to the left, right, or center of a tab stop, or you can align text at a decimal point or insert a bar character. TABLE 3-1 describes the different types of tab stops. You set tabs using the horizontal ruler or the Tabs dialog box. **CASE** ➤ *You use tabs to format the summary information on last minute projects so it is easy to read.*

STEPS

1. **Scroll as needed, then select the five-line list beginning with "Project Dates Cost"**
   Before you set tab stops for existing text, you must select the paragraphs for which you want to set tabs.

2. **Point to the tab indicator 🔲 at the left end of the horizontal ruler**
   The icon that appears in the tab indicator indicates the active type of tab; pointing to the tab indicator displays a ScreenTip with the name of the active tab type. By default, left tab is the active tab type. Clicking the tab indicator scrolls through the types of tabs and indents.

3. **Click the tab indicator to see each of the available tab and indent types, make Left Tab 🔲 the active tab type, click the 1" mark on the horizontal ruler, then click the 3½" mark on the horizontal ruler**
   A left tab stop is inserted at the 1" mark and the 3½" mark on the horizontal ruler. Clicking the horizontal ruler inserts a tab stop of the active type for the selected paragraph or paragraphs.

4. **Click the tab indicator twice so the Right Tab icon ⌐ is active, then click the 5" mark on the horizontal ruler**
   A right tab stop is inserted at the 5" mark on the horizontal ruler, as shown in FIGURE 3-12.

5. **Place the insertion point before Project in the first line in the list, press [Tab], place the insertion point before Dates, press [Tab], place the insertion point before Cost, then press [Tab]**
   Inserting a tab before "Project" left-aligns the text at the 1" mark, inserting a tab before "Dates" left-aligns the text at the 3½" mark, and inserting a tab before "Cost" right-aligns "Cost" at the 5" mark.

6. **Insert a tab at the beginning of each remaining line in the list**
   The paragraphs left-align at the 1" mark.

7. **Insert a tab before each Oct. in the list, then insert a tab before each $ in the list**
   The dates left-align at the 3½" mark. The prices right-align at the 5" mark.

8. **Select the five lines of tabbed text, drag the right tab stop to the 5½" mark on the horizontal ruler, then deselect the text**
   Dragging the tab stop moves it to a new location. The prices right-align at the 5½" mark.

9. **Select the last four lines of tabbed text, click the launcher 🔲 in the Paragraph group, then click the Tabs button at the bottom of the Paragraph dialog box**
   The Tabs dialog box opens, as shown in FIGURE 3-13. You can use the Tabs dialog box to set tab stops, change the position or alignment of existing tab stops, clear tab stops, and apply tab leaders to tabs. **Tab leaders** are lines that appear in front of tabbed text.

10. **Click 3.5" in the Tab stop position list box, click the 2 option button in the Leader section, click Set, click 5.5" in the Tab stop position list box, click the 2 option button in the Leader section, click Set, click OK, deselect the text, then save your changes**
    A dotted tab leader is added before each 3.5" and 5.5" tab stop in the last four lines of tabbed text, as shown in FIGURE 3-14.

Formatting Text and Paragraphs

FIGURE 3-12: **Left and right tab stops on the horizontal ruler**

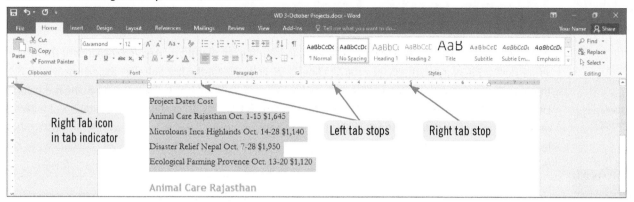

Right Tab icon
in tab indicator

Left tab stops

Right tab stop

FIGURE 3-13: **Tabs dialog box**

Select the tab
stop you want
to modify

Select Leader
options

Apply the selected
settings to the
selected tab stop

Clears the
selected tab stop

Clears all
tab stops

FIGURE 3-14: **Tab leaders**

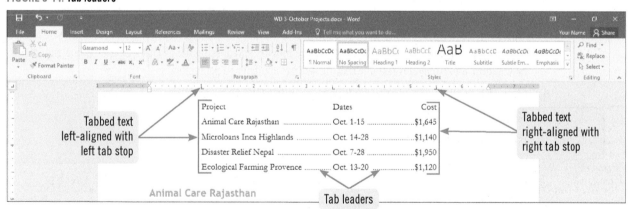

Tabbed text
left-aligned with
left tab stop

Tabbed text
right-aligned with
right tab stop

Tab leaders

TABLE 3-1: **Types of tabs**

tab	use to
⌞ Left tab	Set the start position of text so that text runs to the right of the tab stop as you type
⊥ Center tab	Set the center align position of text so that text stays centered on the tab stop as you type
⌟ Right tab	Set the right or end position of text so that text moves to the left of the tab stop as you type
⊥ Decimal tab	Set the position of the decimal point so that numbers align around the decimal point as you type
⎮ Bar tab	Insert a vertical bar at the tab position

Work with Indents

Learning Outcomes
- Indent a paragraph
- Indent the first line of a paragraph

When you **indent** a paragraph, you move its edge in from the left or right margin. You can indent the entire left or right edge of a paragraph, just the first line, or all lines except the first line. The **indent markers** on the horizontal ruler indicate the indent settings for the paragraph in which the insertion point is located. Dragging an indent marker to a new location on the ruler is one way to change the indentation of a paragraph; changing the indent settings in the Paragraph group on the Layout tab is another; and using the indent buttons in the Paragraph group on the Home tab is a third. TABLE 3-2 describes different types of indents and some of the methods for creating each. **CASE** *You indent several paragraphs in the flyer.*

STEPS

1. **Press [Ctrl][Home], place the insertion point in the italicized paragraph under the title, then click the** Increase Indent button **in the Paragraph group on the Home tab**
   The entire paragraph is indented ½" from the left margin, as shown in FIGURE 3-15. The indent marker also moves to the ½" mark on the horizontal ruler. Each time you click the Increase Indent button, the left edge of a paragraph moves another ½" to the right.

2. **Click the** Decrease Indent button **in the Paragraph group**
   The left edge of the paragraph moves ½" to the left, and the indent marker moves back to the left margin.

3. **Drag the** First Line Indent marker **to the ¼" mark on the horizontal ruler**
   FIGURE 3-16 shows the First Line Indent marker being dragged. The first line of the paragraph is indented ¼". Dragging the First Line Indent marker indents only the first line of a paragraph.

4. **Scroll to the bottom of page 1, place the insertion point in the quotation, click the** Layout tab, **click the** Indent Left text box **in the Paragraph group, type** .5, **click the** Indent Right text box, **type** .5, **then press** [Enter]
   The left and right edges of the paragraph are indented ½" from the margins, as shown in FIGURE 3-17.

5. **Press [Ctrl][Home], place the insertion point in the italicized paragraph, then click the** launcher **in the Paragraph group**
   The Paragraph dialog box opens. You can use the Indents and Spacing tab to check or change the alignment, indentation, and paragraph and line spacing settings applied to a paragraph.

6. **Click the** Special list arrow, **click** (none), **click** OK, **then save your changes**
   The first line indent is removed from the paragraph.

Applying text effects and clearing formatting

The Word Text Effects and Typography feature allows you to add visual appeal to your documents by adding special text effects to text, including outlines, shadows, reflections, and glows. The feature also includes a gallery of preformatted combined text effect styles, called **WordArt**, that you can apply to your text to format it quickly and easily. To apply a WordArt style or a text effect to text, simply select the text, click the Text Effects and Typography button in the Font group on the Home tab, and select a WordArt style from the gallery or point to a type of text effect, such as reflection or shadow, to open a gallery of styles related to that type of text effect. Experiment with combining text effect styles to give your text a striking appearance.

If you are unhappy with the way text is formatted, you can use the Clear All Formatting command to return the text to the default format settings. The default format includes font and paragraph formatting: text is formatted in 11-point Calibri, and paragraphs are left-aligned with 1.08 point line spacing, 8 points of space after, and no indents. To clear formatting from text and return it to the default format, select the text you want to clear, and then click the Clear All Formatting button in the Font group on the Home tab. If you prefer to return the text to the default font and remove all paragraph formatting, making the text 11-point Calibri, left-aligned, single spaced, with no paragraph spacing or indents, select the text and then simply click the No Spacing button in the Styles group on the Home tab.

FIGURE 3-15: Indented paragraph

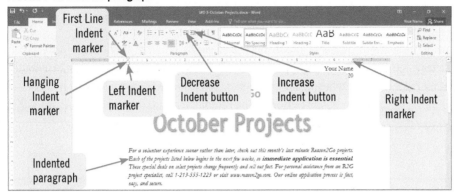

FIGURE 3-16: Dragging the First Line Indent marker

FIGURE 3-17: Paragraph indented from the left and right

TABLE 3-2: Types of indents

indent type: description	to create
Left indent: The left edge of a paragraph is moved in from the left margin	Drag the Left Indent marker □ on the ruler to the right to the position where you want the left edge of the paragraph to align; when you drag the left indent marker, all the indent markers move as one
Right indent: The right edge of a paragraph is moved in from the right margin	Drag the Right Indent marker △ on the ruler to the left to the position where you want the right edge of the paragraph to align
First line indent: The first line of a paragraph is indented more than the subsequent lines	Drag the First Line Indent marker ▽ on the ruler to the right to the position where you want the first line of the paragraph to begin; or activate the First Line Indent marker ▽ in the tab indicator, and then click the ruler at the position where you want the first line of the paragraph to begin
Hanging indent: The subsequent lines of a paragraph are indented more than the first line	Drag the Hanging Indent marker △ on the ruler to the right to the position where you want the hanging indent to begin; or activate the Hanging Indent marker △ in the tab indicator, and then click the ruler at the position where you want the second and remaining lines of the paragraph to begin; when you drag the hanging indent marker, the left indent marker moves with it
Negative indent (or Outdent): The left edge of a paragraph is moved to the left of the left margin	Drag the Left Indent marker □ on the ruler left to the position where you want the negative indent to begin; when you drag the left indent marker, all markers move as one

Add Bullets and Numbering

Learning Outcomes
- Apply bullets or numbering to lists
- Renumber a list
- Change bullet or numbering styles

Formatting a list with bullets or numbering can help to organize the ideas in a document. A **bullet** is a character, often a small circle, that appears before the items in a list to add emphasis. Formatting a list as a numbered list helps illustrate sequences and priorities. You can quickly format a list with bullets or numbering by using the Bullets and Numbering buttons in the Paragraph group on the Home tab. **CASE** *You format the lists in your flyer with numbers and bullets.*

STEPS

1. **Scroll until the** Disaster Relief Nepal heading **is at the top of your screen**

2. **Select the** three-line list **of 3-day add-ons, click the** Home tab, **then click the** Numbering list arrow ▦ ▾ **in the Paragraph group**

   The Numbering Library opens, as shown in FIGURE 3-18. You use this list to choose or change the numbering style applied to a list. You can drag the pointer over the numbering styles to preview how the selected text will look if the numbering style is applied.

3. **Click the numbering style called out in** FIGURE 3-18

   The paragraphs are formatted as a numbered list.

   QUICK TIP
   To remove a bullet or number, select the paragraph(s), then click ▦ ▾ or ▦ ▾.

4. **Place the insertion point after** Pokhara — Valley of Lakes, **press [Enter], then type** Temples of Janakpur

   Pressing [Enter] in the middle of the numbered list creates a new numbered paragraph and automatically renumbers the remainder of the list. Similarly, if you delete a paragraph from a numbered list, Word automatically renumbers the remaining paragraphs.

5. **Click** 1 **in the list**

   Clicking a number in a list selects all the numbers, as shown in FIGURE 3-19.

6. **Click the** Bold button **B** **in the Font group**

   The numbers are all formatted in bold. Notice that the formatting of the items in the list does not change when you change the formatting of the numbers. You can also use this technique to change the formatting of bullets in a bulleted list.

   QUICK TIP
   To use a symbol or a picture for a bullet character, click the Bullets list arrow, click Define New Bullet, and then select from the options in the Define New Bullet dialog box.

7. **Select the list of items under "Last minute participants in the Disaster Relief Nepal project...", then click the** Bullets button ▦ **in the Paragraph group**

   The four paragraphs are formatted as a bulleted list using the most recently used bullet style.

8. **Click a** bullet **in the list to select all the bullets, click the** Bullets list arrow ▦ ▾ **in the Paragraph group, click the** check mark bullet style, **click the** document **to deselect the text, then save your changes**

   The bullet character changes to a check mark, as shown in FIGURE 3-20.

Creating multilevel lists

You can create lists with hierarchical structures by applying a multilevel list style to a list. To create a **multilevel list**, also called an outline, begin by applying a multilevel list style using the Multilevel List list arrow ▦ ▾ in the Paragraph group on the Home tab, then type your outline, pressing [Enter] after each item. To demote items to a lower level of importance in the outline, place the insertion point in the item, then click the Increase Indent button ▦ in the Paragraph group on the Home tab. Each time you indent a paragraph, the item is demoted to a lower level in the outline. Similarly, you can use the Decrease Indent button ▦ to promote an item to a higher level in the outline. You can also create a hierarchical structure in any bulleted or numbered list by using ▦ and ▦ to demote and promote items in the list. To change the multilevel list style applied to a list, select the list, click ▦ ▾ and then select a new style.

FIGURE 3-18: Numbering Library

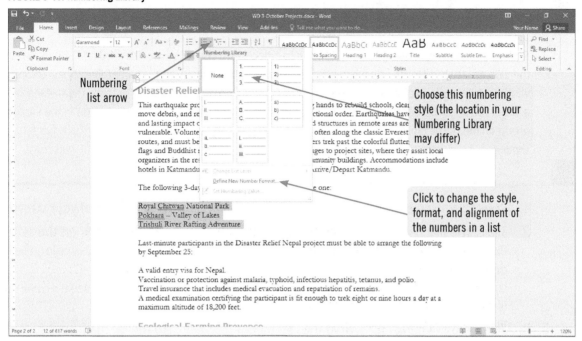

Numbering list arrow

Choose this numbering style (the location in your Numbering Library may differ)

Click to change the style, format, and alignment of the numbers in a list

FIGURE 3-19: Numbered list

Bullets button

Numbers selected in numbered list

FIGURE 3-20: Check mark bullets applied to list

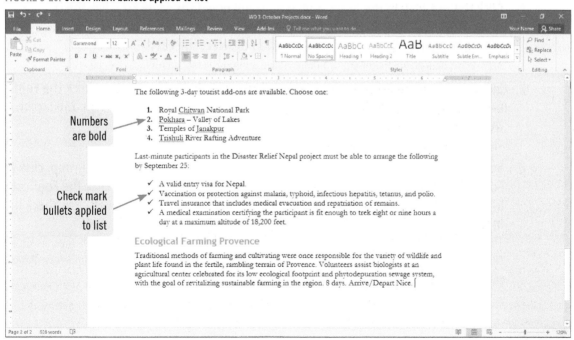

Numbers are bold

Check mark bullets applied to list

Add Borders and Shading

Learning Outcomes
- Apply shading to text
- Apply borders to text
- Highlight text

Borders and shading can add color and splash to a document. **Borders** are lines you add above, below, to the side, or around words or paragraphs. You can format borders using different line styles, colors, and widths. **Shading** is a color or pattern you apply behind words or paragraphs to make them stand out on a page. You apply borders and shading using the Borders button and the Shading button in the Paragraph group on the Home tab. **CASE** ▸ *You enhance the tabbed text of the last minute projects schedule by adding shading to it. You also apply a border around the tabbed text to set it off from the rest of the document.*

STEPS

1. **Press [Ctrl][Home], then scroll down until the tabbed text is at the top of your screen**

2. **Select the** five paragraphs **of tabbed text, click the** Shading list arrow 🔲 ▾ **in the Paragraph group on the Home tab, click the** Green, Accent 6, Lighter 60% **color, then deselect the text**

   Light green shading is applied to the five paragraphs. Notice that the shading is applied to the entire width of the paragraphs, despite the tab settings.

3. **Select the** five paragraphs, **drag the** Left Indent marker 🔲 **to the ¾" mark on the horizontal ruler, drag the** Right Indent marker 🔺 **to the 5¾" mark, then deselect the text**

   The shading for the paragraphs is indented from the left and right, which makes it look more attractive, as shown in FIGURE 3-21.

4. **Select the** five paragraphs, **click the** Bottom Border list arrow 🔲 ▾ **in the Paragraph group, click** Outside Borders, **then deselect the text**

   A black outside border is added around the selected text. The style of the border added is the most recently used border style, in this case the default, a thin black line.

5. **Select the** five paragraphs, **click the** Outside Borders list arrow 🔲 ▾, **click** No Border, **click the** No Border list arrow 🔲 ▾, **then click** Borders and Shading

   The Borders and Shading dialog box opens, as shown in FIGURE 3-22. You use the Borders tab to change the border style, color, and width, and to add boxes and lines to words or paragraphs.

6. **Click the** Box icon **in the Setting section, scroll down the Style list, click the** double-line style, **click the** Color list arrow, **click the** Green, Accent 6, Darker 25% **color, click the** Width list arrow, **click** 1½ pt, **click OK, then deselect the text**

   A 1½-point dark green double-line border is added around the tabbed text.

7. **Select the** five paragraphs, **click the** Bold button 🅱 **in the Font group, click the** Font Color list arrow 🅰 ▾ **in the Font group, click the** Green, Accent 6, Darker 25% **color, then deselect the text**

   The text changes to bold dark green.

8. **Select the** first line **in the tabbed text, click the** launcher 🔲 **in the Font group, click the** Font tab **if it is not the active tab, scroll and click 14 in the Size list, click the** Font color list arrow, **click the** Orange, Accent 2, Darker 25% **color, click the** Small caps check box **in the Effects section, click** OK, **deselect the text, then save your changes**

   The text in the first line of the tabbed text is enlarged and changed to orange small caps, as shown in FIGURE 3-23. When you change text to small caps, the lowercase letters are changed to uppercase letters in a smaller font size.

FIGURE 3-21: Shading applied to the tabbed text

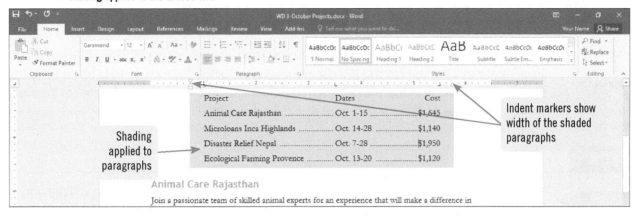

Shading applied to paragraphs

Indent markers show width of the shaded paragraphs

FIGURE 3-22: Borders tab in Borders and Shading dialog box

Select border settings before applying them in the Preview area

Click to change the location of the border relative to the text

Choose a line style

Preview of border settings

Click buttons or edges of preview to apply borders

Choose to apply the settings to a paragraph or to selected text

FIGURE 3-23: Borders and shading applied to the document

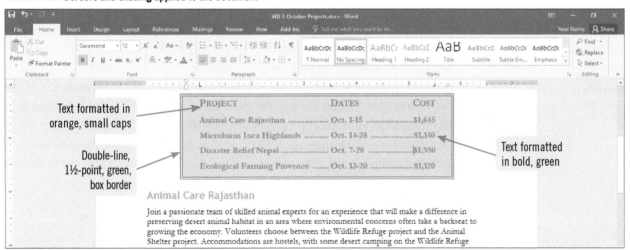

Text formatted in orange, small caps

Double-line, 1½-point, green, box border

Text formatted in bold, green

Word 2016

Highlighting text in a document

The Highlight tool allows you to mark and find important text in a document. **Highlighting** is transparent color that is applied to text using the Highlight pointer. To highlight text, click the Text Highlight Color list arrow in the Font group on the Home tab, select a color, then use the I-beam part of the pointer to select the text you want to highlight. Click to turn off the Highlight pointer. To remove highlighting, select the highlighted text, click then click No Color. Highlighting prints, but it is used most effectively when a document is viewed on screen.

Insert Online Pictures

**Learning
Outcomes**
• Insert images
• Resize images
• Wrap text and
   position images

Clip art is a collection of graphic images that you can insert into a document. Bing Image Search clip art images are images that you can add to a document using the Online Pictures command on the Insert tab. Once you insert a clip art image, you can wrap text around it, resize it, enhance it, and move it to a different location. **CASE** ▸ *You illustrate the second page of the document with an online clip art image.*

STEPS

1. **Scroll to the top of page 2, place the insertion point before** Microloans Inca Highlands, **click the** Insert tab, **then click the** Online Pictures button **in the Illustrations group**
   The Insert Pictures window opens. You can use this to search for images related to a keyword.

2. **Type** Inca **in the Bing Image Search text box, then press** [Enter]
   Images that have the keyword "Inca" associated with them appear in the Bing Image Search window.

3. **Scroll down the gallery of images, click the clip called out in** FIGURE 3-24, **then click** Insert
   The clip is inserted at the location of the insertion point. When a graphic is selected, the active tab changes to the Picture Tools Format tab. This tab contains commands used to adjust, enhance, arrange, and size graphics. The white circles that appear on the square edges of the graphic are the **sizing handles**.

4. **Type** 1.8 **in the Shape Height text box in the Size group on the Picture Tools Format tab, then press** [Enter]
   The size of the graphic is reduced. When you decreased the height of the graphic, the width decreased proportionally. You can also resize a graphic proportionally by dragging a corner sizing handle. Until you apply text wrapping to a graphic, it is part of the line of text in which it was inserted (an **inline graphic**). To move a graphic independently of text, you must make it a **floating graphic**.

5. **Click the** Position button **in the Arrange group, then click** Position in Middle Center with Square Text Wrapping
   The graphic is moved to the middle of the page and the text wraps around it. Applying text wrapping to the graphic made it a floating graphic. A floating graphic can be moved anywhere on a page. You can also wrap text around a graphic using the Layout Options button.

6. **Scroll up until the Microloans Inca Highlands heading is at the top of your screen, position the pointer over the graphic, when the pointer changes to** ⌖ **drag the graphic up and to the right so its edges align with the right margin and the top of the paragraph under the Microloans Inca Highlands heading as shown in** FIGURE 3-25, **then release the mouse button**
   The graphic is moved to the upper-right corner of the page. Green alignment guides may appear to help you align the image with the margins.

7. **Click the** Position button **in the Arrange group, then click** Position in Top Left with Square Text Wrapping
   The graphic is moved to the upper-left corner of the page.

8. **Click the** Picture Effects button **in the Picture Styles group, point to** Shadow, **point to each style to see a preview of the style applied to the graphic, then click** Offset Left
   A shadow effect is applied to the graphic.

9. **Press** [Ctrl][Home], **click the** View tab, **then click the** Multiple Pages button **in the Zoom group to view the completed document as shown in** FIGURE 3-26.

10. **Save your changes, submit the document to your instructor, then close the document and exit Word**

FIGURE 3-24: Insert Pictures window

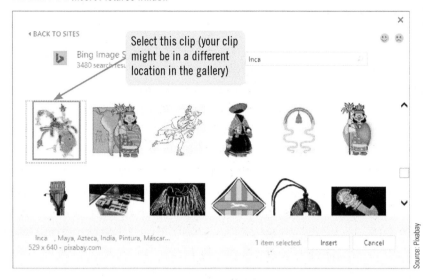

Source: Pixabay

FIGURE 3-25: Graphic being moved to a new location

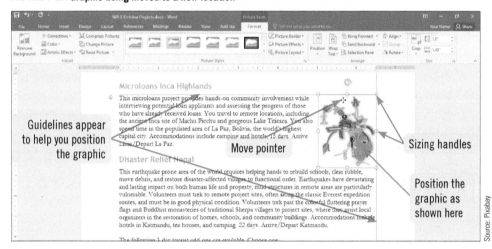

Source: Pixabay

FIGURE 3-26: Completed Document

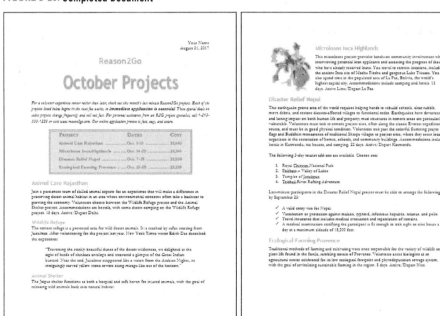

Source: Pixabay

Practice

Concepts Review

Label each element of the Word program window shown in FIGURE 3-27.

FIGURE 3-27

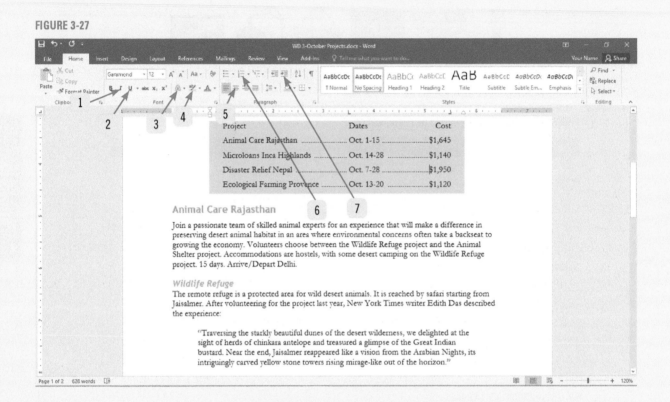

Match each term with the statement that best describes it.

8. Inline graphic

9. Style

10. Shading

11. Border

12. Floating graphic

13. Highlight

14. Point

15. Bullet

a. A graphic symbol that appears at the beginning of a paragraph in a list

b. Transparent color that is applied to text to mark it in a document

c. A set of format settings

d. An image that text wrapping has been applied to

e. An image that is inserted as part of a line of text

f. A line that can be applied above, below, or to the sides of a paragraph

g. A unit of measurement equal to $1/72$ of an inch

h. Color or pattern that is applied behind text to make it look attractive

Formatting Text and Paragraphs

Select the best answer from the list of choices.

16. **Which dialog box is used to change the scale of characters?**
    a. Paragraph
    b. Font
    c. Tabs
    d. Borders and Shading

17. **What is Calibri?**
    a. A font
    b. A style
    c. A text effect
    d. A character format

18. **What is the most precise way to increase the amount of white space between two paragraphs?**
    a. Indent the paragraphs
    b. Change the line spacing of the paragraphs
    c. Change the before spacing for the second paragraph
    d. Change the font size

19. **Which type of indent results in subsequent lines of a paragraph being indented more than the first line?**
    a. Right indent
    b. First line indent
    c. Negative indent
    d. Hanging indent

20. **Which command is used to add a reflection or an outline to text?**
    a. Underline
    b. Text Effects and Typography
    c. Strikethrough
    d. Change Case

Skills Review

1. **Format with fonts.**
   a. Start Word, open the file WD 3-2.docx from the location where you store your Data Files, save it as **WD 3-Manchester EDA Report**, then scroll through the document to get a feel for its contents.
   b. Press [Ctrl][A], then format the text in 12-point Californian FB. Choose a different serif font if Californian FB is not available to you.
   c. Press [Ctrl][Home], format the report title **City of Manchester** in 28-point Berlin Sans FB Demi. Choose a different sans serif font if Berlin Sans FB Demi is not available to you.
   d. Change the font color of the report title to Blue, Accent 5, Darker 25%.
   e. Format the subtitle **Economic Development Authority Report Executive Summary** in 16-point Berlin Sans FB Demi, then press [Enter] before Executive in the subtitle.
   f. Format the heading **Mission Statement** in 14-point Berlin Sans FB Demi with a Gold, Accent 4, Darker 25% font color.
   g. Press [Ctrl][Home], then save your changes to the report.

2. **Copy formats using the Format Painter.**
   a. Use the Format Painter to copy the format of the Mission Statement heading to the following headings: **Guiding Principles, Issues, Proposed Actions**.
   b. Show formatting marks, then format the paragraph under the Mission Statement heading in italic.
   c. Format **Years Population Growth**, the first line in the four-line list under the Issues heading, in bold, small caps, with a Blue, Accent 5, Darker 25% font color.
   d. Change the font color of the next two lines under Years Population Growth to Blue, Accent 5, Darker 25%.
   e. Format the line **Source: Office of State Planning** in italic, then save your changes.

3. **Change line and paragraph spacing.**
   a. Change the line spacing of the three-line list under the first body paragraph to 1.5 lines.
   b. Add 6 points of space after the title City of Manchester. Add 18 points of space before and 6 points of space after the Executive Summary line in the subtitle.
   c. Add 12 points of space after the Mission Statement heading, then add 12 points of space after each additional heading in the report (Guiding Principles, Issues, Proposed Actions).

Skills Review (continued)

    d. Add 6 points of space after each paragraph in the list under the Guiding Principles heading.

    e. Change the line spacing of the four-line list under the Issues heading that begins with Years Population Growth to 1.15.

    f. Add 6 points of space after each paragraph under the Proposed Actions heading.

    g. Press [Ctrl][Home], then save your changes to the report.

4. Align paragraphs.

    a. Press [Ctrl][A] to select the entire document, then justify all the paragraphs.

    b. Center the three-line report title.

    c. Press [Ctrl][End], press [Enter], type your name, press [Enter], type the current date, then right-align your name and the date.

    d. Save your changes to the report.

5. Work with tabs.

    a. Scroll up and select the four-line list of population information under the Issues heading.

    b. Set left tab stops at the 2" mark and the 3¾" mark.

    c. Insert a tab at the beginning of each line in the list.

    d. In the first line, insert a tab before Population. In the second line, insert a tab before 4.5%. In the third line, insert a tab before 53%.

    e. Select the first three lines, then drag the second tab stop to the 3" mark on the horizontal ruler.

    f. Press [Ctrl][Home], then save your changes to the report.

6. Work with indents.

    a. Indent the first line of the paragraph under the Mission Statement heading ½".

    b. Indent the first line of the paragraph under the Guiding Principles heading ½".

    c. Indent the first line of each of the three body paragraphs under the Issues heading ½".

    d. Press [Ctrl][Home], then save your changes to the report.

7. Add bullets and numbering.

    a. Apply bullets to the three-line list under the first body paragraph. Change the bullet style to small black circles if that is not the current bullet symbol.

    b. Change the font color of the bullets to Blue, Accent 5, Darker 25%.

    c. Scroll down until the Guiding Principles heading is at the top of your screen.

    d. Format the six-paragraph list under Guiding Principles as a numbered list.

    e. Format the numbers in 14-point Berlin Sans FB Demi, then change the font color to Blue, Accent 5, Darker 25%.

    f. Scroll down until the Proposed Actions heading is at the top of your screen, then format the paragraphs under the heading as a bulleted list using check marks as the bullet style.

    g. Change the font color of the bullets to Blue, Accent 5, Darker 25%, press [Ctrl][Home], then save your changes to the report.

8. Add borders and shading.

    a. Add a 1-point Blue, Accent 5, Darker 25% bottom border below the Mission Statement heading.

    b. Use the Format Painter or the [F4] keys to add the same border to the other headings in the report (Guiding Principles, Issues, Proposed Actions).

    c. Under the Issues heading, select the first three lines of tabbed text, which are formatted in blue, then apply Gold, Accent 4, Lighter 60% shading to the paragraphs.

    d. Select the first three lines of tabbed text again if necessary, then add a 1½ -point Blue, Accent 5, Darker 25% single line box border around the paragraphs.

    e. Indent the shading and border around the paragraphs 1¾" from the left and 1¾" from the right.

    f. Turn off formatting marks, then save your changes.

Formatting Text and Paragraphs

Skills Review (continued)

9. **Insert online pictures.** *(Note: To complete these steps, your computer must be connected to the Internet.)*

   a. Press [Ctrl][Home], then open the Insert Pictures window.

   b. Search using Bing Image Search to find images related to the keyword **buildings**.

   c. Insert the image shown in FIGURE 3-28. *(Note: Select a different image if this one is not available to you. It is best to select an image that is similar in shape to the image shown in FIGURE 3-28.)*

   d. Use the Shape Width text box in the Size group on the Picture Tools Format tab to change the width of the image to 1.5".

   e. Use the Position command to position the image in the top right with square text wrapping.

   f. Apply an Offset Diagonal Bottom Left shadow style to the image.

   g. View your document in two-page view and compare it to the document shown in FIGURE 3-28. Adjust the size or position of the image as needed to so that your document resembles the document shown in the figure.

   h. Save your changes to the document, submit it to your instructor, close the file, and then exit Word.

FIGURE 3-28

City of Manchester

Economic Development Authority Report

Executive Summary

The City of Manchester Economic Development Authority (EDA) has written an economic policy plan for the city of Manchester. The plan is intended to advance dynamic and interactive discussion. It will be used to continuously assess and foster decision-making about the following in the city of Manchester:

- Development
- Infrastructure
- Quality of life

Mission Statement

The purpose of the EDA is to foster a sustainable economy consistent with the city's planning objectives. The mix of industry, commerce, open space, residential development, and the arts in Manchester results in the city's vitality and an excellent quality of life for its citizens. Maintaining this balance is important.

Guiding Principles

Six basic principles guide Manchester's economic policy. These principles seek to safeguard the special features that give the city its character while embracing appropriate economic opportunities.

1. Manchester should remain a major economic center of the region.
2. Economic activity must respect Manchester's natural, cultural, and historic heritage.
3. A pedestrian-friendly commercial center is essential.
4. Sustained economic prosperity requires a balance between residential development, industrial/commercial development, and open space.
5. Open space in the rural district must be preserved.
6. Investing in the infrastructure is necessary to maintain and expand the existing tax and job base.

Issues

Of Manchester's approximately 64,000 acres of land, 12% is zoned for business, commercial, or industrial use, and 88% for residential development. Historically the city has relied upon business and industry to provide 35%-40% of the tax base, as well as employment opportunities. Non-residential development has traditionally been the backbone of the Manchester economy. Today, however, Manchester does not have a great deal of non-residential development potential.

The population of Manchester is expected to rise dramatically over the next few decades. The following chart shows the expected change:

Years	Population Growth
2020-2040	4.5%
2040-2060	53% (projected)

Source: Office of State Planning

At issue is the city's ability to continue to support increasing public costs (most importantly, education) with a tax base shifting toward residential taxpayers. The EDA believes Manchester should remain the market center of the region and avoid becoming a bedroom community. Manchester has maintained a sense of community in part because more than 50% of working residents are able to earn a living within the city. Jobs must be continuously created to sustain the percentage of residents who live and work in Manchester.

Proposed Actions

✓ Implement a business retention program that focuses on the growth and expansion of businesses already operating in Manchester.

✓ Build a consortium of technical and skill development resources to assist companies with educational and training needs.

✓ Sponsor a green business workshop.

✓ Allocate funds for expanded downtown parking.

✓ Develop a strategic open space plan.

Your Name

Today's Date

Source: Pixabay

Independent Challenge 1

You are an estimator for Sustainable Life Design | Build in Jackson, Illinois. You have drafted an estimate for a home renovation job and you need to format it. It's important that your estimate have a clean, striking design, and reflect your company's professionalism.

a. Start Word, open the file WD 3-3.docx from the drive and folder where you store your Data Files, save it as

FIGURE 3-29

WD 3-Chou Birch Estimate, then read the document to get a feel for its contents. FIGURE 3-29 shows how you will format the letterhead.

b. Select the entire document, change the style to No Spacing, then change the font to 11-point Calibri Light.

c. In the first line of the letterhead, format **Sustainable Life** in 30-point Arial Black, then apply all caps to Life. Format **Sustainable** with the Green, Accent 6, Darker 25% font color, format **LIFE** with the Green, Accent 6 font color, then delete the space between the two words. Format **Design | Build** in 30-point Arial with a Green, Accent 6, Darker 25% font color. (*Hint*: Type 30 in the Font Size text box, then press [Enter].)

d. Format the next line in 10-point Arial with a Green, Accent 6, Darker 25% font color.

e. Center the two-line letterhead.

f. Add a 2¼-point dotted Green, Accent 6, Darker 25% border below the address line paragraph.

g. With the insertion point in the address line, open the Borders and Shading dialog box, click Options to open the Border and Shading Options dialog box, change the Bottom setting to **5** points, then click OK twice to close the dialog boxes and to adjust the location of the border relative to the line of text.

h. Format the title **Proposal of Renovation** in 14-point Arial, then center the title.

i. Format the following headings (including the colons) in 11-point Arial: **Date**, **Work to be performed for and at**, **Scope of work**, **Payment schedule**, and **Agreement**.

j. Select the 14-line list under **Scope of work** that begins with **Demo of all...**, then change the paragraph spacing to add 4 points of space after each paragraph in the list. (*Hint*: Select 0 pt in the After text box, type 4, then press Enter.)

k. With the list selected, set a right tab stop at the 6¼" mark, insert tabs before every price in the list, then apply dotted line tab leaders.

l. Format the list as a numbered list, then apply bold to the numbers.

m. Apply bold and italic to the two lines, **Total estimated job cost...** and **Approximate job time...** below the list.

n. Replace Your Name with your name in the signature block, select the signature block (Respectfully submitted through your name), set a left tab stop at the 3¼" mark, then indent the signature block using tabs.

o. Examine the document carefully for formatting errors, and make any necessary adjustments.

p. Save the document, submit it to your instructor, then close the file and exit Word.

Independent Challenge 2

Your employer, the Mission Center for Contemporary Arts in Guelph, Ontario, is launching a membership drive. Your boss has written the text for a flyer advertising Mission membership, and asks you to format it so that it is eye catching and attractive.

a. Open the file WD 3-4.docx from the drive and folder where you store your Data Files, save it as **WD 3-Mission 2017**, then read the document. FIGURE 3-30 shows how you will format the first several paragraphs of the flyer.

b. Select the entire document, change the style to No Spacing, then change the font to 10-point Calibri Light.

FIGURE 3-30

What we do for ARTISTS

Since 1982, the artist residency program at the Mission Center for Contemporary Arts has supported the work of more than 1500 artists from all over Canada and from 40 other nations. The residency awards include studio and living space, a monthly stipend to help artists with their expenses, and use of specialized equipment for all types of visual and performance art. Each artist gives a public lecture or performance at the Mission.

c. Center the first line, **MEMBERSHIP DRIVE**, and apply shading to the paragraph. Choose a dark custom shading color of your choice for the shading color. (*Hint*: Click More Colors, then select a color from the Standard or Custom tab.) Format the text in 24-point Calibri Light, bold, with a white font color. Expand the character spacing by 10 points. (*Hint*: Use the Advanced tab in the Font dialog box. Set the Spacing to Expanded, and then type **10** in the By text box.)

d. Format the second line, **2017**, in 48-point Broadway, bold. Apply the Fill - White, Outline - Accent 2, Hard Shadow - Accent 2 text effect style to the text. (*Hint*: Use the Text Effects and Typography button.) Expand the character spacing by 10 points, and change the character scale to 250%. Center the line.

e. Format each **What we do for...** heading in 11-point Calibri Light, bold. Change the font color to the same custom color used for shading the title. (*Note*: The color now appears in the Recent Colors section of the Font Color gallery.) Add a single-line ½-point black border under each heading.

f. Format each subheading (**Gallery**, **Lectures**, **Library**, **All members...**, and **Membership Levels**) in 10-point Calibri Light, bold. Add 3 points of spacing before each paragraph. (*Hint*: Select 0 in the Before text box, type 3, then press Enter.)

g. Indent each body paragraph ¼", except for the lines under the **What we do for YOU** heading.

h. Format the four lines under the **All members...** subheading as a bulleted list. Use a bullet symbol of your choice, and format the bullets in the custom font color.

i. Indent the five lines under the **Membership Levels** heading ¼". For these five lines, set left tab stops at the 1¼" mark and the 2¼" mark on the horizontal ruler. Insert tabs before the price and before the word All in each of the five lines.

j. Format the name of each membership level (**Artistic**, **Conceptual**, etc.) in 10-point Calibri Light, bold, italic, with the custom font color.

k. Format the **For more information...** heading in 14-point Calibri Light, bold, with the custom font color, then center the heading.

l. Center the last two lines, replace Your Name with your name, then apply bold to your name.

m. Examine the document carefully for formatting errors, and make any necessary adjustments.

n. Save the flyer, submit it to your instructor, then close the file and exit Word.

Independent Challenge 3

One of your responsibilities as program coordinator at Alpine Vistas Resort is to develop a program of winter outdoor learning and adventure workshops. You have drafted a memo to your boss to update her on your progress. You need to format the memo so it is professional looking and easy to read.

a. Start Word, open the file WD 3-5.docx from the drive and folder where you store your Data Files, then save it as **WD 3-Alpine Vistas Memo**.

b. Select the **Alpine Vistas Resort Memorandum** heading, apply the Quick Style Title to it, then center the heading. (*Hint*: Open the Quick Style gallery, then click the Title style.)

c. In the memo header, replace Today's Date and Your Name with the current date and your name.

d. Select the four-line memo header, set a left tab stop at the ¾" mark, then insert tabs before the date, the recipient's name, your name, and the subject of the memo.

e. Apply the Quick Style Strong to **Date:**, **To:**, **From:**, and **Re:**.

f. Apply the Quick Style Heading 2 to the headings **Overview**, **Workshops**, **Accommodations**, **Fees**, and **Proposed winter programming**.

g. Under the Fees heading, apply the Quick Style Emphasis to the words **Workshop fees** and **Accommodations fees**.

h. On the second page of the document, format the list under the **Proposed winter programming** heading as a multilevel list. FIGURE 3-31 shows the hierarchical structure of the outline. (*Hints*: The list is on pages 2 and 3 so be sure to select the entire list before applying the multilevel style. Apply a multilevel list style, then use the Increase Indent and Decrease Indent buttons to change the level of importance of each item.)

i. Change the outline numbering style to the bullet numbering style shown in FIGURE 3-31 if a different style is used in your outline.

j. Change the font color of each bullet level in the list to a theme font color of your choice. (*Hint*: Select one bullet of each level to select all the bullets at that level, then apply a font color.)

k. Zoom out on the memo so that two pages are displayed in the document window, then, using the Change Case button, change the title Alpine Vistas Resort Memorandum so that only the initial letter of each word is capitalized.

l. Using the Fonts button on the Design tab, change the fonts to a font set of your choice. Choose fonts that allow the document to fit on two pages.

m. Using the Colors button on the Design tab, change the colors to a color palette of your choice.

n. Apply different styles and adjust other formatting elements as necessary to make the memo attractive, eye catching, and readable. The finished memo should fit on two pages.

o. Save the document, submit it to your instructor, then close the file and exit Word.

FIGURE 3-31

Proposed winter programming
- ❖ Skiing, Snowboarding, and Snowshoeing
  - ➤ Skiing and Snowboarding
    - ▪ Cross-country skiing
      - • Cross-country skiing for beginners
      - • Intermediate cross-country skiing
      - • Inn-to-inn ski touring
      - • Moonlight cross-country skiing
    - ▪ Telemarking
      - • Basic telemark skiing
      - • Introduction to backcountry skiing
      - • Exploring on skis
    - ▪ Snowboarding
      - • Backcountry snowboarding
  - ➤ Snowshoeing
    - ▪ Beginner
      - • Snowshoeing for beginners
      - • Snowshoeing and winter ecology
    - ▪ Intermediate and Advanced
      - • Intermediate snowshoeing
      - • Guided snowshoe trek
      - • Above tree line snowshoeing
- ❖ Winter Hiking, Camping, and Survival
  - ➤ Hiking
    - ▪ Beginner
      - • Long-distance hiking
      - • Winter summits
      - • Hiking for women
  - ➤ Winter camping and survival
    - ▪ Beginner
      - • Introduction to winter camping
      - • Basic winter mountain skills
      - • Building snow shelters
    - ▪ Intermediate
      - • Basic winter mountain skills II
      - • Ice climbing
      - • Avalanche awareness and rescue

Independent Challenge 4: Explore

The fonts you choose for a document can have a major effect on the document's tone. Not all fonts are appropriate for use in a business document, and some fonts, especially those with a definite theme, are appropriate only for specific purposes. In this Independent Challenge, you will use font formatting and other formatting features to design a letterhead and a fax coversheet for yourself or your business. The letterhead and coversheet should not only look professional and attract interest, but also say something about the character of your business or your personality. FIGURE 3-32 shows an example of a business letterhead.

a. Start Word, and save a new blank document as **WD 3-Personal Letterhead** to the drive and folder where you store your Data Files.

b. Type your name or the name of your business, your address, your phone number, your fax number, and your website or e-mail address.

c. Format your name or the name of your business in a font that expresses your personality or says something about the nature of your business. Use fonts, font colors, text effects and typography, borders, shading, paragraph formatting, and other formatting features to design a letterhead that is appealing and professional.

d. Save your changes, submit the document to your instructor, then close the file.

e. Open a new blank document, and save it as **WD 3-Personal Fax Coversheet**. Type FAX, your name or the name of your business, your address, your phone number, your fax number, and your website or e-mail address at the top of the document.

f. Type a fax header that includes the following: Date:, To:, From:, Re:, Pages:, and Comments:.

g. Format the information in the fax coversheet using fonts, font effects, borders, paragraph formatting, and other formatting features. Since a fax coversheet is designed to be faxed, all fonts and other formatting elements should be black or grey.

h. Save your changes, submit the document to your instructor, close the file, then exit Word.

FIGURE 3-32

Rebecca Valerino Interior Design
443 Sanchez Street, 6th floor, Santa Fe, NM 87501 Tel: 505-555-9767 Fax: 505-555-2992 www.valerino.com

Visual Workshop

Open the file WD 3-6.docx from the drive and folder where you store your Data Files. Create the menu shown in FIGURE 3-33. (*Hints*: Use the sizing handles to resize the graphic to be approximately 1.4" tall and 6.5" wide. Use Californian FB or a similar font for the text. Add color, bold, and italic as shown in the figure. Change the font size of the café name to 28 points, the font size of Today's Specials to 14 points, the font size of the menu to 12 points, and the font size of the italicized text at the bottom to 10 points. Format the prices using tabs and leader lines. Use paragraph spacing to adjust the spacing between paragraphs so that all the text fits on one page. Make other adjustments as needed so your menu is similar to the one shown in FIGURE 3-33.) Save the menu as **WD 3-Todays Specials**, then submit a copy to your instructor.

FIGURE 3-33

City Beach Café

Today's Specials

Strawberry Summer Salad

Arugula and baby spinach topped with sliced strawberries, goat cheese, sunflower seeds, and croutons, served with a strawberry vinaigrette. Add shrimp or lobster. $9.00

Shrimp and Avocado Salad

Shrimp and avocado salad over mixed greens with sliced tomatoes, cucumbers, and corn salsa, served with cilantro lime vinaigrette. $12.00

Lobster Tacos

Generous chunks of lobster over ginger slaw with chipotle crema and pickled onions. Served with cilantro lime rice and beans. $15.00

Coconut Encrusted Haddock

Filet of haddock lighted breaded with panko and coconut. Oven baked and served with cilantro lime rice and beans and corn on the cob. $16.00

Tropical Grilled Swordfish

Seasoned swordfish grilled and finished with citrus pineapple salsa. Served with cilantro lime rice and beans, and ginger slaw. $18.00

Shrimp Burrito

Tender grilled shrimp served with cilantro rice, black beans, romaine lettuce, cheese, salsa verde, pico de gallo, and corn on the cob. $11.00

Scallop Kebob

Ginger lime drenched scallops grilled and served with tropical macaroni salad, citrus pineapple salsa, and corn on the cob. $15.00

We serve only fresh, local, sustainably farmed and harvested ingredients.

Chef: Your Name

Source: Stocksnap.io

Formatting Documents

CASE You have written and formatted the text for an informational report for Reason2Go volunteers about staying healthy while traveling. You are now ready to format the pages. You plan to organize the text in columns, to illustrate the report with a table, and to add footnotes and a bibliography.

Module Objectives

After completing this module, you will be able to:

- Set document margins
- Create sections and columns
- Insert page breaks
- Insert page numbers
- Add headers and footers
- Insert a table
- Add footnotes and endnotes
- Insert citations
- Manage sources and create a bibliography

Files You Will Need

WD 4-1.docx WD 4-5.docx
WD 4-2.docx WD 4-6.docx
WD 4-3.docx WD 4-7.docx
WD 4-4.docx

Set Document Margins

Learning Outcomes
• Set custom margins
• Change paper size
• Change page orientation

Changing a document's margins is one way to change the appearance of a document and control the amount of text that fits on a page. The **margins** of a document are the blank areas between the edge of the text and the edge of the page. When you create a document in Word, the default margins are 1" at the top, bottom, left, and right sides of the page. You can adjust the size of a document's margins using the Margins command on the Layout tab or using the rulers. **CASE** *The report should be a four-page document when finished. You begin by reducing the size of the document margins so that more text fits on each page.*

STEPS

1. **Start Word, open the file** WD 4-1.docx **from the location where you store your Data Files, then save it as** WD 4-Travel Health 2Go

   The report opens in Print Layout view.

2. **Scroll through the report to get a feel for its contents, then press** [Ctrl][Home]

   The report is currently five pages long. Notice that the status bar indicates the page where the insertion point is located and the total number of pages in the document.

3. **Click the** Layout tab, **then click the** Margins button **in the Page Setup group**

   The Margins menu opens. You can select predefined margin settings from this menu, or you can click Custom Margins to create different margin settings.

4. **Click** Custom Margins

   The Page Setup dialog box opens with the Margins tab displayed, as shown in FIGURE 4-1. You can use the Margins tab to change the top, bottom, left, or right document margin, to change the orientation of the pages from portrait to landscape, and to alter other page layout settings. **Portrait orientation** means a page is taller than it is wide; **landscape orientation** means a page is wider than it is tall. This report uses portrait orientation. You can also use the Orientation button in the Page Setup group on the Layout tab to change the orientation of a document.

5. **Click the** Top down arrow **three times until** 0.7" **appears, then click the** Bottom down arrow **until** 0.7" **appears**

   The top and bottom margins of the report will be .7".

6. **Press** [Tab], **type** .7 **in the Left text box, press** [Tab], **then type** .7 **in the Right text box**

   The left and right margins of the report will also be .7". You can change the margin settings by using the arrows or by typing a value in the appropriate text box.

7. **Click** OK

   The document margins change to .7", as shown in FIGURE 4-2. The location of each margin (right, left, top, and bottom) is shown on the horizontal and vertical rulers at the intersection of the white and shaded areas. You can also change a margin setting by using the ↰ pointer to drag the intersection to a new location on the ruler.

8. **Click the** View tab, **then click the** Multiple Pages button **in the Zoom group**

   The first three pages of the document appear in the document window.

9. **Scroll down to view all five pages of the report, press** [Ctrl][Home], **click the** 100% button **in the Zoom group, then save your changes**

FIGURE 4-1: **Margins tab in Page Setup dialog box**

Default margin settings
Set gutter margin
Select page orientation
Select gutter position
Set mirror margins and other page layout options
Preview of margin settings
Select part of document to apply settings to

FIGURE 4-2: **Report with smaller margins**

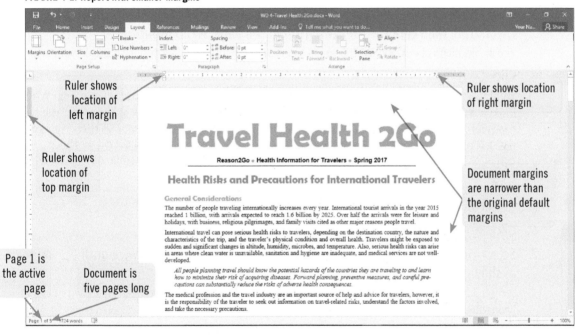

Ruler shows location of left margin
Ruler shows location of top margin
Page 1 is the active page
Document is five pages long
Ruler shows location of right margin
Document margins are narrower than the original default margins

Changing orientation, margin settings, and paper size

By default, the documents you create in Word use an 8½" x 11" paper size in portrait orientation with the default margin settings. You can change the orientation, margin settings, and paper size to common settings using the Orientation, Margins, and Size buttons in the Page Setup group on the Layout tab. You can also adjust these settings and others in the Page Setup dialog box. For example, to change the layout of multiple pages, use the Multiple pages list arrow on the Margins tab to create pages that use mirror margins, that include two pages per sheet of paper, or that are formatted using a book fold. **Mirror margins** are used in a document with facing pages, such as a magazine, where the margins on the left page of the document are a mirror image of the margins on the right page. Documents with mirror margins have inside and outside margins, rather than right and left margins. Another type of margin is a gutter margin, which is used in documents that are bound, such as books. A **gutter** adds extra space to the left, top, or inside margin to allow for the binding. Add a gutter to a document by adjusting the setting in the Gutter position text box on the Margins tab. To change the size of the paper used, use the Paper size list arrow on the Paper tab to select a standard paper size, or enter custom measurements in the Width and Height text boxes.

Create Sections and Columns

Learning Outcomes
- Customize the status bar
- Insert section breaks
- Format text in columns

Dividing a document into sections allows you to format each section of the document with different page layout settings. A **section** is a portion of a document that is separated from the rest of the document by section breaks. **Section breaks** are formatting marks that you insert in a document to show the end of a section. Once you have divided a document into sections, you can format each section with different column, margin, page orientation, header and footer, and other page layout settings. By default, a document is formatted as a single section, but you can divide a document into as many sections as you like. **CASE** *You insert a section break to divide the document into two sections, and then format the text in the second section in two columns. First, you customize the status bar to display section information.*

STEPS

1. **Right-click the** status bar, **click** Section **on the Customize Status Bar menu that opens (if it is not already checked), then click the document to close the menu**
   The status bar indicates the insertion point is located in section 1 of the document.

2. **Click the** Home tab, **then click the** Show/Hide ¶ button ⟦¶⟧ **in the Paragraph group**
   Turning on formatting marks allows you to see the section breaks you insert in a document.

3. **Place the insertion point before the heading** General Considerations, **click the** Layout tab, **then click the** Breaks button **in the Page Setup group**
   The Breaks menu opens. You use this menu to insert different types of section breaks. See TABLE 4-1.

4. **Click** Continuous
   Word inserts a continuous section break, shown as a dotted double line, above the heading. When you insert a section break at the beginning of a paragraph, Word inserts the break at the end of the previous paragraph. The section break stores the formatting information for the previous section. The document now has two sections. Notice that the status bar indicates the insertion point is in section 2.

5. **Click the** Columns button **in the Page Setup group**
   The columns menu opens. You use this menu to format text using preset column formats or to create custom columns.

6. **Click** More Columns **to open the Columns dialog box**

7. **Select** Two **in the Presets section, click the** Spacing down arrow **twice until** 0.3" **appears as shown in** FIGURE 4-3, **then click** OK
   Section 2 is formatted in two columns of equal width with .3" of spacing between, as shown in FIGURE 4-4. Formatting text in columns is another way to increase the amount of text that fits on a page.

8. **Click the** View tab, **click the** Multiple Pages button **in the Zoom group, scroll down to examine all four pages of the document, press** [Ctrl][Home], **then save the document**
   The text in section 2—all the text below the continuous section break—is formatted in two columns. Text in columns flows automatically from the bottom of one column to the top of the next column.

TABLE 4-1: Types of section breaks

section	function
Next page	Begins a new section and moves the text following the break to the top of the next page
Continuous	Begins a new section on the same page
Even page	Begins a new section and moves the text following the break to the top of the next even-numbered page
Odd page	Begins a new section and moves the text following the break to the top of the next odd-numbered page

FIGURE 4-3: Columns dialog box

Select a preset format for columns

Change the number of columns

Set custom widths and spacing for columns

Select to add a line between columns

Select to create columns of equal width

Set space between columns

Preview of current settings

Select part of document to apply format to

FIGURE 4-4: Continuous section break and columns

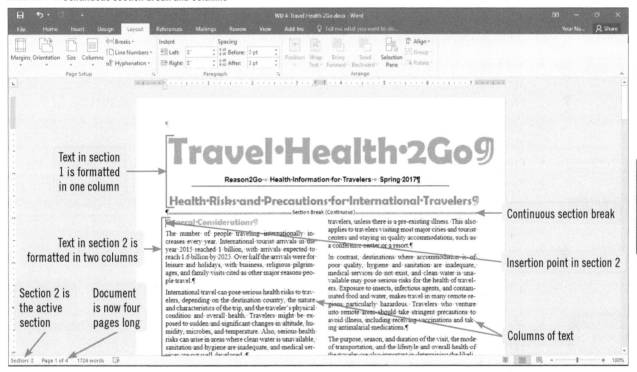

Text in section 1 is formatted in one column

Continuous section break

Text in section 2 is formatted in two columns

Insertion point in section 2

Section 2 is the active section

Document is now four pages long

Columns of text

Changing page layout settings for a section

Dividing a document into sections allows you to vary the layout of a document. In addition to applying different column settings to sections, you can apply different margins, page orientation, paper size, vertical alignment, header and footer, page numbering, footnotes, endnotes, and other page layout settings. For example, if you are formatting a report that includes a table with many columns, you might want to change the table's page orientation to landscape so that it is easier to read. To do this, you would insert a section break before and after the table to create a section that contains only the table, and then you would change the page orientation of the section that contains the table to landscape. If the table does not fill the page, you could also change the vertical alignment of the table so that it is centered vertically on the page. To do this, use the Vertical alignment list arrow on the Layout tab of the Page Setup dialog box.

To check or change the page layout settings for an individual section, place the insertion point in the section, then open the Page Setup dialog box. Select any options you want to change, click the Apply to list arrow, click This section, then click OK. When you select This section in the Apply to list box, the settings are applied to the current section only. When you select This point forward, the settings are applied to the current section and all sections that follow it. If you select Whole document in the Apply to list box, the settings are applied to all the sections in the document. Use the Apply to list arrow in the Columns dialog box or the Footnote and Endnote dialog box to change those settings for a section.

Insert Page Breaks

Learning Outcomes
- Insert and delete page breaks
- Insert a column break
- Balance columns

As you type text in a document, Word inserts an **automatic page break** (also called a soft page break) when you reach the bottom of a page, allowing you to continue typing on the next page. You can also force text onto the next page of a document by using the Breaks command to insert a **manual page break** (also called a hard page break). Another way to control the flow of text is to apply pagination settings using the Line and Page Breaks tab in the Paragraph dialog box. **CASE** *You insert manual page breaks where you know you want to begin each new page of the report.*

STEPS

1. **Click the** 100% **button, scroll to the bottom of page 1, place the insertion point before the heading** Malaria: A Serious..., **click the** Layout tab, **then click the** Breaks button **in the Page Setup group**

   The Breaks menu opens. You also use this menu to insert page, column, and text-wrapping breaks. TABLE 4-2 describes these types of breaks.

2. **Click** Page

   Word inserts a manual page break before "Malaria: A Serious Health Risk for Travelers" and moves all the text following the page break to the beginning of the next page, as shown in FIGURE 4-5.

3. **Scroll down, place the insertion point before the heading** Preventive Options... **on page 2, press and hold** [Ctrl], **then press** [Enter]

   Pressing [Ctrl][Enter] is a fast way to insert a manual page break. The heading is forced to the top of the third page.

4. **Scroll to the bottom of page 3, place the insertion point before the heading** Insurance for Travelers **on page 3, then press** [Ctrl][Enter]

   The heading is forced to the top of the fourth page.

5. **Scroll up, click to the left of the page break on page 2 with the selection pointer** ↗ **to select the page break, then press** [Delete]

   The manual page break is deleted and the text from pages 2 and 3 flows together. You can also use the selection pointer to click to the left of a section or a column break to select it.

6. **Place the insertion point before the heading** Medical Kit... **on page 2, then press** [Ctrl][Enter]

   The heading is forced to the top of the third page.

7. **Click the** View tab, **click the** Multiple Pages button **in the Zoom group, scroll to view all four pages of the document, then save your changes**

   Pages 1, 2, and 3 are shown in FIGURE 4-6. Your screen might show a different number of pages.

Controlling automatic pagination

Another way to control the flow of text between pages (or between columns) is to apply pagination settings to specify where Word positions automatic page breaks. To apply automatic pagination settings, simply select the paragraphs(s) or line(s) you want to control, click the launcher in the Paragraph group on the Home or Layout tab, click the Line and Page Breaks tab in the Paragraph dialog box, and then select one or more of the following settings in the Pagination section before clicking OK.

- Keep with next: Apply to any paragraph you want to appear together with the next paragraph in order to prevent the page or column from breaking between the paragraphs.

- Keep lines together: Apply to selected paragraph or lines to prevent a page or column from breaking in the middle of a paragraph or between certain lines.

- Page break before: Apply to add an automatic page break before a specific paragraph.

- Widow/Orphan control: Turned on by default; ensures at least two lines of a paragraph appear at the top and bottom of every page or column by preventing a page or column from beginning with only the last line of a paragraph (a **widow**), or ending with only the first line of a new paragraph (an **orphan**).

FIGURE 4-5: Manual page break in document

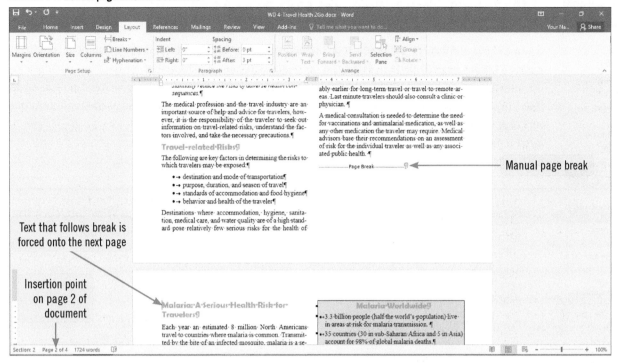

Text that follows break is forced onto the next page

Insertion point on page 2 of document

Manual page break

FIGURE 4-6: Pages 1, 2, and 3

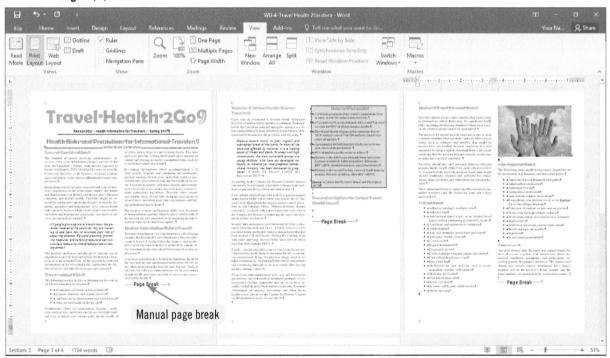

Manual page break

Page Break

Page Break

TABLE 4-2: Types of breaks

break	function
Page	Forces the text following the break to begin at the top of the next page
Column	Forces the text following the break to begin at the top of the next column
Text Wrapping	Forces the text following the break to begin at the beginning of the next line

Formatting Documents

Insert Page Numbers

If you want to number the pages of a multiple-page document, you can insert a page number field to add a page number to each page. A **field** is a code that serves as a placeholder for data that changes in a document, such as a page number or the current date. When you use the Page Number button on the Insert tab to add page numbers to a document, you insert the page number field at the top, bottom, or side of any page, and Word automatically numbers all the pages in the document for you. **CASE** ▶ *You insert a page number field so that page numbers will appear centered between the margins at the bottom of each page in the document.*

STEPS

1. **Press [Ctrl][Home], click the 100% button in the Zoom group on the View tab, click the Insert tab, then click the Page Number button in the Header & Footer group**

   The Page Number menu opens. You use this menu to select the position for the page numbers. If you choose to add a page number field to the top, bottom, or side of a document, a page number will appear on every page in the document. If you choose to insert it in the document at the location of the insertion point, the field will appear on that page only.

2. **Point to Bottom of Page**

   A gallery of formatting and alignment options for page numbers to be inserted at the bottom of a page opens, as shown in FIGURE 4-7.

3. **Scroll down the gallery to view the options, scroll to the top of the gallery, then click Plain Number 2 in the Simple section**

   A page number field containing the number 1 is centered in the Footer area at the bottom of page 1 of the document, as shown in FIGURE 4-8. The document text is gray, or dimmed, because the Footer area is open. Text that is inserted in a Footer area appears at the bottom of every page in a document.

4. **Double-click the document text**

   Double-clicking the document text closes the Footer area. The page number is now dimmed because it is located in the Footer area, which is no longer the active area. When the document is printed, the page numbers appear as normal text. You will learn more about working with the Footer area in the next lesson.

5. **Scroll down the document to see the page number at the bottom of each page**

   Word numbered each page of the report automatically, and each page number is centered at the bottom of the page. If you want to change the numbering format or start page numbering with a different number, you can simply click the Page Number button, click Format Page Numbers, and then choose from the options in the Page Number Format dialog box.

6. **Press [Ctrl][Home], click the View tab, click the Page Width button in the Zoom group, then save the document**

Moving around in a long document

Rather than scrolling to move to a different place in a long document, you can use the Navigation pane to move the insertion point to the top of a specific page. To open the Navigation pane, click the Find button in the Editing group on the Home tab, and then click Pages to display a thumbnail of each page in the document in the Navigation pane. Use the scroll box in the Navigation pane to scroll through the thumbnails. Click a thumbnail in the Navigation pane to move the insertion point to the top of that page in the document window.

FIGURE 4-7: Page Number gallery

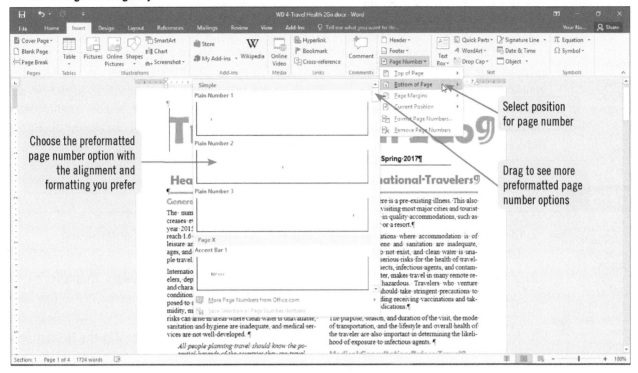

Choose the preformatted page number option with the alignment and formatting you prefer

Select position for page number

Drag to see more preformatted page number options

FIGURE 4-8: Page number in document

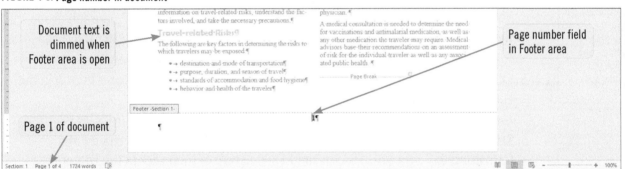

Document text is dimmed when Footer area is open

Page number field in Footer area

Page 1 of document

Inserting Quick Parts

The Word Quick Parts feature makes it easy to insert reusable pieces of content into a document quickly. The **Quick Parts** items you can insert include fields, such as for the current date or the total number of pages in a document; document property information, such as the author and title of a document; and building blocks, which are customized content that you create, format, and save for future use.

To insert a Quick Part into a document at the location of the insertion point, click the Quick Parts button in the Text group on the Insert tab (or, if headers and footers are open, click the Quick Parts button in the Insert group on the Header & Footer Tools Design tab), and then select the type of Quick Part you want to insert. To insert a field into a document, click Field on the Quick Parts menu that opens, click the name of the field you want to insert in the Field dialog box, and then click OK. Field information is updated automatically each time the document is opened or saved.

To insert a document property, point to Document Property on the Quick Parts menu, and then click the property you want to insert. The property is added to the document as a content control and contains the document property information shown in the Properties dialog box. If you did not assign a document property, the content control contains a placeholder, which you can replace with your own text. Once you replace the placeholder text—or edit the document property information that appears in the content control—this text replaces the property information in the Properties dialog box.

To insert a building block, click Building Blocks Organizer on the Quick Parts menu, select the building block you want, and then click Insert. You will learn more about working with building blocks in later lessons.

Add Headers and Footers

A **header** is text or graphics that appears at the top of every page of a document. A **footer** is text or graphics that appears at the bottom of every page. In longer documents, headers and footers often contain the title of the publication or chapter, the name of the author, or a page number. You can add headers and footers to a document by double-clicking the top or bottom margin of a document to open the Header and Footer areas, and then inserting text and graphics into them. You can also use the Header or Footer command on the Insert tab to insert predesigned headers and footers that you can modify with your information. When the header and footer areas are open, the document text is dimmed and cannot be edited. **CASE** *You create a header that includes the name of the report.*

STEPS

1. **Click the** Insert tab, **then click the** Header button **in the Header & Footer group**

   A gallery of built-in header designs opens.

2. **Scroll down the gallery to view the header designs, scroll up the gallery, then click** Blank

   The Header & Footer Tools Design tab opens and is the active tab, as shown in FIGURE 4-9. This tab is available whenever the Header and Footer areas are open.

3. **Type** Reason2Go Health Information for Travelers **in the content control in the Header area**

   This text will appear at the top of every page in the document.

4. **Select the header text (but not the paragraph mark below it), click the** Home tab, **click the** Font list arrow **in the Font group, click** Berlin Sans FB Demi, **click the** Font Color list arrow **A ·, click** Blue, Accent 5, **click the** Center button **in the Paragraph group, click the** Bottom Border button **, then click in the Header area to deselect the text**

   The text is formatted in blue Berlin Sans FB Demi and centered in the Header area with a bottom border.

5. **Click the** Header & Footer Tools Design tab, **then click the** Go to Footer button **in the Navigation group**

   The insertion point moves to the Footer area, where a page number field is centered in the Footer area.

6. **Select the** page number field **in the footer, use the Mini toolbar to change the formatting to** Berlin Sans FB Demi **and** Blue, Accent 5, **then click in the Footer area to deselect the text and field**

   The footer text is formatted in blue Berlin Sans FB Demi.

7. **Click the** Close Header and Footer button **in the Close group, then scroll down until the bottom of page 1 and the top of page 2 appear in the document window**

   The Header and Footer areas close, and the header and footer text is dimmed, as shown in FIGURE 4-10.

8. **Press** [Ctrl][Home]

   The report already includes the company information at the top of the first page, making the header information redundant. You can modify headers and footers so that the header and footer text does not appear on the first page of a document.

9. **Position the pointer over the header text at the top of page 1, then double-click**

   The Header and Footer areas open. The Options group on the Header & Footer Tools Design tab includes options for creating a different header and footer for the first page of a document, and for creating different headers and footers for odd- and even-numbered pages.

10. **Click the** Different First Page check box **to select it, click the** Close Header and Footer button, **scroll to see the header and footer on pages 2, 3, and 4, then save the document**

    The header and footer text is removed from the Header and Footer areas on the first page.

FIGURE 4-9: Header area

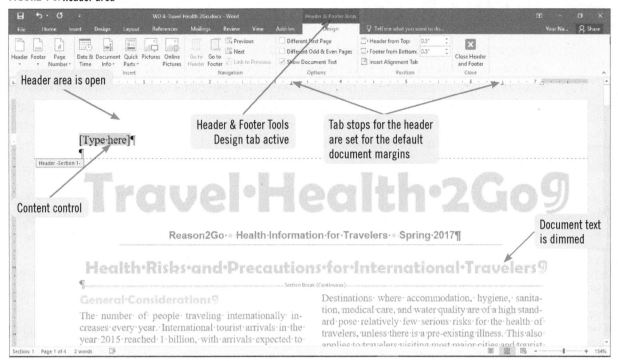

- Header area is open
- Header & Footer Tools Design tab active
- Tab stops for the header are set for the default document margins
- [Type here]¶
- Content control
- Document text is dimmed

FIGURE 4-10: Header and footer in document

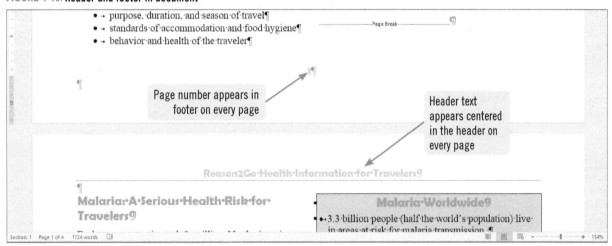

- Page number appears in footer on every page
- Header text appears centered in the header on every page

Adding a custom header or footer to the gallery

When you design a header that you want to use again in other documents, you can add it to the Header gallery by saving it as a building block. **Building blocks** are reusable pieces of formatted content or document parts, including headers and footers, page numbers, and text boxes, that are stored in galleries. Building blocks include predesigned content that comes with Word, as well as content that you create and save for future use. For example, you might create a custom header that contains your company name and logo and is formatted using the fonts, border, and colors you use in all company documents.

To add a custom header to the Header gallery, select all the text in the header, including the last paragraph mark, click the Header button, and then click Save Selection to Header Gallery.

In the Create New Building Block dialog box that opens, type a unique name for the header in the Name text box, click the Gallery list arrow and select the appropriate gallery, verify that the Category is General, and then type a brief description of the new header design in the Description text box. This description appears in a ScreenTip when you point to the custom header in the gallery. When you are finished, click OK. The new header appears in the Header gallery under the General category.

To remove a custom header from the Header gallery, right-click it, click Organize and Delete, make sure the appropriate building block is selected in the Building Blocks Organizer that opens, click Delete, click Yes, and then click Close. You can follow the same process to add or remove a custom footer to the Footer gallery.

Word 2016

Insert a Table

Learning Outcomes
- Create a table
- Delete a table
- Apply a table style

Adding a table to a document is a useful way to illustrate information that is intended for quick reference and analysis. A **table** is a grid of columns and rows that you can fill with text and graphics. A **cell** is the box formed by the intersection of a column and a row. The lines that divide the columns and rows of a table and help you see the grid-like structure of the table are called **borders**. A simple way to insert a table into a document is to use the Insert Table command on the Insert tab. **CASE** *You add a table to page 2 showing the preventive options for serious travel health diseases.*

STEPS

1. **Scroll until the heading** Preventive Options... **is at the top of your document window**

2. **Select the heading** Preventive Options... **and the two paragraph marks below it, click the** Layout tab, **click the** Columns button **in the Page Setup group, click** One, **click the** heading **to deselect the text, then scroll down to see the bottom half of page 2**

   A continuous section break is inserted before the heading and after the second paragraph mark, creating a new section, section 3, as shown in FIGURE 4-11. The document now includes four sections, with the heading Preventive Options... in Section 3. Section 3 is formatted as a single column.

3. **Place the insertion point before the first paragraph mark below the heading, click the** Insert tab, **click the** Table button **in the Tables group, then click** Insert Table

   The Insert Table dialog box opens. You use this dialog box to create a blank table.

4. **Type** 5 **in the Number of columns text box, press [Tab], type** 6 **in the Number of rows text box, make sure the** Fixed column width option button **is selected, then click** OK

   A blank table with five columns and six rows is inserted in the document. The insertion point is in the upper-left cell of the table, and the Table Tools Design tab becomes the active tab.

5. **Click the** Home tab, **click the** Show/Hide ¶ button ¶ **in the Paragraph group, type** Disease **in the first cell in the first row, press [Tab], type** Vaccine, **press [Tab], type** Prophylaxis Drug, **press [Tab], type** Eat and Drink Safely, **press [Tab], type** Avoid Insects, **then press [Tab]**

   Don't be concerned if the text wraps to the next line in a cell as you type. Pressing [Tab] moves the insertion point to the next cell in the row or to the first cell in the next row.

6. **Type** Malaria, **press [Tab][Tab], click the** Bullets list arrow ▤ ▾ **in the Paragraph group, click the** check mark style, **press [Tab][Tab], then click the** Bullets button ▤

   The active bullet style, a check mark, is added to a cell when you click the Bullets button.

7. **Type the text shown in** FIGURE 4-12 **in the table cells**

8. **Click the** Table Tools Layout tab, **click the** AutoFit button **in the Cell Size group, click** AutoFit Contents, **click the** AutoFit button **again, then click** AutoFit Window

   The width of the table columns is adjusted to fit the text and then the window.

9. **Click the** Select button **in the Table group, click** Select Table, **click the** Align Center button ▤ **in the Alignment group, click** Disease **in the table, click the** Select button, **click** Select Column, **click the** Align Center Left button ▤, **then click in the table to deselect the column**

   The text in the table is centered in each cell, and then the text in the first column is left-aligned.

10. **Click the** Table Tools Design tab, **click the** More button ▾ **in the Table Styles group, scroll down, click the** List Table 3 – Accent 5 style, **then save your changes**

    The List Table 3 - Accent 5 table style is applied to the table, as shown in FIGURE 4-13. A **table style** includes format settings for the text, borders, and shading in a table.

FIGURE 4-11: **New section**

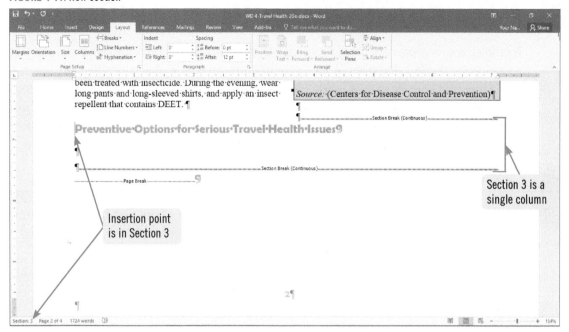

Insertion point is in Section 3

Section 3 is a single column

FIGURE 4-12: **Text in table**

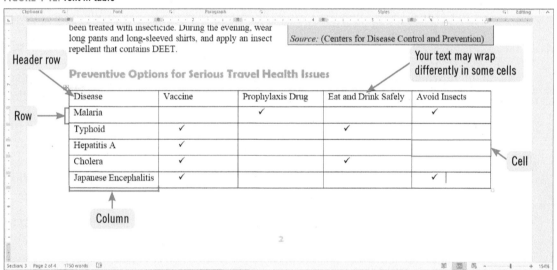

Header row

Row

Column

Your text may wrap differently in some cells

Cell

Preventive Options for Serious Travel Health Issues

Disease	Vaccine	Prophylaxis Drug	Eat and Drink Safely	Avoid Insects
Malaria		✓		✓
Typhoid	✓		✓	
Hepatitis A	✓			
Cholera	✓		✓	
Japanese Encephalitis	✓			✓

FIGURE 4-13: **Completed table**

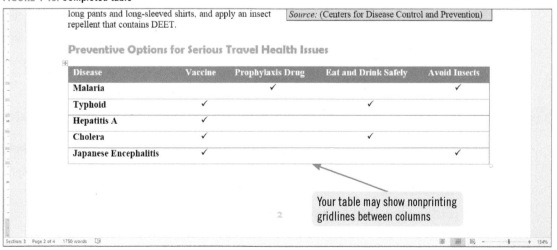

Preventive Options for Serious Travel Health Issues

Disease	Vaccine	Prophylaxis Drug	Eat and Drink Safely	Avoid Insects
Malaria		✓		✓
Typhoid	✓		✓	
Hepatitis A	✓			
Cholera	✓		✓	
Japanese Encephalitis	✓			✓

Your table may show nonprinting gridlines between columns

Add Footnotes and Endnotes

Footnotes and endnotes are used in documents to provide further information, explanatory text, or references for text in a document. A **footnote** or **endnote** is an explanatory note that consists of two linked parts: the **note reference mark** that appears next to text to indicate that additional information is offered in a footnote or endnote, and the corresponding footnote or endnote text. Word places footnotes at the end of each page and endnotes at the end of the document. You insert and manage footnotes and endnotes using the tools in the Footnotes group on the References tab. **CASE** ▶ *You add several footnotes to the report.*

STEPS

> **TROUBLE**
> Scroll up as needed to see the note reference mark; then scroll down to see the footnote.

1. **Press [Ctrl][Home], place the insertion point at the end of the first body paragraph in the second column of text (after "resort."), click the References tab, then click the Insert Footnote button in the Footnotes group**

   A note reference mark, in this case a superscript 1, appears after "resort.", and the insertion point moves below a separator line at the bottom of the page. A note reference mark can be a number, a symbol, a character, or a combination of characters.

2. **Type Behavior is a critical factor. For example, going outdoors in a malaria-endemic area could result in becoming infected., place the insertion point at the end of the second column of text (after "health."), click the Insert Footnote button, then type It is best to consult a travel medicine specialist.**

   The footnote text appears below the separator line at the bottom of page 1, as shown in FIGURE 4-14.

3. **Scroll down until the bottom half of page 3 appears in the document window, place the insertion point at the end of "Medications taken on a regular basis at home" in the second column, click the Insert Footnote button, then type All medications should be stored in carry-on luggage, in their original containers and labeled clearly.**

   The footnote text for the third footnote appears at the bottom of the first column on page 3.

4. **Place the insertion point at the end of "Sunscreen" in the bulleted list in the second column, click the Insert Footnote button, then type SPF 15 or greater.**

   The footnote text for the fourth footnote appears at the bottom of page 3.

5. **Place the insertion point after "Disposable gloves" in the first column, click the Insert Footnote button, type At least two pairs., place the insertion point after "Scissors, safety pins, and tweezers" in the first column, click the Insert Footnote button, then type Pack these items in checked luggage.**

   Notice that when you inserted new footnotes between existing footnotes, Word automatically renumbered the footnotes and wrapped the footnote text to the next column. The new footnotes appear at the bottom of the first column on page 3, as shown in FIGURE 4-15.

6. **Press [Ctrl][Home], then click the Next Footnote button in the Footnotes group**

   The insertion point moves to the first reference mark in the document.

> **QUICK TIP**
> To convert all footnotes to endnotes, click the launcher in the Footnotes group, click Convert, click OK, then click Close.

7. **Click the Next Footnote button twice, press [Delete] to select the number 3 reference mark, then press [Delete] again**

   The third reference mark and associated footnote are deleted from the document and the footnotes are renumbered automatically. You must select a reference mark to delete a footnote; you can not simply delete the footnote text itself.

8. **Press [Ctrl][Home], then save your changes**

FIGURE 4-14: **Footnotes in the document**

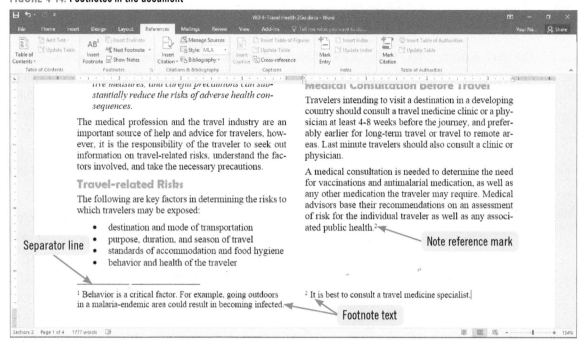

FIGURE 4-15: **Renumbered footnotes in the document**

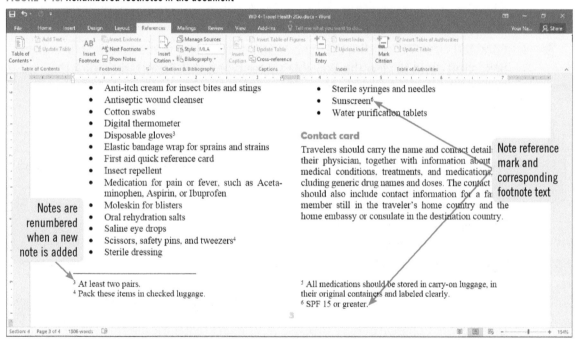

Customizing the layout and formatting of footnotes and endnotes

You can change the location, formatting, and numbering options for footnotes and endnotes in a document using the Footnote and Endnote dialog box. To open the dialog box, click the launcher in the Footnotes group on the References tab. Use the list arrows in the Location section of the dialog box to locate footnotes at the bottom of the page (the default) or directly below the text on a page, and to locate endnotes at the end of a document or at the end of a section. Use the Columns list arrow in the Footnote layout section to format footnote text in one or more columns, or to match section layout (the default). Use the options in the Format section of the dialog box to change the number format of the note reference marks, to use a symbol instead of a character, and to change the numbering of footnotes and endnotes. You can choose to apply the settings to a section or to the document as a whole. When you are finished, click Apply.

Insert Citations

Learning Outcomes
- Add a source to a document
- Insert a citation
- Edit a citation

The Word References feature allows you to keep track of the reference sources you consult when writing research papers, reports, and other documents, and makes it easy to insert a citation in a document. A **citation** is a parenthetical reference in the document text that gives credit to the source for a quotation or other information used in a document. Citations usually include the name of the author and, for print sources, a page number. When you insert a citation you can use an existing source or create a new source. Each time you create a new source, the source information is saved on your computer so that it is available for use in any document. **CASE** ▶ *The report already includes two citations. You add several more citations to the report.*

STEPS

1. **Scroll down, place the insertion point after "people travel" but before the period at the end of the first paragraph in the first column of text, click the** Style list arrow **in the Citations & Bibliography group, then click** MLA Seventh Edition
   You will format the sources and citations in the report using the style recommended by the Modern Language Association (MLA).

QUICK TIP
When you create a new source for a document, it appears automatically in the bibliography when you generate it.

2. **Click the** Insert Citation button **in the Citations & Bibliography group**
   A list of the sources already used in the document opens. You can choose to cite one of these sources, create a new source, or add a placeholder for a source. When you add a new citation to a document, the source is added to the list of master sources that is stored on the computer. The new source is also associated with the document.

3. **Click** Add New Source, **click the** Type of Source list arrow **in the Create Source dialog box, scroll down to view the available source types, click** Report, **then click the** Corporate Author check box
   You select the type of source and enter the source information in the Create Source dialog box. The fields available in the dialog box change, depending on the type of source selected.

QUICK TIP
Only sources that you associate with a document stay with the document when you move it to another computer. The master list of sources remains on the computer where it was created.

4. **Enter the data shown in** FIGURE 4-16 **in the Create Source dialog box, then click** OK
   The citation (World Tourism Organization) appears at the end of the paragraph. Because the source is a print publication, it needs to include a page number.

5. **Click the citation to select it, click the** Citation Options list arrow **on the right side of the citation, then click** Edit Citation
   The Edit Citation dialog box opens, as shown in FIGURE 4-17.

QUICK TIP
You can also choose to add or remove the author, year, or title from a citation.

6. **Type** 19 **in the Pages text box, then click** OK
   The page number 19 is added to the citation.

7. **Scroll down, place the insertion point at the end of the quotation (after ...consequences.), click the** Insert Citation button, **click** Add New Source, **enter the information shown in** FIGURE 4-18, **then click** OK
   A citation for the Web publication that the quotation was taken from is added to the report. No page number is used in this citation because the source is a Web site.

8. **Scroll to the bottom of page 2, click under the table, type** Source:, **italicize** Source:, **click after** Source:, **click the** Insert Citation button, **then click** Johnson, Margaret **in the list of sources**
   The citation (Johnson) appears under the table.

9. **Click the citation, click the** Citation Options list arrow, **click** Edit Citation, **type** 55 **in the Pages text box, click** OK, **then save your changes**
   The page number 55 is added to the citation.

FIGURE 4-16: Adding a Report source

Create Source   ? ✕

Type of Source   Report ▼

Bibliography Fields for MLA

Author	[Edit]
	☑ Corporate Author World Tourism Organization
Title	Tourism Highlights
Year	2017
Publisher	World Tourism Organization
City	Madrid
Report Type	White Paper
Medium	Print

☐ Show All Bibliography Fields

Tag name   Example: Document   **Your tag name may differ**

Wor17 ◄   [OK]   [Cancel]

FIGURE 4-17: Edit Citation dialog box

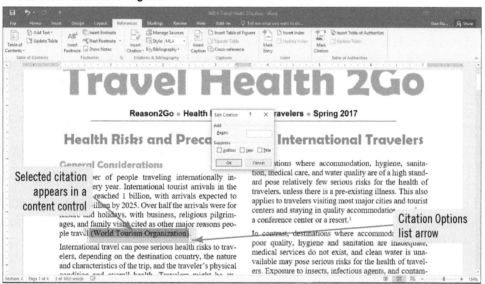

FIGURE 4-18: Adding a Web publication source

Create Source   ? ✕

Type of Source   Document From Web site ▼

Bibliography Fields for MLA

Author	[Edit]
	☑ Corporate Author World Health Organization
Name of Web Page	International Travel and Health 2017 Edition
Name of Web Site	World Health Organization Web site
Year	2017
Month	January
Day	10
Year Accessed	2017
Month Accessed	March
Day Accessed	11
Medium	Web

☐ Show All Bibliography Fields

Tag name   Example: Document

Wor171   [OK]   [Cancel]

Learning
Outcomes
- Add and delete sources
- Edit a source
- Insert a bibliography field

Manage Sources and Create a Bibliography

Many documents require a **bibliography**, a list of sources that you used in creating the document. The list of sources can include only the works cited in your document (a **works cited** list) or both the works cited and the works consulted (a bibliography). The Bibliography feature in Word allows you to generate a works cited list or a bibliography automatically based on the source information you provide for the document. The Source Manager dialog box helps you to organize your sources. **CASE** *You add a bibliography to the report. The bibliography is inserted as a field and it can be formatted any way you choose.*

STEPS

QUICK TIP
You must copy sources from the Master List to the Current List for the sources to be available when you open the document on another computer.

1. **Press [Ctrl][End] to move the insertion point to the end of the document, then click the Manage Sources button in the Citations & Bibliography group**

   The Source Manager dialog box opens, as shown in FIGURE 4-19. The Master List shows the two sources you added and any other sources available on your computer. The Current List shows the sources available in the current document. A check mark next to a source indicates the source is cited in the document. You use the tools in the Source Manager dialog box to add, edit, and delete sources from the lists, and to copy sources between the Master and Current Lists. The sources that appear in the Current List will appear in the bibliography.

2. **Click the Baker, Mary source in the Current List**

   A preview of the citation and bibliographical entry for the source in MLA style appears in the Preview box. You do not want this source to be included in your bibliography for the report.

3. **Click Delete**

   The source is removed from the Current List but remains on the Master List on the computer where it originated.

4. **Click Close, click the Bibliography button in the Citations & Bibliography group, click References, then scroll up to see the heading References at the top of the field**

   A Bibliography field labeled "References" is added at the location of the insertion point. The bibliography includes all the sources associated with the document, formatted in the MLA style for bibliographies. The text in the Bibliography field is formatted with the default styles.

TROUBLE
Don't be concerned if the list of sources becomes gray when you select the heading Bibliography. This simply indicates the Bibliography field is active. Text that is selected is highlighted in dark gray.

5. **Select References; apply the following formats: Berlin Sans FB Demi and the Green, Accent 6 font color; drag down the list of sources to select the entire list and change the font size to 11; then click outside the bibliography field to deselect it**

   The format of the bibliography text now matches the rest of the report.

6. **Press [Ctrl][End], type your name, click the View tab, click Multiple Pages, then scroll up and down to view each page in the report**

   The completed report is shown in FIGURE 4-20.

7. **Save your changes, submit your document, close the file, then exit Word**

Working with Web sources

Publications found on the Web can be challenging to document. Many Web sites can be accessed under multiple domains, URLs change, and electronic publications are often updated frequently, making each visit to a Web site potentially unique. For these reasons, it's best to rely on the author, title, and publication information for a Web publication when citing it as a source in a research document. If possible, you can include a URL as supplementary information only, along with the date the Web site was last updated and the date you accessed the site. Since Web sites are often removed, it's also a good idea to download or print any Web source you use so that it can be verified later.

FIGURE 4-19: **Source Manager dialog box**

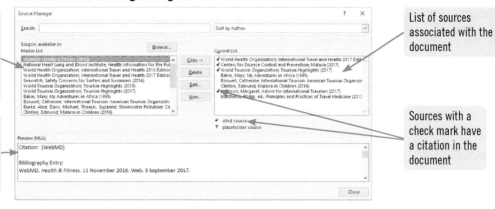

FIGURE 4-20: **Completed report**

Source: Pixabay

Practice

Concepts Review

Label each element shown in FIGURE 4-21.

FIGURE 4-21

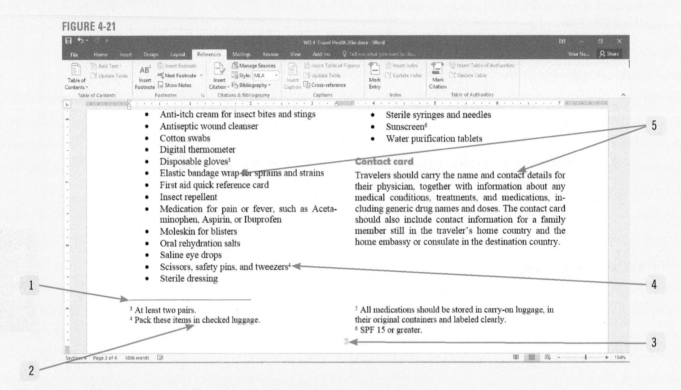

Match each term with the statement that best describes it.

6. **Bibliography**

7. **Header**

8. **Margin**

9. **Table**

10. **Citation**

11. **Manual page break**

12. **Field**

13. **Footer**

14. **Section break**

a. A grid of columns and rows that you can fill with text and graphics

b. A list of the sources used to create a document

c. Text or graphics that appear at the top of every page in a document

d. A formatting mark that forces the text following the mark to begin at the top of the next page

e. Text or graphics that appear at the bottom of every page in a document

f. A placeholder for information that changes

g. A formatting mark that divides a document into parts that can be formatted differently

h. The blank area between the edge of the text and the edge of the page

i. A parenthetical reference in the document text that gives credit to a source

Formatting Documents

Select the best answer from the list of choices.

15. **Which type of break can you insert if you want to force text to begin on the next page?**
    a. Column break
    b. Continuous section break
    c. Next page section break
    d. Text wrapping break

16. **Which type of break do you insert if you want to balance the columns in a section?**
    a. Text wrapping break
    b. Manual page break
    c. Column break
    d. Continuous section break

17. **Which of the following do documents with mirror margins always have?**
    a. Inside and outside margins
    b. Sections
    c. Portrait orientation
    d. Different first page headers and footers

18. **Which of the following cannot be inserted using the Quick Parts command?**
    a. AutoText building block
    b. Page number field
    c. Page break
    d. Document property

19. **Which appears at the end of a document?**
    a. Endnote
    b. Citation
    c. Page break
    d. Footnote

20. **What name describes formatted pieces of content that are stored in galleries?**
    a. Field
    b. Endnote
    c. Property
    d. Building Block

Skills Review

1. **Set document margins.**
   a. Start Word, open the file WD 4-2.docx from the location where you store your Data Files, then save it as **WD 4-Seaside Fitness**.
   b. Change the top and bottom margin settings to Moderate: 1" top and bottom, and .75" left and right.
   c. Save your changes to the document.

2. **Create sections and columns.**
   a. Turn on the display of formatting marks, then customize the status bar to display sections if they are not displayed already.
   b. Insert a continuous section break before the **Welcome to the Seaside Fitness Center** heading.
   c. Format the text in section 2 in two columns, then save your changes to the document.

3. **Insert page breaks.**
   a. Scroll to page 3, then insert a manual page break before the heading **Facilities and Services**. (*Hint*: The page break will appear at the bottom of page 2.)
   b. Scroll down and insert a manual page break before the heading **Membership**, then press [Ctrl][Home].
   c. On page 1, select the heading **Welcome to the Seaside Fitness Center** and the paragraph mark below it, use the Columns button to format the selected text as one column, then center the heading on the page.
   d. Follow the direction in step c to format the heading **Facilities and Services** and the paragraph mark below it on page 3, and the heading **Membership** and the paragraph mark below it on page 4, as one column, with centered text, then save your changes to the document.

4. **Insert page numbers.**
   a. Insert page numbers in the document at the bottom of the page. Select the Plain Number 2 page number style from the gallery.
   b. Close the Footer area, scroll through the document to view the page number on each page, then save your changes to the document.

Skills Review (continued)

5. Add headers and footers.

a. Double-click the margin at the top of a page to open the Header and Footer areas.

b. With the insertion point in the Header area, click the Quick Parts button in the Insert Group on the Header & Footer Tools Design tab, point to Document Property, then click Author.

c. Replace the text in the Author content control with your name, press [End] to move the insertion point out of the content control, then press [Spacebar]. (*Note*: If your name does not appear in the header, right-click the Author content control, click Remove Content Control, then type your name in the header.)

d. Click the Insert Alignment Tab button in the Position group, select the Right option button and keep the alignment relative to the margin, then click OK in the dialog box to close the dialog box and move the insertion point to the right margin.

e. Use the Insert Date and Time command in the Insert group to insert the current date using a format of your choice as static text. (*Hint*: Be sure the Update automatically check box is not checked.)

f. Apply italic to the text in the header.

g. Move the insertion point to the Footer area.

h. Double-click the page number to select it, then format the page number in bold and italic.

i. Move the insertion point to the header on page 1, use the Header & Footer Tools Design tab to create a different header and footer for the first page of the document, type your name in the First Page Header area, then apply italic to your name.

j. Close headers and footers, scroll to view the header and footer on each page, then save your changes to the document.

6. Insert a table.

a. On page 4, double-click the word **Table** at the end of the Membership Rates section to select it, press [Delete], open the Insert Table dialog box, then create a table with two columns and five rows.

b. Apply the List Table 2 table style to the table.

c. Press [Tab] to leave the first cell in the header row blank, then type **Rate**.

d. Press [Tab], then type the following text in the table, pressing [Tab] to move from cell to cell.

Enrollment/Individual	**$100**
Enrollment/Couple	**$150**
Monthly membership/Individual	**$125**
Monthly membership/Couple	**$200**

e. Select the table, use the AutoFit command on the Table Tools Layout tab to select the AutoFit to Contents option, and then select the AutoFit to Window option. (*Note*: In this case, AutoFit to Window fits the table to the width of the column of text.)

f. Save your changes to the document.

7. Add footnotes and endnotes.

a. Press [Ctrl[Home], scroll down, place the insertion point at the end of the first body paragraph, insert a footnote, then type **People who are active live longer and feel better.**

b. Place the insertion point at the end of the first paragraph under the Benefits of Exercise heading, insert a footnote, then type **There are 1,440 minutes in every day. Schedule 30 of them for physical activity.**

c. Place the insertion point at the end of the first paragraph under the Tips for Staying Motivated heading, insert a footnote, type **Always consult your physician before beginning an exercise program.**, then save your changes.

8. Insert citations.

a. Place the insertion point at the end of the second paragraph under the Benefits of Exercise heading (after "down from 52% in 2015" but before the period), then be sure the style for citations and bibliography is set to MLA Seventh Edition.

Skills Review (continued)

b. Insert a citation, add a new source, enter the source information shown in the Create Source dialog box in FIGURE 4-22, then click OK.

c. Place the insertion point at the end of the italicized quotation in the second column of text, insert a citation, then select Jason, Laura from the list of sources.

d. Edit the citation to include the page number **25**.

e. Scroll to page 2, place the insertion point at the end of the "Be a morning exerciser" paragraph but before the ending period, insert a citation for WebMD, then save your changes.

FIGURE 4-22

9. **Manage sources and create a bibliography.**

a. Press [Ctrl][End], then open the Source Manager dialog box.

b. Select the source Health, National Institute of: ... in the Current List, click Edit, click the Corporate Author check box, edit the entry so it reads **National Institute of Health**, click OK, then click Close.

c. Insert a bibliography labeled References.

d. Select References, then change the font to 14-point Tahoma with a black font color. Pages 1 and 4 of the formatted document are shown in FIGURE 4-23.

e. Save your changes to the document, submit it to your instructor, then close the document and exit Word.

FIGURE 4-23

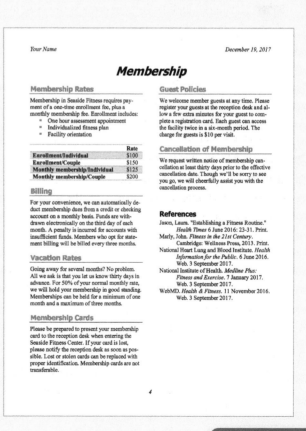

Independent Challenge 1

You are the owner of a small business called Lone Tree Catering. You have begun work on the text for a brochure advertising your business and you are now ready to lay out the pages and prepare the final copy. The brochure will be printed on both sides of an 8½" x 11" sheet of paper, and folded in thirds.

a. Start Word, open the file WD 4-3.docx from the location where you store your Data Files, then save it as **WD 4-Lone Tree Catering**. Read the document to get a feel for its contents.

b. Change the page orientation to landscape, and change all four margins to .6".

c. Format the document in three columns of equal width.

d. Insert a next page section break before the heading **Catering Services**.

e. On page 1, insert column breaks before the headings **Sample Tuscan Banquet Menu** and **Sample Indian Banquet Menu**.

f. Change the column spacing in section 1 (which is the first page) to .4", add lines between the columns on the first page, then select the text in the columns in section 1 and center it.

g. Double-click the bottom margin to open the footer area, create a different header and footer for the first page, then type **Call for custom menus designed to your taste and budget.** in the First Page Footer -Section 1- area.

FIGURE 4-24

h. Center the text in the footer area, format it in 20-point Papyrus, bold, with a Green, Accent 6 font color, then close headers and footers.

i. On page 2, insert a column break before Your Name, then press [Enter] 22 times to move the contact information to the bottom of the second column.

j. Replace Your Name with your name, then center the contact information in the column.

k. Press [Ctrl][End], insert a column break at the bottom of the second column. Type the text shown in FIGURE 4-24 in the third column, then apply the No Spacing style to the text. Refer to the figure as you follow the instructions for formatting the text in the third column.

l. Format Lone Tree Catering in 28-point Papyrus, bold, with a Green, Accent 6 font color.

m. Format the remaining text in 12-point Papyrus with a Green, Accent 6 font color. Center the text in the third column.

n. Insert an online picture of a tree, similar to the tree shown in FIGURE 4-24. Do not be concerned if the image you select is not the same tree image as that shown in the figure. Do not wrap text around the graphic.

o. Resize the graphic and add or remove blank paragraphs in the third column of your brochure so that the spacing between elements roughly matches the spacing shown in FIGURE 4-24.

p. Save your changes, then submit a copy to your instructor. If possible, you can print the brochure with the two pages back to back so that the brochure can be folded in thirds.

q. Close the document and exit Word.

Lone Tree Catering

Complete catering services available for all types of events. Menus and estimates provided upon request.

Source: Openclipart.org

Independent Challenge 2

You work in the Campus Safety Department at Valley State College. You have written the text for an informational flyer about parking regulations on campus, and now you need to format the flyer so it is attractive and readable.

a. Start Word, open the file WD 4-4.docx from the drive and folder where you store your Data Files, then save it as **WD 4-Valley Parking**. Read the document to get a feel for its contents.

b. Change all four margins to .7".

c. Insert a continuous section break before **1. May I bring a car to school?** (*Hint*: Place the insertion point before the word May.)

d. Scroll down and insert a next page section break before **Sample Parking Permit**.

e. Format the text in section 2 in three columns of equal width with .3" of space between the columns.

f. Hyphenate the document using the automatic hyphenation feature. (*Hint*: Use the Hyphenation button in the Page Setup group on the Layout tab.)

g. Add a 3-point dotted-line bottom border to the blank paragraph under Valley State College Department of Campus Safety. (*Hint*: Place the insertion point before the paragraph mark under Valley State College...)

h. Open the Header area, and type your name in the header. Right-align your name, and format it in 10-point Arial.

i. Add the following text to the footer, inserting symbols between words as indicated: **Parking and Shuttle Service Office • 54 Buckley Street • Valley State College • 942-555-2227**. (*Hint*: Click the Symbol command in the Symbols group on the Insert tab to insert a symbol. To find a small circle symbol, be sure the font is set to (normal text) and the subset is set to General Punctuation.)

j. Format the footer text in 9-point Arial Black, and center it in the footer.

k. Apply a 3-point dotted-line border above the footer text. Make sure to apply the border to the paragraph.

l. Add a continuous section break at the end of section 2 to balance the columns in section 2.

m. Place the insertion point on page 2 (which is section 4). Change the left and right margins in section 4 to 1". Also change the page orientation of section 4 to landscape.

n. Change the vertical alignment of section 4 to center. (*Hint*: Use the Vertical Alignment list arrow on the Layout tab in the Page Setup dialog box.)

o. Apply an appropriate table style to the table, such as the style shown in FIGURE 4-25. (*Hint*: Check and uncheck the options in the Table Style Options group on the Table Tools Design tab to customize the style so it enhances the table data.)

p. Save your changes, submit your work, close the document, then exit Word.

FIGURE 4-25

Sample Parking Permit

Valley State College
Office of Parking and Shuttle Service

2017-18 Student Parking Permit

License number:	VT 623 487
Make:	Subaru
Model:	Forester
Year:	2013
Color:	Silver
Permit Issue Date:	September 6, 2017
Permit Expiration Date:	June 4, 2018

Restrictions:
Parking is permitted in the Valley State College Greene Street lot 24 hours a day, 7 days a week. Shuttle service is available from the Greene Street lot to campus from 7 a.m. to 7 p.m. Monday through Friday. Parking is also permitted in any on-campus lot from 4:30 p.m. Friday to midnight Sunday.

Independent Challenge 3

A book publisher would like to publish an article you wrote on stormwater pollution in Australia as a chapter in a forthcoming book called *Environmental Issues for the New Millennium*. The publisher has requested that you format your article like a book chapter before submitting it for publication, and has provided you with a style sheet. According to the style sheet, the citations and bibliography should be formatted in Chicago style. You have already created the sources for the chapter, but you need to insert the citations.

FIGURE 4-26

a. Start Word, open the file WD 4-5.docx from the location where you store your Data Files, then save it as **WD 4-Chapter 8**. You will format the first page as shown in FIGURE 4-26.

b. Change the font of the entire document to 10-point Book Antigua. If this font is not available to you, select a different font suitable for the pages of a book. Change the alignment to justified.

c. Use the Page Setup dialog box to change the paper size to a custom setting of 6" x 9".

d. Create mirror margins. (*Hint*: Use the Multiple pages list arrow.) Change the top and bottom margins to .8", change the inside margin to .4", change the outside margin to .6", and create a .3" gutter to allow room for the book's binding.

e. Change the Zoom level to Page Width, open the Header and Footer areas, then apply the setting to create different headers and footers for odd- and even-numbered pages.

f. In the odd-page header, type **Chapter 8**, insert a symbol of your choice, type **The Silver Creek Catchment and Stormwater Pollution**, then format the header text in 9-point Book Antigua italic and right-align the text.

g. In the even-page header, type your name, then format the header text in 9-point Book Antigua italic. (*Note*: The even-page header should be left-aligned.)

h. Insert a left-aligned page number field in the even-page footer area, format it in 10-point Book Antigua, insert a right-aligned page number field in the odd-page footer area, then format it in 10-point Book Antigua.

i. Format the page numbers so that the first page of your chapter, which is Chapter 8 in the book, begins on page 167. (*Hint*: Select a page number field, click the Page Number button, then click Format Page Numbers.)

j. Go to the beginning of the document, press [Enter] 10 times, type **Chapter 8: The Silver Creek Catchment and Stormwater Pollution**, press [Enter] twice, type your name, then press [Enter] twice.

k. Format the chapter title in 16-point Book Antigua bold, format your name in 14-point Book Antigua, then left-align the title text and your name.

l. Click the References tab, make sure the citations and bibliography style is set to Chicago Sixteenth Edition, place the insertion point at the end of the first body paragraph on page 1 but before the ending period, insert a citation for Alice Burke, et. al., then add the page number **40** to the citation.

m. Add the citations listed in TABLE 4-3 to the document using the sources already associated with the document.

TABLE 4-3

page	location for citation	source	page number
2	End of the first complete paragraph (after ...WCSMP, but before the period)	City of Weston	3
3	End of the first complete paragraph (after ...pollution, but before the colon)	Jensen	135
4	End of first paragraph (after ...health effects, but before the period)	City of Weston	5
4	End of fourth bulleted list item (after 1 month.)	Seawatch	None
5	End of second paragraph (after ...problem arises, but before the period)	Burke, et. al.	55
6	End of paragraph before Conclusion (after ...stormwater system, but before the period)	City of Weston	7
6	End of first paragraph under Conclusion (after ...include, but before the colon)	Jensen	142

Independent Challenge 3 (continued)

n. Press [Ctrl][End], insert a Works Cited list, format the Works Cited heading in 11-point Book Antigua, black font color, bold, then format the list of works cited in 10-point Book Antigua.

o. Scroll to page 4 in the document, place the insertion point at the end of the paragraph above the Potential health effects... heading, press [Enter] twice, type **Table 1: Total annual pollutant loads per year in the Silver Creek Catchment**, press [Enter] twice, then format the text you just typed as bold if it is not bold.

p. Insert a table with four columns and four rows.

q. Type the text shown in FIGURE 4-27 in the table. Do not be concerned when the text wraps to the next line in a cell.

FIGURE 4-27

Area	Nitrogen	Phosphorus	Suspended solids
Silver Creek	9.3 tonnes	1.2 tonnes	756.4 tonnes
Durras Arm	6.2 tonnes	.9 tonnes	348.2 tonnes
Cabbage Tree Creek	9.8 tonnes	2.3 tonnes	485.7 tonnes

r. Apply the Grid Table 1 Light table style. Make sure the text in the header row is bold, then remove any bold formatting from the text in the remaining rows.

s. Use AutoFit to make the table fit the contents, then use AutoFit to make the table fit the window.

t. Save your changes, submit your work, then close the document and exit Word.

Independent Challenge 4: Explore

One of the most common opportunities to use the page layout features of Word is when formatting a research paper. The format recommended by the *MLA Handbook for Writers of Research Papers*, a style guide that includes information on preparing, writing, and formatting research papers, is the standard format used by many schools, colleges, and universities. In this independent challenge, you will research the MLA guidelines for formatting a research paper and use the guidelines you find to format the pages of a sample research report.

a. Use your favorite search engine to search the Web for information on the MLA guidelines for formatting a research report. Use the keywords **MLA Style** and **research paper format** to conduct your search.

b. Look for information on the proper formatting for the following aspects of a research paper: paper size, margins, title page or first page of the report, line spacing, paragraph indentation, and page numbers. Also find information on proper formatting for citations and a works cited page. Print the information you find.

c. Start Word, open the file WD 4-6.docx from the drive and folder where you store your Data Files, then save it as **WD 4-Research Paper**. Using the information you learned, format this document as a research report.

d. Adjust the margins, set the line spacing, and add page numbers to the document in the format recommended by the MLA. Use **The Maori History of New Zealand** as the title for your sample report, use your name as the author name, and use the name of the course you are enrolled in currently as well as the instructor's name for that course. Make sure to format the title page exactly as the MLA style dictates.

e. Format the remaining text as the body of the research report. Indent the first line of each paragraph rather than use quadruple spacing between paragraphs.

f. Create three sources, insert three citations in the document—a book, a journal article, and a Web site—and create a works cited page, following MLA style. If necessary, edit the format of the citations and works cited page to conform to MLA format. (*Note:* For this practice document, you are allowed to make up sources. Never make up sources for real research papers.)

g. Save the document, submit a copy to your instructor, close the document, then exit Word.

Open the file WD 4-7.docx from the location where you store your Data Files, then modify it to create the article shown in FIGURE 4-28. (*Hint*: Change all four margins to .6". Add the footnotes as shown in the figure.) Save the document with the filename **WD 4-Garden**, then print a copy.

FIGURE 4-28

GARDENER'S NOTEBOOK

Preparing a Perennial Garden for Winter

By Your Name

A sense of peace descends when a perennial garden is put to bed for the season. The plants are safely tucked in against the elements, and the garden is ready to welcome the winter. When the work is done, you can sit back and anticipate the bright blooms of spring. Many gardeners are uncertain about how to close a perennial garden. This week's column demystifies the process.

Clean up

Garden clean up can be a gradual process—plants will deteriorate at different rates, allowing you to do a little bit each week.

- Edge beds and borders and remove stakes, trellises, and other plant supports.
- Dig and divide irises, daylilies, and other early bloomers.
- Cut back plants when foliage starts to deteriorate, then rake all debris out of the garden and pull any weeds that remain.

Plant perennials

Fall is the perfect time to plant perennials.[1] The warm, sunny days and cool nights provide optimal conditions for new root growth, without the stress of summer heat.

- Dig deeply and enhance soil with organic matter.
- Use a good starter fertilizer to speed up new root growth and establish a healthy base.
- Untangle the roots of new plants before planting.

- Water after planting as the weather dictates, and keep plants moist for several days.

Add compost

Organic matter is the key ingredient to healthy garden soil. Composting adds nutrients to the soil, helps the soil retain water and nutrients, and keeps the soil well aerated. If you take care of the soil, your plants will become strong and disease resistant.[2]

Before adding compost, use an iron rake to loosen the top few inches of soil. Spread a one to two inch layer of compost over the entire garden—the best compost is made up of yard waste and kitchen scraps—and then refrain from stepping on the area and compacting the soil.

Winter mulch

Winter protection for perennial beds can only help plants survive the winter. Winter mulch prevents the freezing and thawing cycles, which cause plants to heave and eventually die. Here's what works and what doesn't:

- Always apply mulch after the ground is frozen.
- Never apply generic hay because it contains billions of weed seeds. Also, whole leaves and bark mulch hold too much moisture.[3]
- Use a loose material to allow air filtration. Straw and salt marsh hay are excellent choices for mulch.
- Remove the winter mulch in the spring as soon as new growth begins.

---

[1] Fall is also an excellent time to plant shrubs and trees.

[2] You can buy good compost, but it is easy and useful to make it at home. Composting kitchen scraps reduces household garbage by about one-third.

[3] If using leaves, use only stiff leaves, such as Oak or Beech. Soft leaves, such as Maple, make it difficult for air and water to filtrate.

Source: StackSnap

Creating a Presentation in PowerPoint 2016

CASE ▶ Reason2Go (R2G) is a voluntourism company that provides customers a unique experience of traveling to different countries and performing volunteer work. As a marketing representative for R2G, one of your responsibilities is to develop materials that describe the company vision, philosophy, and services. You have been asked to create a presentation using PowerPoint 2016 that describes projects R2G is currently developing in Kenya Africa.

Module Objectives

After completing this module, you will be able to:

- Define presentation software
- Plan an effective presentation
- Examine the PowerPoint window
- Enter slide text

- Add a new slide
- Apply a design theme
- Compare presentation views
- Print a PowerPoint presentation

Files You Will Need

No files needed.

Define Presentation Software

Presentation software (also called presentation graphics software) is a computer program you use to organize and present information to others. Presentations are typically in the form of a slide show. Whether you are explaining a new product or moderating a meeting, presentation software can help you effectively communicate your ideas. You can use PowerPoint to create informational slides that you print or display on a monitor, share in real time on the web, or save as a video for others to watch. **CASE** *You need to start working on your Kenya presentation. Because you are only somewhat familiar with PowerPoint, you get to work exploring its capabilities.* FIGURE 1-1 *shows how a presentation looks printed as handouts.* FIGURE 1-2 *shows how the same presentation might look shared on the Internet with others.*

DETAILS

You can easily complete the following tasks using PowerPoint:

- **Enter and edit text easily**

  Text editing and formatting commands in PowerPoint are organized by the task you are performing at the time, so you can enter, edit, and format text information simply and efficiently to produce the best results in the least amount of time.

- **Change the appearance of information**

  PowerPoint has many effects that can transform the way text, graphics, and slides appear. By exploring some of these capabilities, you discover how easy it is to change the appearance of your presentation.

- **Organize and arrange information**

  Once you start using PowerPoint, you won't have to spend much time making sure your information is correct and in the right order. With PowerPoint, you can quickly and easily rearrange and modify text, graphics, and slides in your presentation.

- **Include information from other sources**

  Often, when you create presentations, you use information from a variety of sources. With PowerPoint, you can import text, photographs, videos, numerical data, and other information from files created in programs such as Adobe Photoshop, Microsoft Word, Microsoft Excel, and Microsoft Access. You can also import information from other PowerPoint presentations as well as graphic images from a variety of sources such as the Internet, other computers, a digital camera, or other graphics programs. Always be sure you have permission to use any work that you did not create yourself.

- **Present information in a variety of ways**

  With PowerPoint, you can present information using a variety of methods. For example, you can print handout pages or an outline of your presentation for audience members. You can display your presentation as an on-screen slide show using your computer, or if you are presenting to a large group, you can use a video projector and a large screen. If you want to reach an even wider audience, you can broadcast the presentation or upload it as a video to the Internet so people anywhere in the world can use a web browser to view your presentation.

- **Collaborate with others on a presentation**

  PowerPoint makes it easy to collaborate or share a presentation with colleagues and coworkers using the Internet. You can use your email program to send a presentation as an attachment to a colleague for feedback. If you have a number of people that need to work together on a presentation, you can save the presentation to a shared workspace such as a network drive or OneDrive so authorized users in your group with an Internet connection can access the presentation.

FIGURE 1-1: **PowerPoint handout**

FIGURE 1-2: **Presentation shared on the Internet**

Using PowerPoint on a touch screen

You can use PowerPoint 2016 on a Windows computer with a touch-enabled monitor or any other compatible touch screen, such as a tablet computer. Using your fingers, you can use typical touch gestures to create, modify, and navigate presentations. To enable touch mode capabilities in PowerPoint, you need to add the Touch Mode button to the Quick Access toolbar. Click the Customize Quick Access Toolbar button, click

Touch/Mouse Mode, click the on the Quick Access toolbar then click Touch. In Touch mode, additional space is added around all of the buttons and icons in the Ribbon and the status bar to make them easier to touch. Common gestures that you can use in PowerPoint include double-tapping text to edit it and tapping a slide then dragging it to rearrange it in the presentation.

Plan an Effective Presentation

Before you create a presentation, you need to have a general idea of the information you want to communicate. PowerPoint is a powerful and flexible program that gives you the ability to start a presentation simply by entering the text of your message. If you have a specific design in mind that you want to use, you can start the presentation by working on the design. In most cases you'll probably enter the text of your presentation into PowerPoint first and then tailor the design to the message and audience. When preparing your presentation, you need to keep in mind not only who you are giving it to, but also how you are presenting it. For example, if you are giving a presentation using a projector, you need to know what other equipment you will need, such as a sound system and a projector. **CASE** ▶ *Use the planning guidelines below to help plan an effective presentation.* FIGURE 1-3 *illustrates a storyboard for a well-planned presentation.*

DETAILS

In planning a presentation, it is important to:

• **Determine and outline the message you want to communicate**

The more time you take developing the message and outline of your presentation, the better your presentation will be in the end. A presentation with a clear message that reads like a story and is illustrated with appropriate visual aids will have the greatest impact on your audience. Start the presentation by providing a general description of the Kenyan projects currently being developed. See FIGURE 1-3.

• **Identify your audience and where and how you are giving the presentation**

Audience and delivery location are major factors in the type of presentation you create. For example, a presentation you develop for a staff meeting that is held in a conference room would not necessarily need to be as sophisticated or detailed as a presentation that you develop for a large audience held in an auditorium. Room lighting, natural light, screen position, and room layout all affect how the audience responds to your presentation. You might also broadcast your presentation over the Internet to several people who view the presentation on their computers in real time. This presentation will be broadcast over the Internet.

• **Determine the type of output**

Output choices for a presentation include black-and-white or color handouts for audience members, on-screen slide show, a video, or an online broadcast. Consider the time demands and computer equipment availability as you decide which output types to produce. Because this presentation will be broadcast over the Internet, the default output settings work just fine.

• **Determine the design**

Visual appeal, graphics, and presentation design work together to communicate your message. You can choose one of the professionally designed themes that come with PowerPoint, modify one of these themes, or create one of your own. You decide to choose one of PowerPoint's design themes for your presentation.

FIGURE 1-3: **Storyboard of the presentation**

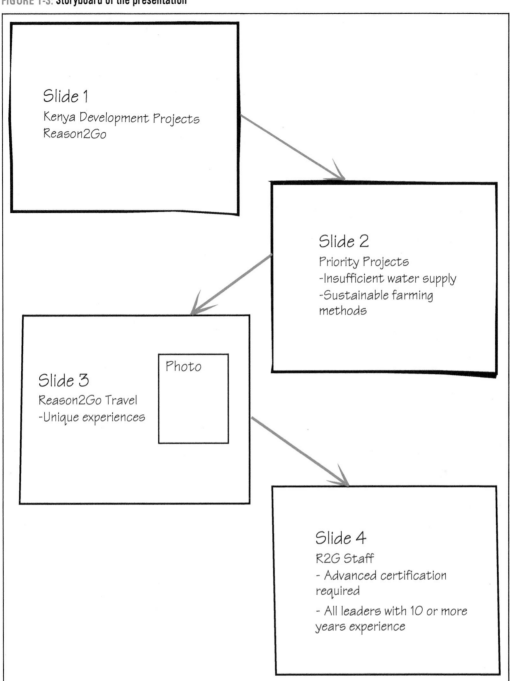

Understanding copyright

Intellectual property is any idea or creation of the human mind. Copyright law is a type of intellectual property law that protects works of authorship, including books, webpages, computer games, music, artwork, and photographs. Copyright protects the expression of an idea, but not the underlying facts or concepts. In other words, the general subject matter is not protected, but how you express it is, such as when several people photograph the same sunset. Copyright attaches to any original work of authorship as soon as it is created, you do not have to register it with the Copyright Office or display the copyright symbol, ©. Fair use is an exception to copyright and permits the public to use copyrighted material for certain purposes without obtaining prior consent from the owner. Determining whether fair use applies to a work depends on its purpose, the nature of the work, how much of the work you want to copy, and the effect on the work's value. Unauthorized use of protected work (such as downloading a photo or a song from the web) is known as copyright infringement and can lead to legal action.

PowerPoint 2016
Module 1

Learning
Outcomes
• Explain PowerPoint
window elements

Examine the PowerPoint Window

When you first start PowerPoint, you have the ability to choose what kind of presentation you want to use to start—a blank one, or one with a preformatted design. You can also open and work on an existing presentation. PowerPoint has different **views** that allow you to see your presentation in different forms. By default, the PowerPoint window opens in **Normal view**, which is the primary view that you use to write, edit, and design your presentation. Normal view is divided into areas called **panes**: the pane on the left, called the **Slides tab**, displays the slides of your presentation as small images, called **slide thumbnails**. The large pane is the Slide pane where you do most of your work on the slide. **CASE** *The PowerPoint window and the specific parts of Normal view are described below.*

STEPS

1. **Start** PowerPoint 2016
   PowerPoint starts and the PowerPoint start screen opens, as shown in FIGURE 1-4.

2. **Click the** Blank Presentation slide thumbnail
   The PowerPoint window opens in Normal view, as shown in FIGURE 1-5.

DETAILS

TROUBLE

If you are unsure how to start PowerPoint, refer to the "Getting Started with Office 2016" Module in this book for specific instructions on how to start the application.

Using Figure 1-5 as a guide, examine the elements of the PowerPoint window, then find and compare the elements described below:

• The **Ribbon** is a wide band spanning the top of the PowerPoint window that organizes all of PowerPoint's primary commands. Each set of primary commands is identified by a **tab**; for example, the Home tab is selected by default, as shown in FIGURE 1-5. Commands are further arranged into **groups** on the Ribbon based on their function. So, for example, text formatting commands such as Bold, Underline, and Italic are located on the Home tab, in the Font group.

• The **Slides tab** is to the left. You can navigate through the slides in your presentation by clicking the slide thumbnails. You can also add, delete, or rearrange slides using this pane.

• The **Slide pane** displays the current slide in your presentation.

• The **Quick Access toolbar** provides access to common commands such as Save, Undo, Redo, and Start From Beginning. The Quick Access toolbar is always visible no matter which Ribbon tab you select. Click the Customize Quick Access Toolbar button to add or remove buttons.

• The **View Shortcuts** buttons on the status bar allow you to switch quickly between PowerPoint views.

• The **Notes button** on the status bar opens the Notes pane and is used to enter text that references a slide's content. You can print these notes and refer to them when you make a presentation or use them as audience handouts. The Notes pane is not visible in Slide Show view.

• The **Comments button** on the status bar opens the Comments pane. In the Comments pane you can create, edit, select, and delete comments.

• The **status bar**, located at the bottom of the PowerPoint window, shows messages about what you are doing and seeing in PowerPoint, including which slide you are viewing and the total number of slides. In addition, the status bar displays the Zoom slider controls, the Fit slide to current window button 🔲, and other functionality information.

• The **Zoom slider** on the lower-right corner of the status bar is used to zoom the slide in and out.

FIGURE 1-4: PowerPoint start screen

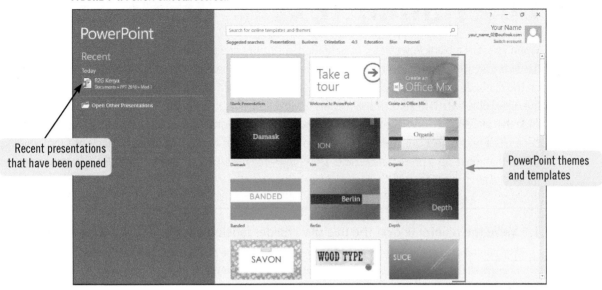

Recent presentations that have been opened

PowerPoint themes and templates

FIGURE 1-5: PowerPoint window in Normal view

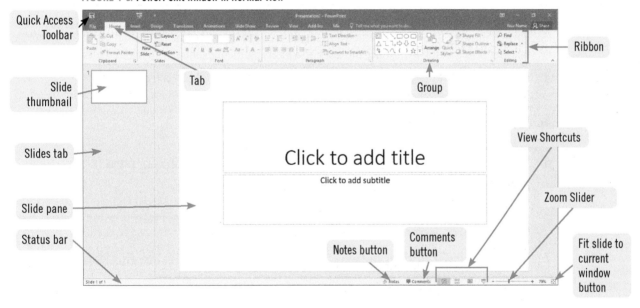

Quick Access Toolbar

Slide thumbnail

Tab

Slides tab

Slide pane

Status bar

Group

Ribbon

View Shortcuts

Zoom Slider

Notes button

Comments button

Fit slide to current window button

Viewing your presentation in gray scale or black and white

Viewing your presentation in gray scale (using shades of gray) or pure black and white is very useful when you are printing a presentation on a black-and-white printer and you want to make sure your presentation prints correctly. To see how your color presentation looks in gray scale or black and white, click the View tab, then click either the Grayscale or Black and White button in the Color/Grayscale group. Depending on which button you select, the Grayscale or the Black and White tab appears, and the Ribbon displays different settings that you can customize. If you don't like the way an individual object looks in black and white or gray scale, you can change its color. Click the object while still in Grayscale or Black and White view, then choose an option in the Change Selected Object group on the Ribbon.

Enter Slide Text

Learning
Outcomes
• Enter slide text
• Change slide text

When you start a blank PowerPoint presentation, an empty title slide appears in Normal view. The title slide has two **text placeholders**—boxes with dotted borders—where you enter text. The top text placeholder on the title slide is the **title placeholder**, labeled "Click to add title". The bottom text placeholder on the title slide is the **subtitle text placeholder**, labeled "Click to add subtitle". To enter text in a placeholder, click the placeholder and then type your text. After you enter text in a placeholder, the placeholder becomes a text object. An **object** is any item on a slide that can be modified. Objects are the building blocks that make up a presentation slide. **CASE** ➤ *Begin working on your presentation by entering text on the title slide.*

STEPS

1. **Move the pointer ⌕ over the title placeholder labeled** Click to add title **in the Slide pane**

   The pointer changes to Ⅰ when you move the pointer over the placeholder. In PowerPoint, the pointer often changes shape, depending on the task you are trying to accomplish.

2. **Click the** title placeholder **in the Slide pane**

   The **insertion point**, a blinking vertical line, indicates where your text appears when you type in the placeholder. A **selection box** with a dashed line border and **sizing handles** appears around the placeholder, indicating that it is selected and ready to accept text. When a placeholder or object is selected, you can change its shape or size by dragging one of the sizing handles. See FIGURE 1-6.

3. **Type** Community Development Projects Kenya

   PowerPoint wraps the text to a second line and then center-aligns the title text within the title placeholder, which is now a text object. Notice the text also appears on the slide thumbnail on the Slides tab.

4. **Click the** subtitle text placeholder **in the Slide pane**

   The subtitle text placeholder is ready to accept text.

5. **Type** Presented by, **then press** [Enter]

   The insertion point moves to the next line in the text object.

6. **Type** Community Health Education, **press** [Enter], **type** Reason2Go, **press** [Enter], **type** Marketing Dept., **press** [Enter], **then type** your name

   Notice the AutoFit Options button ⊞ appears near the text object. The AutoFit Options button on your screen indicates that PowerPoint has automatically decreased the font size of all the text in the text object so it fits inside the text object.

7. **Click the** AutoFit Options button ⊞, **then click** Stop Fitting Text to This Placeholder **on the shortcut menu**

   The text in the text object changes back to its original size and no longer fits inside the text object.

8. **In the subtitle text object, position** Ⅰ **to the right of** Education, **drag left to select the entire line of text, press** [Backspace], **then click outside the text object in a blank area of the slide**

   The Community Health Education line of text is deleted and the AutoFit Options button menu closes, as shown in FIGURE 1-7. Clicking a blank area of the slide deselects all selected objects on the slide.

9. **Click the** Save button 🖫 **on the Quick Access toolbar to open Backstage view, then save the presentation as** PPT 1-R2G **in the location where you store your Data Files**

   In Backstage view, you have the option of saving your presentation to your computer or OneDrive. Notice that PowerPoint automatically entered the title of the presentation as the filename in the Save As dialog box.

FIGURE 1-6: **Title text placeholder selected**

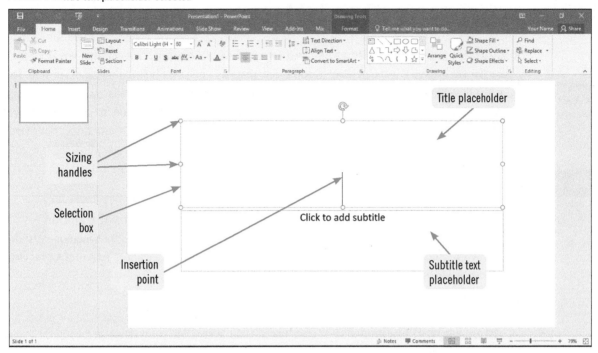

FIGURE 1-7: **Text on title slide**

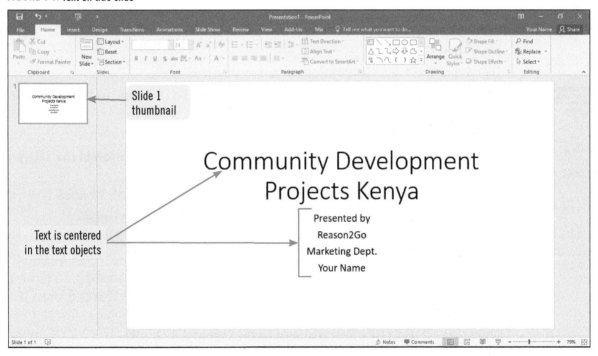

Inking a slide

In Slide View, you can add freehand pen and highlighter marks, also known as **inking**, to the slides of your presentation to emphasize information. To begin inking, go to the slide you want mark up, click the Review tab, then click the Start Inking button in the Ink group. The Pens tab appears on the Ribbon and the Pen tool appears on the slide ready for you to draw using your mouse. To customize your pen, select a different pen color, style, or thickness from options in the Pens group. Click the Highlighter button in the Write group to insert highlighter strokes on your slide. To erase inking on the slide, click the Eraser button in the Write group.

Add a New Slide

Learning
Outcomes
• Add a new slide
• Indent text levels
• Modify slide layout

Usually when you add a new slide to a presentation, you have a pretty good idea of what you want the slide to look like. For example, you may want to add a slide that has a title over bulleted text and a picture. To help you add a slide like this quickly and easily, PowerPoint provides many standard slide layouts. A **slide layout** contains text and object placeholders that are arranged in a specific way on the slide. You have already worked with the Title Slide layout in the previous lesson. In the event that a standard slide layout does not meet your needs, you can modify an existing slide layout or create a new, custom slide layout. **CASE** *To continue developing the presentation, you create a slide that explains the needs in Kenya.*

STEPS

1. **Click the** New Slide button **in the Slides group on the Home tab on the Ribbon**
   A new blank slide (now the current slide) appears as the second slide in your presentation, as shown in FIGURE 1-8. The new slide contains a title placeholder and a content placeholder. A **content placeholder** can be used to insert text or objects such as tables, charts, videos, or pictures. Notice the status bar indicates Slide 2 of 2 and the Slides tab now contains two slide thumbnails.

2. **Type** Priority Projects, **then click the** bottom content placeholder
   The text you typed appears in the title placeholder, and the insertion point is now at the top of the bottom content placeholder.

3. **Type** Well water production, **then press** [Enter]
   The insertion point appears directly below the text when you press [Enter], and a new first-level bullet automatically appears.

4. **Press** [Tab]
   The new first-level bullet is indented and becomes a second-level bullet.

5. **Type** Inadequate water supply, **press** [Enter], **then click the** Decrease List Level button ⇤ **in the Paragraph group**
   The Decrease List Level button changes the second-level bullet into a first-level bullet.

6. **Type** Sustainable farming methods, **then click the** New Slide list arrow **in the Slides group**
   The Office Theme layout gallery opens. Each slide layout is identified by a descriptive name.

7. **Click the** Two Content slide layout, **then type** Unique Travel Experience
   A new slide with a title placeholder and two content placeholders appears as the third slide. The text you typed is the title text for the slide.

8. **Click the left content placeholder, type** Adventurous travel destinations, **press** [Enter], **click the** Increase List Level button ⇥, **type** Serve others in desperate need, **press** [Enter], **then type** Satisfaction of helping your fellow man
   The Increase List Level button moves the insertion point one level to the right.

9. **Click a blank area of the slide, then click the** Save button 🖫 **on the Quick Access toolbar**
   The Save button saves all of the changes to the file. Compare your screen with FIGURE 1-9.

FIGURE 1-8: **New blank slide in Normal view**

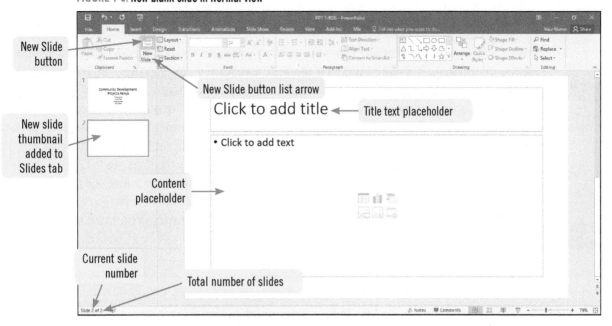

New Slide button

New Slide button list arrow

Title text placeholder

New slide thumbnail added to Slides tab

Content placeholder

Current slide number

Total number of slides

FIGURE 1-9: **New slide with Two Content slide layout**

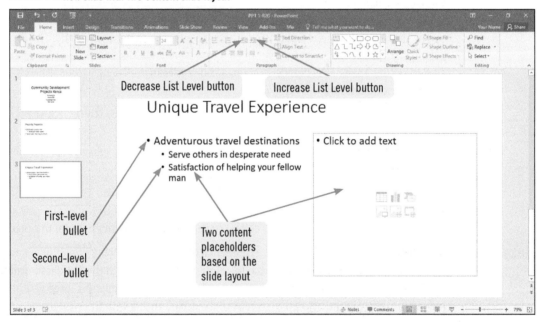

Decrease List Level button

Increase List Level button

First-level bullet

Second-level bullet

Two content placeholders based on the slide layout

Entering and printing notes

You can add notes to your slides when there are certain facts you want to remember during a presentation or when there is additional information you want to hand out to your audience. Notes do not appear on the slides when you run a slide show. Use the Notes pane in Normal view or Notes Page view to enter notes for your slides. To open or close the Notes pane, click the Notes button on the status bar. To enter text notes on a slide, click in the Notes pane, then type. If you want to insert graphics as notes, you must use Notes Page view. To open Notes Page view, click the View tab on the Ribbon, then click the Notes Page button in the Presentation Views group. You can print your notes by clicking the File tab on the Ribbon to open Backstage view. Click Print, click the Full Page Slides list arrow in the Settings group (this button retains the last setting for what was printed previously so it might differ) to open the gallery, and then click Notes Pages. Once you verify your print settings, click the Print button. If you don't enter any notes in the Notes pane, and print the notes pages, the slides print as large thumbnails with blank space below the thumbnails to hand write notes.

Apply a Design Theme

PowerPoint provides many design themes to help you quickly create a professional and contemporary looking presentation. A **theme** includes a set of 12 coordinated colors for text, fill, line, and shadow, called **theme colors**; a set of fonts for titles and other text, called **theme fonts**; and a set of effects for lines and fills, called **theme effects** to create a cohesive look. Each theme has at least four custom coordinated variants that provides you with additional color options. In most cases, you would apply one theme to an entire presentation; you can, however, apply multiple themes to the same presentation. You can use a design theme as is, or you can alter individual elements of the theme as needed. Unless you need to use a specific design theme, such as a company theme or product design theme, it is faster and easier to use one of the themes supplied with PowerPoint. If you design a custom theme, you can save it to use in the future. **CASE** *You decide to change the default design theme in the presentation to a new one.*

STEPS

1. **Click the** Slide 1 thumbnail **on the Slides tab**
   Slide 1, the title slide, appears in the Slide pane.

2. **Click the** Design tab **on the Ribbon, then point to the** Integral theme **in the Themes group, as shown in** FIGURE 1-10
   The Design tab appears, and a Live Preview of the Integral theme is displayed on the selected slide. A **Live Preview** allows you to see how your changes affect the slides before actually making the change. The Live Preview lasts about 1 minute, and then your slide reverts back to its original state. The first (far left) theme thumbnail identifies the current theme applied to the presentation, in this case, the default design theme called the Office Theme. The number of themes you can see in the Themes group depends on your monitor resolution and screen size.

3. **Slowly move your pointer** ⬚ **over the other design themes, then click the** Themes group down scroll arrow
   A Live Preview of the theme appears on the slide each time you pass your pointer over the theme thumbnails, and a ScreenTip identifies the theme names.

4. **Move** ⬚ **over the** design themes, **then click the** Wisp theme
   The Wisp design theme is applied to all the slides in the presentation. Notice the new slide background color, graphic elements, fonts, and text color. You decide this theme isn't right for this presentation.

QUICK TIP
One way to apply multiple themes to the same presentation is to click the Slide Sorter button on the status bar, select a slide or a group of slides, then click the theme.

5. **Click the** More button ⬚ **in the Themes group**
   The Themes gallery window opens. At the top of the gallery window in the This Presentation section is the current theme applied to the presentation. Notice that just the Wisp theme is listed here because when you changed the theme in the last step, you replaced the default theme with the Wisp theme. The Office section identifies all of the standard themes that come with PowerPoint.

6. **Right-click the** Slice theme **in the Office section, then click** Apply to Selected Slides
   The Slice theme is applied only to Slide 1. You like the Slice theme better, and decide to apply it to all slides.

7. **Right-click the** Slice theme **in the Themes group, then click** Apply to All Slides
   The Slice theme is applied to all three slides. Preview the next slides in the presentation to see how it looks.

8. **Click the** Next Slide button ⬚ **at the bottom of the vertical scroll bar**
   Compare your screen to FIGURE 1-11.

9. **Click the** Previous Slide button ⬚ **at the bottom of the vertical scroll bar, then save your changes**

FIGURE 1-10: Slide showing a different design theme

FIGURE 1-11: Presentation with Slice theme applied

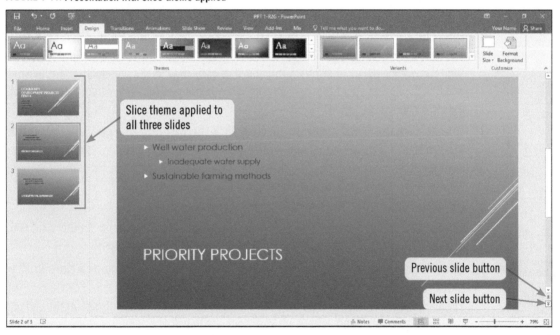

Customizing themes

You are not limited to using the standard themes PowerPoint provides; you can also modify a theme to create your own custom theme. For example, you might want to incorporate your school's or company's colors on the slide background of the presentation or be able to type using fonts your company uses for brand recognition. To change an existing theme, click the View tab on the Ribbon, then click one of the Master buttons in the Master Views group. Click the Theme Colors button, the Theme Fonts button, or the Theme Effects button in the Background group to make changes to the theme, save this new theme for future use by clicking the Themes button in the Edit Themes group, then click Save Current Theme. You also have the ability to create a new font theme or color theme from scratch by clicking the Theme Fonts button or the Theme Colors button and then clicking Customize Fonts or Customize Colors. You work in the Create New Theme Fonts or Create New Theme Colors dialog box to define the custom theme fonts or colors.

Compare Presentation Views

Learning
Outcomes
• Open PowerPoint
views

PowerPoint has six primary views: Normal view, Outline view, Slide Sorter view, Notes Page view, Slide Show view, and Reading view. Each PowerPoint view displays your presentation in a different way and is used for different purposes. Normal view is the primary editing view where you add text, graphics, and other elements to the slides. Outline view is the view you use to focus on the text of your presentation. Slide Sorter view is primarily used to rearrange slides; however, you can also add slide effects and design themes in this view. You use Notes Page view to type notes that are important for each slide. Slide Show view displays your presentation over the whole computer screen and is designed to show your presentation to an audience. Similar to Slide Show view, Reading view is designed to view your presentation on a computer screen. To move easily among the PowerPoint views, use the View Shortcuts buttons located on the status bar and the View tab on the Ribbon. TABLE 1-1 provides a brief description of the PowerPoint views. **CASE** *Examine each of the PowerPoint views, starting with Normal view.*

STEPS

1. **Click the View tab on the Ribbon, then click the Outline View button in the Presentation Views group**

   The presentation text is in the Outline pane on the left side of the window, as shown in FIGURE 1-12. Notice the status bar identifies the number of the slide you are viewing and the total number of slides in the presentation.

2. **Click the small slide icon ▢ next to Slide 2 in the Outline pane, then click the Slide Sorter button ⊞ on the status bar**

   Slide Sorter View opens to display a thumbnail of each slide in the presentation in the window. You can examine the flow of your slides and drag any slide or group of slides to rearrange the order of the slides in the presentation.

3. **Double-click the Slide 1 thumbnail, then click the Reading View button ▦ on the status bar**

   The first slide fills the screen, as shown in FIGURE 1-13. Use Reading view to review your presentation or to show your presentation to someone directly on your computer. The status bar controls at the bottom of the window make it easy to move between slides in this view.

4. **Click the Slide Show button ▱ on the status bar**

   The first slide fills the entire screen now without the title bar and status bar. In this view, you can practice running through your slides as they would appear in a slide show.

QUICK TIP
You can also press
[Enter], [Spacebar],
[Page Up], [Page
Down], or the arrow
keys to advance the
slide show.

5. **Click the left mouse button to advance through the slides one at a time until you see a black slide, then click once more to return to Outline view**

   The black slide at the end of the slide show indicates the slide show is finished. At the end of a slide show, you return to the slide and PowerPoint view you were in before you ran the slide show, in this case, Slide 1 in Outline view.

6. **Click the Notes Page button in the Presentation Views group**

   Notes Page view appears, showing a reduced image of the current slide above a large text placeholder. You can enter text in this placeholder and then print the notes page for your own use.

7. **Click the Normal button in the Presentation Views group, then click the Home tab on the Ribbon**

FIGURE 1-12: **Outline view**

FIGURE 1-13: **Reading view**

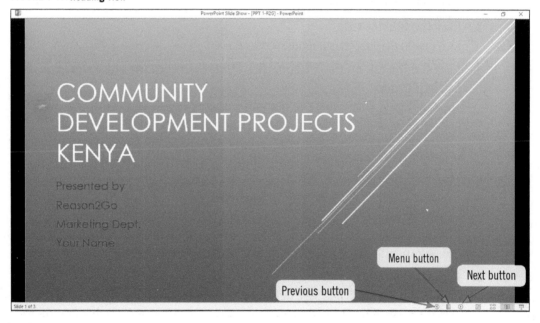

TABLE 1-1: **PowerPoint views**

view name	button	button name	displays
Normal		Normal	The Slide pane and the Slides tab at the same time
Outline View	(no View Shortcuts button)		An outline of the presentation and the Slide pane at the same time
Slide Sorter		Slide Sorter	Thumbnails of all slides
Slide Show		Slide Show	Your presentation on the whole computer screen
Reading View		Reading View	Your presentation in a large window on your computer screen
Notes Page	(no View Shortcuts button)		A reduced image of the current slide above a large text box

Print a PowerPoint Presentation

Learning Outcomes
- Print a presentation
- Set print settings
- Modify color settings

You print your presentation when you want to review your work or when you have completed it and want a hard copy. Reviewing your presentation at different stages of development gives you a better perspective of the overall flow and feel of the presentation. You can also preview your presentation to see exactly how each slide looks before you print the presentation. When you are finished working on your presentation, even if it is not yet complete, you can close the presentation file and exit PowerPoint. **CASE** ▶ *You are done working on the Kenya presentation for now. You save and preview the presentation, then you print the slides and notes pages of the presentation so you can review them later. Before leaving for the day, you close the file and exit PowerPoint.*

STEPS

1. **Click the** Save button 🖫 **on the Quick Access toolbar, click the** File tab **on the Ribbon, then click** Print

   The Print window opens, as shown in FIGURE 1-14. Notice the preview pane on the right side of the window displays the first slide of the presentation. If you do not have a color printer, you will see a grayscale image of the slide.

QUICK TIP

To quickly print the presentation with the current Print options, add the Quick Print button to the Quick Access toolbar.

2. **Click the** Next Page button ▶ **at the bottom of the Preview pane, then click** ▶ **again**

   Each slide in the presentation appears in the preview pane.

3. **Click the** Print button

   Each slide in the presentation prints.

4. **Click the** File tab **on the Ribbon, click** Print, **then click the** Full Page Slides button **in the Settings group**

   The Print Layout gallery opens. In this gallery you can specify what you want to print (slides, handouts, notes pages, or outline), as well as other print options. To save paper when you are reviewing your slides, you can print in handout format, which lets you print up to nine slides per page. The options you choose in the Print window remain there until you change them or close the presentation.

QUICK TIP

To print slides appropriate in size for overhead transparencies, click the Design tab, click the Slide Size button in the Customize group, click Customize Slide Size, click the Slides sized for list arrow, then click Overhead.

5. **Click** 3 Slides, **click the** Color button **in the Settings group, then click** Pure Black and White

   PowerPoint removes the color and displays the slides as thumbnails next to blank lines, as shown in FIGURE 1-15. Using the Handouts with three slides per page printing option is a great way to print your presentation when you want to provide a way for audience members to take notes. Printing pure black-and-white prints without any gray tones can save printer toner.

6. **Click the** Print button

   The presentation prints one page showing all the slides of the presentation as thumbnails next to blank lines.

7. **Click the** File tab **on the Ribbon, then click** Close

   If you have made changes to your presentation, a Microsoft PowerPoint alert box opens asking you if you want to save changes you have made to your presentation file.

8. **Click** Save, **if necessary, to close the alert box**

   Your presentation closes.

9. **Click the** Close button ⊠ **in the Title bar**

   The PowerPoint program closes, and you return to the Windows desktop.

FIGURE 1-14: Print window

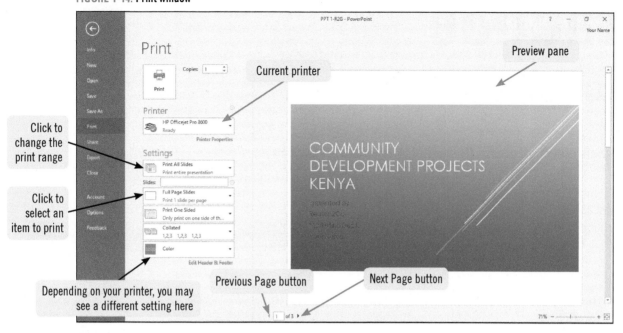

Click to change the print range

Click to select an item to print

Depending on your printer, you may see a different setting here

Current printer

Preview pane

Previous Page button

Next Page button

FIGURE 1-15: Print window with changed settings

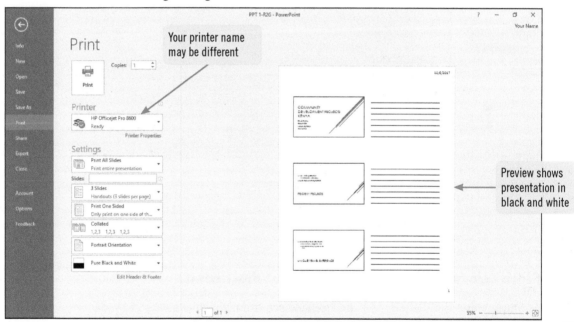

Your printer name may be different

Preview shows presentation in black and white

Microsoft Office Online Apps

Some Office programs, PowerPoint for example, include the capability to incorporate feedback—called online collaboration—across the Internet or a company network. Using **cloud computing** (work done in a virtual environment), you can take advantage of web programs called Microsoft Office Online Apps, which are simplified versions of the programs found in the Microsoft Office 2016 suite. Because these programs are online, they take up no computer disk space and are accessed using Microsoft OneDrive, a free service from Microsoft. Using Microsoft OneDrive, you and your colleagues can create and store documents in the "cloud" and make the documents available to whomever you grant access. To use Microsoft OneDrive, you need to create a free Microsoft account, which you obtain at the Microsoft website.

Practice

Concepts Review

Label each element of the PowerPoint window shown in FIGURE 1-16.

FIGURE 1-16

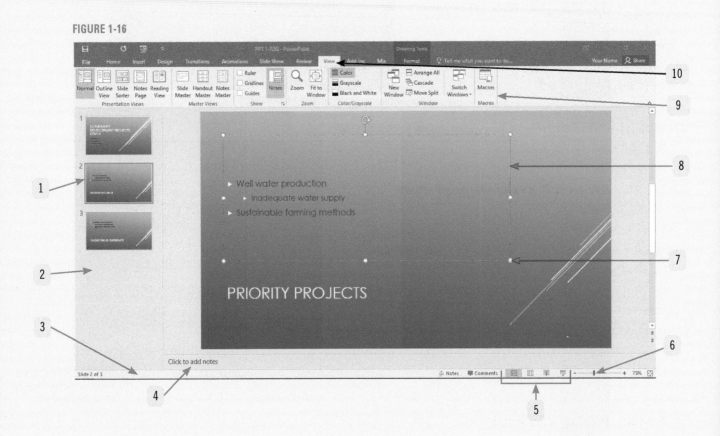

Match each term with the statement that best describes it.

11. **Slide Show view**
12. **Slide Layout**
13. **Inking**
14. **Theme**
15. **Zoom slider**
16. **Text placeholder**

a. Freehand pen and highlighter marks on a slide
b. A view that displays a presentation to show to an audience
c. Allows you to change the size of the slide in the window
d. Set of coordinated colors, fonts, and effects
e. Placeholders arranged in a specific way on the slide
f. Box with dotted border where you enter text

Select the best answer from the list of choices.

17. The view that fills the entire computer screen with each slide in the presentation is called:
    a. Outline view.
    b. Normal view.
    c. Slide Show view.
    d. Fit to window view.

18. You can enter slide text in the Slide Pane and in the _____.
    a. Reading pane
    b. Notes Page view
    c. Outline view
    d. Slides tab

19. What is the function of the slide layout?
    a. Defines how all the elements on a slide are arranged.
    b. Enables you to apply a template to the presentation.
    c. Puts all your slides in order.
    d. Shows you which themes you can apply.

20. Which of the following is not included in a design theme?
    a. Pictures
    b. Normal view
    c. Fonts
    d. Colors

21. Which button indents the insertion point to the right?
    a. Right Indent Level
    b. Increase List Level
    c. Decrease Indent Level
    d. Move Margin

22. Which status bar feature allows you to quickly switch between views?
    a. Zoom Slider
    b. View Shortcuts
    c. Fit slide to current window button
    d. Switch view button

23. What can you drag to adjust the size of an object?
    a. Rotate handle
    b. Object border point
    c. Sizing handle
    d. Selection box

24. What are the basic building blocks of any presentation?
    a. Placeholders
    b. Objects
    c. Slides
    d. Graphics

Skills Review

1. **Examine the PowerPoint window.**
   a. Start PowerPoint, if necessary then open a new blank presentation.
   b. Identify as many elements of the PowerPoint window as you can without referring to the lessons in this module.
   c. Be able to describe the purpose or function of each element.
   d. For any elements you cannot identify, refer to the lessons in this module.

2. **Enter slide text.**
   a. In the Slide pane in Normal view, enter the text **Nelsonville** in the title placeholder.
   b. In the subtitle text placeholder, enter **Wyoming Ghost Town Preservation Society**.
   c. On the next line of the placeholder, enter your name.
   d. Deselect the text object.
   e. Save the presentation using the filename **PPT 1-Nelsonville** to location where you store your Data Files.

Skills Review (continued)

3. Add a new slide.

   a. Create a new slide.

   b. Using FIGURE 1-17, enter text on the slide.

   c. Create another new slide.

   d. Using FIGURE 1-18, enter text on the slide.

   e. Save your changes.

4. Apply a design theme.

   a. Click the Design tab.

   b. Click the Themes group More button, then point to all of the themes.

   c. Locate the Ion Boardroom theme, then apply it to the selected slide.

   d. Select Slide 1.

   e. Locate the Wisp theme, then apply it to Slide 1.

   f. Apply the Wisp theme to all of the slides in the presentation.

   g. Use the Next Slide button to move to Slide 3, then save your changes.

5. Compare presentation views.

   a. Click the View tab, then click the Outline View button in the Presentation Views group.

   b. Click the Slide Sorter button in the Presentation Views group.

   c. Click the Notes Page button in the Presentation Views group, then click the Previous Slide button twice.

   d. Click the Reading View button in the Presentation Views group, then click the Next button on the status bar.

   e. Click the Normal button on the status bar, then click the Slide Show button.

   f. Advance the slides until a black screen appears, then click to end the presentation.

   g. Save your changes.

6. Print a PowerPoint presentation.

   a. Print all the slides as handouts, 3 Slides, in color.

   b. Print the presentation outline.

   c. Close the file, saving your changes.

   d. Exit PowerPoint.

FIGURE 1-17

Nelsonville's Settlers

- First wagon train left Tennessee in Aug. 1854
  - Expedition led by the Thomas Leslie, James Rowley, and Benjamin Lane families
  - 18 separate families made the trip
  - Wagon train split into two groups due to illness
- First wagons arrived in Wyoming Nov. 1854
  - During trip 5 people died and 1 baby delivered
  - Settlers defended themselves against 2 Indian raids in Nebraska
  - Wyoming area settled known by locals as "Four Trees Crossing"

FIGURE 1-18

Nelsonville Hotel & Bar History

- Built by John Nelson in 1868
  - Constructed from local lodgepole and ponderosa pine
  - Sold cattle and land for construction capital
- Continuously operated from 1870 to 1929
  - Featured 14 double rooms and 1 bridal suite
  - Restaurant, bath house, and barber shop eventually added to property
  - Featured gambling tables until 1911

Independent Challenge 1

You work for RuraLink Systems, a business that offers rural broadband Internet service and network server management. One of your jobs at the company is to present the company's services to local government and community meetings. Your boss has asked you to create a company profile presentation that describes company goals and services.

a. Start PowerPoint then open a new blank presentation.

b. In the title placeholder on Slide 1, type **RuraLink Systems**.

c. In the subtitle placeholder, type your name, press [Enter], then type today's date.

d. Apply the Ion Boardroom design theme to the presentation.

e. Save your presentation with the filename **PPT 1-RuraLink** to the location where you store your Data Files.

f. Use FIGURE 1-19 and FIGURE 1-20 to add two more slides to your presentation. (*Hint*: Slide 3 uses the Comparison layout.)

g. Use the buttons on the View tab to switch between all of PowerPoint's views.

h. Print the presentation using handouts, 3 Slides, in black and white.

i. Save and close the file, then exit PowerPoint.

FIGURE 1-19

RuraLink Service Goals

- Prompt & reliable service
- Provide only necessary services to complete job
- Work done on time and within budget
- Comply with all relevant regulatory agencies
- Superior network server management
- 100% Satisfaction guarantee

FIGURE 1-20

Basic Services

Installation Services
- Location assessment
- Free estimates
- 50% off full installation
- Latest technology provided
- Guaranteed workmanship

Client Services
- 24-hr customer service
- 24-hr emergency service
- Complete documentation back-up services available

Independent Challenge 2

You have recently been promoted to sales manager at General Hardwood Industries, which sells and distributes specialty hardwood products used in flooring, cabinets, and furniture. Part of your job is to present company sales figures at a yearly sales meeting. Use the following information as the basis for units of wood sold nationally in your presentation: 501 units cherry, 429 units birch, 95 units hickory, 742 units mahogany, 182 units Brazilian walnut, 401 units American walnut, and 269 units pine. Assume that General Hardwood has five sales regions throughout the country: Pacific Northwest, West, South, Midwest, and Northeast. Also, assume the sales in each region rose between 1.2% and 3.6% over last year, and gross sales reached $31 million. The presentation should have at least five slides.

a. Spend some time planning the slides of your presentation. What is the best way to show the information provided? What other information could you add that might be useful for this presentation?

b. Start PowerPoint.

c. Give the presentation an appropriate title on the title slide, and enter today's date and your name in the subtitle placeholder.

d. Add slides and enter appropriate slide text.

e. On the last slide of the presentation, include the following information:
General Hardwood Industries
"Your specialty hardwood store"

FIGURE 1-21

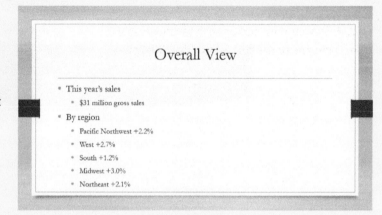

f. Apply a design theme. A typical slide might look like the one shown in FIGURE 1-21.

g. Switch views. Run through the slide show at least once.

h. Save your presentation with the filename **PPT 1-General** where you store your Data Files.

i. Close the presentation and exit PowerPoint.

Independent Challenge 3

You work for Janic Corporation, an international trade company that distributes products made in the Midwest. The marketing manager has asked you to plan and create a PowerPoint presentation that describes the primary products Janic exports and the top 3 importing countries; Saudi Arabia, Mexico, and Japan. Describe the top exports, which include tractors, fresh and frozen pork meat, soybeans, corn, and aircraft engine parts. Use the Internet, if possible, to research information that will help you formulate your ideas. The presentation should have at least five slides.

a. Spend some time planning the slides of your presentation.

b. Start PowerPoint then open a new blank presentation.

c. Give the presentation an appropriate title on the title slide, and enter today's date and your name in the subtitle placeholder.

d. Add slides and enter appropriate slide text.

e. On the last slide of the presentation, type the following information:
Janic Corp.
Est. 1948
Headquarters: Independence, MO

f. Apply a design theme.

g. Switch views. Run through the slide show at least once.

h. Save your presentation with the filename **PPT 1-Janic** to the location where you store your Data Files.

i. Close the presentation and exit PowerPoint.

Independent Challenge 4: Explore

You are a member of the Chattanooga Service Organization (CSO), a non profit organization in Chattanooga, TN. This organization raises money throughout the year to support community needs such as schools, youth organizations, and other worthy causes. This year CSO has decided to support the Penhale Youth Center by hosting a regional barbeque cook-off, called the Ultimate BBQ Cook-Off. The competition includes over 20 cooking teams from a five-state region. Create a presentation that describes the event.

a. Spend some time planning the slides of your presentation. Assume the following: the competition is a 2-day event; event advertising will be multistate wide; musical groups will be invited; there will be events and games for kids; the event will be held at the county fairgrounds. Use the Internet, if possible, to research information that will help you formulate your ideas.

b. Start PowerPoint then open a new blank presentation.

c. Give the presentation an appropriate title on the title slide, and enter your name and today's date in the subtitle placeholder.

d. Add slides and enter appropriate slide text. You must create at least three slides.

e. Apply a Design Theme. Typical slides might look like the ones shown in FIGURE 1-22 and FIGURE 1-23.

f. View the presentation.

g. Save your presentation with the filename **PPT 1-CSO** to the location where you store your Data Files.

h. Close the presentation and exit PowerPoint.

FIGURE 1-22

FIGURE 1-23

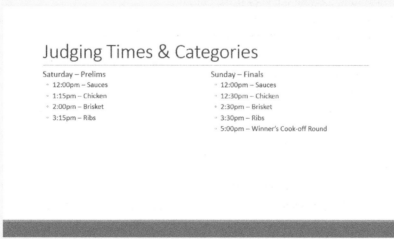

Visual Workshop

Create the presentation shown in FIGURE 1-24 and FIGURE 1-25. Make sure you include your name on the title slide. Save the presentation as **PPT 1-Neptune** to the location where you store your Data Files. Print the slides.

FIGURE 1-24

NEPTUNE INDUSTRIES | Your Name
Senior Project Manager

FIGURE 1-25

PRODUCT OVERVIEW

Product designation: Genford XDS-2000
- Turf reduction device
- Primary guidance system: global positioning system

Systems tested
- Integrated on-board computer system
- Engine and hydraulics
- Turf reduction components
- Obstacle detection system

Modifying a Presentation

CASE ▶ You continue working on your Kenya Africa projects presentation. In this module, you'll enter text using Outline view, then you'll format text, create a SmartArt graphic, draw and modify objects, and add slide footer information in the presentation.

Module Objectives

After completing this module, you will be able to:

- Enter text in Outline view
- Format text
- Convert text to SmartArt
- Insert and modify shapes

- Rearrange and merge shapes
- Edit and duplicate shapes
- Align and group objects
- Add slide footers

Files You Will Need

PPT 2-1.pptx   PPT 2-4.pptx

PPT 2-2.pptx   PPT 2-5.pptx

PPT 2-3.pptx

Enter Text in Outline View

Learning
Outcomes
• Enter text in
Outline view
• Create a new slide

You can enter presentation text by typing directly on the slide in the Slide pane, or, if you need to focus on the text of the presentation, you can enter text in Outline view. Text in Outline view is organized so the headings, or slide titles, appear at the top of the outline. Each subpoint, or each line of bulleted text, appears as one or more indented lines under the title. Each indent in the outline creates another level of bulleted text on the slide. **CASE** *You switch to Outline view to enter text for two more slides for your presentation.*

STEPS

1. **Start PowerPoint, open the presentation** PPT 2-1.pptx **from the location where you store your Data Files, then save it as** PPT 2-R2G.pptx

   A presentation with the new name appears in the PowerPoint window.

2. **Click the** Slide 2 thumbnail **in the Slides tab, click the** New Slide button list arrow **in the Slides group, then click** Title and Content

   A new slide, Slide 3, with the Title and Content layout appears as the current slide below Slide 2.

3. **Click the** View tab **on the Ribbon, then click the** Outline View button **in the Presentation Views group**

   The text of the presentation appears in the Outline pane next to the Slide pane. The slide icon and the insertion point for Slide 3 are highlighted, indicating it is selected and ready to accept text. Text that you enter next to a slide icon becomes the title for that slide.

4. **Type** Water: The Strategic Commodity, **press [Enter], then press [Tab]**

   When you pressed [Enter] after typing the slide title, you created a new slide. However, because you want to enter bulleted text on Slide 3, you then pressed [Tab] so the text you type will be entered as bullet text on Slide 3. See FIGURE 2-1.

5. **Type** Economic efficiency, **press [Enter], type** Social fairness, **press [Enter], type** Sustainability, **press [Enter], type** Population demands, **then press [Enter]**

   Each time you press [Enter], the insertion point moves down one line.

6. **Press** [Shift][Tab]

   Because you are working in Outline view, a new slide with the same layout, Slide 4, is created when you press [Shift][Tab].

7. **Type** Water: Developmental Essentials, **press [Ctrl][Enter], type** Household water safety, **press [Enter], type** Catchment area, **press [Enter], type** Water quality, **press [Enter], then type** Conflict resolution

   Pressing [Ctrl][Enter] while the insertion point is in the title text object moves the cursor into the content placeholder.

8. **Position the pointer on the** Slide 3 icon ⬜ **in the Outline pane**

   The pointer changes to ✛. The Water: The Strategic Commodity slide, Slide 3, is out of order.

9. **Drag** ⬜ **down until a horizontal indicator line appears above the Slide 5 icon, then release the mouse button**

   The third slide moves down and switches places with the fourth slide, as shown in FIGURE 2-2.

10. **Click the** Normal button ▣ **on the status bar, then save your work**

    The Outline pane closes, and the Slides tab is now visible in the window.

FIGURE 2-1: Outline view showing new slide

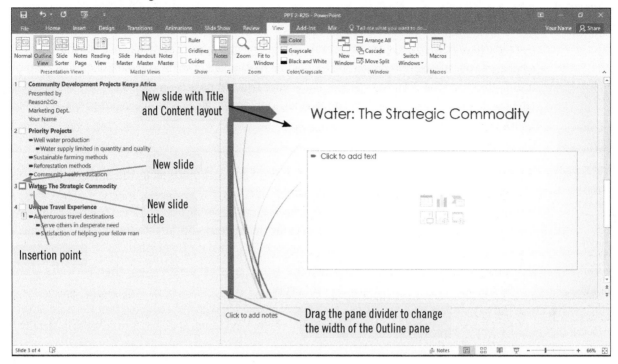

FIGURE 2-2: Outline view showing moved slide

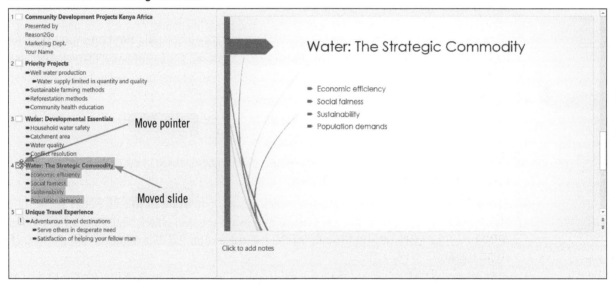

Using proofing tools for other languages

If you have a presentation in another language, how would you check the spelling and grammar of that presentation? Every version of PowerPoint contains a language pack with a primary language, such as English, Italian, or Arabic. Each language pack includes additional languages other than the primary language. For example, the English language pack also includes French and Spanish. So, let's say you have an English version of PowerPoint and you want to check the spelling of a presentation that is written in French. To check the spelling of a French presentation, click a text object on a slide, click the Review tab on the Ribbon, click the Language button in the Language group, then click Set Proofing Language to open the Language dialog box. Click one of the French options from the list, then click OK. Only languages in the list with a spelling symbol are available to use for checking spelling and grammar. Now when you check the spelling, PowerPoint will do so in French. If your version of PowerPoint does not have the language you want to use, you can purchase additional language packs from Microsoft.

Format Text

Once you have entered and edited the text in your presentation, you can modify the way the text looks to emphasize your message. Important text should be highlighted in some way to distinguish it from other text or objects on the slide. For example, if you have two text objects on the same slide, you could draw attention to one text object by changing its color, font, or size. **CASE** ► *You decide to format the text on Slide 5 of the presentation.*

STEPS

QUICK TIP

To show or hide the Mini toolbar, click the File tab on the Ribbon, click Options, then click the Show Mini Toolbar on selection check box.

1. **Click the Home tab on the Ribbon, click the Slide 5 thumbnail in the Slides tab, then double-click Travel in the title text object**

    The word "Travel" is selected, and a Mini toolbar appears above the text. The **Mini toolbar** contains basic text-formatting commands, such as bold and italic, and appears when you select text using the mouse. This toolbar makes it quick and easy to format text, especially when the Home tab is closed.

2. **Move** ⌖ **over the Mini toolbar, click the Font Color list arrow** 🅰▾, **then click the Dark Red color box in the Standard Colors row**

    The text changes color to dark red, as shown in FIGURE 2-3. When you click the Font Color list arrow, the Font Color gallery appears showing the Theme Colors and Standard Colors. ScreenTips help identify font colors. Notice that the Font Color button on the Mini toolbar and the Font Color button in the Font group on the Home tab change color to reflect the new color choice, which is now the active color.

QUICK TIP

To select an unse-lected text object, press [Shift], click the text object, then release [Shift].

3. **Move the pointer over the title text object border until the pointer changes to** ⬍, **then click the border**

    The border changes from a dashed to a solid line as you move the pointer over the text object border. The entire title text object is selected, and changes you make now affect all of the text in the text object. When the whole text object is selected, you can change its size, shape, and other attributes. Changing the color of the text helps emphasize it.

4. **Click the Font Color button** 🅰▾ **in the Font group**

    All of the text in the title text object changes to the current active color, dark red.

QUICK TIP

For more text for-matting options, right-click a text object, then click Format Text Effects to open the Format Shape - Text Options pane.

5. **Click the Font list arrow in the Font group**

    A list of available fonts opens with Century Gothic, the current font used in the title text object, selected at the top of the list in the Theme Fonts section.

6. **Scroll down the alphabetical list, then click Goudy Old Style in the All Fonts section**

    The Goudy Old Style font replaces the original font in the title text object. Notice that as you move the pointer over the font names in the font list the selected text on the slide displays a Live Preview of the available fonts.

7. **Click the Underline button** 🅄 **in the Font group, then click the Increase Font Size button** 🄰ˆ **in the Font group**

    All of the text now displays an underline and increases in size to 40.

8. **Click the Character Spacing button** 🄰⅄▾ **in the Font group, then click Tight**

    The spacing between the letters in the title decreases. Compare your screen to FIGURE 2-4.

9. **Click a blank area of the slide outside the text object to deselect it, then save your work**

    Clicking a blank area of the slide deselects all objects that are selected.

FIGURE 2-3: Selected word with Mini toolbar open

FIGURE 2-4: Formatted text

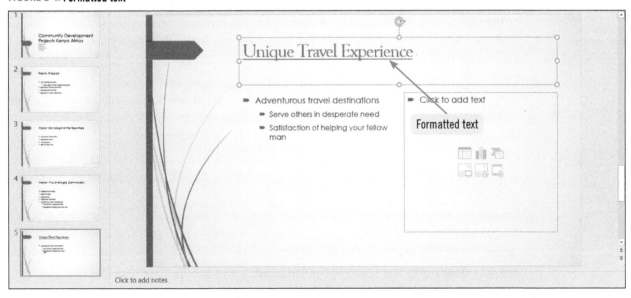

Replacing text and fonts

As you review your presentation, you may decide to replace certain text or fonts throughout the entire presentation using the Replace command. Text can be a word, phrase, or sentence. To replace specific text, click the Home tab on the Ribbon, then click the Replace button in the Editing group. In the Replace dialog box, enter the text you want to replace, then enter the text you want to use as its replacement. You can also use the Replace command to replace one font for another. Simply click the Replace button list arrow in the Editing group, then click Replace Fonts to open the Replace Font dialog box.

Convert Text to SmartArt

Learning
Outcomes
• Create a SmartArt
  graphic
• Modify the
  SmartArt design

Sometimes when you are working with text it just doesn't capture your attention. The ability to convert text to a SmartArt graphic provides a creative way to convey a message using text and graphics. A **SmartArt** graphic is a professional-quality diagram that graphically illustrates text. For example, you can show steps in a process or timeline, show proportional relationships, or show how parts relate to a whole. You can create a SmartArt graphic from scratch or create one by converting existing text you have entered on a slide. **CASE** ▶ *You want the presentation to appear visually dynamic, so you convert the text on Slide 3 to a SmartArt graphic.*

STEPS

1. **Click the** Slide 3 thumbnail **in the Slides tab, click** Household **in the text object, then click the** Convert to SmartArt Graphic button **in the Paragraph group**

   A gallery of SmartArt graphic layouts opens. As with many features in PowerPoint, you can preview how your text will look prior to applying the SmartArt graphic layout by using PowerPoint's Live Preview feature. You can review each SmartArt graphic layout and see how it changes the appearance of the text.

2. **Move** ▷ **over the** SmartArt graphic layouts **in the gallery**

   Notice how the text becomes part of the graphic and the color and font changes each time you move the pointer over a different graphic layout. SmartArt graphic names appear in ScreenTips.

TROUBLE
If the Text pane is not open as shown in Figure 2-5, click the Text pane control on the SmartArt graphic.

3. **Click the** Basic Process layout **in the SmartArt graphics gallery**

   A SmartArt graphic appears on the slide in place of the text object, and the SmartArt Tools Design tab opens on the Ribbon, as shown in FIGURE 2-5. A SmartArt graphic consists of two parts: the SmartArt graphic and a Text pane where you type and edit text. This graphic also has placeholders where you can add pictures to the SmartArt graphic.

4. **Click each** bullet point **in the Text pane, then click the** Text pane control button ▷

   Notice that each time you select a bullet point in the text pane, a selection box appears around the text objects in the SmartArt graphic. The Text pane control opens and closes the Text pane. You can also open and close the Text pane using the Text Pane button in the Create Graphic group.

QUICK TIP
Text objects in the SmartArt graphic can be moved and edited like any other text object in PowerPoint.

5. **Click the** More button ▼ **in the Layouts group, click** More Layouts **to open the Choose a SmartArt Graphic dialog box, click** Matrix, **click the** Basic Matrix layout icon, **then click** OK

   The SmartArt graphic changes to the new graphic layout. You can change how the SmartArt graphic looks by applying a SmartArt Style. A **SmartArt Style** is a preset combination of simple and 3-D formatting options that follows the presentation theme.

6. **Move** ▷ **slowly over the styles in the SmartArt Styles group, then click the** More button ▼ **in the SmartArt Styles group**

   A Live Preview of each style is displayed on the SmartArt graphic. The SmartArt styles are organized into sections; the top group offers suggestions for the best match for the document, and the bottom group shows you all of the possible 3-D styles that are available.

QUICK TIP
Click the Convert button in the Reset group, then click Convert to Text to revert the SmartArt graphic to a standard text object.

7. **Move** ▷ **over the styles in the gallery, click** Intense Effect **in the Best Match for Document section, then click in a blank area of the slide outside the SmartArt graphic**

   Notice how this new style adds a shadow to each object to achieve a dimensional effect. Compare your screen to FIGURE 2-6.

8. **Click the** Slide 4 thumbnail **in the Slides tab, then save your work**

   Slide 4 appears in the Slide pane.

FIGURE 2-5: **Text converted to a SmartArt graphic**

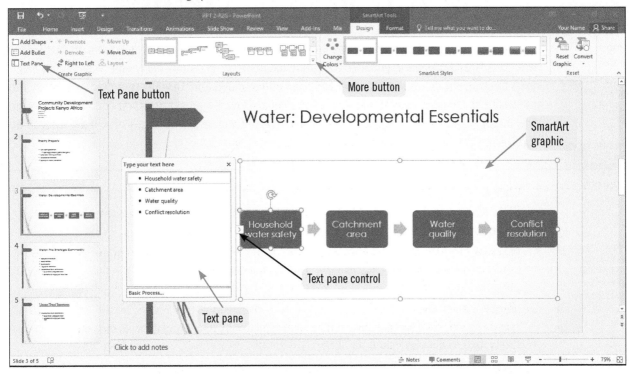

FIGURE 2-6: **Final SmartArt graphic**

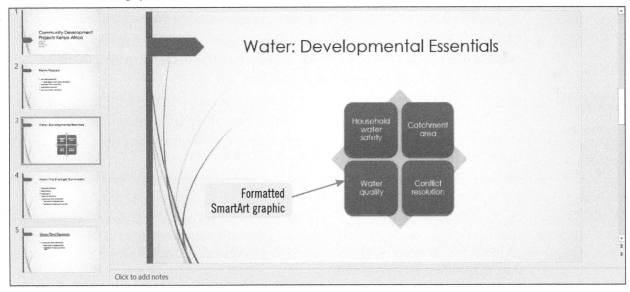

Choosing SmartArt graphics

When choosing a SmartArt graphic to use on your slide, remember that you want the SmartArt graphic to communicate the message of the text effectively; not every SmartArt graphic layout achieves that goal. You must consider the type of text you want to illustrate. For example, does the text show steps in a process, does it show a continual process, or does it show nonsequential information? The answer to this question will dictate the type of SmartArt graphic layout you should choose. Also, the amount of text you want to illustrate will have an effect on the SmartArt graphic layout you choose. Most of the time key points will be the text you use in a SmartArt graphic. Finally, some SmartArt graphic layouts are limited by the number of shapes they can accommodate, so be sure to choose a graphic layout that can illustrate your text appropriately. Experiment with the SmartArt graphic layouts until you find the right one, and have fun in the process!

Insert and Modify Shapes

Learning Outcomes
- Create a shape
- Modify a shape's style

In PowerPoint you can insert many different types of shapes including lines, geometric figures, arrows, stars, callouts, and banners to enhance your presentation. You can modify many aspects of a shape including its fill color, line color, and line style, as well as add shadows and 3-D effects. A quick way to alter the appearance of a shape is to apply a Quick Style. A **Quick Style** is a set of formatting options, including line style, fill color, and effects. **CASE** *You decide to draw some shapes on Slide 4 of your presentation that identify strategies for increasing water supply.*

STEPS

1. **Click the** More button **in the Drawing group, click the** Diamond button **in the Basic Shapes section, then position ╋ in the blank area of Slide 4 below the slide title**
   ScreenTips help you identify the shapes.

2. **Press and hold** [Shift], **drag ╋ down and to the right to create the shape, as shown in** FIGURE 2-7, **release the mouse button, then release** [Shift]
   A diamond shape appears on the slide, filled with the default theme color. Pressing [Shift] while you create the object maintains the object proportions as you change its size. A **rotate handle**—circular arrow—appears on top of the shape, which you can drag to manually rotate the shape. To change the style of the shape, apply a Quick Style from the Shape Styles group.

3. **Click the** Drawing Tools Format tab **on the Ribbon, click the** **in the Shape Styles group, move ╳ over the styles in the gallery to review the effects on the shape, then click** Moderate Effect - Orange, Accent 2
   An orange Quick Style with coordinated gradient fill, line, and shadow color is applied to the shape.

4. **Click the** Shape Outline list arrow **in the Shape Styles group, point to** Weight, **move ╳ over the line weight options to review the effect on the shape, then click** 4½ pt
   The outline weight (or width) increases and is easier to see now.

5. **Click the** Shape Effects button **in the Shape Styles group, point to** Preset, **move ╳ over the effect options to review the effect on the shape, then click** Preset 7
   Lighting and shadow effects are added to the shape to give it a three-dimensional appearance. It is easy to change the shape to any other shape in the shapes gallery.

6. **Click the** Edit Shape button **in the Insert Shapes group, point to** Change Shape **to open the shapes gallery, then click the** Teardrop button **in the Basic Shapes section**
   The diamond shape changes to a teardrop shape and a yellow circle—called an **adjustment handle**—appears in the upper-right corner of the shape. Some shapes have an adjustment handle that can be moved to change the most prominent feature of an object, in this case the end of the teardrop. You can rotate the shape to make the shape look different.

7. **Click the** Rotate button **in the Arrange group, move ╳ over the** rotation options **to review the effect on the shape, then click** Flip Horizontal
   Notice that the adjustment handle is now on the top left of the shape, indicating that the shape has flipped horizontally, or rotated 180 degrees, as shown in FIGURE 2-8. You prefer the diamond shape, and you decide the shape looks better rotated back the way it was before.

8. **Click the** Undo button list arrow **in the Quick Access Toolbar, click** Change Shape, **click a blank area of the slide, then save your work**
   The last two commands you performed are undone, and the shape changes back to a diamond and is flipped back to its original position. Clicking a blank area of the slide deselects all selected objects.

FIGURE 2-7: Diamond shape added to slide

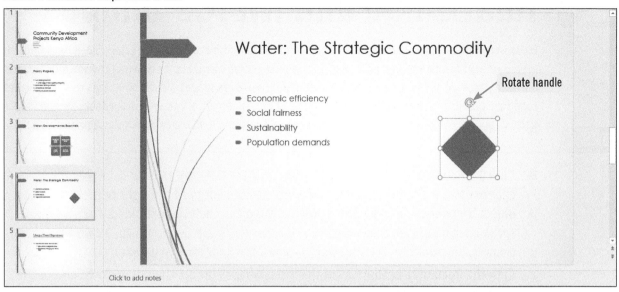

FIGURE 2-8: Rotated teardrop shape

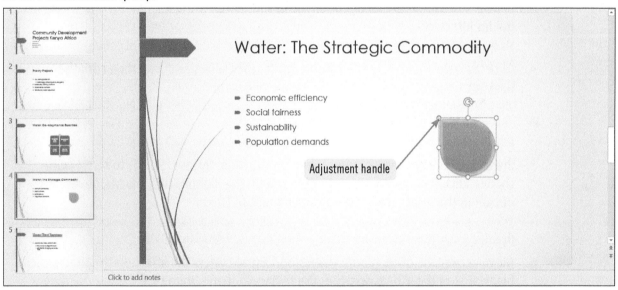

Using the Eyedropper to match colors

As you develop your presentation and work with different shapes and pictures, sometimes from other sources, there may be a certain color that is not in the theme colors of the presentation that you want to capture and apply to objects in your presentation. To capture a color on a specific slide, select any object on the slide, click any button list arrow with a color feature, such as the Shape Fill button or the Shape Outline button on the Drawing Tools Format tab, then click Eyedropper. Move the 🖊 over the color you want to capture and pause, or hover. As you hover over a color, a Live Preview of the color appears and the RGB (Red Green Blue) values, called coordinates, appear in a ScreenTip. Click when you see the color you want to capture. The new color now appears in any color gallery under Recent Colors. If you decide not to capture a new color, press [Esc] to close the Eyedropper without making any change.

Rearrange and Merge Shapes

Learning
Outcomes
• Reorder shapes
• Combine shapes
  together

STEPS

Every object on a slide is placed, or stacked, on the slide in the order it was created, like a deck of cards placed one on top of another. Each object on a slide can be moved up or down in the stack depending on how you want the objects to look on the slide. **Merging** shapes, which combines multiple shapes together, provides you the potential to create unique geometric shapes not available in the Shapes gallery. **CASE** *You create a rectangle shape on Slide 4 and then merge it with the diamond shape.*

1. **Click Economic in the text object, position ⬚ over the right-middle sizing handle, ⬚ changes to ↔, then drag the sizing handle to the left until the right border of the text object is under the middle of the word Strategic in the title text object**

   The width of the text object decreases. When you position ⬚ over a sizing handle, it changes to ↔. This pointer points in different directions depending on which sizing handle it is over.

2. **Click the Rectangle button ⬚ in the Insert Shapes group, then drag down and to the right to create the shape**

   Compare your screen to FIGURE 2-9. A rectangle shape appears on the slide, filled with the default theme color. You can move shapes by dragging them on the slide.

3. **Drag the rectangle shape over the diamond shape, then use the Smart Guides that appear to position the rectangle shape in the center of the diamond shape where the guides intersect**

   Smart Guides help you position objects relative to each other and determine equal distances between objects.

4. **Click the Select button in the Editing group, click Selection Pane, then click the Send Backward button ▼ in the Selection pane once**

   The Selection pane opens on the right side of the window showing the four objects on the slide and the order they are stacked on the slide. The Send Backward and Bring Forward buttons let you change the stacking order. The rectangle shape moves back one position in the stack behind the diamond shape.

5. **Press [SHIFT], click the diamond shape on the slide, release [SHIFT] to select both shapes, click the Drawing Tools Format tab on the Ribbon, click the Merge Shapes button in the Insert Shapes group, then point to Union**

   The two shapes appear to merge, or combine, together to form one shape. The merged shape assumes the theme and formatting style of the rectangle shape because it was selected first.

6. **Move ⬚ over the other merge shapes options to review the effect on the shape, click a blank area of the slide twice, click the rectangle shape, then click the Bring Forward button in the Arrange group on the Drawing Tools Format tab once**

   Each merge option produces a different result. The rectangle shape moves back to the top of the stack. Now, you want to see what happens when you select the diamond shape first before you merge the two shapes together.

7. **Click the diamond shape, press [SHIFT], click the rectangle shape, release [SHIFT], click the Merge Shapes button in the Insert Shapes group, then point to Union**

   The merged shape adopts the theme and formatting style of the diamond shape.

8. **Point to each of the merge shapes options, then click Subtract**

   The two shapes merge into one shape. This merge option deletes the area of all shapes from the first shape you selected, so in this case the area of the rectangle shape is deleted from the diamond shape. The merged shape is identified as Freeform 5 in the Selection pane. See FIGURE 2-10.

9. **Click the Selection Pane button in the Arrange group, click a blank area of the slide, then save your work**

FIGURE 2-9: Rectangle shape added to slide

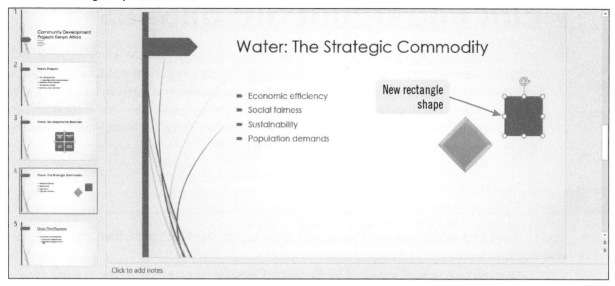

FIGURE 2-10: New Merged shape

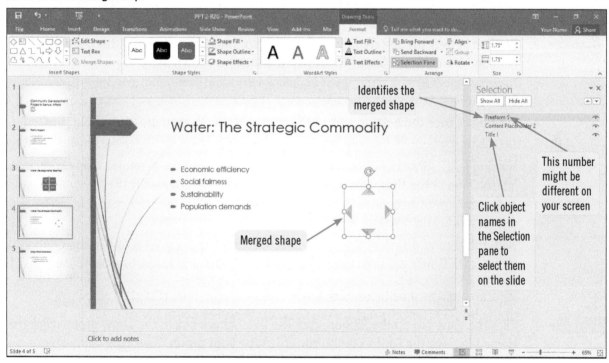

Changing the size and position of shapes

Usually when you resize a shape you can simply drag one of the sizing handles around the outside of the shape, but sometimes you may need to resize a shape more precisely. When you select a shape, the Drawing Tools Format tab appears on the Ribbon, offering you many different formatting options including some sizing commands located in the Size group. The Width and Height commands in the Size group allow you to change the width and height of a shape. You also have the option to open the Format Shape pane, which allows you to change the size of a shape, as well as the rotation, scale, and position of a shape on the slide.

Edit and Duplicate Shapes

Learning Outcomes
• Modify shape, size, and design
• Duplicate shapes

Once you have created a shape you still have the ability to refine its basic characteristics, which helps change the size and appearance of the shape. For example, if you create a shape and it is too large, you can reduce its size by dragging any of its sizing handles. Most PowerPoint shapes can have text attached to them. All shapes can be moved and copied. To help you resize and move shapes and other objects precisely, PowerPoint has rulers you can add to the Slide pane. Rulers display the measurement system your computer uses, either inches or metric measurements. **CASE** ▶ *You want three identical diamond shapes on Slide 4. You first add the ruler to the slide to help you change the size of the diamond shape you've already created, and then you make copies of it.*

STEPS

1. **Right-click a blank area of Slide 4, click** Ruler **on the shortcut menu, then click the bottom part of the** diamond shape **to select it**

   Rulers appear on the left and top of the Slide pane. Unless the ruler has been changed to metric measurements, it is divided into inches with half-inch and eighth-inch marks. Notice the current location of the ⌕ is identified on both rulers by a small dotted red line in the ruler.

2. **Drag the** middle left sizing handle **on the diamond shape to the left approximately ½",
then release the mouse button**

   The diamond shape is now slightly larger in diameter.

   QUICK TIP
   To display or hide gridlines, click the Gridlines check box in the Show group on the View tab.

3. **Position** ⌕ **over the selected** diamond shape **so that it changes to** ⌖, **then drag the** diamond shape **to the Smart Guides on the slide, as shown in** FIGURE 2-11

   PowerPoint uses a series of evenly spaced horizontal and vertical lines—called **gridlines**—to align objects, which force objects to "snap" to the grid.

4. **Position** ⌖ **over the bottom part of the** diamond shape, **then press and hold** [Ctrl]

   The pointer changes to ⌖, indicating that PowerPoint makes a copy of the shape when you drag the mouse.

5. **Holding** [Ctrl], **drag the** diamond shape **to the right until the diamond shape copy is in a blank area of the slide, release the mouse button, then release** [Ctrl]

   An identical copy of the diamond shape appears on the slide and Smart Guides appear above and below the shape as you drag the new shape to the right, which helps you align shapes.

6. **With the** second diamond shape **still selected, click the** Copy list arrow **in the Clipboard group, click** Duplicate, **then move the** duplicated diamond **shape to a blank area of the slide**

   You have duplicated the diamond shape twice and now have three identical shapes on the slide.

   QUICK TIP
   Press and hold [Alt] to temporarily turn the snap-to-grid feature off while dragging objects on the slide or dragging a sizing handle to make precise adjustments.

7. **Click the** View tab **on the Ribbon, click the** Ruler **check box in the Show group, click the** Home tab, **click the** Font Color button ▲ **in the Font group, then type** Rainwater Harvesting

   The ruler closes, and the text you type appears in the selected diamond shape and becomes a part of the shape. Now if you move or rotate the shape, the text moves with it. Compare your screen with FIGURE 2-12.

8. **Click the** left diamond shape, **click** ▲, **type** Salt Removal, **click the** right diamond shape, **click** ▲, **type** Continuous Water Use, **click in a blank area of the slide, then save your work**

   All three diamond shapes include text.

FIGURE 2-11: **Merged shape moved on slide**

FIGURE 2-12: **Duplicated shapes**

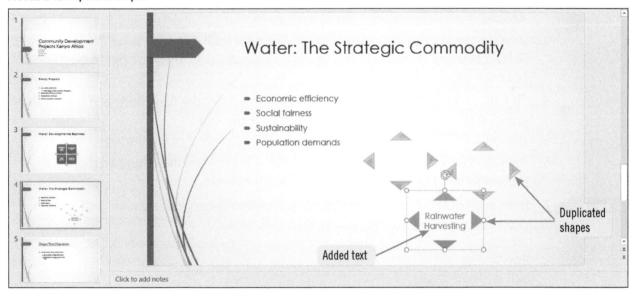

Editing points of a shape

If you want to customize the form (or outline) of any shape in the shapes gallery, you can modify its edit points. To display a shape's edit points, select the shape you want to modify, click the Drawing Tools Format tab on the Ribbon, click the Edit Shape button in the Insert Shapes group, then click Edit Points. Black edit points appear on the shape. To change the form of a shape, drag a black edit point. When you click a black edit point, white square edit points appear on either side of the black edit point, which allow you to change the curvature of a line between two black edit points. When you are finished with your custom shape, you can save it as picture and reuse it in other presentations or other files. To save the shape as a picture, right-click the shape, then click Save as Picture.

PowerPoint 2016

Align and Group Objects

Learning Outcomes
• Move shapes using guides
• Align and group shapes

After you are finished creating and modifying your objects, you can position them accurately on the slide to achieve the look you want. Using the Align commands in the Arrange group, you can align objects relative to each other by snapping them to the gridlines on a slide or to guides that you manually position on the slide. The Group command groups two or more objects into one object, which secures their relative position to each other and makes it easy to edit and move them. **CASE** ▸ *You are ready to position and group the diamond shapes on Slide 4 to finish the slide.*

STEPS

1. **Right-click a blank area of the slide, point to** Grid and Guides **on the shortcut menu, then click** Guides

   The guides appear as dotted lines on the slide and usually intersect at the center of the slide. Guides help you position objects precisely on the slide.

QUICK TIP
To quickly add a new guide to the slide, press [Ctrl], then drag an existing guide. The original guide remains in place. Drag a guide off the slide to delete it.

2. **Position** ⬚ **over the** horizontal guide **in a blank area of the slide, notice the pointer change to** ⥮, **press and hold the mouse button until the pointer changes to a measurement guide box, then drag the** guide **up until the guide position box reads** 1.33

3. **Drag the** vertical guide **to the left until the guide position box reads** .33, **then drag the** Salt Removal shape **so that the top and left edges of the shape touch the guides, as shown in** FIGURE 2-13

   The Salt Removal shape attaches or "snaps" to the guides.

4. **Drag the** Continuous Water Use shape **to the right until it touches a vertical Smart Guide, press and hold** [Shift], **click the** Salt Removal shape, **then release** [Shift]

   Two shapes are now selected.

5. **Click the** Drawing Tools Format tab **on the Ribbon, click the** Align button **in the Arrange group, click** Align Top, **then click a blank area of the slide**

   The right diamond shape moves up and aligns with the other shape along their top edges.

6. **Drag the** Rainwater Harvesting diamond shape **in between the other two shapes, as shown in** FIGURE 2-14

QUICK TIP
To set the formatting of a shape as the default, right-click the shape, then click Set as Default Shape on the Shortcut menu.

7. **Press and hold** [Shift], **click the other two** diamond shapes, **release** [Shift], **click the** Group button **in the Arrange group, then click** Group

   The shapes are now grouped together to form one object without losing their individual attributes. Notice that the sizing handles and rotate handle now appear on the outer edge of the grouped object, not around each individual object.

8. **Drag the** horizontal guide **to the middle of the slide until its guide position box reads** 0.00, **then drag the** vertical guide **to the middle of the slide until its guide position box reads** 0.00

9. **Click the** View tab **on the Ribbon, click the** Guides check box **in the Show group, click a blank area of the slide, then save your work**

   The guides are no longer displayed on the slide.

FIGURE 2-13: **Repositioned shape**

FIGURE 2-14: **Repositioned shapes**

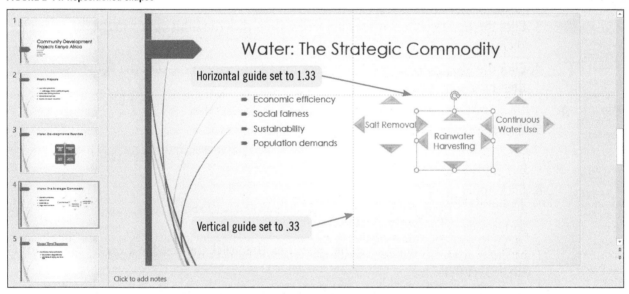

Distributing objects

There are two ways to distribute objects in PowerPoint: relative to each other and relative to the slide edge. If you choose to distribute objects relative to each other, PowerPoint evenly divides the empty space between all of the selected objects. When distributing objects in relation to the slide, PowerPoint evenly splits the empty space from slide edge to slide edge between the selected objects. To distribute objects relative to each other, click the Align button in the Arrange group on the Drawing Tools Format tab, then click Align Selected Objects. To distribute objects relative to the slide, click the Align button in the Arrange group on the Drawing Tools Format tab, then click Align to Slide.

Add Slide Footers

Learning Outcomes
• Add footer text to slides

Footer text, such as a company, school, or product name, the slide number, or the date, can give your slides a professional look and make it easier for your audience to follow your presentation. Slides do not have headers. However, notes or handouts can include both header and footer text. You can review footer information that you apply to the slides in the PowerPoint views and when you print the slides. Notes and handouts header and footer text is visible when you print notes pages, handouts, and the outline. **CASE** ▶ *You add footer text to the slides of the Kenya Africa presentation to make it easier for the audience to follow.*

STEPS

QUICK TIP
The placement of the footer text objects on the slide is dependent on the presentation theme.

1. **Click the** Insert tab **on the Ribbon, then click the** Header & Footer button **in the Text group**

   The Header and Footer dialog box opens, as shown in FIGURE 2-15. The Header and Footer dialog box has two tabs: a Slide tab and a Notes and Handouts tab. The Slide tab is selected. There are three types of footer text, Date and time, Slide number, and Footer. The bold rectangles in the Preview box identify the default position of the three types of footer text placeholders on the slides.

2. **Click the** Date and time check box **to select it**

   The date and time options are now available to select. The Update automatically date and time option button is selected by default. This option updates the date and time to the date and time set by your computer every time you open or print the file.

QUICK TIP
If you want a specific date to appear every time you view or print the presentation, click the Fixed date option button, then type the date in the Fixed text box.

3. **Click the** Update automatically list arrow, **then click the** third option **in the list**

   The month is spelled out in this option.

4. **Click the** Slide number check box, **click the** Footer check box, **click the** Footer text box, **then type your name**

   The Preview box now shows all three footer placeholders are selected.

5. **Click the** Don't show on title slide check box

   Selecting this check box prevents the footer information you entered in the Header and Footer dialog box from appearing on the title slide.

6. **Click** Apply to All

   The dialog box closes, and the footer information is applied to all of the slides in your presentation except the title slide. Compare your screen to FIGURE 2-16.

7. **Click the** Slide 1 thumbnail **in the Slides tab, then click the** Header & Footer button **in the Text group**

   The Header and Footer dialog box opens again.

8. **Click the** Don't show on title slide check box **to deselect it, click the** Footer check box, **then select the text in the Footer text box**

TROUBLE
If you click Apply to All in Step 9, click the Undo button on the Quick Access toolbar and repeat Steps 7, 8, and 9.

9. **Type** Striving Toward a Sustainable Future, **click** Apply, **then save your work**

   Only the text in the Footer text box appears on the title slide. Clicking Apply applies this footer information to just the current slide.

10. **Submit your presentation to your instructor, then exit PowerPoint**

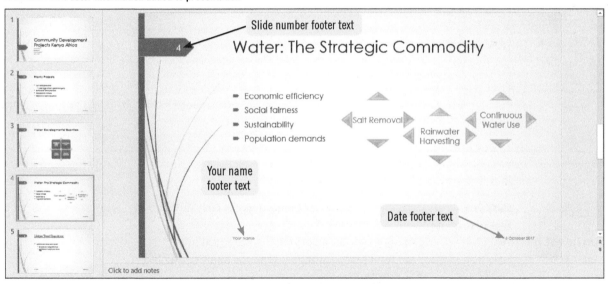

Creating superscript and subscript text

Superscript or subscript text is a number, figure, symbol, or letter that appears smaller than other text and is positioned above or below the normal line of text. A common superscript in the English language is the sign indicator next to number, such as 1st or 3rd. Other examples of superscripts are the trademark symbol^{TM} and the copyright symbol$^{©}$. To create superscript text in PowerPoint, select the text, number, or symbol, then press [CTRL] [SHIFT] [+] at the same time. Probably the most familiar subscript text are the numerals in chemical compounds and formulas, for example, H_2O and CO_2. To create subscript text, select the text, number, or symbol, then press [CTRL] [=] at the same time. To change superscript or subscript text back to normal text, select the text, then press [CTRL] [Spacebar].

Practice

Concepts Review

Label each element of the PowerPoint window shown in FIGURE 2-17.

FIGURE 2-17

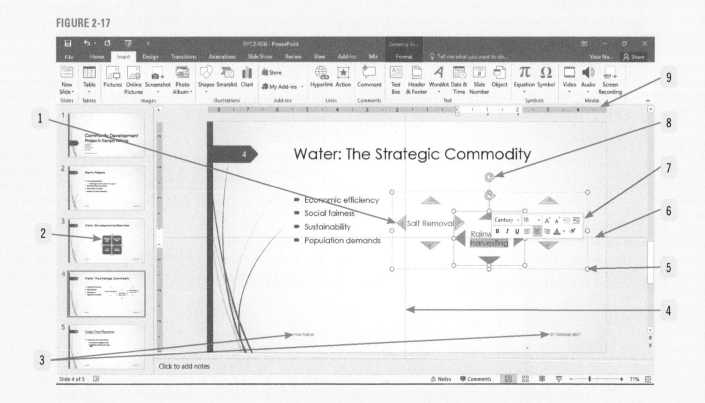

Match each term with the statement that best describes it.

10. **Adjustment handle**
11. **Quick Style**
12. **Rotate handle**
13. **Gridlines**
14. **Merge**
15. **Smart Guides**

a. Evenly spaced horizontal and vertical lines
b. A set of formatting options you apply to an object
c. Combines multiple shapes to create a unique geometric shape
d. Changes the most prominent feature of an object
e. Helps you determine equal distances between objects
f. Drag to turn an object

Select the best answer from the list of choices.

16. What is *not* true about grouped objects?
a. Grouped objects have one rotate handle.
b. Grouped objects act as one object but maintain their individual attributes.
c. Sizing handles appear around the grouped object.
d. Each object is distributed relative to the slide edges.

17. A professional-quality diagram that visually illustrates text best describes which of the following?
a. A SmartArt Style
b. A merged shape
c. A subscript
d. A SmartArt graphic

18. Which of the following statements is *not* true about Outline view?
a. Pressing [Enter] moves the insertion point down one line.
b. Text you enter next to the slide icon becomes a bullet point for that slide.
c. Headings are the same as slide titles.
d. Added slides use the same layout as the previous slide.

19. What do you have to drag to customize the form or outline of a shape?
a. Anchor points
b. Edit points
c. Slide edges
d. Shape area

20. Why would you use the Eyedropper tool?
a. To format an object with a new style
b. To soften the edges of a shape
c. To capture and apply a new color to an object
d. To change the fill color of an object

21. What appears just above text when it is selected?
a. Mini toolbar
b. QuickStyles
c. Adjustment handle
d. AutoFit Options button

22. Which of the following statements about merged shapes is *not* true?
a. Merged shapes can be added to the shapes gallery.
b. A merged shape assumes the theme of the shape that is selected first.
c. The stacking order of shapes changes the way a merged shape looks.
d. A merged shape is a combination of multiple shapes.

Skills Review

FIGURE 2-18

1. Enter text in Outline view.
a. Open the presentation PPT 2-2.pptx from the location where you store your Data Files, then save it as **PPT 2-Inverter**. The completed presentation is shown in FIGURE 2-18.
b. Create a new slide after Slide 2 with the Title and Content layout.
c. Open Outline view, then type **Diffusion Desalinization**.
d. Press [Enter], press [Tab], type **Main Feed**, press [Enter], type **Circulating Pump**, press [Enter], type **Primary Heaters**, press [Enter], then type **Diffusion Tower**.

Modifying a Presentation

Skills Review (continued)

   e. Move Slide 3 below Slide 4, then switch back to Normal view.

   f. Click the Home tab, then save your changes.

2. Format text.

   a. Go to Slide 1, select the name JJ Peterman, then move the pointer over the Mini Toolbar.

   b. Click the Font Color list arrow, then click Green under Standard Colors.

   c. Select the text object, then change all of the text to the color Green.

   d. Click the Font Size list arrow, click 24, then click the Italic button.

   e. Click the Character Spacing button, click Loose, then save your changes.

3. Convert text to SmartArt.

   a. Click the text object on Slide 4.

   b. Click the Convert to SmartArt Graphic button, then apply the Basic Matrix graphic layout to the text object.

   c. Click the More button in the Layouts group, click More Layouts, click Process in the Choose a SmartArt Graphic dialog box, click Accent Process, then click OK.

   d. Click the More button in the SmartArt Styles group, then apply the Intense Effect style from the Best Match for Document group to the graphic.

   e. Close the text pane if necessary, then click outside the SmartArt graphic in a blank part of the slide.

   f. Save your changes.

4. Insert and modify shapes.

   a. Go to Slide 3, then add rulers to the Slide pane.

   b. Click the More button in the Drawing group to open the Shapes gallery, click the Plus button in the Equation Shapes section, press [Shift], then draw a two-inch shape in a blank area of the slide.

   c. On the Drawing Tools Format tab, click the More button in the Shape Styles group, then click Colored Fill – Orange, Accent 3.

   d. Click the Shape Effects button, point to Shadow, then click Offset Diagonal Bottom Left.

FIGURE 2-19

   e. Click the Shape Outline list arrow, then click Black, Text 1, Lighter 15% in the Theme Colors section.

   f. Drag the Plus shape to the small open area in the middle of the diagram, adjust the shape if needed to make it fit in the space as shown in FIGURE 2-19, then save your changes.

5. Rearrange and merge shapes.

   a. Click the title text object on Slide 3, then drag the bottom-middle sizing handle up above the shapes.

   b. Click the More button in the Insert Shapes group, click the Hexagon button in the Basic Shapes section, press and hold [Shift], then draw a 1-inch shape.

   c. Drag the hexagon shape over top of the plus shape and center it, then open the Selection pane.

   d. Send the hexagon shape back one level, press [Shift], click the plus shape, then click the Merge Shapes button in the Insert Shapes group on the Drawing Tools Format tab.

   e. Point to each of the merge shapes options, click a blank area of the slide twice, then click the plus shape.

Skills Review (continued)

   f. Send the plus shape back one level, press [Shift], click the hexagon shape, click the Merge Shapes button, then click Combine.

   g. Close the Selection pane, then save your work.

6. Edit and duplicate shapes.

   a. Select the up-angled shape to the right of the merged shape, then using [Ctrl] make one copy of the shape.

   b. Use Smart Guides to align the new up-angled shape just to the right of the original shape.

   c. Click the Rotate button in the Arrange group, click Flip Vertical, click the Undo button, click the Rotate button, then click Flip Horizontal.

   d. Type **Bypass**, click the up-angled shape to the right of the merged shape, type **Water**, click the down-angled shape to the left of the merged shape, then type **Flow**.

   e. Click the Heat Source arrow shape above the merged shape, then drag the bottom-middle sizing handle down until the arrow touches the merged shape.

   f. Click a blank area of the slide, add the guides to the Slide pane, then save your changes.

7. Align and group objects.

   a. Move the vertical guide to the left until 3.42 appears, drag a selection box to select the five small purple triangle shapes at the bottom of the slide, then click the Drawing Tools Format tab.

   b. Click the Align button in the Arrange group, click Align Middle, click the Align button, then click Distribute Horizontally.

   c. Click the Rotate button in the Arrange group, click Rotate Left 90°, click the Group button in the Arrange group, then click Group.

   d. Move the grouped triangle shape object to the guide in the blank space on the down-angled shape to the left of the merged shape.

   e. Duplicate the grouped triangle shape object, then rotate the new object to the left 90°.

   f. Duplicate the rotated grouped triangle shape object, then move the two new triangle shape objects on the slide as shown in FIGURE 2-20.

   g. Set the guides back to 0.00, remove the guides from your screen, remove the rulers, then save your work.

FIGURE 2-20

8. Add slide footers.

   a. Open the Header and Footer dialog box.

   b. On the Slide tab, click the Date and time check box to select it, then click the Fixed option button.

   c. Add the slide number to the footer, then type your name in the Footer text box.

   d. Apply the footer to all of the slides except the title slide.

   e. Open the Header and Footer dialog box again, then click the Notes and Handouts tab.

   f. Click the Date and time check box, then type today's date in the Fixed text box.

   g. Type the name of your class in the Header text box, then click the Page number check box.

   h. Type your name in the Footer text box.

   i. Apply the header and footer information to all the notes and handouts, then save your changes.

   j. Submit your presentation to your instructor, close the presentation, then exit PowerPoint.

Independent Challenge 1

You are the director of the Center for the Arts in Rapid City, South Dakota, and one of your many duties is to raise funds to cover operation costs. One of the primary ways you do this is by speaking to businesses, community clubs, and other organizations throughout the region. Every year you speak to many organizations, where you give a short presentation detailing what the theater center plans to do for the coming season. You need to continue working on the presentation you started already.

a. Start PowerPoint, open the presentation PPT 2-3.pptx from the location where you store your Data Files, and save it as **PPT 2-Arts**.

b. Use Outline view to enter the following as bulleted text on the Commitment to Excellence slide:

Excellence
Testing
Study
Diligence

c. Apply the Ion design theme to the presentation.

d. Change the font color of each play name on Slide 3 to Gold, Accent 3.

e. Change the bulleted text on Slide 5 to the Trapezoid List SmartArt Graphic, then apply the Polished SmartArt style.

f. Add your name and slide number as a footer on the slides, then save your changes.

g. Submit your presentation to your instructor, close your presentation, then exit PowerPoint.

Independent Challenge 2

You are a manager for J Barrett Inc., a financial services company. You have been asked by your boss to develop a presentation outlining important details and aspects of the mortgage process to be used at a financial seminar.

a. Start PowerPoint, open the presentation PPT 2-4.pptx from the location where you store your Data Files, and save it as **PPT 2-Broker**.

b. Apply the Facet design theme to the presentation.

c. On Slide 3, press [Shift], select the three shapes, Banks, Mortgage Bankers, and Private Investors, release [Shift], then using the Align command align them to their left edges.

d. Select the blank shape, type **Borrower**, press [Shift], select the Mortgage Broker and Mortgage Bankers shapes, release [Shift], then using the Align command distribute them horizontally and align them to the middle.

e. Select all of the shapes, then apply Intense Effect – Orange, Accent 4 from the Shape Styles group.

f. Create a diamond shape, then merge it with the Borrower shape as shown in FIGURE 2-21. (*Hint*: Use the Fragment Merge option.)

g. Using the Arrow shape from the Shapes gallery, draw a 6-pt arrow between all of the shapes. (*Hint*: Draw one arrow shape, change the line weight using the Shape Outline list arrow, then duplicate the shape.)

h. Group all the shapes together.

i. Add the page number and your name as a footer on the notes and handouts, then save your changes.

j. Submit your presentation to your instructor, close your presentation, then exit PowerPoint.

FIGURE 2-21

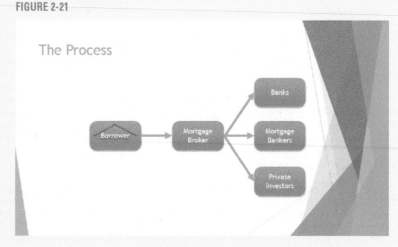

Independent Challenge 3

You are an independent distributor of natural foods in Birmingham, Alabama. Your business, Southern Whole Foods, has grown progressively since its inception 5 years ago, but sales have leveled off over the last 9 months. In an effort to increase your market share, you decide to purchase J&R Foods, a natural food dealer, which would allow your company to expand into surrounding states. Use PowerPoint to develop a presentation you can use to gain a financial backer for the acquisition. Create your own information for the presentation.

a. Start PowerPoint, create a new presentation, then apply the Wood Type design theme to the presentation.

b. Type **A Plan for Growth** as the main title on the title slide, and **Southern Whole Foods** as the subtitle.

c. Save the presentation as **PPT 2-Southern** to the location where you store your Data Files.

d. Add five more slides with the following titles: Slide 2, **Trends**; Slide 3, **Growth**; Slide 4, **Funding**; Slide 5, **History**; Slide 6, **Management Team**.

e. Enter appropriate text into the text placeholders of the slides. Use both the Slide pane and Outline view to enter text.

f. Convert text on one slide to a SmartArt graphic, then apply the SmartArt graphic style Inset Effect.

g. Create two shapes, format the shapes, then merge the shapes together.

h. View the presentation as a slide show, then view the slides in Slide Sorter view.

i. Add the slide number and your name as a footer on the slides, then save your changes.

j. Submit your presentation to your instructor, close your presentation, then exit PowerPoint.

Independent Challenge 4: Explore

Your computer instructor at Basset City College has been asked by the department head to convert her Computer Basics 101 course into an accelerated night course designed for adult students. Your instructor has asked you to help her create a presentation for the class that she can post on the Internet. Most of the basic text information is already on the slides, you primarily need to add a theme and other object formatting.

a. Start PowerPoint, open the presentation PPT 2-5.pptx from the location where you store your Data Files, and save it as **PPT 2-Basset**.

b. Add a new slide after the Course Facts slide with the same layout, type **Course Details** in the title text placeholder, then enter the following as bulleted text in Outline view:
   Information systems
   Networking
   Applied methods
   Technology solutions
   Software design
   Applications

c. Apply the Retrospect design theme to the presentation.

d. Select the title text object on Slide 1 (*Hint*: Press [Shift] to select the whole object), then change the text color to Orange.

e. Change the font of the title text object to Biondi, then decrease the font size to 48.

f. Click the subtitle text object on Slide 1, then change the character spacing to Very Loose.

g. Change the text on Slide 4 to a SmartArt graphic. Use an appropriate diagram type for a list.

h. Change the style of the SmartArt diagram using one of the SmartArt Styles, then view the presentation in Slide Show view.

i. Add the slide number and your name as a footer on the notes and handouts, then save your changes.

j. Submit your presentation to your instructor, close your presentation, then exit PowerPoint.

Visual Workshop

Create the presentation shown in FIGURE 2-22 and FIGURE 2-23. Add today's date as the date on the title slide. Save the presentation as **PPT 2-Nebraska Trade** to the location where you store your Data Files. (*Hint*: The SmartArt style used for the SmartArt is a 3D style.) Review your slides in Slide Show view, then add your name as a footer to the notes and handouts. Submit your presentation to your instructor, save your changes, close the presentation, then exit PowerPoint.

FIGURE 2-22

FIGURE 2-23

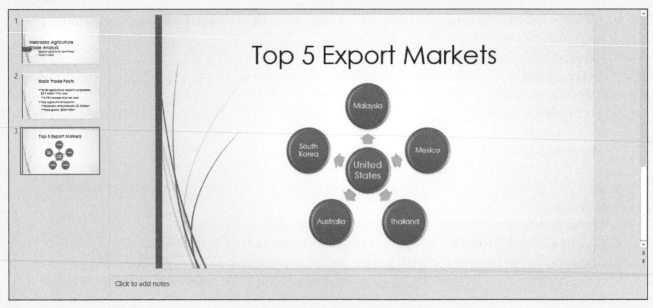

Inserting Objects into a Presentation

CASE ▶ In this module, you continue working on the presentation by inserting text from Microsoft Word. You also add visual elements into the presentation including a photograph, a table, and a chart. You format these objects using PowerPoint's powerful object-editing features.

Module Objectives

After completing this module, you will be able to:

- Insert text from Microsoft Word
- Insert and style a picture
- Insert a text box
- Insert a chart
- Enter and edit chart data
- Insert slides from other presentations
- Insert a table
- Insert and format WordArt

Files You Will Need

PPT 3-1.pptx	PPT 3-10.pptx
PPT 3-2.docx	PPT 3-11.pptx
PPT 3-3.jpg	PPT 3-12.jpg
PPT 3-4.pptx	PPT 3-13.pptx
PPT 3-5.pptx	PPT 3-14.docx
PPT 3-6.docx	PPT 3-15.jpg
PPT 3-7.jpg	PPT 3-16.jpg
PPT 3-8.pptx	PPT 3-17.jpg
PPT 3-9.pptx	PPT 3-18.jpg

Insert Text from Microsoft Word

Learning
Outcomes
• Create slides using
  Outline view
• Move and delete
  slides

It is easy to insert documents saved in Microsoft Word format (.docx), Rich Text Format (.rtf), plain text format (.txt), and HTML format (.htm) into a PowerPoint presentation. If you have an outline saved in a document file, you can import it into PowerPoint to create a new presentation or create additional slides in an existing presentation. When you import a document into a presentation, PowerPoint creates an outline structure based on the styles in the document. For example, a Heading 1 style in the Word document becomes a slide title and a Heading 2 style becomes the first level of text in a bulleted list. If you insert a plain text format document into a presentation, PowerPoint creates an outline based on the tabs at the beginning of the document's paragraphs. Paragraphs without tabs become slide titles, and paragraphs with one tab indent become first-level text in bulleted lists. **CASE** *You have a Microsoft Word document with information about the new Kenyan well project tour that you want to insert into your presentation.*

STEPS

QUICK TIP
While in Normal
view you can click
the Normal button
in the status bar to
go to Outline view.

1. **Start PowerPoint, open the presentation PPT 3-1.pptx from the location where you store your Data Files, save it as PPT 3-R2G, click the View tab on the Ribbon, then click the Outline View button in the Presentation Views group**

2. **Click the Slide 6 icon ▢ in the Outline pane, click the Home tab on the Ribbon, click the New Slide button list arrow in the Slides group, then click Slides from Outline**

   Slide 6 appears in the Slide pane. The Insert Outline dialog box opens. Before you insert an outline into a presentation, you need to determine where you want the new slides to be placed. You want the text from the Word document inserted as new slides after Slide 6.

3. **Navigate to the location where you store your Data Files, click the Word document file PPT 3-2.docx, then click Insert**

   Six new slides (7, 8, 9, 10, 11, and 12) are added to the presentation, and the new Slide 7 appears in the Slide pane. See FIGURE 3-1.

4. **Click the down scroll arrow ▼ in the Outline pane and read the text for all the new slides, then click the Normal button ▤ on the status bar**

   The information on Slides 7 and 12 refer to information not needed for this presentation.

5. **Click the Slide 7 thumbnail in the Slides tab, press [Ctrl], click the Slide 12 thumbnail, then click the Cut button in the Clipboard group**

   Slides 7 and 12 are deleted, and the next slide down (Suggested Itinerary) becomes the new Slide 10 and appears in the Slide pane.

6. **Drag the Slide 10 thumbnail in the Slides tab above Slide 8**

   Slide 10 becomes Slide 8. The inserted slides have a different slide layout and font style than the other slides. You want the text of the inserted outline to adopt the theme fonts of the presentation.

QUICK TIP
You can also use
Slide Sorter view to
move slides around
in the presentation.

7. **Click the Slide 7 thumbnail in the Slides tab, press [Shift], click the Slide 10 thumbnail, release [Shift], click the Reset button in the Slides group, click the Layout button in the Slides group, then click the Title and Content slide layout**

   The new slides now follow the presentation design and font themes. Compare your screen to FIGURE 3-2.

8. **Click the Save button ▤ on the Quick Access toolbar**

FIGURE 3-1: Outline pane showing imported text

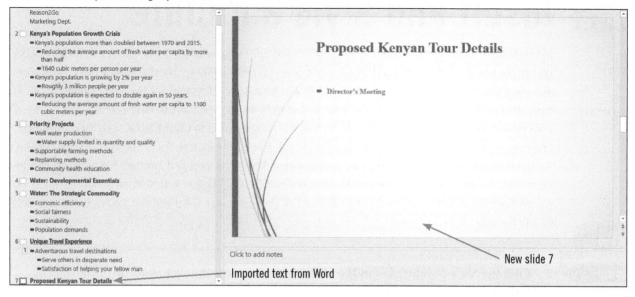

FIGURE 3-2: Slides reset to Wisp theme default settings

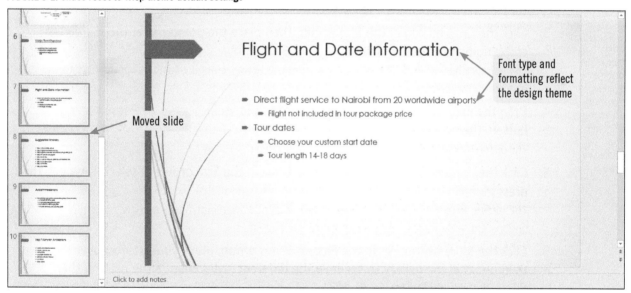

Sending a presentation using email

You can send a copy of a presentation over the Internet to a reviewer to edit and add comments. You can use Microsoft Outlook to send your presentation. Although your email program allows you to attach files, you can send a presentation using Outlook from within PowerPoint. Click the File tab, click Share, click Email in the center pane, then click Send as Attachment. Outlook opens and automatically creates an email with a copy of the presentation attached to it. You can also attach and send a PDF copy or an XPS copy of the presentation using your email program. Both of these file formats preserve document formatting, enable file sharing, and can be viewed online and printed.

Insert and Style a Picture

Learning
Outcomes
• Insert and format
a picture
• Resize and move a
picture

In PowerPoint, a **picture** is defined as a digital photograph, a piece of line art or clip art, or other artwork that is created in another program. PowerPoint gives you the ability to insert different types of pictures including JPEG File Interchange Format and BMP Windows Bitmap files into a PowerPoint presentation. As with all objects in PowerPoint, you can format and style inserted pictures to help them fit the theme of your presentation. You can also hide a portion of the picture you don't want to be seen by **cropping** it. The cropped portion of a picture is still available to you if you ever want to show that part of picture again. To reduce the size of the file you can permanently delete the cropped portion by applying picture compression settings in the Compress Pictures dialog box. **CASE** *In this lesson you insert a JPG file picture taken by an R2G staff member that is saved on your computer. Once inserted, you crop and style it to best fit the slide.*

STEPS

1. **Click the** Slide 6 thumbnail **in the Slides tab, then click the** Pictures icon 🖾 **in the content placeholder on the slide**

   The Insert Picture dialog box opens displaying the pictures available in the default Pictures folder.

2. **Navigate to location where you store your Data Files, select the picture file** PPT 3-3.jpg, **then click** Insert

   The picture fills the content placeholder on the slide, and the Picture Tools Format tab opens on the Ribbon. The picture would look better if you cropped some of the image.

3. **Click the** Crop button **in the Size group, then place the pointer over the** middle-left cropping handle **on the picture**

   The pointer changes to ⊣. When the Crop button is active, cropping handles appear next to the sizing handles on the selected object.

4. **Drag the** middle of the picture **to the right as shown in** FIGURE 3-3, **release the mouse button, then press** [Esc]

   The picture would look better on the slide if it were larger.

5. **Click the** number (3.08) **in the Width text box in the Size group to select it, type** 4, **then press** [Enter]

   The picture height and width increase proportionally. PowerPoint has a number of picture formatting options, and you decide to experiment with some of them.

6. **Click the** More button ⯆ **in the Picture Styles group, move your pointer over the** style thumbnails **in the gallery to see how the different styles change the picture, then click** Bevel Rectangle **(3rd row)**

   The picture now has rounded corners and a background shadow.

7. **Click the** Corrections button **in the Adjust group, move your pointer over the** thumbnails **to see how the picture changes, then click** Sharpen: 25% **in the Sharpen/Soften section**

   The picture clarity is better.

8. **Click the** Artistic Effects button **in the Adjust group, move your pointer over the** thumbnails **to see how the picture changes, then click a blank area of the slide**

   The artistic effects are all interesting, but none of them will work well for this picture.

9. **Drag the** picture **to the center of the blank area of the slide to the right of the text object, click a blank area on the slide, then save your changes**

   Compare your screen to FIGURE 3-4.

FIGURE 3-3: Using the cropping pointer to crop a picture

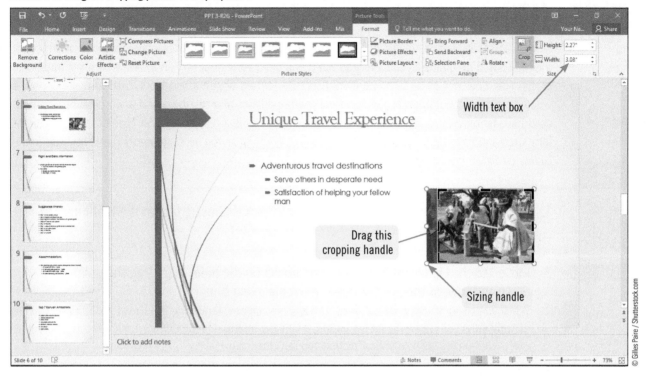

FIGURE 3-4: Cropped and styled picture

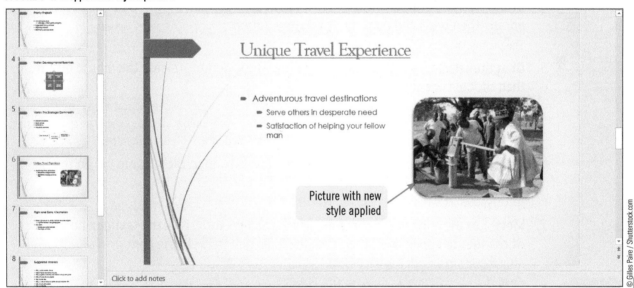

Inserting a screen recording

Using the Screen Recording button in the Media group on the Insert tab, you can record your computer screen with audio and insert the recording to a slide. For example, if you want to make a recording of an Internet video, locate and display the video on your computer screen. In PowerPoint on the slide where you want to insert the recording, click the Screen Recording button. On the toolbar, click the Select Area button, drag a selection box around the video, click the Audio button if necessary, then click the Record button on the toolbar. Click the video play button. When finished recording, click Windows Logo+[Shift]+Q to stop recording. PowerPoint opens and the recording appears on your slide. Click the Play button to review your recording.

PowerPoint 2016

Insert a Text Box

As you've already learned, you enter text on a slide using a title or content placeholder that is arranged on the slide based on a slide layout. Every so often you need additional text on a slide where the traditional placeholder does not place text. There are two types of text boxes: a text label, used for a small phrase where text doesn't automatically wrap inside the boundaries of a text box, and a word-processing box, used for a sentence or paragraph where the text wraps inside a text box. Either type of text box can be formatted and edited just like any other text object. **CASE** *You decide to create a text box next to the picture on Slide 6 and then edit and format the text.*

STEPS

1. **Click the** Slide 6 thumbnail **in the Slides tab, click the** Insert tab **on the Ribbon, then click the** Text Box button **in the Text group**

   The pointer changes to ↓.

2. **Move** ↓ **to the blank area below the text object on the slide, then drag the pointer** + **down and toward the right about 3" to create a text box**

   When you begin dragging, an outline of the text box appears, indicating the size of the text box you are drawing. After you release the mouse button, a blinking insertion point appears inside the text box, in this case a word-processing box, indicating that you can enter text.

3. **Type** Village chief in March 2017 inaugurates new hand pump

   Notice the text box increases in size as your text wraps to additional lines inside the text box. Your screen should look similar to FIGURE 3-5. After entering the text, you decide to edit the sentence.

4. **Drag** I **over the phrase** in March 2017 **to select it, position** ▷ **on top of the selected phrase, then press and hold the** left mouse button

   The pointer changes to ▷.

5. **Drag the selected words to the right of the word "pump", release the mouse button, then click outside the text box**

   A grey insertion line appears as you drag, indicating where PowerPoint places the text when you release the mouse button. The phrase "in March 2017" moves after the word "pump". Notice there is no space between the words "pump" and "in" and the spelling error is identified by a red wavy underline.

6. **Right-click the** red underlined words **in the text box, then click "pump in" on the shortcut menu**

   Space is added between the two words in the text box.

7. **Move** I **to the edge of the text box, which changes to** ⬚, **click the** text box border **(it changes to a solid line), then click the** Italic button *I* **in the Font group**

   All of the text in the text box is italicized.

8. **Click the** Shape Fill list arrow **in the Drawing group, click the** Light Green, Background 2, Darker 10% color box, **click the** Shape Outline list arrow **in the Drawing group, then click the** Dark Red, Accent 1, Lighter 40% color box

   The text object is now filled with a light green color and has a red outline.

9. **Position** ⬚ **over the text box edge, drag the** text box **to the Smart Guide on the slide as shown in** FIGURE 3-6, **then save your changes**

FIGURE 3-5: **New text object**

FIGURE 3-5: **New text object**

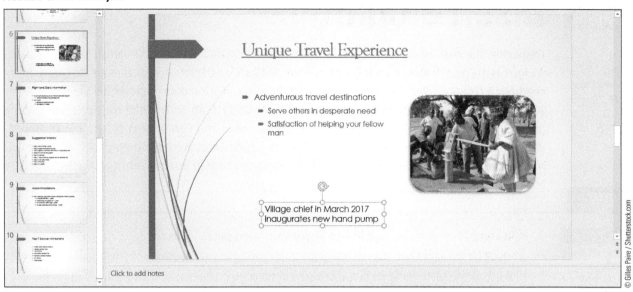

FIGURE 3-6: **Formatted text object**

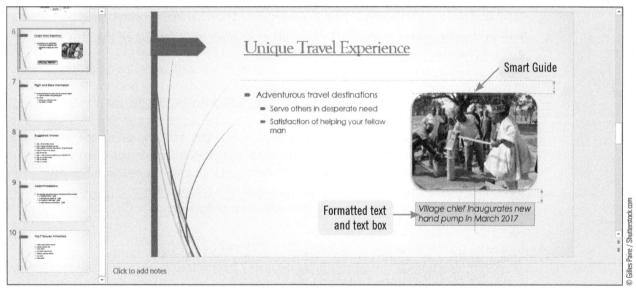

Changing text box defaults

You can change the default formatting characteristics of text boxes you create using the Text Box button on the Insert tab. To change the formatting defaults for text boxes, select an existing formatted text box, or create a new one and format it using any of PowerPoint's formatting commands. When you are ready to change the text box defaults of a text box that is not selected, press [Shift], right-click the formatted text box, release [Shift], then click Set as Default Text Box on the shortcut menu. Any new text boxes you create now will display the formatting characteristics of this formatted text box.

Insert a Chart

Frequently, the best way to communicate numerical information is with a visual aid such as a chart. A **chart** is the graphical representation of numerical data. PowerPoint uses Excel to create charts. Every chart has a corresponding **worksheet** that contains the numerical data displayed by the chart. When you insert a chart object into PowerPoint, you are embedding it. An **embedded object** is one that is a part of your presentation (just like any other object you insert into PowerPoint) except that an embedded object's data source can be opened, in this case using Excel, for editing purposes. Changes you make to an embedded object in PowerPoint using the features in PowerPoint do not affect the data source for the data. **CASE** *You insert a chart on a new slide.*

STEPS

1. **Click the** Slide 2 thumbnail **in the Slides tab, then press** [Enter]

   Pressing [Enter] adds a new slide to your presentation with the slide layout of the selected slide, in this case the Title and Content slide layout.

2. **Click the** Title placeholder, **type** Population Growth Comparison, **then click the** Insert Chart icon ▥ **in the Content placeholder**

   The Insert Chart dialog box opens as shown in FIGURE 3-7. Each chart type includes a number of 2D and 3D styles. The Clustered Column chart is the default 2D chart style. For a brief explanation of common chart types, refer to TABLE 3-1.

3. **Click** OK

   The PowerPoint window displays a clustered column chart below a worksheet with sample data, as shown in FIGURE 3-8. The Chart Tools Design tab on the Ribbon contains commands you use in PowerPoint to work with the chart. The worksheet consists of rows and columns. The intersection of a row and a column is called a **cell**. Cells are referred to by their row and column location; for example, the cell at the intersection of column A and row 1 is called cell A1. Each column and row of data in the worksheet is called a **data series**. Cells in column A and row 1 contain **data series labels** that identify the data or values in the column and row. "Category 1" is the data series label for the data in the second row, and "Series 1" is a data series label for the data in the second column. Cells below and to the right of the data series labels, in the shaded blue portion of the worksheet, contain the data values that are represented in the chart. Cells in row 1 appear in the chart **legend** and describe the data in the series. Each data series has corresponding **data series markers** in the chart, which are graphical representations such as bars, columns, or pie wedges. The boxes with the numbers along the left side of the worksheet are **row headings**, and the boxes with the letters along the top of the worksheet are **column headings**.

4. **Move the pointer over the worksheet, then click cell** C4

   The pointer changes to ✛. Cell C4, containing the value 1.8, is the selected cell, which means it is now the **active cell**. The active cell has a thick green border around it.

5. **Click the** Close button ✕ **on the worksheet title bar, then click the** Quick Layout button **in the Chart Layouts group**

   The worksheet window closes, and the Quick Layout gallery opens.

6. **Move ▷ over the layouts in the gallery, then click** Layout 1

   This new layout moves the legend to the right side of the chart and increases the size of the data series markers.

7. **Click in a blank area of the slide to deselect the chart, then save your changes**

   The Chart Tools Design tab is no longer active.

FIGURE 3-7: Insert Chart dialog box

FIGURE 3-8: Worksheet open showing chart data

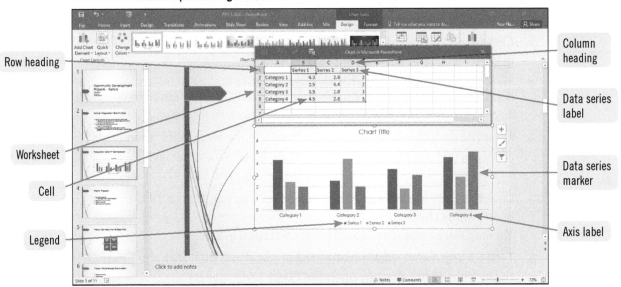

TABLE 3-1: Chart types

chart type	icon looks like	use to
Column		Track values over time or across categories
Line		Track values over time
Pie		Compare individual values to the whole
Bar		Compare values in categories or over time
Area		Show contribution of each data series to the total over time
X Y (Scatter)		Compare pairs of values
Stock		Show stock market information or scientific data
Surface		Show value trends across two dimensions
Radar		Show changes in values in relation to a center point
Combo		Use multiple types of data markers to compare values

PowerPoint 2016

Enter and Edit Chart Data

Learning Outcomes
- Change chart data values and labels
- Format a chart

STEPS

After you insert a chart into your presentation, you need to replace the sample information with the correct data. If you have the data you want to chart in an Excel worksheet, you can import it from Excel; otherwise, you can type your own data into the worksheet on the slide. As you enter data and make other changes in the worksheet, the chart on the slide automatically reflects the new changes. **CASE** *You enter and format population data you have gathered comparing the growth trends of three African countries.*

1. **Click the chart on Slide 3, click the Chart Tools Design tab on the Ribbon, then click the Edit Data button in the Data group**

    The chart is selected and the worksheet opens in a separate window. The information in the worksheet needs to be replaced with the correct data.

2. **Click the Series 1 cell, type Kenya, press [Tab], type Uganda, press [Tab], then type S. Africa**

    The data series labels you enter in the worksheet are displayed in the legend on the chart. Pressing [Tab] moves the active cell from left to right one cell at a time in a row. Pressing [Enter] in the worksheet moves the active cell down one cell at a time in a column.

3. **Click the Category 1 cell, type 1990, press [Enter], type 2000, press [Enter], type 2010, press [Enter], type 2015, then press [Enter]**

    These data series labels appear in the worksheet and along the bottom of the chart on the *x*-axis. The *x*-axis is the horizontal axis also referred to as the **category axis**, and the *y*-axis is the vertical axis also referred to as the **value axis**.

4. **Enter the data shown in FIGURE 3-9 to complete the worksheet, then press [Enter]**

    Notice that the height of each column in the chart, as well as the values along the *y*-axis, adjust to reflect the numbers you typed. You have finished entering the data in the Excel worksheet.

5. **Click the Close button ✕ on the worksheet title bar, then click the Chart Title text box object in the chart**

    The worksheet window closes. The Chart Title text box is selected.

6. **Type 25 Year Trend, click a blank area of the chart, then click the Chart Styles button 🖌 to the right of the chart to open the Chart Styles gallery**

    The Chart Styles gallery opens on the left side of the chart with Style selected.

7. **Scroll down the gallery, click Style 6, click Color at the top of the Chart Styles gallery, then click the Color 3 palette in the Colorful section**

    The new chart style and color gives the column data markers a professional look as shown in FIGURE 3-10.

8. **Click a blank area on the slide, then save the presentation**

    The Chart Styles gallery closes.

FIGURE 3-9: **Worksheet data for the chart**

FIGURE 3-10: **Formatted chart**

Adding a hyperlink to a chart

You can add a hyperlink to any object in PowerPoint, including a chart. Select that chart, click the Insert tab on the Ribbon, then click the Hyperlink button in the Links group. If you are linking to another file, click the Existing File or Web Page button, locate the file you want to link to the chart, then click OK. Or, if you want to link to another slide in the presentation, click the Place in This Document button, click the slide in the list, then click OK. Now, during a slide show you can click the chart to open the linked object. To remove the link, click the chart, click the Hyperlink button in the Links group, then click Remove Link.

Insert Slides from Other Presentations

To save time and energy, you can insert one or more slides you already created in other presentations into an existing presentation or one you are currently working on. One way to share slides between presentations is to open an existing presentation, copy the slides you want to the Clipboard, and then paste them into your open presentation. However, PowerPoint offers a simpler way to transfer slides directly between presentations. By using the Reuse Slides pane, you can insert slides from another presentation or a network location called a Slide Library. A **Slide Library** is folder that you and others can access to open, modify, and review presentation slides. Newly inserted slides automatically take on the theme of the open presentation, unless you decide to use slide formatting from the original source presentation. **CASE** ▶ *You decide to insert slides you created for another presentation into the Kenya presentation.*

STEPS

1. **Click the** Slide 6 thumbnail **in the Slides tab, click the** New Slide list arrow **in the Slides group, then click** Reuse Slides

   The Reuse Slides pane opens on the right side of the pre sentation window.

2. **Click the** Browse button **in the Reuse Slides pane, click** Browse File, **navigate to the location where you store your Data Files, select the presentation file** PPT 3-4.pptx, **then click** Open

   Five slide thumbnails are displayed in the pane with the first slide thumbnail selected as shown in FIGURE 3-11. The slide thumbnails identify the slides in the **source presentation**, PPT 3-4.pptx.

3. **Point to each slide in the Reuse Slides pane list to display a ScreenTip, then click the** Strategies for Managing Water Demand slide

   The new slide appears in the Slides tab and Slide pane as the new Slide 7. Notice the title new slide assumes the design style and formatting of your presentation, which is called the **destination presentation**.

4. **Click the** Keep source formatting check box **at the bottom of the Reuse Slides pane, click the** Water Restructuring Policies slide, **then click the** Keep source formatting check box

   This new slide keeps the design style and formatting of the source presentation.

5. **Click the** Slide 7 thumbnail **in the Slides tab, then click each of the remaining three slides in the Reuse Slides pane**

   Three more slides are inserted into the presentation with the design style and formatting of the destination presentation. You realize that Slides 7 and 11 are not needed for this presentation.

6. **Click the** Slide 11 thumbnail **in the Slides tab, press** [Ctrl], **click the** Slide 7 thumbnail, **release** [Ctrl], **right-click the** Slide 7 thumbnail, **then click** Delete Slide **in the shortcut menu**

   Slides 7 and 11 are deleted.

7. **Click the** Reuse Slides pane Close button ⊠, **click a blank area of the slide, then save the presentation**

   The Reuse Slides pane closes. Compare your screen to FIGURE 3-12.

FIGURE 3-11: Presentation window with Reuse Slides pane open

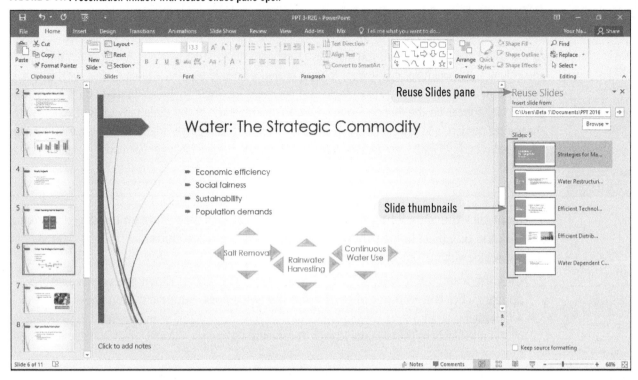

FIGURE 3-12: New slides added to presentation

Working with multiple windows

Another way to work with information in multiple presentations is to arrange the presentation windows on your monitor so you see each window side by side. Open each presentation, click the View tab on the Ribbon in any presentation window, then click the Arrange All button in the Window group. Each presentation you have open is placed next to each other so you can easily drag, or transfer, information between the presentations.

If you are working with more than two open presentations, you can overlap the presentation windows on top of one another. Open all the presentations you want, then click the Cascade Windows button in the Window group. Now you can easily jump from one presentation to another by clicking on the presentation title bar or any part of the presentation window.

Insert a Table

Learning
Outcomes
• Insert a table
• Add text to a table
• Change table size
  and layout

As you create your presentation, you may have some information that would look best organized in rows and columns. For example, if you want to view related data side by side, a table is ideal for this type of information. Once you have created a table, two new tabs, the Table Tools Design tab and the Table Tools Layout tab, appear on the Ribbon. You can use the commands on the table tabs to apply color styles, change cell borders, add cell effects, add rows and columns to your table, adjust the size of cells, and align text in the cells. **CASE** ▶ *You decide a table best illustrates the technology considerations for building a well in Kenya.*

STEPS

1. **Right-click the** Slide 9 thumbnail **in the Slides tab, click** New Slide **on the shortcut menu, click the** title placeholder, **then type** Technology Considerations
   A new slide with the Title and Content layout appears.

2. **Click the** Insert Table icon ▦, **click the** Number of columns down arrow **twice until** 3 **appears, click the** Number of rows up arrow **twice until** 4 **appears, then click** OK
   A formatted table with three columns and four rows appears on the slide, and the Table Tools Design tab opens on the Ribbon. The table has 12 cells. The insertion point is in the first cell of the table and is ready to accept text.

3. **Type** Financial, **press** [Tab], **type** Maintenance, **press** [Tab], **type** Population, **then press** [Tab]
   The text you typed appears in the top three cells of the table. Pressing [Tab] moves the insertion point to the next cell; pressing [Enter] moves the insertion point to the next line in the same cell.

4. **Enter the rest of the table information shown in** FIGURE 3-13
   The table would look better if it were formatted differently.

5. **Click the** More button ▼ **in the Table Styles group, scroll to the bottom of the gallery, then click** Medium Style 3
   The background and text color change to reflect the table style you applied.

6. **Click the** Financial cell in the table, click the Table Tools Layout tab **on the Ribbon, click the** Select button **in the Table group, click** Select Row, **then click the** Center button ☰ **in the Alignment group**
   The text in the top row is centered horizontally in each cell.

7. **Click the** Select button **in the Table group, click** Select Table, **then click the** Center Vertically button ⊟ **in the Alignment group**
   The text in the entire table is aligned in the center of each cell.

8. **Click the** Table Tools Design tab, **click the** Effects button **in the Table Styles group, point to** Cell Bevel, **then click** Soft Round **(2nd row)**
   The 3D effect makes the cells of the table stand out. The table would look better in a different place on the slide.

9. **Place the pointer** ⟡ **over the top edge of the table, drag the table straight down so it is placed as shown in** FIGURE 3-14, **click a blank area of the slide, then save the presentation**
   The slide looks better with more space between the table and the slide title.

FIGURE 3-13: **Inserted table with data**

FIGURE 3-14: **Formatted table**

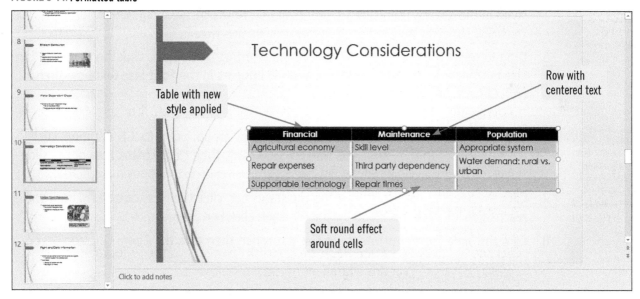

Setting permissions

In PowerPoint, you can set specific access permissions for people who review or edit your work so you have better control over your content. For example, you may want to give a user permission to edit or change your presentation but not allow them to print it. You can also restrict a user by permitting them to view the presentation without the ability to edit or print the presentation, or you can give the user full access or control of the presentation. To use this feature, you first must have access to an information rights management company. Then, to set user access permissions, click the File tab, click the Protect Presentation button, point to Restrict Access, then click an appropriate option.

Insert and Format WordArt

As you work to create an interesting presentation, your goal should include making your slides visually appealing. Sometimes plain text can come across as dull and unexciting in a presentation. **WordArt** is a set of decorative text styles, or text effects, you can apply to any text object to help direct the attention of your audience to a certain piece of information. You can use WordArt in two different ways: you can apply a WordArt text style to an existing text object that converts the text into WordArt, or you can create a new WordArt object. The WordArt text styles and effects include text shadows, reflections, glows, bevels, 3D rotations, and transformations. **CASE** ▸ *Create a new WordArt text object on Slide 4.*

STEPS

1. **Click the** Slide 4 thumbnail **in the Slides tab, click the** Insert tab **on the Ribbon, then click the** WordArt button **in the Text group**

   The WordArt gallery appears displaying 20 WordArt text styles.

2. **Click** Fill – Orange, Accent 2, Outline – Accent 2 **(first row)**

   A text object appears in the middle of the slide displaying sample text with the WordArt style you just selected. The Drawing Tools Format tab is open on the Ribbon.

3. **Click the edge of the** WordArt text object, **then when the pointer changes to** 🕂, **drag the text object to the blank area of the slide**

4. **Click the** More button ▼ **in the WordArt Styles group, move** ▷ **over all of the WordArt styles in the gallery, then click** Gradient Fill – Olive Green, Accent 1, Reflection

   The sample text in the WordArt text object changes to the new WordArt style.

5. **Drag to select the text** Your text here **in the WordArt text object, click the** Decrease Font Size button A˅ **in the Mini toolbar so that** 48 **appears in the Font Size text box, then type** Clean water equals self-reliance

   The text is smaller.

6. **Click the** Text Effects button **in the WordArt Styles group, point to** 3-D Rotation, **click** Off Axis 1 Right **in the Parallel section (second row), then click a blank area of the slide**

   The off-axis effect is applied to the text object. Compare your screen to FIGURE 3-15.

7. **Click the** Reading View button 📖 **on the status bar, click the** Next button ⓘ **until you reach Slide 15, click the** Menu button 🖹, **then click** End Show

8. **Click the** Slide Sorter button 🔡 **on the status bar, then click the** Zoom Out icon ➖ **on the status bar until all 15 slides are visible**

   Compare your screen with FIGURE 3-16.

9. **Click the** Normal button 🖵 **on the status bar, add your name, the slide number and the date as a footer to the slides, save your changes, submit your presentation to your instructor, then exit PowerPoint**

FIGURE 3-15: WordArt inserted on slide

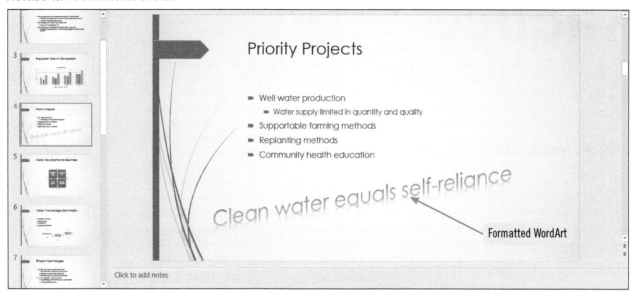

FIGURE 3-16: Completed presentation in Slide Sorter view

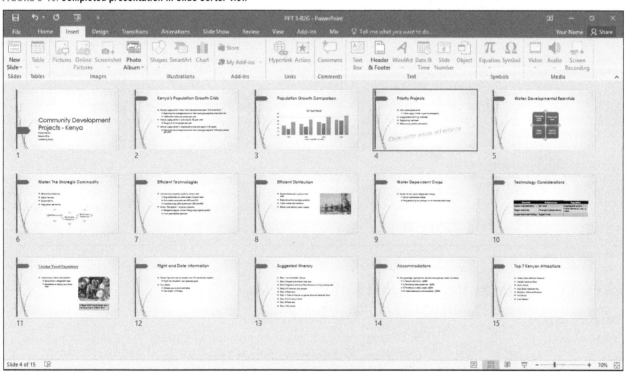

Saving a presentation as a video

You can save your PowerPoint presentation as a full-fidelity video, which incorporates all slide timings, transitions, animations, and narrations. The video can be distributed using a disc, the web, or email. Depending on how you want to display your video, you have three resolution settings from which to choose: Presentation Quality, Internet Quality, and Low Quality. The Large setting, Presentation Quality (1920 X 1080), is used for viewing on a computer monitor, projector, or other high-definition displays. The Medium setting, Internet Quality (1280 X 720), is used for uploading to the web or copying to a standard DVD. The Small setting, Low Quality (852 X 480), is used on portable media players. To save your presentation as a video, click the File tab, click Export, click Create a Video, choose your settings, then click the Create Video button.

Practice

Concepts Review

Label each element of the PowerPoint window shown in FIGURE 3-17.

FIGURE 3-17

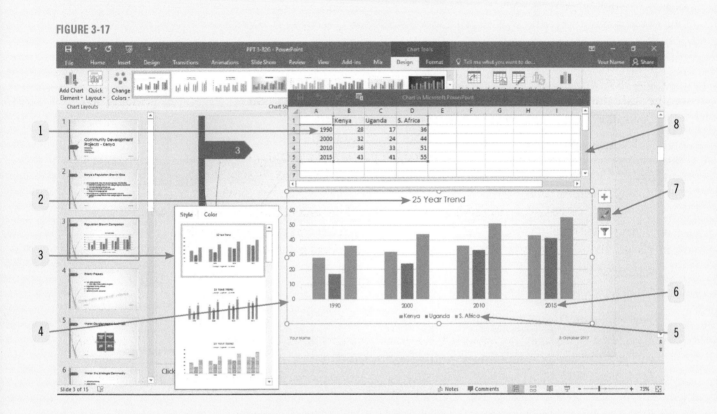

Match each term with the statement that best describes it.

9. **Category axis**
10. **Crop**
11. **Cell**
12. **Value axis**
13. **Chart**

a. The *y*-axis (vertical) in a chart
b. Intersection of a row and column in a worksheet
c. The graphical representation of numerical data
d. The *x*-axis (horizontal) in a chart
e. Hide a portion of a picture

Select the best answer from the list of choices.

14. _____ is the network folder that you can open in the Reuse Slides pane to insert slides from other presentations.

    a. Slide Library   **c.** Export Exchange

    b. Slide Exchange   **d.** Slide Room

15. Use a(n) _____ object to best illustrate information you want to compare side by side.

    a. WordArt   **c.** SmartArt

    b. Table   **d.** Equation

16. An object that has its own data source and becomes a part of your presentation after you insert it best describes which of the following?

    a. Embedded object   **c.** Table

    b. WordArt   **d.** Screenshot

17. Each column and row of data in a worksheet are _____.

    a. Data series labels   **c.** Data series

    b. Headings   **d.** Data markers

18. The slide thumbnails in the Reuse Slides pane identify the slides of the _____ presentation.

    a. destination   **c.** source

    b. default   **d.** open

19. _____ to permanently delete a cropped portion of a picture.

    a. Use the Crop to Fit feature   **c.** Change the picture's artistic effect

    b. Change the aspect ratio   **d.** Apply picture compression

20. _____ is created by inserting text from Word document that does not have tabs.

    a. A new presentation   **c.** A first level text in a bulleted list

    b. A slide title   **d.** A Heading 1 style

Skills Review

1. **Insert text from Microsoft Word.**

    a. Open PPT 3-5.pptx from the location where you store your Data Files, then save it as **PPT 3-Tsar Tour**. You will work to create the completed presentation as shown in FIGURE 3-18.

    b. Click Slide 2 in the Slides tab, then use the Slides from Outline command to insert the file PPT 3-6.docx from the location where you store your Data Files.

    c. In the Slides tab, drag Slide 7 above Slide 6, then delete Slide 9, "Budapest, Hungary".

    d. Select Slides 3, 4, 5, 6, 7, and 8 in the Slides tab, reset the slides to the default theme settings, then save your work.

FIGURE 3-18

Skills Review (continued)

2. Insert and style a picture.

    a. Select Slide 2 in the Slides tab, then insert the picture PPT 3-7.jpg from the location where you store your Data Files.

    b. Crop the right side of the picture up to the building, then increase the size of the picture so it is 5" wide.

    c. Drag the picture to the right so it is in the center of the blank area of the slide.

    d. Click the Color button, change the color tone to Temperature: 11200 K, then save your changes.

3. Insert a text box.

    a. On Slide 2, insert a text box below the picture.

    b. Type **Catherine palace**.

    c. Select the text object, then click the More button in the Shape Styles group on the Drawing Tools Format tab.

    d. Click Moderate Effect – Orange, Accent 5, then fit the text box to the text by dragging its sizing handles.

    e. Center the text object under the picture using Smart Guides.

    f. In the main text object, type the word **on** before the word **Volga**, then move the word **cruise** before the word **on**.

4. Insert a chart.

    a. Create a new slide after Slide 8 with a Title Only layout and title it **Sales by Quarter**.

    b. On the Insert tab, click the Chart button in the Illustrations group, click Pie in the left column, then insert a Pie chart.

    c. Close the worksheet, drag the top-middle sizing handle of the chart down under the slide title, then apply the Layout 1 quick layout to the chart.

5. Enter and edit chart data.

    a. Show the worksheet, enter the data shown in TABLE 3-2 into the worksheet, then close the worksheet.

    b. Type **Tsar River Tour Sales** in the chart title text object.

    c. Click the Chart Styles button next to the chart, then change the chart style to Style 12.

    d. Click Color in the Charts Styles gallery, then change the color to Color 3 in the Colorful section.

    e. Close the Charts Styles gallery, then save your changes.

TABLE 3-2

	Sales
1st Qtr	11
2nd Qtr	31
3rd Qtr	37
4th Qtr	21

6. Insert slides from other presentations.

    a. Go to Slide 8, then open the Reuse Slides pane.

    b. Open PPT 3-8.pptx from the location where you store your Data Files.

    c. Insert the fourth slide thumbnail, insert the second slide thumbnail, and then insert the third slide thumbnail.

    d. Close the Reuse Slides pane, then save your work.

7. Insert a table.

    a. Add a new slide after Slide 11 with the Title and Content layout.

    b. Add the slide title **Stateroom Special Features**.

    c. Insert a table with three columns and four rows.

    d. Enter the information shown in TABLE 3-3, then change the table style to Light Style 2 – Accent 2.

    e. In the Table Tools Layout tab, center the text in the top row.

    f. Open the Table Tools Design tab, click the Effects button, point to Cell Bevel, then apply the Convex effect.

    g. Move the table to the center of the blank area of the slide, then save your changes.

TABLE 3-3

Deluxe Stateroom	Veranda Suite	Master Suite
160 sq. ft.	225 sq. ft.	400 sq. ft.
Private bathroom	Glass sliding door	Queen bed
Large picture window	Walk-in closet	Panoramic veranda

Skills Review (continued)

8. Insert and format WordArt.

a. Go to Slide 5, then, insert a WordArt text object using the style Fill – Yellow, Accent 3, Sharp Bevel.

b. Type **A Golden Ring City**, apply the Triangle Down Transform text effect (first row in the Warp section) to the text object, then move the text object to the middle of the blank area of the slide.

c. View the presentation in Slide Show view, add your name as a footer to all the slides, then save your changes.

d. Submit your presentation to your instructor, close your presentation, and exit PowerPoint.

Independent Challenge 1

You are a financial management consultant for Pitlock, Bryer & Mansouetti, located in Bradenton, Florida. One of your responsibilities is to create standardized presentations on different financial investments for use on the company website. As part of the presentation for this meeting, you insert a chart, add a WordArt object, and insert slides from another presentation.

a. Open PPT 3-9.pptx from the location where you store your Data Files, then save it as **PPT 3-BIP**.

b. Add your name as the footer on all of the slides, then apply the Frame Design Theme.

c. Insert a clustered column chart on Slide 2, then enter the data in TABLE 3-4 into the worksheet.

d. Close the worksheet, format the chart using Style 14, then resize and move the chart to the blank area beside the text object.

e. Type **Annualized Return** in the chart title text object.

f. Open the Reuse Slides pane, open PPT 3-10.pptx from the location where you store your Data Files, then insert Slides 2, 3, and 4.

g. Close the Reuse Slides pane, move Slide 5 above Slide 4, then select Slide 3.

h. Insert a WordArt object using the Fill - Orange, Accent 4, Soft Bevel style, type **Invest early**, press [Enter], type **for**, press [Enter], then type **the long haul**.

i. Click the Text Effects button, point to Transform, then apply the Button text effect from the Follow Path section.

j. Move the WordArt object to a blank area of the slide, click the Text Effects button, point to Shadow, then apply an Outer shadow effect.

k. View the presentation slide show, make any necessary changes, then save your work. See FIGURE 3-19.

l. Submit the presentation to your instructor, then close the presentation, and exit PowerPoint.

TABLE 3-4

	Stocks	Bonds	Mutual funds
1 Year	5.3%	1.9%	3.8%
3 Year	4.8%	3.7%	6.7%
5 Year	3.2%	2.2%	8.3%
10 Year	2.6%	3.4%	7.2%

FIGURE 3-19

Independent Challenge 2

You work for the Boston Port Group in the commercial container division. You have been asked to enhance a marketing presentation that is going to promote the port facilities. You work on completing a presentation by inserting a picture, a text box, and a table.

a. Start PowerPoint, open PPT 3-11.pptx from the location where you store your Data Files, and save it as **PPT 3-Port**.

b. Add your name and today's date to Slide 1 in the Subtitle text box.

c. Apply the Droplet theme to the presentation.

d. On Slide 5, click the Pictures icon in the content placeholder, then insert the file PPT 3-12.jpg from the location where you store your Data Files.

e. Apply the Simple Frame, Black picture style to the picture, click the Color button, then change the color saturation to Saturation: 0%.

f. Change the size of the picture so its width is 5.2" using the Width text box in the Size group.

g. Insert a text box on the slide below the picture, type **Largest volume port on East Coast**, then format the text and text box with three formatting commands.

h. Go to Slide 2, select the picture, click the Picture Effects button, point to Soft Edges, then click 5 Point.

i. Open the Artistic Effects gallery, then apply the Cement effect to the picture.

j. Go to Slide 4, create a new table, then enter the data in TABLE 3-5. Format the table using at least two formatting commands. Be able to identify which formatting commands you applied to the table.

k. View the final presentation in Slide Show view. Make any necessary changes (refer to FIGURE 3-20).

l. Save the presentation, submit the presentation to your instructor, close the file, and exit PowerPoint.

TABLE 3-5

Total	August	September
Total containers	25,524.0	22,417.0
Loaded containers	15,283.0	14,016.0
Empty containers	10,241.0	8,401.0
Total tons	375,240	334,180

FIGURE 3-20

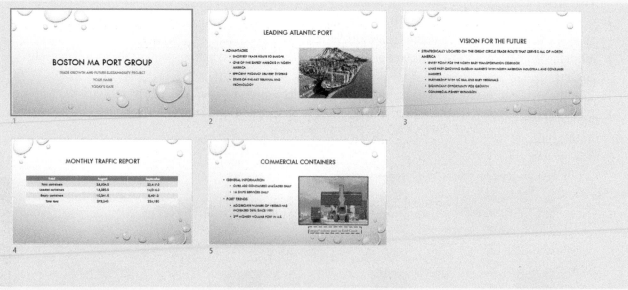

© tcly/Shutterstock; © Prasit Rodphan/Shutterstock

Independent Challenge 3

You work for World Partners Inc., a company that produces instructional software to help people learn foreign languages. Once a year, World Partners holds a meeting with their biggest client, the United States Department of Homeland Security, to brief the government on new products and to receive feedback on existing products. Your supervisor has started a presentation and has asked you to look it over and add other elements to make it look better.

a. Start PowerPoint, open PPT 3-13.pptx from the location where you store your Data Files, and save it as **PPT 3-World**.

b. Add an appropriate design theme to the presentation.

c. Insert the Word outline PPT 3-14.docx after the Product Revisions slide, then reset the new slides to the design theme.

d. Insert and format a text object and a WordArt object.

e. Insert an appropriate table on a slide of your choice. Use your own information, or use text from a bulleted list on one of the slides.

f. Add your name as footer text on the slides, then save the presentation.

g. Submit your presentation to your instructor, close the file, then exit PowerPoint.

Independent Challenge 4: Explore

As an international exchange student at your college, one of your assignments in your Intercultural Communication Studies class is to present information on a student exchange you took last semester. You need to create a pictorial presentation that highlights a trip to a different country. Create a presentation using your own pictures. If you don't have access to any appropriate pictures, use the three pictures provided in the Data Files for this unit: PPT 3-15.jpg, PPT 3-16.jpg, and PPT 3-17.jpg. *(NOTE: To complete steps below, your computer must be connected to the Internet.)*

a. Start PowerPoint, create a new blank presentation, and save it as **PPT 3-Exchange** to the location where you store your Data Files.

b. Locate and insert the pictures you want to use. Place one picture on each slide using the Content with Caption slide layout, then apply a picture style to each picture.

c. Click the Crop list arrow, and use one of the other cropping options to crop a picture.

d. Add information about each picture in the text placeholder, and enter a slide title. If you use the pictures provided, research Costa Rica, using the Internet for relevant information to place on the slides.

e. Apply an appropriate design theme, then apply an appropriate title and your name to the title slide.

FIGURE 3-21

f. View the final presentation slide show (refer to FIGURE 3-21).

g. Add a slide number and your class name as footer text to all of the slides, save your work, then submit your presentation to your instructor.

© Tami Freed/Shutterstock; © Ruth Choi/Shutterstock; © Mihai-Bogdan Lazar/Shutterstock

h. Close the file, and exit PowerPoint.

Visual Workshop

Create a one-slide presentation that looks like FIGURE 3-22. The slide layout used is a specific layout designed for pictures. Insert the picture file PPT 3-18.jpg to complete this presentation. Add your name as footer text to the slide, save the presentation as **PPT 3-TCM** to the location where you store your Data Files, then submit your presentation to your instructor.

FIGURE 3-22

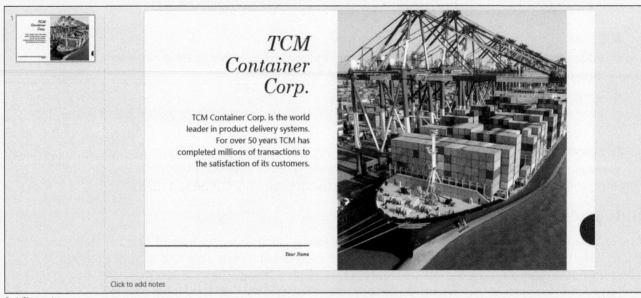

© tcly/Shutterstock

Finishing a Presentation

CASE You have reviewed your work and are pleased with the slides you created so far for the Reason2Go presentation. Now you are ready to add some final enhancements to the slides to make the PowerPoint presentation interesting to watch.

Module Objectives

After completing this module, you will be able to:

- Modify masters
- Customize the background and theme
- Use slide show commands
- Set slide transitions and timings
- Animate objects
- Use proofing and language tools
- Inspect a presentation
- Create an Office Mix

Files You Will Need

PPT 4-1.pptx	PPT 4-6.jpg
PPT 4-2.jpg	PPT 4-7.pptx
PPT 4-3.pptx	PPT 4-8.pptx
PPT 4-4.jpg	PPT 4-9.jpg
PPT 4-5.pptx	PPT 4-10.jpg

Modify Masters

Learning
Outcomes
• Navigate Slide
  Master view
• Add and modify
  a picture

Each presentation in PowerPoint has a set of **masters** that store information about the theme and slide layouts. Masters determine the position and size of text and content placeholders, fonts, slide background, color, and effects. There are three Master views: Slide Master view, Notes Master view, and Handout Master view. Changes made in Slide Master view are reflected on the slides in Normal view; changes made in Notes Master view are reflected in Notes Page view, and changes made in Handout Master view appear when you print your presentation using a handout printing option. The primary benefit to modifying a master is that you can make universal changes to your whole presentation instead of making individual repetitive changes to each of your slides. **CASE** *You want to add the R2G company logo to every slide in your presentation, so you open your presentation and insert the logo on the slide master.*

STEPS

1. **Start PowerPoint, open the presentation PPT 4-1.pptx from the location where you store your Data Files, save the presentation as PPT 4-R2G, then click the View tab on the Ribbon**
   The title slide for the presentation appears.

QUICK TIP
You can press and hold [Shift] and click the Normal button on the status bar to display the slide master.

2. **Click the Slide Master button in the Master Views group, scroll to the top of the Master Thumbnails pane, then click the Wisp Slide Master thumbnail (first thumbnail)**
   The Slide Master view appears with the slide master displayed in the Slide pane as shown in FIGURE 4-1. A new tab, the Slide Master tab, appears next to the Home tab on the Ribbon. The slide master is the Wisp theme slide master. Each theme comes with its own slide master. Each master text placeholder on the slide master identifies the font size, style, color, and position of text placeholders on the slides in Normal view. For example, for the Wisp theme, the Master title placeholder positioned at the top of the slide uses a black, 36 pt, Century Gothic font. Slide titles use this font style and formatting. Each slide master comes with associated slide layouts located below the slide master in the Master Thumbnails pane. Slide layouts follow the information on the slide master, and changes you make are reflected in all of the slide layouts.

QUICK TIP
You can make sure the current master remains with the presentation by clicking the Preserve button in the Edit Master group.

3. **Point to each of the slide layouts in the Master Thumbnails pane, then click the Title and Content Layout thumbnail**
   As you point to each slide layout, a ScreenTip appears identifying each slide layout by name and lists if any slides in the presentation are using the layout. Slides 2–9 and 12–15 are using the Title and Content Layout.

4. **Click the Wisp Slide Master thumbnail, click the Insert tab on the Ribbon, then click the Pictures button in the Images group**
   The Insert Picture dialog box opens.

5. **Select the picture file PPT 4-2.jpg from the location where you store your Data Files, then click Insert**
   The R2G logo picture is placed on the slide master and will now appear on all slides in the presentation. The picture is too large and would look better with a transparent background.

6. **Click 2.45" in the Width text box in the Size group, type 1.75, press [Enter], click the Color button in the Adjust group, then click Set Transparent Color**
   The pointer changes to ⟍.

QUICK TIP
To reset the background color of a picture to its original state, click the Reset Picture button in the Adjust group.

7. **Click the lime green color in the logo picture, drag the logo as shown in FIGURE 4-2, then click a blank area of the slide**
   The picture background color is now transparent.

8. **Click the Normal button ▣ on the status bar, then save your changes**

FIGURE 4-1: Slide Master view

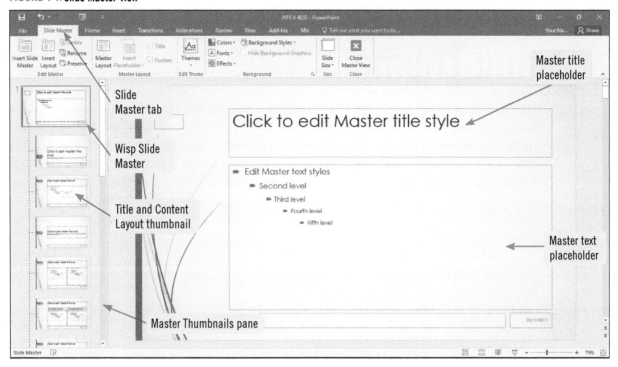

FIGURE 4-2: Picture added to slide master

Create custom slide layouts

As you work with PowerPoint, you may find that you need to develop a customized slide layout. For example, you may need to create a presentation for a client that has a slide that displays four pictures with a caption underneath each picture. To make everyone's job easier, you can create a custom slide layout that includes only the placeholders you need. To create a custom slide layout, open Slide Master view, and then click the Insert Layout button in the Edit Master group. A new slide layout appears below the last layout for the selected master in the Master Thumbnails pane.

You can choose to add several different placeholders including Content, Text, Picture, Chart, Table, SmartArt, Media, and Online Image. Click the Insert Placeholder list arrow in the Master Layout group, click the placeholder you want to add, drag ╋ to create the placeholder, then position the placeholder on the slide. In Slide Master view, you can add or delete placeholders in any of the slide layouts. You can rename a custom slide layout by clicking the Rename button in the Edit Master group and entering a descriptive name to better identify the layout.

Customize the Background and Theme

Learning Outcomes
- Apply a slide background and change the style
- Modify presentation theme

Every slide in a PowerPoint presentation has a **background**, the area behind the text and graphics. You modify the background to enhance the slides using images and color. You can quickly change the background appearance by applying a background style, which is a set of color variations derived from the theme colors. Theme colors determine the colors for all slide elements in your presentation, including slide background, text and lines, shadows, fills, accents, and hyperlinks. Every PowerPoint theme has its own set of theme colors. See TABLE 4-1 for a description of the theme colors. **CASE** *The R2G presentation can be improved with some design enhancements. You decide to modify the background of the slides by changing the theme colors and fonts.*

STEPS

1. **Click the** Design tab **on the Ribbon, then click the** Format Background button **in the Customize group**

   The Format Background pane opens displaying the Fill options. The gradient option button is selected indicating the slide has a gradient background.

2. **Click the** Solid fill option button, **review the slide, click the** Pattern fill option button, **then click the** Dotted diamond **pattern (seventh row)**

   FIGURE 4-3 shows the new background on Slide 1 of the presentation. The new background style covers the slide behind the text and background graphics. **Background graphics** are objects placed on the slide master.

3. **Click the** Hide background graphics check box **in the Format Background pane**

   All of the background objects, which include the R2G logo, the red pentagon shape, and the other colored shapes, are hidden from view, and only the text objects and slide number remain visible.

4. **Click the** Hide background graphics check box, **then click the** Reset Background button **at the bottom of the Format Background pane**

   All of the background objects and the gradient fill slide background appear again as specified by the theme.

5. **Click the** Picture or texture fill option button, **click the** Texture button 🔲, **click** Woven mat (top row), **then drag the** Transparency slider **until 40% is displayed in the text box**

   The new texture fills the slide background behind the background items.

6. **Click the** Format Background pane Close button ⊠, **click the** Slide 3 thumbnail **in the Slides tab, then point to the** black theme variant **in the Variants group**

   The new theme variant changes the color of the shapes on the slide and the background texture. A **variant** is a custom variation of the applied theme, in this case the Wisp theme. Theme variants are similar to the original theme, but they are made up of different complementary colors, slide backgrounds, such as textures and patterns, and background elements, such as shapes and pictures.

7. **Point to the other** variants **in the Variants group, click the** second variant **from the left, then save your work**

   The new variant is applied to the slide master and to all the slides in the presentation. Compare your screen to FIGURE 4-4.

FIGURE 4-3: New background style applied

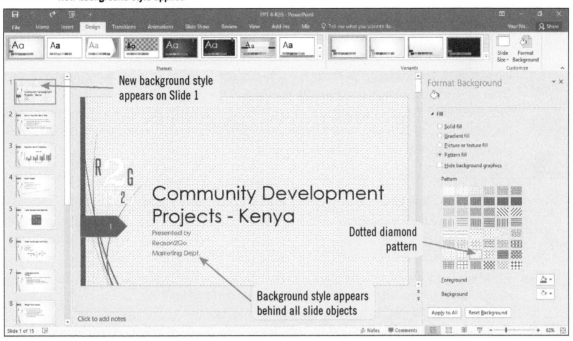

FIGURE 4-4: New theme variant

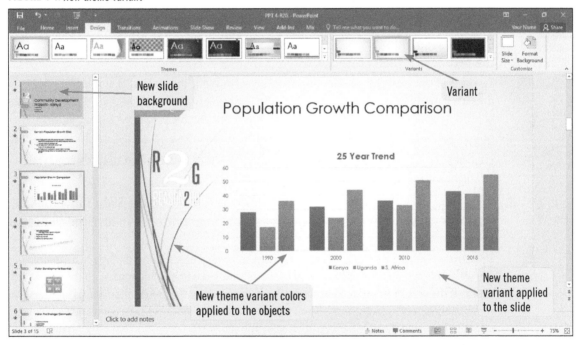

TABLE 4-1: Theme colors

color element	description
Text/Background colors	Contrasting colors for typed characters and the slide background
Accent colors	There are six accent colors used for shapes, drawn lines, and text; the shadow color for text and objects and the fill and outline color for shapes are all accent colors; all of these colors contrast appropriately with background and text colors
Hyperlink color	Colors used for hyperlinks you insert
Followed Hyperlink color	Color used for hyperlinks after they have been clicked

Finishing a Presentation

Use Slide Show Commands

With PowerPoint, Slide Show view is used primarily to deliver a presentation to an audience, either over the Internet using your computer or through a projector connected to your computer. As you've seen, Slide Show view fills your computer screen with the slides of the presentation, showing them one at a time. In Slide Show view, you can draw freehand pen or highlighter strokes, also known as **ink annotations**, on the slide or jump to other slides in the presentation. **CASE** *You run the slide show of the presentation and practice using some of the custom slide show options.*

STEPS

1. **Click the Slide Show button ☐ on the status bar, then press [Spacebar]**
   Slide 3 filled the screen first, and then Slide 4 appears. Pressing [Spacebar] or clicking the left mouse button is an easy way to move through a slide show. See TABLE 4-2 for other basic slide show keyboard commands. You can easily navigate to other slides in the presentation during the slide show.

2. **Move ☐ to the lower-left corner of the screen to display the Slide Show toolbar, click the See all slides button ☐, then click the Slide 2 thumbnail**
   Slide 2 appears on the screen. With the Slide Show toolbar you can emphasize points in your presentation by drawing highlighter strokes on the slide during a slide show.

3. **Click the Pen and laser pointer tools button ☐, on the Slide Show toolbar, then click Highlighter**
   The pointer changes to the highlighter pointer ┃. You can use the highlighter anywhere on the slide.

4. **Drag ┃, to highlight doubled between 1970 and 2015 and double again in 50 years in the text object, then press [Esc]**
   Two lines of text are highlighted as shown in FIGURE 4-5. While the ┃ is visible, mouse clicks do not advance the slide show; however, you can still move to the next slide by pressing [Spacebar] or [Enter]. Pressing [Esc] or [Ctrl][A] while drawing with the highlighter or pen switches the pointer back to ☐.

5. **Right-click anywhere on the screen, point to Pointer Options, click Eraser, the pointer changes to ☐, then click the lower highlight annotation in the text object**
   The highlight annotation on the "double again in 50 years" text is erased.

6. **Press [Esc], click the More slide show options button ☐ on the Slide Show toolbar, click Show Presenter View, then click the Pause the timer button ☐ above the slide as shown in FIGURE 4-6**
   Presenter view is a view that you can use when showing a presentation through two monitors; one that you see as the presenter and one that your audience sees. The current slide appears on the left of your screen (which is the only object your audience sees), the next slide in the presentation appears in the upper-right corner of the screen. Speaker notes, if you have any, appear in the lower-right corner. The timer you paused identifies how long the slide has been viewed by the audience.

7. **Click ☐, click Hide Presenter View, then click the Advance to the next slide button ☐ on the Slide Show toolbar**
   Slide 3 appears.

8. **Press [Enter] to advance through the entire slide show until you see a black slide, then press [Spacebar]**
   If there are ink annotations on your slides, you have the option of saving them when you quit the slide show. Saved ink annotations appear as drawn objects in Normal view.

9. **Click Discard, then save the presentation**
   The highlight ink annotation is deleted on Slide 2, and Slide 3 appears in Normal view.

FIGURE 4-5: Slide 2 in Slide Show view with highlighter drawings

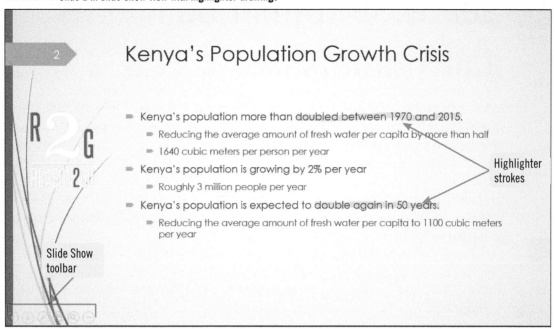

FIGURE 4-6: Slide 2 in Presenter view

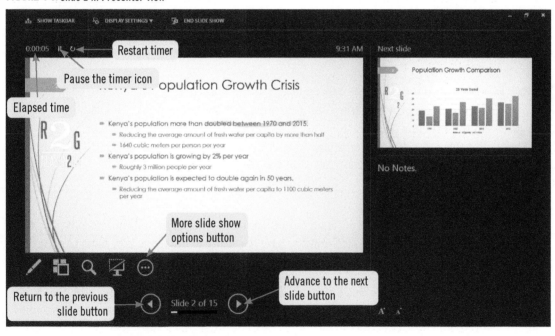

TABLE 4-2: Basic Slide Show view keyboard commands

keyboard commands	description
[Enter], [Spacebar], [PgDn], [N], [down arrow], or [right arrow]	Advances to the next slide
[E]	Erases the ink annotation drawing
[Home], [End]	Moves to the first or last slide in the slide show
[up arrow], [PgUp], or [left arrow]	Returns to the previous slide
[S]	Pauses the slide show when using automatic timings; press again to continue
[B]	Changes the screen to black; press again to return
[Esc]	Stops the slide show

Learning
Outcomes
• Apply and modify
  a transition
• Modify slide
  timings

Set Slide Transitions and Timings

In a slide show, you can determine how each slide advances in and out of view and how long each slide appears on the screen. **Slide transitions** are the visual and audio effects you apply to a slide that determine how each slide moves on and off the screen during the slide show. **Slide timing** refers to the amount of time a slide is visible on the screen. Typically, you set slide timings only if you want the presentation to automatically progress through the slides during a slide show. Setting the correct slide timing, in this case, is important because it determines how much time your audience has to view each slide. Each slide can have a different slide transition and different slide timing. **CASE** ▶ *You decide to set slide transitions and 7-second slide timings for all the slides.*

STEPS

1. **Click the Slide 1 thumbnail in the Slides tab, then click the Transitions tab on the Ribbon**

   Transitions are organized by type into three groups: Subtle, Exciting, and Dynamic Content.

2. **Click the More button ▼ in the Transition to This Slide group, then click Drape in the Exciting section**

   The new slide transition plays on the slide, and a transition icon ⭐ appears next to the slide thumbnail in the Slides tab as shown in FIGURE 4-7. You can customize the slide transition by changing its direction and speed.

   > **QUICK TIP**
   > You can add a sound that plays with the transition from the Sound list arrow in the Timing group.

3. **Click the Effect Options button in the Transition to This Slide group, click Right, click the Duration up arrow in the Timing group until 3.00 appears, then click the Preview button in the Preview group**

   The Drape slide transition now plays from the right on the slide for 3.00 seconds. You can apply this transition with the custom settings to all of the slides in the presentation.

4. **Click the Apply To All button in the Timing group, then click the Slide Sorter button ▦ on the status bar**

   All of the slides now have the customized Drape transition applied to them as identified by the transition icons located below each slide. You also have the ability to determine how slides progress during a slide show—either manually by mouse click or automatically by slide timing.

5. **Click the On Mouse Click check box under Advance Slide in the Timing group to clear the check mark**

   When this option is selected, you would have to click to manually advance slides during a slide show. Now, with this option disabled, you can set the slides to advance automatically after a specified amount of time.

   > **QUICK TIP**
   > Click the transition icon under any slide in Slide Sorter view to see its transition play.

6. **Click the After up arrow in the Timing group, until 00:07.00 appears in the text box, then click the Apply To All button**

   The timing between slides is 7 seconds as indicated by the time under each slide thumbnail in FIGURE 4-8. When you run the slide show, each slide will remain on the screen for 7 seconds. You can override a slide's timing and speed up the slide show by using any of the manual advance slide commands.

7. **Click the Slide Show button 🖵 on the status bar**

   The slide show advances automatically. A new slide appears every 7 seconds using the Drape transition.

8. **When you see the black slide, press [Spacebar], then save your changes**

   The slide show ends and returns to Slide Sorter view with Slide 1 selected.

FIGURE 4-7: **Applied slide transition**

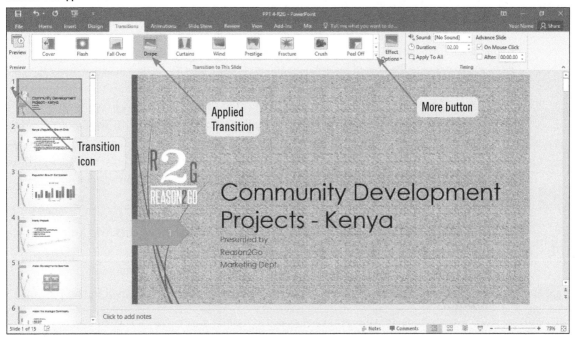

FIGURE 4-8: **Slide sorter view showing applied transition and timing**

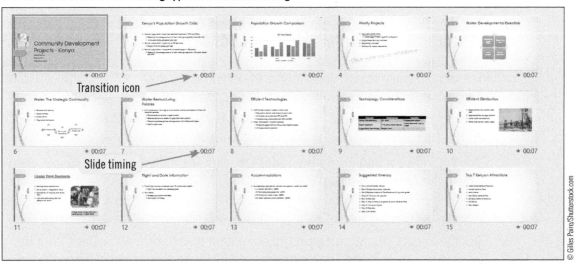

Rehearsing slide show timings

You can set different slide timings for each slide; for example, the title slide can appear for 20 seconds and the second slide for 1 minute. To set timings click the Rehearse Timings button in the Set Up group on the Slide Show tab. Slide Show view opens and the Recording toolbar shown in **FIGURE 4-9** opens. It contains buttons to pause between slides and to advance to the next slide. After opening the Recording toolbar, you can practice giving your presentation by manually advancing each slide in the presentation. When you are finished, PowerPoint displays the total recorded time for the presentation and you have the option to save the recorded timings. The next time you run the slide show, you can use the timings you rehearsed.

FIGURE 4-9: **Recording toolbar**

Animate Objects

Animations let you control how objects and text appear and move on the screen during a slide show and allow you to manage the flow of information and emphasize specific facts. You can animate text, pictures, sounds, hyperlinks, SmartArt diagrams, charts, and individual chart elements. For example, you can apply a Fade animation to bulleted text so each paragraph enters the slide separately from the others. Animations are organized into four categories, Entrance, Emphasis, Exit, and Motion Paths. The Entrance and Exit animations cause an object to enter or exit the slide with an effect. An Emphasis animation causes an object visible on the slide to have an effect and a Motion Path animation causes an object to move on a specified path on the slide. **CASE** > *You animate the text and graphics of several slides in the presentation.*

STEPS

1. **Double-click the** Slide 5 thumbnail **to return to Normal view, click the** Animations tab **on the Ribbon, then click the** SmartArt object

   Text as well as other objects, such as a shape or picture, can be animated during a slide show.

   QUICK TIP
   There are additional
   animation options
   for each animation
   category located at
   the bottom of the
   animations gallery.

2. **Click the** More button �굿 **in the Animation group, then click** Swivel **in the Entrance section**

   Animations can be serious and business-like, or humorous, so be sure to choose appropriate effects for your presentation. A small numeral 1, called an animation tag 1, appears near the object. **Animation tags** identify the order in which objects are animated during slide show.

3. **Click the** Effect Options button **in the Animation group, click** All at Once, **then click the** Duration up arrow **in the Timing group until** 03.00 **appears**

   Effect options are different for every animation, and some animations don't have effect options. Changing the animation timing increases the duration of the animation and gives it a more dramatic effect. Compare your screen to FIGURE 4-10.

4. **Click the** Slide Show button 🖵 **on the status bar until you see Slide 6, then press** [Esc]

   After the slide transition finishes, the shapes object spins twice for a total of three seconds.

5. **Click the** Slide 2 thumbnail **in the Slides tab, click the** bulleted list text object, **then click** Wipe **in the Animation group**

   The text object is animated with the Wipe animation. Each line of text has an animation tag with each paragraph displaying a different number. Accordingly, each paragraph is animated separately.

6. **Click the** Effect Options button **in the Animation group, click** All at Once, **click the** Duration up arrow **in the Timing group until** 02.00 **appears, then click the** Preview **button in the Preview group**

   Notice the animation tags for each line of text in the text object now have the same numeral (1), indicating that each line of text animates at the same time.

   QUICK TIP
   If you want to
   individually animate
   the parts of a
   grouped object, then
   you must ungroup
   the objects before
   you animate them.

7. **Click** Population **in the title text object, click** ⎿ **in the Animation group, scroll down, then click** Shapes **in the Motion Paths section**

   A motion path object appears over the shapes object and identifies the direction and shape, or path, of the animation. When needed, you can move, resize, and change the direction of the motion path. Notice the numeral 2 animation tag next to the title text object indicating that it is animated *after* the bulleted list text object. Compare your screen to FIGURE 4-11.

8. **Click the** Move Earlier button **in the Timing group, click the** Slide Show tab **on the Ribbon, then click the** From Beginning button **in the Start Slide Show group**

   The slide show begins from Slide 1. The animations make the presentation more interesting to view.

9. **When you see the black slide, press** [Enter], **then save your changes**

FIGURE 4-10: Animation applied to SmartArt object

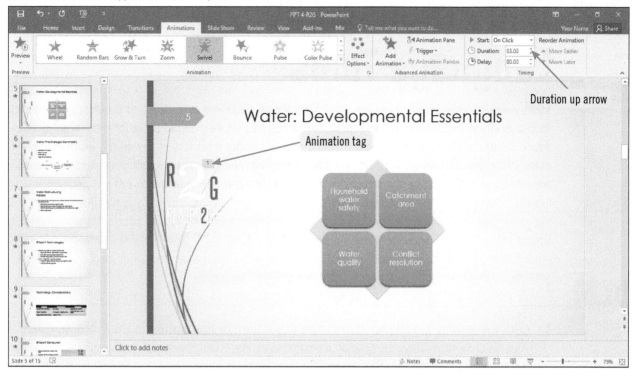

FIGURE 4-11: Motion path applied to title text object

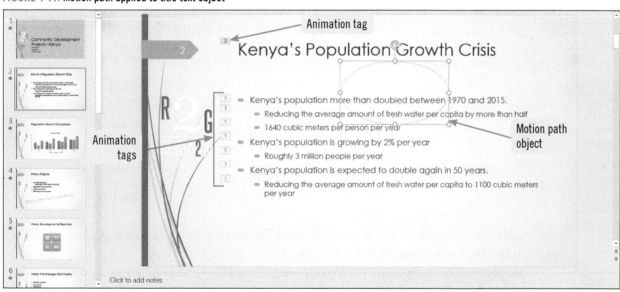

Attaching a sound to an animation

Text or objects that have animation applied can be customized further by attaching a sound for extra emphasis. First, select the animated object, then on the Animations tab, click the Animation Pane button in the Advanced Animation group. In the Animation Pane, click the animation you want to apply the sound to, click the Animation list arrow, then click Effect Options to open the animation effect's dialog box. In the Enhancements section, click the Sound list arrow, then choose a sound. Click OK when you are finished. Now, when you run the slide show, the sound you applied will play with the animation.

Finishing a Presentation

Use Proofing and Language Tools

Learning Outcomes
• Spell check a presentation
• Translate slide text

As your work on the presentation file nears completion, you need to review and proofread your slides thoroughly for errors. You can use the Spell Checker feature in PowerPoint to check for and correct spelling errors. This feature compares the spelling of all the words in your presentation against the words contained in the dictionary. You still must proofread your presentation for punctuation, grammar, and word-usage errors because the Spell Checker recognizes only misspelled and unknown words, not misused words. For example, the spell checker would not identify the word "last" as an error, even if you had intended to type the word "past." PowerPoint also includes language tools that translate words or phrases from your default language into another language using the Microsoft Translator. **CASE** ▶ *You're finished working on the presentation for now, so it's a good time to check spelling. You then experiment with language translation because the final presentation will be translated into different languages.*

STEPS

1. **Click the Review tab on the Ribbon, then click the Spelling button in the Proofing group**
   PowerPoint begins to check the spelling in your presentation. When PowerPoint finds a misspelled word or a word that is not in its dictionary, the Spelling pane opens, as shown in FIGURE 4-12. In this case, the Spell Checker identifies a word on Slide 13, but it does not recognize that is spelled correctly and suggests some replacement words.

2. **Click Ignore All in the Spelling pane**
   PowerPoint ignores all instances of this word and continues to check the rest of the presentation for errors. If PowerPoint finds any other words it does not recognize, either change or ignore them. When the Spell Checker finishes checking your presentation, the Spelling pane closes, and an alert box opens with a message stating the spelling check is complete.

3. **Click OK in the Alert box, then click the Slide 4 thumbnail in the Slides tab**
   The alert box closes. Now you experiment with the language translation feature.

4. **Click the Translate button in the Language group, then click Choose Translation Language**
   The Translation Language Options dialog box opens.

5. **Click the Translate to list arrow, click Czech, then click OK**
   The Translation Language Options dialog box closes.

6. **Click the Translate button in the Language group, click Mini Translator [Czech], click Yes in the alert box, then select the first line of text in the text object**
   The Microsoft Translator begins to analyze the selected text, and a semitransparent Microsoft Translator box appears below the text. The Mini toolbar may also appear above the text.

7. **Move the pointer over the Microsoft Translator box**
   A Czech translation of the text appears as shown in FIGURE 4-13. The translation language setting remains in effect until you reset it.

8. **Click the Translate button in the Language group, click Choose Translation Language, click the Translate to list arrow, click English (United States), click OK, click the Translate button again, then click Mini Translator [English (United States)]**
   The Mini Translator is turned off, and the translation language is restored to the default setting.

FIGURE 4-12: **Spelling pane**

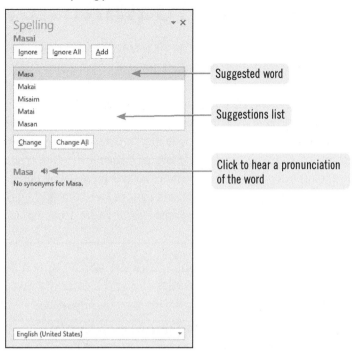

FIGURE 4-13: **Translated text in the Microsoft Translator box**

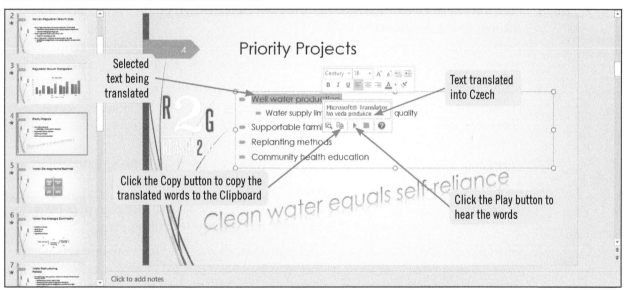

Checking spelling as you type

By default, PowerPoint checks your spelling as you type. If you type a word that is not in the dictionary, a wavy red line appears under it. To correct an error, right-click the misspelled word, then review the suggestions, which appear in the shortcut menu. You can select a suggestion, add the word you typed to your custom dictionary, or ignore it. To turn off automatic spell checking, click the File tab, then click Options to open the PowerPoint Options dialog box. Click Proofing in the left column, then click the Check spelling as you type check box to deselect it. To temporarily hide the wavy red lines, click the Hide spelling and grammar errors check box to select it. Contextual spelling in PowerPoint identifies common grammatically misused words, for example, if you type the word "their" and the correct word is "there," PowerPoint will identify the mistake and place a wavy red line under the word. To turn contextual spelling on or off, click Proofing in the PowerPoint Options dialog box, then click the Check grammar with spelling check box.

Inspect a Presentation

Learning
Outcomes
• Modify document
  properties
• Inspect and
  remove unwanted
  data

Reviewing your presentation can be an important step. You should not only find and fix errors, but also locate and delete confidential company or personal information and document properties you do not want to share with others. If you share presentations with others, especially over the Internet, it is a good idea to inspect the presentation file using the Document Inspector. The **Document Inspector** looks for hidden data and personal information that is stored in the file itself or in the document properties. Document properties, also known as **metadata**, include specific data about the presentation, such as the author's name, subject matter, title, who saved the file last, and when the file was created. Other types of information the Document Inspector can locate and remove include presentation notes, comments, ink annotations, invisible on-slide content, off-slide content, and custom XML data. **CASE** ▶ *You decide to view and add some document properties, inspect your presentation file, and learn about the Mark as Final command.*

STEPS

QUICK TIP
Click the Properties
list button, then click
Advanced Properties
to open the
Properties dialog box
to see or change
more document
properties.

1. **Click the** File tab **on the Ribbon, click the** Add a tag text box **in the Properties section, type** Kenya, water well, **then click the** Add a category text box
   This data provides some descriptive keywords for the presentation.

2. **Type** Proposal, **then click the** Show All Properties link
   The information you enter here about the presentation file can be used to identify and organize your file. The Show All Properties link displays all of the file properties and those you can change. You now use the Document Inspector to search for information you might want to delete in the presentation.

QUICK TIP
If you need to save a
presentation to run
in an earlier version
of PowerPoint, check
for unsupported
features using the
Check Compatibility
feature.

3. **Click the** Check for Issues button, **click** Inspect Document, **then click** Yes **to save the changes to the document**
   The Document Inspector dialog box opens. The Document Inspector searches the presentation file for seven different types of information that you might want removed from the presentation before sharing it.

4. **Make sure all of the check boxes have check marks, then click** Inspect
   The presentation file is reviewed, and the results are shown in FIGURE 4-14. The Document Inspector found items having to do with document properties, which you just entered, and embedded documents which are the pictures in the file. You decide to leave all the document properties alone.

5. **Click** Close, **click the** File tab **on the Ribbon, then click the** Protect Presentation button

6. **Click** Mark as Final, **then click** OK **in the alert box**
   An information alert box opens. Be sure to read the message to understand what happens to the file and how to recognize a marked-as-final presentation. You decide to complete this procedure.

7. **Click** OK, **click the** Home tab **on the Ribbon, then click anywhere in the title text object**
   When you select the title text object, the Ribbon closes automatically and an information alert box at the top of the window notes that the presentation is marked as final, making it a read-only file. Compare your screen to FIGURE 4-15. A **read-only** file is one that can't be edited or modified in any way. Anyone who has received a read-only presentation can only edit the presentation by changing its marked-as-final status. You still want to work on the presentation, so you remove the marked-as-final status.

8. **Click the** Edit Anyway button **in the information alert box, then save your changes**
   The Ribbon and all commands are active again, and the file can now be modified.

FIGURE 4-14: Document Inspector dialog box

FIGURE 4-15: Marked as final presentation

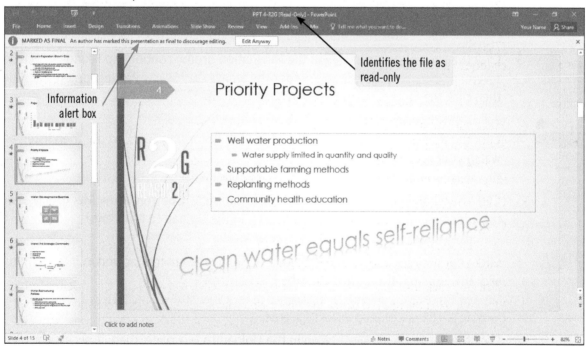

Digitally sign a presentation

What is a digital signature, and why would you want to use one in PowerPoint? A **digital signature** is similar to a handwritten signature in that it authenticates your document; however, a digital signature, unlike a handwritten signature, is created using computer cryptography and is not visible within the presentation itself. There are three primary reasons you would add a digital signature to a presentation: one, to authenticate the signer of the document; two, to ensure that the content of the presentation has not been changed since it was signed; and three, to assure the reader of the origin of the signed document. To add a digital signature, click the File tab on the Ribbon, click the Protect Presentation button, click Add a Digital Signature, then follow the dialog boxes.

Create an Office Mix

Office Mix is a free add-in application developed by Microsoft which, once downloaded from the web, is integrated directly on the PowerPoint Ribbon with its own set of tools located on the Mix tab. Using Office Mix, you create and then insert interactive content onto the slides of your presentation. Content such as a video recording of you giving a presentation, video clips from the web, and interactive quizzes or polls are easy to create. Once you are finished creating your Office Mix, you can publish it to the Office Mix website or the cloud to be shared with others. **CASE** *You decide to create a short recording explaining the chart and introducing a priority project. You then publish the Mix to the Office Mix website. (Note: The Office Mix add-in must be installed from the Office Mix website prior to performing the steps of this lesson.)*

STEPS

1. **Click the** Slide 3 thumbnail **in the Slides tab, click the** Mix tab **on the Ribbon, look over the commands on the Mix tab, then click the** Slide Recording button **in the Record group**
   The Screen Recording view opens as shown in FIGURE 4-16. The Screen Recording view displays the current slide with navigation, recording, and inking tools.

2. **When you are ready to begin recording, click the** Record button **in the Record group, look into your computer's camera, then speak these words into your microphone** "This chart shows the population trends for Kenya, Uganda, and South Africa"
   Your Office Mix recording begins as soon as you click the Record button. If a slide has animations, each animation must be advanced manually during the recording in order to see the animation.

3. **Click the** Next Slide button ➡ **in the Navigation group, continue speaking** "R2G has several priority projects", **drag** ✎ **under the words** Well Water Production **on the slide, then click the** Stop button **in the Navigation group**
   A small speaker appears in the upper right corner of the slide indicating there is a recording on the slide.

4. **Click the** Preview Slide Recording **button in the Recording Tools group, then listen and watch your recording**
   You can move to any slide and preview its recording using the buttons in the Navigation group.

5. **Click the window** Close button, **click the** Upload to Mix button **in the Mix group, read the information, then click the** Next button **in the Upload to Mix pane**
   The Upload to Mix pane displays sign in account methods.

6. **Click your** account button **in the Upload to Mix pane, enter your sign in information, click the** Sign in **button, then click the** Next button
   The new Office Mix is uploaded and published to the Office Mix website. There is a percentage counter showing you the upload and publishing progress.

7. **Click the** Show me my Mix button **in the Upload to Mix pane, then, if necessary, click the** Sign in button **on the webpage that appears**
   The Office Mix webpage appears with the new Office Mix you just created as shown in FIGURE 4-17. On this page you can provide a content description, a category, or a tag, as well as set permissions.

8. **Click** My Mixes **at the top of the window, click the** PPT 4-R2G Play button, **then follow the directions on the screen to watch the Office Mix**
   Each slide in the presentation, including the Office Mix recordings you made on Slide 3 and 4, appears.

9. **Click** Your Name **at the top of the window, click** sign out, **click your** web browser Close button, **click the** Close button **in the Upload to Mix pane, save your changes, submit your presentation to your instructor, then exit PowerPoint**

FIGURE 4-16: **Office Mix screen recording view**

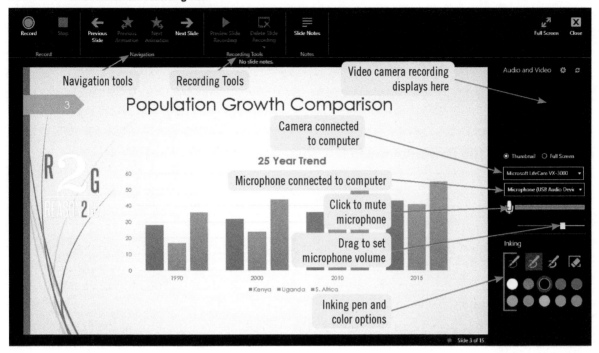

FIGURE 4-17: **Office Mix webpage**

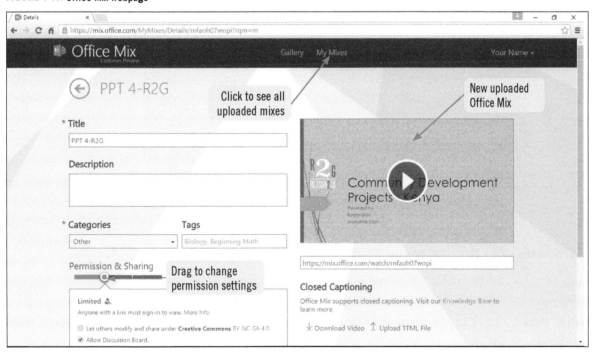

Inserting a multiple choice interactive quiz

Using the Mix tab, you can create a custom interactive quiz that can be presented in Slide Show view or uploaded to the Office Mix website to share with others. On the Mix tab, click the Quizzes Videos Apps button in the Insert group. In the Lab Office Add-ins dialog box, click Multiple Choice Quiz, then click Trust It. A multiple choice quiz object appears on your slide with blank text boxes that you fill out with a quiz question and answers. Be sure to enter the correct answer in the light green answer text box, then add as many other possible answers as you like. You can customize your question by shuffling the answer every time the question is opened, limiting the number of answer attempts, and allowing more than one right answer.

Practice

Concepts Review

Label each element of the PowerPoint window shown in FIGURE 4-18.

FIGURE 4-18

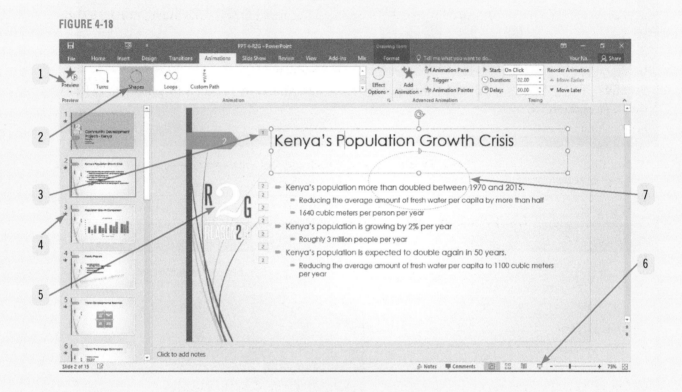

Match each term with the statement that best describes it.

8. Masters

9. Background

10. Presenter view

11. Slide timing

12. Office Mix

13. Ink annotations

a. The area behind the text and graphics

b. Drawings on slide created during slide show

c. A special view that you use when showing a presentation on two monitors

d. Add-in application you use to create interactive content

e. Determines how long slide is visible on screen

f. Slides that store theme and placeholder information

Select the best answer from the list of choices.

14. What determines the position and size of text and content placeholders and the slide background of a presentation?
    a. Home tab
    b. Background
    c. Master
    d. Normal view

15. Apply this to your presentation to quickly modify the applied theme.
    a. Office Mix
    b. Background
    c. Animation
    d. Variant

16. Freehand pen and highlighter strokes are also known as _____.
    a. ink annotations
    b. pictures
    c. markings
    d. scribbles

17. A slide _____ is a special visual effect that determines how a slide moves during a slide show.
    a. annotation
    b. view
    c. background
    d. transition

18. Set slide _____ to make your presentation automatically progress through the slides during a slide show.
    a. animations
    b. timings
    c. hyperlinks
    d. recordings

19. Animation _____ identify the order in which objects are animated during a slide show.
    a. tags
    b. paths
    c. thumbnails
    d. schemes

20. A _____ file is one that can't be edited or modified in any way.
    a. signed
    b. final
    c. read-only
    d. saved

Skills Review

1. **Modify masters.**
   a. Open the presentation PPT 4-3.pptx from the location where you store your Data Files, then save the presentation as **PPT 4-Dual Arm**.
   b. Open Slide Master view using the View tab, then click the Circuit Slide Master thumbnail.
   c. Insert the picture PPT 4-4.jpg, then set the background color to transparent.
   d. Resize the picture so it is 1.0" wide.
   e. Drag the picture to the upper-right corner of the slide to align with the top of the Title text object, then deselect the picture.
   f. Switch to Normal view, then save your changes.

2. **Customize the background and theme.**
   a. Click the Design tab, then click the second variant from the left.
   b. Go to Slide 4, then open the Format Background pane.
   c. Click the Solid fill option button, then click Gold, Accent 1, Darker 25%.
   d. Set the Transparency to 30%, close the Format Background pane then save your changes.

Skills Review (continued)

3. Use slide show commands.

   a. Open Slide Show view, then go to Slide 1 using the See all slides button on the Slide Show toolbar.

   b. Use the Pen ink annotation tool to circle the slide title.

   c. Go to Slide 2, then use the Highlighter to highlight four points in the bulleted text on the slide.

   d. Erase two highlight annotations on the bulleted text, then press [Esc].

   e. Open Presenter view, then stop the timer.

   f. Advance the slides to Slide 5, then click the Zoom into the slide button (now called the Zoom out button) on the Slide Show toolbar, then click in the center of the graph.

   g. Click the Zoom into the slide button, then return to Slide 1.

   h. Hide Presenter view, advance through the slide show, save your ink and highlight annotations, then save your work.

4. Set slide transitions and timings.

   a. Go to Slide Sorter view, click the Slide 1 thumbnail, then apply the Fall Over transition to the slide.

   b. Change the effect option to Right, change the duration to 2.50, then apply to all the slides.

   c. Change the slide timing to 5 seconds, then apply to all of the slides.

   d. Switch to Normal view, view the slide show, then save your work.

5. Animate objects.

   a. Go to Slide 3, click the Animations tab, then select both arrows on the slide. (*Hint*: Use SHIFT to select both arrows.)

   b. Apply the Wipe effect to the objects, click the Effect Options button, then apply the From Top effect.

   c. Select the lower two box shapes, apply the Random Bars animation, then preview the animations.

   d. Change the effect options to Vertical, then preview the animations.

   e. Select the top two box shapes, apply the Shape animation, click the Effect Options button, then click Box.

   f. Click the Move Earlier button in the Timing group until the two top box shape animation tags display 1.

   g. Preview the animations, then save your work.

6. Use proofing and language tools.

   a. Check the spelling of the document, and change any misspelled words. Ignore any words that are correctly spelled but that the spell checker doesn't recognize. There is one misspelled word in the presentation.

   b. Go to Slide 6, then set the Mini Translator language to Thai.

   c. View the Thai translation of text on Slide 6.

   d. Choose one other language (or as many as you want), translate words or phrases on the slide, reset the default language to English (United States), turn off the Mini Translator, then save your changes.

7. Inspect a presentation.

   a. On the File tab in the Properties section, type information of your choosing in the Tags and Categories text fields.

   b. Open the Document Inspector dialog box.

   c. Make sure the Off-Slide Content check box is selected, then inspect the presentation.

   d. Delete the off-slide content, then close the dialog box. Save your changes.

8. Create an Office Mix.

   a. Go to Slide 2, open the Mix tab, then click the Slide Recording button.

   b. Click the Record button, speak these words into your microphone, "Here you see the typical applications for the new R2G series dual robotic arm," use your pen to underline the slide title, then click the Stop button.

   c. Preview your slide recording, then close the window.

   d. Click the Upload to Mix button, sign in to your account, then upload your new mix to the Office Mix website.

   e. Watch the Office Mix, sign out of your account, then close the webpage window.

   f. Close the Upload to Mix pane, then save your work.

Skills Review (continued)

g. Switch to Slide Sorter view, then compare your presentation to FIGURE 4-19.

h. Submit your presentation to your instructor, then close the presentation.

FIGURE 4-19

Independent Challenge 1

You work for World International Studies Program (WISP) as a study consultant. You have been working on a presentation that describes a new study program developed in Russia. You need to finish up what you have been working on by adding transitions, timings, and animation effects to the presentation.

a. Open the file PPT 4-5.pptx from the location where you store your Data Files, and save the presentation as **PPT 4-WISP**.

b. Add the slide number and your name as the footer on all slides, except the title slide.

c. Open Slide Master view, click the Celestial Slide Master thumbnail, insert the picture PPT 4-6.jpg, then resize the picture so it is 1.5" wide.

d. Click the Color button, then click the Purple, Accent color 1 Dark in the Recolor section.

e. Move the picture to the top left corner of the slide, then close Slide Master view.

f. Apply the Shape animation to the title text on each slide.

g. Apply the Float In animation to the bulleted text objects on each slide.

h. Apply the Shape animation to the picture on Slide 3, then change the effect option to Box.

i. Apply the Vortex slide transition, apply a 5-second slide timing, then apply to all of the slides.

j. Check the spelling of the presentation, save your changes, then view the presentation in Slide Show view.

k. Submit your presentation to your instructor, close the presentation, then exit PowerPoint.

Independent Challenge 2

You are a development engineer at Adtec Global Systems, Inc., a manufacturer of civilian drone technology located in Phoenix, Arizona. Adtec designs and manufactures personal drone systems largely used in the movie industry and in commercial agricultural business. You need to finish the work on a quarterly presentation that outlines the progress of the company's newest technologies by adding animations, customizing the background, and using the Document Inspector.

a. Open the file PPT 4-7.pptx from the location where you store your Data Files, and save the presentation as **PPT 4-Adtec**.

Independent Challenge 2 (continued)

b. Apply an appropriate design theme, then apply a gradient fill slide background to the title slide using the Format Background pane.

c. Apply the Airplane slide transition to all slides, apply the Shape animation to the following objects: the bulleted text on Slide 2 and the table on Slide 4, then change the Effect options on the table to a box shape with an out direction.

d. Use the Microsoft Translator to translate the bulleted text on Slide 2 using two different languages.

e. Run the Document Inspector with all options selected, identify what items the Document Inspector finds, close the Document Inspector dialog box, then review the slides to find the items.

f. Add a slide at the end of the presentation that identifies the items the Document Inspector found.

g. Run the Document Inspector again, and remove all items except the document properties.

h. View the slide show, and make ink annotations to the slides. Save the annotations at the end of the slide show.

i. Add your name as a footer to all slides, check the spelling, fix any misspellings, then save your work.

j. Submit your presentation to your instructor, then close the presentation and exit PowerPoint.

Independent Challenge 3

You work for Buffington, Genung, O'Lynn & Associates, a full-service investment and pension firm. Your manager wants you to create a presentation on pension plan options. You completed adding the information to the presentation, now you need to add a design theme, format information to highlight important facts, add animation effects, and add slide timings.

a. Open the file PPT 4-8.pptx from the location where you store your Data Files, and save the presentation as **PPT 4-Invest**.

b. Apply an appropriate design theme, then apply a theme variant.

c. Apply animation effects to the following objects: the shapes on Slide 3 and the bulleted text on Slide 4. View the slide show to evaluate the effects you added, and make adjustments as necessary.

d. Convert the text on Slide 5 to a Circle Relationship SmartArt graphic (found in the Relationship category).

e. Apply the Inset SmartArt style to the SmartArt graphic, then change its color to Dark 2 Fill.

f. Go to Slide 3, align the Sector and Quality arrow shapes to their bottoms, then align the Allocation and Maturity arrow shapes to their right edges.

g. On Slides 6 and 7, change the table style format to Themed Style 1 - Accent 2, and adjust the tables.

h. Apply a 7-second timing to Slides 3–7 and a 5-second timing to Slides 1 and 2.

i. Add your name as a footer to the slides, check the spelling, then save your work. An example of a finished presentation is shown in FIGURE 4-20.

j. Submit your presentation to your instructor, then close the presentation and exit PowerPoint.

FIGURE 4-20

Independent Challenge 4: Explore

You work for the Office of Veterans Affairs at your college. Create a basic presentation that you can publish to the Office Mix website that describes the basic services offered by the school to service members. (*Note: To complete this Independent Challenge, you may need to be connected to the Internet.*)

a. Plan and create the slide presentation that describes the veteran services provided by the college. To help create content, use your school's website or use the Internet to locate information at another college. The presentation should contain at least six slides.

b. Use an appropriate design theme then change the theme variant.

c. Add one or more photographs to the presentation, then style and customize at least one photo.

d. Save the presentation as **PPT 4-Vet** to the location where you store your Data Files.

e. Add slide transitions and animation effects to the presentation. View the slide show to evaluate the effects you added.

f. Go to Slide 5, translate the last line of text in the bulleted text box into Greek, then click the Copy button on the Microsoft Translator box.

g. Insert a new text box on Slide 5, paste the Greek text into the text box, then drag the Greek text box below the bulleted text box.

h. Change the language in the Microsoft translator back to English, then turn off the Microsoft Translator.

i. Add the slide number and your name as a footer to the slides, check the spelling, inspect the presentation, then save your work.

j. Make an Office Mix of this presentation, then upload it to the Office Mix website. Make sure to include information in your recording on at least 2 slides and use the pen to make ink annotations on your slides.

k. Submit your presentation to your instructor, then exit PowerPoint. An example of a finished presentation is shown in FIGURE 4-21.

FIGURE 4-21

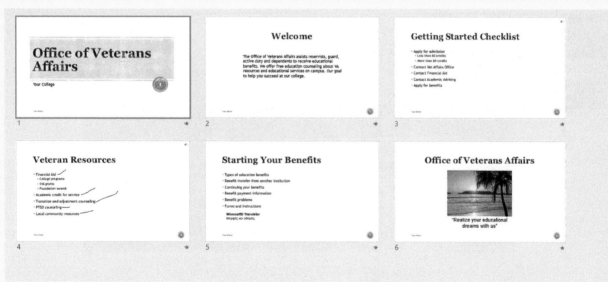

Visual Workshop

Create a presentation that looks like FIGURE 4-22, and FIGURE 4-23, which shows two slides with a specific slide layout, slide background, theme, and theme variant. Insert pictures **PPT 4-9** and **PPT 4-10** to the slides, then insert the picture **PPT 4-6** to the presentation slide master. (*Hint*: the slide master picture background is transparent.) Add your name as footer text to the slide, save the presentation as **PPT 4-Corp** to the location where you store your Data Files, then submit your presentation to your instructor.

© Prasit Rodphan/Shutterstock.com

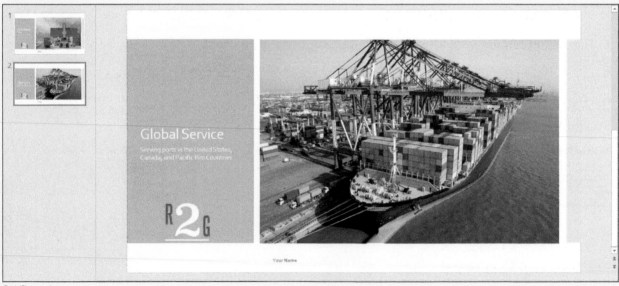

© tcly/Shutterstock.com

Getting Started with Excel 2016

CASE You have been hired as an assistant at Reason2Go (R2G), a company that allows travelers to make a difference in the global community through voluntourism, while having a memorable vacation experience. You report to Yolanda Lee, the vice president of finance. As Yolanda's assistant, you create worksheets to analyze data from various divisions of the company, so you can help her make sound decisions on company expansion, investments, and new voluntourism opportunities.

Module Objectives

After completing this module, you will be able to:

- Understand spreadsheet software
- Identify Excel 2016 window components
- Understand formulas
- Enter labels and values and use the AutoSum button

- Edit cell entries
- Enter and edit a simple formula
- Switch worksheet views
- Choose print options

Files You Will Need

EX 1-1.xlsx   EX 1-4.xlsx
EX 1-2.xlsx   EX 1-5.xlsx
EX 1-3.xlsx

Understand Spreadsheet Software

Learning Outcomes
- Describe the uses of Excel
- Define key spreadsheet terms

Microsoft Excel is the electronic spreadsheet program within the Microsoft Office suite. An **electronic spreadsheet** is an app you use to perform numeric calculations and to analyze and present numeric data. One advantage of a spreadsheet program over pencil and paper is that your calculations are updated automatically, so you can change entries without having to manually recalculate. TABLE 1-1 shows some of the common business tasks people accomplish using Excel. In Excel, the electronic spreadsheet you work in is called a **worksheet**, and it is contained in a file called a **workbook**, which has the file extension .xlsx. **CASE** *At R2G, you use Excel extensively to track finances and manage corporate data.*

DETAILS

When you use Excel, you have the ability to:

- **Enter data quickly and accurately**

  With Excel, you can enter information faster and more accurately than with pencil and paper. FIGURE 1-1 shows a payroll worksheet created using pencil and paper. FIGURE 1-2 shows the same worksheet created using Excel. Equations were added to calculate the hours and pay. You can use Excel to recreate this information for each week by copying the worksheet's structure and the information that doesn't change from week to week, then entering unique data and formulas for each week.

- **Recalculate data easily**

  Fixing typing errors or updating data is easy in Excel. In the payroll example, if you receive updated hours for an employee, you just enter the new hours and Excel recalculates the pay.

- **Perform what-if analysis**

  The ability to change data and quickly view the recalculated results gives you the power to make informed business decisions. For instance, if you're considering raising the hourly rate for an entry-level tour guide from $12.50 to $15.00, you can enter the new value in the worksheet and immediately see the impact on the overall payroll as well as on the individual employee. Any time you use a worksheet to ask the question "What if?" you are performing **what-if analysis**. Excel also includes a Scenario Manager where you can name and save different what-if versions of your worksheet.

- **Change the appearance of information**

  Excel provides powerful features, such as the Quick Analysis tool, for making information visually appealing and easier to understand. Format text and numbers in different fonts, colors, and styles to make it stand out.

- **Create charts**

  Excel makes it easy to create charts based on worksheet information. Charts are updated automatically in Excel whenever data changes. The worksheet in FIGURE 1-2 includes a 3-D pie chart.

- **Share information**

  It's easy for everyone at R2G to collaborate in Excel using the company intranet, the Internet, or a network storage device. For example, you can complete the weekly payroll that your boss, Yolanda Lee, started creating. You can also take advantage of collaboration tools such as shared workbooks so that multiple people can edit a workbook simultaneously.

- **Build on previous work**

  Instead of creating a new worksheet for every project, it's easy to modify an existing Excel worksheet. When you are ready to create next week's payroll, you can open the file for last week's payroll, save it with a new filename, and modify the information as necessary. You can also use predesigned, formatted files called **templates** to create new worksheets quickly. Excel comes with many templates that you can customize.

FIGURE 1-1: Traditional paper worksheet

Reason2Go
Project Leader Divison Payroll Calculator

Name	Hours	O/T Hrs	Hrly Rate	Reg Pay	O/T Pay	Gross Pay
Brucker, Pieter	40	4	16.75	670	134	804
Cucci, Lucia	35	0	12	420	0	420
Klimt, Gustave	40	2	13.25	530	53	583
Lafontaine, Jeanne	29	0	15.25	442.25	0	442.25
Martinez, Juan	37	0	13.2	488.4	0	488.4
Mioshi, Keiko	39	0	21	819	0	819
Shernwood, Burt	40	0	16.75	670	0	670
Strano, Riccardo	40	8	16.25	650	260	910
Wadsworth, Alice	40	5	13.25	530	132.5	662.5
Yamamoto, Johji	38	0	15.5	589	0	589

FIGURE 1-2: Excel worksheet

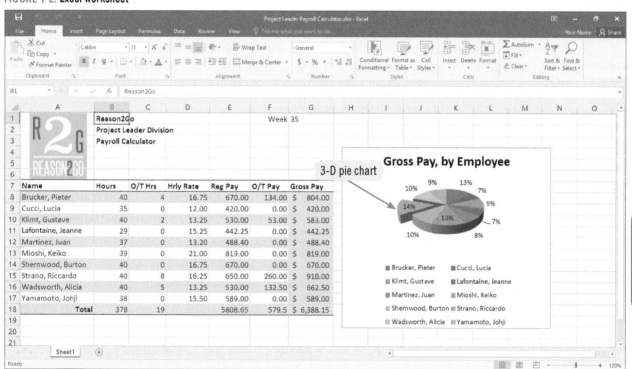

TABLE 1-1: Business tasks you can accomplish using Excel

you can use spreadsheets to	by
Perform calculations	Adding formulas and functions to worksheet data; for example, adding a list of sales results or calculating a car payment
Represent values graphically	Creating charts based on worksheet data; for example, creating a chart that displays expenses
Generate reports	Creating workbooks that combine information from multiple worksheets, such as summarized sales information from multiple stores
Organize data	Sorting data in ascending or descending order; for example, alphabetizing a list of products or customer names, or prioritizing orders by date
Analyze data	Creating data summaries and short lists using PivotTables or AutoFilters; for example, making a list of the top 10 customers based on spending habits
Create what-if data scenarios	Using variable values to investigate and sample different outcomes, such as changing the interest rate or payment schedule on a loan

Identify Excel 2016 Window Components

Learning
Outcomes
• Open and save an
  Excel file
• Identify Excel
  window elements

To start Excel, Microsoft Windows must be running. Similar to starting any app in Office, you can use the Start button on the Windows taskbar, the Start button on your keyboard, or you may have a shortcut on your desktop you prefer to use. If you need additional assistance, ask your instructor or technical support person. **CASE** *You decide to start Excel and familiarize yourself with the worksheet window.*

STEPS

QUICK TIP

For more information on starting a program or opening and saving a file, see the module "Getting Started with Microsoft Office 2016."

1. **Start Excel, click** Open Other Workbooks **on the navigation bar, click** This PC, **then click** Browse **to open the Open dialog box**

2. **In the Open dialog box, navigate to the location where you store your Data Files, click** EX 1-1.xlsx, **then click** Open

   The file opens in the Excel window.

3. **Click the** File tab, **click** Save As **on the navigation bar, then click** Browse **to open the Save As dialog box**

TROUBLE

If you don't see the extension .xlsx on the filenames in the Save As dialog box, don't worry; Windows can be set up to display or not to display the file extensions.

4. **In the Save As dialog box, navigate to the location where you store your Data Files if necessary, type** EX 1-Project Leader Payroll Calculator **in the File name text box, then click** Save

   Using FIGURE 1-3 as a guide, identify the following items:

   • The **Name box** displays the active cell address. "A1" appears in the Name box.
   • The **formula bar** allows you to enter or edit data in the worksheet.
   • The **worksheet window** contains a grid of columns and rows. Columns are labeled alphabetically and rows are labeled numerically. The worksheet window can contain a total of 1,048,576 rows and 16,384 columns. The intersection of a column and a row is called a **cell**. Cells can contain text, numbers, formulas, or a combination of all three. Every cell has its own unique location or **cell address**, which is identified by the coordinates of the intersecting column and row. The column and row indicators are shaded to make identifying the cell address easy.
   • The **cell pointer** is a dark rectangle that outlines the cell you are working in. This cell is called the **active cell**. In FIGURE 1-3, the cell pointer outlines cell A1, so A1 is the active cell. The column and row headings for the active cell are highlighted, making it easier to locate.
   • **Sheet tabs** below the worksheet grid let you switch from sheet to sheet in a workbook. By default, a workbook file contains one worksheet—but you can have as many sheets as your computer's memory allows, in a workbook. The New sheet button to the right of Sheet 1 allows you to add worksheets to a workbook. **Sheet tab scrolling buttons** let you navigate to additional sheet tabs when available.
   • You can use the **scroll bars** to move around in a worksheet that is too large to fit on the screen at once.
   • The **status bar** is located at the bottom of the Excel window. It provides a brief description of the active command or task in progress. **The mode indicator** in the lower-left corner of the status bar provides additional information about certain tasks.

5. **Click cell** A4

   Cell A4 becomes the active cell. To activate a different cell, you can click the cell or press the arrow keys on your keyboard to move to it.

QUICK TIP

The button that displays in the bottom-right corner of a range is the Quick Analysis tool.

6. **Click cell** B5, **press and hold the mouse button, drag ⊕ to cell** B14, **then release the mouse button**

   You selected a group of cells and they are highlighted, as shown in FIGURE 1-4. A selection of two or more cells such as B5:B14 is called a **range**; you select a range when you want to perform an action on a group of cells at once, such as moving them or formatting them. When you select a range, the status bar displays the average, count (or number of items selected), and sum of the selected cells as a quick reference.

FIGURE 1-3: **Open workbook**

FIGURE 1-4: **Selected range**

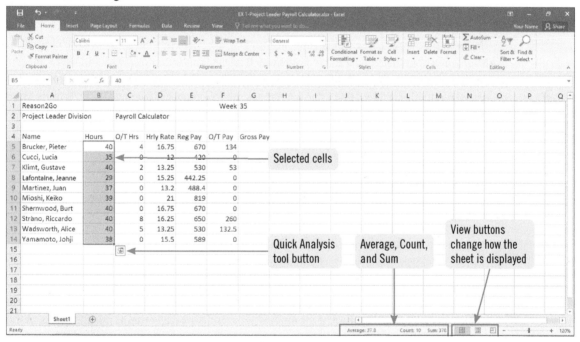

Using OneDrive and Office Online

If you have a Microsoft account, you can save your Excel files and photos in OneDrive, a cloud-based service from Microsoft. When you save files in OneDrive, you can access them on other devices—such as a tablet or smartphone. OneDrive is available as an app on smartphones and tablets, making access simple. You can open files to view them on any device, and you can even make edits to them using **Office Online**, which includes simplified versions of the apps found in the Office 2016 suite. Because Office Online is web-based, the apps take up no computer disk space and you can use them on any Internet-connected device.

Understand Formulas

Learning
Outcomes
• Explain how a
  formula works
• Identify Excel
  arithmetic operators

Excel is a truly powerful program because users at every level of mathematical expertise can make calculations with accuracy. To do so, you use formulas. A **formula** is an equation in a worksheet. You use formulas to make calculations as simple as adding a column of numbers, or as complex as creating profit-and-loss projections for a global corporation. To tap into the power of Excel, you should understand how formulas work. **CASE** *Managers at R2G use the Project Leader Payroll Calculator workbook to keep track of employee hours prior to submitting them to the Payroll Department. You'll be using this workbook regularly, so you need to understand the formulas it contains and how Excel calculates the results.*

STEPS

1. **Click cell E5**

   The active cell contains a formula, which appears on the formula bar. All Excel formulas begin with the equal sign (=). If you want a cell to show the result of adding 4 plus 2, the formula in the cell would look like this: =4+2. If you want a cell to show the result of multiplying two values in your worksheet, such as the values in cells B5 and D5, the formula would look like this: =B5*D5, as shown in FIGURE 1-5. While you're entering a formula in a cell, the cell references and arithmetic operators appear on the formula bar. See TABLE 1-2 for a list of commonly used arithmetic operators. When you're finished entering the formula, you can either click the Enter button on the formula bar or press [Enter].

2. **Click cell F5**

   This cell contains an example of a more complex formula, which calculates overtime pay. At R2G, overtime pay is calculated at twice the regular hourly rate times the number of overtime hours. The formula used to calculate overtime pay for the employee in row 5 is:

   O/T Hrs times (2 times Hrly Rate)

   In the worksheet cell, you would enter: =C5*(2*D5), as shown in FIGURE 1-6. The use of parentheses creates groups within the formula and indicates which calculations to complete first—an important consideration in complex formulas. In this formula, first the hourly rate is multiplied by 2, because that calculation is within the parentheses. Next, that value is multiplied by the number of overtime hours. Because overtime is calculated at twice the hourly rate, managers are aware that they need to closely watch this expense.

DETAILS

In creating calculations in Excel, it is important to:

• **Know where the formulas should be**

  An Excel formula is created in the cell where the formula's results should appear. This means that the formula calculating Gross Pay for the employee in row 5 will be entered in cell G5.

• **Know exactly what cells and arithmetic operations are needed**

  Don't guess; make sure you know exactly what cells are involved before creating a formula.

• **Create formulas with care**

  Make sure you know exactly what you want a formula to accomplish before it is created. An inaccurate formula may have far-reaching effects if the formula or its results are referenced by other formulas, as shown in the payroll example in FIGURE 1-6.

• **Use cell references rather than values**

  The beauty of Excel is that whenever you change a value in a cell, any formula containing a reference to that cell is automatically updated. For this reason, it's important that you use cell references in formulas, rather than actual values, whenever possible.

• **Determine what calculations will be needed**

  Sometimes it's difficult to predict what data will be needed within a worksheet, but you should try to anticipate what statistical information may be required. For example, if there are columns of numbers, chances are good that both column and row totals should be present.

FIGURE 1-5: Viewing a formula

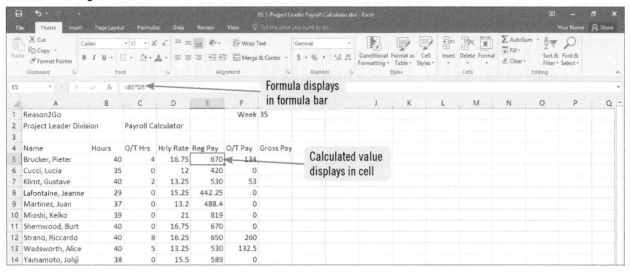

Formula displays in formula bar

Calculated value displays in cell

FIGURE 1-6: Formula with multiple operators

Formula to calculate overtime pay

TABLE 1-2: Excel arithmetic operators

operator	purpose	example
+	Addition	=A5+A7
-	Subtraction or negation	=A5-10
*	Multiplication	=A5*A7
/	Division	=A5/A7
%	Percent	=35%
^ (caret)	Exponent	=6^2 (same as 6^2)

Enter Labels and Values and Use the AutoSum Button

Learning Outcomes
- Build formulas with the AutoSum button
- Copy formulas with the fill handle

To enter content in a cell, you can type in the formula bar or directly in the cell itself. When entering content in a worksheet, you should start by entering all the labels first. **Labels** are entries that contain text and numerical information not used in calculations, such as "2019 Sales" or "Travel Expenses". Labels help you identify data in worksheet rows and columns, making your worksheet easier to understand. **Values** are numbers, formulas, and functions that can be used in calculations. To enter a calculation, you type an equal sign (=) plus the formula for the calculation; some examples of an Excel calculation are "=2+2" and "=C5+C6". Functions are built-in formulas; you learn more about them in the next module. **CASE** ▸ *You want to enter some information in the Project Leader Payroll Calculator workbook and use a very simple function to total a range of cells.*

STEPS

1. **Click cell A15, then click in the formula bar**

    Notice that the **mode indicator** on the status bar now reads "Edit," indicating you are in Edit mode. You are in Edit mode any time you are entering or changing the contents of a cell.

2. **Type Totals, then click the Enter button ✓ on the formula bar**

    Clicking the Enter button accepts the entry. The new text is left-aligned in the cell. Labels are left-aligned by default, and values are right-aligned by default. Excel recognizes an entry as a value if it is a number or it begins with one of these symbols: +, -, =, @, #, or $. When a cell contains both text and numbers, Excel recognizes it as a label.

3. **Click cell B15**

    You want this cell to total the hours worked by all the trip advisors. You might think you need to create a formula that looks like this: =B5+B6+B7+B8+B9+B10+B11+B12+B13+B14. However, there's an easier way to achieve this result.

4. **Click the AutoSum button Σ in the Editing group on the Home tab on the Ribbon**

    The SUM function is inserted in the cell, and a suggested range appears in parentheses, as shown in FIGURE 1-7. A **function** is a built-in formula; it includes the **arguments** (the information necessary to calculate an answer) as well as cell references and other unique information. Clicking the AutoSum button sums the adjacent range (that is, the cells next to the active cell) above or to the left, although you can adjust the range if necessary by selecting a different range before accepting the cell entry. Using the SUM function is quicker than entering a formula, and using the range B5:B14 is more efficient than entering individual cell references.

5. **Click ✓ on the formula bar**

    Excel calculates the total contained in cells B5:B14 and displays the result, 378, in cell B15. The cell actually contains the formula =SUM(B5:B14), and the result is displayed.

6. **Click cell C13, type 6, then press [Enter]**

    The number 6 replaces the cell's contents, the cell pointer moves to cell C14, and the value in cell F13 changes.

7. **Click cell C18, type Average Gross Pay, then press [Enter]**

    The new label is entered in cell C18. The contents appear to spill into the empty cells to the right.

8. **Click cell B15, position the pointer on the lower-right corner of the cell (the fill handle) so that the pointer changes to +, drag + to cell G15, then release the mouse button**

    Dragging the fill handle across a range of cells copies the contents of the first cell into the other cells in the range. In the range B15:G15, each filled cell now contains a function that sums the range of cells above, as shown in FIGURE 1-8.

9. **Save your work**

Getting Started with Excel 2016

FIGURE 1-7: Creating a formula using the AutoSum button

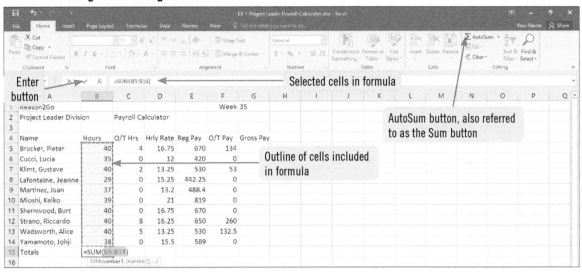

Enter button

Selected cells in formula =SUM(B5:B14)

AutoSum button, also referred to as the Sum button

Outline of cells included in formula

FIGURE 1-8: Results of copied SUM functions

	A	B	C	D	E	F	G
1	Reason2Go					Week 35	
2	Project Leader Division		Payroll Calculator				
3							
4	Name	Hours	O/T Hrs	Hrly Rate	Reg Pay	O/T Pay	Gross Pay
5	Brucker, Pieter	40	4	16.75	670	134	
6	Cucci, Lucia	35	0	12	420	0	
7	Klimt, Gustave	40	2	13.25	530	53	
8	Lafontaine, Jeanne	29	0	15.25	442.25	0	
9	Martinez, Juan	37	0	13.2	488.4	0	
10	Mioshi, Keiko	39	0	21	819	0	
11	Shernwood, Burt	40	0	16.75	670	0	
12	Strano, Riccardo	40	8	16.25	650	260	
13	Wadsworth, Alice	40	6	13.25	530	159	
14	Yamamoto, Johji	38	0	15.5	589	0	
15	Totals	378	20	153.2	5808.65	606	0
16							

B15 =SUM(B5:B14)

Auto Fill options button

Navigating a worksheet

With over a million cells available in a worksheet, it is important to know how to move around in, or **navigate**, a worksheet. You can use the arrow keys on the keyboard , ↑ , ↓ , → , or ← to move one cell at a time, or press [Page Up] or [Page Down] to move one screen at a time. To move one screen to the left, press [Alt][Page Up]; to move one screen to the right, press [Alt][Page Down]. You can also use the mouse pointer to click the desired cell. If the desired cell is not visible in the worksheet window, use the scroll bars or use the Go To command by clicking the Find & Select button in the Editing group on the Home tab on the Ribbon. To quickly jump to the first cell in a worksheet, press [Ctrl][Home]; to jump to the last cell, press [Ctrl][End].

Edit Cell Entries

Learning
Outcomes
• Edit cell entries in
the formula bar
• Edit cell entries in
the cell

You can change, or **edit**, the contents of an active cell at any time. To do so, double-click the cell, and then click in the formula bar or just start typing. Excel switches to Edit mode when you are making cell entries. Different pointers, shown in TABLE 1-3, guide you through the editing process. **CASE** *You noticed some errors in the worksheet and want to make corrections. The first error is in cell A5, which contains a misspelled name.*

STEPS

1. **Click cell A5, then click to the right of P in the formula bar**

   As soon as you click in the formula bar, a blinking vertical line called the **insertion point** appears on the formula bar at the location where new text will be inserted. See FIGURE 1-9. The mouse pointer changes to I when you point anywhere in the formula bar.

2. **Press [Delete], then click the Enter button ✓ on the formula bar**

   Clicking the Enter button accepts the edit, and the spelling of the employee's first name is corrected. You can also press [Enter] or [Tab] to accept an edit. Pressing [Enter] to accept an edit moves the cell pointer down one cell, and pressing [Tab] to accept an edit moves the cell pointer one cell to the right.

QUICK TIP

On some keyboards, you might need to press an [F-Lock] key to enable the function keys.

3. **Click cell B6, then press [F2]**

   Excel switches to Edit mode, and the insertion point blinks in the cell. Pressing [F2] activates the cell for editing directly in the cell instead of the formula bar. Whether you edit in the cell or the formula bar is simply a matter of preference; the results in the worksheet are the same.

QUICK TIP

The Undo button allows you to reverse up to 100 previous actions, one at a time.

4. **Press [Backspace], type 8, then press [Enter]**

   The value in the cell changes from 35 to 38, and cell B7 becomes the active cell. Did you notice that the calculations in cells B15 and E15 also changed? That's because those cells contain formulas that include cell B6 in their calculations. If you make a mistake when editing, you can click the Cancel button ✕ on the formula bar *before* pressing [Enter] to confirm the cell entry. The Enter and Cancel buttons appear only when you're in Edit mode. If you notice the mistake *after* you have confirmed the cell entry, click the Undo button ↶ ▾ on the Quick Access toolbar.

QUICK TIP

You can use the keyboard to select all cell contents by clicking to the right of the cell contents in the cell or formula bar, pressing and holding [Shift], then pressing [Home].

5. **Click cell A9, then double-click the word Juan in the formula bar**

   Double-clicking a word in a cell selects it. When you selected the word, the Mini toolbar automatically displayed.

6. **Type Javier, then press [Enter]**

   When text is selected, typing deletes it and replaces it with the new text.

7. **Double-click cell C12, press [Delete], type 4, then click ✓**

   Double-clicking a cell activates it for editing directly in the cell. Compare your screen to FIGURE 1-10.

8. **Save your work**

Recovering unsaved changes to a workbook file

You can use Excel's AutoRecover feature to automatically save (Autosave) your work as often as you want. This means that if you suddenly lose power or if Excel closes unexpectedly while you're working, you can recover all or some of the changes you made since you saved it last. (Of course, this is no substitute for regularly saving your work: this is just added insurance.) To customize the AutoRecover settings, click the File tab, click Options, then click

Save. AutoRecover lets you decide how often and into which location it should Autosave files. When you restart Excel after losing power, a Document Recovery pane opens and provides access to the saved and Autosaved versions of the files that were open when Excel closed. You can also click the File tab, click Open on the navigation bar, then click any file in the Recover Unsaved Workbooks list to open Autosaved workbooks.

FIGURE 1-9: Worksheet in Edit mode

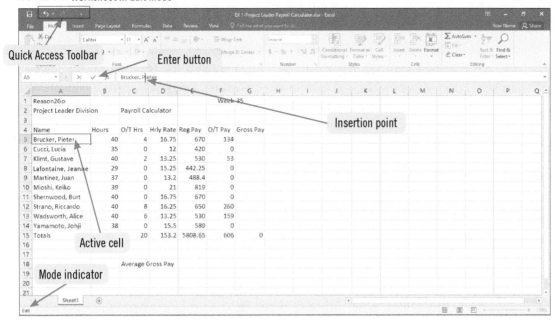

FIGURE 1-9: Worksheet in Edit mode

FIGURE 1-10: Edited worksheet

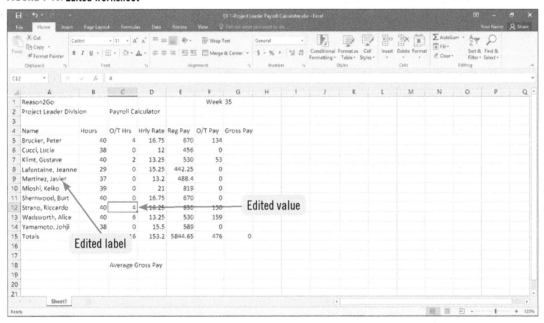

TABLE 1-3: Common pointers in Excel

name	pointer	use to	visible over the
Normal		Select a cell or range; indicates Ready mode	Active worksheet
Fill handle		Copy cell contents to adjacent cells	Lower right corner of the active cell or range
I-beam		Edit cell contents in active cell or formula bar	Active cell in Edit mode or over the formula bar
Move		Change the location of the selected cell(s)	Perimeter of the active cell(s)
Copy		Create a duplicate of the selected cell(s)	Perimeter of the active cell(s) when [Ctrl] is pressed
Column resize		Change the width of a column	Border between column heading indicators

Enter and Edit a Simple Formula

You use formulas in Excel to perform calculations such as adding, multiplying, and averaging. Formulas in an Excel worksheet start with the equal sign (=), also called the **formula prefix**, followed by cell addresses, range names, values, and **calculation operators**. Calculation operators indicate what type of calculation you want to perform on the cells, ranges, or values. They can include **arithmetic operators**, which perform mathematical calculations (see TABLE 1-2 in the "Understand Formulas" lesson); **comparison operators**, which compare values for the purpose of true/false results; **text concatenation operators**, which join strings of text in different cells; and **reference operators**, which enable you to use ranges in calculations. **CASE** *You want to create a formula in the worksheet that calculates gross pay for each employee.*

STEPS

1. **Click cell G5**

   This is the first cell where you want to insert the formula. To calculate gross pay, you need to add regular pay and overtime pay. For employee Peter Brucker, regular pay appears in cell E5 and overtime pay appears in cell F5.

2. **Type =, click cell E5, type +, then click cell F5**

   Compare your formula bar to FIGURE 1-11. The blue and red cell references in cell G5 correspond to the colored cell outlines. When entering a formula, it's a good idea to use cell references instead of values whenever you can. That way, if you later change a value in a cell (if, for example, Peter's regular pay changes to 690), any formula that includes this information reflects accurate, up-to-date results.

3. **Click the Enter button ☑ on the formula bar**

   The result of the formula =E5+F5, 804, appears in cell G5. This same value appears in cell G15 because cell G15 contains a formula that totals the values in cells G5:G14, and there are no other values at this time.

4. **Click cell F5**

   The formula in this cell calculates overtime pay by multiplying overtime hours (C5) times twice the regular hourly rate (2*D5). You want to edit this formula to reflect a new overtime pay rate.

5. **Click to the right of 2 in the formula bar, then type .5 as shown in FIGURE 1-12**

   The formula that calculates overtime pay has been edited.

6. **Click ☑ on the formula bar**

   Compare your screen to FIGURE 1-13. Notice that the calculated values in cells G5, F15, and G15 have all changed to reflect your edits to cell F5.

7. **Save your work**

Understanding named ranges

It can be difficult to remember the cell locations of critical information in a worksheet, but using cell names can make this task much easier. You can name a single cell or range of contiguous, or touching, cells. For example, you might name a cell that contains data on average gross pay "AVG_GP" instead of trying to remember the cell address C18. A named range must begin with a letter or an underscore. It cannot contain any spaces or be the same as a built-in name, such as a function or another object (such as a different named range) in the workbook. To name a range, select the cell(s) you want to name, click the Name box in the formula bar, type the name you want to use, then press [Enter]. You can also name a range by clicking the Formulas tab, then clicking the Define Name button in the Defined Names group. Type the new range name in the Name text box in the New Name dialog box, verify the selected range, then click OK. When you use a named range in a formula, the named range appears instead of the cell address. You can also create a named range using the contents of a cell already in the range. Select the range containing the text you want to use as a name, then click the Create from Selection button in the Defined Names group. The Create Names from Selection dialog box opens. Choose the location of the name you want to use, then click OK.

FIGURE 1-11: Simple formula in a worksheet

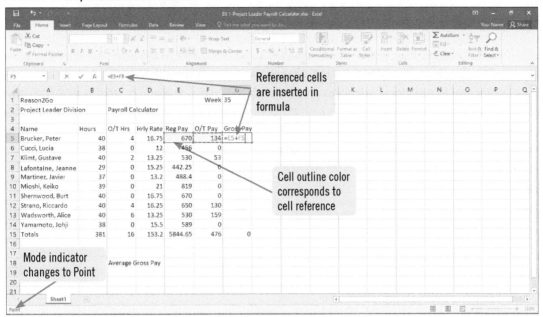

FIGURE 1-12: Edited formula in a worksheet

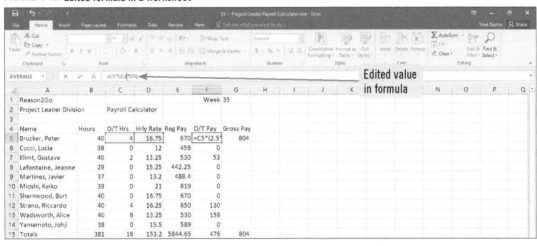

FIGURE 1-13: Edited formula with changes

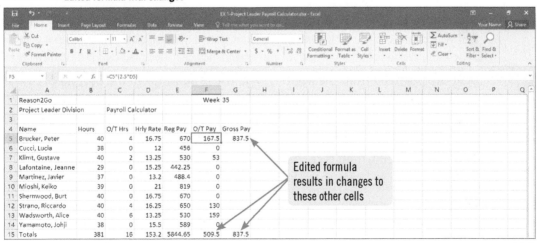

Excel 2016

Switch Worksheet Views

Learning Outcomes
• Change worksheet views
• Create a header/footer
• Select a range

You can change your view of the worksheet window at any time, using either the View tab on the Ribbon or the View buttons on the status bar. Changing your view does not affect the contents of a worksheet; it just makes it easier for you to focus on different tasks, such as entering content or preparing a worksheet for printing. The View tab includes a variety of viewing options, such as View buttons, zoom controls, and the ability to show or hide worksheet elements such as gridlines. The status bar offers fewer View options but can be more convenient to use. **CASE** *You want to make some final adjustments to your worksheet, including adding a header so the document looks more polished.*

STEPS

QUICK TIP

Although a worksheet can contain more than a million rows and thousands of columns, the current document contains only as many pages as necessary for the current project.

1. **Click the View tab on the Ribbon, then click the Page Layout button in the Workbook Views group**

   The view switches from the default view, Normal, to Page Layout view. **Normal view** shows the worksheet without including certain details like headers and footers, or tools like rulers and a page number indicator; it's great for creating and editing a worksheet, but may not be detailed enough when you want to put the finishing touches on a document. **Page Layout view** provides a more accurate view of how a worksheet will look when printed, as shown in FIGURE 1-14. The margins of the page are displayed, along with a text box for the header. A footer text box appears at the bottom of the page, but your screen may not be large enough to view it without scrolling. Above and to the left of the page are rulers. Part of an additional page appears to the right of this page, but it is dimmed, indicating that it does not contain any data. A page number indicator on the status bar tells you the current page and the total number of pages in this worksheet.

2. **Move the pointer ⟍ over the header *without clicking***

   The header is made up of three text boxes: left, center, and right. Each text box is outlined in green as you pass over it with the pointer.

QUICK TIP

You can change header and footer information using the Header & Footer Tools Design tab that opens on the Ribbon when a header or footer is active. For example, you can insert the date by clicking the Current Date button in the Header & Footer Elements group, or insert the time by clicking the Current Time button.

3. **Click the left header text box, type Reason2Go, click the center header text box, type Project Leader Payroll Calculator, click the right header text box, then type Week 35**

   The new text appears in the text boxes, as shown in FIGURE 1-15. You can also press the [Tab] key to advance from one header box to the next.

4. **Select the range A1:G2, then press [Delete]**

   The duplicate information you just entered in the header is deleted from cells in the worksheet.

5. **Click the View tab if necessary, click the Ruler check box in the Show group, then click the Gridlines check box in the Show group**

   The rulers and the gridlines are hidden. By default, gridlines in a worksheet do not print, so hiding them gives you a more accurate image of your final document.

6. **Click the Page Break Preview button 🗒 on the status bar**

   Your view changes to Page Break Preview, which displays a reduced view of each page of your worksheet, along with page break indicators that you can drag to include more or less information on a page.

QUICK TIP

Once you view a worksheet in Page Break Preview, the page break indicators appear as dotted lines after you switch back to Normal view or Page Layout view.

7. **Drag the pointer ⇕ from the bottom page break indicator to the bottom of row 20**

   See FIGURE 1-16. When you're working on a large worksheet with multiple pages, sometimes you need to adjust where pages break; in this worksheet, however, the information all fits comfortably on one page.

8. **Click the Page Layout button in the Workbook Views group, click the Ruler check box in the Show group, then click the Gridlines check box in the Show group**

   The rulers and gridlines are no longer hidden. You can show or hide View tab items in any view.

9. **Save your work**

FIGURE 1-14: Page Layout view

Turns ruler on/off

Workbook Views group

Turns gridlines on/off

Vertical ruler

Horizontal ruler

Header text box

Additional dimmed page

Current page and total number of pages

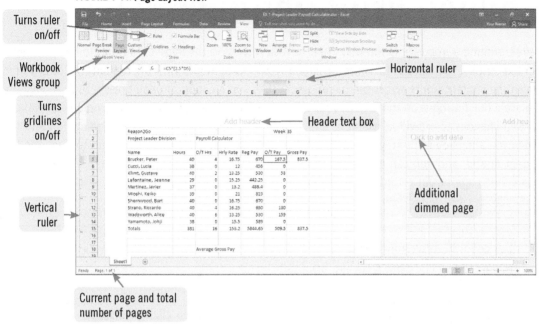

FIGURE 1-15: Header text entered

Header & Footer Tools Design tab

Header text boxes

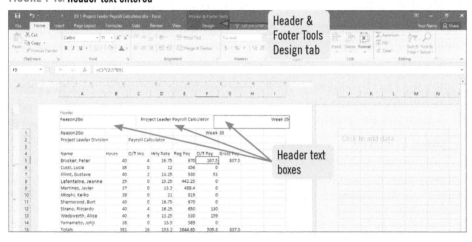

FIGURE 1-16: Page Break Preview

Blue outline indicates print area

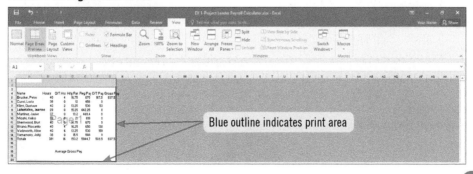

Choose Print Options

Before printing a document, you may want to review it using the Page Layout tab to fine-tune your printed output. You can use tools on the Page Layout tab to adjust print orientation (the direction in which the content prints across the page), paper size, and location of page breaks. You can also use the Scale to Fit options on the Page Layout tab to fit a large amount of data on a single page without making changes to individual margins, and to turn gridlines and column/row headings on and off. When you are ready to print, you can set print options such as the number of copies to print and the correct printer, and you can preview your document in Backstage view using the File tab. You can also adjust page layout settings from within Backstage view and immediately see the results in the document preview. **CASE** *You are ready to prepare your worksheet for printing.*

STEPS

1. **Click cell A20, type your name, then click ✓**

2. **Click the Page Layout tab on the Ribbon**
   Compare your screen to FIGURE 1-17. The solid outline indicates the default **print area**, the area to be printed.

3. **Click the Orientation button in the Page Setup group, then click Landscape**
   The paper orientation changes to **landscape**, so the contents will print across the length of the page instead of across the width. Notice how the margins of the worksheet adjust.

4. **Click the Orientation button in the Page Setup group, then click Portrait**
   The orientation returns to **portrait**, so the contents will print across the width of the page.

5. **Click the Gridlines View check box in the Sheet Options group on the Page Layout tab, click the Gridlines Print check box to select it if necessary, then save your work**
   Printing gridlines makes the data easier to read, but the gridlines will not print unless the Gridlines Print check box is checked.

6. **Click the File tab, click Print on the navigation bar, then select an active printer if necessary**
   The Print tab in Backstage view displays a preview of your worksheet exactly as it will look when it is printed. To the left of the worksheet preview, you can also change a number of document settings and print options. To open the Page Setup dialog box and adjust page layout options, click the Page Setup link in the Settings section. Compare your preview screen to FIGURE 1-18. You can print from this view by clicking the Print button, or return to the worksheet without printing by clicking the Back button ⬅. You can also print an entire workbook from the Backstage view by clicking the Print button in the Settings section, then selecting the active sheet or entire workbook.

7. **Compare your settings to FIGURE 1-18, then click the Print button**
   One copy of the worksheet prints.

8. **Submit your work to your instructor as directed, then exit Excel**

Printing worksheet formulas

Sometimes you need to keep a record of all the formulas in a worksheet. You might want to do this to see exactly how you came up with a complex calculation, so you can explain it to others. To prepare a worksheet to show formulas rather than results when printed, open the workbook containing the formulas you want to print. Click the Formulas tab, then click the Show Formulas button in the Formula Auditing group to select it. When the Show Formulas button is selected, formulas rather than resulting values are displayed in the worksheet on screen and when printed. (The Show Formulas button is a toggle: click it again to hide the formulas.)

FIGURE 1-17: Worksheet with Portrait orientation

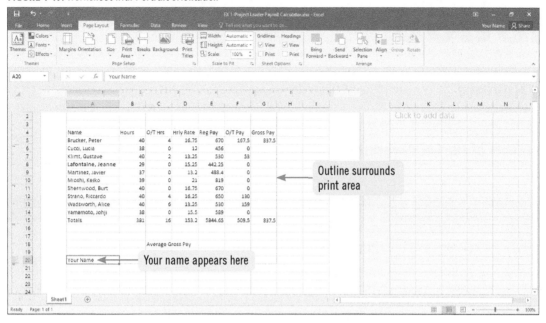

Outline surrounds print area

Your name appears here

FIGURE 1-18: Worksheet in Backstage view

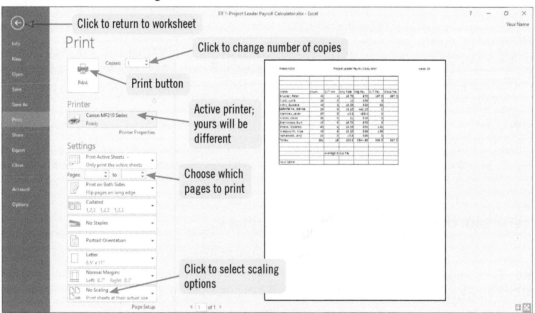

Click to return to worksheet

Click to change number of copies

Print button

Active printer; yours will be different

Choose which pages to print

Click to select scaling options

Scaling to fit

If you have a large amount of data that you want to fit to a single sheet of paper, but you don't want to spend a lot of time trying to adjust the margins and other settings, you have several options. You can easily print your work on a single sheet by clicking the No Scaling list arrow in the Settings section on the Print place in Backstage view, then clicking Fit Sheet in One Page. Another method for fitting worksheet content onto one page is to click the Page Layout tab, then change the Width and Height settings in the Scale to Fit group each to 1 Page. You can also use the Fit to option in the Page Setup dialog box to fit a worksheet on one page. To open the Page Setup dialog box, click the dialog box launcher in the Scale to Fit group on the Page Layout tab, or click the Page Setup link in the Print place in Backstage view. Make sure the Page tab is selected in the Page Setup dialog box, then click the Fit to option button.

Practice

Concepts Review

Label the elements of the Excel worksheet window shown in FIGURE 1-19.

FIGURE 1-19

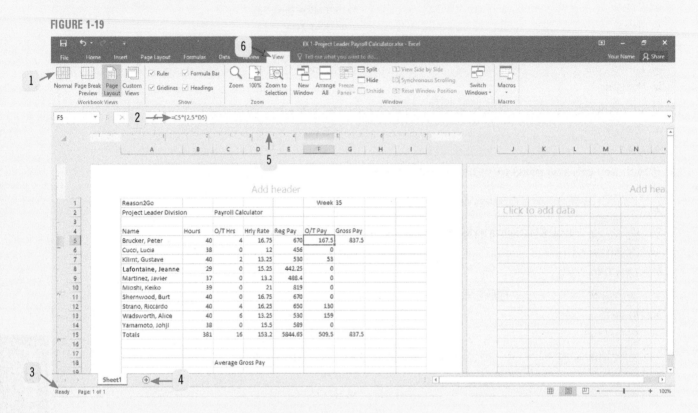

Match each term with the statement that best describes it.

7. **Name box**
8. **Workbook**
9. **Formula prefix**
10. **Orientation**
11. **Cell**
12. **Normal view**

a. Part of the Excel program window that displays the active cell address
b. Default view in Excel
c. Direction in which contents of page will print
d. Equal sign preceding a formula
e. File consisting of one or more worksheets
f. Intersection of a column and a row

Select the best answer from the list of choices.

13. **Which feature could be used to print a very long worksheet on a single sheet of paper?**
    a. Show Formulas
    b. Scale to Fit
    c. Page Break Preview
    d. Named Ranges

14. **In which area can you see a preview of your worksheet?**
    a. Page Setup
    b. Backstage view
    c. Printer Setup
    d. View tab

15. **A selection of multiple cells is called a:**
    a. Group.
    b. Range.
    c. Reference.
    d. Package.

16. **Using a cell address in a formula is known as:**
    a. Formularizing.
    b. Prefixing.
    c. Cell referencing.
    d. Cell mathematics.

17. **Which worksheet view shows how your worksheet will look when printed?**
    a. Page Layout
    b. Data
    c. Review
    d. View

18. **Which key can you press to switch to Edit mode?**
    a. [F1]
    b. [F2]
    c. [F4]
    d. [F6]

19. **In which view can you see the header and footer areas of a worksheet?**
    a. Normal view
    b. Page Layout view
    c. Page Break Preview
    d. Header/Footer view

20. **Which view shows you a reduced view of each page of your worksheet?**
    a. Normal
    b. Page Layout
    c. Thumbnail
    d. Page Break Preview

21. **The maximum number of worksheets you can include in a workbook is:**
    a. 3.
    b. 250.
    c. 255.
    d. Unlimited.

Skills Review

1. **Understand spreadsheet software.**
   a. What is the difference between a workbook and a worksheet?
   b. Identify five common business uses for electronic spreadsheets.
   c. What is what-if analysis?

2. **Identify Excel 2016 window components.**
   a. Start Excel.
   b. Open EX 1-2.xlsx from the location where you store your Data Files, then save it as **EX 1-Weather Data**.
   c. Locate the formula bar, the Sheet tabs, the mode indicator, and the cell pointer.

3. **Understand formulas.**
   a. What is the average high temperature of the listed cities? (*Hint*: Select the range B5:G5 and use the status bar.)
   b. What formula would you create to calculate the difference in altitude between Atlanta and Dallas? Enter your answer (as an equation) in cell D13.

Skills Review (continued)

4. Enter labels and values and use the AutoSum button.

   a. Click cell H8, then use the AutoSum button to calculate the total snowfall.

   b. Click cell H7, then use the AutoSum button to calculate the total rainfall.

   c. Save your changes to the file.

5. Edit cell entries.

   a. Use [F2] to correct the spelling of SanteFe in cell G3 (the correct spelling is Santa Fe).

   b. Click cell A17, then type your name.

   c. Save your changes.

6. Enter and edit a simple formula.

   a. Change the value 41 in cell C8 to **52**.

   b. Change the value 37 in cell D6 to **35.4**.

   c. Select cell J4, then use the fill handle to copy the formula in cell J4 to cells J5:J8.

   d. Save your changes.

7. Switch worksheet views.

   a. Click the View tab on the Ribbon, then switch to Page Layout view.

   b. Add the header **Average Annual Weather Data** to the center header text box.

   c. Add your name to the right header box.

   d. Delete the contents of cell A17.

   e. Delete the contents of cell A1.

   f. Save your changes.

8. Choose print options.

   a. Use the Page Layout tab to change the orientation to Portrait.

   b. Turn off gridlines by deselecting both the Gridlines View and Gridlines Print check boxes (if necessary) in the Sheet Options group.

   c. Scale the worksheet so all the information fits on one page. If necessary, scale the worksheet so all the information fits on one page. (*Hint*: Click the Width list arrow in the Scale to Fit group, click 1 page, click the Height list arrow in the Scale to Fit group, then click 1 page.) Compare your screen to FIGURE 1-20.

   d. Preview the worksheet in Backstage view, then print the worksheet.

   e. Save your changes, submit your work to your instructor as directed, then close the workbook and exit Excel.

FIGURE 1-20

	Atlanta	Boston	Dallas	Orlando	Phoenix	Santa Fe	Total	Average
Altitude	1050	20	430	91	1110	7000		1616.83
High Temp	89	69	96	82	86	70		82
Low Temp	33.5	44	35.4	62	59	43		46.15
Rain (in.)	50.19	42.53	21.32	47.7	7.3	14	183.04	30.5067
Snow (in.)	0	52	6	0	0	32	90	15

Average Annual Weather Data   Your Name

Alt. Diff. ->   Atlanta & Dallas   620

Independent Challenge 1

A real estate development company has hired you to help them make the transition to using Excel in their office. They would like to list properties they are interested in acquiring in a workbook. You've started a worksheet for this project that contains labels but no data.

a. Open the file EX 1-3.xlsx from the location where you store your Data Files, then save it as **EX 1-Real Estate Acquisitions**.

b. Enter the data shown in TABLE 1-4 in columns A, C, D, and E (the property address information should spill into column B).

TABLE 1-4

Property Address	Price	Bedrooms	Bathrooms	Area
1507 Pinon Lane	575000	4	2.5	NE
32 Zanzibar Way	429000	3	4	SE
60 Pottery Lane	526500	2	2	NE
902 Excelsior Drive	315000	4	3	NW

c. Use Page Layout view to create a header with the following components: the title **Real Estate Acquisitions** in the center and your name on the right.

d. Create formulas for totals in cells C6:E6.

e. Save your changes, then compare your worksheet to FIGURE 1-21.

f. Submit your work to your instructor as directed.

g. Close the worksheet and exit Excel.

FIGURE 1-21

Independent Challenge 2

You are the general manager for Luxury Motors, a high-end auto reseller. Although the company is just five years old, it is expanding rapidly, and you are continually looking for ways to save time. You recently began using Excel to manage and maintain data on inventory and sales, which has greatly helped you to track information accurately and efficiently.

a. Start Excel.

b. Save a new workbook as **EX 1-Luxury Motors** in the location where you store your Data Files.

c. Switch to an appropriate view, then add a header that contains your name in the left header text box and the title **Luxury Motors** in the center header text box.

Independent Challenge 2 (continued)

d. Using FIGURE 1-22 as a guide, create labels for at least seven car manufacturers and sales for three months. Include other labels as appropriate. The car make should be in column A and the months should be in columns B, C, and D. A Total row should be beneath the data, and a Total column should be in column E.

FIGURE 1-22

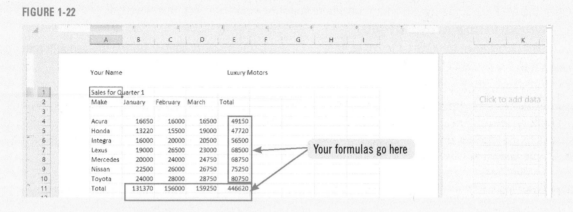

e. Enter values of your choice for the monthly sales for each make.

f. Add formulas in the Total column to calculate total quarterly sales for each make. Add formulas at the bottom of each column of values to calculate the total for that column. Remember that you can use the AutoSum button and the fill handle to save time.

g. Save your changes, preview the worksheet in Backstage view, then submit your work to your instructor as directed.

h. Close the workbook and exit Excel.

Independent Challenge 3

This Independent Challenge requires an Internet connection.

Your company, which is headquartered in Paris, is planning to open an office in New York City. You think it would be helpful to create a worksheet that can be used to convert Celsius temperatures to Fahrenheit, to help employees who are unfamiliar with this type of temperature measurement.

a. Start Excel, then save a blank workbook as **EX 1-Temperature Conversions** in the location where you store your Data Files.

b. Create column headings using FIGURE 1-23 as a guide. (*Hint:* You can widen column B by clicking cell B1, clicking the Format button in the Cells group on the Home tab, then clicking AutoFit Column Width.)

FIGURE 1-23

c. Create row labels for each of the seasons.

d. In the appropriate cells, enter what you determine to be a reasonable indoor temperature for each season.

e. Use your web browser to find out the conversion rate for Fahrenheit to Celsius. (*Hint:* Use your favorite search engine to search on a term such as **temperature conversion formula**.)

Independent Challenge 3 (continued)

f. In the appropriate cells, create a formula that calculates the conversion of the Fahrenheit temperature you entered into a Celsius temperature.

g. In Page Layout View, add your name and the title **Temperature Conversions** to the header.

h. Save your work, then submit your work to your instructor as directed.

i. Close the file, then exit Excel.

Independent Challenge 4: Explore

You've been asked to take over a project started by a co-worker whose Excel skills are not as good as your own. The assignment was to create a sample invoice for an existing client. The invoice will include personnel hours, supplies, and sales tax. Your predecessor started the project, including layout and initial calculations, but she has not made good use of Excel features and has made errors in her calculations. Complete the worksheet by correcting the errors and improving the design. Be prepared to discuss what is wrong with each of the items in the worksheet that you change.

a. Start Excel, open the file EX 1-4.xlsx from the location where you store your Data Files, then save it as **EX 1-Improved Invoice**.

b. There is an error in cell E5: please use the Help feature to find out what is wrong. If you need additional assistance, search Help on *overview of formulas*.

c. Correct the error in the formula in cell E5, then copy the corrected formula into cells E6:E7.

d. Correct the error in the formula in cell E11, then copy the corrected formula into cells E12 and E13.

e. Cells E8 and E14 also contain incorrect formulas. Cell E8 should contain a formula that calculates the total personnel expense, and cell E14 should calculate the total supplies used.

f. Cell G17 should contain a formula that adds the Invoice subtotal (total personnel and total supplies).

g. Cell G18 should calculate the sales tax by multiplying the Subtotal (G17) and the sales tax (cell G18).

h. The Invoice Total (cell G19) should contain a formula that adds the Invoice subtotal (cell G17) and Sales tax (cell G18).

i. Add the following to cell A21: **Terms**, then add the following to cell B21: **Net 10**.

j. Switch to Page Layout view and make the following changes to the Header: Improved Invoice for Week 22 (in the left header box), Client ABC (in the center header box), and your name (in the right header box).

k. Delete the contents of A1:A2, switch to Normal view, then compare your worksheet to FIGURE 1-24.

l. Save your work.

FIGURE 1-24

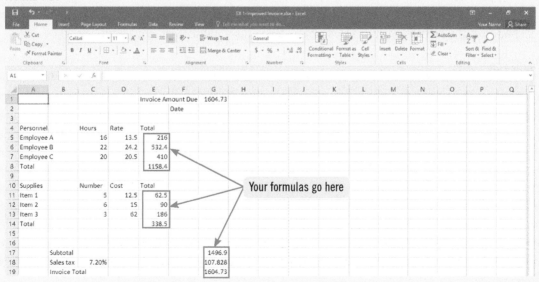

Excel 2016

Visual Workshop

Open the file EX 1-5.xlsx from the location where you store your Data Files, then save it as **EX 1-Project Tools**. Using the skills you learned in this module, modify your worksheet so it matches FIGURE 1-25. Enter formulas in cells D4 through D13 and in cells B14 and C14. Use the AutoSum button and fill handle to make entering your formulas easier. Add your name in the left header text box, then print one copy of the worksheet with the formulas displayed.

FIGURE 1-25

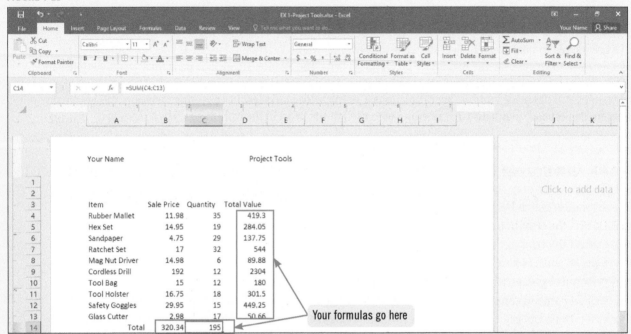

Getting Started with Excel 2016

Working with Formulas and Functions

CASE Yolanda Lee, the vice president of finance at Reason2Go, needs to analyze tour expenses for the current year. She has asked you to prepare a worksheet that summarizes this expense data and includes some statistical analysis. She would also like you to perform some what-if analysis, to see what quarterly expenses would look like with various projected increases.

Module Objectives

After completing this module, you will be able to:

- Create a complex formula
- Insert a function
- Type a function
- Copy and move cell entries
- Understand relative and absolute cell references
- Copy formulas with relative cell references
- Copy formulas with absolute cell references
- Round a value with a function

Files You Will Need

EX 2-1.xlsx   EX 2-3.xlsx

EX 2-2.xlsx   EX 2-4.xlsx

Create a Complex Formula

A **complex formula** is one that uses more than one arithmetic operator. You might, for example, need to create a formula that uses addition and multiplication. In formulas containing more than one arithmetic operator, Excel uses the standard **order of precedence** rules to determine which operation to perform first. You can change the order of precedence in a formula by using parentheses around the part you want to calculate first. For example, the formula =4+2*5 equals 14, because the order of precedence dictates that multiplication is performed before addition. However, the formula =(4+2)*5 equals 30, because the parentheses cause 4+2 to be calculated first. **CASE** *You want to create a formula that calculates a 20% increase in tour expenses.*

STEPS

1. **Start Excel, open the file EX 2-1.xlsx from the location where you store your Data Files, then save it as EX 2-R2G Tour Expense Analysis**

2. **Select the range B4:B11, click the Quick Analysis tool 📑 that appears below the selection, then click the Totals tab**

   The Totals tab in the Quick Analysis tool displays commonly used functions, as seen in FIGURE 2-1.

3. **Click the AutoSum button Σ in the Quick Analysis tool**

   The newly calculated value displays in cell B12 and has bold formatting automatically applied, helping to set it off as a sum. This shading is temporary, and will not appear after you click a cell.

4. **Click cell B12, then drag the fill handle to cell E12**

   The formula in cell B12, as well as the bold formatting, is copied to cells C12:E12.

5. **Click cell B14, type =, click cell B12, then type +**

   In this first part of the formula, you are inserting a reference to the cell that contains total expenses for Quarter 1.

6. **Click cell B12, then type *.2**

   The second part of this formula adds a 20% increase (B12*.2) to the original value of the cell (the total expenses for Quarter 1).

7. **Click the Enter button ✓ on the formula bar**

   The result, 42749.58, appears in cell B14.

8. **Press [Tab], type =, click cell C12, type +, click cell C12, type *.2, then click ✓**

   The result, 42323.712, appears in cell C14.

9. **Drag the fill handle from cell C14 to cell E14, then save your work**

   The calculated values appear in the selected range, as shown in FIGURE 2-2. Dragging the fill handle on a cell copies the cell's contents or continues a series of data (such as Quarter 1, Quarter 2, etc.) into adjacent cells. This option is called **Auto Fill**.

Using Add-ins to improve worksheet functionality

Excel has more functionality than simple and complex math computations. Using the My Add-ins feature (found in the Add-ins group in the Insert tab), you can insert an add-in into your worksheet that accesses the web and adds functionality. Many of the add-ins are free or available for a small fee and can be used to create an email, appointment, meeting, contact, or task, or be a reference source, such as the Mini Calendar or Date Picker. When you click the My Add-ins button list arrow, you'll see any Recently Used Add-ins. Click See All to display the featured Add-ins for Office and to go to the Store to view available add-ins. When you find one you want, make sure you're logged in to Office.com, click the add-in, click Trust It, and the add-in will be installed. Click the My Add-ins button and your add-in should display under Recently Used Add-ins. Click it, then click Insert. The add-in will display in the Recently Used Add-ins pane when you click the My Add-ins button.

FIGURE 2-1: Totals tab in the Quick Analysis tool

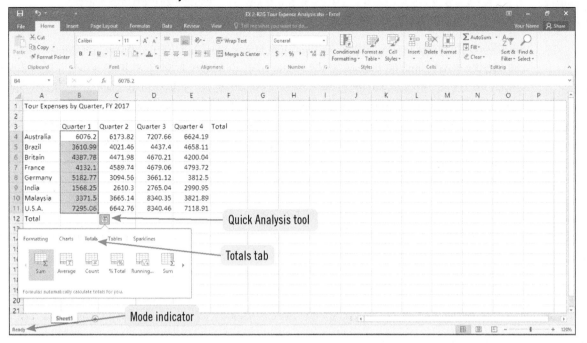

FIGURE 2-2: Results of copied formulas

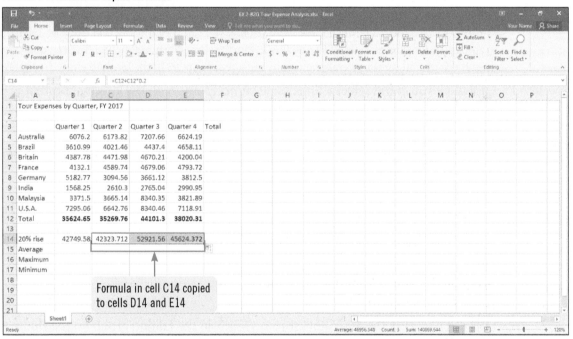

Reviewing the order of precedence

When you work with formulas that contain more than one operator, the order of precedence is very important because it affects the final value. If a formula contains two or more operators, such as 4+.55/4000*25, Excel performs the calculations in a particular sequence based on the following rules: Operations inside parentheses are calculated before any other operations. Reference operators (such as ranges) are calculated first. Exponents are calculated next, then any multiplication and division—progressing from left to right. Finally, addition and subtraction are calculated from left to right. In the example 4+.55/4000*25, Excel performs the arithmetic operations by first dividing .55 by 4000, then multiplying the result by 25, then adding 4. You can change the order of calculations by using parentheses. For example, in the formula (4+.55)/4000*25, Excel would first add 4 and .55, then divide that amount by 4000, then finally multiply by 25.

Insert a Function

Learning
Outcomes
• Use the Insert
Function button
• Select a range for
use in a function
• Select a function
from the AutoSum
list arrow

Functions are predefined worksheet formulas that enable you to perform complex calculations easily. You can use the Insert Function button on the formula bar to choose a function from a dialog box. You can quickly insert the SUM function using the AutoSum button on the Ribbon, or you can click the AutoSum list arrow to enter other frequently used functions, such as **AVERAGE**. You can also use the Quick Analysis tool to calculate commonly used functions. Functions are organized into categories, such as Financial, Date & Time, and Statistical, based on their purposes. You can insert a function on its own or as part of another formula. For example, you have used the SUM function on its own to add a range of cells. You could also use the SUM function within a formula that adds a range of cells and then multiplies the total by a decimal. If you use a function alone, it always begins with an equal sign (=) as the formula prefix. **CASE** *You need to calculate the average expenses for the first quarter of the year and decide to use a function to do so.*

STEPS

QUICK TIP

When using the Insert Function button or the AutoSum list arrow, it is not necessary to type the equal sign (=); Excel adds it as necessary.

1. **Click cell B15**

   This is the cell where you want to enter a calculation that averages expenses per country for the first quarter.

2. **Click the Insert Function button** f_x **on the formula bar**

   An equal sign (=) is inserted in the active cell and in the formula bar, and the Insert Function dialog box opens, as shown in FIGURE 2-3. In this dialog box, you specify the function you want to use by clicking it in the Select a function list. The Select a function list initially displays recently used functions. If you don't see the function you want, you can click the Or select a category list arrow to choose the desired category. If you're not sure which category to choose, you can type the function name or a description in the Search for a function field. The AVERAGE function is a statistical function, but you don't need to open the Statistical category because this function already appears in the Most Recently Used category.

QUICK TIP

To learn about a function, click it in the Select a function list. The arguments and format required for the function appear below the list.

3. **Click AVERAGE in the Select a function list if necessary, read the information that appears under the list, then click OK**

   The Function Arguments dialog box opens, in which you define the range of cells you want to average.

QUICK TIP

When selecting a range, remember to select all the cells between and including the two references in the range.

4. **Click the Collapse button** 🔳 **in the Number1 field of the Function Arguments dialog box, select the range B4:B11 in the worksheet, then click the Expand button** 🔳 **in the Function Arguments dialog box**

   Clicking the Collapse button minimizes the dialog box so that you can select cells in the worksheet. When you click the Expand button, the dialog box is restored, as shown in FIGURE 2-4. You can also begin dragging in the worksheet to automatically minimize the dialog box; after you select the desired range, the dialog box is restored.

5. **Click OK**

   The Function Arguments dialog box closes, and the calculated value is displayed in cell B15. The average expenses per country for Quarter 1 is 4453.0813.

6. **Click cell C15, click the AutoSum list arrow** Σ ⏷ **in the Editing group on the Home tab, then click Average**

   A ScreenTip beneath cell C15 displays the arguments needed to complete the function. The text "number1" is in boldface, telling you that the next step is to supply the first cell in the group you want to average.

7. **Select the range C4:C11 in the worksheet, then click the Enter button** ✓ **on the formula bar**

   The average expenses per country for the second quarter appear in cell C15.

8. **Drag the fill handle from cell C15 to cell E15**

   The formula in cell C15 is copied to the rest of the selected range, as shown in FIGURE 2-5.

9. **Save your work**

FIGURE 2-3: Insert Function dialog box

FIGURE 2-4: Expanded Function Arguments dialog box

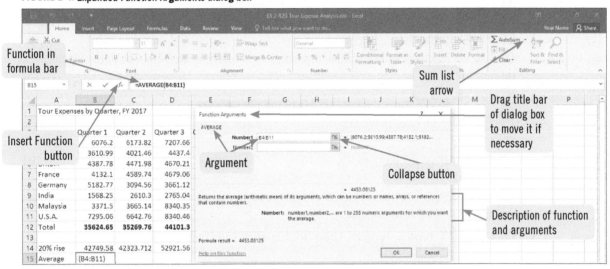

FIGURE 2-5: Average functions used in worksheet

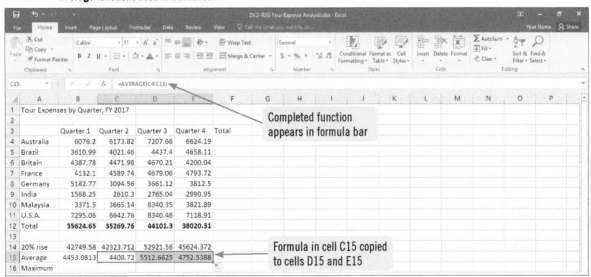

Type a Function

Learning
Outcomes
• Select a function
  by typing
• Use AutoComplete
  to copy formulas

In addition to using the Insert Function dialog box, the AutoSum button, or the AutoSum list arrow on the Ribbon to enter a function, you can manually type the function into a cell and then complete the arguments needed. This method requires that you know the name and initial characters of the function, but it can be faster than opening several dialog boxes. Experienced Excel users often prefer this method, but it is only an alternative, not better or more correct than any other method. The Excel **Formula AutoComplete** feature makes it easier to enter function names by typing, because it suggests functions depending on the first letters you type. **CASE** *You want to calculate the maximum and minimum quarterly expenses in your worksheet, and you decide to manually enter these statistical functions.*

STEPS

1. **Click cell B16, type =, then type m**

   Because you are manually typing this function, it is necessary to begin with the equal sign (=). The Formula AutoComplete feature displays a list of function names beginning with "M" beneath cell B16. Once you type an equal sign in a cell, each letter you type acts as a trigger to activate the Formula AutoComplete feature. This feature minimizes the amount of typing you need to do to enter a function and reduces typing and syntax errors.

2. **Click MAX in the list**

   Clicking any function in the Formula AutoComplete list opens a ScreenTip next to the list that describes the function.

QUICK TIP
When you select the function, a ScreenTip automatically displays more detailed information about the function.

3. **Double-click MAX**

   The function is inserted in the cell, and a ScreenTip appears beneath the cell to help you complete the formula. See FIGURE 2-6.

4. **Select the range B4:B11, as shown in FIGURE 2-7, then click the Enter button ✓ on the formula bar**

   The result, 7295.06, appears in cell B16. When you completed the entry, the closing parenthesis was automatically added to the formula.

5. **Click cell B17, type =, type m, then double-click MIN in the list of function names**

   The MIN function appears in the cell.

6. **Select the range B4:B11, then press [Enter]**

   The result, 1568.25, appears in cell B17.

7. **Select the range B16:B17, then drag the fill handle from cell B17 to cell E17**

   The maximum and minimum values for all of the quarters appear in the selected range, as shown in FIGURE 2-8.

8. **Save your work**

Using the COUNT and COUNTA functions

When you select a range, a count of cells in the range that are not blank appears in the status bar. You can use this information to determine things such as how many team members entered project hours in a worksheet. For example, if you select the range A1:A5 and only cells A1, A4, and A5 contain data, the status bar displays "Count: 3." To count nonblank cells more precisely, or to incorporate these calculations in a worksheet, you can use the COUNT and COUNTA functions. The COUNT function returns the number of cells in a range that contain numeric data, including numbers, dates, and formulas. The COUNTA function returns the number of cells in a range that contain any data at all, including numeric data, labels, and even a blank space. For example, the formula =COUNT(A1:A5) returns the number of cells in the range that contain numeric data, and the formula =COUNTA(A1:A5) returns the number of cells in the range that are not empty. If you use the COUNT functions in the Quick Analysis tool, the calculation is entered in the cell immediately beneath the selected range.

FIGURE 2-6: **MAX function in progress**

13					
14	20% rise	42749.58	42323.712	52921.56	45624.372
15	Average	4453.0813	4408.72	5512.6625	4752.5388
16	Maximum	=MAX(			
17	Minimum	MAX(**number1**, [number2], ...)			

FIGURE 2-7: **Completing the MAX function**

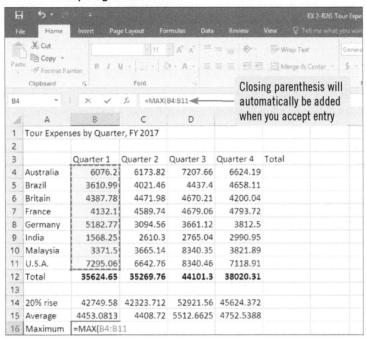

FIGURE 2-8: **Completed MAX and MIN functions**

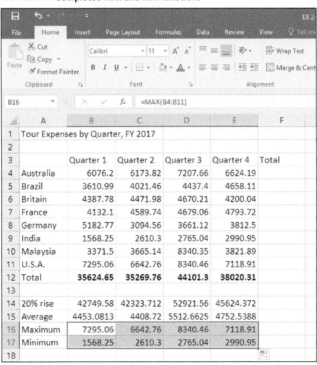

Copy and Move Cell Entries

There are three ways you can copy or move cells and ranges (or the contents within them) from one location to another: the Cut, Copy, and Paste buttons on the Home tab on the Ribbon; the fill handle in the lower-right corner of the active cell or range; or the drag-and-drop feature. When you copy cells, the original data remains in the original location; when you cut or move cells, the original data is deleted from its original location. You can also cut, copy, and paste cells or ranges from one worksheet to another. **CASE** *In addition to the 20% rise in tour expenses, you also want to show a 30% rise. Rather than retype this information, you copy and move selected cells.*

STEPS

1. **Select the range B3:E3, then click the Copy button 🖺 in the Clipboard group on the Home tab**

   The selected range (B3:E3) is copied to the **Clipboard**, a temporary Windows storage area that holds the selections you copy or cut. A moving border surrounds the selected range until you press [Esc] or copy an additional item to the Clipboard.

2. **Click the launcher 🖪 in the Clipboard group**

   The Office Clipboard opens in the Clipboard task pane, as shown in FIGURE 2-9. When you copy or cut an item, it is cut or copied both to the Clipboard provided by Windows and to the Office Clipboard. Unlike the Windows Clipboard, which holds just one item at a time, the Office Clipboard contains up to 24 of the most recently cut or copied items from any Office program. Your Clipboard task pane may contain more items than shown in the figure.

3. **Click cell B19, then click the Paste button in the Clipboard group**

   A copy of the contents of range B3:E3 is pasted into the range B19:E19. When pasting an item from the Office Clipboard or Clipboard into a worksheet, you only need to specify the upper left cell of the range where you want to paste the selection. Notice that the information you copied remains in the original range B3:E3; if you had cut instead of copied, the information would have been deleted from its original location once it was pasted.

4. **Press [Delete]**

   The selected cells are empty. You have decided to paste the cells in a different row. You can repeatedly paste an item from the Office Clipboard as many times as you like, as long as the item remains in the Office Clipboard.

5. **Click cell B20, click the first item in the Office Clipboard, then click the Close button ✕ on the Clipboard task pane**

   Cells B20:E20 contain the copied labels.

6. **Click cell A14, press and hold [Ctrl], point to any edge of the cell until the pointer changes to ⬚, drag cell A14 to cell A21, release the mouse button, then release [Ctrl]**

   The copy pointer ⬚ continues to appear as you drag, as shown in FIGURE 2-10. When you release the mouse button, the contents of cell A14 are copied to cell A21.

7. **Click to the right of 2 in the formula bar, press [Backspace], type 3, then click the Enter button ✓**

8. **Click cell B21, type =, click cell B12, type *1.3, click ✓ on the formula bar, then save your work**

   This new formula calculates a 30% increase of the expenses for Quarter 1, though using a different method from what you previously used. Anything you multiply by 1.3 returns an amount that is 130% of the original amount, or a 30% increase. Compare your screen to FIGURE 2-11.

FIGURE 2-9: Copied data in Office Clipboard

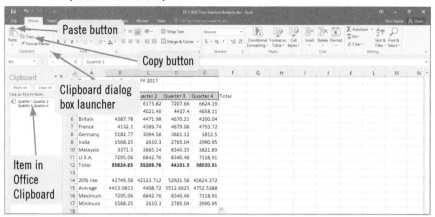

FIGURE 2-10: Copying cell contents with drag-and-drop

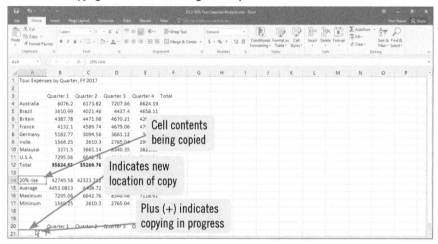

FIGURE 2-11: Formula entered to calculate a 30% increase

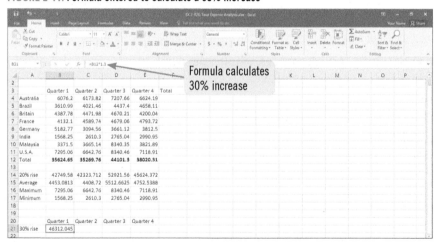

Inserting and deleting selected cells

As you add formulas to your workbook, you may need to insert or delete cells. When you do this, Excel automatically adjusts cell references to reflect their new locations. To insert cells, click the Insert list arrow in the Cells group on the Home tab, then click Insert Cells. The Insert dialog box opens, asking if you want to insert a cell and move the current active cell down or to the right of the new one. To delete one or more selected cells, click the Delete list arrow in the Cells group, click Delete Cells, and in the Delete dialog box, indicate which way you want to move the adjacent cells. When using this option, be careful not to disturb row or column alignment that may be necessary to maintain the accuracy of cell references in the worksheet. Click the Insert button or Delete button in the Cells group to insert or delete a single cell.

Learning
Outcomes
• Identify cell
referencing
• Identify when to
use absolute or
relative cell
references

Understand Relative and Absolute Cell References

As you work in Excel, you may want to reuse formulas in different parts of a worksheet to reduce the amount of data you have to retype. For example, you might want to include a what-if analysis in one part of a worksheet showing a set of sales projections if sales increase by 10%. To include another analysis in another part of the worksheet showing projections if sales increase by 50%, you can copy the formulas from one section to another and simply change the "1" to a "5". But when you copy formulas, it is important to make sure that they refer to the correct cells. To do this, you need to understand the difference between relative and absolute cell references. **CASE** *You plan to reuse formulas in different parts of your worksheets, so you want to understand relative and absolute cell references.*

DETAILS

Consider the following when using relative and absolute cell references:

• **Use relative references when you want to preserve the relationship to the formula location**

When you create a formula that references another cell, Excel normally does not "record" the exact cell address for the cell being referenced in the formula. Instead, it looks at the relationship that cell has to the cell containing the formula. For example, in FIGURE 2-12, cell F5 contains the formula: =SUM(B5:E5). When Excel retrieves values to calculate the formula in cell F5, it actually looks for "the four cells to the left of the formula," which in this case is cells B5:E5. This way, if you copy the cell to a new location, such as cell F6, the results will reflect the new formula location and will automatically retrieve the values in cells B6, C6, D6, and E6. These are **relative cell references**, because Excel is recording the input cells *in relation to* or *relative to* the formula cell.

In most cases, you want to use relative cell references when copying or moving, so this is the Excel default. In FIGURE 2-12, the formulas in cells F5:F12 and cells B13:F13 contain relative cell references. They total the "four cells to the left of" or the "eight cells above" the formulas.

• **Use absolute cell references when you want to preserve the exact cell address in a formula**

There are times when you want Excel to retrieve formula information from a specific cell, and you don't want the cell address in the formula to change when you copy it to a new location. For example, you might have a price in a specific cell that you want to use in all formulas, regardless of their location. If you use relative cell referencing, the formula results would be incorrect, because the formula would reference a different cell every time you copy it. Therefore, you need to use an **absolute cell reference**, which is a reference that does not change when you copy the formula.

You create an absolute cell reference by placing a $ (dollar sign) in front of both the column letter and the row number of the cell address. You can either type the dollar sign when typing the cell address in a formula (for example, "=C12*B16") or you can select a cell address on the formula bar and then press [F4], and the dollar signs are added automatically. FIGURE 2-13 shows formulas containing both absolute and relative references. The formulas in cells B19 to E26 use absolute cell references to refer to a potential sales increase of 50%, shown in cell B16.

FIGURE 2-12: Formulas containing relative references

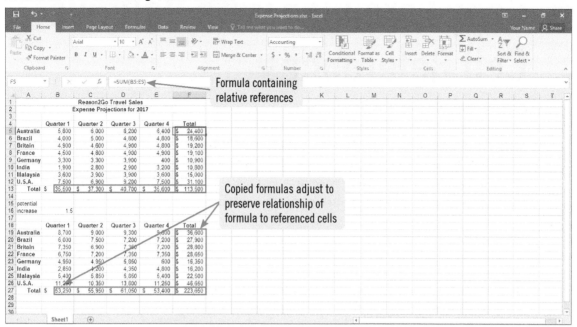

Formula containing relative references

Copied formulas adjust to preserve relationship of formula to referenced cells

FIGURE 2-13: Formulas containing absolute and relative references

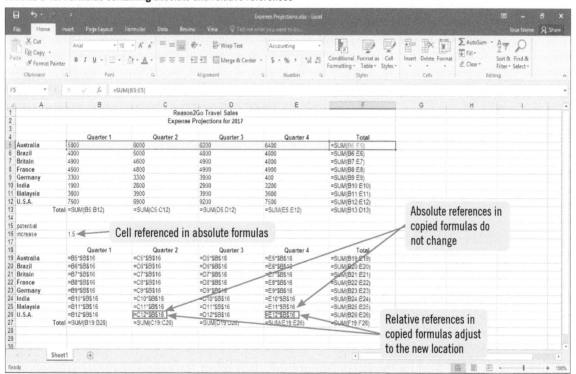

Absolute references in copied formulas do not change

Cell referenced in absolute formulas

Relative references in copied formulas adjust to the new location

Using a mixed reference

Sometimes when you copy a formula, you want to change the row reference, but keep the column reference the same. This type of cell referencing combines elements of both absolute and relative referencing and is called a **mixed reference**. For example, when copied, a formula containing the mixed reference C$14 would change the column letter relative to its new location, but not the row number. In the mixed reference $C14, the column letter would not change, but the row number would be updated relative to its location. Like an absolute reference, a mixed reference can be created by pressing the [F4] function key with the cell reference selected. With each press of the [F4] key, you cycle through all the possible combinations of relative, absolute, and mixed references (C14, C14, C$14, and $C14).

Copy Formulas with Relative Cell References

Learning
Outcomes
• Copy and Paste
formulas with
relative cell
references
• Examine Auto Fill
and Paste Options
• Use the Fill button

Copying and moving a cell allow you to reuse a formula you've already created. Copying cells is usually faster than retyping the formulas in them and helps to prevent typing errors. If the cells you are copying contain relative cell references and you want to maintain the relative referencing, you don't need to make any changes to the cells before copying them. **CASE** *You want to copy the formula in cell B21, which calculates the 30% increase in quarterly expenses for Quarter 1, to cells C21 through E21. You also want to create formulas to calculate total expenses for each tour country.*

STEPS

1. **Click cell B21 if necessary, then click the Copy button 📋 in the Clipboard group on the Home tab**

   The formula for calculating the 30% expense increase during Quarter 1 is copied to the Clipboard. Notice that the formula =B12*1.3 appears in the formula bar, and a moving border surrounds the active cell.

QUICK TIP

To paste only specific components of a copied cell or range, click the Paste list arrow in the Clipboard group, then click Paste Special. You can selectively copy formats, formulas, values, comments, and validation rules; transpose columns and rows; paste a link; or add, subtract, multiply, or divide using the Paste Special dialog box.

2. **Click cell C21, then click the Paste button 📋 *(not the list arrow)* in the Clipboard group**

   The formula from cell B21 is copied into cell C21, where the new result of 45850.688 appears. Notice in the formula bar that the cell references have changed so that cell C12 is referenced instead of B12. This formula contains a relative cell reference, which tells Excel to substitute new cell references within the copied formulas as necessary. This maintains the same relationship between the new cell containing the formula and the cell references within the formula. In this case, Excel adjusted the formula so that cell C12—the cell reference nine rows above C21—replaced cell B12, the cell reference nine rows above B21.

3. **Drag the fill handle from cell C21 to cell E21**

   A formula similar to the one in cell C21 now appears in cells D21 and E21. After you use the fill handle to copy cell contents, the **Auto Fill Options button** appears, as shown in FIGURE 2-14. You can use the Auto Fill Options button to fill the cells with only specific elements of the copied cell if you wish.

4. **Click cell F4, click the AutoSum button Σ in the Editing group, then click the Enter button ✔ on the formula bar**

5. **Click 📋 in the Clipboard group, select the range F5:F6, then click 📋**

   See FIGURE 2-15. After you click the Paste button, the **Paste Options button** appears.

6. **Click the Paste Options button 📋 (Ctrl)▾ adjacent to the selected range**

   You can use the Paste options list to paste only specific elements of the copied selection if you wish. The formula for calculating total expenses for tours in Britain appears in the formula bar. You would like totals to appear in cells F7:F11. The Fill button in the Editing group can be used to copy the formula into the remaining cells.

7. **Press [Esc] to close the Paste Options list, then select the range F6:F11**

8. **Click the Fill button 🔽 in the Editing group, then click Down**

   The formulas containing relative references are copied to each cell. Compare your worksheet to FIGURE 2-16.

9. **Save your work**

FIGURE 2-14: Formula copied using the fill handle

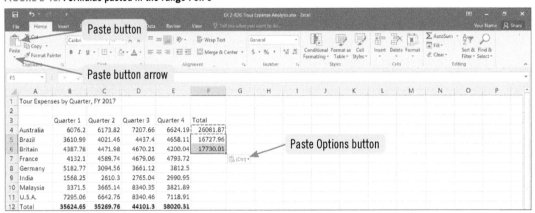

FIGURE 2-15: Formulas pasted in the range F5:F6

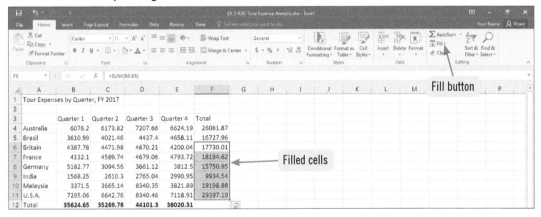

FIGURE 2-16: Formula copied using Fill Down

Using Paste Preview

You can selectively copy formulas, values, or other choices using the Paste list arrow, and you can see how the pasted contents will look using the Paste Preview feature. When you click the Paste list arrow, a gallery of paste option icons opens. When you point to an icon, a preview of how the content will be pasted using that option is shown in the worksheet. Options include pasting values only, pasting values with number formatting, pasting formulas only, pasting formatting only, pasting transposed data so that column data appears in rows and row data appears in columns, and pasting with no borders (to remove any borders around pasted cells).

Copy Formulas with Absolute Cell References

Learning Outcomes
• Create an absolute cell reference
• Use the fill handle to copy absolute cell references

When copying cells, you might want one or more cell references in a formula to remain unchanged. In such an instance, you need to apply an absolute cell reference before copying the formula to preserve the specific cell address when the formula is copied. You create an absolute reference by placing a dollar sign ($) before the column letter and row number of the address (for example, A1). **CASE** *You need to do some what-if analysis to see how various percentage increases might affect total expenses. You decide to add a column that calculates a possible increase in the total tour expenses, and then change the percentage to see various potential results.*

STEPS

1. **Click cell G1, type Change, then press [Enter]**

2. **Type 1.1, then press [Enter]**
   You store the increase factor that will be used in the what-if analysis in this cell (G2). The value 1.1 can be used to calculate a 10% increase: anything you multiply by 1.1 returns an amount that is 110% of the original amount.

3. **Click cell H3, type What if?, then press [Enter]**

4. **In cell H4, type =, click cell F4, type *, click cell G2, then click the Enter button ✓ on the formula bar**
   The result, 28690.1, appears in cell H4. This value represents the total annual expenses for Australia if there is a 10% increase. You want to perform a what-if analysis for all the tour countries.

5. **Drag the fill handle from cell H4 to cell H11**
   The resulting values in the range H5:H11 are all zeros, which is not the result you wanted. Because you used relative cell addressing in cell H4, the copied formula adjusted so that the formula in cell H5 is =F5*G3; because there is no value in cell G3, the result is 0, an error. You need to use an absolute reference in the formula to keep the formula from adjusting itself. That way, it will always reference cell G2.

6. **Click cell H4, press [F2] to change to Edit mode, then press [F4]**
   When you press [F2], the range finder outlines the arguments of the equation in blue and red. The insertion point appears next to the G2 cell reference in cell H4. When you press [F4], dollar signs are inserted in the G2 cell reference, making it an absolute reference. See FIGURE 2-17.

7. **Click ✓, then drag the fill handle from cell H4 to cell H11**
   Because the formula correctly contains an absolute cell reference, the correct values for a 10% increase appear in cells H4:H11. You now want to see what a 20% increase in expenses looks like.

8. **Click cell G2, type 1.2, then click ✓**
   The values in the range H4:H11 change to reflect the 20% increase. Compare your worksheet to FIGURE 2-18.

9. **Save your work**

FIGURE 2-17: Absolute reference created in formula

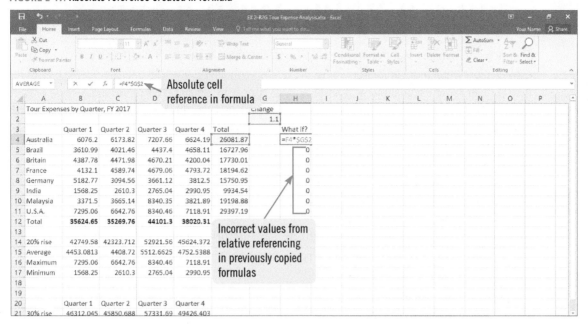

FIGURE 2-18: What-if analysis with modified change factor

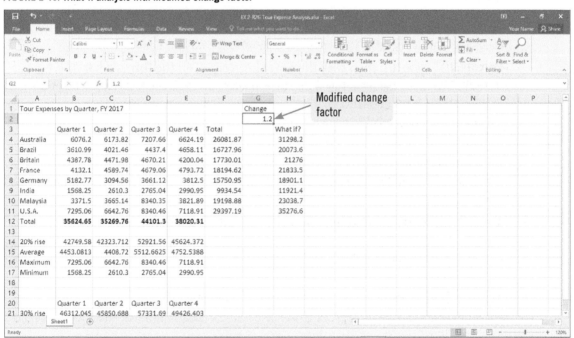

Using the fill handle for sequential text or values

Often, you need to fill cells with sequential text: months of the year, days of the week, years, or text plus a number (Quarter 1, Quarter 2,...). For example, you might want to create a worksheet that calculates data for every month of the year. Using the fill handle, you can quickly and easily create labels for the months of the year just by typing "January" in a cell. Drag the fill handle from the cell containing "January" until you have all the monthly labels you need. You can also easily fill cells with a date sequence by dragging the fill handle on a single cell containing a date. You can

fill cells with a number sequence (such as 1, 2, 3,...) by dragging the fill handle on a selection of two or more cells that contain the sequence. To create a number sequence using the value in a single cell, press and hold [Ctrl] as you drag the fill handle of the cell. As you drag the fill handle, Excel automatically extends the existing sequence into the additional cells. (The content of the last filled cell appears in the ScreenTip.) To choose from all the fill series options for the current selection, click the Fill button in the Editing group on the Home tab, then click Series to open the Series dialog box.

Round a Value with a Function

Learning
Outcomes
• Use Formula
AutoComplete to
insert a function
• Copy an edited
formula

The more you explore features and tools in Excel, the more ways you'll find to simplify your work and convey information more efficiently. For example, cells containing financial data are often easier to read if they contain fewer decimal places than those that appear by default. You can round a value or formula result to a specific number of decimal places by using the ROUND function. **CASE** *In your worksheet, you'd like to round the cells showing the 20% rise in expenses to show fewer digits; after all, it's not important to show cents in the projections, only whole dollars. You want Excel to round the calculated value to the nearest integer. You decide to edit cell B14 so it includes the ROUND function, and then copy the edited formula into the other formulas in this row.*

STEPS

1. **Click cell B14, then click to the right of = in the formula bar**

   You want to position the function at the beginning of the formula, before any values or arguments.

2. **Type RO**

   Formula AutoComplete displays a list of functions beginning with RO beneath the formula bar.

3. **Double-click ROUND in the functions list**

   The new function and an opening parenthesis are added to the formula, as shown in FIGURE 2-19. A few additional modifications are needed to complete your edit of the formula. You need to indicate the number of decimal places to which the function should round numbers, and you also need to add a closing parenthesis around the set of arguments that comes after the ROUND function.

4. **Press [END], type ,0), then click the Enter button ✓ on the formula bar**

   The comma separates the arguments within the formula, and 0 indicates that you don't want any decimal places to appear in the calculated value. When you complete the edit, the parentheses at either end of the formula briefly become bold, indicating that the formula has the correct number of open and closed parentheses and is balanced.

5. **Drag the fill handle from cell B14 to cell E14**

   The formula in cell B14 is copied to the range C14:E14. All the values are rounded to display no decimal places. Compare your worksheet to FIGURE 2-20.

6. **Scroll down so row 25 is visible, click cell A25, type your name, then click ✓**

7. **Save your work, preview the worksheet in the Print place in Backstage view, then submit your work to your Instructor as directed**

8. **Exit Excel**

Using Auto Fill options

When you use the fill handle to copy cells, the Auto Fill Options button appears. Auto Fill options differ depending on what you are copying. If you had selected cells containing a series (such as "Monday" and "Tuesday") and then used the fill handle, you would see options for continuing the series (such as "Wednesday" and "Thursday") or for simply pasting the copied cells. Clicking the Auto Fill Options button opens a list that lets you choose from the following options: Copy Cells, Fill Series (if applicable), Fill Formatting Only, Fill Without Formatting, or Flash Fill. Choosing Copy Cells means that the cell's contents and its formatting will be copied. The Fill Formatting Only option copies only the formatting attributes, but not cell contents. The Fill Without Formatting option copies the cell contents, but no formatting attributes. Copy Cells is the default option when using the fill handle to copy a cell, so if you want to copy the cell's contents and its formatting, you can ignore the Auto Fill Options button. The Flash Fill option allows you to create customized fill ranges on the fly, such as 2, 4, 6, 8, 10, by entering at least two values in a pattern: Excel automatically senses the pattern.

FIGURE 2-19: **ROUND function added to an existing formula**

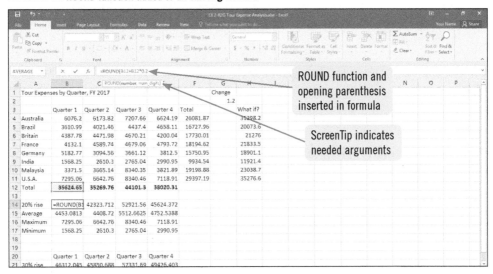

ROUND function and opening parenthesis inserted in formula

ScreenTip indicates needed arguments

FIGURE 2-20: **Completed worksheet**

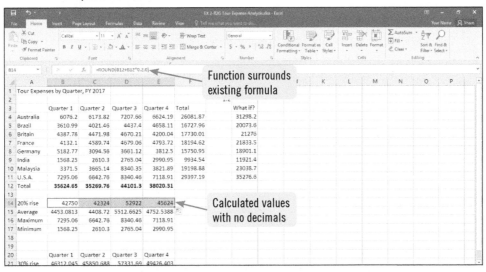

Function surrounds existing formula

Calculated values with no decimals

Creating a new workbook using a template

Excel **templates** are predesigned workbook files intended to save time when you create common documents such as balance sheets, budgets, or time cards. Templates contain labels, values, formulas, and formatting, so all you have to do is customize them with your own information. Excel comes with many templates, and you can also create your own or find additional templates on the web. Unlike a typical workbook, which has the file extension .xlsx, a template has the extension .xltx. To create a workbook using a template, click the File tab, then click New on the navigation bar. The New place in Backstage view displays thumbnails of some of the many templates available. The Blank workbook template is selected by default and is used to create a blank workbook with no content or special formatting. To select a different template, click one of the selections in the New place, view the preview, then click Create. FIGURE 2-21 shows an example. (Your available templates may differ.) When you click

Create, a new workbook is created based on the template; when you save the new file in the default format, it has the regular .xlsx extension. To save a workbook of your own as a template, open the Save As dialog box, click the Save as type list arrow, then change the file type to Excel Template.

FIGURE 2-21: **Previewing the Budget Planner template**

Excel 2016

Practice

Concepts Review

Label each element of the Excel worksheet window shown in FIGURE 2-22.

FIGURE 2-22

Match each term or button with the statement that best describes it.

8. Launcher
9. Fill handle
10. Drag-and-drop method
11. Formula AutoComplete
12. [Delete] key

a. Clears the contents of selected cells
b. Item on the Ribbon that opens a dialog box or task pane
c. Lets you move or copy data from one cell to another without using the Clipboard
d. Displays an alphabetical list of functions from which you can choose
e. Lets you copy cell contents or continue a series of data into a range of selected cells

Select the best answer from the list of choices.

13. You can use any of the following features to enter a new function *except*:
    a. Insert Function button.
    b. Formula AutoComplete.
    c. AutoSum list arrow.
    d. Clipboard.

14. Which key do you press and hold to copy while dragging and dropping selected cells?
    a. [Alt]
    b. [Ctrl]
    c. [F2]
    d. [Tab]

15. What type of cell reference is C$19?
    a. Relative
    b. Absolute
    c. Mixed
    d. Certain

16. Which key do you press to convert a relative cell reference to an absolute cell reference?
    a. [F2]
    b. [F4]
    c. [F5]
    d. [F6]

17. What type of cell reference changes when it is copied?
    a. Circular
    b. Absolute
    c. Relative
    d. Specified

Skills Review

1. Create a complex formula.

    a. Open EX 2-2.xlsx from the location where you store your Data Files, then save it as **EX 2-Construction Supply Company Inventory**.
    b. Select the range B4:B8, click the Totals tab in the Quick Analysis tool, then click the AutoSum button.
    c. Use the fill handle to copy the formula in cell B9 to cells C9:E9.
    d. In cell B11, create a complex formula that calculates a 30% decrease in the total number of cases of pylons.
    e. Use the fill handle to copy this formula into cell C11 through cell E11.
    f. Save your work.

2. Insert a function.

    a. Use the AutoSum list arrow to create a formula in cell B13 that averages the number of cases of pylons in each storage area.
    b. Use the Insert Function button to create a formula in cell B14 that calculates the maximum number of cases of pylons in a storage area.
    c. Use the AutoSum list arrow to create a formula in cell B15 that calculates the minimum number of cases of pylons in a storage area.
    d. Save your work.

Skills Review (continued)

3. Type a function.

   a. In cell C13, type a formula that includes a function to average the number of cases of bricks in each storage area. (*Hint*: Use Formula AutoComplete to enter the function.)

   b. In cell C14, type a formula that includes a function to calculate the maximum number of cases of bricks in a storage area.

   c. In cell C15, type a formula that includes a function to calculate the minimum number of cases of bricks in a storage area.

   d. Save your work.

4. Copy and move cell entries.

   a. Select the range B3:F3.

   b. Copy the selection to the Clipboard.

   c. Open the Clipboard task pane, then paste the selection into cell B17.

   d. Close the Clipboard task pane, then select the range A4:A9.

   e. Use the drag-and-drop method to copy the selection to cell A18. (*Hint*: The results should fill the range A18:A23.)

   f. Save your work.

5. Understand relative and absolute cell references.

   a. Write a brief description of the difference between relative and absolute references.

   b. List at least three situations in which you think a business might use an absolute reference in its calculations. Examples can include calculations for different types of worksheets, such as time cards, invoices, and budgets.

6. Copy formulas with relative cell references.

   a. Calculate the total in cell F4.

   b. Use the Fill button to copy the formula in cell F4 down to cells F5:F8.

   c. Select the range C13:C15.

   d. Use the fill handle to copy these cells to the range D13:F15.

   e. Save your work.

7. Copy formulas with absolute cell references.

   a. In cell H1, change the existing value to **1.575**.

   b. In cell H4, create a formula that multiplies F4 and an absolute reference to cell H1.

   c. Use the fill handle to copy the formula in cell H4 to cells H5 and H6.

   d. Use the Copy and Paste buttons to copy the formula in cell H4 to cells H7 and H8.

   e. Change the amount in cell H1 to **2.5**.

   f. Save your work.

Skills Review (continued)

8. Round a value with a function.

    a. Click cell H4.

    b. Edit this formula to include the ROUND function showing zero decimal places.

    c. Use the fill handle to copy the formula in cell H4 to the range H5:H8.

    d. Enter your name in cell A25, then compare your work to FIGURE 2-23.

    e. Save your work, preview the worksheet in Backstage view, then submit your work to your instructor as directed.

    f. Close the workbook, then exit Excel.

FIGURE 2-23

Independent Challenge 1

You are thinking of starting a small coffee shop where locals can gather. Before you begin, you need to evaluate what you think your monthly expenses will be. You've started a workbook, but need to complete the entries and add formulas.

a. Open EX 2-3.xlsx from the location where you store your Data Files, then save it as **EX 2-Coffee Shop Expenses**.

b. Make up your own expense data, and enter it in cells B4:B10. (Monthly sales are already included in the worksheet.)

c. Create a formula in cell C4 that calculates the annual rent.

d. Copy the formula in cell C4 to the range C5:C10.

e. Move the label in cell A15 to cell A14.

f. Create formulas in cells B11 and C11 that total the monthly and annual expenses.

g. Create a formula in cell C13 that calculates annual sales.

h. Create a formula in cell B14 that determines whether you will make a profit or loss, then copy the formula into cell C14.

i. Copy the labels in cells B3:C3 to cells E3:F3.

j. Type **Projected Increase** in cell G1, then type **.2** in cell H2.

k. Create a formula in cell E4 that calculates an increase in the monthly rent by the amount in cell H2. You will be copying this formula to other cells, so you'll need to use an absolute reference.

l. Create a formula in cell F4 that calculates the increased annual rent expense based on the calculation in cell E4.

m. Copy the formulas in cells E4:F4 into cells E5:F10 to calculate the remaining monthly and annual expenses.

n. Create a formula in cell E11 that calculates the total monthly expenses, then copy that formula to cell F11.

o. Copy the contents of cells B13:C13 into cells E13:F13.

p. Create formulas in cells E14 and F14 that calculate profit/loss based on the projected increase in monthly and annual expenses.

q. Change the projected increase to **.17**, then compare your work to the sample in FIGURE 2-24.

r. Enter your name in a cell in the worksheet.

s. Save your work, preview the worksheet in Backstage view, submit your work to your instructor as directed, close the workbook, and exit Excel.

FIGURE 2-24

	A	B	C	D	E	F	G	H	I
1	Estim	Your formulas go here (your formula results will differ)	C				Projected Increase		
2			enses					0.17	
3		Monthly	Annually		Monthly	Annually			
4	Rent	2500	30000		2925	35100			
5	Supplies	1600	19200		1872	22464			
6	Milk	3600	43200		4212	50544			
7	Sugar	1300	15600		1521	18252			
8	Pastries	850	10200		994.5	11934			
9	Coffee	600	7200		702	8424			
10	Utilities	750	9000		877.5	10530			
11	Total	11200	134400		13104	157248			
12									
13	Sales	24500	294000		23000	276000			
14	Profit/Loss	13300	159600		9896	118752			

Independent Challenge 2

The Office Specialists Center is a small, growing business that rents small companies space and provides limited business services. They have hired you to organize their accounting records using Excel. The owners want you to track the company's expenses. Before you were hired, one of the bookkeepers began entering last year's expenses in a workbook, but the analysis was never completed.

a. Start Excel, open EX 2-4.xlsx from the location where you store your Data Files, then save it as **EX 2-Office Specialists Center Finances**. The worksheet includes labels for functions such as the average, maximum, and minimum amounts of each of the expenses in the worksheet.

b. Think about what information would be important for the bookkeeping staff to know.

c. Using the Quick Analysis tool, create a formula in the Quarter 1 column that uses the SUM function, then copy that formula into the Total row for the remaining quarters.

d. Use the SUM function to create formulas for each expense in the Total column.

e. Create formulas for each expense and each quarter in the Average, Maximum, and Minimum columns and rows using the method of your choice.

f. Compare your worksheet to the sample shown in FIGURE 2-25.

g. Enter your name in cell A25, then save your work.

h. Preview the worksheet, then submit your work to your instructor as directed.

i. Close the workbook and exit Excel.

FIGURE 2-25

	A	B	C	D	E	F	G	H	I	J
1	Office Specialists Center									
2										
3	Operating Expenses for 2017									
4										
5	Expense	Quarter 1	Quarter 2	Quarter 3	Quarter 4	Total	Average	Maximum	Minimum	
6	Rent	10240	10240	10240	10240	40960	10240	10240	10240	
7	Utilities	9500	8482	7929	8596	34507	8626.75	9500	7929	
8	Payroll	24456	27922	26876	30415	109669	27417.3	30415	24456	
9	Insurance	9000	8594	8472	8523	34589	8647.25	9000	8472	
10	Education	4000	4081	7552	5006	20639	5159.75	7552	4000	
11	Inventory	15986	14115	14641	15465	60207	15051.8	15986	14115	
12	Total	**73182**	**73434**	**75710**	**78245**					
13										
14	Average	12197	12239	12618.3	13040.8		Your formulas go here			
15	Maximum	24456	27922	26876	30415					
16	Minimum	4000	4081	7552	5006					

Independent Challenge 3

As the accounting manager of a locally owned food co-op with multiple locations, it is your responsibility to calculate accrued sales tax payments on a monthly basis and then submit the payments to the state government. You've decided to use an Excel workbook to make these calculations.

a. Start Excel, then save a new, blank workbook to the drive and folder where you store your Data Files as **EX 2-Food Co-op Sales Tax Calculations**.

b. Decide on the layout for all columns and rows. The worksheet will contain data for six stores, which you can name by store number, neighborhood, or another method of your choice. For each store, you will calculate total sales tax based on the local sales tax rate. You'll also calculate total tax owed for all six locations.

c. Make up sales data for all six stores.

d. Enter the rate to be used to calculate the sales tax, using your own local rate.

e. Create formulas to calculate the sales tax owed for each location. If you don't know the local tax rate, use **6.5%**.

f. Create a formula to total all the accrued sales tax.

g. Use the ROUND function to eliminate any decimal places in the sales tax figures for each location and in the total due.

h. Add your name to the header, then compare your work to the sample shown in FIGURE 2-26.

i. Save your work, preview the worksheet, and submit your work to your instructor as directed.

j. Close the workbook and exit Excel.

FIGURE 2-26

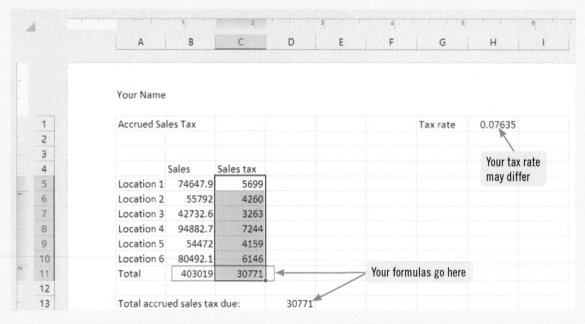

Independent Challenge 4: Explore

So many friends have come to you for help in understanding the various fees associated with purchasing a home that you've decided to create a business that specializes in helping first-time home-buyers. Your first task is to create a worksheet that clearly shows all the information a home buyer will need. Some fees are based on a percentage of the purchase price, and others are a flat fee; overall, they seem to represent a substantial amount above the purchase prices you see listed. A client has seen five houses so far that interest her; one is easily affordable, and the remaining four are all nice, but increasingly more expensive. You decide to create an Excel workbook to help her figure out the real cost of each home.

a. Find out the typical cost or percentage rate of at least three fees that are usually charged when buying a home and taking out a mortgage. (*Hint*: If you have access to the Internet, you can research the topic of home buying on the web, or you can ask friends about standard rates or percentages for items such as title insurance, credit reports, and inspection fees.)

b. Start Excel, then save a new, blank workbook to the location where you store your Data Files as **EX 2-Home Purchase Fees Worksheet**.

c. Create labels and enter data for at least five homes. If you enter this information across the columns in your worksheet, you should have one column for each house, with the purchase price in the cell below each label. Be sure to enter a different purchase price for each house.

d. Create labels for the Fees column and for an Amount or Rate column. Enter the information for each of the fees you have researched.

e. In each house column, enter formulas that calculate the fee for each item. The formulas (and use of absolute or relative referencing) will vary depending on whether the charges are a flat fee or based on a percentage of the purchase price. Make sure that the formulas for items that are based on a percentage of the purchase price (such as the fees for the Title Insurance Policy, Loan Origination, and Underwriter) contain absolute references. A sample of what your workbook might look like is shown in FIGURE 2-27.

f. Total the fees for each house, then create formulas that add the total fees to the purchase price.

g. Enter a title for the worksheet and include your client's name (or use Client 1) in the header.

h. Enter your name in the header, save your work, preview the worksheet, then submit your work to your instructor as directed.

i. Close the file and exit Excel.

FIGURE 2-27

Visual Workshop

Create the worksheet shown in FIGURE 2-28 using the skills you learned in this module. Save the workbook as **EX 2-Monthly Expenses** to the location where you store your Data Files. Enter your name and worksheet title in the header as shown, hide the gridlines, preview the worksheet, and then submit your work to your instructor as directed. (*Hint:* Change the Zoom factor to 90% by using the Zoom out button.)

FIGURE 2-28

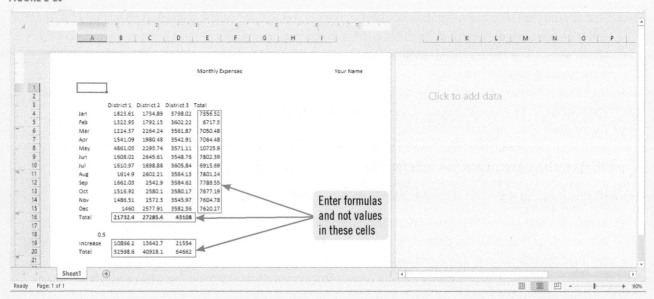

Formatting a Worksheet

CASE ▶ The marketing managers at Reason2Go have requested data from all R2G locations for advertising expenses incurred during the first quarter of this year. Mary Watson has created a worksheet listing this information. She asks you to format the worksheet to make it easier to read and to call attention to important data.

Module Objectives

After completing this module, you will be able to:

- Format values
- Change font and font size
- Change font styles and alignment
- Adjust column width
- Insert and delete rows and columns

- Apply colors, patterns, and borders
- Apply conditional formatting
- Rename and move a worksheet
- Check spelling

Files You Will Need

EX 3-1.xlsx   EX 3-4.xlsx
EX 3-2.xlsx   EX 3-5.xlsx
EX 3-3.xlsx

Format Values

The **format** of a cell determines how the labels and values look—for example, whether the contents appear boldfaced, italicized, or with dollar signs and commas. Formatting changes only the appearance of a value or label; it does not alter the actual data in any way. To format a cell or range, first you select it, then you apply the formatting using the Ribbon, Mini toolbar, or a keyboard shortcut. You can apply formatting before or after you enter data in a cell or range. **CASE** *Mary has provided you with a worksheet that details advertising expenses, and you're ready to improve its appearance and readability. You start by formatting some of the values so they are displayed as currency, percentages, and dates.*

STEPS

1. **Start Excel, open the file** EX 3-1.xlsx **from the location where you store your Data Files, then save it as** EX 3-R2G Advertising Expenses

   This worksheet is difficult to interpret because all the information is crowded and looks the same. In some columns, the contents appear cut off because there is too much data to fit given the current column width. You decide not to widen the columns yet, because the other changes you plan to make might affect column width and row height. The first thing you want to do is format the data showing the cost of each ad.

2. **Select the range D4:D32, then click the** Accounting Number Format button $ **in the Number group on the Home tab**

   The default Accounting **number format** adds dollar signs and two decimal places to the data, as shown in FIGURE 3-1. Formatting this data in Accounting format makes it clear that its values are monetary values. Excel automatically resizes the column to display the new formatting. The Accounting and Currency number formats are both used for monetary values, but the Accounting format aligns currency symbols and decimal points of numbers in a column.

3. **Select the range F4:H32, then click the** Comma Style button **in the Number group**

   The values in columns F, G, and H display the Comma Style format, which does not include a dollar sign but can be useful for some types of accounting data.

4. **Select the range J4:J32, click the** Number Format list arrow, **click** Percentage, **then click the** Increase Decimal button **in the Number group**

   The data in the % of Total column is now formatted with a percent sign (%) and three decimal places. The Number Format list arrow lets you choose from popular number formats and shows an example of what the selected cell or cells would look like in each format (when multiple cells are selected, the example is based on the first cell in the range). Each time you click the Increase Decimal button, you add one decimal place; clicking the button twice would add two decimal places.

5. **Click the** Decrease Decimal button **in the Number group** twice

   Two decimal places are removed from the percentage values in column J.

6. **Select the range B4:B31, then click the** launcher **in the Number group**

   The Format Cells dialog box opens with the Date category already selected on the Number tab.

7. **Select the first** 14-Mar-12 format **in the Type list box as shown in** FIGURE 3-2, **then click** OK

   The dates in column B appear in the 14-Mar-12 format. The second 14-Mar-12 format in the list (visible if you scroll down the list) displays all days in two digits (it adds a leading zero if the day is only a single-digit number), while the one you chose displays single-digit days without a leading zero.

8. **Select the range C4:C31, right-click the** range, **click Format Cells on the shortcut menu, click** 14-Mar **in the Type list box in the Format Cells dialog box, then click** OK

   Compare your worksheet to FIGURE 3-3.

9. **Press** [Ctrl][Home], **then save your work**

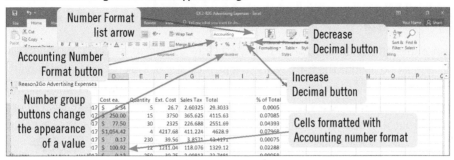

FIGURE 3-1: Accounting number format applied to range

FIGURE 3-2: Format Cells dialog box

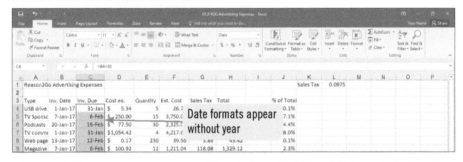

FIGURE 3-3: Worksheet with formatted values

Formatting as a table

Excel includes 60 predefined **table styles** to make it easy to format selected worksheet cells as a table. You can apply table styles to any range of cells that you want to format quickly, or even to an entire worksheet, but they're especially useful for those ranges with labels in the left column and top row, and totals in the bottom row or right column. To apply a table style, select the data to be formatted or click anywhere within the intended range (Excel can automatically detect a range of cells filled with data), click the Format as Table button in the Styles group on the Home tab, then click a style in the gallery, as shown in **FIGURE 3-4**. Table styles are organized in three categories: Light, Medium, and Dark. Once you click a style, Excel asks you to confirm the range selection, then applies the style. Once you have formatted a range as a table, you can use Live Preview to preview the table in other styles by pointing to any style in the Table Styles gallery.

FIGURE 3-4: Table Styles gallery

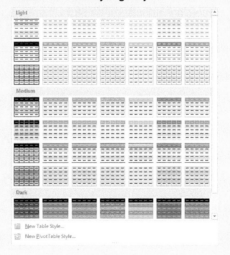

Change Font and Font Size

Learning
Outcomes
• Change a font
• Change a font size
• Use the Mini
  toolbar

A **font** is the name for a collection of characters (letters, numbers, symbols, and punctuation marks) with a similar, specific design. The **font size** is the physical size of the text, measured in units called points. A **point** is equal to 1/72 of an inch. The default font and font size in Excel is 11-point Calibri. TABLE 3-1 shows several fonts in different font sizes. You can change the font and font size of any cell or range using the Font and Font Size list arrows. The Font and Font Size list arrows appear on the Home tab on the Ribbon and on the Mini toolbar, which opens when you right-click a cell or range. CASE ▶ *You want to change the font and font size of the labels and the worksheet title so that they stand out more from the data.*

STEPS

1. **Click the** Font list arrow **in the Font group on the Home tab, scroll down in the Font list to see an alphabetical listing of the fonts available on your computer, then click** Times New Roman, **as shown in** FIGURE 3-5

   The font in cell A1 changes to Times New Roman. Notice that the font names on the list are displayed in the font they represent.

2. **Click the** Font Size list arrow **in the Font group, then click** 20

   The worksheet title appears in 20-point Times New Roman, and the Font and Font Size list boxes on the Home tab display the new font and font size information.

3. **Click the** Increase Font Size button A^ **in the Font group twice**

   The font size of the title increases to 24 point.

4. **Select the range** A3:J3, **right-click, then click the** Font list arrow **on the Mini toolbar**

   The Mini toolbar includes the most commonly used formatting tools, so it's great for making quick formatting changes.

5. **Scroll down in the Font list and click** Times New Roman, **click the** Font Size list arrow **on the Mini toolbar, then click** 14

   The Mini toolbar closes when you move the pointer away from the selection. Compare your worksheet to FIGURE 3-6. Notice that some of the column labels are now too wide to appear fully in the column. Excel does not automatically adjust column widths to accommodate cell formatting; you have to adjust column widths manually. You'll learn to do this in a later lesson.

6. **Save your work**

TABLE 3-1: **Examples of fonts and font sizes**

font	12 point	24 point
Calibri	Excel	Excel
Playbill	Excel	Excel
Comic Sans MS	Excel	Excel
Times New Roman	Excel	Excel

FIGURE 3-5: Font list

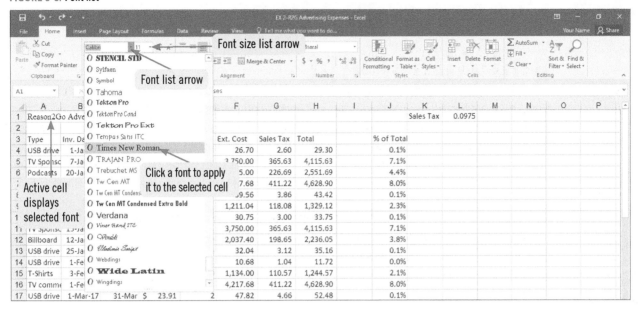

FIGURE 3-6: Worksheet with formatted title and column labels

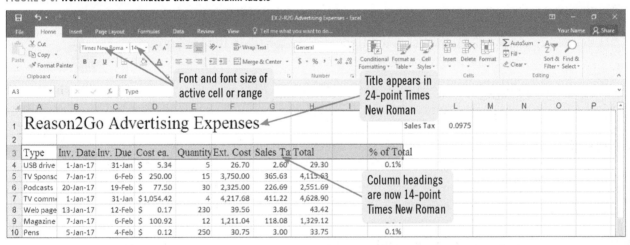

Inserting and adjusting online pictures and other images

You can illustrate your worksheets using online pictures and other images. Office.com makes many photos and animations available for your use. To add a picture to a worksheet, click the Online Pictures button in the Illustrations group on the Insert tab. The Insert Pictures window opens. Here you can search for online pictures (or Clip Art) from a variety of popular sources such as Facebook and Flickr, through the Bing search engine, or on OneDrive. To search, type one or more **keywords** (words related to your subject) in the appropriate Search text box, then press [Enter]. For example, pictures that relate to the keyword house in a search of Office.com appear in the Office.com window, as shown in FIGURE 3-7. When you double-click the image you want in the window, the image is inserted at the location of the active cell. To add images on your computer (or computers on your network) to a worksheet, click the Insert tab on the Ribbon, then click the Pictures button in the Illustrations group. Navigate to

the file you want, then click Insert. To resize an image, drag any corner sizing handle. To move an image, point inside the clip until the pointer changes to ⁺⁺, then drag it to a new location.

FIGURE 3-7: Results of Online Picture search

Learning
Outcomes
• Apply formatting
• Use the Format
  Painter
• Change cell
  alignment

Change Font Styles and Alignment

Font styles are formats such as bold, italic, and underlining that you can apply to affect the way text and numbers look in a worksheet. You can also change the **alignment** of labels and values in cells to position them in relation to the cells' edges—such as left-aligned, right-aligned, or centered. You can apply font styles and alignment options using the Home tab, the Format Cells dialog box, or the Mini toolbar. See TABLE 3-2 for a description of common font style and alignment buttons that are available on the Home tab and the Mini toolbar. Once you have formatted a cell the way you want it, you can "paint" or copy the cell's formats into other cells by using the Format Painter button in the Clipboard group on the Home tab. This is similar to using copy and paste, but instead of copying cell contents, it copies only the cell's formatting. **CASE** *You want to further enhance the worksheet's appearance by adding bold and underline formatting and centering some of the labels.*

STEPS

1. **Press [Ctrl][Home], then click the Bold button B in the Font group on the Home tab**
   The title in cell A1 appears in bold.

2. **Click cell A3, then click the Underline button U in the Font group**
   The column label is now underlined.

3. **Click the Italic button I in the Font group, then click B**
   The heading now appears in boldface, underlined, italic type. Notice that the Bold, Italic, and Underline buttons in the Font group are all selected.

4. **Click the Italic button I to deselect it**
   The italic font style is removed from cell A3, but the bold and underline font styles remain.

5. **Click the Format Painter button in the Clipboard group, then select the range B3:J3**
   The formatting in cell A3 is copied to the rest of the column labels. To paint the formats on more than one selection, double-click the Format Painter button to keep it activated until you turn it off. You can turn off the Format Painter by pressing [Esc] or by clicking . You decide the title would look better if it were centered over the data columns.

6. **Select the range A1:H1, then click the Merge & Center button in the Alignment group**
   The Merge & Center button creates one cell out of the eight cells across the row, then centers the text in that newly created, merged cell. The title "Reason2Go Advertising Expenses" is centered across the eight columns you selected. To split a merged cell into its original components, select the merged cell, then click the Merge & Center button to deselect it. Occasionally, you may find that you want cell contents to wrap within a cell. You can do this by selecting the cells containing the text you want to wrap, then clicking the Wrap Text button in the Alignment group on the Home tab on the Ribbon.

7. **Select the range A3:J3, right-click, then click the Center button on the Mini toolbar**
   Compare your screen to FIGURE 3-8. Although they may be difficult to read, notice that all the headings are centered within their cells.

8. **Save your work**

FIGURE 3-8: Worksheet with font styles and alignment applied

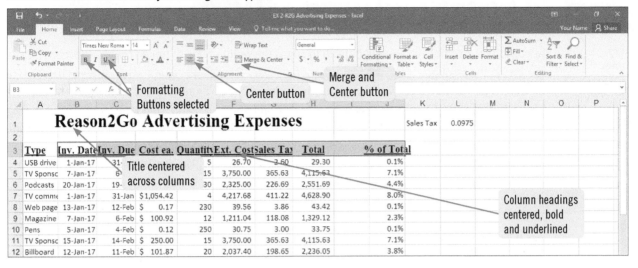

TABLE 3-2: Common font style and alignment buttons

button	description
B	Bolds text
I	Italicizes text
U	Underlines text
	Centers text across columns, and combines two or more selected, adjacent cells into one cell
	Aligns text at the left edge of the cell
	Centers text horizontally within the cell
	Aligns text at the right edge of the cell
	Wraps long text into multiple lines

Excel 2016

Rotating and indenting cell entries

In addition to applying fonts and font styles, you can rotate or indent data within a cell to further change its appearance. You can rotate text within a cell by altering its alignment. Click the Home tab, select the cells you want to modify, then click the launcher in the Alignment group to open the Alignment tab of the Format Cells dialog box. Click a position in the Orientation box or type a number in the Degrees text box to rotate text from its default horizontal orientation, then click OK. You can indent cell contents using the Increase Indent button in the Alignment group, which moves cell contents to the right one space, or the Decrease Indent button, which moves cell contents to the left one space.

Adjust Column Width

Learning Outcomes
- Change a column width by dragging
- Resize a column with AutoFit
- Change the width of multiple columns

As you format a worksheet, you might need to adjust the width of one or more columns to accommodate changes in the amount of text, the font size, or font style. The default column width is 8.43 characters, a little less than 1". With Excel, you can adjust the width of one or more columns by using the mouse, the Format button in the Cells group on the Home tab, or the shortcut menu. Using the mouse, you can drag or double-click the right edge of a column heading. The Format button and shortcut menu include commands for making more precise width adjustments. TABLE 3-3 describes common column formatting commands. **CASE** *You have noticed that some of the labels in columns A through J don't fit in the cells. You want to adjust the widths of the columns so that the labels appear in their entirety.*

STEPS

1. **Position the mouse pointer on the line between the column A and column B headings until it changes to ╫**

   See FIGURE 3-9. The **column heading** is the box at the top of each column containing a letter. Before you can adjust column width using the mouse, you need to position the pointer on the right edge of the column heading for the column you want to adjust. The cell entry "TV commercials" is the widest in the column.

2. **Click and drag the ╫ to the right until the column displays the "TV commercials" cell entries fully (approximately 15.29 characters, 1.23", or 112 pixels)**

   As you change the column width, a ScreenTip is displayed listing the column width. In Normal view, the ScreenTip lists the width in characters and pixels; in Page Layout view, the ScreenTip lists the width in inches and pixels.

3. **Position the pointer on the line between columns B and C until it changes to ╫, then double-click**

   Double-clicking the right edge of a column heading activates the **AutoFit** feature, which automatically resizes the column to accommodate the widest entry in the column. Column B automatically widens to fit the widest entry, which is the column label "Inv. Date".

4. **Use AutoFit to resize columns C, D, and J**

5. **Select the range E5:H5**

   You can change the width of multiple columns at once, by first selecting either the column headings or at least one cell in each column.

6. **Click the Format button in the Cells group, then click Column Width**

   The Column Width dialog box opens. Column width measurement is based on the number of characters that will fit in the column when formatted in the Normal font and font size (in this case, 11-point Calibri).

7. **Drag the dialog box by its title bar if its placement obscures your view of the worksheet, type 11 in the Column width text box, then click OK**

   The widths of columns E, F, G, and H change to reflect the new setting. See FIGURE 3-10.

8. **Save your work**

TABLE 3-3: Common column formatting commands

command	description	available using
Column Width	Sets the width to a specific number of characters	Format button; shortcut menu
AutoFit Column Width	Fits to the widest entry in a column	Format button; mouse
Hide & Unhide	Hides or displays hidden column(s)	Format button; shortcut menu
Default Width	Resets column to worksheet's default column width	Format button

FIGURE 3-9: Preparing to change the column width

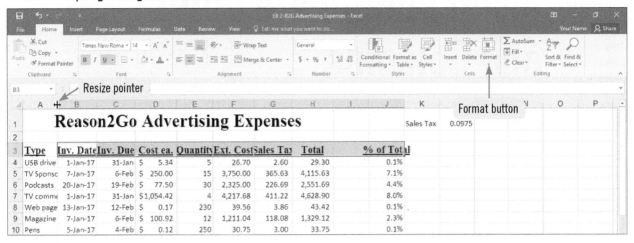

FIGURE 3-10: Worksheet with column widths adjusted

Changing row height

Changing row height is as easy as changing column width. Row height is calculated in points, the same units of measure used for fonts. The row height must exceed the size of the font you are using. Normally, you don't need to adjust row heights manually, because row heights adjust automatically to accommodate font size changes. If you format something in a row to be a larger point size, Excel adjusts the row to fit the largest point size in the row. However, you have just as many options for changing row

height as you do column width. Using the mouse, you can place the ✚ pointer on the line dividing a row heading from the heading below, and then drag to the desired height; double-clicking the line AutoFits the row height where necessary. You can also select one or more rows, then use the Row Height command on the shortcut menu, or click the Format button on the Home tab and click the Row Height or AutoFit Row Height command.

Insert and Delete Rows and Columns

Learning
Outcomes
• Use the Insert
  dialog box
• Use column and
  row heading
  buttons to insert
  and delete

As you modify a worksheet, you might find it necessary to insert or delete rows and columns to keep your worksheet current. For example, you might need to insert rows to accommodate new inventory products or remove a column of yearly totals that are no longer necessary. When you insert a new row, the row is inserted above the cell pointer and the contents of the worksheet shift down from the newly inserted row. When you insert a new column, the column is inserted to the left of the cell pointer and the contents of the worksheet shift to the right of the new column. To insert multiple rows, select the same number of row headings as you want to insert before using the Insert command. **CASE** *You want to improve the overall appearance of the worksheet by inserting a row between the last row of data and the totals. Also, you have learned that row 27 and column J need to be deleted from the worksheet.*

STEPS

1. Right-click cell A32, then click Insert on the shortcut menu

The Insert dialog box opens. See FIGURE 3-11. You can choose to insert a column or a row; insert a single cell and shift the cells in the active column to the right; or insert a single cell and shift the cells in the active row down. An additional row between the last row of data and the totals will visually separate the totals.

QUICK TIP

To insert a single row or column, right-click the row heading immediately below where you want the new row, or right-click the column heading to the right of where you want the new column, then click Insert on the shortcut menu.

2. Click the Entire row option button, then click OK

A blank row appears between the Billboard data and the totals, and the formula result in cell E33 has not changed. The Insert Options button appears beside cell A33. Pointing to the button displays a list arrow, which you can click and then choose from the following options: Format Same As Above (the default setting, already selected), Format Same As Below, or Clear Formatting.

3. Click the row 27 heading

All of row 27 is selected, as shown in FIGURE 3-12.

QUICK TIP

If you inadvertently click the Delete list arrow instead of the button itself, click Delete Sheet Rows in the menu that opens.

4. Click the Delete button in the Cells group; *do not click the list arrow*

Excel deletes row 27, and all rows below it shift up one row. You must use the Delete button or the Delete command on the shortcut menu to delete a row or column; pressing [Delete] on the keyboard removes only the *contents* of a selected row or column.

5. Click the column J heading

The percentage information is calculated elsewhere and is no longer necessary in this worksheet.

QUICK TIP

After inserting or deleting rows or columns in a worksheet, be sure to proof formulas that contain relative cell references.

6. Click the Delete button in the Cells group

Excel deletes column J. The remaining columns to the right shift left one column.

7. Use AutoFit to resize columns F and H, then save your work

---

Hiding and unhiding columns and rows

When you don't want data in a column or row to be visible, but you don't want to delete it, you can hide the column or row. To hide a selected column, click the Format button in the Cells group on the Home tab, point to Hide & Unhide, then click Hide Columns. A hidden column is indicated by a dark green vertical line in its original position. This green line disappears when you click elsewhere in the worksheet. You can display a hidden column by selecting the columns on either side of the hidden column, clicking the Format button in the Cells group, pointing to Hide & Unhide, and then clicking Unhide Columns. (To hide or unhide one or more rows, substitute Hide Rows and Unhide Rows for the Hide Columns and Unhide Columns commands.)

FIGURE 3-12: **Worksheet with row 27 selected**

Adding and editing comments

Much of your work in Excel may be in collaboration with teammates with whom you share worksheets. You can share ideas with other worksheet users by adding comments within selected cells. To include a comment in a worksheet, click the cell where you want to place the comment, click the Review tab on the Ribbon, then click the New Comment button in the Comments group. You can type your comments in the resizable text box that opens containing the computer user's name. A small, red triangle appears in the upper-right corner of a cell containing a comment. If comments are not already displayed in a workbook, other users can point to the triangle to display the comment. To see all worksheet comments, as shown in FIGURE 3-13, click the Show All Comments button in the Comments group. To edit a comment, click the cell containing the comment, then click the Edit Comment button in the Comments

group. To delete a comment, click the cell containing the comment, then click the Delete button in the Comments group.

FIGURE 3-13: **Comments displayed in a worksheet**

	A	B	C	D
21	TV Sponsor	1-Feb-16	2-Mar	Food Network
22	Newspaper	25-Feb-16	26-Mar	Village Reader
23	Web page ads	10-Mar-16	9-Apr	Advertising Concepts
24	TV Sponsor	15-Feb-16	16-Mar	Food Network
25	Pens	15-Mar-16	14-Apr	Mass Appeal, Inc.
26	TV commercials	1-Mar-16	31-Mar	Discovery Channel
27	Podcasts	20-Mar-16	19-Apr	iPodAds
28	Newspaper	1-Apr-16	1-May	University Voice
29	Podcasts	10-Mar-16	10-May	iPodAds
30	Billboard	28-Mar-16	27-Apr	Advertising Concepts

Harriet McDonald:
I think this will turn out to be a very good decision.

Will Moss:
Should we continue with this market, or expand to other types of publications?

Apply Colors, Patterns, and Borders

Learning
Outcomes
• Use Live Preview
  to apply color
  to cells
• Format cells using
  the shortcut menu
• Apply a border
  and pattern to
  a cell

You can use colors, patterns, and borders to enhance the overall appearance of a worksheet and make it easier to read. You can add these enhancements by using the Borders, Font Color, and Fill Color buttons in the Font group on the Home tab of the Ribbon and on the Mini toolbar, or by using the Fill tab and the Border tab in the Format Cells dialog box. You can open the Format Cells dialog box by clicking the dialog box launcher in the Font, Alignment, or Number group on the Home tab, or by right-clicking a selection, then clicking Format Cells on the shortcut menu. You can apply a color to the background of a cell or a range or to cell contents (such as letters and numbers), and you can apply a pattern to a cell or range. You can apply borders to all the cells in a worksheet or only to selected cells to call attention to selected information. To save time, you can also apply **cell styles**, predesigned combinations of formats. **CASE** *You want to add a pattern, a border, and color to the title of the worksheet to give the worksheet a more professional appearance.*

STEPS

1. **Select cell A1, click the Fill Color list arrow** 🎨 **in the Font group, then hover the pointer over the Turquoise, Accent 2 color (first row, sixth column from the left)**
   See FIGURE 3-14. Live Preview shows you how the color will look *before* you apply it. (Remember that cell A1 spans columns A through H because the Merge & Center command was applied.)

2. **Click the Turquoise, Accent 2 color**
   The color is applied to the background (or fill) of this cell. When you change fill or font color, the color on the Fill Color or Font Color button changes to the last color you selected.

3. **Right-click cell A1, then click Format Cells on the shortcut menu**
   The Format Cells dialog box opens.

4. **Click the Fill tab, click the Pattern Style list arrow, click the 6.25% Gray style (first row, sixth column from the left), then click OK**

5. **Click the Borders list arrow** ⊞ **in the Font group, then click Thick Bottom Border**
   Unlike underlining, which is a text-formatting tool, borders extend to the width of the cell, and can appear at the bottom of the cell, at the top, on either side, or on any combination of the four sides. It can be difficult to see a border when the cell is selected.

6. **Select the range A3:H3, click the Font Color list arrow** 🅰 **in the Font group, then click the Blue, Accent 1 color (first Theme Colors row, fifth column from the left) on the palette**
   The new color is applied to the labels in the selected range.

7. **Select the range J1:K1, click the Cell Styles button in the Styles group, click the Neutral cell style (first row, fourth column from the left) in the gallery, then AutoFit column J**
   The font and color change in the range, as shown in FIGURE 3-15.

8. **Save your work**

FIGURE 3-14: Live Preview of fill color

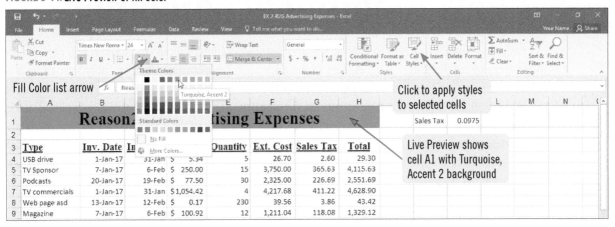

Fill Color list arrow

Click to apply styles to selected cells

Live Preview shows cell A1 with Turquoise, Accent 2 background

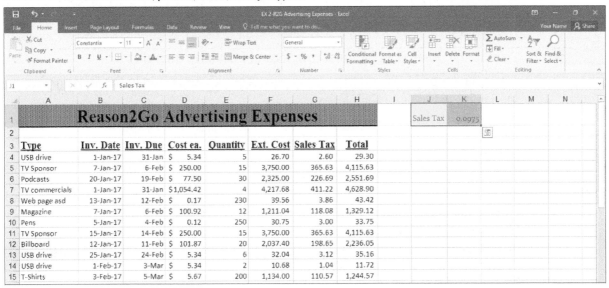

Working with themes and cell styles

Using themes and cell styles makes it easier to ensure that your worksheets are consistent. A **theme** is a predefined set of formats that gives your Excel worksheet a professional look. Formatting choices included in a theme are colors, fonts, and line and fill effects. To apply a theme, click the Themes button in the Themes group on the Page Layout tab to open the Themes gallery, as shown in FIGURE 3-16, then click a theme in the gallery. **Cell styles** are automatically updated if you change a theme. For example, if you apply the 20% - Accent1 cell style to cell A1 in a worksheet that has no theme applied, the fill color changes to light blue with no pattern, and the font changes to Calibri. If you change the theme of the worksheet to Ion Boardroom, cell A1's fill color changes to red and the font changes to Century Gothic, because these are the new theme's associated formats.

FIGURE 3-16: Themes gallery

Apply Conditional Formatting

Learning Outcomes
- Create conditional formatting in a range
- Change formatting and parameters in conditional formatting

So far, you've used formatting to change the appearance of different types of data, but you can also use formatting to highlight important aspects of the data itself. For example, you can apply formatting that changes the font color to red for any cells where the value is greater than $100 and to green where the value is below $50. This is called **conditional formatting** because Excel automatically applies different formats to data if the data meets conditions you specify. The formatting is updated if you change data in the worksheet. You can also copy conditional formats the same way you copy other formats. **CASE** *Mary is concerned about advertising costs exceeding the yearly budget. You decide to use conditional formatting to highlight certain trends and patterns in the data so that it's easy to spot the most expensive advertising.*

STEPS

1. **Select the range H4:H30, click the** Conditional Formatting button **in the Styles group on the Home tab, point to** Data Bars, **then point to the** Light Blue Data Bar **(second row, second from left)**

   Data bars are colored horizontal bars that visually illustrate differences between values in a range of cells. Live Preview shows how this formatting will appear in the worksheet, as shown in FIGURE 3-17.

2. **Point to the** Green Data Bar **(first row, second from left), then click it**

3. **Select the range F4:F30, click the** Conditional Formatting button **in the Styles group, then point to** Highlight Cells Rules

   The Highlight Cells Rules submenu displays choices for creating different formatting conditions. For example, you can create a rule for values that are greater than or less than a certain amount, or between two amounts.

4. **Click** Between **on the submenu**

   The Between dialog box opens, displaying input boxes you can use to define the condition and a default format (Light Red Fill with Dark Red Text) selected for cells that meet that condition. Depending on the condition you select in the Highlight Cells Rules submenu (such as "Greater Than" or "Less Than"), this dialog box displays different input boxes. You define the condition using the input boxes and then assign the formatting you want to use for cells that meet that condition. Values used in input boxes for a condition can be constants, formulas, cell references, or dates.

5. **Type** 2000 **in the first text box, type** 4000 **in the second text box, click the** with list **arrow, click** Light Red Fill, **compare your settings to** FIGURE 3-18, **then click** OK

   All cells with values between 2000 and 4000 in column F appear with a light red fill.

6. **Click cell** E7, **type** 3, **then press** [Enter]

   When the value in cell E7 changes, the formatting also changes because the new value meets the condition you set. Compare your results to FIGURE 3-19.

7. **Press** [Ctrl][Home] **to select cell A1, then save your work**

FIGURE 3-17: Previewing data bars in a range

FIGURE 3-18: Between dialog box

FIGURE 3-19: Worksheet with conditional formatting

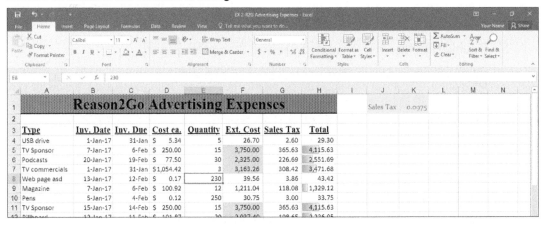

Managing conditional formatting rules

If you create a conditional formatting rule and then want to change a condition, you don't need to create a new rule; instead, you can modify the rule using the Rules Manager. Click the Conditional Formatting button in the Styles group, then click Manage Rules. The Conditional Formatting Rules Manager dialog box opens. Select the rule you want to edit, click Edit Rule, and then modify the settings in the Edit the Rule Description area in the Edit Formatting Rule dialog box. To change the formatting for a rule, click the Format Style button in the Edit the Rule Description area, select the formatting styles you want the text to have, then click OK three times to close the Format Cells dialog box, the Edit Formatting Rule dialog box, and the Conditional Formatting Rules Manager dialog box. The rule is modified, and the new conditional formatting is applied to the selected cells. To delete a rule, select the rule in the Conditional Formatting Rules Manager dialog box, then click the Delete Rule button.

Rename and Move a Worksheet

Learning Outcomes
- Rename a sheet
- Apply color to a sheet tab
- Reorder sheets in a workbook

By default, an Excel workbook initially contains one worksheet named Sheet1, although you can add sheets at any time. Each sheet name appears on a sheet tab at the bottom of the worksheet. When you open a new workbook, the first worksheet, Sheet1, is the active sheet. To move from sheet to sheet, you can click any sheet tab at the bottom of the worksheet window. The sheet tab scrolling buttons, located to the left of the sheet tabs, are useful when a workbook contains too many sheet tabs to display at once. To make it easier to identify the sheets in a workbook, you can rename each sheet and add color to the tabs. You can also organize them in a logical way. For instance, to better track performance goals, you could name each workbook sheet for an individual salesperson, and you could move the sheets so they appear in alphabetical order. **CASE** *In the current worksheet, Sheet1 contains information about actual advertising expenses. Sheet2 contains an advertising budget, and Sheet3 contains no data. You want to rename the two sheets in the workbook to reflect their contents, add color to a sheet tab to easily distinguish one from the other, and change their order.*

STEPS

1. **Click the Sheet2 tab**

   Sheet2 becomes active, appearing in front of the Sheet1 tab; this is the worksheet that contains the budgeted advertising expenses. See FIGURE 3-20.

2. **Click the Sheet1 tab**

   Sheet1, which contains the actual advertising expenses, becomes active again.

3. **Double-click the Sheet2 tab, type Budget, then press [Enter]**

   The new name for Sheet2 automatically replaces the default name on the tab. Worksheet names can have up to 31 characters, including spaces and punctuation.

4. **Right-click the Budget tab, point to Tab Color on the shortcut menu, then click the Bright Green, Accent 4, Lighter 40% color (fourth row, third column from the right) as shown in** FIGURE 3-21

5. **Double-click the Sheet1 tab, type Actual, then press [Enter]**

   Notice that the color of the Budget tab changes depending on whether it is the active tab; when the Actual tab is active, the color of the Budget tab changes to the green tab color you selected. You decide to rearrange the order of the sheets so that the Budget tab is to the left of the Actual tab.

6. **Click the Budget tab, hold down the mouse button, drag it to the left of the Actual tab, as shown in** FIGURE 3-22, **then release the mouse button**

   As you drag, the pointer changes to ▨, the sheet relocation pointer, and a small, black triangle just above the tabs shows the position the moved sheet will be in when you release the mouse button. The first sheet in the workbook is now the Budget sheet. See FIGURE 3-23. You can move multiple sheets by pressing and holding [Shift] while clicking the sheets you want to move, then dragging the sheets to their new location.

7. **Click the Actual sheet tab, click the Page Layout button ▦ on the status bar to open Page Layout view, enter your name in the left header text box, then click anywhere in the worksheet to deselect the header**

8. **Click the Page Layout tab on the Ribbon, click the Orientation button in the Page Setup group, then click Landscape**

9. **Right-click the Sheet3 tab, click Delete on the shortcut menu, press [Ctrl][Home], then save your work**

FIGURE 3-20: **Sheet tabs in workbook**

Sheet1 tab   Sheet2 tab

FIGURE 3-21: **Tab Color palette**

Sheet2 renamed

FIGURE 3-22: **Moving the Budget sheet**

Sheet relocation pointer

FIGURE 3-23: **Reordered sheets**

Budget sheet comes
before Actual sheet

Copying, adding, and deleting worksheets

There are times when you may want to copy a worksheet. For example, a workbook might contain a sheet with Quarter 1 expenses, and you want to use that sheet as the basis for a sheet containing Quarter 2 expenses. To copy a sheet within the same workbook, press and hold [Ctrl], drag the sheet tab to the desired tab location, release the mouse button, then release [Ctrl]. A duplicate sheet appears with the same name as the copied sheet followed by "(2)" indicating that it is a copy. You can then rename the sheet to a more meaningful name. To copy a sheet to a different workbook, both the source and destination workbooks must be open. Select the sheet to copy or move, right-click the sheet tab, then click Move or Copy in the shortcut menu. Complete the information in the Move or Copy dialog box. Be sure to click the Create a copy check box if you are copying rather than moving the worksheet. Carefully check your calculation results whenever you move or copy a worksheet. You can add multiple worksheets to a workbook by clicking the Home tab on the Ribbon, pressing and holding [Shift], then clicking the number of existing worksheet tabs that correspond with the number of sheets you want to add, clicking the Insert list arrow in the Cells group on the Home tab, then clicking Insert Sheet. You can delete multiple worksheets from a workbook by clicking the Home tab, pressing and holding [Shift], clicking the sheet tabs of the worksheets you want to delete, clicking the Delete list arrow in the Cells group on the Home tab, then clicking Delete Sheet.

Check Spelling

Learning Outcomes
- Describe how spell checking works
- Change the spelling using a suggestion
- Replace a word using Find & Select

Excel includes a spell checker to help you ensure that the words in your worksheet are spelled correctly. The spell checker scans your worksheet, displays words it doesn't find in its built-in dictionary, and suggests replacements when they are available. To check all of the sheets in a multiple-sheet workbook, you need to display each sheet individually and run the spell checker for each one. Because the built-in dictionary cannot possibly include all the words that anyone needs, you can add words to the dictionary, such as your company name, an acronym, or an unusual technical term. Once you add a word or term, the spell checker no longer considers that word misspelled. Any words you've added to the dictionary using Word, Access, or PowerPoint are also available in Excel. **CASE** *Before you distribute this workbook to Mary, you check the spelling.*

STEPS

QUICK TIP
The Spelling dialog box lists the name of the language currently being used in its title bar.

1. **Click the Review tab on the Ribbon, then click the Spelling button in the Proofing group**

   The Spelling: English (United States) dialog box opens, as shown in FIGURE 3-24, with "asd" selected as the first misspelled word in the worksheet, and with "ads" selected in the Suggestions list as a possible replacement. For any word, you have the option to Ignore this case of the flagged word, Ignore All cases of the flagged word, Change the word to the selected suggestion, Change All instances of the flagged word to the selected suggestion, or add the flagged word to the dictionary using Add to Dictionary.

2. **Click Change**

   Next, the spell checker finds the word "Podacsts" and suggests "Podcasts" as an alternative.

3. **Verify that the word Podcasts is selected in the Suggestions list, then click Change**

   When no more incorrect words are found, Excel displays a message indicating that the spell check is complete.

4. **Click OK**

5. **Click the Home tab, click Find & Select in the Editing group, then click Replace**

   The Find and Replace dialog box opens. You can use this dialog box to replace a word or phrase. It might be a misspelling of a proper name that the spell checker didn't recognize as misspelled, or it could simply be a term that you want to change throughout the worksheet. Mary has just told you that each instance of "Billboard" in the worksheet should be changed to "Sign."

6. **Type Billboard in the Find what text box, press [Tab], then type Sign in the Replace with text box**

   Compare your dialog box to FIGURE 3-25.

7. **Click Replace All, click OK to close the Microsoft Excel dialog box, then click Close to close the Find and Replace dialog box**

   Excel has made two replacements.

8. **Click the File tab, click Print on the navigation bar, click the No Scaling setting in the Settings section on the Print tab, then click Fit Sheet on One Page**

9. **Click the Return button ⊙ to return to your worksheet, save your work, submit it to your instructor as directed, close the workbook, then exit Excel**

   The completed worksheet is shown in FIGURE 3-26.

Emailing a workbook

You can send an entire workbook from within Excel using your installed email program, such as Microsoft Outlook. To send a workbook as an email message attachment, open the workbook, click the File tab, then click Share on the navigation bar. With the Email option selected in the Share section in Backstage view, click Send as Attachment in the right pane. An email message opens in your default email program with the workbook automatically attached; the filename appears in the Attached field. Complete the To and optional Cc fields, include a message if you wish, then click Send.

FIGURE 3-24: **Spelling: English (United States) dialog box**

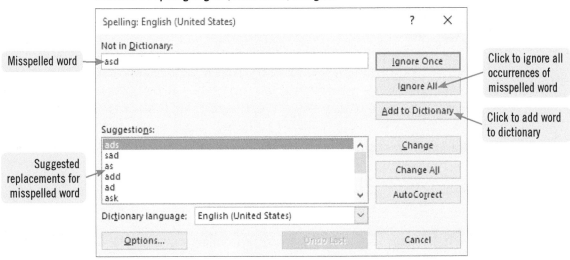

Misspelled word

Suggested replacements for misspelled word

Click to ignore all occurrences of misspelled word

Click to add word to dictionary

FIGURE 3-25: **Find and Replace dialog box**

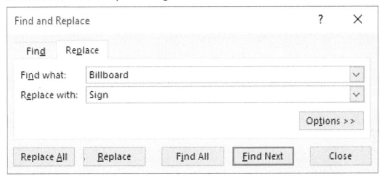

FIGURE 3-26: **Completed worksheet**

Your Name

Reason2Go Advertising Expenses

Sales Tax 0.0975

Type	Inv. Date	Inv. Due	Cost ea.	Quantity	Ext. Cost	Sales Tax	Total
USB drive	1-Jan-17	31-Jan	$ 5.34	5	26.70	2.60	29.30
TV Sponsor	7-Jan-17	6-Feb	$ 250.00	15	3,750.00	365.63	4,115.63
Podcasts	20-Jan-17	19-Feb	$ 77.50	30	2,325.00	226.69	2,551.69
TV commercials	1-Jan-17	31-Jan	$ 1,054.42	3	3,163.26	308.42	3,471.68
Web page ads	13-Jan-17	12-Feb	$ 0.17	230	39.56	3.86	43.42
Magazine	7-Jan-17	6-Feb	$ 100.92	12	1,211.04	118.08	1,329.12
Pens	5-Jan-17	4-Feb	$ 0.12	250	30.75	3.00	33.75
TV Sponsor	15-Jan-17	14-Feb	$ 250.00	15	3,750.00	365.63	4,115.63
Sign	12-Jan-17	11-Feb	$ 101.87	20	2,037.40	198.65	2,236.05
USB drive	25-Jan-17	24-Feb	$ 5.34	6	32.04	3.12	35.16
USB drive	1-Feb-17	3-Mar	$ 5.34	2	10.68	1.04	11.72
T-Shirts	3-Feb-17	5-Mar	$ 5.67	200	1,134.00	110.57	1,244.57
TV commercials	1-Feb-17	3-Mar	$ 1,054.42	4	4,217.68	411.22	4,628.90
USB drive	1-Mar-17	31-Mar	$ 23.91	2	47.82	4.66	52.48
Web page ads	28-Feb-17	30-Mar	$ 0.17	275	47.30	4.61	51.91
Magazine	27-Feb-17	29-Mar	$ 100.92	12	1,211.04	118.08	1,329.12
Podcasts	22-Feb-17	24-Mar	$ 77.50	30	2,325.00	226.69	2,551.69
TV Sponsor	1-Feb-17	3-Mar	$ 250.00	30	7,500.00	731.25	8,231.25
USB drive	25-Feb-17	27-Mar	$ 5.34	6	32.04	3.12	35.16
Web page ads	10-Mar-17	9-Apr	$ 0.17	275	47.30	4.61	51.91
TV Sponsor	15-Feb-17	17-Mar	$ 250.00	25	6,250.00	609.38	6,859.38
Pens	15-Mar-17	14-Apr	$ 0.12	250	30.75	3.00	33.75
TV commercials	1-Mar-17	31-Mar	$ 1,054.44	4	4,217.76	411.23	4,628.99
Podcasts	20-Mar-17	19-Apr	$ 75.50	30	2,265.00	220.84	2,485.84
USB drive	21-Mar-17	20-Apr	$ 5.34	2	10.68	1.04	11.72
Podcasts	23-Mar-17	22-Apr	$ 77.50	30	2,325.00	226.69	2,551.69
Sign	28-Mar-17	27-Apr	$ 101.87	20	2,037.40	198.65	2,236.05
			$ 4,933.90	1783	50,075.20	4,882.33	54,957.53

Practice

Concepts Review

Label each element of the Excel worksheet window shown in FIGURE 3-27.

FIGURE 3-27

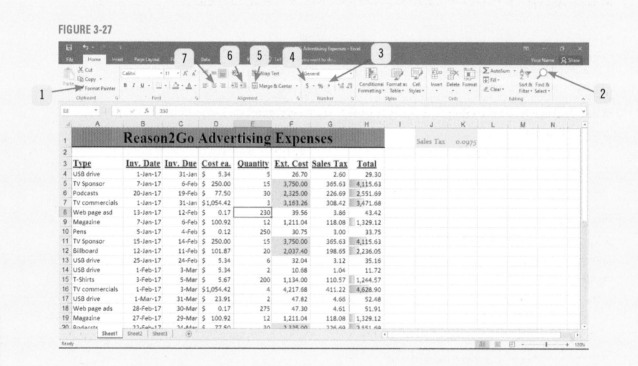

Match each command or button with the statement that best describes it.

8. Spelling button	**a.** Checks for apparent misspellings in a worksheet
9. $	**b.** Adds dollar signs and two decimal places to selected data
10. 🖌 ▾	**c.** Displays fill color options for a cell
11. [Ctrl][Home]	**d.** Moves cell pointer to cell A1
12. ⊞	**e.** Centers cell contents across multiple cells
13. Conditional formatting	**f.** Changes formatting of a cell that meets a certain rule

Select the best answer from the list of choices.

14. **Which of the following is an example of Accounting number format?**
    a. 5555
    c. 55.55%
    b. $5,555.55
    d. 5,555.55

15. **What is the name of the feature used to resize a column to accommodate its widest entry?**
    a. AutoFormat
    c. AutoResize
    b. AutoFit
    d. AutoRefit

16. **Which button copies multiple formats from selected cells to other cells?**
    a. ↶
    c. A̿
    b. ⌟
    d. ⚟

17. **Which button increases the number of decimal places in selected cells?**
    a. ←.0 .00
    c. ⇥
    b. .00 →.0
    d. ⇤

18. **Which button removes the italic font style from selected cells?**
    a. *I*
    c. *I*
    b. **B**
    d. U̲

19. **What feature is used to delete a conditional formatting rule?**
    a. Rules Reminder
    c. Condition Manager
    b. Conditional Formatting Rules Manager
    d. Format Manager

Skills Review

1. **Format values.**
   a. Start Excel, open the file EX 3-2.xlsx from the location where you store your Data Files, then save it as **EX 3-Health Insurance Premiums**.
   b. Use the Sum function to enter a formula in cell B10 that totals the number of employees.
   c. Create a formula in cell C5 that calculates the monthly insurance premium for the accounting department. (*Hint*: Make sure you use the correct type of cell reference in the formula. To calculate the department's monthly premium, multiply the number of employees by the monthly premium in cell B14.)
   d. Copy the formula in cell C5 to the range C6:C10.
   e. Format the range C5:C10 using Accounting number format.
   f. Change the format of the range C6:C9 to the Comma Style.
   g. Reduce the number of decimals in cell B14 to 0 using a button in the Number group on the Home tab.
   h. Save your work.

2. **Change font and font sizes.**
   a. Select the range of cells containing the column labels (in row 4).
   b. Change the font of the selection to Times New Roman.
   c. Increase the font size of the selection to 12 points.
   d. Increase the font size of the label in cell A1 to 14 points.
   e. Save your changes.

3. **Change font styles and alignment.**
   a. Apply the bold and italic font styles to the worksheet title in cell A1.
   b. Use the Merge & Center button to center the Health Insurance Premiums label over columns A–C.
   c. Apply the italic font style to the Health Insurance Premiums label.
   d. Add the bold font style to the labels in row 4.
   e. Use the Format Painter to copy the format in cell A4 to the range A5:A10.
   f. Apply the format in cell C10 to cell B14.
   g. Change the alignment of cell A10 to Align Right using a button in the Alignment group.

Skills Review (continued)

    h. Select the range of cells containing the column labels, then center them.

    i. Remove the italic font style from the Health Insurance Premiums label, then increase the font size to 14.

    j. Move the Health Insurance Premiums label to cell A3, remove the Merge & Center format, then add the bold and underline font styles.

    k. Save your changes.

4. Adjust column width.

    a. Resize column C to a width of 10.71 characters.

    b. Use the AutoFit feature to resize columns A and B.

    c. Clear the contents of cell A13 (do not delete the cell).

    d. Change the text in cell A14 to **Monthly Premium**, then change the width of the column to 25 characters.

    e. Save your changes.

5. Insert and delete rows and columns.

    a. Insert a new row between rows 5 and 6.

    b. Add a new department, **Donations**, in the newly inserted row. Enter **6** as the number of employees in the department.

    c. Copy the formula in cell C7 to C6.

    d. Add the following comment to cell A6: **New department**. Display the comment, then drag to move it out of the way, if necessary.

    e. Add a new column between the Department and Employees columns with the title **Family Coverage**, then resize the column using AutoFit.

    f. Delete the Legal row from the worksheet.

    g. Move the value in cell C14 to cell B14.

    h. Save your changes.

6. Apply colors, patterns, and borders.

    a. Add Outside Borders around the range A4:D10.

    b. Add a Bottom Double Border to cells C9 and D9 (above the calculated employee and premium totals).

    c. Apply the Aqua, Accent 5, Lighter 80% fill color to the labels in the Department column (do not include the Total label).

    d. Apply the Orange, Accent 6, Lighter 60% fill color to the range A4:D4.

    e. Change the color of the font in the range A4:D4 to Red, Accent 2, Darker 25%.

    f. Add a 12.5% Gray pattern style to cell A1.

    g. Format the range A14:B14 with a fill color of Dark Blue, Text 2, Lighter 40%, change the font color to White, Background 1, then apply the bold font style.

    h. Save your changes.

7. Apply conditional formatting.

    a. Select the range D5:D9, then create a conditional format that changes cell contents to green fill with dark green text if the value is between 150 and 275.

    b. Select the range C5:C9, then create a conditional format that changes cell contents to red text if the number of employees exceeds 10.

    c. Apply a purple gradient-filled data bar to the range C5:C9. (*Hint*: Click Purple Data Bar in the Gradient Fill section.)

    d. Use the Rules Manager to modify the conditional format in cells C5:C9 to display values greater than 10 in bold dark red text.

    e. Save your changes.

8. Rename and move a worksheet.

    a. Name the Sheet1 tab **Insurance Data**.

    b. Add a sheet to the workbook, then name the new sheet **Employee Data**.

    c. Change the Insurance Data tab color to Red, Accent 2, Lighter 40%.

Skills Review (continued)

d. Change the Employee Data tab color to Aqua, Accent 5, Lighter 40%.

e. Move the Employee Data sheet so it comes before (to the left of) the Insurance Data sheet.

f. Make the Insurance Data sheet active, enter your name in cell A20, then save your work.

9. Check spelling.

a. Move the cell pointer to cell A1.

b. Use the Find & Select feature to replace the Accounting label with **Accounting/Legal**.

c. Check the spelling in the worksheet using the spell checker, and correct any spelling errors if necessary.

d. Save your changes, then compare your Insurance Data sheet to FIGURE 3-28.

e. Preview the Insurance Data sheet in Backstage view, submit your work to your instructor as directed, then close the workbook and exit Excel.

FIGURE 3-28

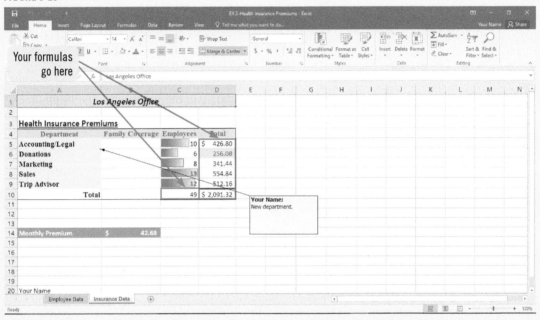

Independent Challenge 1

You run a freelance accounting business, and one of your newest clients is Fresh To You, a small local grocery store. Now that you've converted the store's accounting records to Excel, the manager would like you to work on an analysis of the inventory. Although more items will be added later, the worksheet has enough items for you to begin your modifications.

a. Start Excel, open the file EX 3-3.xlsx from the location where you store your Data Files, then save it as **EX 3-Fresh To You Inventory**.

b. Create a formula in cell E4 that calculates the value of the items in stock based on the price paid per item in cell B4. Format the cell in the Comma Style.

c. In cell F4, calculate the sale value of the items in stock using an absolute reference to the markup value shown in cell H1.

d. Copy the formulas created above into the range E5:F14; first convert any necessary cell references to absolute so that the formulas work correctly.

e. Apply bold to the column labels, and italicize the inventory items in column A.

f. Make sure that all columns are wide enough to display the data and labels.

g. Format the values in the Sale Value column as Accounting number format with two decimal places.

h. Format the values in the Price Paid column as Comma Style with two decimal places.

Independent Challenge 1 (continued)

i. Add a row under Cheddar Cheese for **Whole Wheat flour**, price paid **0.95**, sold by weight (**pound**), with **23** on hand. Copy the appropriate formulas to cells E7:F7.

j. Verify that all the data in the worksheet is visible and formulas are correct. Adjust any items as needed, and check the spelling of the entire worksheet.

k. Use conditional formatting to apply yellow fill with dark yellow text to items with a quantity of less than 25 on hand.

l. Use an icon set of your choosing in the range D4:D14 to illustrate the relative differences between values in the range.

m. Add an outside border around the data in the Item column (*do not* include the Item column label).

n. Delete the row containing the Resource Coffee - decaf entry.

o. Enter your name in an empty cell below the data, then save the file. Compare your worksheet to the sample in FIGURE 3-29.

p. Preview the worksheet in Backstage view, submit your work to your instructor as directed, close the workbook, then exit Excel.

FIGURE 3-29

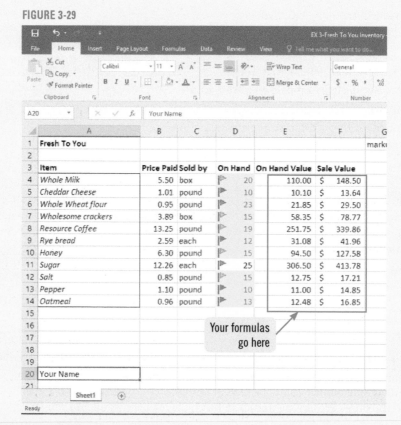

Independent Challenge 2

You volunteer several hours each week with the Assistance League of San Antonio, and you are in charge of maintaining the membership list. You're currently planning a mailing campaign to members in certain regions of the city. You also want to create renewal letters for members whose membership expires soon. You decide to format the list to enhance the appearance of the worksheet and make your upcoming tasks easier to plan.

a. Start Excel, open the file EX 3-4.xlsx from the location where you store your Data Files, then save it as **EX 3-Memphis Assistance League**.

b. Remove any blank columns.

c. Create a conditional format in the Zip Code column so that entries greater than 38249 appear in light red fill with dark red text.

d. Make all columns wide enough to fit their data and labels. (*Hint*: You can use any method to size the columns.)

e. Use formatting enhancements, such as fonts, font sizes, font styles, and fill colors, to make the worksheet more attractive.

Independent Challenge 2 (continued)

f. Center the column labels.

g. Use conditional formatting so that entries for Year of Membership Expiration that are between 2021 and 2023 appear in green fill with bold black text. (*Hint*: Create a custom format for cells that meet the condition.)

h. Adjust any items as necessary, then check the spelling.

i. Change the name of the Sheet1 tab to one that reflects the sheet's contents, then add a tab color of your choice.

j. Enter your name in an empty cell, then save your work.

k. Preview the worksheet, make any final changes you think necessary, then submit your work to your instructor as directed. Compare your work to the sample shown in FIGURE 3-30.

l. Close the workbook, then exit Excel.

FIGURE 3-30

Independent Challenge 3

Advantage Calendars is a Dallas-based printer that prints and assembles calendars. As the finance manager for the company, one of your responsibilities is to analyze the monthly reports from the five district sales offices. Your boss, Joanne Bennington, has just asked you to prepare a quarterly sales report for an upcoming meeting. Because several top executives will be attending this meeting, Joanne reminds you that the report must look professional. In particular, she asks you to highlight the fact that the Northeastern district continues to outpace the other districts.

a. Plan a worksheet that shows the company's sales during the first quarter. Assume that all calendars are the same price. Make sure you include the following:

- The number of calendars sold (units sold) and the associated revenues (total sales) for each of the five district sales offices. The five sales districts are Northeastern, Midwestern, Southeastern, Southern, and Western.

- Calculations that show month-by-month totals for January, February, and March, and a 3-month cumulative total.

- Calculations that show each district's share of sales (percent of Total Sales).

- Labels that reflect the month-by-month data as well as the cumulative data.

- Formatting enhancements such as data bars that emphasize the recent month's sales surge and the Northeastern district's sales leadership.

b. Ask yourself the following questions about the organization and formatting of the worksheet: What worksheet title and labels do you need, and where should they appear? How can you calculate the totals? What formulas can you copy to save time and keystrokes? Do any of these formulas need to use an absolute reference? How do you show dollar amounts? What information should be shown in bold? Do you need to use more than one font? Should you use more than one point size?

c. Start Excel, then save a new, blank workbook as **EX 3-Advantage Calendars** to the location where you store your Data Files.

Independent Challenge 3 (continued)

d. Build the worksheet with your own price and sales data. Enter the titles and labels first, then enter the numbers and formulas. You can use the information in TABLE 3-4 to get started.

TABLE 3-4

Advantage Calendars										
1st Quarter Sales Report										
		January		February		March		Total		
Office	Price	Units Sold	Sales	Units Sold	Sales	Units Sold	Sales	Units Sold	Sales	Total % of Sales
Northeastern										
Midwestern										
Southeastern										
Southern										
Western										

e. Add a row beneath the data containing the totals for each column.

f. Adjust the column widths as necessary.

g. Change the height of row 1 to 33 points.

h. Format labels and values to enhance the look of the worksheet, and change the font styles and alignment if necessary.

i. Resize columns and adjust the formatting as necessary.

j. Add data bars for the monthly Units Sold columns.

k. Add a column that calculates a 25% increase in total sales dollars. Use an absolute cell reference in this calculation. (*Hint*: Make sure that the current formatting is applied to the new information.)

l. Delete the contents of cells J4:K4 if necessary, then merge and center cell I4 over column I:K.

m. Add a bottom double border to cells I10:L10.

n. Enter your name in an empty cell.

o. Check the spelling in the workbook, change to a landscape orientation, save your work, then compare your work to FIGURE 3-31.

p. Preview the worksheet in Backstage view, then submit your work to your instructor as directed.

q. Close the workbook file, then exit Excel.

FIGURE 3-31

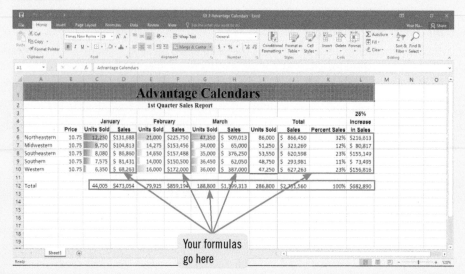

Formatting a Worksheet

Independent Challenge 4: Explore

This Independent Challenge requires an Internet connection.

Your corporate relocation company helps employees to settle quickly and easily into new cities around the world. Your latest client plans to send employees to seven different countries. All employees will receive the same weekly budget in American currency. You need to create a worksheet to help all the employees understand the currency conversion rates in the different countries so that they can plan their spending effectively.

a. Start Excel, then save a new, blank workbook as **EX 3-Foreign Currency Rates** to the location where you store your Data Files.

b. Add a title at the top of the worksheet.

c. Think of seven countries that each use a different currency, then enter column and row labels for your worksheet. (*Hint:* You may wish to include row labels for each country, plus column labels for the country, the $1 equivalent in native currency, the total amount of native currency employees will have in each country, and the name of each country's monetary unit.)

d. Decide how much money employees will bring to each country (for example, $1,000), and enter that in the worksheet.

e. Use your favorite search engine to find your own information sources on currency conversions for the countries you have listed.

f. Enter the cash equivalent to $1 in U.S. dollars for each country in your list.

g. Create an equation that calculates the amount of native currency employees will have in each country, using an absolute cell reference in the formula.

h. Format the entries in the column containing the native currency $1 equivalent as Number number format with three decimal places, and format the column containing the total native currency budget with two decimal places, using the correct currency number format for each country. (*Hint:* Use the Number tab in the Format cells dialog box; choose the appropriate currency number format from the Symbol list.)

i. Create a conditional format that changes the font style and color of the calculated amount in the $1,000 US column to light red fill with dark red text if the amount exceeds **1000** units of the local currency.

j. Merge and center the worksheet title over the column headings.

k. Add any formatting you want to the column headings, and resize the columns as necessary.

l. Add a background color to the title and change the font color if you choose.

m. Enter your name in the header of the worksheet.

n. Spell check the worksheet, save your changes, compare your work to FIGURE 3-32, then preview the worksheet, and submit your work to your instructor as directed.

o. Close the workbook and exit Excel.

FIGURE 3-32

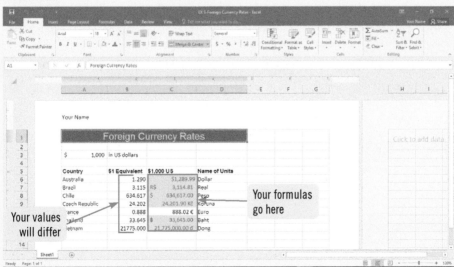

Visual Workshop

Open the file EX 3-5.xlsx from the location where you store your Data Files, then save it as **EX 3-London Employees**. Use the skills you learned in this module to format the worksheet so it looks like the one shown in FIGURE 3-33. Create a conditional format in the Level column so that entries greater than 3 appear in light red fill with dark red text. Create an additional conditional format in the Review Cycle column so that any value equal to 3 appears in black fill with white bold text. Replace the Accounting department label with **Legal**. (*Hint*: The only additional font used in this exercise is 18-point Times New Roman in row 1.) Enter your name in the upper-right part of the header, check the spelling in the worksheet, save your changes, then submit your work to your instructor as directed. (*Hint*: To match the figure exactly, remember to match the zoom level.)

FIGURE 3-33

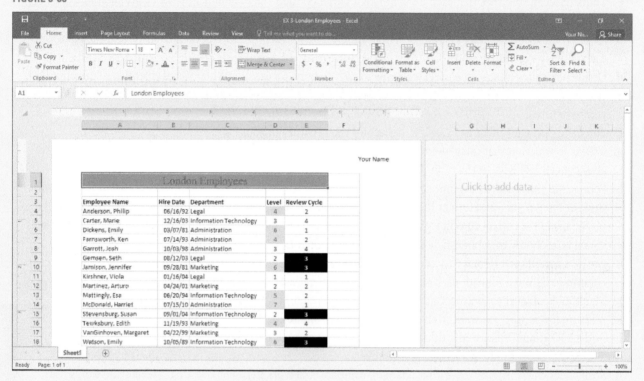

Working with Charts

CASE At the upcoming annual meeting, Yolanda Lee wants to discuss spending patterns at Reason2Go. She asks you to create a chart showing the trends in company expenses over the past four quarters.

Module Objectives

After completing this module, you will be able to:

- Plan a chart
- Create a chart
- Move and resize a chart
- Change the chart design

- Change the chart format
- Format a chart
- Annotate and draw on a chart
- Create a pie chart

Files You Will Need

EX 4-1.xlsx	EX 4-4.xlsx
EX 4-2.xlsx	EX 4-5.xlsx
EX 4-3.xlsx	EX 4-6.xlsx

Plan a Chart

Learning
Outcomes
• Prepare to create
  a chart
• Identify chart
  elements
• Explore common
  chart types

Before creating a chart, you need to plan the information you want your chart to show and how you want it to look. Planning ahead helps you decide what type of chart to create and how to organize the data. Understanding the parts of a chart makes it easier to format and change specific elements so that the chart best illustrates your data. **CASE** ▸ *In preparation for creating the chart for Yolanda's presentation, you identify your goals for the chart and plan its layout.*

DETAILS

Use the following guidelines to plan the chart:

- **Determine the purpose of the chart, and identify the data relationships you want to communicate graphically**

  You want to create a chart that shows quarterly tour expenses for each country where Reason2Go provides tours. This worksheet data is shown in FIGURE 4-1. You also want the chart to illustrate whether the quarterly expenses for each country increased or decreased from quarter to quarter.

- **Determine the results you want to see, and decide which chart type is most appropriate**

  Different chart types display data in distinctive ways. For example, a pie chart compares parts to the whole, so it's useful for showing what proportion of a budget amount was spent on tours in one country relative to what was spent on tours in other countries. A line chart, in contrast, is best for showing trends over time. To choose the best chart type for your data, you should first decide how you want your data displayed and interpreted. TABLE 4-1 describes several different types of charts you can create in Excel and their corresponding buttons on the Insert tab on the Ribbon. Because you want to compare R2G tour expenses in multiple countries over a period of four quarters, you decide to use a column chart.

- **Identify the worksheet data you want the chart to illustrate**

  Sometimes you use all the data in a worksheet to create a chart, while at other times you may need to select a range within the sheet. The worksheet from which you are creating your chart contains expense data for each of the past four quarters and the totals for the past year. You will need to use all the quarterly data except the quarterly totals.

- **Understand the elements of a chart**

  The chart shown in FIGURE 4-2 contains basic elements of a chart. In the figure, R2G tour countries are on the horizontal axis (also called the **x-axis**) and expense dollar amounts are on the vertical axis (also called the **y-axis**). The horizontal axis is also called the **category axis** because it often contains the names of data groups, such as locations, months, or years. The vertical axis is also called the **value axis** because it often contains numerical values that help you interpret the size of chart elements. (3-D charts also contain a **z-axis**, for comparing data across both categories and values.) The area inside the horizontal and vertical axes is the **plot area**. The **tick marks**, on the vertical axis, and **gridlines** (extending across the plot area) create a scale of measure for each value. Each value in a cell you select for your chart is a **data point**. In any chart, a **data marker** visually represents each data point, which in this case is a column. A collection of related data points is a **data series**. In this chart, there are four data series (Quarter 1, Quarter 2, Quarter 3, and Quarter 4). Each is made up of column data markers of a different color, so a **legend** is included to make it easy to identify them.

FIGURE 4-1: **Worksheet containing expense data**

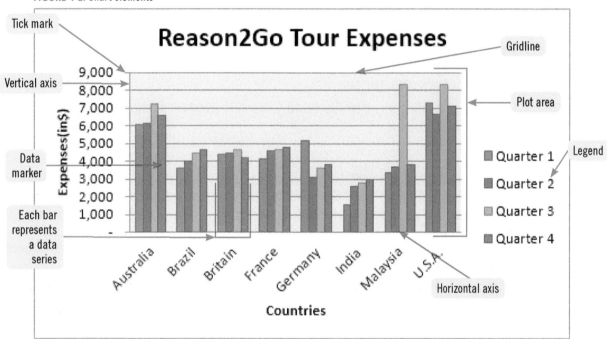

FIGURE 4-2: **Chart elements**

TABLE 4-1: **Common chart types**

type	button	description
Column		Compares data using columns; the Excel default; sometimes referred to as a bar chart in other spreadsheet programs
Line		Compares trends over even time intervals; looks similar to an area chart, but does not emphasize total
Pie		Compares sizes of pieces as part of a whole; used for a single series of numbers
Bar		Compares data using horizontal bars; sometimes referred to as a horizontal bar chart in other spreadsheet programs
Area		Shows how individual volume changes over time in relation to total volume
Scatter		Compares trends over uneven time or measurement intervals; used in scientific and engineering disciplines for trend spotting and extrapolation
Combo		Displays two or more types of data using different chart types; illustrates mixed or widely varying types of data

Create a Chart

Learning Outcomes
• Create a chart
• Switch a chart's columns/rows
• Add a chart title

To create a chart in Excel, you first select the range in a worksheet containing the data you want to chart. Once you've selected a range, you can use The Quick Analysis tool or the Insert tab on the Ribbon to create a chart based on the data in the range. **CASE** *Using the worksheet containing the quarterly expense data, you create a chart that shows how the expenses in each country varied across the quarters.*

STEPS

QUICK TIP
When charting data for a particular time period, make sure that all series are for the same time period.

1. **Start Excel, open the file** EX 4-1.xlsx **from the location where you store your Data Files, then save it as** EX 4-R2G Quarterly Tour Expenses

   You want the chart to include the quarterly tour expenses values, as well as quarter and country labels. You don't include the Total column and row because the figures in these cells would skew the chart.

2. **Select the range** A4:E12, **click the** Quick Analysis tool 📧 **in the lower-right corner of the range, then click** Charts

   The Charts tab on the Quick Analysis tool recommends commonly used chart types based on the range you have selected. The Charts tab also includes a More Charts button for additional chart types, such as stock charts for charting stock market data.

QUICK TIP
To base a chart on data in nonadjacent ranges, press and hold [Ctrl] while selecting each range, then use the Insert tab to create the chart.

3. **On the** Charts tab, **verify that** Clustered Column **is selected, as shown in** FIGURE 4-3, **then click** Clustered Column

   The chart is inserted in the center of the worksheet, and two contextual Chart Tools tabs appear on the Ribbon: Design and Format. On the Design tab, which is currently active, you can quickly change the chart type, chart layout, and chart style, and you can swap how the columns and rows of data in the worksheet are represented in the chart. When seen in the Normal view, three tools display to the right of the chart: these enable you to add, remove, or change chart elements ➕, set a style and color scheme 🖌, and filter the results shown in a chart 🔻. Currently, the countries are charted along the horizontal x-axis, with the quarterly expense dollar amounts charted along the y-axis. This lets you easily compare the quarterly expenses for each country.

4. **Click the** Switch Row/Column button **in the Data group on the Chart Tools Design tab**

   The quarters are now charted along the x-axis. The expense amounts per country are charted along the y-axis, as indicated by the updated legend. See FIGURE 4-4.

5. **Click the** Undo button ↩ ▾ **on the Quick Access Toolbar**

   The chart returns to its original design.

QUICK TIP
You can also triple-click to select the chart title text.

6. **Click the** Chart Title placeholder **to show the text box, click anywhere in the** Chart Title text box, **press [Ctrl][A] to select the text, type** R2G Quarterly Tour Expenses, **then click anywhere in the chart to deselect the title**

   Adding a title helps identify the chart. The border around the chart and the **sizing handles**, the small series of dots at the corners and sides of the chart's border, indicate that the chart is selected. See FIGURE 4-5. Your chart might be in a different location on the worksheet and may look slightly different; you will move and resize it in the next lesson. Any time a chart is selected, as it is now, a blue border surrounds the worksheet data range on which the chart is based, a purple border surrounds the cells containing the category axis labels, and a red border surrounds the cells containing the data series labels. This chart is known as an **embedded chart** because it is inserted directly in the current worksheet and doesn't exist in a separate file. Embedding a chart in the current sheet is the default selection when creating a chart, but you can also embed a chart on a different sheet in the workbook, or on a newly created chart sheet. A **chart sheet** is a sheet in a workbook that contains only a chart that is linked to the workbook data.

7. **Save your work**

FIGURE 4-3: Charts tab in Quick Analysis tool

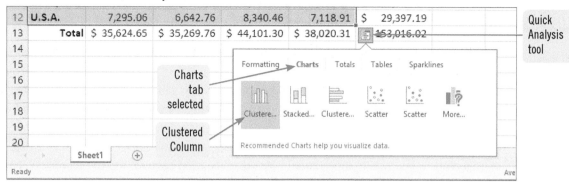

FIGURE 4-4: Clustered Column chart with different configuration of rows and columns

FIGURE 4-5: Chart with original configuration restored and title added

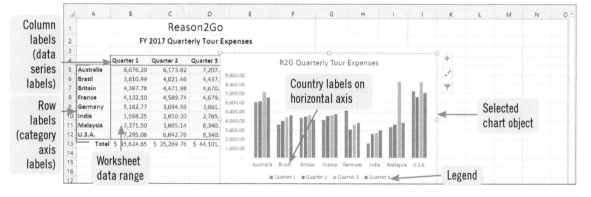

Creating sparklines

You can quickly create a miniature chart called a **sparkline** that serves as a visual indicator of data trends. You can create a sparkline by selecting a range of data, clicking the Quick Analysis tool, clicking the Sparklines tab, then clicking the type of sparkline you want. (The sparkline appears in the cell immediately adjacent to the selected range.) You can also select a range, click the Insert tab, then click the Line, Column, or Win/Loss button in the Sparklines group. In the Create Sparklines dialog box that opens, enter the cell in which you want the sparkline to appear,

then click OK. FIGURE 4-6 shows a sparkline created in a cell. Any changes to data in the range are reflected in the sparkline. To delete a selected sparkline from a cell, click the Clear button in the Group group on the Sparkline Tools Design tab.

FIGURE 4-6: Sparklines in a cell

Move and Resize a Chart

Learning Outcomes
- Reposition a chart
- Resize a chart
- Modify a legend
- Modify chart data

A chart is an **object**, or an independent element on a worksheet, and is not located in a specific cell or range. You can select an object by clicking it; sizing handles around the object indicate it is selected. (When a chart is selected in Excel, the Name box, which normally tells you the address of the active cell, tells you the chart number.) You can move a selected chart anywhere on a worksheet without affecting formulas or data in the worksheet. Any data changed in the worksheet is automatically updated in the chart. You can even move a chart to a different sheet in the workbook, and it will still reflect the original data. You can resize a chart to improve its appearance by dragging its sizing handles. You can reposition chart objects (such as a title or legend) to predefined locations using commands using the Chart Elements button or the Add Chart Element button on the Chart Tools Design tab, or you can freely move any chart object by dragging it or by cutting and pasting it to a new location. When you point to a chart object, the name of the object appears as a ScreenTip. **CASE** > *You want to resize the chart, position it below the worksheet data, and move the legend.*

STEPS

1. **Make sure the chart is still selected, then position the pointer over the chart**

   The pointer shape ⁺ᵏ indicates that you can move the chart. For a table of commonly used object pointers, refer to TABLE 4-2.

2. **Position ⁺ᵏ on a blank area near the upper-left edge of the chart, press and hold the left mouse button, drag the chart until its upper-left corner is at the upper-left corner of cell A16, then release the mouse button**

   When you release the mouse button, the chart appears in the new location.

3. **Scroll down so you can see the whole chart, position the pointer on the right-middle sizing handle until it changes to ↔, then drag the right border of the chart to the right edge of column G**

   The chart is widened. See FIGURE 4-7.

4. **Position the pointer over the upper-middle sizing handle until it changes to ↕, then drag the top border of the chart to the top edge of row 15**

5. **Position the pointer over the lower-middle sizing handle until it changes to ↕, then drag the bottom border of the chart to the bottom border of row 26**

   You can move any object on a chart. You want to align the top of the legend with the top of the plot area.

6. **Click the Quick Layout button in the Chart Layouts group of the Chart Tools Design tab, click Layout 1 (in the upper-left corner of the palette), click the legend to select it, press and hold [Shift], drag the legend up using ⁺ᵏ so the dotted outline is approximately 1/4" above the top of the plot area, then release [Shift]**

   When you click the legend, sizing handles appear around it and "Legend" appears as a ScreenTip when the pointer hovers over the object. As you drag, a dotted outline of the legend border appears. Pressing and holding the [Shift] key holds the horizontal position of the legend as you move it vertically. Although the sizing handles on objects within a chart look different from the sizing handles that surround a chart, they function the same way.

7. **Click cell A12, type United States, click the Enter button ✓ on the formula bar, use AutoFit to resize column A, then save your work**

   The axis label changes to reflect the updated cell contents, as shown in FIGURE 4-8. Changing any data in the worksheet modifies corresponding text or values in the chart. Because the chart is no longer selected, the Chart Tools tabs no longer appear on the Ribbon.

FIGURE 4-7: **Moved and resized chart**

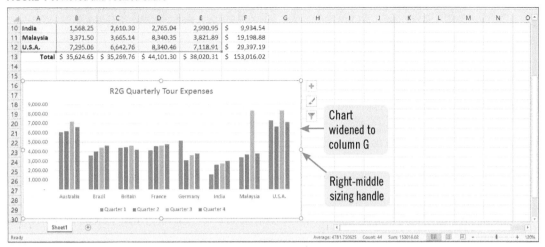

FIGURE 4-8: **Worksheet with modified legend and label**

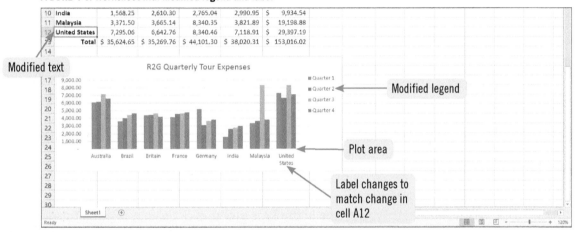

TABLE 4-2: **Common object pointers**

name	pointer	use	name	pointer	use
Diagonal resizing	⬈ or ⬊	Change chart shape from corners	I-beam	I	Edit object text
Draw	+	Draw an object	Move	⊹	Move object
Horizontal resizing	⇔	Change object width	Vertical resizing	↕	Change object height

Moving an embedded chart to a sheet

Suppose you have created an embedded chart that you decide would look better on a chart sheet or in a different worksheet. You can make this change without recreating the entire chart. To do so, first select the chart, click the Chart Tools Design tab, then click the Move Chart button in the Location group. The Move Chart dialog box opens. To move the chart to its own chart sheet, click the New sheet option button, type a name for the new sheet if desired, then click OK. If the chart is already on its own sheet or you want to move it to a different existing sheet, click the Object in option button, click the desired worksheet, then click OK.

Change the Chart Design

Learning Outcomes
- Change the chart design
- Change the chart type
- Apply a chart style

Once you've created a chart, you can change the chart type, modify the data range and column/row configuration, apply a different chart style, and change the layout of objects in the chart. The layouts in the Chart Layouts group on the Chart Tools Design tab offer arrangements of objects in your chart, such as its legend, title, or gridlines; choosing one of these layouts is an alternative to manually changing how objects are arranged in a chart. **CASE** *You discovered that the data for Malaysia and the United States in Quarter 3 is incorrect. After the correction, you want to see how the data looks using different chart layouts and types.*

STEPS

1. **Click cell D11, type 5568.92, press [Enter], type 7107.09, then press [Enter]**
   In the chart, the Quarter 3 data markers for Malaysia and the United States reflect the adjusted expense figures. See FIGURE 4-9.

2. **Select the chart by clicking a blank area within the chart border, click the Chart Tools Design tab on the Ribbon, click the Quick Layout button in the Chart Layouts group, then click Layout 3**
   The legend moves to the bottom of the chart. You prefer the original layout.

3. **Click the Undo button ↶ ⌄ on the Quick Access Toolbar, then click the Change Chart Type button in the Type group**
   The Change Chart Type dialog box opens, as shown in FIGURE 4-10. The left pane of the dialog box lists the available categories, and the right pane shows the individual chart types. A pale gray border surrounds the currently selected chart type.

4. **Click Bar in the left pane of the Change Chart Type dialog box, confirm that the first Clustered Bar chart type is selected in the right pane, then click OK**
   The column chart changes to a clustered bar chart. See FIGURE 4-11. You decide to see how the data looks in a three-dimensional column chart.

5. **Click the Change Chart Type button in the Type group, click Column in the left pane of the Change Chart Type dialog box, click 3-D Clustered Column (fourth from the left in the top row) in the right pane, verify that the left-most 3-D chart is selected, then click OK**
   A three-dimensional column chart appears. You notice that the three-dimensional column format gives you a sense of volume, but it is more crowded than the two-dimensional column format.

6. **Click the Change Chart Type button in the Type group, click Clustered Column (first from the left in the top row) in the right pane of the Change Chart Type dialog box, then click OK**

7. **Click the Style 3 chart style in the Chart Styles group**
   The columns change to lighter shades of color. You prefer the previous chart style's color scheme.

8. **Click ↶ ⌄ on the Quick Access Toolbar, then save your work**

Creating a combo chart

A **combo chart** presents two or more charts in one; a column chart with a line chart, for example. This type of chart is helpful when charting dissimilar but related data. For example, you can create a combo chart based on home price and home size data, showing home prices in a column chart and related home sizes in a line chart. Here a **secondary axis** (such as a vertical axis on the right side of the chart) would supply the scale for the home sizes.

To create a combo chart, select all the data you want to plot, click the Combo chart button 📊 ⌄ in the Charts group in the Insert tab, click a suggested type or Create Custom Combo Chart, supply additional series information if necessary, then click OK. To change an existing chart to a combo chart, select the chart, click Change Chart Type in the Type group on the Chart Tools Design tab, then follow the same procedure.

FIGURE 4-9: **Worksheet with modified data**

FIGURE 4-10: **Change Chart Type dialog box**

FIGURE 4-11: **Column chart changed to bar chart**

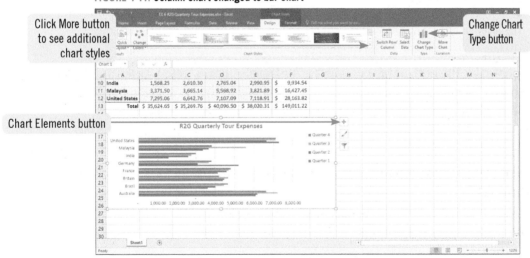

Working with a 3-D chart

Excel includes two kinds of 3-D chart types. In a true 3-D chart, a third axis, called the **z-axis**, lets you compare data points across both categories and values. The z-axis runs along the depth of the chart, so it appears to advance from the back of the chart. To create a true 3-D chart, look for chart types that begin with "3-D," such as 3-D Column. In a 3-D chart, data series can sometimes obscure other columns or bars in the same chart, but you can rotate the chart to obtain a better view. Right-click the chart, then click 3-D Rotation. The Format Chart Area pane opens with the 3-D Rotation category active. The 3-D Rotation options let you change the orientation and perspective of the chart area, plot area, walls, and floor. The 3-D Format category lets you apply three-dimensional effects to selected chart objects. (Not all 3-D Rotation and 3-D Format options are available on all charts.)

Change the Chart Format

Learning Outcomes
- Change the gridlines display
- Add axis titles
- Change the border color
- Add a shadow to an object

While the Chart Tools Design tab contains preconfigured chart layouts you can apply to a chart, the Chart Elements button makes it easy to add, remove, and modify individual chart objects such as a chart title or legend. Using options on this shortcut menu (or using the Add Chart Element button on the Chart Tools Design tab), you can also add text to a chart, add and modify labels, change the display of axes, modify the fill behind the plot area, create titles for the horizontal and vertical axes, and eliminate or change the look of gridlines. You can format the text in a chart object using the Home tab or the Mini toolbar, just as you would the text in a worksheet. **CASE** ▶ *You want to change the layout of the chart by creating titles for the horizontal and vertical axes. To improve the chart's appearance, you'll add a drop shadow to the chart title.*

STEPS

1. **With the chart still selected, click the** Add Chart Element button **in the Chart Layouts group on the Chart Tools Design tab, point to** Gridlines, **then click** Primary Major Horizontal **to deselect it**

   The gridlines that extend from the value axis tick marks across the chart's plot area are removed as shown in FIGURE 4-12.

2. **Click the** Chart Elements button ⊞ **in the upper-right corner** *outside* **the chart border, click the** Gridlines arrow, **click** Primary Major Horizontal, **click** Primary Minor Horizontal, **then click** ⊞ **to close the Chart Elements fly-out menu**

   Both major and minor gridlines now appear in the chart. **Major gridlines** represent the values at the value axis tick marks, and **minor gridlines** represent the values between the tick marks.

QUICK TIP

You can move any title to a new position by clicking one of its edges, then dragging it.

3. **Click** ⊞, **click the** Axis Titles checkbox **to select all the axis titles options, triple-click the** vertical axis title **on the chart, then type** Expenses (in $)

   Descriptive text on the category axis helps readers understand the chart.

QUICK TIP

You can also edit text in a chart or axis title by positioning the pointer over the selected title until it changes to I, clicking the title, then editing the text.

4. **Triple-click the** horizontal axis title **on the chart, then type** Tour Countries

   The text "Tour Countries" appears on the horizontal axis, as shown in FIGURE 4-13.

5. **Right-click the** horizontal axis labels ("Australia", "Brazil", etc.), **click** Font **on the shortcut menu, click the** Latin text font list arrow **in the Font dialog box, click** Times New Roman, **click the** Size down arrow **until 8 is displayed, then click** OK

   The font of the horizontal axis labels changes to Times New Roman, and the font size decreases, making more of the plot area visible.

QUICK TIP

You can also apply a border to a selected chart object by clicking the Shape Outline list arrow on the Chart Tools Format tab, and then selecting from the available options.

6. **Right-click the** vertical axis labels, **then click** Reset to Match

7. **Right-click the** Chart Title ("R2G Quarterly Tour Expenses"), **click** Format Chart Title **on the shortcut menu, click the** Border arrow ▶ **in the Format Chart Title pane to display the options if necessary, then click the** Solid line option button **in the pane**

   A solid border appears around the chart title with the default blue color.

QUICK TIP

You can also apply a shadow to a selected chart object by clicking the Shadow arrow, then clicking a shadow effect.

8. **Click the** Effects button ◻ **in the Format Chart Title pane, click** Shadow, **click the** Presets list arrow, **click** Offset Diagonal Bottom Right **in the Outer group (first row, first from the left), click the** Format Chart Title pane Close button ✕, **then save your work**

   A blue border with a drop shadow surrounds the title. Compare your work to FIGURE 4-14.

FIGURE 4-12: **Gridlines removed from chart**

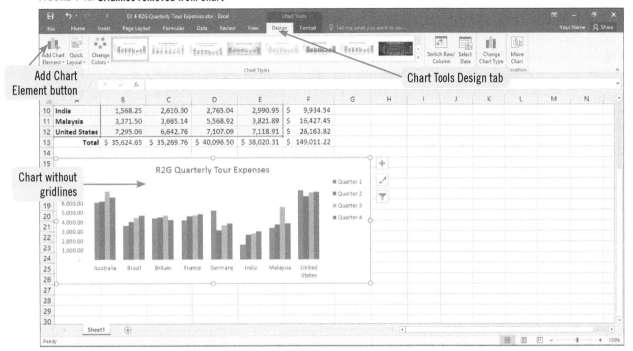

FIGURE 4-13: **Axis titles added to chart**

FIGURE 4-14: **Enhanced chart**

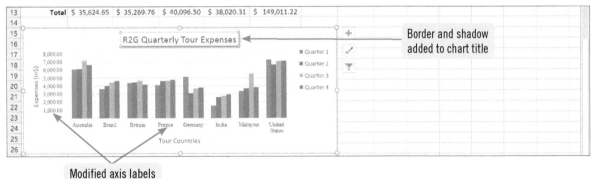

Adding data labels to a chart

There are times when your audience might benefit by seeing data labels on a chart. These labels appear next to the data markers in the chart and can indicate the series name, category name, and/or the value of one or more data points. Once your chart is selected, you can add this information to your chart by clicking the Chart Elements button in the upper-right corner outside the selected chart, clicking the Data Labels arrow, and then clicking a display option for the data labels. Once you have added the data labels, you can format them or delete individual data labels. To delete a data label, select it and then press [Delete].

Format a Chart

Learning Outcomes
- Change the fill of a data series
- Use Live Preview to see a new data series color
- Apply a style to a data series

Formatting a chart can make it easier to read and understand. Many formatting enhancements can be made using the Chart Tools Format tab. You can change the fill color for a specific data series, or you can apply a shape style to a title or a data series using the Shape Styles group. Shape styles make it possible to apply multiple formats, such as an outline, fill color, and text color, all with a single click. You can also apply different fill colors, outlines, and effects to chart objects using arrows and buttons in the Shape Styles group. **CASE** *You want to use a different color for one data series in the chart and apply a shape style to another, to enhance the look of the chart.*

STEPS

QUICK TIP

You can change the chart type of a selected data series by clicking the Chart Tools Design tab on the Ribbon, clicking the Change Chart Type button in the Type group, selecting a chart type for that data series, then clicking OK.

1. **With the chart selected, click the Chart Tools Format tab on the Ribbon, then click any column in the Quarter 4 data series**

   Handles appear on each column in the Quarter 4 data series, indicating that the entire series is selected.

2. **Click the Shape Fill list arrow in the Shape Styles group on the Chart Tools Format tab**

3. **Click Orange, Accent 6 (first row, 10th from the left) as shown in FIGURE 4-15**

   All the columns for the series become orange, and the legend changes to match the new color. You can also change the color of selected objects by applying a shape style.

4. **Click any column in the Quarter 3 data series**

   Handles appear on each column in the Quarter 3 data series.

QUICK TIP

To apply a WordArt style to a text object (such as the chart title), select the object, then click a style in the WordArt Styles group on the Chart Tools Format tab.

5. **Click the More button ⬇ on the Shape Styles gallery, then** *hover the pointer* **over the Moderate Effect – Olive Green, Accent 3 shape style (fifth row, fourth from the left) in the gallery, as shown in FIGURE 4-16**

   Live Preview shows the data series in the chart with the shape style applied.

6. **Click the Subtle Effect – Olive Green, Accent 3 shape style**

   The style for the data series changes, as shown in FIGURE 4-17.

7. **Save your work**

Previewing a chart

To print or preview just a chart, select the chart (or make the chart sheet active), click the File tab, then click Print on the navigation bar. To reposition a chart by changing the page's margins, click the Show Margins button ⊞ in the lower-right corner of the Print tab to display the margins in the preview. You can drag the margin lines to the exact settings you want; as the margins change, the size and placement of the chart on the page change too.

FIGURE 4-15: New shape fill applied to data series

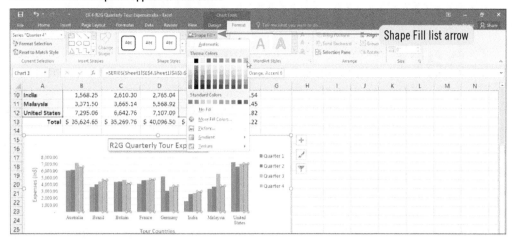

FIGURE 4-16: Live Preview of new style applied to data series

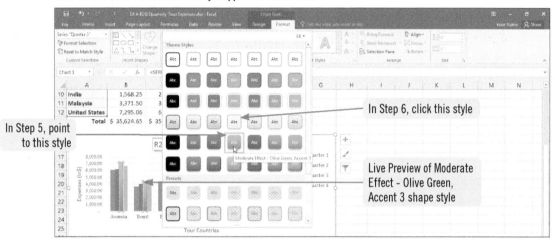

FIGURE 4-17: Style of data series changed

Changing alignment and angle in axis labels and titles

The buttons on the Chart Tools Design tab provide a few options for positioning axis labels and titles, but you can customize their position and rotation to exact specifications using the Format Axis pane or Format Axis Title pane. With a chart selected, right-click the axis text you want to modify, then click Format Axis or Format Axis Title on the shortcut menu. In the pane that opens, click the Size & Properties button, then select the appropriate option. You can also create a custom angle by clicking the Custom angle up and down arrows. When you have made the desired changes, close the pane.

Annotate and Draw on a Chart

Learning
Outcomes
• Type text in a text box
• Draw an arrow on a chart
• Modify a drawn object

You can use text annotations and graphics to point out critical information in a chart. **Text annotations** are labels that further describe your data. You can also draw lines and arrows that point to the exact locations you want to emphasize. Shapes such as arrows and boxes can be added from the Illustrations group on the Insert tab or from the Insert Shapes group on the Chart Tools Format tab on the Ribbon. The Insert group is also used to insert pictures into worksheets and charts. **CASE** ▶ *You want to call attention to the Germany tour expense decrease, so you decide to add a text annotation and an arrow to this information in the chart.*

STEPS

1. **With the chart selected and the** Chart Tools Format tab **active, click the** Text Box **button** 🄰 **in the Insert Shapes group, then move the pointer over the worksheet**

   The pointer changes to ↓, indicating that you will insert a text box where you next click.

2. **Click to the** right of the chart **(anywhere** *outside* **the chart boundary)**

   A text box is added to the worksheet, and the Drawing Tools Format tab appears on the Ribbon so that you can format the new object. First you need to type the text.

3. **Type** Great Improvement

   The text appears in a selected text box on the worksheet, and the chart is no longer selected, as shown in FIGURE 4-18. Your text box may be in a different location; this is not important because you'll move the annotation in the next step.

4. **Point to an edge of the text box so that the pointer changes to** �'▸, **drag the** text box **into the chart to the left of the chart title, as shown in** FIGURE 4-19, **then release the mouse button**

   The text box is a text annotation for the chart. You also want to add a simple arrow shape in the chart.

5. **Click the** chart **to select it, click the** Chart Tools Format tab, **click the** Arrow button ◥ **in the Insert Shapes group, then move the pointer over the text box on the chart**

   The pointer changes to ✛, and the status bar displays "Click and drag to insert an AutoShape." When ✛ is over the text box, black handles appear around the text in the text box. A black handle can act as an anchor for the arrow.

6. **Position** ✛ **on the** black handle **to the right of the "t" in the word "improvement" (in the text box), press and hold the** left mouse button, **drag the** line **to the** Quarter 2 column **for the Germany category in the chart, then release the mouse button**

   An arrow points to the Quarter 2 expense for Germany, and the Drawing Tools Format tab displays options for working with the new arrow object. You can resize, format, or delete it just like any other object in a chart.

7. **Click the** Shape Outline list arrow **in the Shape Styles group, click the** Automatic color, **click the** Shape Outline list arrow **again, point to** Weight, **then click** 1½ pt

   Compare your finished chart to FIGURE 4-20.

8. **Save your work**

FIGURE 4-18: **Text box added**

Drawing
Tools
Format tab

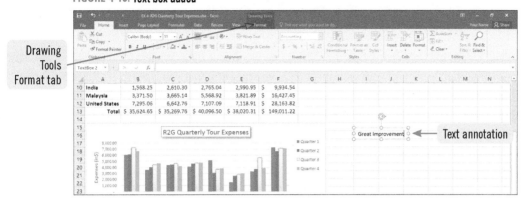

Text annotation

FIGURE 4-19: **Text annotation on the chart**

Text annotation

FIGURE 4-20: **Arrow shape added to chart**

Arrow drawn
and formatted

Adding SmartArt graphics

In addition to charts, annotations, and drawn objects, you can create a variety of diagrams using SmartArt graphics. **SmartArt graphics** are available in List, Process, Cycle, Hierarchy, Relationship, Matrix, Pyramid, Picture, and Office.com categories. To insert SmartArt, click the Insert a SmartArt Graphic button in the Illustrations group on the Insert tab to open the Choose a SmartArt Graphic dialog box. Click a SmartArt category in the left pane, then click a layout for the graphic in the right pane. The right pane shows sample layouts for the selected SmartArt, as shown in **FIGURE 4-21**. The SmartArt graphic appears in the worksheet as an embedded object with sizing handles. Depending on the type of SmartArt graphic you selected, a text pane opens next to the graphic; you can enter text into the graphic using the text pane or by typing directly in the shapes in the diagram.

FIGURE 4-21: **Choose a SmartArt Graphic dialog box**

Create a Pie Chart

Learning
Outcomes
• Create a pie chart
• Explode a pie
  chart slice

You can create multiple charts based on the same worksheet data. While a column chart may illustrate certain important aspects of your worksheet data, you may find that you want to create an additional chart to emphasize a different point. Depending on the type of chart you create, you have additional options for calling attention to trends and patterns. For example, if you create a pie chart, you can emphasize one data point by **exploding**, or pulling that slice away from, the pie chart. When you're ready to print a chart, you can preview it just as you do a worksheet to check the output before committing it to paper. You can print a chart by itself or as part of the worksheet. **CASE** *At an upcoming meeting, Yolanda plans to discuss the total tour expenses and which countries need improvement. You want to create a pie chart she can use to illustrate total expenses. Finally, you want to fit the worksheet and the charts onto one worksheet page.*

STEPS

1. **Select the range A5:A12, press and hold [Ctrl], select the range F5:F12, click the** Insert tab, **click the** Insert Pie or Doughnut Chart button **in the Charts group, then click** 3-D Pie **in the chart gallery**

   The new chart appears in the center of the worksheet. You can move the chart and quickly format it using a chart layout.

2. **Drag the** chart **so its upper-left corner is at the upper-left corner of cell** G1, **click the** Quick Layout button **in the Chart Layouts group of the Chart Tools Design tab, then click** Layout 2

   The chart is repositioned on the page, and its layout changes so that a chart title is added, the percentages display on each slice, and the legend appears just below the chart title.

3. **Select the** Chart Title text, **then type** R2G Total Expenses, by Country

4. **Click the slice for the** India data point, **click it again so it is the only slice selected, right-click it, then click** Format Data Point

   The Format Data Point pane opens, as shown in FIGURE 4-22. You can use the Point Explosion slider to control the distance a pie slice moves away from the pie, or you can type a value in the Point Explosion text box.

5. **Double-click** 0 **in the** Point Explosion text box, **type** 40, **then click the** Close button ☒

   Compare your chart to FIGURE 4-23. You decide to preview the chart and data before you print.

6. **Click cell A1, switch to** Page Layout view, **type your name in the left header text box, then click cell** A1

   You decide the chart and data would fit better on the page if they were printed in landscape orientation.

7. **Click the** Page Layout tab, **click the** Orientation button **in the Page Setup group, then click** Landscape

8. **Click the** File tab, **click** Print **on the navigation bar, verify that the correct printer is selected, click the** No Scaling setting **in the Settings section on the Print tab, then click** Fit Sheet on One Page

   The data and chart are positioned horizontally on a single page, as shown in FIGURE 4-24. The printer you have selected may affect the appearance of your preview screen.

9. **Save and close the workbook, submit your work to your instructor as directed, then exit Excel**

FIGURE 4-22: Format Data Point pane

Point Explosion slider

Point Explosion text box

FIGURE 4-23: Exploded pie slice

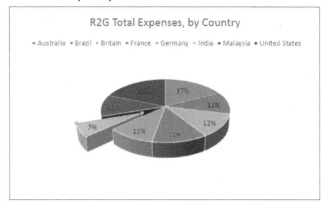

FIGURE 4-24: Preview of worksheet with charts in Backstage view

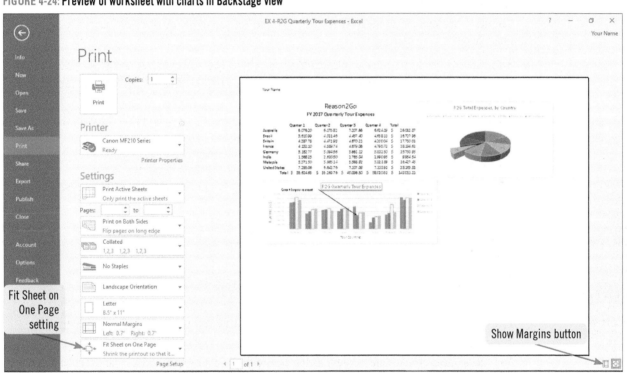

Fit Sheet on One Page setting

Show Margins button

Using the Insert Chart dialog box to discover new chart types

Excel 2016 includes five new chart types. You can explore these charts by clicking the Insert tab on the Ribbon, clicking Recommended Charts, then clicking the All Charts tab in the Insert Chart dialog box. Near the bottom of the list in the left panel are the new chart types: Treemap (which has nine variations), Sunburst, Histogram, Box & Whisker, and Waterfall. If cells are selected prior to opening the Insert Chart dialog box, you will see a sample of the chart type when you click each chart type; the sample will be magnified when you hover the mouse over the sample. The Treemap and Sunburst charts both offer visual comparisons of relative sizes. The Histogram looks like a column chart, but each column (or bin) represents a range of values. The Box & Whisker chart shows distribution details as well as the mean, quartiles, and outliers. The Waterfall chart shows results above and below an imaginary line.

Practice

Concepts Review

Label each element of the Excel chart shown in FIGURE 4-25.

FIGURE 4-25

Match each chart type with the statement that best describes it.

7. Combo   a. Displays different chart types within one chart

8. Pie   b. Compares trends over even time intervals

9. Area   c. Compares data using columns

10. Column   d. Compares data as parts of a whole

11. Line   e. Shows how volume changes over time

Select the best answer from the list of choices.

12. **Which tab on the Ribbon do you use to create a chart?**
    a. Design
    b. Insert
    c. Page Layout
    d. Format

13. **A collection of related data points in a chart is called a:**
    a. Data series.
    b. Data tick.
    c. Cell address.
    d. Value title.

14. **The object in a chart that identifies the colors used for each data series is a(n):**
    a. Data marker.
    b. Data point.
    c. Organizer.
    d. Legend.

15. **How do you move an embedded chart to a chart sheet?**
    a. Click a button on the Chart Tools Design tab.
    b. Drag the chart to the sheet tab.
    c. Delete the chart, switch to a different sheet, then create a new chart.
    d. Use the Copy and Paste buttons on the Ribbon.

16. **Which is *not* an example of a SmartArt graphic?**
    a. Sparkline
    b. Basic Matrix
    c. Organization Chart
    d. Basic Pyramid

17. **Which tab appears only when a chart is selected?**
    a. Insert
    b. Chart Tools Format
    c. Review
    d. Page Layout

Skills Review

1. **Plan a chart.**
   a. Start Excel, open the Data File EX 4-2.xlsx from the location where you store your Data Files, then save it as **EX 4-Software Usage Polling Results**.
   b. Describe the type of chart you would use to plot this data.
   c. What chart type would you use to compare the number of Excel users in each type of business?

2. **Create a chart.**
   a. In the worksheet, select the range containing all the data and headings.
   b. Click the Quick Analysis tool.
   c. Create a Clustered Column chart, then add the chart title **Software Usage, by Business** above the chart.
   d. If necessary, click the Switch Row/Column button so the business type (Accounting, Advertising, etc.) appears as the x-axis.
   e. Save your work.

Skills Review (continued)

3. Move and resize a chart.

  a. Make sure the chart is still selected, and close any open panes if necessary.

  b. Move the chart beneath the worksheet data.

  c. Widen the chart so it extends to the right edge of column H.

  d. Use the Quick Layout button in the Chart Tools Design tab to move the legend to the right of the charted data. (*Hint*: Use Layout 1.)

  e. Resize the chart so its bottom edge is at the top of row 25.

  f. Save your work.

4. Change the chart design.

  a. Change the value in cell B3 to **8**. Observe the change in the chart.

  b. Select the chart.

  c. Use the Quick Layout button in the Chart Layouts group on the Chart Tools Design tab to apply the Layout 10 layout to the chart, then undo the change.

  d. Use the Change Chart Type button on the Chart Tools Design tab to change the chart to a Clustered Bar chart.

  e. Change the chart to a 3-D Clustered Column chart, then change it back to a Clustered Column chart.

  f. Save your work.

5. Change the chart layout.

  a. Use the Chart Elements button to turn off the primary major horizontal gridlines in the chart.

  b. Change the font used in the horizontal and vertical axis labels to Times New Roman.

  c. Turn on the primary major gridlines for both the horizontal and vertical axes.

  d. Change the chart title's font to Times New Roman if necessary, with a font size of 20.

  e. Insert **Business** as the primary horizontal axis title.

  f. Insert **Number of Users** as the primary vertical axis title.

  g. Change the font size of the horizontal and vertical axis titles to 10 and the font to Times New Roman, if necessary.

  h. Change "Personnel" in the worksheet column heading to **Human Resources**, then AutoFit column D, and any other columns as necessary.

  i. Change the font size of the legend to 14.

  j. Add a solid line border in the default color and a (preset) Offset Diagonal Bottom Right shadow to the chart title.

  k. Save your work.

6. Format a chart.

  a. Make sure the chart is selected, then select the Chart Tools Format tab, if necessary.

  b. Change the shape fill of the Excel data series to Dark Blue, Text 2.

  c. Change the shape style of the Excel data series to Subtle Effect – Orange, Accent 6.

  d. Save your work.

7. Annotate and draw on a chart.

  a. Make sure the chart is selected, then create the text annotation **Needs more users**.

  b. Position the text annotation so the word "Needs" is just below the word "Software" in the chart title.

  c. Select the chart, then use the Chart Tools Format tab to create a 1½ pt weight dark blue arrow that points from the bottom center of the text box to the Excel users in the Human Resources category.

  d. Deselect the chart.

  e. Save your work.

Skills Review (continued)

8. Create a pie chart.

  a. Select the range A1:F2, then create a 3-D Pie chart.

  b. Drag the 3-D pie chart beneath the existing chart.

  c. Change the chart title to **Excel Users**.

  d. Apply the Style 7 chart style to the chart, then apply Layout 6 using the Quick Layout button.

  e. Explode the Human Resources slice from the pie chart at **25%**.

  f. In Page Layout view, enter your name in the left section of the worksheet header.

  g. Preview the worksheet and charts in Backstage view, make sure all the contents fit on one page, then submit your work to your instructor as directed. When printed, the worksheet should look like FIGURE 4-26. (Note that certain elements such as the title may look slightly different when printed.)

  h. Save your work, close the workbook, then exit Excel.

FIGURE 4-26

Your Name

	Accounting	Advertising	Human Resources	Law Firm	Medical Lab
Excel	37	16	5	11	38
Word	8	35	20	25	10
PowerPoint	17	15	15	7	3
Access	20	5	2	10	10
Publisher	2	15	22	15	25

Independent Challenge 1

You are the operations manager for the Chicago Arts Alliance. Each year the group revisits the number and types of activities they support to better manage their budgets. For this year's budget, you need to create charts to document the number of events in previous years.

a. Start Excel, open the file EX 4-3.xlsx from the location where you store your Data Files, then save it as **EX 4-Chicago Arts Alliance**.

b. Take some time to plan your charts. Which type of chart or charts might best illustrate the information you need to display? What kind of chart enhancements do you want to use? Will a 3-D effect make your chart easier to understand?

c. Create a Clustered Column chart for the data.

d. Change at least one of the colors used in a data series.

e. Make the appropriate modifications to the chart to make it visually attractive and easier to read and understand. Include a legend to the right of the chart, and add chart titles and horizontal and vertical axis titles using the text shown in TABLE 4-3.

TABLE 4-3

title	text
Chart title	Chicago Arts Alliance Events
Vertical axis title	Number of Events
Horizontal axis title	Types of Events

f. Create at least two additional charts for the same data to show how different chart types display the same data. Reposition each new chart so that all charts are visible in the worksheet. One of the additional charts should be a pie chart for an appropriate data set; the other is up to you.

g. Modify each new chart as necessary to improve its appearance and effectiveness. A sample worksheet containing three charts based on the worksheet data is shown in FIGURE 4-27.

h. Enter your name in the worksheet header.

i. Save your work. Before printing, preview the worksheet in Backstage view, then adjust any settings as necessary so that all the worksheet data and charts will print on a single page.

j. Submit your work to your instructor as directed.

k. Close the workbook, then exit Excel.

FIGURE 4-27

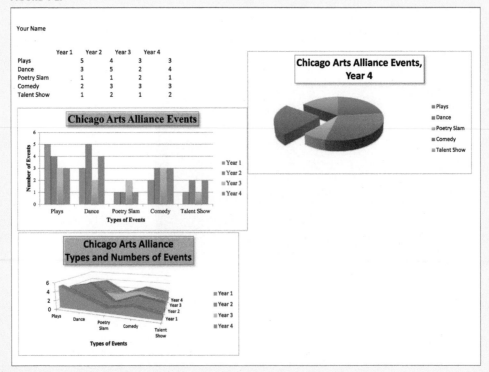

Independent Challenge 2

You work at Canine Companions, a locally owned dog obedience school. One of your responsibilities at the school is to manage the company's sales and expenses using Excel. As part of your efforts, you want to help the staff better understand and manage the school's largest sources of both expenses and sales. To do this, you've decided to create charts using current operating expenses including rent, utilities, and payroll. The manager will use these charts at the next monthly meeting.

a. Start Excel, open EX 4-4.xlsx from the location where you store your Data Files, then save it as **EX 4-Canine Companions Expense Analysis**.

b. Decide which data in the worksheet should be charted. What chart types are best suited for the information you need to show? What kinds of chart enhancements are necessary?

c. Create a 3-D Clustered Column chart in the worksheet showing the expense data for all four quarters. (*Hint*: The expense categories should appear on the x-axis. Do not include the totals.)

d. Change the vertical axis labels (Expenses data) so that no decimals are displayed. (*Hint*: Use the Number category in the Format Axis pane.)

e. Using the sales data, create two charts on this worksheet that compare the sales amounts. (*Hint*: Move each chart to a new location on the worksheet, then deselect it before creating the next one.)

f. In one chart of the sales data, add data labels, then add chart titles as you see fit.

g. Make any necessary formatting changes to make the charts look more attractive, then enter your name in a worksheet cell.

h. Save your work.

i. Preview each chart in Backstage view, and adjust any items as needed. Fit the worksheet to a single page, then submit your work to your instructor as directed. A sample of a printed worksheet is shown in FIGURE 4-28.

j. Close the workbook, then exit Excel.

FIGURE 4-28

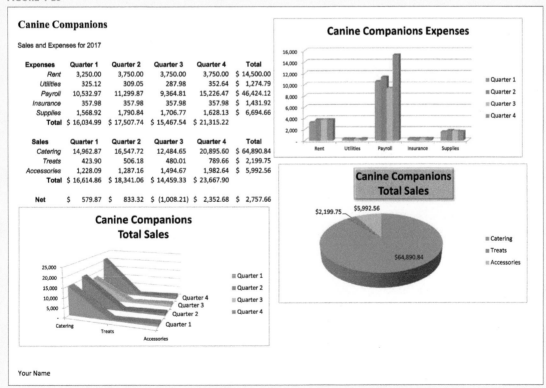

Independent Challenge 3

You are working as an account representative at a clothing store called Zanzibar. You have been examining the advertising expenses incurred recently. The CEO wants to examine expenses designed to increase sales and has asked you to prepare charts that can be used in this evaluation. In particular, you want to see how dollar amounts compare among the different expenses, and you also want to see how expenses compare with each other proportional to the total budget.

a. Start Excel, open the Data File EX 4-5.xlsx from the location where you store your Data Files, then save it as **EX 4-Zanzibar Advertising Expenses**.

b. Identify three types of charts that seem best suited to illustrate the data in the range A16:B24. What kinds of chart enhancements are necessary?

c. Create at least two different types of charts that show the distribution of advertising expenses. (*Hint*: Move each chart to a new location on the same worksheet.) One of the charts should be a 3-D pie chart.

d. In at least one of the charts, add annotated text and arrows highlighting important data, such as the largest expense.

e. Change the color of at least one data series in at least one of the charts.

f. Add chart titles and category and value axis titles where appropriate. Format the titles with a font of your choice. Apply a shadow to the chart title in at least one chart.

g. Add your name to a section of the header, then save your work.

h. Explode a slice from the 3-D pie chart.

i. Add a data label to the exploded pie slice.

j. Preview the worksheet in Backstage view. Adjust any items as needed. Be sure the charts are all visible on one page. Compare your work to the sample in FIGURE 4-29.

k. Submit your work to your instructor as directed, close the workbook, then exit Excel.

FIGURE 4-29

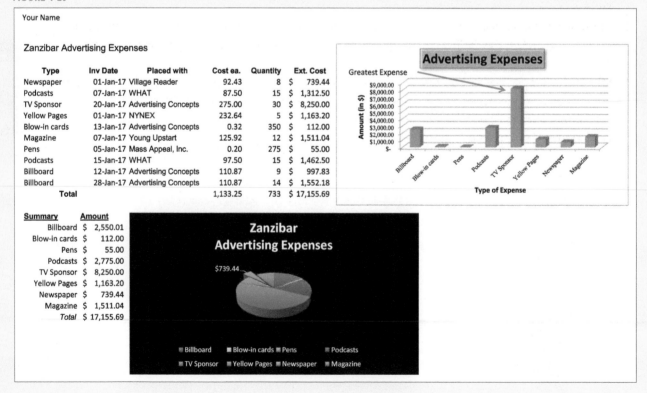

Independent Challenge 4: Explore

This Independent Challenge requires an Internet connection.

All the years of hard work and saving money have paid off, and you have decided to purchase a home. You know where you'd like to live, and you decide to use the web to find out more about houses that are currently available. A worksheet would be a great place to compare the features and prices of potential homes.

a. Start Excel, then save a new, blank workbook as **EX 4-My New House** to the location where you save your Data Files.

b. Decide on where you would like to live, and use your favorite search engine to find information sources on homes for sale in that area. (*Hint*: Try using realtor.com or other realtor-sponsored sites.)

c. Determine a price range and features within the home. Find data for at least five homes that meet your location and price requirements, and enter them in the worksheet. See TABLE 4-4 for a suggested data layout.

TABLE 4-4

suggested data layout					
Location					
Price range					
	House 1	House 2	House 3	House 4	House 5
Asking price					
Bedrooms					
Bathrooms					
Year built					
Size (in sq. ft.)					

d. Format the data so it looks attractive and professional.

e. Create any type of column chart using only the House and Asking Price data. Place it on the same worksheet as the data. Include a descriptive title.

f. Change the colors in the chart using the chart style of your choice.

g. Enter your name in a section of the header.

h. Create an additional chart: a combo chart that plots the asking price on one axis and the size of the home on the other axis. (*Hint*: Use the Tell me what you want to do text box above the Ribbon to get more guidance on creating a Combo Chart.)

i. Save the workbook. Preview the worksheet in Backstage view and make adjustments if necessary to fit all of the information on one page. See FIGURE 4-30 for an example of what your worksheet might look like.

j. Submit your work to your instructor as directed.

k. Close the workbook, then exit Excel.

FIGURE 4-30

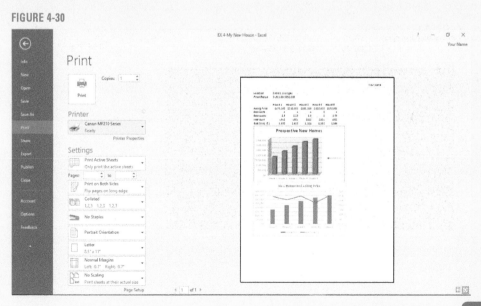

Visual Workshop

Open the Data File EX 4-6.xlsx from the location where you store your Data Files, then save it as **EX 4-Estimated Cost Center Expenses**. Format the worksheet data so it looks like FIGURE 4-31, then create and modify two charts to match the ones shown in the figure. You will need to make formatting, layout, and design changes once you create the charts. (*Hint*: The shadow used in the 3-D pie chart title is made using the Outer Offset Diagonal Top Right shadow.) Enter your name in the left text box of the header, then save and preview the worksheet. Submit your work to your instructor as directed, then close the workbook and exit Excel.

FIGURE 4-31

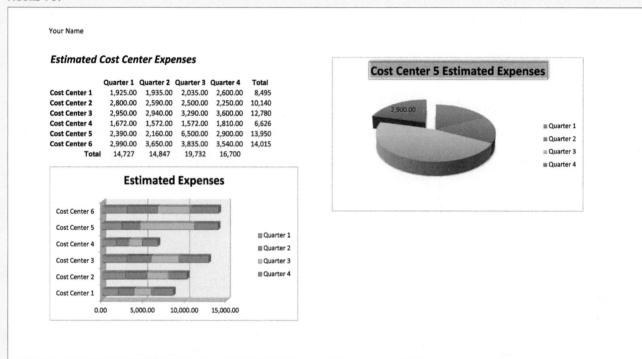

Integrating Word and Excel

CASE ▶ You are working as an operations assistant to Kevin Lawrence, the vice president of Operations for R2G. Kevin has asked you to explore the integration capabilities of Office 2016. First, you create a report in Word that includes values and a chart created in Excel, and then you embed a paragraph of text created in Word into an Excel worksheet.

Module Objectives

After completing this module, you will be able to:

- Integrate data between Word and Excel
- Copy data from Excel to Word
- Copy a chart from Excel to Word
- Create linked objects
- Embed a Word file in Excel

Files You Will Need

INT 1-1.xlsx	INT 1-9.docx
INT 1-2.docx	INT 1-10.xlsx
INT 1-3.xlsx	INT 1-11.xlsx
INT 1-4.docx	INT 1-12.docx
INT 1-5.xlsx	INT 1-13.xlsx
INT 1-6.docx	INT 1-14.docx
INT 1-7.xlsx	INT 1-15.xlsx
INT 1-8.docx	INT 1-16.docx

Learning
Outcomes
• Define copy/paste,
link, and embed
integration
options

Integrate Data Between Word and Excel

Microsoft Office programs are designed to work together through a process called **integration**. When you integrate data from multiple Office programs, you work with both a source file and a destination file. The **source file** is the file from which the information is copied or used. The **destination file** is the file that receives the copied information. You can choose from three integration methods: pasting, linking, and embedding. **CASE** *As an operations assistant, you often create documents such as reports and price lists that include data from both Word and Excel. You decide to review some of the ways in which you integrate data between the two programs.*

DETAILS

You can integrate Word and Excel by:

• **Copying and pasting data from the Clipboard**
You use the Copy and Paste commands to duplicate **objects** such as text selections, numbers (called values in Excel), and pictures from one program and place them into another program. After you copy and paste an object, changes that you make to the object in the source file do not appear in the destination file. The report shown in FIGURE 1-1 was created in Word and includes two objects that were copied from Excel—the photograph that appears to the right of the document title and the shaded table under the document subtitle.

• **Linking data**
Sometimes you want to connect the data that is included in two or more files. For example, suppose you copy the contents of a cell containing a formula from an Excel worksheet and paste it into a Word document. When you change the formula values in Excel, you want the corresponding values to change in the Word document. To create a **link** between data in two files, you select one of the link options that appears when you either click the Paste button list arrow or view options in the Paste Special dialog box. You use the term **linked object** to refer to the connected data. In the report shown in FIGURE 1-1, the value "90" is a linked object. If this percentage changes in the Excel worksheet, the linked percentage in the Word document also changes.

• **Copying and pasting charts**
When you copy a chart from Excel and paste it into Word using the Paste command, Word automatically creates a link between the pasted chart and the original chart. In the report shown in FIGURE 1-1, the column chart was copied from Excel and pasted into the Word document. When the chart values are updated in Excel, the same chart values are updated in the chart copied to Word. You can also copy a chart from the source file and then paste it into the destination file as an object that is not linked.

• **Embedding a Word file in Excel**
You can **embed**, or place an unlinked copy of, the contents of a Word file into an Excel worksheet. You edit the embedded object by double-clicking it and using Word program tools to change text and formatting. This process changes the embedded copy of the Word object in Excel, but does not affect the original source document you created in Word. Similarly, any changes to the source Word document are not reflected in the embedded copy in Excel. In the price list shown in FIGURE 1-2, the text that describes the R2G tours was inserted in Excel as an embedded Word file.

FIGURE 1-1: Word report with objects copied from Excel

Table object copied from Excel

Photograph copied from Excel

Chart linked to Excel source chart

90% value is a linked object

FIGURE 1-2: Price list with embedded Word file

Embedded text inserted directly from a Word file

Understanding object linking and embedding (OLE)

The term **object linking and embedding (OLE)** refers to the technology that Microsoft uses to let you integrate data between programs. You create an object in one program, and then you can choose to either link the object to or embed it in another program. The difference between linking and embedding relates to where the object is stored and how you update the object after you place it in a document. A linked object in a destination file is an image of an object contained in a source file, not a copy of it. Both objects share a single source, which means you make changes to an object only in the source file.

When you embed an object that you created in another program, you include a copy of the object in a destination file. To update the object, you double-click it in the destination file and then use the tools of the source program to make changes. You cannot edit the source object using the tools of the destination program.

Copy Data from Excel to Word

Learning
Outcomes
• Switch between
  Word and Excel
• Copy objects to
  the clipboard
• Paste Excel objects
  into Word

You use the Copy and Paste commands when you want to copy an item from one program to another program. The item might be a line of text, a selection of cells, or an object such as a chart or a picture. The procedure is the same as the one you use to copy and paste an object from one location in a document to another location in the same document. By default, an object copied from one program to another program retains the formatting of the original object and is not linked to the original object. The exception occurs when you copy and paste a chart, which you will learn about in the next lesson. **CASE** ▶ *Kevin Lawrence, the vice president of Operations at R2G, has provided you with an Excel worksheet containing survey data from the Southeast Asia and Oceania Regional Headquarters and created a report in Word that describes the survey results. He asks you to copy two objects from the Excel worksheet and paste them into the Word report.*

STEPS

QUICK TIP
After you open Data
Files for this unit,
click Enable Editing if
prompted.

1. **Start Excel, open the file** INT 1-1.xlsx **from the location where you store your Data Files, then save it as** INT 1-Customer Survey Data

   The values in the range B7:F10 represent the total number of responses in each of the four rating categories for the volunteer experiences that R2G operated in Southeast Asia and Oceania.

2. **Start Word, open the file** INT 1-2.docx **from the location where you store your Data Files, then save it as** INT 1-Customer Survey Report

   The Word report contains text that describes the results of the survey.

3. **Move the mouse pointer over the** Excel program button **on the taskbar, as shown in** FIGURE 1-3, **then click the** Excel program button **to switch to Excel**

   When you point to the Excel program button, a picture of the worksheet and the filename appear.

TROUBLE
If items already
appear in the
Clipboard task pane,
click Clear All.

4. **On the Home tab, click the** dialog box launcher 🔲 **in the Clipboard group**

   The Clipboard task pane opens to the left of the worksheet window. You use the Clipboard when you want to copy and paste more than one item from one program to another program. You can "collect" up to 24 items on the Clipboard and then switch to the other program to paste them.

5. **Click the photograph, click the** Copy button **in the Clipboard group, select the range A4:B4, then click the** Copy button

   Both items now appear on the Clipboard, as shown in FIGURE 1-4. When you place multiple items on the Clipboard, newer items appear at the top of the list and older items move down.

6. **Click the** Word program button **on the taskbar, click the** dialog box launcher 🔲 **in the Clipboard group, verify that the Insertion point appears to the left of the title, then click the photograph on the Clipboard**

7. **Click in the blank space below the subtitle Southeast Asia and Oceania, click** Total Tours 100 **on the Clipboard, then click the** Close button ✖ **on the Clipboard task pane**

   You pasted the object as a table below the document subtitle. When you use the Copy and Paste commands, the default setting is for the copied object to retain the formatting applied to it in the source file.

8. **Click the photograph in the Word document, click the** Layout Options button 🖼 **in the upper-right corner of the photograph, click the** Square option 🔲, **then drag the photograph to the right of the first paragraph using the green alignment guides, as shown in** FIGURE 1-5

9. **Click anywhere in the document to deselect the photograph, then save the document**

FIGURE 1-3: Word and Excel on the taskbar

Filename and picture of the Excel file

Word program button

Excel program button

FIGURE 1-4: Two items collected on the Clipboard

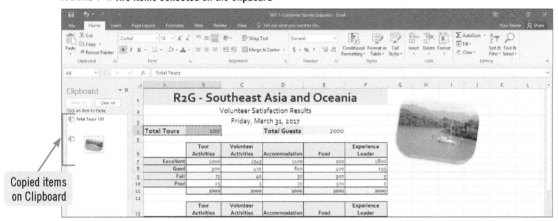

Copied items on Clipboard

FIGURE 1-5: Picture positioned in the Word report

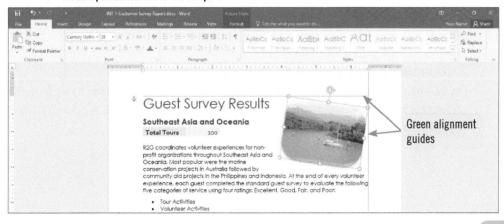

Green alignment guides

Copy a Chart from Excel to Word

Learning Outcomes
• Copy a chart
• View Paste options
• Update a linked chart

You use the Copy and Paste tools to create a link between a chart in Excel and the same chart pasted into a document in Word. When you change the data in the Excel source file, the linked data also changes in the Word destination file. By default, the copied chart will be linked to the chart in the Excel report. However, it will be formatted with the same theme applied to the destination document. **CASE** *You need to copy a column chart representing survey results from Excel and paste it into the Word report.*

STEPS

1. **Click the Excel program button on the taskbar, then close the Clipboard task pane**

2. **Scroll down to view the column chart, click an edge of the chart to select it, then click the Copy button in the Clipboard group**

   The chart in Excel is formatted with the colors of the Banded theme.

3. **Switch to Word, click below the second paragraph (which ends with "January 2018"), then click the Paste button in the Clipboard group**

   The chart appears in the Word document formatted with the colors of the Slice theme, because this theme was already applied to the Word document. The Paste Options button appears in the lower-right corner of the chart.

4. **Click the Paste Options button 📋 (Ctrl)▾ outside the lower-right corner of the pasted chart, as shown in FIGURE 1-6**

   A selection of paste options appears. By default, the option Use Destination Theme & Link Data is selected. The Word document is the destination file and is formatted with the Slice theme. The Excel document is the source file and is formatted with the Banded theme. As a result, the Slice theme applied to the Word file is applied to the chart. TABLE 1-1 describes the five options available for pasting a copied chart.

5. **Move the mouse over each of the five Paste Options buttons to view how the formatting of the chart changes depending on which button is selected, then click the Use Destination Theme & Link Data button 📋**

6. **Switch to Excel, then note the position of the bars for the Food category in the column chart**

   At present, the Poor column (pink) is quite high compared to the Poor columns for the other categories.

7. **Scroll up, click cell E8, type 700, press [Enter], click cell E10, type 200, then press [Enter] and scroll down to the chart**

   In the chart, the Good column (lime green) in the Food category has grown, and the Poor column has shrunk.

8. **Switch to Word, click the chart, click the Chart Tools Design tab, then click the Refresh Data button in the Data group**

   As shown in FIGURE 1-7, the bars for the Food category in the column chart change in the linked chart to reflect the changes you made to the chart in Excel.

9. **Save the document, switch to Excel, then save the workbook**

FIGURE 1-6: Paste Options

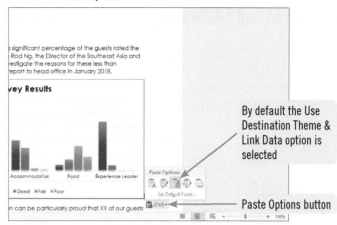

By default the Use Destination Theme & Link Data option is selected

Paste Options button

FIGURE 1-7: Linked chart updated in Word

Columns updated

TABLE 1-1: Paste options for charts

Paste Options button	button name	description
	Use Destination Theme & Embed Workbook	The pasted chart is not linked to the source document, and the pasted chart assumes the formatting of the destination document
	Keep Source Formatting & Embed Workbook	The pasted chart is not linked to the source document, and the pasted chart keeps the same formatting as the source document
	Use Destination Theme & Link Data	This button is selected by default when a chart is pasted into the destination document; the theme of the destination document is applied to the chart, and the chart is linked to the object in the source document
	Keep Source Formatting & Link Data	The pasted chart is linked to the source document, so any changes made to the chart in the source document will be made to the copied chart in the Word document; in addition, the formatting of the source document is retained
	Picture	The chart is pasted as a picture that cannot be modified, and uses the same formatting as the chart in the source document

Create Linked Objects

**Learning
Outcomes**
- Use Paste Special
  to create a link
- Update a linked
  object

To link data other than a chart, you use the Copy button and the Paste Special command to create a link between the source file and the destination file. **CASE** ▶ *You need your report to include a value that represents the average customer ratings. You decide to link the report to the source file data so you can update the data in both files when new information becomes available.*

STEPS

1. **In Excel, click cell G14, type the formula =AVERAGE(B14:F14), press [Enter], click cell G14, then drag its fill handle to cell G17 to enter the remaining three percentages**
   The value "56%" appears in cell G14. This value indicates that, on average, 56% of the responses were Excellent. Only 3% of the responses were Poor.

2. **Click cell F18, type Good/Excellent, press [Tab], type the formula =G14+G15 in cell G18, then press [Enter]**
   The value "87%" appears in cell G18, indicating that 87% of guests rated their R2G volunteer experience as Good or Excellent.

3. **Click cell G18, click the Copy button in the Clipboard group, switch to Word, then select XX that appears following the phrase "can be particularly proud that" in the last paragraph**
   You will paste the contents of cell G18 from Excel over the "XX" in Word.

4. **Click the Paste list arrow in the Clipboard group, then move your mouse over each of the six options to view how the pasted object will appear in the document**
   Two options allow linking—Link & Keep Source Formatting and Link & Merge Formatting. However, both options also insert a line break, so you look for additional paste options in the Paste Special dialog box.

5. **Click Paste Special**
   The Paste Special dialog box opens, as shown in FIGURE 1-8. In this dialog box, you have more options for pasting the value and for controlling its appearance in the destination file.

6. **Click the Paste link option button, click Unformatted Text, click OK, then press [Spacebar] once to add a space after "87%" if necessary**
   The percentage, 87%, appears in the Word document. You decide to test the link.

7. **Switch to Excel, click cell E7, type 500, press [Enter], click cell E9, type 600, then press [Enter]**
   The Good/Excellent rating in cell G18 is now 90%.

8. **Switch to Word, right-click 87%, then click Update Link**
   The value 90% appears. The final document is shown in FIGURE 1-9.

9. **Type your name where indicated in the Word footer, save the document, switch to Excel, type your name where indicated in cell A37, save the workbook, submit your files to your instructor, then close the files**
   If you print the Excel workbook, make sure you fit it on one page.

FIGURE 1-8: **Paste Special dialog box**

FIGURE 1-9: **Completed report**

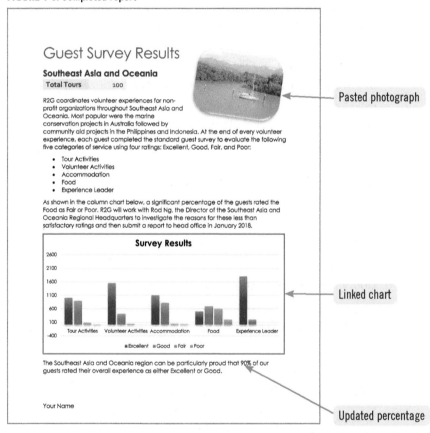

Opening linked files and reestablishing links to charts

When you open a Word file that contains links from an Excel file, a dialog box opens with a message telling you that the document contains links that may refer to other files. The message also asks if you want to update this document with the data from the linked file. Click Yes to update the document with data from the linked file. If you want to change information in both the Excel file and the Word file, you need to open the Excel workbook first, followed by the Word document.

If you make a change to a linked chart in the Excel file, you need to refresh the chart data in Word. To do so, click the chart in Word, click the Chart Tools Design tab, then click the Refresh Data button in the Data group. You also need to manually update any other links by right-clicking the link in Word and then clicking Update Link.

Embed a Word File in Excel

Learning
Outcomes
• Insert a Word file
  as an object
• Edit the Word file
  in Excel

You can embed an entire file that you create in one Office program into a document created in another Office program. You can then edit the embedded file by double-clicking it in the destination program to open the source program. You use the tools of the source program to make changes. TABLE 1-2 summarizes the four ways in which you integrated data between Word and Excel in this module. **CASE** *You have created a price list in Excel that lists the wildlife and marine conservation experiences offered in Southeast Asia and Oceania, but before you distribute it at an upcoming meeting, you decide to include some explanatory text that you have stored in a Word document.*

STEPS

1. **In Excel, open the file INT 1-3.xlsx from the location where you store your Data Files, then save it as INT 1-Wildlife Conservation Price List; in Word, open the file INT 1-4.docx from the location where you store your Data Files, save it as INT 1-Wildlife Conservation, then close the document**

TROUBLE
If the Object button is not visible on the Ribbon, click the down arrow in the Text group.

2. **In Excel, click cell G3, click the Insert tab, then click the Object button ▢ in the Text group**

   The Object dialog box opens. Here you can choose to either create a new object or insert an object from a file.

3. **Click the Create from File tab, click Browse, navigate to where you stored the INT 1-Wildlife Conservation file if necessary, double-click INT 1-Wildlife Conservation, then click OK**

   The text from the Word document appears in a box that starts in cell G3. When you insert an object from another program such as Word, you sometimes need to reposition the current worksheet contents to accommodate the inserted object.

4. **Select the range A4:D20, move the mouse pointer over any border of the selection to show the ✥, then drag the selection down to cell A18**

5. **Move the mouse pointer over the border of the box containing the Word text to show the ✥ pointer, drag the selection to cell A3, click a blank cell, then compare your screen to FIGURE 1-10**

6. **Double-click the box containing the Word text**

   Because the object is embedded, the Word Ribbon and tabs appear within the Excel window. As a result, you can use the tools from the source program (Word) to edit the text. The title bar shows "Document in INT 1-Wildlife Conservation Price List.xlsx - Excel" because you are working within the destination file to edit the embedded object.

7. **Click the Select button in the Editing group, click Select All, click the dialog box launcher ⬚ in the Paragraph group, select the contents of the Left text box in the Indentation section, type .2, press [Tab], type .2 in the Right text box, then click OK**

8. **Select 10 in the first line of paragraph 2, type 13, compare the edited object to FIGURE 1-11, then click outside the object to return to Excel**

   The embedded object is updated in Excel. The text in the source file is not updated because the source file is not linked to the destination file.

9. **Click the File tab, click Print, click Page Setup, click the Margins tab, click the Horizontally check box, click OK, then click ⬅ to return to the workbook**

   The embedded Word object and Excel data are centered between the left and right margins of the page.

10. **Type your name where indicated in cell A34, save the workbook, submit your files to your instructor, then close the workbook and exit Word and Excel**

FIGURE 1-10: Embedded Word file positioned in Excel

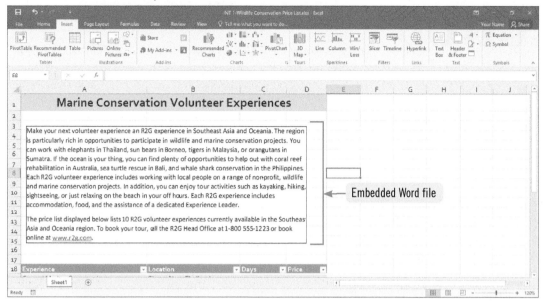

FIGURE 1-11: Embedded object updated in Excel

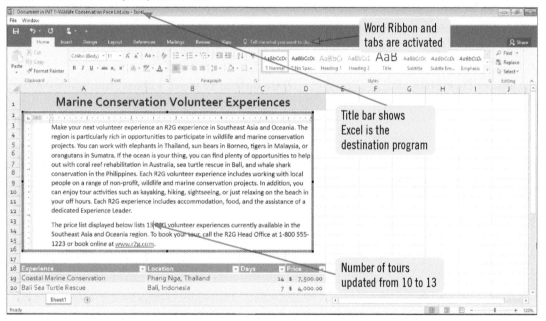

TABLE 1-2: Module 1 integration tasks

object	command	source program	destination program	result	connection	page no.
Cells	Copy/Paste	Excel	Word	Object with Excel formatting	Pasted: no link	4
Chart	Copy/Paste	Excel	Word	Object with Word formatting	Linked	6
Cell	Copy/Paste Special/Paste link	Excel	Word	Formatting varies depending on the formatting option chosen in the Paste Special dialog box	Linked	8
File	Insert/Object/ Create from File	Word	Excel	Text box containing the Word file: to update, double-click and use Word tools within the Excel destination file	Embedded: no link	10

Practice

Concepts Review

Match each term with the statement that best describes it.

1. Embedded file
2. Paste Special
3. Destination file
4. Source file
5. Linked object

a. An unlinked copy of a file placed into another file and then activated by double-clicking

b. The file containing information that is copied and often linked to a different file

c. Within a document, an element that maintains a connection to a different file

d. Used to create and format a connection between objects copied from one file to another file

e. The file that receives the information copied from a different file

Select the best answer from the list of choices.

6. Which of the following objects is, by default, pasted as a link in the destination file?
   a. Excel chart pasted into Word
   b. Word text pasted into Excel
   c. Excel values pasted into Word
   d. Picture pasted from Excel to Word

7. Use the Keep Source Formatting & _____ Data option to paste a chart that you wish to connect with the source document.
   a. Embed
   b. Paste
   c. Link File
   d. Link

8. By default, what theme is applied to a chart when it is copied from Excel and pasted into Word?
   a. The theme used in the source file (Excel)
   b. The Word 2016 theme
   c. The theme used in the destination file (Word)
   d. No theme is applied.

9. In which group on the Excel Ribbon do you find the option to embed an entire file?
   a. Insert
   b. Clipboard
   c. Text
   d. Links

Skills Review

1. **Copy data from Excel to Word.**
   a. Start Excel, open the file INT 1-5.xlsx from the location where you store your Data Files, then save it as **INT 1-Humanities Data**.
   b. Start Word, open the file INT 1-6.docx from the location where you store your Data Files, then save it as **INT 1-Humanities Report**.
   c. Switch to Excel, open the Clipboard task pane, then, if there are items on the Clipboard, click Clear All.
   d. Copy the contents of cell A1 to the Clipboard.
   e. Select the range A4:A7, then copy the contents to the Clipboard.
   f. Switch to Word, open the Clipboard task pane, paste the Humanities object at the top of the document (at the current position of the insertion point), then press [Enter] to add an additional blank line.
   g. Paste the subject areas object on the blank line below the first paragraph.
   h. Close the Clipboard task pane, then save the document.

Skills Review (continued)

2. Copy a chart from Excel to Word.

   a. Switch to Excel, close the Clipboard task pane, then copy the bar chart.

   b. Switch to Word, then paste the bar chart below the second paragraph of text (which ends with "and State scores").

   c. Switch to Excel, then note the position of the bars for Literature.

   d. Change the value in cell C4 to **70**, then switch to Word.

   e. Click the chart, refresh the data, if necessary, then save the document.

   f. Switch to Excel, then save the workbook.

3. Create linked objects.

   a. In Excel, enter the formula **=B4-C4** in cell D4.

   b. Use the Fill handle to copy the formula to the range D5:D7.

   c. Select the range A3:D7, copy it, switch to Word, then use the Paste Special command to paste the cells as a link below paragraph 3 (which ends with "state-wide"), using the Formatted Text (RTF) selection in the Paste Special dialog box.

   d. In Excel, copy cell D7, switch to Word, then use Paste Special to paste the cell over "XX" in the last paragraph as a link using the Unformatted Text option in the Paste Special dialog box. Add a space after the linked object if necessary.

   e. In Excel, change the value in cell B7 to **90**.

   f. In Word, refresh the chart if necessary.

   g. Update the link in the table and the link in the last paragraph so that "20" appears in both places.

   h. Enter your name where indicated in the footer in Word, save the Word report, compare your document to FIGURE 1-12, submit your file to your instructor, then close the document.

   i. In Excel, enter your name in cell A26, save the workbook, submit the file to your instructor, then close the workbook.

4. Embed a Word file in Excel.

   a. In Excel, open the file INT 1-7.xlsx from the location where you store your Data Files, then save it as **INT 1-Art Course Revenue**.

   b. In Word, open the file INT 1-8.docx from the location where you store your Data Files, save it as **INT 1-Art Courses**, then close it.

   c. In Excel, in cell H4, insert the Word file INT 1-Art Courses.docx as an embedded file.

   d. Select the range A6:F16, then move it to cell A14.

   e. Position the box containing the Word text so its upper-left corner is in cell A3.

   f. Change "XX" to **$65** in paragraph 1, then change "ZZ" in paragraph 1 to **80%**.

   g. Click outside the embedded object to return to Excel, compare your screen to FIGURE 1-13, enter your name in cell A24, save the workbook, submit the file to your instructor, then close the workbook and exit Word and Excel.

FIGURE 1-12

FIGURE 1-13

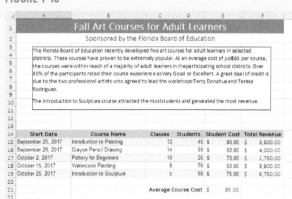

Independent Challenge 1

As a member of the Wolf Island Arts Commission in Alaska, you are responsible for compiling the minutes of the commission's quarterly meetings. You have already written most of the text required for the minutes. Now you need to insert data from Excel that shows how much money was raised from various fund-raising activities.

a. Start Word, open the file INT 1-9.docx from the location where you store your Data Files, save it as **INT 1-Wolf Island Arts Commission Minutes**, start Excel, open the file INT 1-10.xlsx from the location where you store your Data Files, then save it as **INT 1-Wolf Island Data**.

b. In Excel, open the Clipboard task pane, clear all items if necessary, then copy the photograph and cell A2.

c. In Word, open the Clipboard task pane, paste the photograph at the top of the Word document, change the text wrapping of the picture to Square, then position the photograph to the right of the first paragraph.

d. Click to the left of "Approval of Minutes," then paste cell A2.

e. Copy the Fundraising Revenue chart from Excel, then paste it in the appropriate area in the Word document.

f. In Excel, change the number of participants in the plant sale to **1000**; then in Word, refresh the data in the chart if necessary. The Plant Sale slice should be 60%.

g. In Excel, copy the contents of cell E7, switch to Word, select "XX" in the paragraph below the chart, view the paste options, then paste the value as a link using the Unformatted Text selection in the Paste Special dialog box. Add a space if necessary.

h. In Excel, click cell G7, then calculate the total funds raised by adding the contents of the range B7:F7.

i. In cell B8, enter the formula **=B7/G7**, use [F4] to make cell G7 absolute, then copy the formula to the range C8:F8.

j. Copy cell E8, switch to Word, select "ZZ" in the paragraph below the chart, then paste the value as a link using the Unformatted Text selection, adding a space if necessary.

k. In Excel, change the number of participants in the plant sale to **1200**; then in Word, verify the Plant Sale slice changed to 64% and the links updated to $60,000 and 64%. If the links do not update automatically, right-click them and click Update Link in the Word document.

l. Type your name in the Word footer, then save the Word document and Excel workbook, submit the files to your instructor, then close them.

Independent Challenge 2

You work at a summer camp in Montana that provides teens with training programs in digital literacy and community service. You have collected data about the camp enrollment from 2014 to 2019 in an Excel workbook. Now you need to prepare the workbook for distribution at an upcoming meeting with local businesspeople who are interested in sponsoring the camp. You want to include text in the workbook that you have stored in a Word document.

a. Start Excel, open the file INT 1-11.xlsx from the location where you store your Data Files, then save it as **INT 1-High Plains Camp Data**.

b. Start Word, open the file INT 1-12.docx from the location where you store your Data Files, save it as **INT 1-High Plains Camp Information**, then close it.

c. In a blank area of the Excel worksheet, insert the Camp Information file as an embedded object.

d. Adjust the positions of the Excel data and the box containing the Word text so the Word text appears above the Excel data and below the title.

e. In Excel, calculate the total enrollment for the Digital Literacy and Community Service programs in the appropriate cells.

f. To the right of "Community Service," enter and format **Total** to match the formatting for "Digital Literacy" and "Community Service," then calculate the total enrollment for both programs for each year and the total for all programs in all years.

Independent Challenge 2 (continued)

g. Copy the Total enrollment value, edit the embedded Word document so the text is indented by .3" from the left and right margins, then paste the correct total enrollment figure to replace "XX" using the Keep Text Only paste option.

h. Enter your name in cell A22 in Excel, save the Excel workbook, submit the file to your instructor, then close the workbook and exit Excel.

Independent Challenge 3

You own Garden Artist, a landscaping business in Portland, Oregon. You have entered your projected income and expenses in Excel. Now you need to link objects to the company's sales summary in Word.

a. Start Excel, open the file INT 1-13.xlsx from the location where you store your Data Files, then save it as **INT 1-Garden Artist Sales Data**.

b. In cell B14, calculate the Cost of Sales by multiplying the Sales Amount by 60%. (*Hint*: In your formula, multiply the value in cell B6 times .6.) Copy the formula to the range C14:E14.

c. In cell B16, calculate the total profit or loss by subtracting the total expenses from the total income for the month, then copy the formula to the range C16:F16. You should see $66,800 in cell F16.

d. Save the workbook, start Word, open the file INT 1-14.docx from the location where you store your Data Files, then save it as **INT 1-Garden Artist Sales Report**.

e. Select EXPENSES in the paragraph under Projected Expenses, switch to Excel, then copy the value in cell F15 and paste it as a link and as Unformatted Text in Word.

f. Use the same procedure to copy the INCOME and PROFIT amounts from Excel to the appropriate locations in the Word document. Make sure you paste the copied values as links in Unformatted Text.

g. Copy the pie chart from Excel, and paste it into the Word document below the first paragraph after Projected Expenses. Center the pie chart.

h. In Excel, note the percentages in the pie chart (for example, the April slice is 35%), then increase the salaries expense for June to **15,000** and for July to **12,000**.

i. Change the salaries for both April and May to **20,000**. Note how the April slice is now 32%.

j. In Word, update all three links, and verify that the April slice is now 32%.

k. In Excel, open the Clipboard task pane, then copy the heading in cell A1 to the Clipboard.

l. In Word, open the Clipboard task pane, paste the heading at the top of the page and center it, then change the font to Arial Black, the font size to 22 point, and the font color to Dark Green, Accent 2, Darker 25%.

m. Add your name to the document footer, compare the completed sales report to FIGURE 1-14, save the Word file, submit the file to your instructor, then close the Word file.

n. In Excel, enter your name in cell A35, save the workbook, submit the file to your instructor, then close the workbook.

FIGURE 1-14

Garden Artist

Lana Warren, our accountant at Garden Artist, has projected the income and expenses for our landscaping business for the months of April through July.

Projected Expenses

The total projected expenses is $117,200.00 for April through July. The pie chart below displays a breakdown of expenses by total amount.

Breakdown of Monthly Expenses

· April · May · June · July

14%

32%

19%

35%

In order to help decrease our expenses, Elisa Jefferson, one of our own staff members, will create a series of brochures to advertise our products and services, thereby cutting our advertising expenses by 30%.

Projected Income

The total projected income is $174,000.00 for April through July. The projected profit for Garden Artist is $56,800.00 from April through July. We plan to increase sales by charging a higher rate for our landscaping services in April and May, our busiest months.

Your Name

Visual Workshop

Using the Data Files INT 1-15.xlsx and INT 1-16.docx, create the price list shown in FIGURE 1-15. Use formulas to calculate the prices for two-packs and four-packs. Save the workbook as **INT 1-Great Organics Price List**, and save the Word document as **INT 1-Great Organics Information**. Embed the Word document into the Excel worksheet, position the inserted file and the price list in Excel as shown in FIGURE 1-15, then format the embedded Word object as shown in FIGURE 1-15. (*Hint*: The indentation on both sides of the text is .3, and the font size is 12 point.) Add your name to the Excel worksheet, save all files, submit them to your instructor, then close all files.

FIGURE 1-15

Glossary

3D printer Deposits multiple layers of material (typically heated plastic) onto a surface. To achieve the desired shape, the tool head may travel in a different direction as each layer is applied.

Absolute cell reference In a formula, a cell address that refers to a specific cell and does not change when you copy the formula; indicated by a dollar sign before the column letter and/or row number. *See also* Relative cell reference.

Accessories Simple Windows application programs (apps) that perform specific tasks, such as the Calculator accessory for performing calculations. Also called Windows accessories.

Account Log-on information including ISP, email address, and password for each person using Outlook; used to create folders in Outlook for contacts, email, and schedules. *See* also Personal account.

Action Center Opened by clicking the Notifications button on the right side of the taskbar; shows notifications, tips, and reminders. Contains Quick Actions buttons for commonly-used Windows settings.

Active The currently available document, program, or object; on the taskbar, when more than one program is open, the button for the active program appears slightly lighter.

Active cell The cell in which you are currently working.

Active window The window you are currently using; if multiple windows are open, the window in front of other open windows.

Add-in Software that works with an installed app to extend its features.

Add-ins Small programs available from the online Office Store that allow you to access information on the web without having to leave Word.

Address A sequence of drive and folder names that describes a folder's or file's location in the file hierarchy; the highest hierarchy level is on the left, with lower hierarchy levels separated by the ➤ symbol to its right.

Address bar In a window, the area just below the Ribbon that shows the file hierarchy, or address of the files that appear in the file list below it; the address appears as a series of links you can click to navigate to other locations on your computer.

Address book A stored list of names and email addresses that you can access through an email program such as Outlook to address messages.

Adjustment handle A small yellow handle that changes the appearance of an object's most prominent feature.

Align To place objects' edges or centers on the same plane.

Alignment The placement of cell contents in relation to a cell's edges; for example, left-aligned, centered, or right-aligned.

Alignment command A command used in Layout or Design View for a form or report to left-, center-, or right-align a value within its control using the Align Left, Center, or Align Right buttons on the Home tab. In Design View, you can also align the top, bottom, right, or left edge of selected controls using the Align button.

Alternate Back Color property A property that determines the alternating background color of the selected section in a form or report.

Anchoring A layout positioning option that allows you to tie controls together so you can work with them as a group.

AND criteria Criteria placed in the same row of the query design grid. All criteria on the same row must be true for a record to appear on the resulting datasheet.

Animation emphasis effect In Sway, a special effect you can apply to an object to animate it.

Animation tag Identifies the order an object is animated on a slide during a slide show.

App An application program; Windows 10 apps are smaller apps available at the Windows store. Desktop apps, such as Microsoft Office, are more full-featured programs and are available from many software companies.

App window The window that opens after you start an app, showing you the tools you need to use the program and any open program documents.

Application developer The person responsible for building and maintaining tables, queries, forms, and reports for all of the database users.

Application program Any program that lets you work with files or create and edit files such as graphics, letters, financial summaries, and other useful documents, as well as view Web pages on the Internet and send and receive e-mail. Also called an app.

Appointment In the Outlook Calendar, an activity that does not involve inviting other people or scheduling resources.

Argument Information that a function uses to create the final answer. Multiple arguments are separated by commas. All of the arguments for a function are surrounded by a single set of parentheses.

Arithmetic operators In a formula, symbols that perform mathematical calculations, such as addition (+), subtraction (–), multiplication (*), division (/), or exponentiation (^).

Attachment A file, such as a picture, audio clip, video clip, document, worksheet, or presentation, that is sent in addition to the email message composed by typing in the message window.

AutoComplete A feature that automatically suggests text to insert.

AutoCorrect A feature that automatically detects and corrects typing errors, minor spelling errors, and capitalization, and inserts certain typographical symbols as you type.

AutoFill Feature activated by dragging the fill handle; copies a cell's contents or continues a series of entries into adjacent cells.

AutoFill Options button Button that appears after using the fill handle to copy cell contents; enables you to choose to fill cells with specific elements (such as formatting) of the copied cell if desired.

AutoFit A feature that automatically adjusts the width of a column or the height of a row to accommodate its widest or tallest entry.

Automatic page break A page break that is inserted automatically at the bottom of a page.

AutoNumber A field data type in which Access enters a sequential integer for each record added into the datasheet. Numbers cannot be reused even if the record is deleted.

Avg function A built-in Access function used to calculate the average of the values in a given field.

Background The area behind the text and graphics on a slide.

Background graphic An object placed on the slide master

Background image An image that fills an entire form or report, appearing "behind" the other controls; also sometimes called a watermark.

Backstage view View that appears when the File tab is clicked as shown. The navigation bar on the left side contains commands to perform actions common to most Office programs, such as opening a file, saving a file, and closing the file.

Backup A duplicate copy of a file that is stored in another location.

Backward-compatible Software feature that enables documents saved in an older version of a program to be opened in a newer version of the program.

Bibliography A list of sources that you consulted or cited while creating a document.

Blind courtesy copy (Bcc) A way to send an email message to recipients when the sender does not want to reveal who has received courtesy copies.

Blog An informal journal that is created by an individual or a group and available to the public on the Internet; short for weblog.

Blogger The person who creates and maintains a blog.

Bluetooth A type of wireless technology that uses short range radio waves. A Bluetooth device must first be "paired" with a computer so that it knows to trust that particular device.

Bold Formatting applied to text to make it thicker and darker.

Border A line that can be added above, below, or to the sides of a paragraph, text, or table cell; a line that divides the columns and rows of a table.

Bound control A control used in either a form or report to display data from the underlying field; used to edit and enter new data in a form.

Building block Reusable piece of formatted content or document part that is stored in a gallery.

Bullet A small graphic symbol used to identify an item in a list.

Business Intelligence tools Excel features for gathering and analyzing data to answer sophisticated business questions.

Button A small rectangle you can click in order to issue a command to an application program.

Calculation A new value that is created by an expression in a text box on a form or report.

Calculation operators Symbols in a formula that indicate what type of calculation to perform on the cells, ranges, or values.

Calendar In Outlook, provides a convenient way to manage appointments and events.

Calendar Picker A pop-up calendar from which you can choose dates for a date field.

Canvas In the Paint accessory, the area in the center of the app window that you use to create drawings.

Card A section for a particular type of content in a Sway presentation.

Case sensitive An application program's (app's) ability to differentiate between uppercase and lowercase letters; usually used to describe how an operating system evaluates passwords that users type to gain entry to user accounts.

Categories In Outlook, a feature used to tag items so you can track and organize them by specific criteria.

Category axis Horizontal axis in a chart, usually containing the names of data categories; in a 2-dimensional chart, also known as the x-axis.

Cell The box formed by the intersection of a table row and table column.

Cell address The location of a cell, expressed by cell coordinates; for example, the cell address of the cell in column A, row 1 is A1.

Cell pointer Dark rectangle that outlines the active cell.

Cell styles Predesigned combinations of formats based on themes that can be applied to selected cells to enhance the look of a worksheet.

Center Alignment in which an item is centered between the margins.

Character spacing Formatting that changes the width or scale of characters, expands or condenses the amount of space between characters, raises or lowers characters relative to the line of text, and adjusts kerning (the space between standard combinations of letters).

Chart A graphical representation of numerical data from a worksheet. Chart types include 2-D and 3-D column, bar, pie, area, and line charts.

Chart sheet A separate sheet in a workbook that contains only a chart, which is linked to the workbook data.

Charts Pictorial representations of worksheet data that make it easier to see patterns, trends, and relationships; *also called* graphs.

Check box A box that turns an option on when checked or off when unchecked.

Citation A parenthetical reference in the document text that gives credit to the source for a quotation or other information used in a document.

Click To quickly press and release the left button on the pointing device; also called single-click. The touch-screen equivalent is a tap on the screen.

Click and Type A feature that allows you to automatically apply the necessary paragraph formatting to a table, graphic, or text when you insert the item in a blank area of a document in Print Layout or Web Layout view.

Click and Type pointer A pointer used to move the insertion point and automatically apply the paragraph formatting necessary to insert text at that location in the document.

Clip A media file, such as a graphic, sound, animation, or movie.

Clip art A collection of graphic images that can be inserted into documents, presentations, Web pages, spreadsheets, and other Office files.

Clipboard A temporary storage area for items that are cut or copied from any Office file and are available for pasting. *See* Office Clipboard and System Clipboard.

Close button In a Windows title bar, the rightmost button; closes the open window, app, and/or document.

Cloud computing When data, applications, and resources are stored on servers accessed over the Internet or a private internal network rather than on a local computer.

Cloud storage location File storage locations on the World Wide Web, such as Windows OneDrive or Dropbox.

Column break A break that forces text following the break to begin at the top of the next column.

Column heading The box containing the column letter on top of the columns in the worksheet.

Column separator The thin line that separates field names to the left or right in a datasheet or the query design grid.

Combination chart Two charts in one, such as a column chart combined with a line chart, that together graph related but dissimilar data.

Combo box A bound control used to display a drop-down list of possible entries for a field. You can also type an entry from the keyboard into the control so it is a "combination" of the list box and text box controls.

Command An instruction to perform a task, such as opening a file or emptying the Recycle Bin.

Comments button A button on the PowerPoint status bar in Normal view allows you to open the Comments pane where you can create, edit, select, and delete comments.

Comparison operators In a formula, symbols that compare values for the purpose of true/false results.

Compatibility The ability of different programs to work together and exchange data.

Complex formula A formula that uses more than one arithmetic operator.

Computer network The hardware and software that make it possible for two or more computers to share information and resources.

Conditional formatting A type of cell formatting that changes based on the cell's value or the outcome of a formula.

Contact Group A named subset of the people in your Outlook Contacts folder, the named group includes the email addresses for all people in the group so you can send a message or invitation to everyone in the group at once. *See* also Distribution list.

Contacts In Outlook, all information related to people, such as business associates and personal friends.

Content control An interactive object that is embedded in a document you create from a template and that expedites your ability to customize the document with your own information.

Content placeholder A placeholder that is used to enter text or objects such as clip art, charts, or pictures.

Contextual tab A tab that appears only when a specific task can be performed; contextual tabs appear in an accent color and close when no longer needed.

Continuous section break A break that begins a new section on the same page.

Control Any element on a form or report such as a label, text box, line, or combo box. Controls can be bound, unbound, or calculated.

Control Source property A property of a bound control in a form or report that determines the field to which the control is connected.

Conversations Emails that discuss a common subject or thread.

Copy To make a duplicate copy of a file, folder, or other object that you want to store in another location.

Copy and paste To move text or graphics using the Copy and Paste commands.

Cortana The digital personal assistant that comes with Windows 10 and Windows phones; can search, give you reminders, alarms, directions, news, weather, and more.

Courtesy copy (Cc) In email, a way to send a message to a recipient who needs to be aware of the correspondence between the sender and the recipients but who is not the primary recipient of the message.

Creative Commons license A public copyright license that allows the free distribution of an otherwise copyrighted work.

Criteria Entries (rules and limiting conditions) that determine which records are displayed when finding or filtering records in a datasheet or form, or when building a query.

Criteria syntax Rules by which criteria need to be entered. For example, text criteria syntax requires that the criteria are surrounded by quotation marks (" "). Date criteria are surrounded by pound signs (#).

Crop To hide part of an object by using the Cropping tool or to delete a part of a picture.

Current record The record that has the focus or is being edited.

Cut To remove an item from a document and place it on the Clipboard.

Cut and paste To move text or graphics using the Cut and Paste commands.

Data marker

Data marker A graphical representation of a data point in a chart, such as a bar or column.

Data point Individual piece of data plotted in a chart.

Data series The selected range in a worksheet whose related data points Excel converts into a chart.

Data series label Text in the first row and column of a worksheet that identifies data in a chart.

Data series marker A graphical representation of a data series, such as a bar or column.

Data type A required property for each field that defines the type of data that can be entered in each field. Valid data types include AutoNumber, Short Text, Long Text, Number, Currency, Yes/No, Date/Time, and Hyperlink.

Database designer The person responsible for building and maintaining tables, queries, forms, and reports.

Database user The person primarily interested in entering, editing, and analyzing the data in the database.

Datasheet A spreadsheet-like grid that displays fields as columns and records as rows.

Datasheet View A view that lists the records of an object in a datasheet. Tables, queries, and most form objects have a Datasheet View.

Date function A built-in Access function used to display the current date on a form or report; enter the Date function as Date().

Date Navigator A monthly calendar in the To-Do Bar that gives you an overview of the month.

Default In an app window or dialog box, a value that is automatically set; you can change the default to any valid value.

Delete To permanently remove an item from a document.

Deleted Items The folder that stores items when you delete or erase a message from any email folder, which means a deleted item, such as an email or contact card, is actually stored rather than being immediately and permanently deleted. *Also called* Trash folder.

Design View A view in which the structure of an object can be manipulated. Every Access object (table, query, form, report, macro, and module) has a Design View.

Desktop apps Application programs (apps), such as Microsoft Word, that are full-featured and that are often purchased, either from the Windows Store or from a software developer; also called traditional apps.

Destination file In integration, the file that receives the copied information. A Word file that contains an Excel file is the destination file.

Destination presentation The presentation you insert slides to when you reuse slides from another presentation.

Device A hardware component that is part of your computer system, such as a disk drive, a pointing device, or a touch screen device.

Dialog box A window with controls that lets you tell Windows how you want to complete an application program's (app's) command.

Dialog box launcher An icon you can click to open a dialog box or task pane from which to choose related commands.

Digital signature A way to authenticate a presentation files using computer cryptography. A digital signature is not visible in a presentation.

Distribute To evenly divide the space horizontally or vertically between objects relative to each other or the slide edges.

Distribution list A collection of contacts to whom you want to send the same messages; makes it possible for you to send a message to the same group without having to select each contact in the group. *See also* Contact Group.

Docs.com A Microsoft website designed for sharing Sway sites.

Document The electronic file you create using Word.

Document Inspector A PowerPoint feature that examines a presentation for hidden data or personal information.

Document properties Details about a file, such as author name or the date the file was created, that are used to describe, organize, and search for files.

Document window The portion of a application program's (app's) window in which you create the document; displays all or part of an open document.

Documents folder The folder on your hard drive used to store most of the files you create or receive from others; might contain subfolders to organize the files into smaller groups.

Double-click To quickly press and release or click the left button on the pointing device twice. The touch-screen equivalent is a double-tap on the screen.

Draft view A view that shows a document without margins, headers and footers, or graphics.

Drafts The folder that stores unfinished messages that you can finish writing at a later time; many email programs automatically save unsent messages at regular intervals in the Drafts folder as a safety measure.

Drag To point to an object, press and hold the left button on the pointing device, move the object to a new location, and then release the left button. Touch-screen users can press and hold a location, then move along the screen with a finger or stylus.

Drag and drop To move text or a graphic by dragging it to a new location using the mouse.

Drawing canvas In OneNote, a container for shapes and lines.

Drive A physical location on your computer where you can store files.

Drive name A name for a drive that consists of a letter followed by a colon, such as C: for the hard disk drive.

Drop cap A large dropped initial capital letter that is often used to set off the first paragraph of an article.

Dropbox A free online storage site that lets you transfer files that can be retrieved by other people you invite. *See also* Cloud storage location.

Edit To make a change to the contents of an active cell.

Edit mode The mode in which Access assumes you are trying to edit a particular field, so keystrokes such as [Ctrl][End], [Ctrl][Home], [↓], and [↑] move the insertion point within the field.

Edit record symbol A pencil-like symbol that appears in the record selector box to the left of the record that is currently being edited in either a datasheet or a form.

Electronic mail (email) The technology that makes it possible for you to send and receive messages through the Internet.

Electronic spreadsheet A computer program used to perform calculations and analyze and present numeric data.

Email message A message sent using email technology.

Email software A computer program that enables you to send and receive email messages over a network, within an intranet, and through the Internet.

Embed Placement of an object such as a text selection, value, or picture created in a source file into a destination file. An embedded object is edited by opening it in the destination file and then using the tools of the source file to make changes. These changes appear only in the embedded object in the destination file.

Embedded chart A chart displayed as an object in a worksheet.

Embedded object An object that is created in one application and inserted to another; can be edited using the original program file in which they were created.

Emoticon A symbol created by combining keyboard characters; used to communicate feelings in emails.

Endnote Text that provides additional information or acknowledges sources for text in a document and that appears at the end of a document.

Error indicator An icon that automatically appears in Design View to indicate some type of error. For example, a green error indicator appears in the upper-left corner of a text box in Form Design View if the text box Control Source property is set to a field name that doesn't exist.

Even page section break A break that begins a new section on the next even-numbered page.

Event In the Outlook Calendar, an activity that lasts 24 hours or longer.

Exploding Visually pulling a slice of a pie chart away from the whole pie chart in order to add emphasis to the pie slice.

Expression A combination of values, functions, and operators that calculates to a single value. Access expressions start with an equal sign and are placed in a text box in either Form Design View or Report Design View.

Field A code that serves as a placeholder for data that changes in a document, such as a page number.

Field list A list of the available fields in the table or query that the field list represents. Also, a pane that opens in Access and lists the database tables and the fields they contain.

Field name The name given to each field in a table.

Field selector The button to the left of a field in Table Design View that indicates the currently selected field. Also the thin gray bar above each field in the query grid.

File A collection of information stored on your computer, such as a letter, video, or app.

File Explorer A Windows app that allows you to navigate your computer's file hierarchy and manage your files and folders.

File extension A three- or four-letter sequence, preceded by a period, at the end of a filename that identifies the file as a particular type of document; for example, documents in the Rich Text Format have the file extension .rtf.

File hierarchy The tree-like structure of folders and files on your computer.

File list A section of a window that shows the contents of the folder or drive currently selected in the Navigation pane.

File management The ability to organize folders and files on your computer.

File syncing Changes to files stored in the Cloud are automatically synced to all devices.

File tab Provides access to Backstage view and the Word Options dialog box.

Filename A unique, descriptive name for a file that identifies the file's content.

Filter A way to temporarily display only those records that match given criteria.

Filter By Form A way to filter data that allows two or more criteria to be specified at the same time.

Filter By Selection A way to filter records for an exact match.

First line indent A type of indent in which the first line of a paragraph is indented more than the subsequent lines.

Flag A method of coding email messages by assigning different flags to the messages to categorize them or indicate their level of importance for follow up.

Flash Fill A feature that lets you fill a range of text based on samples existing in the current worksheet.

Floating graphic A graphic to which text wrapping has been applied, making the graphic independent of text and able to be moved anywhere on a page.

Focus The property that indicates which field would be edited if you were to start typing.

Folder An electronic container that helps you organize your computer files, like a cardboard folder on your desk; it can contain subfolders for organizing files into smaller groups.

Folder name A unique, descriptive name for a folder that helps identify the folder's contents.

Font The typeface or design of a set of characters (letters, numbers, symbols, and punctuation marks).

Font effect Font formatting that applies a special effect to text, such as small caps or superscript.

Font size The size of characters, measured in units called points.

Font style Format such as bold, italic, and underlining that can be applied to change the way characters look in a worksheet or chart.

Footer Information, such as text, a page number, or a graphic, that appears at the bottom of every page in a document or a section.

Footnote Text that provides additional information or acknowledges sources for text in a document and that appears at the bottom of the page on which the note reference mark appears.

Foreign key field In a one-to-many relationship between two tables, the foreign key field is the field in the "many" table that links the table to the primary key field in the "one" table.

Form An Access object that provides an easy-to-use data entry screen that generally shows only one record at a time.

Form section A location in a form that contains controls. The section in which a control is placed determines where and how often the control prints.

Form View View of a form object that displays data from the underlying recordset and allows you to enter and update data.

Form Wizard An Access wizard that helps you create a form.

Format The appearance of a cell and its contents, including font, font styles, font color, fill color, borders, and shading. *See also* Number format.

Format Painter A feature used to copy the format settings applied to the selected text to other text you want to format the same way.

Formatting Enhancing the appearance of information through font, size, and color changes.

Formatting marks Nonprinting characters that appear on screen to indicate the ends of paragraphs, tabs, and other formatting elements.

Formula A set of instructions used to perform one or more numeric calculations, such as adding, multiplying, or averaging, on values or cells.

Formula bar The area above the worksheet grid where you enter or edit data in the active cell.

Formula prefix An arithmetic symbol, such as the equal sign (=), used to start a formula.

Forwarding Sending an email message you have received to someone else.

Free response quiz A type of Office Mix quiz containing questions that require short answers.

Function A special, predefined formula that provides a shortcut for a commonly used or complex calculation, such as SUM (for calculating a sum) or FV (for calculating the future value of an investment).

Gallery A collection of choices you can browse through to make a selection. Often available with Live Preview.

Gesture An action you take with your finger (or fingers) directly on the screen, such as tapping or swiping.

Graphic image *See* Image.

Gridlines Evenly spaced horizontal and vertical lines on the slide that help you align objects.

Group A PowerPoint feature in which you combine multiple objects into one object.

Grouping A way to sort records in a particular order, as well as provide a section before and after each group of records.

Groups Areas of the Ribbon that arrange commands based on their function, for example, text formatting commands such as Bold, Underline, and Italic are located on the Home tab, in the Font group.

Gutter Extra space left for a binding at the top, left, or inside margin of a document.

Hanging indent A type of indent in which the second and subsequent lines of a paragraph are indented more than the first.

Hard disk A built-in, high-capacity, high-speed storage medium for all the software, folders, and files on a computer. Also called a hard drive.

Hard page break *See* Manual page break.

have not yet been sent.

Header Information, such as text, a page number, or a graphic, that appears at the top of every page in a document or a section.

Highlighted Describes the changed appearance of an item or other object, usually a change in its color, background color, and/or border; often used for an object on which you will perform an action, such as a desktop icon.

Highlighting Transparent color that can be applied to text to call attention to it.

Horizontal ruler A ruler that appears at the top of the document window in Print Layout, Draft, and Web Layout view.

Horizontal scroll bar *See* Scroll bar.

Hub A pane in Microsoft Edge that provides access to favorite websites, a reading list, browsing history, and downloaded files.

Hyperlink Text or a graphic that opens a file, Web page, or other item when clicked. *Also called* a link.

I-beam pointer The pointer used to move the insertion point and select text.

Icon A small image that represents an item, such as the Recycle Bin on your Windows desktop; you can rearrange, add, and delete desktop icons.

Image A nontextual piece of information such as a picture, piece of clip art, drawn object, or graph. Because images are graphical (andnot numbers or letters), they are sometimes referred to as graphical images.

Inactive window An open window you are not currently using; if multiple windows are open, the window(s) behind the active window.

Inbox An email folder that stores all incoming email.

Indent The space between the edge of a line of text or a paragraph and the margin.

Indent marker A marker on the horizontal ruler that shows the indent settings for the active paragraph.

Infinity symbol The symbol that indicates the "many" side of a one-to-many relationship.

Ink annotations A freehand drawing on the screen in Slide Show view made by using the pen or highlighter tool.

Ink to Math tool The OneNote tool that converts handwritten mathematical formulas to formatted equations or expressions.

Ink to Text tool The OneNote tool that converts inked handwriting to typed text.

Inked handwriting In OneNote, writing produced when using a pen tool to enter text.

Inking Freehand pen and highlighter marks you can draw on a slide in Normal view to emphasize information.

Inking toolbar In Microsoft Edge, a collection of tools for annotating a webpage.

Inline graphic A graphic that is part of a line of text.

Insertion point A blinking vertical line that appears when you click in a text box; indicates where new text will be inserted.

Integrate To incorporate a document and parts of a document created in one program into another program; for example, to incorporate an Excel chart into a PowerPoint slide, or an Access table into a Word document.

Integration Term used to describe the process of combining objects and data from two or more applications. For example, a report created in Word can include a chart copied from Excel, or a presentation created in PowerPoint can include a table copied from Access.

Interface The look and feel of a program; for example, the appearance of commands and the way they are organized in the program window.

Is Not Null A criterion that finds all records in which any entry has been made in the field.

Is Null A criterion that finds all records in which no entry has been made in the field.

Italic Formatting applied to text to make the characters slant to the right.

Join line The line identifying which fields establish the relationship between two related tables. Also called a link line.

Junk email Unwanted email that arrives from unsolicited sources. *Also called* spam. Also a default folder in Outlook for junk email.

Justify Alignment in which an item is flush with both the left and right margins.

Key symbol The symbol that identifies the primary key field in each table.

Keyboard shortcut A combination of keys or a function key that can be pressed to perform a command.

Keyword A descriptive word or phrase you enter to obtain a list of results that include that word or phrase. *Also called* shortcut key.

Label control An unbound control that displays text to describe and clarify other information on a form or report.

Label Wizard A report wizard that precisely positions and sizes information to print on a vast number of standard business label specifications.

Labels Descriptive text or other information that identifies data in rows, columns, or charts, but is not included in calculations.

Landscape Page orientation in which the contents of a page span the length of a page rather than its width, making the page wider than it is tall.

Landscape orientation Page orientation in which the page is wider than it is tall.

Launch To open or start a program on your computer.

Launcher An icon you click to open a dialog box or task pane.

Layout A way to group several controls together on a form or report to more quickly add, delete, rearrange, resize, or align controls.

Layout View An Access view that lets you make some design changes to a form or report while you are browsing the data.

Left function An Access function that returns a specified number of characters, starting with the left side of a value in a Text field.

Left indent A type of indent in which the left edge of a paragraph is moved in from the left margin.

Left-align Alignment in which the item is flush with the left margin.

Legend Text box feature in a chart that provides an explanation about the data presented in a chart.

Like operator An operator used in a query to find values in a field that match the pattern you specify.

Line spacing The amount of space between lines of text.

Link A connection created between a source file and a destination file. When an object created in a source file is inserted into or copied to a destination file, any changes made to the object in the source file also appear in the object contained in the destination file.

Link line The line identifying which fields establish the relationship between two related tables.

Linked object An object such as a text selection, value, or picture that is contained in a destination file and linked to a source file. When a change is made to the linked object in the source file, the change also occurs in the linked object in the destination file.

List box A box that displays a list of options from which you can choose (you may need to scroll and adjust your view to see additional options in the list).

Live Preview A feature that lets you point to a choice in a gallery or palette and see the results in the document or object without actually clicking the choice.

Live tile Updated, "live" content that appears on some apps' tiles on the Windows Start menu, including the Weather app and the News app.

Lock screen The screen that appears when you first start your computer, or after you leave it unattended for a period of time, before the sign-in screen.

Log in To select a user account name when a computer starts up, giving access to that user's files. Also called sign in.

Logical view The datasheet of a query is sometimes called a logical view of the data because it is not a copy of the data, but rather, a selected view of data from the underlying tables.

Macro An Access object that stores a collection of keystrokes or commands such as those for printing several reports in a row or providing a toolbar when a form opens.

Mail In Outlook, lets you manage all email.

Major gridlines In a chart, the gridlines that represent the values at the tick marks on the value axis.

Manual page break A page break inserted to force the text following the break to begin at the top of the next page.

Map It An Outlook feature on a Contact card that lets you view a contact's address on a map.

Margin The blank area between the edge of the text and the edge of a page.

Masters One of three views that stores information about the presentation theme, fonts, placeholders, and other background objects. The three master views are Slide Master view, Handout Master view, and Notes Master view.

Maximize button On the right side of a window's title bar, the center button of three buttons; used to expand a window so that it fills the entire screen. In a maximized window, this button changes to a Restore button.

Maximized window A window that fills the desktop.

Meeting In the Outlook Calendar, an activity you invite people to or reserve resources for.

Menu A list of related commands.

Merge A feature in PowerPoint used to combine multiple shapes together; provides you a way to create a variety of unique geometric shapes that are not available in the Shapes gallery.

Message body In an email message, where you write the text of your message.

Message header Contains the basic information about a message including the sender's name and email address, the names and email addresses of recipients and Cc recipients, a date and time stamp, and the subject of the message.

Message threading Allows you to navigate through a group of messages, seeing all replies and forwards from all recipients; includes all emails that discuss a common subject.

Metadata Another name for document properties that includes the author name, the document subject, the document title, and other personal information.

Microsoft account A web service that lets users sign on to one web address so they can use Windows 10 computers as well as Outlook com.

Microsoft Edge New in Windows 10, the Microsoft Web browser that is intended to replace Internet Explorer.

Microsoft OneDrive A Microsoft Web site where you can obtain free file storage space, using your own account, that you can share with others; you can access OneDrive from a laptop, tablet computer, or smartphone.

Microsoft OneNote Mobile app The lightweight version of Microsoft OneNote designed for phones, tablets, and other mobile devices.

Microsoft Store A website, accessible from the Store icon in the Windows 10 taskbar, where you can purchase and download apps, including games, productivity tools, and media software.

Microsoft Windows 10 An operating system.

Mini toolbar A small toolbar that appears next to selected text that contains basic text-formatting commands.

Minimize button On the right side of a window's title bar, the leftmost button of three buttons; use to reduce a window so that it only appears as an icon on the taskbar.

Minimized window A window that is visible only as an icon on the taskbar.

Minor gridlines In a chart, the gridlines that represent the values between the tick marks on the value axis.

Mirror margins Margins used in documents with facing pages, where the inside and outside margins are mirror images of each other.

Mixed reference Cell reference that combines both absolute and relative cell addressing.

Mode indicator An area on the left end of the status bar that indicates the program's status. For example, when you are changing the contents of a cell, the word 'Edit' appears in the mode indicator.

Module An Access object that stores Visual Basic programming code that extends the functions of automated Access processes.

Mouse pointer A small arrow or other symbol on the screen that you move by manipulating the pointing device; also called a pointer.

Move To change the location of a file, folder, or other object by physically placing it in another location.

Multilevel list A list with a hierarchical structure; an outline.

Multiuser A characteristic that means more than one person can enter and edit data in the same Access database at the same time.

Name box Box to the left of the formula bar that shows the cell reference or name of the active cell.

Name property A property that uniquely identifies each object and control on a form or report.

Navigate To move around in a worksheet; for example, you can use the arrow keys on the keyboard to navigate from cell to cell, or press [Page Up] or [Page Down] to move one screen at a time.

Navigate down To move to a lower level in your computer's file hierarchy.

Navigate up To move to a higher level in your computer's file hierarchy.

Navigation buttons Buttons in the lower-left corner of a datasheet or form that allow you to quickly navigate between the records in the underlying object as well as add a new record.

Navigation mode A mode in which Access assumes that you are trying to move between the fields and records of the datasheet (rather than edit a specific field's contents), so keystrokes such as [Ctrl][Home] and [Ctrl][End] move you to the first and last field of the datasheet.

Navigation Pane A pane in the Access program window that provides a way to move between objects (tables, queries, forms, reports, macros, and modules) in the database.

Negative indent A type of indent in which the left edge of a paragraph is moved to the left of the left margin. *Also called* outdent.

Next page section break A break that begins a new section on the next page.

Normal style The default style for text and paragraphs in Word.

Normal view Default worksheet view that shows the worksheet without features such as headers and footers; ideal for creating and editing a worksheet, but may not be detailed enough when formatting a document.

Note In OneNote, a small window that contains text or other types of information.

Note reference mark A mark (such as a letter or a number) that appears next to text to indicate that additional information is offered in a footnote or endnote.

Notebook In OneNote, the container for notes, drawings, and other content.

Notes In Outlook, the electronic version of the sticky notes you buy at your local stationery store; a convenient way to quickly jot down a reminder or an idea.

Notes button A button on the status bar in PowerPoint that opens the Notes pane.

Notes Page view A presentation view that displays a reduced image of the current slide above a large text box where you can type notes.

Notes pane The area in Normal view that shows speaker notes for the current slide; also in Notes Page view, the area below the slide image that contains speaker notes.

Notification area An area on the right side of the Windows 10 taskbar that displays the current time as well as icons representing selected information; the Notifications button displays pop-up messages when a program on your computer needs your attention. Click the Notifications button to display the Action Center. *See also* Action Center.

Number format A format applied to values to express numeric concepts, such as currency, date, and percentage.

Object A table, query, form, report, macro, or module in an Access database.

Object Linking and Embedding (OLE) The term used to refer to the technology Microsoft uses to allow the integration of data between programs. The difference between linking and embedding relates to where the object is stored and how the object is updated after placement in a document. A linked object in a destination file is an image of an object contained in a source file. Both objects share a single source, which means the object is updated only in the source file.

Odd page section break A break that begins a new section on the next odd-numbered page.

Office Clipboard A temporary storage area shared by all Office programs that can be used to cut, copy, and paste multiple items within and between Office programs. The Office Clipboard can hold up to 24 items collected from any Office program. *See also* System Clipboard.

Office Mix A free add-in application integrated to the PowerPoint Ribbon that allows you to create interactive content.

Office Online Apps Versions of the Microsoft Office applications with limited functionality that are available online from Microsoft OneDrive. Users can view documents online and then edit them in the browser using a selection of functions.

Off-site backup Duplicate storage of computer data at a remote location other than your home or office. The backup may be stored on a removable hard drive or sent over the Internet to a Cloud service.

OneDrive An online storage and file sharing service. Access to OneDrive is through a Microsoft account.

One-to-many line The line that appears in the Relationships window and shows which field is duplicated between two tables to serve as the linking field. The one-to-many line displays a "1" next to the field that serves as the "one" side of the relationship and displays an infinity symbol next to the field that serves as the "many" side of the relationship when referential integrity is specified for the relationship. Also called the one-to-many join line.

One-to-many relationship The relationship between two tables in an Access database in which a common field links the tables together. The linking field is called the primary key field in the "one" table of the relationship and the foreign key field in the "many" table of the relationship.

Online collaboration The ability to incorporate feedback or share information across the Internet or a company network or intranet.

Open To use one of the methods for opening a document to retrieve it and display it in the document window.

Operating system A program that manages the complete operation of your computer and lets you interact with it.

Option button A small circle in a dialog box that you click to select only one of two or more related options.

OR criteria Criteria placed on different rows of the query design grid. A record will be selected for the resulting datasheet if it is true for any single row.

Order of precedence Rules that determine the order in which operations are performed within a formula containing more than one arithmetic operator.

Orphan The first line of a paragraph when it appears alone at the bottom of a page.

Orphan record A record in the "many" table of a one-to-many relationship that doesn't have a matching entry in the linking field of the "one" table. Orphan records cannot be created if referential integrity is enforced on a relationship.

Outbox A temporary storage folder for email messages that have not yet been sent.

Outdent *See* Negative indent.

Outline view A view in PowerPoint where you can enter text on slides in outline form. Includes three areas. The Outline pane where you enter text, the Slide pane for the main slide, and the Notes pane where you enter notes.

Outlook Today A feature in Outlook that shows your day at a glance, like an electronic version of a daily planner book; when it is open, you can see what is happening in the Calendar, Tasks, and Messages for the day.

Padding The space between controls.

Page In OneNote, a workspace for inserting notes and other content, similar to a page in a physical notebook.

Page break *See* Automatic page break or Manual page break.

Page Break Preview A worksheet view that displays a reduced view of each page in your worksheet, along with page break indicators that you can drag to include more or less information on a page.

Page Layout view Provides an accurate view of how a worksheet will look when printed, including headers and footers.

Pane A section of a window, such as the Navigation pane in the File Explorer window.

Paragraph spacing The amount of space between paragraphs.

Password A special sequence of numbers and letters that users can employ to control who can access the files in their user account area; keeping the password private helps keep users' computer information secure.

Paste To place a copied item from the Clipboard to a location in a document.

Paste Options button Button that appears onscreen after pasting content; enables you to choose to paste only specific elements of the copied selection, such as the formatting or values, if desired.

Path An address that describes the exact location of a file in a file hierarchy; shows the folder with the highest hierarchy level on the left and steps through each hierarchy level toward the right. Locations are separated by small triangles or by backslashes.

Peek A feature in Outlook that opens a small window when you mouse over an event, task, or some activity and shows you a snapshot of the details for the item.

People In Outlook, where you manage all your business and personal contact information.

People Pane Available in several Outlook views; shows you any social media information available for the person sending the current message and included files, appointments, and notes related to that person.

Personal account In Outlook, identifies you as a user with information such as your email address and password, the type of Internet service provider (ISP) you are using, and the incoming and outgoing email server address for your ISP. *See also* Account.

Photos app A Windows 10 app that lets you view and organize your pictures.

Picture A digital photograph, piece of line art, or other graphic that is created in another program and is inserted into PowerPoint.

Pixel (picture element) One pixel is the measurement of one picture element on the screen.

Plot area In a chart, the area inside the horizontal and vertical axes.

Point A unit of measure used for font size and row height. One point is equal to 1/72nd of an inch.

Pointer *See* Mouse pointer.

Pointing device A device that lets you interact with your computer by controlling the movement of the mouse pointer on your computer screen; examples include a mouse, trackball, touchpad, pointing stick, on-screen touch pointer, or a tablet.

Pointing device action A movement you execute with your computer's pointing device to communicate with the computer; the five basic pointing device actions are point, click, double-click, drag, and right-click.

Portrait Page orientation in which the contents of a page span the width of a page, so the page is taller than it is wide.

Portrait orientation A printout that is 8.5 inches wide by 11 inches tall.

Power button The physical button on your computer that turns your computer on.

PowerPoint window A window that contains the running PowerPoint application including the Ribbon, panes, and tabs.

Presentation software A software program used to organize and present information typically as part of an electronic slide show.

Presenter view A PowerPoint view you access while in Slide Show view. Typically you use this view when showing a presentation through two monitors, one that you see as the presenter and one that the audience sees.

Preview pane A pane on the right side of a File Explorer window that shows the actual contents of a selected file without opening an app; might not work for some types of files, such as databases.

Previewing Prior to printing, seeing onscreen exactly how the printed document will look.

Primary key field A field that contains unique information for each record. A primary key field cannot contain a null entry.

primary recipient of the message.

Print area The portion of a worksheet that will be printed; can be defined by selecting a range and then using the Print Area button on the Page Layout tab.

Print Layout view A view that shows a document as it will look on a printed page.

Print Preview An Access view that shows you how a report or other object will print on a sheet of paper.

Program A set of instructions written for a computer, such as an operating system program or an application program; also called an application or an app.

Property A characteristic that further defines a field (if field properties), control (if control properties), section (if section properties), or object (if object properties).

Property Sheet A window that displays an exhaustive list of properties for the chosen control, section, or object on a form or report.

Query An Access object that provides a spreadsheet-like view of the data, similar to that in tables. It may provide the user with a subset of fields and/or records from one or more tables. Queries are created when the user has a "question" about the data in the database.

Query design grid The bottom pane of the Query Design View window in which you specify the fields, sort order, and limiting criteria for the query.

Query Design View The window in which you develop queries by specifying the fields, sort order, and limiting criteria that determine which fields and records are displayed in the resulting datasheet.

Quick Access buttons Buttons that appear at the bottom of the Windows Action Center; single-click to perform common actions such as turning WiFi on or off.

Quick Access toolbar A customizable toolbar that contains buttons you can click to perform frequently used commands.

Quick Access view A list of frequently-used folders and recently used files that appears when you first open File Explorer.

Quick Analysis tool An icon that is displayed below and to the right of a range that lets you easily create charts and other elements.

Quick Part A reusable piece of content that can be inserted into a document, including a field, document property, or a preformatted building block.

Quick Style Determines how fonts, colors, and effects of the theme are combined and which color, font, and effect is dominant. A Quick Style can be applied to shapes or text.

RAM **(Random Access Memory)** The storage location that is part of every computer, that temporarily stores open apps and document data while a computer is on.

Range A selection of two or more cells, such as B5:B14.

Read Mode view A document view that hides the tabs and Ribbon and is useful for reading long documents.

Reading view In Microsoft Edge, the display of a webpage that removes ads and most graphics and uses a simple format for the text.

Read-only An object property that indicates whether the object can read and display data, but cannot be used to change (write to) data.

Record A row of data in a table.

Record source The table or query that defines the field and records displayed in a form or report.

Recycle Bin A desktop object that stores folders and files you delete from your hard drive(s) and enables you to restore them.

Reference operators In a formula, symbols which enable you to use ranges in calculations.

Referential integrity A set of Access rules that govern data entry and help ensure data accuracy. Setting referential integrity on a relationship prevents the creation of orphan records.

Relational database software Software such as Access that is used to manage data organized in a relational database.

Relative cell reference In a formula, a cell address that refers to a cell's location in relation to the cell containing the formula and that automatically changes to reflect the new location when the formula is copied or moved; default type of referencing used in Excel worksheets. *See also* Absolute cell reference.

Removable storage Storage media that you can easily transfer from one computer to another, such as DVDs, CDs, or USB flash drives.

Report An Access object that creates a professional printout of data that may contain such enhancements as headers, footers, and calculations on groups of records.

Report Wizard An Access wizard that helps you create a report.

Responsive design A way to provide content so that it adapts appropriately to the size of the display on any device.

Restore Down button On the right side of a maximized window's title bar, the center of three buttons; use to reduce a window to its last non-maximized size. In a restored window, this button changes to a Maximize button.

Ribbon In many Microsoft app windows, a horizontal strip near the top of the window that contains tabs (pages) of grouped command buttons that you click to interact with the app.

Ribbon Display Options button A button on the title bar that is used to use to hide or show the Ribbon and the Ribbon tabs and commands.

Rich Text Format (RTF) The file format that the WordPad app uses to save files.

Right indent A type of indent in which the right edge of a paragraph is moved in from the right margin.

Right-align Alignment in which an item is flush with the right margin.

Right-click To press and release the right button on the pointing device; use to display a shortcut menu with commands you issue by left-clicking them.

Rotate handle A small round arrow at the top of a selected object that you can drag to turn the selected object.

Row heading The box containing the row number to the left of the row in a worksheet.

RTF *See* Rich Text Format.

Rule In Outlook, enables you to organize your email by setting parameters for incoming email; for example, you can specify that all email from a certain person goes into the folder for a specific project.

Ruler A vertical or horizontal guide that appears in Form and Report Design View to help you position controls.

Sandbox A computer security mechanism that helps to prevent attackers from gaining control of a computer.

Sans serif font A font (such as Calibri) whose characters do not include serifs, which are small strokes at the ends of letters.

Save To store a file permanently on a disk or to overwrite the copy of a file that is stored on a disk with the changes made to the file.

Save As Command used to save a file for the first time or to create a new file with a different filename, leaving the original file intact.

Save As command A command on the File tab that saves the entire database (and all objects it contains) or only the current object with a new name.

Screen capture An electronic snapshot of your screen, as if you took a picture of it with a camera, which you can paste into a document.

Screen clipping In OneNote, an image copied from any part of a computer screen.

Screen recording In Office Mix, a video you create by capturing your desktop and any actions performed on it.

ScreenTip A label that identifies the name of the button or feature, briefly describes its function, conveys any keyboard shortcut for the command, and includes a link to associated help topics, if any.

Scroll To use the scroll bars or the arrow keys to display different parts of a document in the document window.

Scroll arrow A button at each end of a scroll bar for adjusting your view in a window in small increments in that direction.

Scroll bar A vertical or horizontal bar that appears along the right or bottom side of a window when there is more content than can be displayed within the window, so that you can adjust your view.

Scroll bars Bars on the right edge (vertical scroll bar) and bottom edge (horizontal scroll bar) of the document window that allow you to move around in a document that is too large to fit on the screen at once.

Scroll box A box in a scroll bar that you can drag to display a different part of a window.

Search criteria Descriptive text that helps identify the application program (app), folder, file, or Web site you want to locate when conducting a search.

Search Tools tab A tab that appears in the File Explorer window after you click the Search text box; lets you specify a specific search location, limit your search, repeat previous searches, save searches, and open a folder containing a found file.

Secondary axis In a combination chart, an additional axis that supplies the scale for one of the chart types used.

Section A location of a form or report that contains controls. The section in which a control is placed determines where and how often the control prints.

Section break A formatting mark inserted to divide a document into sections.

Section tab In OneNote, a divider for organizing a notebook.

Select To change the appearance of an item by clicking, double-clicking, or dragging across it, to indicate that you want to perform an action on it.

Select pointer The mouse pointer shape that looks like a white arrow pointing toward the upper-left corner of the screen.

Selection box A dashed border that appears around a text object or placeholder, indicating that it is ready to accept text.

Selection pointer A pointer used to click a button or another element of the Word program window.

Sent Items When you send an email message, a copy of the message is stored in this folder to help you track the messages you send out.

Serif font A font (such as Times New Roman) whose characters include serifs, which are small strokes at the ends of letters.

Service provider The organization or company that provides email or Internet access.

Shading A background color or pattern that can be applied to text, tables, or graphics.

Share button A button on the Ribbon that is used to save a document to the Cloud.

Sheet tab scrolling buttons Allow you to navigate to additional sheet tabs when available; located to the left of the sheet tabs.

Sheet tabs Identify the sheets in a workbook and let you switch between sheets; located below the worksheet grid.

Shortcut An icon that acts as a link to an app, file, folder, or device that you use frequently.

Shortcut key *See* Keyboard shortcut.

Shortcut menu A menu of context-appropriate commands for an object that opens when you right-click that object.

Shut down To exit the operating system and turn off your computer.

Sign in To select a user account name when a computer starts up, giving access to that user's files. Also called log in.

Simple Query Wizard An Access wizard that prompts you for information it needs to create a new query.

Single-click *See* Click.

Single-factor authentication Security protocol in which an individual provides only one credential (password) to verify their identity.

Sizing handles Small series of dots at the corners and edges of a chart indicating that the chart is selected; drag to resize the chart.

Slide layout This determines how all of the elements on a slide are arranged, including text and content placeholders.

Slide Library A folder that you and others can access to open, modify, and review presentation slides.

Slide Notes In Office Mix, the written and displayed version of notes typically used to recite narration while creating a slide recording.

Slide pane The main section of Normal view that displays the current slide.

Slide recording In Office Mix, a video you create by recording action with a webcam, a camera attached or built into a computer.

Slide Show view A view that shows a presentation as an electronic slide show; each slide fills the screen.

Slide Sorter view A view that displays a thumbnail of all slides in the order in which they appear in a presentation; used to rearrange slides and slide transitions.

Slide thumbnail *See* Thumbnail.

Slide timing The amount of time each slide is visible on the screen during a slide show.

Slide transition The special effect that moves one slide off the screen and the next slide on the screen during a slide show. Each slide can have its own transition effect.

Slides tab On the left side of the Normal view, displays the slides in the presentation as thumbnails.

Smart Guides A feature in PowerPoint used to help position objects relative to each other and determine equal distances between objects.

SmartArt A professional quality graphic diagram that visually illustrates text.

SmartArt graphics Predesigned diagram types for the following types of data: List, Process, Cycle, Hierarchy, Relationship, Matrix, and Pyramid.

SmartArt Style A pre-set combination of formatting options that follows the design theme that you can apply to a SmartArt graphic.

Snap assist feature The Windows 10 feature that lets you drag a window to the left or right side of the screen, where it "snaps" to fill that half of the screen and displays remaining open windows as thumbnails you click to fill the other half.

Soft page break *See* Automatic page break.

Sort Change the order of, such as the order of files or folders in a window, based on criteria such as date, file size, or alphabetical by filename.

Source file In integration, the file from which the information is copied or used. An Excel file that is inserted into a file that contains a Word report is the source file.

Source presentation The presentation you insert slides from when you reuse slides from another presentation.

Spam Unwanted email that arrives from unsolicited sources. *Also called* junk email.

Spamming The sending of identical or near-identical unsolicited messages to a large number of recipients. Many email programs have filters that identify this email and place it in a special folder.

Sparkline A quick, simple chart located within a cell that serves as a visual indicator of data trends.

Spin box A text box with up and down arrows; you can type a setting in the text box or click the arrows to increase or decrease the setting.

Split form A form split into two panes; the upper pane allows you to display the fields of one record in any arrangement, and the lower pane maintains a datasheet view of the first few records.

SQL (Structured Query Language) A language that provides a standardized way to request information from a relational database system.

Start button A clickable button at in the lower left corner of the Windows 10 screen that you click to open the Start menu.

Start menu Appears after you click the Start button; provides access to all programs, documents, and settings on the computer.

Status bar The bar at the bottom of the Word program window that shows information about the document, including the current page number, the total number of pages in a document, the document word count, and the on/off status of spelling and grammar checking, and contains the view buttons, the Zoom level button and the Zoom slider.

Storyline In Sway, the workspace for assembling a presentation.

Style A named collection of character and paragraph formats that are stored together and can be applied to text to format it quickly.

Subdatasheet A datasheet that is nested within another datasheet to show related records. The subdatasheet shows the records on the "many" side of a one-to-many relationship.

Subfolder A folder within another folder.

Subject line Meaningful text in the subject text box of an email message providing recipients with an idea of the message content.

Subscript A font effect in which text is formatted in a smaller font size and placed below the line of text.

Subtitle text placeholder A box on the title slide reserved for subpoint text.

Suite A group of programs that are bundled together and share a similar interface, making it easy to transfer skills and program content among them.

Sum function A mathematical function that totals values in a field.

Superscript A font effect in which text is formatted in a smaller font size and placed above the line of text.

Sway site A website Sway creates to share and display a Sway presentation.

Symbol A special character that can be inserted into a document using the Symbol command.

Sync In OneNote, to save a new or updated notebook so that all versions of the notebook, such as a notebook on OneDrive and a copy on a hard drive, have the same contents.

Syntax Rules for entering information such as query criteria or property values.

System Clipboard A clipboard that stores only the last item cut or copied from a document. See also Clipboard and Office Clipboard.

System on a Chip (SoC) Consolidates the functions of the CPU, graphics and sound cards, memory, and more onto a single silicon chip. This miniaturization allows devices to become increasingly compact.

T

Tab A page in an application program's Ribbon, or in a dialog box, that contains a group of related commands and settings.

Tab Index property A form property that indicates the numeric tab order for all controls on the form that have the Tab Stop property set to Yes.

Tab leader A line that appears in front of tabbed text.

Tab order property A form property that determines the sequence in which the controls on the form receive the focus when the user presses [Tab] or [Enter] in Form view.

Tab stop A location on the horizontal ruler that indicates where to align text.

Tab Stop property A form property that determines whether a field accepts focus.

Table A collection of records for a single subject, such as all of the customer records; the fundamental building block of a relational database because it stores all of the data.

Table Design View A view of a table that provides the most options for defining fields.

Table styles Predesigned formatting that can be applied to a range of cells or even to an entire worksheet; especially useful for those ranges with labels in the left column and top row, and totals in the bottom row or right column. See also Table.

Tabs Organizational unit used for commands on the Ribbon. The tab names appear at the top of the Ribbon and the active tab appears in front.

Task In Outlook, an item in Tasks.

Task view A new Windows 10 area, accessible from the Task view button on the taskbar, that lets you switch applications and create multiple desktops (also called virtual desktops).

Taskbar The horizontal bar at the bottom of the Windows 10 desktop; displays icons representing apps, folders, and/or files on the left, and the Notification area, containing the date and time and special program messages, on the right.

Tasks In Outlook, the electronic to-do list, whereby each task has a subject, a start and end date, priority, and a description.

Tell Me box A text box on the Ribbon that is used to find a command or access the Word Help system.

Template A predesigned, formatted file that serves as the basis for a new workbook; Excel template files have the file extension .xltx.

Text Align property A control property that determines the alignment of text within the control.

Text annotations Labels added to a chart to draw attention to or describe a particular area.

Text box An area in a Windows program that you click to enter text.

Text concatenation operators In a formula, symbols used to join strings of text in different cells.

Text effect Formatting that applies a visual effect to text, such as a shadow, glow, outline, or reflection.

Text placeholder A box with a dotted border and text that you replace with your own text.

Text wrapping Formatting applied to a graphic to make it a floating graphic.

Text wrapping break Forces the text following the break to begin at the beginning of the next line.

Theme A predefined set of colors, fonts, line and fill effects, and other formats that can be applied to an Access database and give it a consistent, professional look.

Theme colors The set of 12 coordinated colors that make up a PowerPoint presentation; a theme assigns colors for text, lines, fills, accents, hyperlinks, and background.

Theme effects The set of effects for lines and fills.

Theme fonts The set of fonts for titles and other text.

Thumbnail A small image of a slide. Thumbnails are visible on the Slides tab and in Slide Sorter view.

Tick marks Notations of a scale of measure on a chart axis.

Tile A shaded rectangle on the Windows 10 Start menu that represents an app. See also App and Application program.

Title bar Appears at the top of every Office program window; displays the document name and program name.

Title placeholder A box on a slide reserved for the title of a presentation or slide.

Title slide The first slide in a presentation.

To Do tag In OneNote, an icon that helps you keep track of your assignments and other tasks.

Toggle button A button that turns a feature on and off.

Toolbar In an application program, a set of buttons, lists, and menus you can use to issue program commands.

Trash folder *See* Deleted Items folder.

Two-factor authentication (2FA) Security protocol in which an individual provides two credentials (often a pre-established password plus a one-time, randomly-generated code sent to a mobile phone) to verify their identity.

Ultraportable computer A type of laptop that is generally smaller and less powerful.

Unbound control A control that does not change from record to record and exists only to clarify or enhance the appearance of the form, using elements such as labels, lines, and clip art.

Universal apps *See* Windows 10 apps.

USB (Universal Serial Bus) Data communications standard designed to replace the need for earlier interfaces such as parallel and serial ports.

USB flash drive A removable storage device for folders and files that you plug into a USB port on your computer; makes it easy to transport folders and files to other computers. Also called a pen drive, flash drive, jump drive, keychain drive, or thumb drive.

User account A special area in a computer's operating system where users can store their own files and preferences.

User interface A collective term for all the ways you interact with a software program.

Username The first part of an email address that identifies the person who receives the email that is sent to this email address.

Vacation response An automatically-generated email message you can have sent in response to received emails when you are away; most email programs allow you to create a vacation response.

Value axis In a chart, the axis that contains numerical values; in a 2-dimensional chart, also known as the y-axis.

Values Numbers, formulas, and functions used in calculations.

Variant A custom variation of the applied theme that uses different colors, fonts, and effects.

Vertical alignment The position of text in a document relative to the top and bottom margins.

Vertical ruler A ruler that appears on the left side of the document window in Print Layout view.

Vertical scroll bar *See* scroll bar.

View Each Access object has different views for different purposes. For example, you work with data in Datasheet View. You modify the design of the object in Layout and Design Views. You preview a printout in Print Preview. Common views include Datasheet View for a table or query, or Design View for any Access object.

View buttons Buttons on the status bar that are used to change document views.

View Shortcuts The buttons at the bottom of the PowerPoint window on the status bar that you click to switch among views.

Wearables Computer devices that may be worn on a person's wrist or incorporated into clothing.

Web Layout view A view that shows a document as it will look when viewed with a Web browser.

Web Note In Microsoft Edge, an annotation on a webpage.

Web-based email Web site that provides free email addresses and service.

What-if analysis A decision-making tool in which data is changed and formulas are recalculated, in order to predict various possible outcomes.

Widow The last line of a paragraph when it is carried over to the top of the following page, separate from the rest of the paragraph.

Wildcard A special character used in criteria to find, filter, and query data. The asterisk (*) stands for any group of characters. For example, the criteria I* in a State field criterion cell would find all records where the state entry was IA, ID, IL, IN, or Iowa. The question mark (?) wildcard stands for only one character.

Window A rectangular-shaped work area that displays an app or a collection of files, folders, and Windows tools.

Window control buttons The set of three buttons on the right side of a window's title bar that let you control the window's state, such as minimized, maximized, restored to its previous open size, or closed.

Windows 10 apps Apps (application programs) for Windows 10 that often have a single purpose, such as Photos, News, or OneDrive.

Windows 10 desktop An electronic work area that lets you organize and manage your information, much like your own physical desktop.

Windows 10 UI The Windows 10 user interface. *See also* User interface.

Windows accessories Application programs (apps), such as Paint or WordPad, that come with the Windows 10 operating system.

Windows Action Center A pane that appears in the lower right corner of the Windows 10 screen that lets you quickly view system notifications and selected settings; also has Quick Action buttons to perform common actions in one click.

Windows app Small program available for free or for purchase in the Windows Store; can run on Windows desktops, laptops, tablets, and phones.

Windows Search The Windows feature that lets you look for files and folders on your computer storage devices; to search, type text in the Search text box in the title bar of any open window, or click the Start button and type text in the search text box.

Word art A drawing object that contains text formatted with special shapes, patterns, and orientations.

Word processing program A software program that includes tools for entering, editing, and formatting text and graphics.

Word program window The window that contains the Word program elements, including the document window, Quick Access toolbar, Ribbon, and status bar.

Word wrap A feature that automatically moves the insertion point to the next line as you type.

WordArt A set of decorative styles or text effects that is applied to text.

Workbook A collection of related worksheets contained within a single file which has the file extension xlsx.

Works cited A list of sources that you cited while creating a document.

Worksheet A single sheet within a workbook file; also, the entire area within an electronic spreadsheet that contains a grid of columns and rows.

Worksheet window Area of the program window that displays part of the current worksheet; the worksheet window displays only a small fraction of the worksheet, which can contain a total of 1,048,576 rows and 16,384 columns.

X-axis The horizontal axis in a chart; because it often shows data categories, such as months or locations, *also called* Category axis.

XML Acronym that stands for eXtensible Markup Language, which is a language used to structure, store, and send information.

Y-axis The vertical axis in a chart; because it often shows numerical values, *also called* Value axis.

Z-axis The third axis in a true 3-D chart, lets you compare data points across both categories and values.

Zoom level button A button on the status bar that is used to change the zoom level of the document in the document window.

Zoom slider A slider on the status bar that is dragged to enlarge or decrease the display size of the document in the document window.

Zooming A feature that makes screen information appear larger but shows less of it on screen at once, or shows more of a document on screen at once but at a reduced size; does not affect actual document size.

Zooming in A feature that makes a printout appear larger but shows less of it on screen at once; does not affect the actual size of the printout.

Zooming out A feature that shows more of a printout on screen at once but at a reduced size; does not affect the actual size of the printout.

Index

G

X

Y

Z